Lecture Notes in Computer Science   12219

More information about this series at http://www.springer.com/series/7409

Gabriela Viale Pereira · Marijn Janssen ·
Habin Lee · Ida Lindgren ·
Manuel Pedro Rodríguez Bolívar ·
Hans Jochen Scholl · Anneke Zuiderwijk (Eds.)

Electronic Government

19th IFIP WG 8.5 International Conference, EGOV 2020
Linköping, Sweden, August 31 – September 2, 2020
Proceedings

 Springer

Editors
Gabriela Viale Pereira 🆔
Danube University Krems
Krems, Austria

Habin Lee 🆔
Brunel University London
Uxbridge, UK

Manuel Pedro Rodríguez Bolívar 🆔
University of Granada
Granada, Spain

Anneke Zuiderwijk 🆔
Delft University of Technology
Delft, The Netherlands

Marijn Janssen 🆔
Delft University of Technology
Delft, The Netherlands

Ida Lindgren 🆔
Linköping University
Linköping, Sweden

Hans Jochen Scholl 🆔
University of Washington
Seattle, WA, USA

ISSN 0302-9743   ISSN 1611-3349   (electronic)
Lecture Notes in Computer Science
ISBN 978-3-030-57598-4   ISBN 978-3-030-57599-1   (eBook)
https://doi.org/10.1007/978-3-030-57599-1

LNCS Sublibrary: SL3 – Information Systems and Applications, incl. Internet/Web, and HCI

This Springer imprint is published by the registered company Springer Nature Switzerland AG
The registered company address is: Gewerbestrasse 11, 6330 Cham, Switzerland

Preface

The EGOV-CeDEM-ePart 2020 presents the third-year edition after the merger of the IFIP WG 8.5 Electronic Government (EGOV), the IFIP WG 8.5 IFIP Electronic Participation (ePart), and the Conference for E-Democracy and Open Government Conference (CeDEM). The merged conference is dedicated to the broader area of electronic government, open government, smart governance, e-democracy, policy informatics, and electronic participation. Scholars from around the world have attended this premier academic forum for a long time, which has given EGOV a worldwide reputation as one of the leading conferences in the research domains of electronic, open, and smart government, as well as electronic participation.

Due to the pandemic, this year's conference was held from August 31 to September 2, as a digital conference. The original hosts at Linköping University, Sweden, supported the organization, and all presentations and discussions, workshops keynotes, and panels were held online. Despite the disappointment of not being able to host the conference locally, the conference was a huge success.

The call for papers attracted completed research papers, work-in-progress papers on ongoing research (including doctoral papers), project and case descriptions, as well as workshop and panel proposals. The submissions were assessed through a double-blind peer-review process, with at least two reviewers per submission, and the acceptance rate was 39%. The conference tracks present advances in the socio-technological domain of the public sphere, demonstrating cutting-edge concepts, methods, and styles of investigation by multiple disciplines. The papers were distributed over the following tracks:

- General E-Government and E-Governance Track
- General E-Democracy and eParticipation Track
- AI, Data Analytics, and Automated Decision Making Track
- Smart Cities (Government, Communities and Regions) Track
- Social Media Track
- Social Innovation Track
- Open Data: Social and Technical Aspects Track
- Digital Society Track
- Cybersecurity Track
- Legal Informatics Track
- Practitioners' Track

Among the full research paper submissions, 30 papers (empirical and conceptual) from the general E-Government and E-Governance track, as well as the tracks on Smart Cities, AI, and Open Data were accepted for this year's Springer LNCS EGOV proceedings (vol. 12219), whereas another 11 papers of completed research papers from the General ePart Track, as well as the tracks on Social Media, Legal Informatics, Digital Society, and Social Innovation, went into the LNCS ePart proceedings (vol. 12220). The papers included in this volume have been clustered under the following headings:

- E-Government Foundations
- E-Government Services and Open Government
- Open Data: Social and Technical Aspects
- AI, Data Analytics, and Automated Decision Making
- Smart Cities

As in the previous years and per the recommendation of the Paper Awards Committee under the leadership of Noella Edelmann, Danube University Krems, Austria, and Evangelos Kalampokis from the University of Macedonia, Greece, the IFIP EGOV-CeDEM-ePart 2020 Conference Organizing Committee grants outstanding paper awards in three distinct categories:

- The most interdisciplinary and innovative research contribution
- The most compelling critical research reflection
- The most promising practical concept

The winners in each category were announced during an awards ceremony held at the conference.

Many people make large events like this conference happen. We thank the members of the Program Committee and the additional reviewers for their great efforts in reviewing the submitted papers. We would like to express our gratitude to Ida Lindgren, Ulf Melin, and the team from Linköping University (LiU) for hosting the conference. Although disappointed from not being able to host it locally, they made the conference a success. LiU conducts world-leading, boundary-crossing research in fields that include materials science, IT, and hearing. In the same spirit, the university offers many innovative educational programs, frequently with a clear professional focus and leading to qualification as, for example, doctors, teachers, economists, and engineers. LiU was granted university status in 1975 and today has 32,000 students and 4,000 employees. The students are among the most desirable in the labor market, and international rankings consistently place LiU as a leading global university. The EGOV 2020 conference was hosted by the Division of Information Systems and Digitalization, at the Department of Management and Engineering, which is one of the most visible digital government research constellations in Europe and well-known for extensive research collaborations with a focus on public sector organizations and their digitalization in Sweden and beyond. We are looking forward having our conference in Linköping in the near future and having the opportunity to visit this excellent research group.

September 2020

Gabriela Viale Pereira
Marijn Janssen
Habin Lee
Ida Lindgren
Manuel Pedro Rodríguez Bolívar
Hans Jochen Scholl
Anneke Zuiderwijk

Organization

Conference Lead Organizer

Marijn Janssen — Delft University of Technology, The Netherlands

General E-Government and E-Governance Track

Gabriela Viale Pereira — Danube University Krems, Austria
Ida Lindgren — Linköping University, Sweden
Hans Jochen Scholl — University of Washington, USA

General E-Democracy and eParticipation Track

Noella Edelmann — Danube University Krems, Austria
Peter Parycek — Fraunhofer Fokus, Germany, and Danube-University Krems, Austria
Robert Krimmer — Tallinn University of Technology, Estonia

Smart Cities (Government, Communities and Regions) Track

Manuel Pedro Rodríguez Bolívar — University of Granada, Spain
Karin Axelsson — Linköping University, Sweden
Nuno Lopes — DTx: Digital Transformation Colab, Portugal

AI, Data Analytics, and Automated Decision Making Track

Habin Lee — Brunel University London, UK
Euripidis Loukis — University of the Aegean, Greece
Evangelos Kalampokis — University of Macedonia, Greece

Social Media Track

Sarah Hoffmann — University of Agder, Norway
Marius Rohde Johannessen — University of South-Eastern Norway, Norway
Panos Panagiotopoulos — Queen Mary University of London, UK

Social Innovation Track

Csaba Csaki — Corvinus Business School, Hungary
Gianluca Misuraca — European Commission, Joint Research Centre, Spain
Marijn Janssen — Delft University of Technology, The Netherlands

Open Data: Social and Technical Aspects Track

Anneke Zuiderwijk	Delft University of Technology, The Netherlands
Ramon Gil-Garcia	University at Albany, USA
Efthimios Tambouris	University of Macedonia, Greece

Digital Society

Thomas Lampoltshammer	Danube University Krems, Austria
Christian Østergaard Madsen	IT University of Copenhagen, Denmark
Katarina L. Gidlund	Mid Sweden University, Sweden

Cybersecurity Track

Natalia Kadenko	Delft University of Technology, The Netherlands
Marijn Janssen	Delft University of Technology, The Netherlands

Legal Informatics Track

Peter Parycek	Fraunhofer Fokus, Germany
Anna-Sophie Novak	Danube University Krems, Austria

Practitioners' Track

Francesco Mureddu	The Lisbon Council, Belgium
Peter Reichstädter	Austrian Parliament, Austria
Francesco Molinari	Politecnico di Milano, Italy
Morten Meyerhoff Nielsen	United Nations University, Portugal

Chair of Outstanding Papers Awards

Noella Edelmann	Danube University Krems, Austria
Evangelos Kalampokis	University of Macedonia, Greece

PhD Colloquium Chairs

Gabriela Viale Pereira	Danube University Krems, Austria
J. Ramon Gil-Garcia	University at Albany, SUNY, USA
Ida Lindgren	Linköping University, Sweden

Program Committee

Suha Alawadhi	Kuwait University, Kuwait
Karin Ahlin	Mid Sweden University, Sweden
Valerie Albrecht	Danube University Krems, Austria

Laura Alcaide-Muñoz	University of Granada, Spain
Karin Axelsson	Linköping University, Sweden
Ana Alice Baptista	University of Minho, Portugal
Flavia Bernardini	Universidade Federal Fluminense, Brazil
Lasse Berntzen	University of South-Eastern Norway, Norway
Radomir Bolgov	Saint Petersburg State University, Russia
Walter Castelnovo	University of Insubria, Italy
Alexopoulos Charalampos	University of the Aegean, Greece
Youngseok Choi	University of Southampton, UK
Wichian Chutimaskul	King Mongkut's University of Technology Thonburi, Thailand
Antoine Clarinval	Université de Namur, Belgium
Andreiwid Sheffer Corrêa	Federal Institute of Sao Paulo, Brazil
J. Ignacio Criado	Universidad Autónoma de Madrid, Spain
Joep Crompvoets	KU Leuven, Belgium
Jonathan Crusoe	Linköpings Universitet, Sweden
Frank Danielsen	University of Agder, Norway
Lieselot Danneels	KU Leuven, Belgium
Athanasios Deligiannis	International Hellenic University, Greece
Edna Dias Canedo	Universidade de Brasília, Brazil
Bettina Distel	Universität Münster, Germany
Noella Edelmann	Danube University Krems, Austria
Margarita Fourer	Danube University Krems, Austria
Luz Maria Garcia	Universidad de la Sierra Sur, Mexico
Elisabeth Gebka	University of Namur, Belgium
J. Ramon Gil-Garcia	University at Albany, USA
Malin Granath	Linköping University, Sweden
Stefanos Gritzalis	University of Piraeus, Greece
Christine Große	Mid Sweden University, Sweden
Martijn Hartog	Delft University of Technology, The Netherlands
Marcia Hino	FGV/EAESP, Brazil
Roumiana Ilieva	Technical University of Sofia, Bulgaria
Marijn Janssen	Delft University of Technology, The Netherlands
Marius Rohde Johannessen	University of South-Eastern Norway, Norway
Gustaf Juell-Skielse	Stockholm University, Sweden
Yury Kabanov	National Research University, Russia
Natalia Kadenko	Delft University of Technology, The Netherlands
Evangelos Kalampokis	CERTH, Greece
Eleni Kanellou	NTUA, Greece
Evika Karamagioli	Université Paris 8, France
Areti Karamanou	University of Macedonia, Greece
Ilka Kawashita	University of Minho, Portugal
Jongwoo Kim	Hanyang University, South Korea
Fabian Kirstein	Fraunhofer Institute, Germany
Thomas Lampoltshammer	Danube University Krems, Austria
Habin Lee	Brunel University, UK

Hong Joo Lee	The Catholic University of Korea, South Korea
Johan Linåker	Lund University, Sweden
Ida Lindgren	Linköping University, Sweden
Nuno Lopes	DTx: Digital Transformation Colab, Portugal
Euripidis Loukis	University of the Aegean, Greece
Rui Pedro Lourenço	INESC Coimbra, Portugal
Nikolaos Loutas	European Commission, Belgium
Edimara Luciano	Pontifical Catholic University of Rio Grande do Sul, Brazil
Luis F. Luna-Reyes	University at Albany, SUNY, USA
Bjorn Lundell	University of Skövde, Sweden
Ahmad Luthfi	Delft University of Technology, The Netherlands
Johan Magnusson	University of Gothenburg, Sweden
Ricardo Matheus	Delft University of Technology, The Netherlands
Keegan Mcbride	Tallinn University of Technology, Estonia
John McNutt	University of Delaware, USA
Rony Medaglia	Copenhagen Business School, Denmark
Fritz Meiners	Fraunhofer Institute, Germany
Ulf Melin	Linkoping University, Sweden
Tobias Mettler	University of Lausanne, Switzerland
Gianluca Misuraca	European Commission, Belgium
Michael Möstl	Donau-Universität Krems, Austria
Alessia Caterina Neuroni	Bern University of Applied Sciences, Switzerland
Mille Nielsen	IT University of Copenhagen, Denmark
Anastasija Nikiforova	University of Latvia, Latvia
Anna-Sophie Novak	Danube University Krems, Austria
Panos Panagiotopoulos	Queen Mary University of London, UK
Darcy Parks	Linköping University, Sweden
Sergio Picazo-Vela	Universidad de las Americas Puebla, Mexico
Luiz Pereira Pinheiro Junior	Universidade Positivo, Brazil
Kerley Pires	United Nations University, Portugal
Vigan Raca	Independent
Nicolau Reinhard	University of São Paulo, Brazil
Taiane Ritta Coelho	Federal University of Parana, Brazil
Manuel Pedro Rodríguez Bolívar	University of Granada, Spain
Alexander Ronzhyn	University of Koblenz-Landau, Germany
Athanasia Routzouni	University of the Aegean, Greece
Boriana Rukanova	Delft University of Technology, The Netherlands
Per Runeson	Lund University, Sweden
Rodrigo Sandoval-Almazan	Universidad Autonoma del Estado de Mexico, Mexico
Hans J Scholl	University of Washington, USA
Hendrik Scholta	University of Munster, Germany
Judith Schossböck	Danube University Krems, Austria
Luiza Schuch de Azambuja	Tallinn University of Technology, Estonia
Johanna Sefyrin	Linköping University, Sweden

Tobias Siebenlist	Heinrich Heine University Düsseldorf, Germany
Anthony Simonofski	KU Leuven, Belgium
Fredrik Söderström	Linköpings Universitet, Sweden
Karin Steiner	Danube University Krems, Austria
Leif Sundberg	Mid Sweden University, Sweden
Iryna Susha	Örebro University, Sweden
Proscovia Svärd	Mid Sweden University, Sweden
Efthimios Tambouris	University of Macedonia, Greece
Luca Tangi	Politecnico di Milano, Italy
Konstantinos Tarabanis	University of Macedonia, Greece
Lörinc Thurnay	Danube University Krems, Austria
Jolien Ubacht	Delft University of Technology, The Netherlands
Mathias Van Compernolle	Ghent University, Belgium
Marco Velicogna	IRSIG-CNR, Italy
Gabriela Viale Pereira	Danube University Krems, Austria
Shefali Virkar	Danube University Krems, Austria
Frederika Welle Donker	Knowledge Centre Open Data, The Netherlands
Guilherme Wiedenhöft	Federal University of Rio Grande, Brazil
Elin Wihlborg	Linkoping University, Sweden
Maija Ylinen	Tampere University of Technology, Finland
Chien-Chih Yu	National ChengChi University, China
Thomas Zefferer	A-SIT Plus GmbH, Austria
Anneke Zuiderwijk	Delft University of Technology, The Netherlands

Additional Reviewers

Alizée Francey
Auriane Marmier
Colin van Noordt
Dimitris Zeginis
Gianluigi Viscusi
Jaewon Choi
Junyeong Lee
Karl Kristian Larsson

Mariana Gustafsson
Ruth Angelie Cruz
Sangwook Ha
Silvia Lips
Yannis Charalabidis
Yingying Gao
Yu-lun Liu

Contents

Open Data: Social and Technical Aspects

AI, Data Analytics, and Automated Decision Making

Smart Cities

E-Government Foundations

Between Overexploitation and Underexploitation of Digital Opportunities – A Case Study with Focus on Affordances and Constraints

Göran Goldkuhl[1,2]([✉]) [iD]

[1] Department of Management Engineering, Linköping University, Linköping, Sweden
goran.goldkuhl@liu.se
[2] Department of Informatics Media, Uppsala University, Uppsala, Sweden

Abstract. Several policies for e-government, both on national and supranational levels, express visions and claims for more advanced exploitation of digital opportunities. The paper contributes through a problematization of the idea of utilizing digital opportunities and a conceptualization of this into the polarity of overexploitation vs. underexploitation of digital opportunities. It is based on a qualitative and diagnostic case study on the digitalization of medical certificates and theoretically informed by affordance theory and activity theory. Digital arrangements in the case study are investigated and different types of digital affordances and constraints are revealed. There are examples of surplus of affordances (i.e. overexploitation), lack of affordances and affordances with embedded constraints (i.e. underexploitation), and useful affordances (i.e. adequate exploitation). The application of the affordance and constraint concepts is, in the paper, done through a two-step staging: 1) General characteristics of digital technology give affordances for design. 2) The resulting digital artifacts will have different properties and these properties give affordances but also constraints for use. The resulting conceptualizations are discussed in relation to normative, regulative and other institutional aspects concerning digitalization in the public sector. This is conceptualized in a graphical model describing policy and other pre-conditions, designed digital artifacts, and workpractice effects.

Keywords: E-government · Affordance · Constraint · Policy · Digital opportunity

1 Introduction

There is a strong claim, among both practitioners and scholars, for increased exploitation of digital opportunities in public administration. In policy planning for e-government development, there exist visions and claims for better utilization of opportunities that digital technology offers. This can be seen in policy documents both on national and supranational levels. There exist several EU policy documents that argue for more advanced

G. Viale Pereira et al. (Eds.): EGOV 2020, LNCS 12219, pp. 3–14, 2020.
https://doi.org/10.1007/978-3-030-57599-1_1

exploitation of digital opportunities such as the Tallinn Declaration that states "we are yet to seize the full potential of the digital transformation in our administrations as well as at the EU level" [9]. Another policy document argues for "embracing creative disruption from technology ... packaged in new digital government offerings" [7] as an important design principle for overcoming barriers of innovation in public administration. One policy example on the national level is the national agenda for digitalization in the public sector of Sweden. There is an enounced objective to reach e-government of world-class: "Sweden should be best in the world at using the opportunities of digitalization." [36]. This objective, originally formulated in 2011, has recurrently been expressed in several policy reports; e.g. [37]. There is a clear competitive reasoning behind this vision; to be one of the best. The recurring benchmarks of e-government maturity [1] seem to be a driver for this kind of thinking. There exist international benchmarks such as the United Nation's e-Government Development Index [39] and the European Commission's eGovernment Benchmark [8].

In the scholarly literature, there exist several proposals for stage models [e.g. 22, 25, 26] of egov evolution. These models describe stages of different maturity layers, where more advanced layers are presumed to be better. However, as noted [4], "these stages ... do in fact mainly assume that the level of technological sophistication can be an indicator of success".

This paper addresses this issue of exploitation of digital opportunities in e-government. The main inquiry question is: *In what ways are digital opportunities utilized?* This is based on a knowledge interest in relationships between digital policies and digital realizations. This is an area that is considered as under-researched [4, 21]. The paper contributes to this discourse through a problematization of the idea of utilizing digital opportunities and a conceptualization of this into the polarity of overexploitation vs. underexploitation of digital opportunities. It does so, empirically informed by a qualitative and diagnostic case study on the digitalization of medical certificates and theoretically informed by affordance theory [11] and activity theory [24, 43].

2   Research Approach

This presented research is a "slice" of a larger research endeavor on the governance of multi-organizational digital artifacts in public administration. A research team has studied the relations between different policies and the realization and use of digital artifacts. Several qualitative case studies have been conducted. In the first stage of the research, eight case studies were conducted in parallel. In a later stage of research, another case study was performed based on results from the previous empirical studies. The case studies were based on a general research interest in relations and possible tensions between a policy level and the actual artifact level [14]. The focus was on complex multi-organizational digital artifacts in the public sector [18].

The presented research is based on the last case study. Several purposes guided this specific case study on the digitalization of medical certificates. It aimed at 1) an evaluation of the digitalization of medical certificates (primary target group: those responsible for these digital artifacts), 2) an application and assessment of a multi-dimensional evaluation approach with digital medical certificates as the evaluation object (target groups:

scholars and practitioners interested in methods for evaluation of digital artifacts), and 3) abstracted (case study-based) knowledge on complex multi-organizational digital artifacts in the public sector (target groups: scholars and practitioners interested in policies and the realization of digital artifacts in the public sector). The sliced research presented in this paper is part of the third purpose.

The case study research was conducted through a continual alternation between 1) an empirical and diagnostic inquiry of digital medical certificates and 2) theorizing with qualitative data analysis, reflection, and abstraction [13, 41]. In the empirical part, we mainly used the following methods for collection/generation of data: Interviewing and workshops with knowledgeable practitioners, document studies, and inspections and explorations of the focused digital artifacts [15, 31]. In these studies of digital artifacts, we acted as potential users and collected empirical data concerning digital functionality, interactivity, and information. Screenshots were generated and also annotated with comments on critical concerns. We used a multi-dimensional evaluation approach that guided an alternating focus on dimensions such as stakeholders, digital work processes, digital functionality, digitalized information, digital interaction, interoperability in digital landscapes, goals and values, and laws and regulations [18]. The generation and analysis of data were initially performed in an inductive manner close to the ideals of grounded theory [3]. We aimed at discovery of new knowledge rather than driven by certain hypotheses. This quest for discovery and novel knowledge comprised an open-minded approach in data generation (in order to *see new things*) and data analysis (in order to *create a new understanding*) through interpretation and abstraction leading to new categories [17].

However, the generation and analysis data were not conducted by the researchers as "blank slates". The evaluation approach with its different dimensions and concepts guided the generation and analysis of data. This means that this type of pre-understanding had an influence on the knowledge development process [17]. Later in the data analysis and abstraction process, new categories and conjectures emerged. For this presented slice of research, the inquiry question was formulated: *In what ways are digital opportunities utilized?* The formulation of this inquiry question was based on 1) findings and insights from the case study and 2) our general knowledge interest on the potential influence from policies with an aim to "maximize" the utilization of digital opportunities (see discussion in Sect. 1). The formulation of this inquiry question was guided by an identified problematic situation in the empirical practice and not by spotting gaps in the literature [3, 6, 40]. Based on these emergent insights and the formulated inquiry question, the analysis turned from an inductive to an abductive manner [16, 38, 40]. Appropriate theoretical assistance was sought for. Through previous acquaintance with affordance theory [12], this theory was found suitable as a theoretical lens for further analysis. Further theorizing was conducted partially as a problematization of the dictum of maximizing the utilization of digital opportunities. "The more – the better" can be challenged. Affordance theory was found useful for this further theorizing. Through a conceptual analysis of affordance theory, a need was found to complement this through the addition of views from activity theory.

3 Theoretical Lens: Affordance Theory and Activity Theory

Affordance theory was originally formulated by Gibson [11]. It is considered as an ecological theory of perception. The main idea is that the environment of humans (and other species) is perceived in terms of *what it affords for action*. This means that affordances are properties of the environment in relation to actors. They are not just physical properties of things. The difference between affordances and pure physical properties is described by Gibson [11, p 127]. A floor is stand-on-able, walk-on-able and run-over-able when recognizing what it affords. These affordances are of course based on certain physical properties (e.g. the floor being horizontal, flat, extended and rigid).

However, affordances should not be seen as subjective or mental constructs as Gibson emphasizes. The affordances are in the external objects – but these properties are relational properties, i.e. they exist in relation to an observer/actor. "These positive and negative affordances are properties of things taken with reference to an observer but not properties of the experiences of the observer" [11, p 137].

Affordance theory has attracted interest in information systems research. This comprises both issues of human-computer interaction [e.g. 12, 19, 20, 30, 32] and broader IS issues [e.g. 20, 22, 27, 35]. The general view of affordances in digital technology is that *digitalized artifacts have properties that are relational to their users* and that these properties *provide* (= afford) *action possibilities to the user*. Affordances need to be both *informative* (visible and understandable) and *operational* (accessible and executable) to the user; see [12, 19]. This paper leans more to the HCI tradition [12, 19, 30] of employment of the affordance notion than the broader IS orientation. This follows from the close empirical investigation of the digital artifacts' functionality and interactivity as mentioned in Sect. 2 above [15, 31].

According to Gibson [11], there exist also negative affordances. These are properties in the environment that can be seen as aggravating or preventing actions. To consider an affordance as negative can, however, be seen as confusing. This terminological problem has been discussed by [42, 45]. Volkoff and Strong [42] express this conceptual and terminological issue in the following way: "A different question relates to whether affordances can be both enabling and constraining, or whether affordances are only enabling, and constraints are different." Zammuto et al. [45 p 752] argue for an inclusive notion of affordance covering both positive and constraining functions: "An affordance perspective recognizes how the materiality of an object favors, shapes, or invites, and at the same time constrains, a set of specific uses." A way to dig deeper into this conceptual/terminological controversy is to turn to etymology. The etymological meaning of the word "afford", coming from the Middle English word "aforth", is "to put forth, contribute; further, advance" (Online Etymology). A lexical definition of "further" is "to help the progress of something so that it is more likely to be successful" (MacMillan Dictionary). Based on these etymological and lexical definitions, a "negative affordance" seems to be close to a self-contradiction. Conceptually, there is thus a need for a theoretical complement to affordance theory.

Activity theory can contribute to such distinctions through its concept of mediated action [43]. Within this theoretical tradition, Kuutti [24] emphasizes that "the tool is at the same time both enabling and limiting". This means that tools (like digital artifacts) have properties that afford/enable actions but also properties that constrain and sometimes prevent actions. All such artifact properties have the function of mediating/directing actions in certain ways. The key theoretical concept of affordance is thus here complemented with the concepts of constraint and prevention. These different concepts are used, and thus illustrated, in the theoretical reasoning on findings from the performed case study (Sect. 5 below).

4   Case Study Description: Digitalization of Medical Certificates

The case study covers digital artifacts related to doctors' issuing of medical certificates and the transfer of those certificates to patients, their employers and the Social Insurance Agency (SIA), that manages sickness benefit cases. A medical certificate, issued by a doctor, is needed by citizens/employees to prove a legitimate sickness leave to the employer and to SIA. There exist several related digital artifacts in this digital landscape of medical certificates and sickness management. DigCert is a healthcare system containing digital support for issuing, storage and transfer of certificates. MyCert is a module in the national health portal where each citizen/patient can manage his/her medical certificates. One possibility is to print the certificate for delivery to the employer. There exist several digital artifacts at SIA; one e-service for patients' submission of sickness benefit applications and an internal case handling system for sickness benefits.

Before the digitalization, the medical certificates were issued using paper forms. This form was provided by the Social Insurance Agency to healthcare organizations. The doctor handed over the issued medical certificate to the patient who was responsible to distribute it (or copies) to the employer and to SIA. There are still some doctors that use this old form and procedure.

When investigating the digital solution, we found that were three different ways to transfer the digital medical certificate from healthcare to SIA for their case handling. 1) Since there exist restrictive privacy regulations in Sweden, it was not permitted for healthcare to just distribute the medical certificate to SIA. An explicit consent from the patient was needed. If this was given and then recorded by the doctor in DigCert, the issued medical certificate could be transferred digitally to SIA. 2) Another way to transfer the certificate digitally was by the patient through the use of MyCert. After selecting a specific certificate in the web application, the patient can initiate a digital transfer to SIA. 3) The first two weeks of sick leave are paid by the employer. After this period, the patient/employee needs to apply to SIA for sickness benefits. This can be done digitally by the patient through SIA:s e-service. In this application process, the medical certificate can be digitally retrieved from DigCert and attached to the application.

The case handling process of sickness benefits at SIA is substantially facilitated by receiving the medical certificate in a digital format. This was a strong motivating force in the design of digital solutions. Therefore, these three alternative ways of digital transfer were designed and implemented. However, these digital solutions have given dysfunctional effects. These three digital transfer solutions are built on different communication logics. The first two are based on a push-logic. In these situations, the medical certificates are digitally pushed from the healthcare organization to SIA before any sickness benefits application is submitted. If the patient/employee gets well during the first two weeks, there is no need to submit any benefits application to SIA. In these situations, SIA receives medical certificates that have no function for their case handling. However, they cannot just throw them away. According to regulations, SIA must open a case and try to reach the health insured/patient and ask for a sickness benefits application. This is a totally unnecessary administration that costs time and money. The third situation builds on a pull-logic. The digital medical certificate is submitted together with a sickness benefits application.

One important element in the digitalization of medical certificates was the introduction of a decision support in the DigCert's digital service for doctors issuing of certificates. This is a health-insurance decision support containing a repository of medical diagnoses and recommended periods of sick leave for each diagnosis. These standards guide the doctor to select an appropriate sickness leave period. If the doctor issues a period that deviates from the standard period, the doctor is prompted by the digital service to motivate such a deviation.

5   Findings and Discussion

5.1   Overexploitation vs. Underexploitation of Digital Opportunities

In the analysis of this case, it was discovered that some parts of the digital artifacts could be characterized as *overexploitation* of digital opportunities, while others could be seen as *underexploitation* of such opportunities. These categories were generated through a cross-data analysis, which is an analysis tactic of grounded theory [3]. Through a "constant comparison" of different data items and generated categories looking for similarities and differences, new categories can emerge. What is here called overexploited and underexploited digital opportunities are ascribed features of digital artifacts. They are characterized as such in relation to (policy) expectations on digital artifacts. The artifact features were thus seen in relation to pre-conditional policy formulations, such as visions for "world-class" utilization of digital opportunities as expressed in national digital agendas [36, 37]. However, these characterizations were also made through an assessment of the effects of the artifact features. The identification of dysfunctional effects influenced the way these features were conceived of and thus that they were characterized as a deviation from an appropriate exploitation of digital opportunities. A contextual analysis was thus necessary to formulate these categories of overexploited and underexploited digital opportunities, i.e. looking "backward" to policy pre-conditions and "forward" to effects in the digitalized workpractice.

Overexploitation means that a quest to exploit digital opportunities can sometimes be pushed too far. One such example is the design of three variants of digital transfer processes of the medical certificate from healthcare to the Social Insurance Agency. This means identifying opportunities with digital technologies and then exaggerating the use of such opportunities. Three alternative ways of transfer were designed to ensure that SIA receives the medical certificate in a digital format. As described above (in the case study description, Sect. 4), these alternative transfer ways had dysfunctional effects.

The case shows several examples of the contrary, i.e. what is here called digital underexploitation. A retained form thinking is one such example. The earlier paper form for medical certificates has heavily influenced the interaction design of a digital certificate form. This has meant a lack of communicative renewal. The digital form for issuing a medical certificate is lacking in precision and clarity (e.g. insufficient explanations, contradictions, unnecessary linguistic variation, work-language imperfections). Another example of such a digital underexploitation is that digital communication has been optimized to one stakeholder/recipient (SIA). There is a lack of adaptation of communication to other recipients (the patient and the employer). This comprises 1) information content not adapted (through information deficiencies and information surpluses) to different recipients and 2) a lack of seamless digital transfer to employers.

The case shows also examples of *adequate exploitation of digital opportunities*. One such example is the introduction of the health-insurance decision support with standardized sickness leave periods. The designers have here utilized the possibility to embed a digital repository into the issuing service of medical certificates. This decision support/repository can be continually updated with changed health-insurance considerations and it is well integrated into the certificate service with a digital retrieval function that is easy for the doctors to manage.

5.2 Affordances, Constraints and Other Pre-conditions for Design and Use

Digital technology affords generally different opportunities, such as programmability and digitization of information with efficient capture, storage, processing, transfer and presentation of such information [44]. These features give *affordances for design*. However, the design of digital artifacts in workpractices (such as handling of medical certificates) is influenced by many other circumstances. There are digital policies with appeals to more fully exploit digital opportunities. There are also specific needs and different circumstances in the actual workpractice that influence the design (issues concerning healthcare, employment, and health-insurance). The workpractice situation of medical certificates management frames the design of digital artifacts. The main requirements for the digital design are obtained from conceptions of objectives, problems, and work-processes in these workpractices. The substance for the digital design (as values, stakeholder roles, work-language, procedures) emanates from the related practices of healthcare and health-insurance. One important concern in this case (as in most other egov areas) is the regulative background of extant legislation [2, 23]. It is said that there exist more than Swedish 70 laws/statutes that have relevance for medical certificates. Digital design is thus a choice of what kind of digital opportunities to utilize [10].

The design outcome will be an amalgamation of these different affordances, constraints and other pre-conditions (Fig. 1). The designed digital artifacts (as a networked digital arrangement) with different properties give *affordances for use in workpractice contexts*. Some of the characteristics of the designed digital artifacts do, however, not provide any desired action possibilities. In this actual case there exist:

1. A surplus of affordances, as three ways of digital transfer of certificates that give dysfunctional effects such as unnecessary excess work.
2. Affordances with embedded constraints, as unclear instructions in the certificate form that entail risks for incomplete or deficient medical certificates.
3. A lack of affordances, as no adaptation to employers that may generate extra work for patients and also intrude patient/employee privacy.

4. Useful affordances, as the use of the health-insurance decision support for guidance to set adequate sick leave periods.

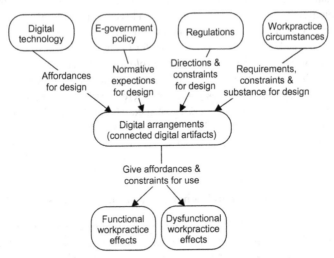

Fig. 1. Pre-conditions for digital design and digital arrangements as pre-conditions for workpractice use and effects.

A main formulated category, based on this case study, is *degree of digital exploitation*. This is an attributive construct as being a property class of digital arrangements. The degree of digital exploitation, as described above, varies between overexploited digital opportunity (1), adequately exploited digital opportunity (4), and underexploited digital opportunity (2, 3). What has been clear through this case study is the necessity to analyze these kinds of phenomena relationally; i.e. both to antecedents and to consequences. The digital arrangement with its properties (affordances, constraints, and lack of affordances) are *pre-conditions* for digital use in workpractices. They are also "*post-conditions*"; in this case, results of design practices. Obviously, there are important differences between the separate design practices leading to the different kinds of digital properties. In (1) and (4), an *exploitive strategy* has been applied implying a design where digital opportunities were utilized to create something novel in the practices of medical certificate management. In (1), the design has given full priority to the objective to have medical certificates in digital format while neglecting other consequences. Three different ways were designed in order to ensure medical certificates in digital format. The other two (2, 3) are results from a *conversion strategy*, where features of previous paper-based practices are sustained.

The application of the affordance concept is, in this analysis, done through a two-step staging: 1) General characteristics of digital technology give *affordances for design*. Different digital options of a general character can be utilized in designing and such digital opportunities can be utilized in different ways and degrees. The implemented egov artifacts for use are results of diverse design practices where digital opportunities have been exploited differently. 2) The resulting digital artifacts will have different properties and these properties give *affordances but also constraints for use.* Digital properties will not only enable actions but they also direct, constrain and prevent different actions following the synthesized view of affordance theory and activity theory (Sect. 3). Such digital affordances and constraints will thus influence the actions of different users/stakeholders.

The model in Fig. 1 is influenced by the policy/design/effect (PDE) model [14]. The PDE model describes efficacy linkages from policy expectations (P) to the designing activities leading to designed artifacts (D) and further to the use of these artifacts and subsequent effects (E). In the new model (Fig. 1), an expansion has been made to include other aspects than only a policy influence as in the original model. Policy was already, in the PDE model [14], given a broad interpretation covering policy statements, values and regulations (as legally codified values). However, in this new and enhanced model other aspects are included as influencing design processes: General properties of digital technology that give affordances for design and the specific subject matter of addressed workpractices that frames the design process. This enhanced model could still be called PDE model, but with another elucidation: "Pre-conditions/Design/Effects".

Related thinking about egov evolution can be found in the Technology Enactment Model [10] and variants/modifications of this [5, 28]. The institutional character of 1) governmental activities and 2) the use of egov artifacts is emphasized in these models. This applies also to the enhanced PDE model. There are, however, some important differences that need to be noted. In Technology Enactment Model, there is a differentiation between objective technology and enacted technology. Enacted technology is considered as the, by its users, appropriated digital artifact; i.e. what it is actually used for, following the theoretical views from [33]. Objective technology has, unfortunately, fluid meanings in the Technology Enactment Model. In some places, it seems to mean general characteristics of information technology and sometimes an implemented digital artifact as such. In the PDE model, there is an important difference between 1) digital technology with general characteristics giving affordances for digital design and 2) specific digital artifacts. "Technology" is never used to mean specific digital artifacts as can be the case in [10, 33]. An implemented digital artifact gives affordances and constraints for use. How these affordances and constraints are utilized, followed and appropriated by a user corresponds to "enacted technology" in the Technology Enactment Model. In the PDE model, institutional elements are not put in one "box". There are different institutional elements in the listed pre-conditions. "Egov policy" contains normative expectations from policy-makers. "Regulations" cover all kinds of laws and statutes that pertain to the addressed workpractices. These are two pivotal parts of institutions following [35]. "Workpractice circumstances" include other institutional elements that govern the kinds of workpractices addressed. There will be relational elements (such as stakeholder roles), linguistic elements (concepts and vocabulary), performative elements (established processes and procedures), and also normative elements (specific workpractice values). Such institutional elements may, through design processes, be inscribed in the digital artifacts and thus substantially affect its use and give practice impacts. The digital artifacts will be *mediators of the institutional pre-conditions* through its use.

6 Conclusion

This paper has contributed a conceptualization of the utilization of digital opportunities in e-government through the polarity of overexploitation vs. underexploitation. The conceptual development was based on a theoretical lens of affordances and constraints. This has been further theorized through the enhancement of a conceptual model (PDE) of Preconditions for design, Designed digital artifacts, and Effects that arise from their uses. Besides these obvious conceptual contributions that could influence further empirical and theoretical studies, the conducted inquiry demonstrates a way to research e-government with the following traits: a qualitative case study with a combination of inductive investigation aiming for discovery, evaluation of findings and use of a synthesized theoretical lens for conceptual development. This proposed case study approach involves also an alternation between three different foci in empirical inquiry, data analysis, and conceptualization: 1) different features of designed and used digital arrangements (i.e. connected digital artifacts), 2) a "backward" analysis revealing the rationale for design and other kinds of pre-conditions for design, and 3) a forward analysis clarifying both functional and dysfunctional effects from the use of digital arrangements. See Fig. 1 for illustration; start with the center (1) and move backward to pre-conditions for design (2) and forward to effects from use (3).

Based on this inquiry the following advice can be given to practice: A challenge in this context is to achieve a balanced digital exploitation where you do not overexploit or underexploit the digital opportunities. The dictum should be: *Exploit digital opportunities in a balanced way to reach real improvements in workpractices.* An evaluation of how digital opportunities are utilized should not stop until an assessment of effects on workpractices and stakeholders is completed.

Acknowledgments. The empirical and theoretical work presented in this paper has benefited from close cooperation with my research colleague Annie Röstlinger. I am also grateful to informants from the public agencies for providing good empirical access. Parts of this research work has been financially supported by the Swedish Governmental Agency for Innovation Systems (VINNOVA).

References

1. Berntzen, L., Olsen, M.G.: Benchmarking e-government. a comparative review of three international benchmarking studies. In: Third International Conference on Digital Society. IEEE (2009)
2. Contini, F., Cordella, A.: Assembling law and technology in the public sector: the case of e-justice reforms. In: Proceedings Digital Government Research 2015, pp. 124–132, ACM (2015)
3. Corbin, J., Strauss, A.: Basics of qualitative research. Techniques and procedures for developing Grounded Theory, 3rd edn, Sage, Thousand Oaks (2008)
4. Cordella, A.: E-government success: how to account for ICT, administrative rationalization, and institutional change. In: Gil-Garcia, R. (eds.) E-Government Success Factors and Measure, IGI, Hershey (2013)
5. Cordella, A., Iannacci, F.: Information systems in the public sector: the e-Government enactment framework. J. Strategic. Inf. Syst. **19**, 52–66 (2010)

6. Dewey, J.: Logic: The Theory of Inquiry. Henry Holt, New York (1938)
7. EC: Powering European public sector innovation: Towards a new architecture, European Commission (2013)
8. EC: eGovernment Benchmark 2018, European Commission (2018)
9. EU: Tallinn Declaration on eGovernment; European Union (2017)
10. Fountain, J.: Building the Virtual State. Information Technology and Institutional Change. Brooking Institution Press, Washington (2001)
11. Gibson, J.: The Ecological Approach to Visual Perception. Houghton Mifflin, Boston (1979)
12. Goldkuhl, G.: Actability theory meets affordance theory: clarifying HCI in IT usage situations. In: Proceedings of ECIS-2008, Galway (2008)
13. Goldkuhl, G.: The research practice of practice research: theorizing and situational inquiry. Syst. Signs Actions 5(1), 7–29 (2011)
14. Goldkuhl, G.: From policy to design and effects: a framework for e-government research. In: The 9th Scandinavian Workshop on E-Government, Copenhagen (2012)
15. Goldkuhl, G.: The generation of qualitative data in information systems research: the diversity of empirical research methods. Communications of AIS 44, Article 28 (2019)
16. Goldkuhl, G., Cronholm, S.: Adding theoretical grounding to grounded theory – towards Multi-grounded theory. Int. J. Qual. Methods 9(2), 187–205 (2010)
17. Goldkuhl, G., Cronholm, S.: Grounded theory in information systems research – from themes in IS discourse to possible developments. In: Proceedings ICIS-2019, Munich (2019)
18. Goldkuhl, G., Röstlinger, A.: Governance of shared digital artifacts in the public sector: a multi-dimensional approach. In: The 15th Scandinavian Workshop on E-Government, Copenhagen (2018)
19. Hartson, R.: Cognitive, physical, sensory, and functional affordances in interaction design. Behav. Inform. Technol. 22(5), 315–338 (2003)
20. Hutchby, I.: Conversation and Technology. From the Telephone to the Internet. Polity, Cambridge (2001)
21. Jæger, B., Löfgren, K.: The history of the future: changes in Danish e-government strategies 1994–2010. Inf. Polity 15, 253–269 (2010)
22. Kim, D.-Y., Grant, G.: E-government maturity model using the capability maturity model integration. J. Syst. Inf. Technol. 12(3), 230–244 (2010)
23. Knackstedt, R., Eggert, M., Heddier, M., Chasin, F., Becker, J.: The relationship of IS and law – the perspective of and implications for IS research. In: ECIS-2013 Proceedings, Utrecht (2013)
24. Kuutti, K.: Activity theory as a potential framework for human-computer interaction research. In: Nardi, B.A. (ed.) Context and consciousness. Activity theory and human-computer interaction, MIT Press, Cambridge (1996)
25. Layne, K., Lee, J.: Developing fully functional E-government: a four-stage model. Govern. Inf. Q. 18(2), 122–136 (2001)
26. Lee, J.: 10 year retrospect on stage models of e-Government: a qualitative meta-synthesis. Govern. Inf. Q. 27, 220–230 (2010)
27. Leonardi, P.: When flexible routines meet flexible technologies: affordance, constraint, and the imbrication of human and material agencies. MIS Q. 35(1), 147–167 (2011)
28. Luna-Reyez, L., Gil-Garcia, R.: Digital government transformation and internet portals: the co-evolution of technology, organizations, and institutions. Govern. Inf. Q. 31, 545–555 (2014)
29. Markus, L., Silver, M.: A foundation for the study of IT effects: a new look at DeSanctis and Poole's concepts of structural features and spirit. J. AIS 9(10/11), 609–632 (2008)
30. McGrenere, J., Ho, W.: Affordances: clarifying and evolving a concept. In: Proceedings of Graphics Interface, Montreal (2000)
31. Nielsen, J.: Usability Engineering. Academic Press, San Diego (1993)

32. Norman, D.: The Psychology of Everyday Things. Basic Books, New York (1988)
33. Orlikowski, W.: The duality of technology: Rethinking the concept of technology in organizations. Organ. Sci. **3**(3), 398–429 (1992)
34. Pozzi, G., Pigni, F., Vitari, C.: Affordance theory in the IS discipline: a review and synthesis of the literature. In: AMCIS-2014 Proceedings (2014)
35. Scott, W.: Institutions and Organizations, 4th edn. SAGE, Thousand Oaks (2014)
36. Swedish Government: It i människans tjänst – en digital agenda för Sverige, Report N2011.12, Government Offices of Sweden (2011). [in Swedish]
37. Swedish Government: För digitalisering i tiden. Slutbetänkande av Digitaliseringskommissionen, SOU 2016:89, Swedish Governmental Inquiries (2016). [in Swedish]
38. Thornberg, R.: Informed grounded theory. Scand. J. Educ. Res. **56**(3), 243–259 (2012)
39. UN: United Nations E-Government Survey 2018, United Nations (2018)
40. Van Maanen, J., Sørensen, J., Mitchell, T.: The interplay between theory and method. Acad. Manag. Rev. **32**(4), 1145–1154 (2007)
41. VanWynsberghe, R., Khan, S.: Redefining case study. Int. J. Qual. Methods **6**(2), 80–94 (2007)
42. Volkoff, O., Strong, D.: Affordance theory and how to use it in IS research. In: The Routledge Companion to Management Information Systems, pp. 232–245, Routledge (2017)
43. Wertsch, J.: Mind as Action. Oxford University Press, New York (1998)
44. Yoo, Y., Henfridsson, O., Lyytinen, K.: The new organizing logic of digital innovation: an Agenda for information systems research. Inf. Syst. Res. **21**(4), 724–735 (2010)
45. Zammuto, R., Griffith, T., Majchrzak, A., Dougherty, D., Faraj, S.: Information technology and the changing fabric of organization. Organ. Sci. **18**(5), 749–762 (2007)

Developing an Analytical Framework for Analyzing and Comparing National E-Government Strategies

Sara Hofmann[1]([✉]), Christian Østergaard Madsen[2], and Bettina Distel[3]

[1] University of Agder, Postboks 422, 4604 Kristiansand, Norway
sara.hofmann@uia.no
[2] IT University Copenhagen, Rued Langgaards Vej 7, 2300 Copenhagen, Denmark
[3] University of Münster, Leonardo-Campus 3, 48149 Münster, Germany

Abstract. Across the world, e-government strategies are developed for the effective digitalization of the public sector. They offer governments a framework for dealing with challenges such as technical and legal interoperability and collaboration between public and private sector stakeholders, and for promoting a future vision for a digital public sector. Since e-government strategies are policy document and, thus, likely to convey biased perspectives, analyses of these strategies can yield insights into these biases and different perspectives on public sector digitalization. Until now, there has been no widely recognized framework for systematically analyzing e-government strategies. Based on literature and by applying our findings to the Danish and German e-government strategies, we have developed a novel analytical framework for comprehensively analyzing and comparing national e-government strategies. The framework focuses on the strategies' role, their function, and their specific content, such as strategic goals and measures to implement e-government. Analyzing and comparing both countries as a proof of concept shows fundamental differences in the level of digitalization and the implementation of e-government. This article contributes to both research and practice by presenting a comprehensive framework for analyzing national e-government strategies and by discussing their context-sensitivity.

Keywords: E-government strategy · Digital government strategy · Policy analysis

1 Introduction

Digital technologies offer important opportunities for achieving efficiency gains and improving service levels in public sector administration [1–3]. Moreover, through the successful strategic implementation of emerging technologies, public digitalization can contribute to addressing societal issues such as an aging population, improving healthcare, and creating business opportunities [4–6]. However, digital technologies also bring challenges. For instance, governments must protect their information and citizens against

© IFIP International Federation for Information Processing 2020
Published by Springer Nature Switzerland AG 2020
G. Viale Pereira et al. (Eds.): EGOV 2020, LNCS 12219, pp. 15–28, 2020.
https://doi.org/10.1007/978-3-030-57599-1_2

hacker attacks and misinformation, and they must ensure that public employees and citizens have the necessary skills and are motivated to use the digital services offered [3, 7]. Finally, the successful implementation of digital technologies requires attention to numerous other areas, i.e. the national context, technical and legal interoperability, and collaboration between public and private sector stakeholders [3].

Digital strategies offer governments a framework to address these issues and promote their vision for utilizing digital technologies. The national digital strategies were not created for research purposes, but with the explicit purpose of promoting public sector digitalization. As policy documents, they are interesting, precisely because they are not neutral, but rather present a biased view on a specific topic [8]. Thus, a comparative analysis of national digital strategies may yield important insight into these biases and different perspectives on public sector digitalization.

We find Denmark and Germany to be interesting countries for such a comparative analysis. On the one hand, the two countries have many similarities. They are neighbors, industrialized, wealthy, welfare states, with large public sectors. In terms of e-government implementation and adoption, however, they are vastly different. Denmark is a frontrunner, while Germany continuously lacks behind in service offers and adoption rates despite having Europe's largest national economy [9]. German delegates regularly visit Danish e-government decision makers to learn from their experiences, and Denmark has even institutionalized a digitalization ambassador in the Danish embassy in Berlin.

There are numerous non-peer reviewed studies, which compare and rank e-government adoption in different countries [9–11]. Similarly, several studies analyze e-government strategies from developing countries. However, there are few studies, which analyze and compare national e-government strategies in industrialized countries. Recently, a framework by Rose et al. [12] has become popular for analyzing values in e-government policy documents [13–15]. But, to the best of our knowledge, there is no recent widely recognized framework for analyzing and comparing other elements of national e-government strategies. To address these gaps in the extant literature, we have conducted a study, with two specific research goals:

1. Develop an analytical framework for comparing national e-government strategies.
2. Apply the framework to the Danish and German e-government strategies as a proof of concept.

This paper is structured as follows: The next section presents previous studies on e-government and digital strategies and background information. Then we present the method we applied to develop the analytical framework, followed by the analytical framework itself. We then offer a proof-of-concept by briefly presenting our comparative analysis of the Danish and German e-government strategies. Finally, we offer concluding remarks, discuss the limitations of our study and suggest future studies.

2 Background on E-Government Strategies

2.1 E-Government Strategies

Sandoval-Almazán et al. distinguish between (national) digital government strategies, which operate at the societal level, and enterprise or e-government strategies, which operate at the organizational level [3]. A national digital strategy is a framework for the use of digital technologies for governments and in society. It represents *"a general vision of how information technology should be utilized to support social and economic development of the society as a whole, as well as focusing on benefitting specific subsets of the society"* (p. 10). National digital strategies are linked to the UN millennium goals such as gender equality and literacy. When developing such strategies, representatives from the public and private sectors and from the civil society often collaborate. In contrast, a digital government, e-government, or enterprise strategy, deals with applying IT in the public sector. Such a strategy concerns *"the internal use of information technologies aimed at creating more efficient government and improved delivery of government services."* (p. 14). The 'internal' perspective can refer to one government organization, or a nationwide level, i.e., the whole public sector of a nation.

We searched for studies analyzing and/or comparing e-government strategies, in general, and from Germany and Denmark specifically. The search was conducted in May 2019 and updated in March 2020 using Publish and Perish with Google Scholar as search engine. The keywords used were Danish, Denmark, German, Germany, digital government, e-government, strategy, policy analysis, and comparison.

Many of the identified studies include e-government strategies and similar policy papers in their analyses, but few present in-depth analyses of the national e-government strategies as texts. In 2003, Chadwick and May presented an analysis of policy documents on public sector digitalization comparing the US, EU, and the UK [2]. We have not identified any recent studies, which analyze and compare national e-government strategies as texts through qualitative or quantitative content analysis. Rather, scholars have analyzed the strategies by other means, such as by interviewing and surveying policymakers [16, 17], by describing the goals and key topics therein at a high level of abstraction (i.e. in headlines) [18], or indirectly by presenting data analyses from other sources [19], such as consultancy companies and international rankings of countries according to the availability and diffusion of e-government services [9].

While such comparisons can be useful, they are unfit for our research purposes. The international e-government rankings are frequently criticized by scholars [20] because they have not been subject to peer-review, and because both methodology and the underlying data is often black-boxed and not available for closer inspection. According to Blaikie such tertiary data – which has been generated and analyzed by another researcher – should be treated with caution because of the risk for *"unintentional or deliberate distortion"* [21]. We also found that several of the identified studies merely reproduced the strategies' overtly optimistic presentation of e-government by repeating a list of benefits, without any form of critical reflection.

2.2 The Danish and the German E-Government Strategy

We consider Sandoval-Almazán et al.'s classification of strategies in the public sector as a continuum ranging from national digital strategies on the one end to e-government enterprise strategies on the other end. The strategies of Denmark and Germany we have analyzed can be classified in between the two extreme cases. Neither do they discuss the general use of digital technologies in a society as a whole nor are they limited to the internal use of digital technologies within the public sector or a public sector organization. Rather, both strategies deal with the use of digital technologies, its technical and social antecedents and consequences both within public sector organizations and beyond that, thus extending the understanding of e-government enterprise strategies. However, their focus is clearly limited to the interaction between public sector and further stakeholders, thus limiting the boundaries to public sector services and thereby staying below the general use of digital technologies as proclaimed in national digital strategies.

The Danish digitalization strategy 'A Stronger and More Secure Digital Denmark' is the fifth document in a row of strategies, with the first strategy being published in 2001, the penultimate in 2011. Although each of the strategies can be considered individually and sets new priorities, together they form a single digitalization program for Denmark. The latest strategy of 2016 was developed by the Danish Agency for Digitalization as a cooperation of all federal levels, i.e., the national government, the local government, and the Danish regions together authored the strategy. The strategy is 60 pages long, graphically prepared and follows a uniform design as a brochure.

It opens with an introductory section on the overall mission pursued with the strategy, a short outline of current developments that require further digitalization within the public sector, and a short positioning of the strategy within the overall Danish digitalization program. Afterwards, the vision and goals of the strategy are stated. Specifically, the Danish strategy aims i) for "digital solutions [that are...] easy-to-use, quick and [that] ensure high quality", ii) for "digitisation [that...] provide[s] good conditions for growth", and iii) for "security and confidence" [22, p. 15]. The strategy's main part divides each goal into three sub-goals and lists the specific initiatives and measures planned to achieve each goal. The strategy concludes with an outlook on how it can be further developed.

The German National E-Government Strategy was published in 2015 as an amendment of the original strategy of 2011 and is authored by the IT Planning Council. The council coordinates the digitalization efforts of all federal levels in Germany and, thus, coordinates e-government projects across the levels. Being an amendment to the original one, the current version of the German e-government strategy does not set a new focus but deepens and extends the program of its predecessor. The strategy is presented in text form, with one figure summarizing the strategy's main goals and related actions.

The German strategy starts with a foreword, highlighting the how and why of its development. The second section focuses on current developments that challenge the German public sector and that can be addressed through further digitalization. In addition, it also contains a separate section on its role for e-government activities and projects in Germany. Afterwards, the five guiding principles of the strategy are introduced, namely i) "Usefulness [of e-government] for citizens, businesses and public administrations", ii) "Cost-effectiveness, efficiency and performance [of e-government]", iii) "Information security and data protection", iv) ensuring "Transparency and participation in society", and finally, v) ensuring "Innovation and sustainability" [23, p. 7]. In the subsequent section, each of these principles is divided into several goals and a set of accompanying initiatives and measures to reach these goals. The strategy concludes with an exhaustive glossary of main terms and projects mentioned in the strategy.

Although there is a rich literature and many empirical studies of e-government from Germany, we have not identified studies, which analyze the national German e-government strategy as a policy document. The five Danish national e-government strategies from 2001–2016 have, however, been subject to several studies.

Jæger and Löfgren present an in-depth, theoretically guided analysis [24]. They present direct quotes from the strategies to back up their claims, and find, that the democratic ideals, which initially informed e-government policies, have been sidelines in favor of managerial and efficiency ideals. This echoes Chadwick and May [2], who found similar developments in e-government strategies from the US, UK and EU [2]. Similarly, Scupola [25], along with Meyerhof and Yasuka [26], present the historical development of e-government in Denmark based on analysis of policy document and interviews with key stakeholders. Jansen, Berger and Goldkuhl compare the three Scandinavian countries' e-government strategies with an emphasis on secure digital post [27]. They find that the countries' strategies offer three remarkably different approaches to digital post adoption from coercion (Denmark), to nudging (Norway) to voluntary (Sweden). Joseph and Avdic compare EU fact-sheets of Nordic countries' e-government policies [28]. Schou and Hjelholt have conducted several analyses of the e-government strategies, informed by a critical realist, post-marxist perspective [29–31]. Their studies revolve around the construction of the digital citizen, and how the strategies treat socially excluded groups. Persson et al. apply Rose et al.'s e-government value framework [12] to guide their analysis of two e-government strategies from 1994 and 2016 [13]. They find little development over the years, although values concerning citizen engagement have declined.

3 Method for Developing the Analytical Framework

The analytical framework for comparing national e-government strategies was developed in a two-stage process. First, we identified relevant prior literature (see Sect. 2) on which the analytical framework and its specific categories is based. Second, the resulting framework was applied to the strategies (see Sect. 5) and iteratively refined.

The comparison of the national e-government strategies requires an interpretation of its contents, wherefore a *qualitative content analysis* was conducted. Commonly, three different types of (qualitative) content analyses are differentiated that serve specific purposes [13]. The conventional content analysis is used to inductively analyze the material, whereas the directed content analysis makes use of predefined categories when interpreting the data. Finally, the summative content analysis is used to understand the context in which words or concepts are used. For our purposes, the second variation, the directed content analysis, is most appropriate as several studies especially on the Danish e-government strategies already exist. The directed content analysis as presented by Hsieh and Shannon [32] widely corresponds to the structuring content analysis by Mayring [33], who also proposes a detailed process model for this kind of content analysis, which we follow in our work (see Fig. 1).

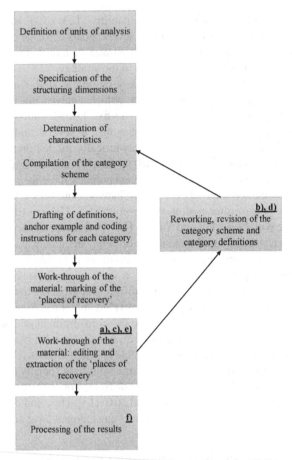

Fig. 1. Methodological process model based on [33]

First, the analysis starts with deciding on the **units of analysis**, which in the present study are the written national e-government strategies of Denmark and Germany in their latest versions. Second, based on the above identified prior research, we derived a **set of relevant categories** for the strategies' assessment with a total of six overarching categories, namely contextualization and self-understanding of the strategy, goals of the strategy, actions of the strategy, stakeholders, public service areas and technologies, national context, and conditions and consequences of e-government. For each of these categories, we derived sub-categories either from prior literature or inductively through a first informal test coding. The third and fourth step in this process include **compiling the preliminary category scheme** and to decide on a first version of **definitions, anchor examples,** and **coding instructions**. In a first **work-through** (a) (see Fig. 1) of the strategies, this version of our coding scheme was used to code both strategies and re-define all categories, examples, definitions and coding instructions. This was done by identifying all relevant statements in the strategies and assigning them to one or more sub-categories according to the coding instructions. The results and all coded segments were discussed in a workshop with all three researchers, where differences in the coding strategy, unclear or imprecise definitions were discussed, and the **category scheme was reworked** (b). These steps were followed by another work-through and a second workshop during which the researchers agreed on a final coding scheme which, finally, was applied to both strategies by one researcher (c−e). During the **processing of the results**, the last step as proposed by [33], the categories were re-grouped into five main categories (see Sect. 4) although the content did not change any more (f). The final coding scheme is presented in the following section. Table 1 contains a summary of all categories and sub-categories and shows which sub-categories were derived from literature and which were derived inductively from the material.

4 Presentation of Analytical Framework for Analyzing E–Government Strategies

As described above, we have iteratively developed the analysis framework, starting from literature and enhancing it by inductive development of further categories. Our main literature sources for developing the categories are the compendium "Building Digital Government Strategies" by Sandoval-Almazán et al. [3] and the "Recommendation of the Council on Digital Government Strategies" published by the OECD [34].

Table 1 gives an overview of our coding categories.

Table 1. Analytical framework

Category	Description
1. Contextualization and self-understanding of the strategy	
a. Authors	Who are the authors of the strategy?
b. Audience of the strategy	Does the strategy explicitly mention the audience? Whom?
c. Role of the strategy	What does the strategy say about how it should be applied?
d. Plan for further development of the strategy[a]	Does the strategy mention how it will be expanded in the future? How?
e. Legal activities/framework	What laws/legal frameworks are mentioned in the strategy that influence or are influenced by the strategy and its goals?
f. Definition of main terms[a]	Are main terms explicitly defined, e.g. in a glossary or in the text?
2. Goals and actions of the strategy	
a. Strategic goals	What overall high-level goals does the strategy mention?

(*continued*)

Table 1. (*continued*)

Category	Description
b. SMART goals[a]	What SMART (specific, measurable, applicable, reachable and/or time-bound) goals are mentioned in the strategy?
c. Explicit tasks[a]	What tasks to implement are explicitly mentioned in the strategy?
d. Implicit tasks[a]	What tasks that would be required to implement the strategy are implicitly mentioned in the strategy?
3. Stakeholders, public service areas and technologies	
a. Stakeholders	What stakeholders that influence or are being influenced are mentioned in the strategy?
b. Public service areas	What specific public areas does the digital strategy concern?
c. Technologies (what is the 'e')[a]	What specific technologies that are used or to be used by the public sector are mentioned in the strategy?
4. National context	
a. National context	What country-specific context does the strategy mention?
5. Conditions and consequences of e-government	
a. Risks, considerations, barriers, requirements, and challenges	What factors does the strategy mention that need to be considered to increase and promote the use of e-government?
b. Societal challenges[a]	What society-wide factors does the strategy mention that challenge or are challenged by e-government?
c. Negative consequences of e-government[a]	What negative consequences of e-government does the strategy mention?
d. Positive consequences of e-government[a]	What positive consequences of e-government does the strategy mention?

[a] categories marked with an asterisk were added inductively during coding

Contextualization and Self-understanding of the Strategy. The first main category describes how the strategy understands itself and how it is put into legal context. It is important that a responsible body is identified for ensuring the implementation of the overall strategy, which needs to be coordinated among different levels of the public sector. Furthermore, the relevant stakeholders and different levels of public sector organizations should deliver their input to the development of the strategy [34]. Since these roles are often difficult to comprehend from an outside perspective, it makes sense to identify the *authors of the strategy (1a)* as well as the *audience of the strategy (1b).*

While the first are responsible for developing and publishing the strategy, the latter are those for whom the strategy is written. In an ideal case, an e-government strategy should be applied in every public sector decision and the interplay between this strategy and other public sector strategies should be taken into account and aligned [34]. Thus, it is important to identify the *role of the strategy (1c)*, referring to any information that mentions how the strategy should be applied. During our coding, we added the category *plan for further development of the strategy (1d)* that explains how the strategy is supposed to be further developed in the future. An e-government strategy can be one in a row of several subsequent strategies or might need to be regularly revised. Since in e-government processes, often several government agencies are involved, new forms of interaction require substantial institutional changes including laws, rules, and norms [3]. Therefore, these regulations might need to be adjusted in order to implement an e-government strategy, which can require reviewing existing legal and regulatory frameworks. The category *legal activities/frameworks (1e)* captures the legal framework that influence or are influenced by the e-government strategy. Finally, we added the category *definition of main terms (1f)*, where important concepts are described, e.g. in a glossary. This can be relevant for understanding the terminology used in a strategy and it can give hints as to the audience of the strategy.

Goals and Actions of the Strategy. The second main category describes the goals of the strategy and the actions required to reach the goals. The application of technology is no goal in itself. Before developing a roadmap for using technology, it is therefore crucial to understand and define the problems that need to be solved by e-government [3]. These problems can then be formulated into *strategic goals (2a)*, which are the overall high-level goals a strategy contains. The OECD, for example, defines main goals of an e-government strategy as "greater transparency, openness and inclusiveness of government processes and operations" [34, p. 6]. In addition to strategic goals, we also came across *SMART goals (2b)* in the strategies, which refer to operational goals including specific, measurable, achievable, realistic, or time-bound elements. Furthermore, we identified more operationalizable tasks. On the one hand, strategies can contain *explicit tasks (2c)*, i.e., activities that according to the strategy need to be carried out to implement the goals. On the other hand, they can refer to *implicit tasks (2d)*, which are implicitly indicated.

Stakeholders, Public Service Areas and Technologies. The third main category includes the stakeholders, the public service areas and the technologies that are mentioned in the strategy. For every e-government project, it is important to understand the involved or affected *stakeholders (3a)* because the success of e-government endeavors depends heavily on their support and adoption of the solutions [3, 34]. These stakeholders can be internal or external. During coding, we identified the category *public service areas (3b)*, which categorizes specific domains or contexts that the strategy mentions. These areas indicate areas of prioritization for the years to come or show projects that have been successful during the past. In addition to stakeholders and service areas, technologies are acknowledged as important key driver to create and improve innovation and public service delivery [34]. Therefore, the final sub-category refers to the *technologies (3c)* that, according to the strategy, are used or to be used.

National Context (4). The fourth category describes if the e-government strategy mentions a country-specific context. It is important to understand that e-government as such and e-government strategies are highly context-dependent and that it is not possible to transfer solutions from one country one on one to any other context [35]. E-government projects are, for example, highly dependent on the country's or municipality's economic situation as well as the political structures and environment [3].

Conditions and Consequences of E-Government. The fifth and final main category describes the conditions and consequences of e-government that need to be considered according to the strategy. Using digital technologies in the public sector can evoke several risks such as security and privacy issues that need to be overcome by a strategy [34]. The first sub-category *risks, considerations, barriers, requirements or challenges for e-government* (5a), therefore, refers to aspects that need to be considered or overcome in order to increase and implement e-government. In addition to these specific individual, technical or organizational aspects, we identified *societal challenges* (5b), which describe society-wide challenges that influence or are influenced by e-government. Finally, we coded *negative consequences* (5c) and *positive consequences* (5d) of e-government that are mentioned by the strategy.

5 Application of Analytical Framework to the Danish and German E-Government Strategies

After developing the final set of categories, we coded the Danish and the German e-government strategies to get a proof of concept of our analytical framework. This section contains an excerpt of the analysis. Besides the analysis of the content of both strategies, we also counted how often the categories were coded in each strategy in order to assess the importance given each category within the strategies.

Contextualization and Self-understanding of the Strategy. This category was coded 26 times in the Danish and 32 times in the German strategy. Both strategies clearly describe the *role of the strategy (1a)* but differ in how they do so. The statements coded in the Danish strategy integrate the current strategy into the overall Danish digitalization program. Thus, the role of the Danish strategy is not restricted to specific goals in a given timeframe but explicitly includes previous strategies and their goals as well. In contrast, the German strategy is more focused on itself. The statements show that the strategy's role is to underline the IT planning council's mandate to coordinate the development of e-government in Germany. In addition, some statements indicate that the strategy follows existing strategies of other organizations in structure and content. Rather than setting the course of digitalization for the upcoming years – as the Danish strategy – the German strategy is formulated as a guiding framework that aims at ensuring the effectiveness and efficiency of administrative processes.

Goals and Actions of the Strategy. In the Danish strategy, 186 segments were coded, in contrast to 69 in the German strategy. The Danish strategy mentions several *strategic goals (2a)* such as the creation of growth and value, especially for businesses, through digitalization, ensuring and enhancing current security standards in order to safe-guard the strong confidence of the Danish society in the public sector digitalization, increasing and enhancing the user-friendliness of digital government services, and increasing the transparency of the public sector, for example, to disclose how sensitive data of citizens and businesses is processed. The German strategy has similar strategic goals, namely usefulness of e-services; cost-effectiveness, efficiency, and performance; information security and data protection; transparency and participation in society; innovation and sustainability. However, the themes running through all goals differ from those identified as underlying the Danish strategic goals and we only find two of these underlying themes. *First,* the strategy focuses on increasing user-friendliness for all users of public administrations, i.e. citizens, businesses, and public administrations, by providing e-services. This theme emerges in all specific goals of the strategy and is strongly focused on developing client-centric e-services and enabling democratic participation, without specifically addressing efficiency or effectiveness as can be seen in the Danish strategy. *Second,* the strategic goals focus on reaching and sustaining a high level of security and stability of technical infrastructures. This theme is focused on internal processes and the creation and maintenance of technical cooperation, i.e. interoperability of systems between the federal levels.

Stakeholder, Public Service Areas, and Technologies. In the Danish strategy, we coded 148 instances for the third category and 45 instances for the German strategy. Both strategies identify similar *stakeholders (3a).* These include stakeholders from the public sector such as public sector employees, ministries and agencies or the public sector in general, stakeholders from the private sector, and stakeholders from the civil society such as citizens or stakeholder organizations. In the Danish strategy, the stakeholders in the citizen category are sometimes concretized and referred to as 'Danes', 'parents', 'elderly' or even more concretely 'young people released from prison'. The German strategy further includes research organizations as potential stakeholders. In both strategies, especially the stakeholder groups from the public and the private sector are ascribed an active role in the sense that they need to cooperate or perform certain activities in order to increase e-government activities. Citizens, in contrast, are mainly presented as passive stakeholders who can benefit from digital services.

National Context (4). We identified 31 instances of the national context in the Danish and one instance in the German strategy, showing a much stronger emphasis on context in the Danish strategy. Interestingly, these contextual factors cover quite different areas. Some areas, such as adoption rates, and the development of digital infrastructure, are generally objective and quantitative, while others such as the importance of high levels of trust, the nature of collaboration and pragmatism, are more subjective and qualitative. One of these sub-themes also, quite directly, concerns the importance of the history of the strategies and the iterative approach to digitalization. This, by extension, highlights the important role of the authors of the strategy, especially the Digitalization Agency. In contrast, the only point where the German strategy mentions a national context is a reference to Germany's federal structure.

Conditions and Consequences of E-Government. The Danish e-government strategy contains two instances of *negative consequences (5c)* from digitalization. These concern the increased vulnerability, which digitalization entails, due to the interconnectedness of the IT systems and increased risk of cybercrime. The latter may not only lead to economic damage, but also to a loss of public trust in IT. The German strategy does not mention any negative consequences of e-government. In contrast, we coded 72 instances of *positive consequences (5d)* in the Danish e-government strategy, and seven instances of positive consequences in the German strategy. In terms of the number of instances coded, it is clear, that the strategies have a much stronger focus on the potentially positive than negative consequences.

6 Discussion and Conclusion

In this article, we developed an analytical framework for national e-government strategies and applied this framework to the Danish and German e-government strategies as a proof of concept. Based on prior research on e-government strategies and amended by induction, we developed a framework of five overarching categories that describes the role, function and specific contents of (national) e-government strategies. We applied the analytical framework to the German and Danish national e-government strategies. Our analysis and comparison suggest that the strategies differ fundamentally but are both characterized by the respective national context: Denmark has a long tradition of digitalization and the strategy is part of an overarching vision of digitalization that spans decades. The German strategy is much more influenced by the status quo of digitalization and – conceived merely as an amendment of the original strategy – might be the beginning of a comparable development.

Our study offers several contributions to e-government practice. First, the framework highlights the context-sensitivity of e-government strategies. Therefore, policymakers should be cautious before attempting to transfer strategies and best practices from one context to another. Our study is – to the best of our knowledge – the first to analyze the national German e-government strategy as a policy document through content analysis and compare it to the Danish strategy. This comparison shows fundamental differences in how policymakers conceptualize e-government, and in how e-government strategies are used as tools to implement e-government. Further, we find that, systematically analyzing and comparing strategies with this framework can disclose otherwise hidden or only implicitly described conceptualizations of the functions of IT in the public sector, the roles the stakeholders play or should play, their duties and the bigger picture policy-makers actually aim for. We find that the framework is suitable to analyze strategies on all federal levels and allows for international comparisons. Our study also offers contribution to e-government research. We have developed a framework to analyze e-government strategies and tested it on two such strategies.

The focus of the study was on two wealthy, developed economies with differing levels of e-government adoption. While the chosen cases already provide rich insights into the development and implementation of e-government strategies, we suggest widening the scope of our framework by applying it to countries with lower e-government maturity. We would like to invite researchers to use our framework and apply it to other e-government strategies. Such additional analyses and comparison can add to the understanding of how e-government is perceived and developed across the world. Rather than focusing on one particular application area such as digital post or the presence of certain (public) values in the strategies, our approach is holistic, and seeks to describe the strategies as a whole through five large aspects. These aspects can be analyzed in-depth on their own or be compared. By focusing on various aspects and their relation to one another, we can address the criticism by Jaeger and Löfgren that *"literature tends to take on policy-makers' cognitive and normative positions as factual propositions, where these positions are treated as explicit and objective realities"* [24, p. 253].

Acknowledgements. The study was funded by the German National Centre for E-Government (NEGZ). Christian Ø. Madsen's research is funded by the Research Centre for Government IT, which is a collaboration between the IT University of Copenhagen, the Danish Agency for Digitisation, and the self-owned institution ATP. The Research Centre's external funding partners were not involved in the development of the research questions presented herein, nor the analysis, discussion, or presentation of the study's results.

References

1. Lindgren, I., Madsen, C.Ø., Hofmann, S., Melin, U.: Close encounters of the digital kind: a research agenda for the digitalization of public services. Gov. Inf. Q. **36**(3), 427–436 (2019)
2. Chadwick, A., May, C.: Interaction between states and citizens in the age of the internet: "e-government" in the United States, Britain, and the European Union. Governance-an Int. J. Policy Adm. **16**, 271–300 (2003)
3. Sandoval-Almazán, R., et al.: Building Digital Government Strategies. PAIT, vol. 16. Springer, Cham (2017). https://doi.org/10.1007/978-3-319-60348-3
4. Niehaves, B.: Iceberg ahead: on electronic government research and societal aging. Gov. Inf. Q. **28**, 310–319 (2011)
5. Bertot, J.C., Gorham, U., Jaeger, P.T., et al.: Big data, open government and e-government: Issues, policies and recommendations. Inf. Polity **19**, 5–16 (2014)
6. Heitmueller, A., Henderson, S., Warburton, W., et al.: Developing public policy to advance the use of big data in health care. Health Aff. **33**, 1523–1530 (2014)
7. Bertot, J.C., Jaeger, P.T.: The e-government paradox: better customer service doesn't necessarily cost less. Gov. Inf. Q. **25**, 149–154 (2008)
8. Bryman, A.: Social Research Methods, 5th edn. Oxford University Press, Oxford (2016)
9. European Commission: The digital economy and society index (DESI) (2019)
10. Ayanso, A., Chatterjee, D., Cho, D.I.: E-government readiness index: a methodology and analysis. Gov. Inf. Q. **28**, 522–532 (2011)
11. Codagnone, C., Misuraca, G., Savoldelli, A., Lupianez-Villanueva, F.: Institutional isomorphism, policy networks, and the analytical depreciation of measurement indicators: the case of the EU e-government benchmarking. Telecommun. Policy **39**, 305–319 (2015)
12. Rose, J., Persson, J.S., Heeager, L.T., Irani, Z.: Managing e-government: value positions and relationships. Inf. Syst. J. **25**, 531–571 (2015)
13. Persson, J.S., Reinwald, A., Skorve, E., Nielsen, P.A.: Value positions in e-government strategies: something is (not) changing in the state of Denmark. In: Proceedings 25th European Conference Information System ECIS, pp. 904–917 (2017)
14. Sundberg, L.: Value positions and relationships in the Swedish digital government. Adm. Sci. **9**, 1–16 (2019)

15. Toll, D., Lindgren, I., Melin, U., Madsen, C.Ø.: Artificial intelligence in Swedish policies: values, benefits, considerations and risks. In: Lindgren, I. (ed.) EGOV 2019. LNCS, vol. 11685, pp. 301–310. Springer, Cham (2019). https://doi.org/10.1007/978-3-030-27325-5_23
16. Deakins, E., Dillon, S., Chen, W.: A comparison between e-government practices in Taiwan and New Zealand. Commun. ICISA **1**, 1–24 (2007)
17. Weerakkody, V., Jones, S., Olsen, E.: E-government: a comparison of strategies in local authorities in the UK and Norway. In: 3rd European Mediterranean Middle East Conference Information System (EMCIS 2006), pp. 1–15 (2006)
18. Rodousakis, N., Mendes, A.: The development of inclusive e-government in Austria and Portugal: a comparison of two success stories. Eur. J. Soc. Sci. Res. **21**, 283–316 (2008)
19. He, W., Sun, L.: Comparison of e-government strategy between Chinese and foreign nations: content, model and characteristics. In: 2011 International Conference on Business Management and Electronic Information, vol. 2, pp. 186–190 (2011)
20. Bannister, F.: The curse of the benchmark: an assessment of the validity and value of e-government comparisons. Int. Rev. Adm. Sci. **73**, 171–188 (2007)
21. Blaikie N.: Designing Social Research. Polity (2012)
22. The Danish Government: The digital strategy - a stronger and more secure digital Denmark (2016)
23. IT-Planungsrat: National e-government strategy update (2015)
24. Jæger, B., Löfgren, K.: The history of the future: changes in Danish e-government strategies 1994–2010. Inf. Polity Int. J. Gov. Democr. Inf. Age **15**, 253–269 (2010)
25. Scupola, A.: A case study of digital transformation of Danish public services : actors and policies. In: 2018 11th CMI International Conference: Prospects and Challenges Towards Developing a Digital Economy within the EU, pp. 14–18 (2018)
26. Meyerhoff, M., Yasuoka, M.: An analysis of the Danish approach to eGovernment benefit realisation. In: Internet Technologies Society 2014 Conference Proceedings, pp. 47–58 (2014)
27. Jansen, A., Berger, J.B., Goldkuhl, G.: First choice, free choice or no choice - differences in secure digital post in the Scandinavian countries. Electronic Government Electron Participation Joint Proceeding Ongoing Research Project IFIP WG 8.5 EGOV ePart vol.23, pp. 135–143 (2016)
28. Joseph, S., Avdic, A.: Where do the nordic nations' strategies take e-government? Electron. J. e-Government **14**, 2–16 (2016)
29. Jannick, S., Hjelholt, M.: Digitalizing the welfare state: citizenship discourses in Danish digitalization strategies from 2002 to 2015. Crit. Policy Stud. (2017)
30. Hjelholt, M., Schou, J.: Digital lifestyles between solidarity, discipline and neoliberalism: on the historical transformations of the Danish it political field from 1994 to 2016. TripleC **15**, 370–389 (2017)
31. Hjelholt, M., Schou, J.: Digital citizenship and neoliberalization: governing digital citizens in Denmark. Citizsh. Stud. **22**, 507–522 (2018)
32. Hsieh, H.-F., Shannon, S.E.: Three approaches to qualitative content analysis. Qual. Health Res. **15**, 1277–1288 (2005)
33. Mayring, P.: Qualitative Inhaltsanalyse. Beltz, Weinheim; Basel, Grundlagen und Techniken (2015)
34. OECD recommendation of the council on digital government strategies (2014)
35. Heeks, R.: e-Government as a carrier of context. J. Public Policy **25**, 51–74 (2005)

A Pathology of Public Sector IT Governance: How IT Governance Configuration Counteracts Ambidexterity

Johan Magnusson[1,2]([⊠]), Jwan Khisro[1], and Ulf Melin[3]

[1] Swedish Center for Digital Innovation, University of Gothenburg, Gothenburg, Sweden
johan.magnusson@gu.se
[2] Kristiania University College, Oslo, Norway
[3] Linköping University, Linköping, Sweden

Abstract. Public sector organizations are invariable stuck in a contortionist position in regards to how they approach digitalization. Centralized delivery models for IT drive efficiency in the short term, but at the same time they have been identified to potentially counter-act innovation. This study utilizes an interpretative case study of 21 Swedish public agencies and their centralized IT function to analyze how existing IT governance configuration impacts organizational ambidexterity. The empirical base consists of 31 interviews and studies of secondary material in the form of steering documents. The findings show that IT Governance is experienced as decreasing the level of innovation in the organization and hence negatively impacting ambidexterity by systematically skewing the balance between efficiency and innovation. These findings are discussed in relation to previous research, and propositions for future research for better understanding IT governance configuration in the context of ambidexterity are presented and discussed.

Keywords: Ambidexterity · IT governance · Public sector

1 Introduction

In the past all the people who tried to build a science of the normal without being careful to start from the pathological [...] have ended up in often ridiculous failures. [1, p. 285]

Digitalization involves the utilization of digital technologies in the parallel strive for efficiency and innovation [2]. As such, a public sector organization set on a path of digitalization needs to balance these two intentions and make sure that the appropriate pre-requisites are in place that avoids trade-offs [3]. Unfortunately, with the long-term dominance of bureaucratic governance models [4], the bulk of existing governance and control is geared for efficiency rather than innovation [5]. Hence, IT governance legacy has been identified as a constricting factor for achieving ambidexterity [6–8].

G. Viale Pereira et al. (Eds.): EGOV 2020, LNCS 12219, pp. 29–41, 2020.
https://doi.org/10.1007/978-3-030-57599-1_3

Ambidexterity, here referred to as the simultaneous handling of established business activities and rapidly changing new activities [9], infers that the organization needs to strive for an instrumental balance between efficiency and innovation in its digital initiatives. In terms of the link to organizational ambidexterity, we follow [10] and equate exploitation with efficiency, through seeing it as continuous improvements of existing services and processes. Exploration is equated with innovation through seeing it as initiatives for the acquisition and development of radically new knowledge and service concepts.

In line with recent findings from the field of organizational ambidexterity [11] balance is regarded as a dynamic process rather than a fixed state. Any public sector organization striving for sustainable advantage and performance needs to continually re-balance between efficiency and innovation. In times of increased dynamism in the environment, more emphasis (i.e. more resources) have to be devoted to innovation than in times of decreased dynamism [12]. Hence, an organization acting in an environment with shifts in dynamism needs to be equipped with not only capabilities for efficiency and innovation, but also for balancing [13]. In other words, instances of IT governance configurations that "tip the scale" through a built-in balancing bias may be referred to as pathological in that they counteract the long-term intent of the organization.

Most sectors have experienced an increase in dynamism through emergent digitalization [14]. The once relatively stable expectations of the customers are increasingly becoming influenced by digital services from challenging actors, where the pace of new services as well as the ease-of-access drives the industry towards increased digital intensity [8]. At the same time, governance in said organizations is designed to counteract risk and fluctuations over time, resulting in a sub-optimal fit [15].

In lieu of this, there is a need for increased knowledge in terms of how existing governance practices counteract organizations' abilities to realize the benefits of digitalization. Through understanding the limitations of existing governance, i.e. the *pathology* of IT governance to return to the opening quote, we hope to inform future research and practice. Provided this rationale, the research question that this paper addresses is:

> *How do current configurations of IT Governance impact organizational ambidexterity?*

This answers the calls from research such as [4] and [8] on the need for new types of IT governance that do not counter-act the need for agility and pace in digital development. The study was operationalized through an interpretative qualitative case study conducted in the spring of 2019. The organization in question, the County Administrative Boards of Sweden, is a collection of 21 public agencies with a centralized provisioning and joint governance of IT.

This paper is organized accordingly: After this brief introduction, we continue with the precursory findings and theoretical framing, addressing issues such as the governance of IT in the public sector and ambidexterity. This is followed by the research approach and results, where the findings are presented in conjunction with the identified themes of counteracting governance and propositions for future research. After this, we discuss the findings and said propositions, as well as implications for practice.

2 Precursory Findings and Theoretical Framing

2.1 IT Governance

IT Governance, here understood in line with Weill and Ross [16] as the decision-rights and accountabilities for IT-related investments, has a long line of inquiry dating back to the 1960's. Starting from the turn of the millennium, there was an increased emphasis on understanding the intricate integration of issues of IT in the general governance of the organization [17]. This in turn spiked a re-visiting of contingency studies for normative contributions into how IT Governance should be designed [18]. Despite being a rich and popular field, IT Governance has been criticized by several authors for an over emphasis on formal controls [5], a functional perspective on IT [3] and its isomorphic tendencies where firms display increasing similarities in their governance configurations despite having widely different operational logics [6].

More recent contributions to the study of IT Governance have explored the new types of control that may be aspirational. In [19], this is re-conceptualized following a liberalist approach where IT Governance is continued to be treated according to an internal market logic. In [8], the functional perspective is replaced with a platform approach focused on services rather than assets, resulting in what the researchers deem a better fit with practice. Core to the stream of research within IT Governance is the perception of governance as manifested in a set of mechanisms [17]. Through focusing on the contingencies for particular configurations of mechanisms, research has explored the combination of structures, process and relational mechanisms as advocated by [18, 20, 21].

In line with Wiener et al. [5], the notion of control configuration has been criticized for not amply considering the enactment of governance. As noted by [13], it is not merely in the design of organization and governance that we govern, but ultimately through how these frameworks are *enacted* by front-line managers. In this study, we posit that despite governance enactment being a promising path of inquiry, this does not mean that additional studies of IT Governance mechanisms and their configuration are not warranted.

2.2 Organizational Ambidexterity and Analytical Framework

Following the organizational ambidexterity stream of research, we acknowledge that organizations that wish to achieve long-term performance and relevance to its stakeholders need to balance between exploration and exploitation [9, 12]. This means that in order to achieve long-term success, organizations need to be ambidextrous, i.e. equipped with the capability to dynamically balance between exploration and exploitation over time [11, 13]. Following [10] as well as [22] operationalization, we equate exploration with innovation and exploitation with efficiency. In relation to digitalization, researchers such as [23] have called for "digital ambidexterity", i.e. the capability to dynamically balance the intent and focus of their consummate digital initiatives in terms of efficiency and innovation.

From the organizational ambidexterity perspective, initiatives directed towards exploitation (i.e. efficiency) versus exploration (i.e. innovation) together form a consummate whole. In other words, efficiency and innovation are discriminate constructs, without overlay, resulting in the assumption that when combined, said initiatives equate the total body of resources of the organization. To summarize, there are two theoretical assumptions (TA) that form the basis for our argumentation in this paper:

TA1: Ambidexterity is a measure of the dynamic balancing between efficiency and innovation.

TA2: The level of innovation and efficiency are mutually exclusive, i.e. an increase in the level of innovation will invariably lead to a proportionate decrease in efficiency.

These two theoretical assumptions are combined into an analytical framework as seen in Fig. 1 under Results.

3 Method

The researchers were contacted by the County Administrative Boards of Sweden (CAB) in the fall of 2018 for a potential commissioned research project underlying this paper. After initial discussions concerning a potential research collaboration and the challenges identified by the representatives of the organization, the focus fell on how IT was currently governed. With this being in line with the research interests of the involved researchers, the case was selected on account of fit and convenience. We designed a qualitative, interpretative case study [24] to address the research need. CAB consists of 21 independent agencies with a total of 6.000 employees. The agencies are distributed across Sweden and are tasked with weighing in on decisions related to a wide are issues such as fishery, agriculture, environment, housing et cetera. They are Sweden's oldest agencies, dating back to the 1600s, and in the event of a major crisis such as war they are designed to function as self-governed and -sufficient kingdoms [25].

Since 2009, CAB has employed a centralized and standardized delivery model for IT in the form of a shared service center. The founding idea was to create economies of scale and facilitate homogenization in terms of quality of service between the different geographical areas in Sweden. The central IT department is seated in Gothenburg with three smaller branches scattered throughout Sweden. CAB adheres to a supply/demand configuration with organizational entities devoted to supply and demand management. In terms of portfolios, there are two (development and maintenance), with resources distributed with a lion share in maintenance.

Data was collected in two forms. First, steering documents and secondary material was collected (a total of 35 documents, including IT strategy, Digital strategy, governance setup et cetera). The selection of this data was done in close dialogue with the steering group from CAB, with the explicit intent of gathering data of relevance to understanding the current setup of IT Governance. Second, a total of 31 interviews were conducted with a total of 21 respondents during the spring of 2019. 24 interviews were conducted with individuals from the Shared Service Center (SSC), and seven interviews with people from operations in roles from all hierarchical levels. Each semi-structured interview was conducted by at least two individuals, and all interviews were sound-recorded and fully transcribed. The respondents were asked for consent on using the interviews for continued research, and promised anonymity. Using multiple empirical sources is clearly in line with qualitative and interpretative research [24]. Interviewing respondents face-to-face also gave us a good opportunity to ask follow-up questions and be open for emerging thoughts and responses, enriching the data utilized in this paper. The interview transcripts were coded using the qualitative analysis software Nvivo Pro in two iterations [26]. The first iteration of coding was done inductively, looking for themes in the responses. This resulted in a total of seven identified themes. The second iteration looked for second-order constructs, resulting in four constructs which form the basis for our presentation of results below. The analysis followed an integrated and iterative approach to analysis [24, 27].

4   Results

CAB is unanimously presented by respondents' through the interviews as an organization with a very low level of innovation. There are substantial shortcomings in the innovation capabilities displayed in the empirical material, and the respondents are clear in identifying current configurations of governance as the main rationale behind an expressed lack of innovation. In order to attain ambidexterity, a substantial re-balancing towards innovation is needed and acknowledged by the respondents. Figure 1 summarizes the identified themes in relation to the analytical framework.

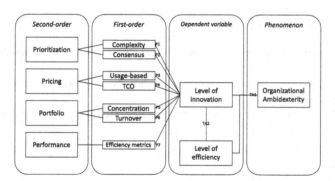

Fig. 1. Summary of research findings

The study identified four overarching second-order themes as constraining factors for ambidexterity (Fig. 1). These are presented below in conjunction with the empirical data, along with propositions for future research expanding on the identified relationships with ambidexterity.

4.1   Prioritization

Prioritization refers to the process through which new investments associated with IT are handled in the organization. As such, the process is signified by being highly complex and cumbersome (multiple steps), and, building on consensus as a pre-requisite for go-ahead on investments.

"I don't think any other agency has an as-a-complex governance model as we do." County Governor

In terms of the *complexity* identified in the case, the primary driver of complexity is the underlying model for how an investment gets prioritized and approved. CAB works with a standardized model (PM3) and the associated process has 25 steps. The result is a process where the high workload for associated documentation and the long lead-times result in stagnation.

"It takes too long for them (suggestions) to reach those higher levels. Employees cannot push ideas all the way up to decisions. It is too difficult simply, it takes too long." Employee, general organization.

In addition to this, there is a built-in need for consensus regarding all digital initiatives to gain approval. This consensus goes all the way up to the CEO level, where all 21 CEOs have to be in accord in terms of which investments to fund.

"So, if we are going to start a new project, the whole group of governors, 21 of them need to be in a consensus decision." Manager form the budget group.

The result is a growing inertia in the organization, where digital investments take a long time to push through to an investment decision.

"You can say we´re sometimes paralyzed by our own rules, laws and regulations" Employee, general organization.

On the basis of these findings, we have identified two propositions for future research:

P1: The level of complexity in the prioritization process for IT-related investments will negatively influence the level of innovation.
P2: The level of required consensus in the prioritization process for IT-related investments will negatively influence the level of innovation.

4.2 Pricing

Pricing refers to how IT cost is allocated through charge-back in the form of internal pricing for IT-related products and services. With 50% of the operating budget for the SSC being based on direct funding through sent invoices, the pricing of said services fills two functions. First and foremost, it is employed to create organizational transparency for the resources spent on IT, i.e. legitimacy. Second, it is designed to factor in cost-drivers for the SSC, resulting in plannability and credibility in financial control.

"IT cost is split per user, because in the end it is the user, that creates the cost. If there weren't a user, there wouldn't any cost. It is fair handling of IT cost." Chief Strategy Officer.

"60% of all the funds of the IT part is based on users and that is not supporting, let's say the development, because we are using more and more IT, the best business is requesting more and more as well" Chief Information Officer.

"But if we do not have usage-based pricing, that would mean that people would start using IT much more!" Manager, field-notes from final presentation of findings.

As seen in the three quotes, pricing is paradoxical based on both IT-use being a sound basis for assessing true cost, and through cost directly influencing decreased use of IT. The CAB digital strategy is clear in stipulating that everything that can be digitalized should, and hence there is an inherent conflict between the pricing model and the strategic intent. If the use of IT is assumed to provide increasing returns, then the organization (according to the second quote) should aim for a pricing model that does not promote short-term activity related to decreased use of IT. At the same time, the pricing model is institutionalized and widely accepted in the organization, having been around in a stable form for the past five years. As noted by the department managers, it provides them as customers with transparency, and also with increased plannability in terms of cost.

"...this is quite [a] complex [system] but it is actually working well, and it gives transparency..." Department manager.

From the SSCs perspective, the pricing model works as a basis for managing demand in the organization with the intent of plannability and efficiency. Provided the model, they are equipped with a method that reduces variability and fluctuations for 50% of their operating budget, with clear early warning signals as noted by the Financial controller:

"So, we are just working to figure out a mechanism that we can get an early warning if we expect to see significant changes in volumes coming here." Financial controller.

In relation to plannability and the high dependency for the SSC on the revenue generated through the internal billing system, the organization applies a model for total cost of ownership (TCO) over five years in all its digital initiatives. This means that for an investment to be prioritized, it has to be fully funded in terms of both development and maintenance. With the organization working with a significant legacy environment, this results in the maintenance cost for new development of technologies that do not fit the existing legacy will be significant. This places a significant deterrent to new initiatives, where the actual development costs are relatively small compared to the maintenance cost. Pricing new development according to this model results in significant cost hurdles. At the same time, the organization does not manage additional cost attributable to aging legacy, whereby there are no signals in terms of when modernization of the infrastructure is warranted from a development cost perspective.

On the basis of these findings, we have identified two propositions for future research:

P3: The use of usage-based pricing for IT cost charge-back will negatively influence the level of innovation.
P4: The use of total cost of ownership as a basis for prioritization of IT-related investments will negatively influence the level of innovation.

4.3 Portfolio

Portfolio refers to how the total amount of IT-related projects and assets that are jointly managed (bundled). CAB manages two parallel portfolios, one for maintenance and one for development. As seen in the study, there is lacking plannability on account of money being sparse and short-term. This results in the organization not amply managing the lifecycle of its systems in the portfolios.

> *"We work in cycles that are too short. As of now, we procure new applications and systems simply because we have the money for it. Then we use it for a while and eventually a forget about it and buy a new one instead." Employee, IT-department.*

The lack of lifecycle management also results in the organization not amply addressing the need for decommissioning systems in a timely manner. CAB lacks an overview of the total amount of systems, as well as the age of said systems. Without this information, there is little insight into what systems should be decommissioned versus modernized versus maintained.

At the same time, the lack of oversight and transparency in both lifecycle and the content of the portfolios results in a problem with amply meeting the demands from the business side. As noted above, there are significant lags in the process from ideation to actual deployment, which results in significant frustration from the business side.

On the basis of these findings, we have identified two propositions for future research:

P5: The level of concentration of the IT portfolio will negatively influence the level of innovation.
P6: A low rate of turnover over time in the IT portfolio will negatively influence the level of innovation.

4.4 Performance

Performance refers to how the performance of the IT function in the CAB is measured and managed.

> *"So, I think it is important for us to show that we all the time more efficient in IT department to leverage the economy of scale because that the mission given to us and we try to optimize our IT all the time." Chief Information Officer.*

As noted by the CIO in the quote above, the IT department is deeply rooted in a perception that they should be as efficient as possible. This is also visible in the performance reporting done, where the sole focus lies in staying on-par with budget. Through this, the idea of the IT department being proactive in meeting new demands from the business becomes counter-productive to the performance on what they are measured. Increased fluctuations of demand would invariably lead to a decrease in efficiency.

> *"It's deeply rooted in our DNA to be reactive, not proactive and I think that's not good. The CABs do not need the reactive IT, they need proactive IT." Chief Strategy Officer.*

At the same time, this reactiveness is experienced as something that goes against both sound economic thinking (i.e. straining resources) and the experienced value of the IT department as noted by the Head of Strategy. Several respondents identified the opportunity cost of not amply being responsive towards new demands from the business, at least in the longer run. The focus on merely cost in the short-run is highlighted as a counter-productive practice in the long-run, where the organization is now striving for expanding the performance measurement and management with functional metrics such as SLA compliance et cetera.

"So, I guess cause you talked about that the mission is focused a lot on delivering cost efficient services to users... ...we made some SLAs but we presented them to a small group (3 people)... and there has been very low interest from the other 20 counties...." Department manager, user support.

On the basis of these findings, we have identified one proposition for future research:

P7: A sole function on efficiency metrics for performance management of the IT function will negatively influence the level of innovation.

5 Discussion

This paper has sought to answer the question of how IT Governance configuration impacts ambidexterity in a public sector organization. As the findings show, there are multiple instances of configurations that have a negative impact on the level of innovation, hence acting as a bias for increased efficiency at the expense of innovation. This phenomenon has previously been addressed as an efficiency creep [4] or increased emphasis on exploitation [3, 28], yet our paper is the first to identify specific configurations in IT Governance that act as mechanisms for said biases. This is important as an original result within the e-government field in this paper.

Prioritization acts as a deterrent for innovation and hence shifts the emphasis in ambidexterity towards efficiency. Both the level of complexity in the and the requirement for consensus at the two upper levels of management act in direct conflict with the underlying digital strategy of the agencies. Any new digital initiative needs to be chaperoned through a prioritization process placing high demands in terms of work-load for the champion of the investment. At the same time, the requirement for consensus places high demands on political activities. These challenges have previously been identified in the literature [19], yet propositions 1 and 2 need to be further addressed. Considering the context of Scandinavian public sector, the value of consensus and democracy, are really important values in institutional life.

In regards to the issue of pricing, previous literature has identified a need for increased transparency in IT costing [29]. The underlying rationale is that if there is a clear line of sight between the cost driver (use) and the cost (price) then the organization will be equipped with decreasing cost. Unfortunately, the underlying assumption of this is that the value of use may be less than the cost, and that the value of use is strictly contained within the P&L of the user. Both of these may be seen as troubling (and/or dated) assumptions. With the value of IT often being organizational wide, and the digital strategy of the case organizations being one of increased digitalization this is found to be counteracted by the pricing scheme. Previous literature is full of critical reflections on pricing IT services, yet full charge-back is still the dominant model in practice [30], whereby we conclude that there is a need for research into propositions 3 and 4.

Pertaining to the issue of the portfolio, the expressed dilapidate state of the existing legacy environment is a constant area of concern for the case organizations. At the same time, it is symptomatic of a governance that traditionally has been geared towards maintaining legacy rather than addressing requirements for modernization. All processes found in Prioritization and Pricing act to conserve and counteract investments that would decrease the digital heritage [7, 31]. As such, the lack of insight into the turnover of systems, the age of systems et cetera is problematic since it does not provide the organization with signals of necessary re-investments [5]. Provided this, we see the need for additional research into propositions 5 and 6.

Lastly, the existing performance measurement and management of the IT function in the public agencies was found to be directly counteracting innovation. With the IT function solely measured on efficiency metrics, i.e. keeping its budget, any type of innovation initiative will invariably negatively impact the efficiency of the function. All new projects are deemed a risk in relation to fulfilling the core objective, i.e. delivering standardized services to operations. Hence, we see a need for additional research, within the e-government and the IS fields, into proposition 7.

With this study focused on understanding the impact of governance configurations on ambidexterity, said seven propositions become instrumental for increasing our insight into a potential pathology of IT Governance. Core to our reasoning has been the necessity for a configuration of governance that is aligned with the underlying strategic positioning of not only the organization(s), but also the intended use of digital initiatives in the quest for digitalization [18, 22, 32]. Here, we believe that the case may be illustrative of potential draw-backs of a governance geared for IT in a time when digitalization was not a core strategic objective for the organization. Hence, for organizations that strive for digitalization, previous research [2, 3, 8] would warrant an increased emphasis on ambidexterity. We hope that the propositions presented in this paper may act as a source of inspiration for future research. There are three main implications for practice. First, organizations that aspire for ambidexterity should strive to avoid the identified IT Governance configurations or at least be aware of the potential shortcomings. Second, there are clear identified trade-offs between efficiency and innovation that should be avoided, whereby the ambidextrous balancing point needs to be used as a strategic mechanism. Knowing which levels of innovation are aspirational for the organization at any given point in time will aid the IT department in configuring their IT Governance so that it is aligned with the organization's objectives. Third, with this balancing point being dynamic, i.e. shifting over time, there is a need for increasing the fluidity of IT Governance mechanisms, where a certain amount of flexibility should be built into the design. For additional insights into this in relation to new demands placed on the organization by digital transformation, see [33] and [34].

With this being a first attempt at a structured investigation into the pathology of IT Governance, it is off course laden with limitations. We acknowledge that the single-case study approach, despite being rich and deep, utilized places significant limitations if one aims for statistical generalizability of our findings [35]. At the same time, with this being an exploratory study, we deem the approach to be justifiable and acknowledge analytical generalizability. More studies are needed and we hope to see research into the phenomenon in the future. Another limitation lies in the choice of a collection of agencies with a centralized IT function. This is, in the Swedish context, an outlier. At the same time, the current push for digital centralization [36] within the Swedish context will require learning from previous centralized approaches, and here we believe that our study may form the basis for insight. In terms of the transferability of findings between both the private and the public sector and across national boundaries, we are aware of the limitations as put forth in [37].

6 Conclusion

This study has aimed at exploring how current configurations of IT Governance impact ambidexterity in organizations. We have studied this through a case study of 21 agencies in Sweden, with a centralized IT function. Through the study, we identified four areas and seven underlying configurations of IT Governance that were found to be skewing the ambidextrous balance towards efficiency rather than innovation, despite the organization expressing a need for increased innovation. We refer to these findings, and the propositions derived through them as a step towards a pathology of IT Governance, i.e. an attempt at understanding how certain configurations may act as deterrents for achieving the strategic objectives of organizations.

References

1. Canguilhem, G.: The Normal and the Pathological. Zone Books, New York (2016)
2. Yoo, Y., Henfridsson, O., Lyytinen, K.: Research commentary—the new organizing logic of digital innovation: an agenda for information systems research. Inf. Syst. Res. 21(4), 724–735 (2010)
3. Gregory, R.W., Keil, M., Muntermann, J., Mähring, M.: Paradoxes and the nature of ambidexterity in IT transformation programs. Inf. Syst. Res. 26(1), 57 (2015)
4. Magnusson, J., Koutsikouri, D., Päivärinta, T.: Efficiency creep and shadow innovation: ambidextrous IT governance in the public sector. Eur. J. Inf. Syst. (2020, in press)
5. Wiener, M., Mähring, M., Remus, U., Saunders, C.S.: Control configuration and control enactment in information systems projects: review and expanded theoretical framework. MIS Q. 40(3), 741–774 (2016)
6. Magnusson, J., Bygstad, B.: Why I act differently: studying patterns of legitimation among CIOs through motive talk. Inf. Technol. People 26(3), 265–282 (2013)
7. Magnusson, J., Nilsson, A., Kizito, M.: Enacting digital ambidexterity: the case of the swedish public sector. In: AMCIS Conference Proceedings, Cancun, Mexico (2019)
8. Gregory, R.W., Kaganer, E., Henfridsson, O., Ruch, T.J.: IT consumerization and the transformation of IT governance. MIS Q. 42(4), 1225–1253 (2018)
9. March, J.G.: Exploration and exploitation in organizational learning. Organ. Sci. 2(1), 71–87 (1991)
10. Benner, M.J., Tushman, M.L.: Exploitation, exploration, and process management: the productivity dilemma revisited. Acad. Manag. Rev. 28(2), 238–256 (2003)

11. Luger, J., Raisch, S., Schimmer, M.: Dynamic balancing of exploration and exploitation: the contingent benefits of ambidexterity. Organ. Sci. **29**(3), 449–470 (2018)
12. Raisch, S., Birkinshaw, J.: Organizational ambidexterity: antecedents, outcomes, and moderators. J. Manag. **34**(3), 375–409 (2008)
13. Zimmermann, A., Raisch, S., Cardinal, L.B.: Managing persistent tensions on the frontline: a configurational perspective on ambidexterity. J. Manage. Stud. **55**(5), 739–769 (2018)
14. Hinings, B., Gegenhuber, T., Greenwood, R.: Digital innovation and transformation: an institutional perspective. Inf. Organ. **28**(1), 52–61 (2018)
15. Mergel, I., Gong, Y., Bertot, J.: Agile government: systematic literature review and future research. Gov. Inf. Q. **35**(4), 291–298 (2018)
16. Weill, P., Ross, J.: A matrixed approach to designing IT governance. MIT Sloan Manag. Rev. **46**(2), 26 (2005)
17. De Haes, S., Van Grembergen, W.: An exploratory study into IT governance implementations and its impact on business/IT alignment. Inf. Syst. Manag. **26**(2), 123–137 (2009)
18. Wu, S.P.J., Straub, D.W., Liang, T.P.: How information technology governance mechanisms and strategic alignment influence organizational performance: insights from a matched survey of business and IT managers. MIS Q. **39**(2), 497–518 (2015)
19. Leclercq-Vandelannoitte, A., Bertin, E.: From sovereign IT governance to liberal IT governmentality? A Foucauldian analogy. Eur. J. Inf. Syst. **27**(3), 326–346 (2018)
20. Schlosser, F., Beimborn, D., Weitzel, T., Wagner, H.T.: Achieving social alignment between business and IT–an empirical evaluation of the efficacy of IT governance mechanisms. J. Inf. Technol. **30**(2), 119–135 (2015)
21. Tonelli, A.O., de Souza Bermejo, P.H., Dos Santos, P.A., Zuppo, L., Zambalde, A.L.: IT governance in the public sector: a conceptual model. Inf. Syst. Front. **19**(3), 593–610 (2017)
22. Xue, L., Ray, G., Sambamurthy, V.: Efficiency or innovation: how do industry environments moderate the effects of firms IT asset portfolio? MIS Q. **36**(2) (2012)
23. Piccinini, E., Hanelt, A., Gregory, R., Kolbe, L.: Transforming industrial business: the impact of digital transformation on automotive organizations. In: Proceedings of the International Conference for Information Systems, Fort Worth, Texas, US (2015)
24. Walsham, G.: Interpretive case studies in IS research: nature and method. Eur. J. Inf. Syst. **4**(2), 74–81 (1995)
25. www.lansstyrelsen.se. Accessed Mar 2020
26. Silverman, D.: Interpreting Qualitative Data. SAGE Publications Limited, London (2019)
27. Eisenhardt, K.M.: Building theories from case study research. Acad. Manag. Rev. **14**(4), 532–550 (1989)
28. Mithas, S., Rust, R.T.: How information technology strategy and investments influence firm performance: conjecture and empirical evidence. MIS Q. **40**(1) (2016)
29. Myers, N., Starliper, M.W., Summers, S.L., Wood, D.A.: The impact of shadow IT systems on perceived information credibility and managerial decision making. Acc. Horiz. **31**(3), 105–123 (2017)
30. Cokins, G.: The top seven trends in management accounting. EDPACS **53**(4), 1 (2016)
31. Rolland, K.H., Mathiassen, L., Rai, A.: Managing digital platforms in user organizations: the interactions between digital options and digital debt. Inf. Syst. Res. **29**(2), 419–443 (2018)
32. Banker, R.D., Hu, N., Pavlou, P.A., Luftman, J.: CIO reporting structure, strategic positioning, and firm performance. MIS Q. **35**, 487–504 (2011)
33. Berente, N., Lyytinen, K., Yoo, Y., King, J.L.: Routines as shock absorbers during organizational transformation: Integration, control, and NASA's enterprise information system. Organ. Sci. **27**(3), 551–572 (2016)
34. Yeow, A., Soh, C., Hansen, R.: Aligning with new digital strategy: a dynamic capabilities approach. J. Strateg. Inf. Syst. **27**(1), 43–58 (2018)

35. Eisenhardt, K.M., Graebner, M.E.: Theory building from cases: opportunities and challenges. Acad. Manag. J. **50**(1), 25–32 (2007)
36. www.digg.se. Accesses Mar 2020
37. Bannister, F.: The curse of the benchmark: an assessment of the validity and value of e-government comparisons. Int. Rev. Admin. Sci. **73**(2), 171 (2007)

Barriers and Drivers of Digital Transformation in Public Organizations: Results from a Survey in the Netherlands

Luca Tangi[1(✉)] ⓘ, Marijn Janssen[2] ⓘ, Michele Benedetti[1] ⓘ, and Giuliano Noci[1]

[1] Department of Management, Economics, and Industrial Engineering, Politecnico di Milano, Milan, Italy
{luca.tangi,michele.benedetti,giuliano.noci}@polimi.it
[2] Faculty of Technology, Policy and Management, Delft University of Technology, Delft, The Netherlands
m.f.w.h.a.janssen@tudelft.nl

Abstract. The introduction of ICT is requiring public administrations to transform their organizations to take advantage of these technologies. Despite its significance, no studies so far collected quantitative evidence on (i) how and the extent to which this transformation is currently underway and (ii) which drivers and barriers are hindering and leading this transformation process. This article aims at filling this gap by surveying Dutch public administrations. In total, 46 responses from different organizations were collected that provide insight into their transformation efforts. Findings show that digital transformation efforts had only a partial impact at the organizational level: processes, employees' duties and tasks and information systems are going through a deep transformation, whereas the social system seems to be less affected by the transformation process. Moreover, the analysis results suggest that external drivers are the main motivation for organizational transformation, and that expected internal barriers do not *de facto* result in digital transformation. These counterintuitive results suggest that in public administrations only exogenous input result in a sense of urgency and that the perceived barriers to transformation can be overcome if there is sufficient external pressure.

Keywords: Organizational transformation · Transformational government · Socio-technical theory · Barriers and drivers · E-government

1 Introduction

New digital technologies promise a more efficient public administration as well as a more effective service provision [1, 2]. However, the achievement of this promise gets often stuck on embedded norms, bureaucracy, processes, and structure [3]. The linkage between the introduction of ICT and the organizational transformation process is unavoidable: the pervasiveness of ICT in public affairs is forcing public agencies not to reduce the introduction of ICT to a mere dematerialization, i.e. substituting a physical

© IFIP International Federation for Information Processing 2020
Published by Springer Nature Switzerland AG 2020
G. Viale Pereira et al. (Eds.): EGOV 2020, LNCS 12219, pp. 42–56, 2020.
https://doi.org/10.1007/978-3-030-57599-1_4

means with digital ones, rather to pursue a necessary (and complex) process of organizational revision for letting the new digital technologies be institutionalized and routinized [4, 5]. Newer technologies should mean newer management, newer competences, newer organizational and inter-organizational structures [6] and often they require a radical change, asking for a disruption of the status quo and the standard operating procedures, by experimenting and iterating with technologies that are not part of the standard toolkit of public administrations [7]. The latter is often referred as transformation. Transformation entails a change in the whole organization, i.e. processes, employees' duties and tasks, information systems, organizational culture and behaviors, and the hierarchical structure. ICT has the potential to impact all those elements [3]. However, so far, the if, how and under which conditions the transformation took place is still unclear.

Some studies explore transformational efforts being undertaken by governments on all levels [8–10], while others highlight a lack of empirical evidence that real public sector transformation has taken place [11]. Moreover, all studies conducted so far are based on case studies, leaving a lack of understanding on the depth and the widespread of this ongoing transformation in the public sector. The cases often show that there are many impediments that complicate transformation as well as many drivers that foster it. Literature deeply investigates barriers and drivers, and categorizes them in different ways (see for example [12, 13]). This literature suggests that these elements have an influence on transformation. However, despite such literature deploying consolidated claims, there is a lack of research that quantitatively test the extent to which they influence the transformation. A quantitative analysis will cast light on the topic exploring if and which of the barriers, drivers and transformation processes observed with case studies can be reliable on a large scale.

This article aims to understand the depth of technology-driven public sector transformation and if and the extent to which barriers and drivers condition this transformation. For this, we review the literature and develop a conceptual model. This model is used to conduct a survey. Finally, conclusions are drawn.

2   Literature Review and Conceptual Model

Previous researches stated that organizational transformation is a necessary condition to realize ICT potential, as well as one of the main challenges public administrations are facing nowadays [3, 9]. On the other side, scholars so far identified several barriers and drivers that can foster or hinder this transformation process. However, only a few attempts have been made to construct and test a model that can explain this transformation [9]. Therefore, we define a model (Fig. 1) that on the one hand aims at assessing the level of ICT-embedded transformation (dependent variables) and, on the other hand the drivers and barriers that can enable or block it (independent variables). In doing that, we rely on the existing literature for grounding on a solid theoretical background each element that feed the design of the overall model and the hypotheses statement.

Fig. 1. Framework of analysis

2.1 Organizational Transformation

Organizations are complex systems that can be considered as the ensemble of five differ-ent elements: process, people, culture, structure and information system [3, 9]. Scholars unanimously agree that those elements are interdependent, therefore a change in one of them can cause changes in the others [3, 14, 15]. The five elements are described in Table 1. The Table provides also a list of examples on the impacts of ICT for each element.

According to the socio-technical theory those five elements can be grouped into two independent but interactive macro-systems that compose the organization [14]:

- the *technical system*, composed by those elements necessary to transform input into output (process, tasks, duties, information system).
- the *social system* that is concerned with all those elements that are related to the environment the technical system in embedded in, the organizational culture and values, and the authority structure.

The introduction of ICT has a direct effect on the technical system. However, previous studies demonstrate that the success of technology implementation is fastly tightened to a change also in the social system [3]. In fact, when organizations design a project that pursues a change only in the technical system, they are more likely to encounter failure [14].

Therefore, the introduction of ICT in an organization is supposed to have an impact on the organization as a whole [3]. Hence, we collect evidence taking into consideration all the five elements that characterize it, without assuming any *ex-ante* hypothesis about the type of relation between them [3, 10, 15, 16]. Thus, we state the following proposition (we do not articulate it as a hypothesis due to the absence of a quantitative method to test it):

P1. Transformation results in changes in the whole organization, impacting all the five elements that ensemble it.

When discussing organizational change, the first variable necessary to consider is the organization size. We intuitively expect that, as for other types of organizational change, bigger organizations are less flexible and more bureaucratic and therefore the transformation process is more complex and organizations are subject to minor changes.

Table 1. Elements of organizational transformation

Element	Description	Literature examples
Process	The set of activities to transform an input in output and to manage and control the entire process	[3, 15, 16]
People	Employees' duties and tasks and, therefore, in the competences needed	[3, 15]
Culture	Endorsed values and personal and collective behaviors	[3, 15, 16]
Structure	The organizational structure, i.e. the level of centralization/decentralization of responsibilities, the hierarchical structure and the degrees of flexibility	[3, 15]
Information system	The technological systems employed for managing the activities, i.e. all the software, hardware and the integration between them	[15]

H1. The size of the organization negatively influences the level of organizational transformation.

2.2 Barriers and Drivers

When approaching a complex process of organizational transformation led by new digital technologies, several barriers can come about and hinder the change [13]. Based on literature, barriers are divided into two categories: structural barriers and cultural barriers. *Structural barriers* comprehend organizational and managerial factors intrinsic to the characteristics of the organization, whereas *cultural barriers* comprehend behaviors of the employees that can hinder the change. Table 2 resumes the identified barriers.

As stated by previous studies, the listed barriers block or hinder the transformation process [13, 15]. In order verify those statements on a large scale, we formulate the following hypotheses.

H2. Structural barriers negatively influence the depth of ICT-embedded organizational transformation
H3. Cultural barriers negatively influence the depth of ICT-embedded organizational transformation

On the other side, literature identifies also several factors that encourage change. We divided the drivers into two categories: internal and external. On the one hand, internal drivers analyze the presence in the organization of elements (like a charismatic leader or some inefficiencies) that make the change more urgent. On the other hand, the urgency of change can come also from outside the organization (external drivers) for example from the pressure of external stakeholder or legal obligations. Table 3 summarizes the identified drivers.

Table 2. Barriers to ICT-embedded organizational transformation

Category	Barrier	Literature examples
Structural barriers	Lack of managerial support	[4, 17, 18]
	Lack of political support	[4, 17, 18]
	Lack of available skills	[12, 19, 20]
	Shortage of personnel	[12, 19, 20]
	Organizational complexity	[13, 21]
	Lack of coordination among the departments/areas of the organization	[16, 19, 22]
Cultural barriers	Resistance to change	[15, 16]
	Bureaucratic culture	[13, 23]
	Fear of innovation	[23]

Table 3. Drivers to ICT-embedded organizational transformation

Category	Barrier	Literature examples
Internal drivers	Strength of internal leadership	[3, 24]
	Internal dissatisfaction about the *status quo*	[8, 12]
	Expected benefits for the administration	[20]
External drivers	Expected benefits for external actors (stakeholders and/or final users)	[23]
	External pressure	[9, 25]
	External legal obligations	[9]

Following the same logic adopted for the barriers, we formulate the following hypotheses.

H4. Internal drivers positively influence the depth of ICT-embedded organizational transformation
H5. External drivers positively influence the depth of ICT-embedded organizational transformation

3   Research Approach

3.1   Survey Design

For testing the hypotheses, a questionnaire was developed and delivered to Dutch public managers. Barriers, drivers and the transformation process are intangible factors, therefore can be assessed only directly asking them to public managers.

The questionnaire was designed following the model presented in Fig. 1. The questionnaire had two sections to make it easier for reading and completing. Section A includes the questions related to the conceptual model. Three questions were defined (in Appendix I the questionnaire):

- questions 1 aims at measuring the dependent variable, i.e. the depth of organizational transformation (process, people, culture, structure, information system). For each element the level of agreement on the impact of ICT was questioned with a 5-point Likert scale.
- question 2 measures the barriers. For each barrier the level of agreement on how this barrier hinders the transformation process that goes along with the introduction of ICT was questioned with a 5-point Likert scale.
- question 3 measures the drivers. For each driver the level of agreement on how this driver pushes the transformation process that goes along with the introduction of ICT was questioned with a 5-point Likert scale.

In section A the respondents were clearly asked to consider the characteristics and the changes in the whole organization over the past couple of years.

Section B asked for demographic information in the form of multiple-choice questions. The section investigates the characteristics of the organization, such as type of administration, number of employees.

The survey was circulated by the Dutch association of municipalities (VNG) and the innovation vehicle of the Dutch government (deDigiCampus.nl). Before sending the survey, a pilot test with a first round of interviews involving 4 public managers was conducted for verifying the intelligibility and the completeness of the questionnaire. After that, the questionnaire was revised and a second pilot test was run with the Dutch association of municipalities for ensuring the goodness of the changes.

The survey was conducted between January and March 2020. At the beginning of February, a recall was made to increase the number of respondents.

The Netherlands were selected for this study due to their high level of e-government maturity and the variety in approaches taken as a decentralized unitary state. This country is enumerated among the "fruitful eGovernment" countries with a high level of digitization and ICT penetration [26]. The Netherlands is the constituent country of the Kingdom of Netherlands, which has also island territories located in the Caribbean. The major political institutions in the country are the monarchy, the parliament, the judiciary and the cabinet. Other levels of government include the municipalities, the provinces, and the water-board. These have their own elected council. Each of them decide on adopting their own technology. The municipalities collaborate in the association of municipalities to focus their efforts and share experiences. Nevertheless, each municipality can choose their own approach to digital transformation. Thanks to the stable relation of the authors with VNG and the deDigiCampus we had the opportunity to have a preferential communication channel for obtaining a large number of responses by public managers.

3.2 Sample and Methods

In total 48 responses were collected, 2 of them were discarded due to incompleteness. Table 4 shows the characteristics of the sample. Firstly, some descriptive statistics were analyzed. Before testing the hypothesis, looking at all the items singularly allows the collection of some more qualitative insight for discussing P1 and identify the more relevant barriers and drivers. Next, a t-test was run for testing H1. Simple regression was run in order to test the hypotheses from 2 to 4.

Table 4. Descriptive statistics of the sample

Element	Mean	Frequency	Percent
Size	<2000 employees	29	63,0
	>2000 employees	17	37,0
Type of administration	Administrative organization	8	17,4
	Ministry	4	8,7
	Municipality	27	58,7
	Other	1	2,2
	Other government	4	8,7
	Regional administration	2	4,3
Role	Director	5	10,9
	Other	9	19,6
	Public manager	13	28,3
	Public servant	19	41,3
Year of experience in the public sector	<5 years	2	4,3
	≥5 years	44	95,7
Year of experience in the current administration	<2 years	3	6,5
	≥2 years	43	93,5

4 Results

4.1 Organizational Transformation

Before testing the hypotheses, exploratory analysis was conducted to explain and discuss the extent to which ICT is leading to a transformation. We firstly took into consideration the five elements that characterize an organization (process, people, culture, structure and information system) in order to understand which of the elements are more impacted by the introduction of ICTs. Table 5 shows the results in terms of mean and standard deviation.

Table 5. ICT-embedded organizational transformation – exploratory results

Element	Mean	Std. dev.
Process	3,66	1,28
People	3,39	1,08
Culture	2,75	0,99
Structure	2,82	1,10
Information system	3,84	1,10

Table 5 offers some quantitative evidence that partially confirms P1: on average, respondents stated that ICTs are transforming the organizations in terms of processes, people and information systems (all the means above 3 out of 5). Moreover, ICTs seems on average less impactful on organizational culture and structure.

The t-test for testing H1 was conducted including only the technical system, i.e. the elements that resulted impacted by the introduction of ICTs (process, people and information system). Those elements were aggregated into an overall indicator summing them together and dividing them by the maximum score achievable (15 out of 15). Appendix II shows the reliability test. The administrations were divided into two categories with respect to their number of employees. Due to the structural characteristics of the Netherlands, the threshold was identified as 2000 employees. The test confirms H1 for both categories. Table 6 and 7 show the results of the test.

Table 6. Organizational transformation and size of the administration – mean and std. dev.

Category	N	Mean	Std. dev.
>2000 employees	29	0,7586	0,18131
≤2000 employees	17	0,6353	0,20438

Table 7. Organizational transformation and size of the administration – t-test

	Levene's test F	Levene's test Sig.	t	df	Sig. (2-tailed)
Equal variances assumed	0,449	0,506	2,132	44	0,039*

Note: *$p < 0.05$, **$p < 0.01$, ***$p < 0.001$

4.2 Organizational Transformation Barriers and Drivers

For the correlation test we aggregated structural barriers, cultural barriers, external drivers and internal drivers into the four overall indicators. In this way summing the single items together and dividing them by the maximum score achievable. In order to be coherent with the previous analysis the depth of organizational transformation was calculated by taking into consideration only the technical system. However, similar results would have been achieved taking when taking into consideration the social system.

Table 8 shows the descriptive statistics of the sample, Table 9 summarizes the results of the analysis. H2, H3 are rejected, H4 could not be tested, due to reliability issues of the overall indicator (see Appendix II), and H5 is confirmed.

The results show that the only independent variable having an impact on the depth of organizational transformation is the external drivers (except for the size of the administration). Public administrations that feel the pressure of an organizational transformation from outside are the ones that have recognized the most an organizational transformation led by the introduction of ICT.

Table 8. Barriers and drivers – descriptive statistics

	Minimum	Maximum	Mean	Std. deviation
SB_Skills	2,00	5,00	3,8261	0,87697
SB_Personnel	1,00	5,00	3,4348	1,00338
SB_PolSupport	1,00	5,00	3,5217	1,06956
SB_ManagSupport	1,00	5,00	3,6087	1,14462
SB_Complexity	1,00	5,00	4,0000	1,07497
SB_Coordination	2,00	5,00	4,2391	0,84813
SB_TOT	**0,47**	**0,97**	**0,7543**	**0,12036**
CB_Resistance	2,00	5,00	3,6304	1,01890
CB_Culture	2,00	5,00	3,8696	0,95705
CB_Fear	2,00	5,00	3,6087	0,99952
CB_TOT	**0,40**	**1,00**	**0,7406**	**0,15411**
ID_Leader	1,00	5,00	3,0870	1,07137
ID_Dissatisfaction	1,00	5,00	2,9565	1,11468
ID_IntBenefit	1,00	5,00	3,6087	0,90623
ID_TOT	**0,20**	**0,87**	**0,6435**	**0,14888**
ED_ExtBenefit	1,00	5,00	3,5870	1,02363
ED_Pressure	1,00	5,00	3,3913	0,99952
ED_Obligation	1,00	5,00	3,5217	1,13017
ED_TOT	**0,20**	**1,00**	**0,7000**	**0,16375**

Table 9. Organizational transformation – regression results

	Unstandardized coefficients		Standardized coefficients	t	Sig.
	B	Std. error	Beta		
(Constant)	0,345	0,252		1,370	0,178
CB_TOT	−0,174	0,232	−0,107	−0,751	0,457
SB_TOT	0,148	0,197	0,116	0,752	0,456
ED_TOT	0,629	0,172	0,523	3,666	0,001***
EMP2	−0,135	0,051	−0,336	−2,628	0,012*

Note: $*p < 0.05$, $**p < 0.01$, $***p < 0.001$

5 Discussion

Firstly, our study quantitative tested and confirmed that the introduction of ICTs is often combined with a transformation of the whole organization (P1). Going deeper into this evidence, the results show that the technical system of an organization (process, people and IS) is the most impacted by the introduction of ICT. On the other side, the social system (culture and structure) is less affected by this transformation.

This evidence corroborates the validity of the socio-technical theory [14] also in a digital setting. The social system is the one with a slower reaction time: change the organizational culture and the entire structure of a public administration it's a longer and more difficult process [27]. We can therefore hypothesize a two-step ICT-embedded organizational transformation: firstly, ICT transforms the technical system of an organization, secondly (temporarily speaking) the social one. The same phenomenon could be explained using the terminology suggested by Mergel et al. [25]: *digitalization* to define the change that involves a transformation existing processes and forms and *digital transformation* for emphasizing cultural and organizational change.

Adopting this classification, the results shows that, in the Netherlands, i.e. one of the country with the highest level of e-government digital maturity, public administrations are going through the digitalization process (i.e. a change in the technical system), while the digital transformation one (i.e. a change in the social system) is still in an embryonic phase.

On the other side, the Netherlands are a country where, on average, public administrations have a high level of complexity, due *in primis* to their large size. The results show, confirming H1, that the size of the administration is correlated with the depth of organizational transformation: for big and complex administrations the transformation process is less clear than in the smaller ones.

The second step includes in the analysis drivers and barriers. Firstly, a descriptive look to the data collected confirm the existing literature on the presence of structural and cultural barriers that curb the transformation (both above 0.7). The size of the Dutch Public Administration can explain why a lack of coordination and organizational complexity are the ones with a higher score (respectively 4.2 and 4.0). Instead, between the cultural barriers, bureaucratic culture has been identified as the most relevant impediment to face (3.9).

However, the evidence from the correlation analysis (Table 9) denies that the presence of those barriers has a relation with the depth of organizational transformation, influenced instead only by external drivers (H5). This result is partially in contrast with previous studies: even if public managers recognize the presence of barriers that obstruct the transformation process [13, 15], the study demonstrates that the deepness of the transformation is not related with the strength of those barriers. We are aware that this result might be influenced by the limited number of observations and self-selection bias. However, this counterintuitive evidence gives room to some further considerations and hypotheses to explain the obtained results.

External factors have a positive effect on the depth of the transformation. Administrations that feel the pressure (or the obligation) to change are the ones who also declare a higher degree of organizational transformation. This evidence can be explained by the nature of the public sector itself. The absence of the need of and pressure for being profitable or the risk of going bankrupt might make public servants less sensitive for internal pressures, whereas a request from the outside the administration is viewed as urgent. A direct consequence of that is the deployment of ICT as an instrument for improving services and participation, requests that come directly from the final users or from national and supra-national institutes, and less as an instrument to answer to internal needs and foster internal efficiency. Public servants initiate transformation due to outside pressures, and do not initiate this for solving internal issues or to obtain benefits for their own organization.

6   Conclusion and Further Research

Transformation in government to gain the benefits from digitalization is a key issue for most governments. Public Administrations are realizing that ICT cannot be reduced to a mere dematerialization of existing procedures and services, but, on the contrary, it must be combined with a change of the entire organization. Despite a general agreement among scholars on it, no studies quantitatively tested and analyzed the phenomenon so far. This article fills in this gap by conducting a survey in the Netherlands. The results show that ICTs are transforming organizations, and, in particular, they are transforming what the socio-technical theory defines as the technical system of an organization, i.e. processes, employees' duties and tasks, information systems. However, in contrary to the expectations this transformation is not hindered by those barriers that the existing literature identifies as an obstacle to the transformation process. Also transformation is not driven by internal organizational needs. Instead, external pressures towards change are the primary driver of organizational transformation.

Such evidence gives room to several further research avenues. First of all, the study focuses on a single country, characterized by a high maturity in terms of ICT implementation in the public sector. Delivering the same survey to a different country will dive deeper into the phenomenon, understanding if the results can be generalized also in other contexts. Moreover, the counterintuitive evidence of no correlation between the barriers and the depth of organizational transformation calls for further analysis to better understand the reasons behind these results. Further studies should design a more complex and comprehensive model, including more elements to better explain the phenomenon.

Appendix I – Questionnaire

1. From an organizational perspective, so far digitalization in your organization transformed: (1- strongly disagree; 5 - strongly agree):

   – Processes (reengineering of the existing processes, process management and control)
   – People (duties, tasks, complexity of work, competences)
   – Culture (endorsed values, personal and collective behavior)
   – Structure (standardization, centralization/decentralization, hierarchy, external relationships, flexibility)
   – Information Systems (IS) (introduction of new IS, replacing of the existing ones, integration amongst different IS, interoperability, IT infrastructure)

2. In your organization, the organizational transformation process that goes along with digitalization is hindered by: (1- strongly disagree; 5 - strongly agree)

   – Lack of available skills
   – Shortage of personnel
   – Lack of political support
   – Lack of managerial support
   – Organizational complexity
   – Lack of coordination among the departments/areas of the organization
   – Resistance to change
   – Bureaucratic culture
   – Fear of innovation

3. In your organization the organizational transformation process that goes along with digitalization is pushed by: (1- strongly disagree; 5 - strongly agree)

   – Strength of internal leadership
   – Internal dissatisfaction about the *status quo*
   – Expected benefits for the administration
   – Expected benefits for external actors (stakeholders and/or final users)
   – External pressure
   – External legal obligations

4. Public Administration:

   – Ministry
   – Administrative Organization

- Regional Administration
- Municipality
- Other government
- Private company
- Other (specify).

5. Number of employees of the Administration:

- ≤20
- 21–100
- 101–400
- 401–2000
- >2000

6. Role:

- Politician
- Director
- Pubic Manager
- Public Servant
- Other (specify)

7. Years of experience in the public sector:

- Less than 5 years
- More than 5 years

8. Years of work in the current organization:

- Less than 2 years
- More than 2 years

Appendix II – Reliability Test

	N. of item	Cronbach's alpha
OT_TOT	5	0,866
OT_Tecnical System	3	0,840
SB_TOT	6	0,646
CB_TOT	3	0,668
ED_TOT	3	0,674
ID_TOT	3	0,536

Note. ID_TOT was excluded from the regression analysis due to the low Cronbach's alpha. Cronbach's alpha higher than 0.6 was considered acceptable, due to the exploratory nature of the study

References

1. Margetts, H., Dunleavy, P.: The second wave of digital-era governance: a quasi-paradigm for government on the web. Philos. Trans. R. Soc. A Math. Phys. Eng. Sci. **371**(1987), 1–17 (2013)
2. Dunleavy, P., Margetts, H., Bastow, S., Tinkler, J.: New public management is dead - long live digital-era governance. J. Public Adm. Res. Theor. **16**(3), 467–494 (2006)
3. Nograšek, J., Vintar, M.: E-government and organisational transformation of government: black box revisited? Gov. Inf. Q. **31**(1), 108–118 (2014)
4. Fountain, J.E.: Public sector: early stage of a deep transformation. In: Litan, R., Rivlin, A. (eds.) The Economic Payoff from the Internet Revolution, pp. 235–268. Brookings Institution Press, Washington, D.C. (2001)
5. Hughes, O.: Public Management And Administration: An Introduction. MacMillan Education (2018)
6. Yildiz, M.: E-government research: reviewing the literature, limitations, and ways forward. Gov. Inf. Q. **24**(3), 646–665 (2007)
7. Pollitt, C.: Advanced Introduction To Public Management and Administration. Edward Elgar, Cheltenham (2016)
8. Weerakkody, V., Dhillon, G.: Moving from e-government to t-government: a study of process reengineering challenges in a UK local authority context. Int. J. Electron. Gov. Res. **4**(4), 1–16 (2008)
9. Pedersen, K.: E-government transformations: challenges and strategies. Transform. Gov. People Process Policy **12**(1), 84–109 (2018)
10. Weerakkody, V., El-Haddadeh, R., Sabol, T., Ghoneim, A., Dzupka, P.: E-government implementation strategies in developed and transition economies: a comparative study. Int. J. Inf. Manage. **32**(1), 66–74 (2012)
11. Coursey, D., Norris, D.F.: Models of e-government: Are they correct? an empirical assessment. Public Adm. Rev. **68**(3), 523–536 (2008)
12. Moon, M.J.: The evolution of e-government amoung municipalities: rhetoric or reality? Public Adm. Rev. **62**(4), 424–433 (2002)
13. van Veenstra, A.F., Klievink, B., Janssen, M.: Barriers and impediments to transformational government: insights from literature and practice. Electron. Gov. Int. J. **8**(2/3), 226–241 (2011)
14. Bostrom, R.P., Heinen, J.S.: MIS problems and failures: a socio- technical perspective. MIS Q. **1**(3), 17–32 (1977)
15. Al-Emadi, A., Anouze, A.L.: Grounded theory analysis of successful implementation of e-government projects: exploring perceptions of e-government authorities. Int. J. Electron. Gov. Res. **14**(1), 23–52 (2018)
16. Weerakkody, V., El-Haddadeh, R., Sivarajah, U., Omar, A., Molnar, A.: A case analysis of e-government service delivery through a service chain dimension. Int. J. Inf. Manage. **47**, 233–238 (2019)
17. Gascó, M.: New technologies and institutional change in public administration. Soc. Sci. Comput. Rev. **21**(1), 6–14 (2003)
18. Ashaye, O.R., Irani, Z.: The role of stakeholders in the effective use of e-government resources in public services. Int. J. Inf. Manage. **49**, 253–270 (2019)

19. Ebrahim, Z., Irani, Z.: E-government adoption: architecture and barriers. Bus. Process Manag. J. **11**(5), 589–611 (2005)
20. Wirtz, B.W., Langer, P.F.: Public multichannel management – an integrated framework of off- and online multichannel government services. Public Organ. Rev. **17**(4), 563–580 (2017)
21. Eynon, R., Dutton, W.H.: Barriers to networked governments: evidence from Europe. Prometheus **25**(3), 225–242 (2007)
22. Janssen, M., Cresswell, A.M.: An enterprise application integration methodology for e-government. J. Enterp. Inf. Manag. **18**(5), 531–547 (2005)
23. Meijer, A.J.: E-governance innovation: barriers and strategies. Gov. Inf. Q. **32**(2), 198–206 (2015)
24. Mohammad, K.: E-leadership: the emerging new leadership for the virtual organization. J. Manag. Sci. **3**(1), 1–21 (2009)
25. Mergel, I., Edelmann, N., Haug, N.: Defining digital transformation: results from expert interviews. Gov. Inf. Q. **36**(4), 1–16 (2019)
26. European Commission, eGovernment Benchmark 2019: trust in government is increasingly important for people (2019)
27. Williamson, Ó.: Transaction cost economics: how it works; where it is headed. Entomol. Exp. Appl. **146**, 23–58 (1998)

E-Government Services and Open Government

Smart Policing: A Critical Review of the Literature

Muhammad Afzal[✉] and Panos Panagiotopoulos

Queen Mary University of London, London, UK
{m.afzal,p.panagiotopoulos}@qmul.ac.uk

Abstract. Smart policing refers to the application of data-driven approaches by police authorities. Although the concept is not new, the vast availability of potentially relevant data sources in policing calls for a critical and consolidated review of the literature. To synthesise the evidence on smart policing, we present a systematic review of 112 articles across all relevant disciplines. Earlier work has concentrated on social media communications or predictive policing while this review identifies several new applications associated with new forms of data and their corresponding roles to policing. We develop a framework to show the connections between smart use of data and police approaches and strategies. We discuss how smart policing can be an area of increased interest in digital government and public management research.

Keywords: Smart policing · Big data · Systematic review

1 Introduction

The data-driven transformation of policing or smart policing has not received much attention in digital government research. Current approaches have concentrated on policing using social media sources [1, 2] and, to a lesser extent, on the predictive capabilities of new tools to enable police authorities to better allocate resources [3]. New forms of data are becoming the cornerstone of policing in many more transformative ways that remain less explored. These new applications at the intersection of data and policing include crime analytics, predictive crime profiling, network analysis of criminal gangs and intelligence using a variety of new sources of data.

Beyond the emphasis on new forms of data, smart policing is a newly established concept that encompasses innovative strategies, collaborations, interagency sharing and research partnerships to exploit data-driven approaches and digital tools [4, 5]. As with business and public policy applications of big data and data analytics, smart policing presumes the integration of various sources from which raw data can be converted into meaningful and actionable information [6]. Large volumes of data offer great potential for policing, but critical questions arise as to how policing has been transformed through use of data. No review has yet synthesised the evidence on smart policing to provide an integrated perspective and establish the connections between data applications and

© IFIP International Federation for Information Processing 2020
Published by Springer Nature Switzerland AG 2020
G. Viale Pereira et al. (Eds.): EGOV 2020, LNCS 12219, pp. 59–70, 2020.
https://doi.org/10.1007/978-3-030-57599-1_5

the strategies and functions of policing. As new data-driven applications have been reshaping the landscape of smart policing quite rapidly in recent years making the need for a contemporary approach even more evident.

The systematic review presented in this paper seeks to achieve the above aims while focusing on the public management implications of smart policing. Following a more detailed background, we explain how the review was conducted and present the findings structured around four main themes that correspond to the four main sources of data in smart policing. The contribution is summarised in the form of an analytical framework that outlines the main approaches to smart policing and leads to implications for future research on the topic.

2   Conceptual Background on Smart Policing

Advanced statistical techniques and large data streams from multiple sources have long been used by police authorities. Starting from the digitisation of police records in the 1970s, most US police departments were using computers and databases for operational allocations as well as strategic decisions by the early 1990s [7]. A significant milestone of data-driven police management came in the 1990s with the use of *CompStat* and *Crime Analysis* [8, 9]. CompStat was deployed both as an accountability tool and an initial approach to operational management via problem-oriented policing that advocates the use of data to identify crime hotspots [8, 9]. While used to evaluate performance of operational commanders, CompStat raised the first issues of data quality and validity leading to changes in the practices of rigorous data collection by field officers. Following its great success to control crime in New York, CompStat was adopted throughout the US while crime analysis in the form of hotspot policing diffused throughout the western democracies by the early 2000s.

More recently, the full range of technologies associated with big data, analytics and new data sources have been introduced in the context of policing. Two major data-related developments are the automated generation of data from surveillance technologies and crowdsourced data from social networks and information sharing sites [10]. Police authorities have been building their expertise on surveillance and monitoring technologies in the wake of 9/11, for example, CCTVs, smart phones, automated number plate readers, dash-board cameras and body-worn video cameras [11, 12]. These real-time sensors can continuously collect large amounts of data in urban environments on the movement of people, traffic flows and violations and changes in environmental indicators like heat, sound or pollution [6].

Crowdsourced data from open information sources – mainly social media – have resulted in new sources of big data streams of text, photos and videos that can be translated into factual information as well as collective opinions, emotions, perceptions and reactions regarding any place, person, current and future events [13]. For example, over 18 terabytes of data were collected and analysed by the French police in the 2015 Paris attacks [14]. In the 2011 riots in the UK, social media data were used as an ample and cost-effective source of intelligence during extensive public disorder [1, 15].

These and several more critical events and case studies have demonstrated the practical relevance of data in policing. However, many questions remain about how large volumes of new data sources have changed policing. One of the reasons is that the literature on policing is fragmented either across the different data applications or policing approaches and terminologies like hotspot policing, problem-oriented policing, intelligence-led policing and predictive policing [16]. Other reviews related to the topic have focused on the emerging area of predictive policing [3] or the use of social media by police authorities [2]. We aim to further develop the concept of smart policing as the synthesis of how policing is changing with smart use of data and assess the whole range of applications and potential impacts of data in policing. To synthesise the literature and provide new insights, we view data applications across the core functions of policing that have been established in the relevant literature as: (1) order maintenance (suppressing riots, preserving public peace and protecting morals); (2) law enforcement (crime prevention and investigation, traffic enforcement, stop-and-frisk operations, raids, patrols, arrests, searches and seizures etc.); and (3) service provision (police officer working as disaster manager, probation worker, social worker, school worker, security manager etc.) [17].

3 Methodology

The systematic review was conducted to collate the empirical evidence surrounding different approaches to data and policing in a systematic, transparent and auditable manner [18]. Searches were conducted in the three most prominent social science databases (EbscoHost, Scopus and Web of Science) using a combination of domain and concept terms. The concept terms covered data-related keywords while the domain terms ensured the relevance of the articles to policing. The following terms were used to search within title, abstract and article keywords: (police OR policing) AND (smart OR intelligence OR algorith* OR predictive OR analytics OR "data science" OR "data driven" OR "big data" OR AI OR "social media"). The search was limited to peer-reviewed academic articles published in English within 2009–2019.

A total of 4,502 articles were initially obtained and reduced to 2,856 after removing duplicates across the databases. A further 2,366 articles were manually removed after the titles and abstracts were screened for relevance to use of data in policing. The remaining 490 articles were further screened on reading the full text with the following criteria: (1) clear focus on data uses within police departments or agencies (2) at least some empirical data or application context provided – studies relying only on conceptual and theoretical foundations were excluded (3) studies focusing only on social media communication and digital engagement without direct relevance to data aspects were excluded. The final selection included 112 articles for the full review.

Initially, the articles were analysed structurally on the basis of author, title, year, journal, context, article type (empirical or conceptual), area of research focus, research question, methods and level of analysis. Then the articles were openly coded with NVivo 12 for: sources of data, analytical techniques (including applications and products), policing activities and outputs. Themes were compared and grouped as follows: (1) sources of data under Kitchin's [19] typology, (2) analytical techniques were inductively grouped under roles to policing (3) policing activities under Braga & Schnell's [20] intervention dimensions (environmental, enforcement and community outreach) and (4) outputs under core policing functions (order maintenance, law enforcement, service provision) [17]. These four analytical dimensions were integrated to develop the framework shown in Fig. 1 and identify research gaps as discussed in the next sections.

4   Findings

Data-driven policing has recently sparked major interest with 40% of the articles appearing in 2018 or 2019. The articles were published in various academic disciplines mostly concentrated in policing and criminology journals (53) followed by sociology and culture (22), information technology and information systems (16), public policy and administration (3) and others (18). The majority of application contexts are concentrated in the US (43 articles) followed by the UK (19), Europe (18), Canada (10), Australia (6) and Asia/Africa (6). The studies include qualitative (71) and quantitative (41) research methods with over half of the latter (23) using data from the US.

The framework of smart policing shown in Fig. 1 maps the different dimensions starting from the three types of data in policing. *Directed data* are intentionally captured either by police officers (crime and disorder records, offender profiles, service calls, community intelligence, warrants and summons) or by other public and private organizations (weather patterns, socio-demographics, lighting, infrastructure conditions, school schedules, traffic patterns, emergency calls). *Automated data* are inherently collected by a device or system used by police or public like smart CCTVs, police body worn cameras, dash-board cameras, automatic number plate readers (ANPR), smart phones, smart cards, environmental sensors etc. [6]. *Crowdsourced data* are created through open source devices, platforms or systems with the greatest volume generated by social networking sites like Facebook, Twitter and Instagram [13].

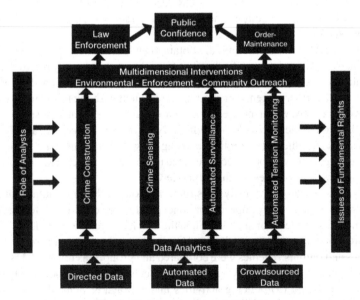

Fig. 1. Framework of smart policing

Various analytical approaches have been adopted for information extraction from these data for *crime construction, crime sensing, automated surveillance* and *automated tension monitoring* as explained below and summarized in Table 1. These emerging "smart roles" of data are transforming the policing functions of law enforcement and order-maintenance and can have positive as well as adverse impacts on public confidence. Surprisingly, the role of data vis-à-vis third core function of service provision remains unexplored in literature and is, accordingly, not reflected in the framework.

4.1 Crime Construction

Crime construction employs directed data to proactively visualize crime incidents and enable prioritising targets and reallocating resources for crime prevention. We distinguish two main applications based on *exploratory* (e.g. spatial analysis, time-series analysis and graph theory) and *predictive analytics* (machine learning and other forecasting techniques) in accordance with policing literature [16].

Exploratory analytics include crime mapping, criminal profiling and gang analysis. Exploratory crime mapping uses primary directed data (reported crime and disorders events or calls for service) to map out areas into hotspots with high victimization risk or crime density [21]. Exploratory profiling employs the primary offender data to identify the most harmful offenders to create deterrence by conditioning police surveillance and arrest efforts. For example, Philadelphia police estimates the harm scores of violent crime offenders by aggregating the weighted scores of static factors like gravity of offence, severity of sentence and time decay [22]. In the case of gangs, network analysis is a better approach to identify influential targets, for instance, using capital scores and other network metrics [23]. However, network analysis suffers on account of missing links arising from untraced and unreported cases.

Our knowledge of the effectiveness of exploratory analytics has been reported based on aggregate crime statistics. Massarotti's [41] longitudinal and Rydberg's [42] quasi experimental evaluations of crime mapping approaches to patrolling found no significant decrease in property crime (burglary, motor vehicle theft and robbery) and violent crime respectively. A range of other studies have reported decreases in violent crime, property crime, gun violence, services calls and other indicators at varying levels [20, 43, 44]. However, these studies have not yet applied more robust methods like balanced random design and their effects are usually reported only in hotspot areas.

Predictive analytics include predictive crime mapping and profiling. Predictive crime mapping applies forecasting models on micro-locations of crimes called prospective or dynamic hot spots [24]. The commonly used techniques are near repeats models (spatio-temporal features of crime data) and risk terrain model (spatial risk zones using socio-demographic features) [25]. Mapping and database extraction tools that apply these techniques have usually developed as an outcome of police-private collaboration (e.g. PredPol, PRECOBs-Enterprise, HunchLab, BlueCRUSH) [25, 26]. Predictive profiling incorporates static and dynamic risk factors to predict future offending tendency of a person by calculating their predictive risk scores. Such automated risk-assessment tools include ProKid (Dutch police), HART (Durham Constabulary, UK) and Strategic Subjects List (Chicago police) [27–29].

Evaluations of predictive mapping and profiling have shown mixed effects [25] Mohler's [24] found a 7.4% reduction in violent and property crime in predicted hotspots

Table 1. Summary of new roles of data in smart policing

Smart roles	Approaches and illustrative examples
Crime construction	• *Exploratory crime mapping*: historical crime data to map out areas (hotspots) with above average crime rates for multi-dimensional interventions to prevent crime and enhance collective efficacy (MAPS, GeoDash etc.) [21] • *Exploratory profiling* uses harm score estimation to generates harm scores of chronic offenders of gun violence based upon offence gravity, sentence severity and time decay functions for enforcement intervention to prevent crime [22] • *Network analysis* calculates network capital from gang-related data for targeting the most instrumental criminals for their apprehension [23] • *Predictive crime mapping* applies machine learning tools (near repeats & risk terrain analysis) to directed data to forecast crime patterns for directed patrolling to prevent crime (e.g. PredPol, HunchLab etc.) [24–26] • *Predictive profiling* applies machine learning techniques to risk factors (e.g. socio-demographics) to forecast probability of offending or victimization for enforcement intervention to create deterrence (ProKid, HART etc.) [27–29]
Crime sensing	• *Signal crimes and disorders* employs geocoded data of crimes and disorders collected from "neighbourhood sentinels" or social media data to generate area signal profiles for enforcement intervention to reduce crime, social harm and public mistrust (e.g., iNSI, ePOOLICE etc.) [30–32]
Automated surveillance	• *Sensor alerting* uses threshold-logic rules, optical character recognition and acoustics correlations for raising flags from data of CCTVs, environmental sensors to improve response times for crime prevention [6, 33, 34] • *Automated pattern recognition* produces spatio-temporal and routing patterns from ANPR data to help predict the locations of suspected vehicles to track and arrest wanted criminals [6, 35] • *Radio-cell analysis* employs data-mining techniques to crime and social unrest coded grid-cell connection data for clustering and pattern recognition to detect suspects for crime investigation (e.g., eFAS) [36] • *Social mapping* includes temporal mapping, facial mapping, relational mapping and sentiment analysis of social media data for crime investigation (e.g.,EU Virtuoso) [32, 37]

(continued)

Table 1. (*continued*)

Smart roles	Approaches and illustrative examples
Automated tension monitoring	• *Tension monitoring analytics* applies a mix of natural language processes, deep learning and network analysis techniques to social media data for grading social cohesion and identifying tension spikes and influential actors to maintain public order (e.g., COSMOS, HaterNet) [13, 38–40]

as compared to exploratory hotspots through directed patrolling. Brantingham [45] found no evidence of racial bias in arrest patterns while Saunders [29] found a 6.8% increased crime risk in enforcement intervention of Strategic Subjects List. Besides, the literature posits an increase in police craft due to increased citizen interaction through directed patrolling in previously untraversed areas [46].

4.2 Crime Sensing

Crime sensing involves the proactive gathering of community intelligence from public and social media to develop signals of crime and disorder to design appropriate strategies through resource reallocation and involvement of other stakeholders beyond relying on public complaints.

Signal crimes perspectives (SCP) employs community intelligence to develop an area signal profile based upon the crime and disorder events affecting public perceptions [30, 31]. The data are proactively collected by computer-assisted personal interviewing software (like i-NSI) and geocoded onto the neighbourhood maps to develop area signal profiles comprising crime, fear-and-avoidance and societal-tension hotspots [30, 31]. Using SCP, the Lancashire police (UK) detected signals of antisocial behaviour, tensions between residents groups and a range of other violations [30]. The Sutton police's (London) use of SCP-based spatio-temporal reallocation of foot and vehicle patrols resulted in 28% decrease of signal events in the risk perception hot spots [31].

Social media users also act as sensors of crime while behaving as victims, witnesses or offenders. An analysis of London-tagged Twitter data in 2013–2014 revealed that the tweet frequency and broken windows indicators were significantly associated with reported burglary, criminal damage and violence [47]. The ePOOLICE system is another example of identification of crime patterns of human smuggling and drug trafficking through integration of police and social media data [32].

4.3 Automated Surveillance

Automated surveillance applies data mining tools and visual analytics to automated and crowdsourced data for law enforcement through real-time monitoring and for prosecution through generation of new forms of evidence. The literature has identified four new approaches of automated surveillance:

Sensor alerting uses video analytics, optical character recognition and acoustics correlations for generating alerts from CCTVs, environmental sensors, ANPRs and shotspotters [6]. Using sensor alerting, the Camden Police (New Jersey, USA) managed to reduce response times by half and overall crime by 40% between 2013 and 2014 [33]. The use of smart CCTV for traffic enforcement in Shanghai significantly increased seat belt compliance from 60.8% to 84.9% between 2015 and 2017 [34].

Automated pattern recognition produces time-and-place and routing patterns which help predict the future locations of suspected or under-watch vehicles [6]. This has helped New York police to trace court absconders, prevent kidnappings and arrest chronic robbers red-handedly [6, 35].

Radio-cell analysis is used to mine mobile phone connection data to identify suspicious connections involved in rioting and heinous crimes (murder and kidnapping) [36]. Human investigators further probe these suspicious connections for establishing links with crime or rioting. The German police used one such application to sort out and charge 379 suspicious individuals from 153,622 connections during the Dresden riots (2011) [36].

Social mapping involves extraction and analysis of social media data related to a suspected individual, group or event during criminal investigations. Data is extracted through manual searching, automated searching (through web crawlers like NiceTrack, EU Virtuoso, RIOT), lawful interception (using deep pocket inspection) and targeted interception (installing Trojan on targeted device) [32, 37]. The data are analysed through: temporal mapping (like Facebook timeline); facial mapping (photos and images in conjunction with facial recognition technology using data mining tools); relational mapping (connection and communication patterns); and sentiment mapping (the language in posts and responses) [37]. For instance, the Vancouver police collaborated with Insurance Corporation of British Columbia to use facial recognition technology for online identification of suspects involved in riots (2011) [37].

4.4 Automated Tension Monitoring

Automated tension monitoring applies tension monitoring analytics to crowdsourced data, mainly social media, for assessing communal tension level and identification of groups and actors involved in sparking social unrest and hatred.

Tension monitoring analytics is a combination of data mining tools (like natural language processing-NLP) and machine learning techniques (like double deep learning and formal concept analysis) [13, 38–40]. The Cardiff Online Social Media Laboratory (COSMOS), an online tension monitoring engine, uses NLP techniques of membership categorization analysis and conversation analysis, measured the community tension following a racial abuse incident between two football players, Suarez and Evra (2011), with an overall accuracy of 0.87 and spike accuracy of 0.97 [12]. Other data mining tools include Naives Bayes and Support Vector Machines that are not able to consistently detect tension spikes [38]. ATHENA, an European crisis management system, uses formal concept analysis for clustering of data and NLP for measuring the sentiment score as positive, negative or neutral [40]. HaterNet, a Spanish hate speech detection system, uses double deep learning for clustering, NLP for classification of tweets and social network analysis for pattern, actor and community identification through word clouds, ranked graphs and clustering respectively [39]. EMOTIVE, the UK project, uses NLP to assess the mood of nation from Twitter data [32].

5 Discussion and Conclusion

The systematic review substantiates the significance of data as central force in smart policing, highlights the major analytical approaches and outlines their smart roles. Together with the framework, the review helps to confine the opaque smart policing terminology to more focused processes (data analytics, smart functions and multi-pronged interventions) leading to outputs (law enforcement and order-maintenance) and outcomes (public confidence and collective efficacy). The review further consolidates the literature across existing multidisciplinary studies that have tackled the data aspects of policing in various ways and methods.

Data appears to be the real precursor of major shift from reactive policing (arrest and random patrolling) to proactive policing (directed patrolling, deterrence, target hardening and community outreach) through efficient reallocation and utilization of resources for law enforcement and order-maintenance thereby improving public confidence, collective efficacy and police craft. In parallel, automated and crowd-sourced data are spurring a radical shift from streel level policing to screen-level policing [48]. The emergence of various applications is pushing towards system-level policing though currently their use is limited to assist human decision making [6, 48].

The findings further reveal how smart policing is transforming police authorities as public management organisations although our knowledge of these aspects is too limited. New roles and skillsets within police departments have not been explored because of issues like deputing of lackadaisical sworn officers as analysts, cultural repulsion of civilian analysts, obscurity of analysts' roles, police managers' inadequate analytical skills, limited training opportunities etc. [46, 49]. Moreover, computers and smart technologies are expensive and upgrading drains the budgets. For instance, 85% of London Metropolitan police's ICT budget in 2012 was consumed in maintenance of 40-year-old computers and redundant ICT systems making patrol officers dependent on radio calls for on-field verifications [5]. Also, data incompleteness, accuracy, overload and sharing issues persist despite the emergence of fusion centres in US [50]. The precision of crime construction is dependent upon liberal public reporting often thwarted by economic risks associated with hot areas [51]. Human interpretation is critical as crime construction and sensing do not explain underlying social complexities and are being theoretically challenged on ethnic and racial grounds though literature fails to support empirically [2, 51].

The review has certain limitations associated with coverage as it focuses solely on the data dimensions of core policing functions to overcome the opacity of smart policing. It does not fully capture the police management practices involved in translating the data-related processes into practice in the real-world scenarios.

Several gaps and limitations in the literature can be identified from the review as the areas can attract more attention by digital government and public management researchers. Current impact evaluations lack rigorous research designs because of unbalanced designs, non-random assignments, dearth of longitudinal studies, omission of displacement effects and use of generic measures like service calls and property crime.

Most evaluation studies have also been conducted in the US or used US-based data with additional evidence coming almost exclusively from the developed world. This offers a unique opportunity for further investigations as police authorities in many developing countries tend to face extreme budget constraints and low police-public trust.

In terms of connecting smart policing to established police approaches and strategies, the framework provides a point of reference for future research. While automated surveillance and tension monitoring are well-known applications, no formal empirical evaluations have yet examined their effects on law enforcement and order-maintenance while the literature argues that they raise issues of fundamental rights like civil liberties, privacy and proportionality [32]. The smart use of data vis-à-vis service provision remains less explored despite the fact that earlier research found that about one-third of street-level work is occupied with providing assistance to weak, ill, drunk and vulnerable citizens, and dealing with emergency (like fire, tree down, accidents) and lost person or property [17]. Finally, there is a dearth of empirical studies exploring the impact of new forms of data on the working styles and discretion of street level officers and their coping strategies. Smart policing approaches might be legitimising police discretion or even possibly increasing their accountability while police managers are faced with trade-offs of resource diversion and screen-level versus street-level policing [46].

References

1. Hu, X., Rodgers, K., Lovrich, N.P.: "We are more than crime fighters": social media images of police departments. Police Q. **21**, 544–572 (2018)
2. de Graaf, G., Meijer, A.: Social media and value conflicts: an explorative study of the dutch police. Public Adm. Rev. **79**, 82–92 (2019)
3. Meijer, A., Wessels, M.: Predictive policing: review of benefits and drawbacks. Int. J. Public Adm. **42**, 1031–1039 (2019)
4. Coldren, J.R., Huntoon, A., Medaris, M.: Introducing smart policing: foundations, principles, and practice. Police Q. **16**, 275–286 (2013)
5. Biggs, J., Bacon, G.: Smart Policing: How the Metropolitan Police Service Can Make Better Use of Technology (2013)
6. Levine, E.S., Tisch, J., Tasso, A., Joy, M.: The New York City Police Department's Domain Awareness System. Interfaces (Providence) **47**, 70–84 (2017)
7. Northrop, A., Kraemer, K.L., King, J.L.: Police use of computers. J. Crim. Justice. **23**, 259–275 (1995)
8. Weisburd, D., Mastrofski, S.D., McNally, A.M., Greenspan, R., Willis, J.J.: Reforming to preserve: compstat and strategic problem solving in american policing. Criminol. Public Policy. **2**, 421–456 (2003)
9. Manning, P.: The Technology of Policing: Crime Mapping, Information Technology, and the Rationality of Crime Control. New York University Press (2008)
10. Broeders, D., Schrijvers, E., van der Sloot, B., van Brakel, R., de Hoog, J., Hirsch Ballin, E.: Big Data and security policies: towards a framework for regulating the phases of analytics and use of big data. Comput. Law Secur. Rev. **33**, 309–323 (2017)
11. Ferguson, A.G.: Big data surveillance: the convergence of big data and law enforcement. In: Gray, D., Henderson, S.E. (eds.) The Cambridge Handbook of Surveillance Law, pp. 171–197. Cambridge University Press, Cambridge (2017)
12. Rogers, C., Scally, E.J.: Police use of technology: insights from the literature. Int. J. Emerg. Serv. **7**, 100–110 (2018)

13. Williams, M.L., Edwards, A., Housley, W., Burnap, P., Rana, O., Avis, N., Morgan, J., Sloan, L.: Policing cyber-neighbourhoods: tension monitoring and social media networks. Polic. Soc. **23**, 461–481 (2013)
14. Kubler, K.: State of urgency: Surveillance, power, and algorithms in France's state of emergency. Big Data Soc. **4**, (2017). https://doi.org/10.1177/2053951717736338
15. Dencik, L., Hintz, A., Carey, Z.: Prediction, pre-emption and limits to dissent: social media and big data uses for policing protests in the United Kingdom. New Media Soc. **20**, 1433–1450 (2018)
16. Santos, R.B.: The effectiveness of crime analysis for crime reduction: cure or diagnosis? J. Contemp. Crim. Justice **30**, 147–168 (2014)
17. Wilson, J.Q.: Varieties of Police Behavior: The Management of Law and Order in Eight Communities. Harvard University Press, Cambridge (1968)
18. Okoli, C., Schabram, K.: A Guide to Conducting a Systematic Literature Review of Information Systems Research. (2010)
19. Kitchin, R.: The Data Revolution: Big Data, Open Data. Data Infrastructures & Their Consequences. Sage Publications Ltd, London (2014)
20. Braga, A.A., Schnell, C.: Evaluating place-based policing strategies: lessons learned from the smart policing initiative in boston. Police Q. **16**, 339–357 (2013)
21. Ariel, B., Weinborn, C., Sherman, L.W.: "Soft" policing at hot spots—do police community support officers work? a randomized controlled trial. J. Exp. Criminol. **12**(3), 277–317 (2016). https://doi.org/10.1007/s11292-016-9260-4
22. Ratcliffe, J.H., Kikuchi, G.: Harm-focused offender triage and prioritization: a philadelphia case study. Polic. An. Int. J. Police Strateg. Manag. **42**, 59–73 (2019)
23. Hashimi, S., Bouchard, M.: On to the next one? Using social network data to inform police target prioritization. Polic. An Int. J. Police Strateg. Manag. **40**, 768–782 (2017)
24. Mohler, G.O., Short, M.B., Malinowski, S., Johnson, M., Tita, G.E., Bertozzi, A.L., Brantingham, P.J.: Randomized controlled field trials of predictive policing. J. Am. Stat. Assoc. **110**, 1399–1411 (2015)
25. Moses, L.B., Chan, J.: Algorithmic prediction in policing: assumptions, evaluation, and accountability. Polic. Soc. **28**, 806–822 (2018)
26. Benbouzid, B.: To predict and to manage. Predictive policing in the United States. Big Data Soc. **6** (2019)
27. Wientjes, J., Delsing, M., Cillessen, A., Janssens, J., Scholte, R.: Identifying potential offenders on the basis of police records: development and validation of the ProKid risk assessment tool. J. Criminol. Res. POLICY Pract. **3**, 249–260 (2017)
28. Oswald, M., Grace, J., Urwin, S., Barnes, G.C.: Algorithmic risk assessment policing models: lessons from the Durham HART model and "Experimental" proportionality. Inf. Commun. Technol. Law. **27**, 223–250 (2018)
29. Saunders, J., Hunt, P., Hollywood, J.S.: Predictions put into practice: a quasi-experimental evaluation of Chicago's predictive policing pilot. J. Exp. Criminol. **12**(3), 347–371 (2016). https://doi.org/10.1007/s11292-016-9272-0
30. Innes, M., Abbott, L., Lowe, T., Roberts, C.: Seeing like a citizen: field experiments in "community intelligence-led policing". Police Pract. Res. An Int. J. **10**, 99–114 (2009)
31. Lowe, T., Innes, M.: Can we speak in confidence? Community intelligence and neighbourhood policing v2.0. Polic. Soc. **22**, 295–316 (2012)
32. Edwards, L., Urquhart, L.: Privacy in public spaces: what expectations of privacy do we have in social media intelligence? Int. J. Law Inf. Technol. **24**, 279–310 (2016)
33. Wiig, A.: Secure the city, revitalize the zone: Smart urbanization in Camden. New Jersey. Environ. Plan. C-Politics Sp. **36**, 403–422 (2018)
34. Li, Q., Peng, J., Chen, T., Yu, Y., Hyder, A.A.: Seatbelt wearing rate in a Chinese city: results from multi-round cross-sectional studies. Accid. Anal. Prev. **121**, 279–284 (2018)

35. Levine, E.S., Tisch, J.S.: Analytics in action at the new york city police department's counterterrorism bureau. Mil. Oper. Res. **19**, 5 + (2014)
36. Paasche, T.F.: Coded police territories: detective software' investigates. Area. **45**, 314–320 (2013)
37. Trottier, D.: 'Fear of contact': police surveillance through social networks. Eur. J. Cult. Polit. Sociol. **4**, 457–477 (2017)
38. Burnap, P., Rana, O.F., Avis, N., Williams, M., Housley, W., Edwards, A., Morgan, J., Sloan, L.: Detecting tension in online communities with computational Twitter analysis. Technol. Forecast. Soc. Change **95**, 96–108 (2015)
39. Pereira-Kohatsu, J.C., Quijano-Sánchez, L., Liberatore, F., Camacho-Collados, M.: Detecting and monitoring hate speech in twitter. Sensors (Switzerland). **19** (2019)
40. Domdouzis, K., Akhgar, B., Andrews, S., Gibson, H., Hirsch, L.: A social media and crowd-sourcing data mining system for crime prevention during and post-crisis situations. J. Syst. Inf. Technol. **18**, 364–382 (2016)
41. Massarotti, M.: Intelligence-led policing: the evaluation of the denver police department's policy. J. Appl. Secur. Res. **7**, 268–283 (2012)
42. Rydberg, J., McGarrell, E.F., Norris, A., Circo, G.: A quasi-experimental synthetic control evaluation of a place-based police-directed patrol intervention on violent crime. J. Exp. Criminol. **14**(1), 83–109 (2018). https://doi.org/10.1007/s11292-018-9324-8
43. Bond, B.J., Hajjar, L.M.: Measuring congruence between property crime problems and response strategies: enhancing the problem-solving process. Police Q. **16**, 323–338 (2013)
44. Uchida, C.D., Swatt, M.L.: Operation LASER and the effectiveness of hotspot patrol: a panel analysis. Police Q. **16**, 287–304 (2013)
45. Brantingham, P.J., Valasik, M., Mohler, G.O.: Does predictive policing lead to biased arrests? results from a randomized controlled trial. Stat. Public Policy. **5**, 1–6 (2018)
46. Ratcliffe, J.H., Taylor, R.B., Fisher, R.: Conflicts and congruencies between predictive policing and the patrol officer's craft. Polic. Soc. 1–17 (2019)
47. Williams, M.L., Burnap, P., Sloan, L.: Crime sensing with big data: The affordances and limitations of using open-source communications to estimate crime patterns. Br. J. Criminol. **57**, 320–340 (2017)
48. Bovens, M., Zouridis, S.: From street-level to system-level bureaucracies: how information and communication technology is transforming administrative discretion and constitutional control. Public Adm. Rev. **62**, 174–184 (2002)
49. Belur, J., Johnson, S.: Is crime analysis at the heart of policing practice? A case study. Polic. Soc. **28**, 768–786 (2018)
50. Taylor, R.W., Russell, A.L.: The failure of police "fusion" centers and the concept of a national intelligence sharing plan. Police Pract. Res. **13**, 184–200 (2012)
51. Galdon Clavell, G.: Exploring the ethical, organisational and technological challenges of crime mapping: a critical approach to urban safety technologies. Ethics Inf. Technol. **20**(4), 265–277 (2018). https://doi.org/10.1007/s10676-018-9477-1

Utilizing an Investment Instrument for Digital Transformation: A Case Study of a Large Swedish Municipality

Jwan Khisro[(⊠)]

Swedish Center for Digital Innovation, University of Gothenburg, Gothenburg, Sweden
jwan.khisro@ait.gu.se

Abstract. The digital transformation of the public sector constitutes a major challenge for public sector organizations and governments alike. At the core of this transformation lies the increased emphasis on utilizing digital solutions to develop and deliver services that assure the continued relevance of the public sector. This study aims to explore how municipalities are utilizing the investment instrument for digital transformation. The Precursory findings present the digital transformation of the public sector and the role of investments in the public sector digital transformation. The research is based on a qualitative case study with an inductive approach. Key was to discover the practitioners' perspectives on how they perceive the investment instrument for digital transformation. The findings show that municipalities manage digital transformation in a short term perspective as an operating expenses (OPEX) rather than in a long-term capital expenditures (CAPEX) perspective to finance digital transformation.

Keywords: Digital transformation · Investment · Public sector · Operating expense · Capital expenditure

1 Introduction

The digital transformation of the public sector constitutes a major challenge for public sector organizations and governments alike (Yoo et al. 2010; Vial 2019; Mergel et al. 2019). At the core of this transformation lies the increased emphasis on utilizing digital solutions to develop and deliver services that assure the continued relevance of the public sector (Janssen and Van Der Voort 2016). At the same time, there is a lack of pace in initiating digital initiatives in the sector (Fehér and Szabó 2018). The public sector is Vial 2019 as "digital sclerosis" by Andersen et al. (2020). Part of this lacking ability for swift action in regards to digital transformation is attributable to existing IT Governance configurations. IT Governance practices are dominated by a logic where the IT function as a central actor in any digitalization initiative is poised to counteract any shift in demand from the internal users. As noted in a study of two large agencies, Magnusson et al. (2020) identified fundamental challenges with the existing configuration of IT Governance. They are tasked with delivering IT to the users with the highest level of efficiency,

© IFIP International Federation for Information Processing 2020
Published by Springer Nature Switzerland AG 2020
G. Viale Pereira et al. (Eds.): EGOV 2020, LNCS 12219, pp. 71–81, 2020.
https://doi.org/10.1007/978-3-030-57599-1_6

and hence measures have been put in place to make sure that there is no fluctuation in demand of new services which would negatively affect the internal efficiency of the IT function (Magnusson et al. 2020). In this situation, digital initiatives are predominantly treated as operating expenses (OPEX) for the users. If a new initiative is required, the full cost of the new initiative will need to be funded through OPEX by the initiating party. In a situation where the underlying infrastructure is under heavy duress and to a large extent obsolete and non-purposive for modern technologies (Riksrevisionen 2019), a substantial amount of funding is needed for not only the initiative itself, but also the underlying infrastructure. This creates a threshold for new initiatives, while at the same time counteracting the long-term development of the infrastructure.

From the literature on the capital structure of the firm (Miller 1988; Gomes 2001; Hilary et al. 2019), prior research has identified a need for balancing investments i.e. capital expenditures (CAPEX) with the use of OPEX to fund new initiatives (Memuleti-won et al. 2018; Vartiainen et al. 2019). For example, funding of assets that will have a long economic lifespan and give returns over longer periods of time such as infras-tructural elements should be handled as investments, whereas short-term initiatives, for instance an application for Covid-19 reporting, would be handled as spend. With the existing funding models for digital initiatives in the public sector almost completely void of capital expenditure (CAPEX) funding (Magnusson et al. 2020), there is a dis-crepancy between theory and practice that warrants additional studies. On the basis of this rationale, this study aims to explore:

How are municipalities utilizing the investment instrument for digital transformation?

The research question is answered through a case study of a large, Swedish munici-pality currently in the midst of a major digital transformation program. The case study was initiated in 2018, and has involved several iterations addressing different research questions. For this particular study, a series of directed interviews were conducted in the spring of 2020.

The paper is organized accordingly: After the Introduction, an overview of the Pre-cursory findings within both the digital transformation of the public sector and the role of investments in this context is presented. This is followed by the Method, which describes the choice of scientific approach, the interviews and method of analysis. The Results is then presented, followed by the Discussion where the findings are analyzed and dis-cussed in relation to previous literature. The Conclusion section provides an answer to the research question. Finally, suggestions for future study are presented.

2   Precursory Findings

2.1   Digital Transformation of the Public Sector

Digital transformation is the profound and accelerating change of business processes, ser-vices and structures, workforce competencies, corporate culture, and partner ecosystems, laws, and regulations, to fully leverage the opportunities brought by digital technologies and their impact across society in a strategic way (Brynjolfsson and McAfee 2011; Gray and Rumpe 2017; Vial 2019). In the literature digital transformation is understood and articulated as a multi-dimensional phenomenon driven by increasing technology use, politics and society (Vial 2019). Currently, it is used synonymously with digitization and digitalization but its meaning and use is not always articulated. Reflecting on Vial's (2019) observation that digital transformation is quite different from IT-enabled transformation, makes it clear that it is a complex and disruptive process (Kane et al. 2019), involving a range of actors and blurred boundaries (Nambisan et al. 2017).

Fulfilling digital transformation in the public sector entails new ways of working with stakeholders, building frameworks of service delivery and creating new forms of relationships and new financial frameworks (European Commission 2013, 2018). From this perspective, digital transformation is challenging for public sector organizations, not the least municipalities.

There is little research that provides insights into how public administrators approach digital transformation initiatives in terms of actual practices that relate to different agendas (Mergel et al. 2019). Frennert (2019) argues that municipalities' budget and strategic planning model is set for up to several years in advance, making technological changes hard to accommodate which in turn may lead to missed opportunities or to procuring irrelevant technologies. Also, costs of technology and insufficient knowledge of digitalization may continue to negatively affect the inclusion of digitalization (Noh 2019). Recent literature also highlights internal conditions including culture, individual competencies and mindset as important for digital transformation (Mergel et al. 2019).

2.2 The Role of Investments in the Public Sector Digital Transformation

Digital investments have a long track-record of study within the area of IT-related investments. Since the advent of IT, researchers and practitioners alike have tried to analyze how digital initiatives for instance technologies and systems impact performance (Dehning and Richardson 2002; Peppard and Ward 2005; Goldfinch 2007).

As noted by Bannister and Remenyi (2000), the research has largely been made more difficult with the very nature of the impacts of IT as problematic to delineate in both time and space. The overarching debate concerning the value of digital investments is one that stands between research that finds positive performance effects of investments (Brynjolfsson and Hitt 1996; Pang et al. 2014; Goh and Arenas 2020), opposed to the ones that find negative performance effects (Chae et al. 2018; Ho et al. 2017). In other words, research displays conflicting results, which has been argued to be an effect of a lack of disaggregation of the digital initiative as such, where it may be too large an object to derive sound findings from (Ho et al. 2017).

An alternative perspective to the role of digital investments would be one that questions the very basics for what is perceived as an investment. Within accounting, an investment is an instrument where capital i.e. own or loans is utilized in order to assure future earnings (Gomes 2001). In other words, there is a sharp delineation between what constitutes spend and investment. This sharp delineation is predominantly void in the literature concerning it-related investments, and in most studies the IT-budget equates to the total amount of IT investment in an organization. This low level of construct validity concerning investment in the prior research may be one source for discrepancy in the findings.

Investments are used to accrue costs over the expected financial lifetime of the investment object. To do so, excess capital is used to cover the investment, resulting in capital expenditures CAPEX instead of operating expenses OPEX. The past decade has seen an unprecedented shift away from CAPEX as a means to fund digital initiatives, partly an effect of new operating models for IT (Magnusson et al. 2020) in combination with increased cloud delivery of software (Schneider and Sunajev 2016).

Prior research in finance has acknowledged the double-edged sword of CAPEX based funding. This is addressed in the literature on the capital structure of the firm (Miller 1988), where an over-emphasis on e.g. loans blocks future opportunities for maneuverability through lock-in effects that come with the financial lifetime of the investment objects being substantial (Tanzi and Davoodi 1998; Hilary et al. 2019). At present, there is no oversight of the capital balance in relation to digital initiatives in the public sector. At the same time, there is a high level of isomorphism between digital funding models among the organizations in the sector, and that the predominant funding model in Sweden is one solely based on OPEX (Magnusson et al. 2020). This raises the question if this hypothesized capital structure with full CAPEX and no OPEX is suboptimal, and increased insight into the use of investments to fund digital transformation is warranted (Hilary et al. 2019).

3   Method

The research is based on a qualitative case study with an inductive approach, which is appropriate considering the explorative character of the study. Key was to discover the practitioners' perspectives on how they perceive the investment instrument for digital transformation (Creswell 2014; Yin 2017).

The setting for the study is a large Swedish municipality with a total of 100,000 citizens, 9,000 employees and an operating budget of € 600M (ekonomifakta.se). The rationale was quite a new digital agenda initiative with substantial allocated resources in the organization. This permitted a long-term commitment with the organization, which gives added value in terms of easy access to the investment budget development process, rich data collection and thus, an opportunity to illustrate municipality investment practice regarding digital elements.

3.1   Interviews

After discussions with representatives from the municipality IT department, the interviewees were selected according to their engagement in the investment practice (see Table 1). They all took a special interest in digital transformation. Eight semi-structured interviews through five physical meetings in the workplace and three online meetings were conducted. Each interview ranged from approximately 45 to 60 min and was recorded on the author's computer and then anonymized, as accepted by all interviewees upon asking. The recorded material was then transcribed verbatim in Swedish and then translated into English.

Table 1. Interviewee's position, organization and responsibility in the municipality.

Position	Organization	Responsibility
Finance director	Municipality	Link up feasibility studies, decision making, financial monitoring, effects and future needs
Finance administrator	Municipality	Accounting and estimate future financial costs
Finance manager of Children and Education	Municipality	Authorize investments
Municipality accountant	Municipality	Following up of investment budget
Assistant municipality chief executive	Municipality	Analysis of investment needs
Controller	Municipality energy company	Profitability calculation and assessment of budget and forecasts
Unit manager	Municipality water company	Coordinate investments and make sure they are in line with budget
Section manager	Municipality building company	Communicate needs concerning buildings

3.2 Method of Analysis

Braun and Clarke's (2006) phases of thematic analysis were utilized as a method to shift from raw interview material to themes. The analytical process started with carefully reading and re-reading the transcribed interviews and noting initial ideas in order to be familiar with the depth and breadth of the interview material. Codes were colored which yielded initial codes for instance regulation, digital investment, prioritization and digital elements. Similar codes were then grouped together and sorted into initial themes such as understanding digital transformation, improving the prioritizing process and configuring the investment budget. Finally, four overarching themes were chosen; (1) Investments are made in a traditional way, (2) IT service handels the digital transformation, (3) Digital transformation is not well understood and (4) Prioritizing is not an easy task.

4   Results

The results present how municipalities are utilizing the investment instrument for digital transformation. It is structured according to the inductively identified themes. Each theme is described and illustrated through extracts from the transcripts.

Investments Are Made in a Traditional Way

"We invest in a traditional way." (Finance director)

Traditionally, the investment budget process starts by each administration making a plan of their local needs. It is then presented to the central building strategist who makes a further needs analysis for the municipality based on demographic development for each couple of years. The politicians then decide what investments should go ahead based on what has been suggested by the municipality. In addition, the municipality has a real estate strategy, plans for local needs and for local destruction, goals- and resource plan, guidelines and financial control rules. These documents are worked together with rules used for following up, keeping and not overspending the budget. Then there are accounting laws and The Committee for municipality accounting recommendations. The Finance administrator elucidated sometimes they are not only in need of money but of staff who can manage and implement the investments. Moreover, there is a need to consider a line between what is investment and what is not. The Finance director added that they check if previous decisions need implementation or not. What does the demographic development look like? i.e. to create an understanding of the business environment and maybe reconsider previous decisions in order to make new ones. Generally speaking, preschool or school places need, that may exist because that can be evaluated based on issues of the work environment and it can be based on social aspects, i.e. on the citizens in the municipality. They have not come up with great innovation ideas in the municipality when it comes to investments.

"Right now, there are no digital elements in the investment budget. I think it's because the organization is digitally immature." (Assistant council chief executive)

There is a clear vision and plan for traditional investments in buildings and streets. The results demonstrated that digital elements are excluded from the investment budgets of the municipality. Instead, digital elements in particular and digitalization in general is completely funded through operating expenses (OPEX), i.e. a small centralized budget for digital transformation and decentralized funding utilized for buying centrally delivered services from the IT function. This result goes with Hilary et al. (2019) who emphasized the need for increased insight into the use of investments to fund digital transformation is warranted.

IT Service Handels the Digital Transformation

"The problem is that the municipality has an internal IT service and we rent the services available. The problem is that we cannot make investment without it being an ongoing cost." (Finance manager of Children and Education)

Digital transformation was not understood as an investment per-se and thus, not included in the investment budget. Rather, they referred to it as a "service budget". Inclusion of digital transformation initiatives in the municipal investment budget ranges between 0 to 0,5%. Digital infrastructural elements for instance cameras, sensors, wifi or broadband are not included. All of the interviewees agreed on the need to increase the assigned budget for digital transformation. There is also a need to know what digital legacy they can leave aside.

> *"Out of the total investment budget there is 0,5% digitalization allocation. It does not include cameras, sensors, WIFI or broadband." (Finance administrator)*

The budget allocated for digital transformation is used for leasing. Thus, there is a need for real digital investments. They need to be a natural part of future budgets as any other investment such as water and electricity. The interviewees mentioned the rapidly increasing development process and digital element costs as obstacles for utilizing the investment instrument for digital transformation. They are not considered in the budgetary framework which is a risk factor. Digital elements are in a separate budget as operating expenses (OPEX) with a very small sum of money. Together with the leasing status, this creates consequences for digital transformation. These findings are compatible with Magnusson et al. (2020) that the past decade has seen an unprecedented shift away from CAPEX as a means to fund digital initiatives, partly an effect of new operating models for information technology (Magnusson et al. 2020). Thus, it is not investment at all rather it is solely a support service. To utilize investment instruments for digital transformation is not an easy mission.

Digital Transformation is Not Well Understood

> *"You have to define digitalization to me because we end up in that type of discussion in the municipality" (Finance director)*
>
> *"It is lack of knowledge about new technology" (Section manager)*
>
> *"The politicians must understand the need and that is a huge pedagogical task" (Assistant council chief executive)*

According to theory, digital transformation is a multi-dimensional phenomenon driven by increasing technology use (Vial 2019) with a complex and disruptive process (Kane 2019) involving a range of actors and blurred boundaries (Nambisan et al. 2017). The results demonstrated there are misconceptions and a lack of a common understanding of the digital transformation. The Finance director focused on that more narrowly by insisting on cultural challenges more than technical challenges such as new work processes and the ability to change when they adopt a new system.

> *"To create a mental journey that is changing their work habits is not easy at all. In the end, it is very much about people and their relations in the business." (Finance director)*

This goes with Mergel et al. (2019), who highlighted internal conditions including culture, individual competencies and mindset as important for digital transformation. On the other hand, the Finance administrator believed that digitalization can solve all present and future problems. The result also demonstrated there is a lack of knowledge about new technologies and thus, little understanding of its opportunities (Brynjolfsson and McAfee 2011; Gray and Rumpe 2017). Thus, understanding of the concept and the new technology as such is not sufficient. There is also a need for user education and training of skills in order to have a mental and cultural change as well (Frennert 2019; Noh 2019). Thus, common understanding of the concept, new technology and knowledge transfer are fundamental dilemmas of the investment instrument because they determine the resources needed and its realization.

Prioritizing is Not an Easy Task

"So, the question is, do we make the right priorities?" (Controller)

The interviewees were very preoccupied by prioritizing. The Finance director focused on the issue in more detail and expressed the need for a priority model "as it is now a bit subjective to make priorities." The lack of a clear prioritizing process could be due to time or lack of skills. Thus, they end up prioritizing discussion every second year. They need to put all investments against each other in order to be able to prioritize. The issue is they have reduced the investment budget which is a challenge that's becoming hard to make priorities. The Section manager stated that they have a mission to prioritize investments generally for all the administrations. Together, they decide what is most important, but it is just about a new building. The local steering committee has to make such priorities. Then they should analyze what creates the most value and what should be prioritized.

"We need to have a better method for how to make priorities i.e. what creates the most value versus how much resources are needed." (Municipality accountant)

"We must have traditional investments put in contrast to digital investments to get the most benefit in the end." (The Assistant council chief executive)

However, the investment budget is based on a structured and democratic needs analysis. Prioritization risks emphasizing doing things right rather than doing the right thing (Drucker 1995) i.e. there is a risk that innovation is easily neglected. The organization therefore needs to have better control of the balance between doing things right and doing the right thing.

5   Discussion

From the result it is clear that the municipality underutilize the investment instrument for digital transformation. There is a restrictive attitude towards including digital elements in municipal investment budgets as they are included and managed through the IT service budget with clear restrictions on how much this budget may contain. Thus, at present there is a separation and lack of a municipal common investment budget earmarked for digital transformation. This leads to a dependence on the IT service department. It is strengthened while at the same time stuck in a type of IT governance that counteracts fluctuations in business and long-term perspective. This has been particularly identified as an inhibitory factor for digital transformation (Magnusson et al. 2020) as it results in a one-sided focus on management and maintenance at the expense of innovation. Digital transformation is thus managed with a short-term perspective. The consequence of using operating expenses (OPEX) rather than capital expenditures (CAPEX) to finance digital transformation, leads to difficulties in a long-term perspective. Digital technology creates options in the future rather than direct benefit, financing via operating means creates a reluctance and inability to handle larger efforts with more long-term benefits. This is in harmony with Gomes (2001) who mentioned an investment is an instrument where capital i.e. own or loans is utilized in order to assure future earnings. Further, there is no regular follow up for increased inclusion of digital elements, for instance hardware, software, equipment and even education costs in municipal investment instruments. The effect of not seeing digital elements as investment objects makes it difficult to prioritize and calculate the benefits. The reason being inadequate consensus on what digital transformation is and what it includes (Frennert 2019). Thus, it generates a silo situation that contradicts a long-term perspective. Indeed, there is no capital expenditures (CAPEX) for digital transformation.

Indisputable, the current situation leads to difficulties in utilizing the investment instrument for digital transformation and thus, for value creation. Instead, the focus is kept on managing urgent costs issues here and now. For each administration, thus, the consequence of this will be a breakdown of the municipality's overall digital transformation, and an inability to find synergies between digital initiatives. Thus, there is a risk of losing out on long-term perspectives associated with the building and maintenance of an appropriate investment instrument.

6   Conclusion and Future Research

The study showed the municipality manages digital transformation in a short term perspective as an operating expenses rather than in a long-term capital expenditure perspective to finance digital transformation. In other words, the municipality is not utilizing their investment instrument for digital transformation. This causes inefficiencies in the creation of digital services, and hinders the adoption pace of digitalization. In order to reach successful digital transformation there is thus a need for a better balance between efficiency and innovation.

The implications for research are that digital transformation needs to be regarded as a natural part of both an investment instrument i.e. capital expenditures and maintenance and development of digital elements i.e. operating expenses (OPEX). The implications for practice are to create a better common understanding of the meaning of digital transformation as it would facilitate considering it as an investment and adjusting policies accordingly. This is in accordance with Mergel et al. (2019) who argued there is little research that provides insights into how public administrators approach digital transformation initiatives in terms of actual practices that relate to different agendas.

This study is the first step in addressing the broader and deeper understanding of investment instrument practice for digital transformation. It has studied one large municipality; a future study could be to further investigate several municipalities in a longitudinal study and could include citizen perspective as well. This study has opened the door to future investigations into how digital elements can be a homogen part of the investment budget. Another future study could be about how municipalities balance efficiency and innovation through the investment instrument.

References

Andersen, K.N., Lee, J., Henriksen, H.Z.: Digital Sclerosis? Wind of change for government and the employees. Digit. Gov.: Res. Pract. **1**(1), 1–14 (2020). https://doi.org/10.1145/3360000

Bannister, F., Remenyi, D.: Acts of faith: instinct, value and IT investment decisions. J. Inf. Technol. **15**(3), 231–241 (2000)

Brynjolfsson, E., McAfee, A.: Race Against the Machine: How the Digital Revolution is Accelerating Innovation, Driving Productivity, and Irreversibly Transforming Employment and the Economy. Digital Frontier Press, Lexington (2011)

Braun, V., Clarke, V.: Using thematic analysis in psychology. Qual. Res. Psychol. **3**(2), 77–101 (2006). https://doi.org/10.1191/1478088706qp063oa

Brynjolfsson, E., Hitt, L.: Paradox lost? Firm-level evidence on the returns to information systems spending. Manag. Sci. **42**(4), 541–558 (1996)

Chae, H.C., Koh, C.E., Park, K.O.: Information technology capability and firm performance: role of industry. Inf. Manag. **55**(5), 525–546 (2018). https://doi.org/10.1016/j.im.2017.10.001

Creswell, J.W.: Research Design: Qualitative, Quantitative, and Mixed Methods Approaches, 4th edn. Sage Publications, Los Angeles (2014)

Dehning, B., Richardson, V.J.: Returns on investments in information technology: a research synthesis. J. Inf. Syst. **16**(1), 7–30 (2002)

Drucker, P.F.: People and Performance: The Best of Peter Drucker on Management. Routledge, Abingdon (1995)

Ekonomifakta home page. https://www.ekonomifakta.se/Fakta/Regional-statistik/Alla-lan/Vaster norrlands-lan/Sundsvall/. Accessed 21 Feb 2020

European Commission. High Level Group on the Modernisation of Higher Education. Report to the European commission on improving the quality of teaching and learning in Europe's higher education institutions. Publications Office of the European Union (2013)

European Commission 2018. In: The New European Community, pp. 85–132. Routledge (2018)

Fehér, P., Szabó, Z.: December. Digitalization in the Public Sector–Findings of a Hungarian Survey. In: 2018 12th International Conference on Software, Knowledge, Information Management & Applications (SKIMA), pp. 1–6. IEEE (2018). https://doi.org/10.1109/skima.2018.8631534

Frennert, S.: Lost in digitalization? Municipality employment of welfare technologies. Disabil. Rehab. Assist. Technol. **14**(6), 635–642 (2019). https://doi.org/10.1080/17483107.2018.149 6362

Goh, J.M., Arenas, A.E.: IT value creation in public sector: how IT-enabled capabilities mitigate tradeoffs in public organisations. Eur. J. Inf. Syst., 1–19 (2020). https://doi.org/10.1080/096 0085x.2019.1708821

Gray, J., Rumpe, B.: Models for the digital transformation. Softw. Syst. Model. **16**(2), 307–308 (2017). https://doi.org/10.1007/s10270-017-0596-7

Gomes, J.F.: Financing investment. Am. Econ. Rev. **91**(5), 1263–1285 (2001)

Goldfinch, S.: Pessimism, computer failure, and information systems development in the public sector. Public Adm. Rev. **67**(5), 917–929 (2007)

Hilary, G., Ma, M.S., Yan, W.: Opening the black box of capital investment: the roles of capital expenditure budget and execution. In: Wenjia, Opening the Black Box of Capital Investment: The Roles of Capital Expenditure Budget and Execution (2019). http://dx.doi.org/10.2139/ssrn. 3347421

Ho, J., Tian, F., Wu, A., Xu, S.X.: Seeking value through deviation? Economic impacts of IT overinvestment and underinvestment. Inf. Syst. Res. **28**(4), 850–862 (2017). https://doi.org/10.1287/isre.2017.0710

Janssen, M., Van Der Voort, H.: Adaptive governance: towards a stable, accountable and responsive government (2016). https://doi.org/10.1016/j.giq.2016.02.003

Kane, G.: The technology fallacy: people are the real key to digital transformation. Res. Technol. Manag. **62**(6), 44–49 (2019). https://doi.org/10.1080/08956308.2019.1661079

Magnusson, J., Koutsikouri, D., Päivärinta, T.: Efficiency creep and shadow innovation: enacting ambidextrous IT governance in the public sector. Eur. J. Inf. Syst. (2020). https://doi.org/10.1080/0960085x.2020.1740617

Memuletiwon, D.T., et al.: Virtualization: an innovative way to reducing CAPEX and OPEX for control systems. In: Offshore Technology Conference (2018). https://doi.org/10.4043/289 98-ms

Mergel, I., Edelmann, N., Haug, N.: Defining digital transformation: results from expert interviews. Gov. Inf. Q. **36**(4), 101385 (2019). https://doi.org/10.1016/j.giq.2019.06.002

Miller, M.H.: The Modigliani-Miller propositions after thirty years. J. Econ. Perspect. **2**(4), 99–120 (1988)

Nambisan, S., Lyytinen, K., Majchrzak, A., Song, M.: Digital innovation management: reinventing innovation management research in a digital world. MIS Q. **41**(1), 223–238 (2017)

Noh, Y.: A comparative study of public libraries' contribution to digital inclusion in Korea and the United States. J. Librarianship Inf. Sci. **51**(1), 59–77 (2019). https://doi.org/10.1177/096 1000616668571

Pang, M.S., Lee, G., DeLone, W.H.: IT resources, organizational capabilities, and value creation in public-sector organizations: a public-value management perspective. J. Inf. Technol. **29**(3), 187–205 (2014)

Peppard, J., Ward, J.: Unlocking sustained business value from IT investments. Calif. Manag. Rev. **48**(1), 52–70 (2005)

Yin, R.K.: Case Study Research and Applications: Design and Methods. Sage Publications, Thousand Oaks (2017)

Riksrevisionen. Drift och underhåll av statliga vägar – betydligt dyrare än väntat. ISBN 978-91-7086-532-9. RiR 2019:24. Tryck: Riksdagens interntryckeri, Stockholm (2019)

Schneider, S., Sunyaev, A.: Determinant factors of cloud-sourcing decisions: reflecting on the IT outsourcing literature in the era of cloud computing. J. Inf. Technol. **31**(1), 1–31 (2016). https://doi.org/10.1057/jit.2014.25

Tanzi, V., Davoodi, H.: Corruption, public investment, and growth. In: Shibata, H., Ihori, T. (eds.) The Welfare State, Public Investment, and Growth, pp. 41–60. Springer, Tokyo (1998). https://doi.org/10.1007/978-4-431-67939-4_4

Vial, G.: Understanding digital transformation: a review and a research agenda. J. Strateg. Inf. Syst. (2019). https://doi.org/10.1016/j.jsis.2019.01.003

Vartiainen, E., Masson, G., Breyer, C., Moser, D., Román Medina, E.: Impact of weighted average cost of capital, capital expenditure, and other parameters on future utility-scale PV levelised cost of electricity. Prog. Photovolt.: Res. Appl. (2019) https://doi.org/10.1002/pip.3189

Yoo, Y., Henfridsson, O., Lyytinen, K.: Research commentary—the new organizing logic of digital innovation: an agenda for information systems research. Inf. Syst. Res. **21**(4), 724–735 (2010). https://doi.org/10.1287/isre.1100.0322

Service Quality Through Government Proactivity: The Concept of Non-interaction

Peter Kuhn[(⊠)] 📵 and Dian Balta

fortiss GmbH, Research Institute of the Free State of Bavaria for Software-Intensive Systems and Services, Munich, Germany
pkuhn@fortiss.org

Abstract. In the course of digitalization, governments increasingly aim at improving service quality for their users. To support this aim, government proactivity is considered a suitable approach: reduction of interactions or even non-interaction between users and government. While government proactivity can be crucial for improving the service quality perceived by its users, there is a lacking of understanding how exactly non-interaction interplays with service quality. Understanding this interplay is important, given that for some services non-interaction might also decrease service quality: for instance, non-interactive student loans spare the user the application but at the same time cause automatic debt. We introduce the purpose of an interaction as a lens to help understand this interplay. The lens utilizes the fact that the purpose of an interaction has to be fulfilled also in a proactive, non-interactive version of the service. We operationalize the lens by proposing two groups of interaction purposes and integrating them with service quality dimensions in an analysis framework. The framework can be used to analyze individual services towards their service quality in a proactive, non-interactive version of the service. Our work contributes to theory by developing a set of interaction purposes to study service interactions and the qualitative interplay of non-interaction and service quality on a service level. Based on an exemplary application of the service *free school transport*, we demonstrate how government service designers can adapt the framework into a tool for the evaluation and design of individual services.

Keywords: Proactive government · Service quality · User-government interactions · Interaction purpose

1 Introduction

Digitalization transforms the way governments deliver public services [1]. Higher service quality, often in terms of efficiency and user-centricity is considered a main objective in this transformation by governments (e.g. [2]). A particular approach that intensively gains traction is proactive government services (e.g. [3]). Proactive services are initiated and delivered by governments proactively i.e. without help of its users [4] and are

G. Viale Pereira et al. (Eds.): EGOV 2020, LNCS 12219, pp. 82–95, 2020.
https://doi.org/10.1007/978-3-030-57599-1_7

realized by a fundamental shift in how government works: instead of pulling applications and information from the user, proactive governments push, i.e. automatically and autonomously deliver, services to the user [5]. Hence, proactive governments are considered the next step in government development and the maturity of governments that are proactive is considered the highest [4, 6].

From a user perspective, proactive governments result in reduction or complete absence of interactions to obtain a specific service [7]. Given that interactions such as filling and filing forms are considered cumbersome by users [4] their reduction or complete absence potentially has positive effects on service quality. Arguably, non-interaction can be considered a major factor determining the perception of public service and should be a focus of government efforts to increase service quality.

Despite the suggested importance of non-interaction between users and governments for high-quality service provision, the extant body of research is still lacking a thorough understanding of the interplay of non-interaction and service quality. This is especially relevant because fewer interactions not necessarily result in better service quality. For instance, proactive, non-interactive public student loans in Germany would spare the beneficiary the application effort, but also cause him or her an automatic debt that has to be paid back later. In an attempt to study the current role of interactions in public services, Lindgren et al. [8] compare main characteristics of traditional and digital public service interactions – e.g. purpose and communication – in order to understand digitalization effects. However, these considerations are of limited use for non-interactive services which – by definition – have neither analogue nor digital interactions. Also, not all digital interactions are the same and, thus, their interplay with service quality might differ. A conceptualization of service interactions on a less generic level, which allows for defining a continuum towards non-interaction is lacking.

Based on these considerations, we address the following research questions:

- What is a comprehensive conceptualization of interactions to study the interplay of non-interaction with service quality?
- How can this concept be operationalized in order to analyse services towards improved service quality?

We introduce the interaction purpose as a lens to help understand the interplay between non-interaction and service quality. The lens utilizes the fact that the purpose of an interaction has to be fulfilled also in a proactive, non-interactive version of the service and, thus, allows to study the effects of reducing interactions on service. To this end, we propose a categorization of interactions by their purpose and build an analysis framework for the analysis of services and their quality in the continuum towards non-interaction. To demonstrate the applicability of the framework, we apply it to exemplary services and discuss the findings.

2 Theoretical Background

Proactivity in government is a relatively new focus of e-government literature. The first section of this chapter will give an overview over the existing work and elaborate on how user-government interactions are discussed in this context. The idea of proactive governments is directly connected to the aim of making public services "better" for its users. The question of what makes a service "good" is discussed in the literature under the term "service quality" and will be summarized in the second section of this chapter. Again we will especially elaborate on the interaction perspective in service quality literature.

2.1 Proactive Government and Public Services

The notion of proactivity in government has been a topic of research in the context of public services from different perspectives and for different aspects [4–7]. Proactive service provision by governments can be defined as delivering "a service to a citizen when a life event occurs, without the citizen having to request the service" [4]. A government that delivers proactive services is considered user-friendly and improving service quality, since it supplies a service to the user (user-centric) instead of just approving it (government-centric) [4].

The implementation of proactive services has so far been studied from a conceptual perspective and on a government level. Some authors ([4, 5, 9–11]) find challenges and requirements from technical and organizational perspectives but stay on a generic level. For instance, in the stage model of Scholta et al. [4] proactive service delivery affects the storage and use of data inside government. Linder et al. [5] investigate use cases and finds that technology is an enabler for proactive services.

Three levels of proactivity can be distinguished for governments [4, 6]: A reactive government that is not proactive at all, an attentive government that has some proactive aspects, and the fully proactive government that is proactive in all aspects. In a continuous interpretation, proactivity of a service can be seen as inversely proportional to the interaction effort for the user to get the service [7]. Completely proactive services in the spirit of this interpretation are therefore non-interactive, i.e. do not require user-government interaction from user to government whatsoever.

However, the implementation of non-interaction in public services should also consider the user perspective [12, 13]. Non-interactive services are not necessarily positive for the perceived quality of a service by its user. As elaborated in the introduction, services like student loans not only cause benefits but also obligations. To the best of our knowledge, the interplay of non-interaction and service quality has not been extensively studied yet.

2.2 Service Quality

The user's perception of public services has been widely studied in service quality literature [14]. The quality of a service can be defined as the gap between user expectation and perceived performance [15] and was conceptualized in numerous models and dimensions [12, 16–23].

Papadomichelaki and Mentzas [18] propose the e-GovQual, a multiple-item scale for measuring service quality in e-Government. Following the authors, the quality of a service can be measured along the dimensions efficiency, trust, reliability and citizen support [18]. *Efficiency* considers the ease of use, content and functionality of a service.

This includes how findable, organized and how self-explanatory the service is. *Trust* focuses on privacy and security. Exemplary aspects of this dimension are the protection of personal information and the secure transmission of data. *Reliability* touches on correct and immediate performance. I.e. the unrestricted access and speedy executing of a service. *Citizen support* is about the responsiveness and problem solving capacity of a service. The ability of a user to get help when needed and a prompt reply by the government are part of this dimension.

Information exchange and its design play an important role for perceived service quality [24, 25]. For example the design of forms has a distinct effect on service quality [26]. Consequently, the interactions necessary for this information exchange are a perspective on services that has been used in service quality literature. Arias and Maçada [14] find that ease of interaction and service interaction are independent variables which have been proposed to influence service quality. Sá et al. [19] define a service as the entirety of all interactions and Wimmer [27] defines user-government interactions as a layer of public e-services. For the assessment of service quality Jansen and Ølnes [12] synthesize different categorizations of interactions in literature and use them in their assessment framework. However, to the best of our knowledge, the exact interplay of reducing interactions of a public service and its service quality has not been studied yet.

3 Research Approach

The research described in this paper was conducted as a qualitative study [28] based on a use case in a research project with the city of Munich and using an argumentative-deductive approach [29]. We chose this approach for two reasons. First, during the research project, in their role as scientific consultants, the authors of this paper were involved in dialogical action. This allowed for an in-depth study of a single case. Second, we aimed at the constructive development of a theory-based concept combining interpretation of work as well as practical inquiry, which motivated the argumentative-deductive approach [29]. In the following sections we describe the case background as well as the literature review, data collection and analysis that fuelled the iterative process in more detail.

3.1 Case Background

As many cities in Germany, the city of Munich, state of Bavaria, gradually implements digital public services. To this end, the current approach is to provide forms online. Using the german electronic ID and providing electronic payment options, this allows citizens and businesses to apply for public services online. So far the number of digital services is still small, but will continuously increase over the next months and years.

While offering online forms can make applying for public services more efficient and comfortable, the potential of digitalization goes far beyond digital forms. This is why the city of Munich puts effort into increasing service quality to the full extent. Given the novelty of many aspects of this topic in the administration, the city decided to include scientific consulting to help ensure the accordance of their efforts with scientific findings. The goal of the consulting was to provide the city with guidelines for improving service quality. In the course of the scientific consulting the authors were in regular contact to members of a strategic unit within the IT-department of the city which is responsible for the conceptualization of digital services. We had access to relevant documents and contact persons in- and outside the IT department. This provided the opportunity to constantly evaluate our argumentative-deductive findings with experts form practice.

3.2 Literature Review, Data Collection and Analysis

We conducted a hermeneutic literature review [30] to study the theoretical foundations. As elaborated in the above chapter this includes previous work on proactive government and service quality, both with a focus on interactions. For literature on proactivity we used the work of Scholta et al. [4] as a starting point; on service quality the literature review by Arias and Maçada [14].

Based on the theoretical foundations we designed the data collection consisting of two rounds of interviews with domain and digitalization experts from the case municipality and four other municipalities, a workshop and a final interview. The experts for the interviews were selected for their knowledge of a specific service in depth (experts from case municipality) and their experience with a broad range of different public services from an administrative perspective (experts from other municipalities). The case municipality experts are responsible for the review, decision and processing of applications for their respective services. The other four experts have different roles in designing and implementing high-quality e-government services in their respective municipalities. The interviews lasted between 40 and 120 min and were recorded and transcribed if agreed by the expert. For the 4 interviews without recording, notes were taken and converted into minutes. The transcriptions as well as the minutes were sent to the experts for feedback and approval. After the feedback was integrated, the documents were coded by two scientists independently. The data collection was concluded by a 45 min workshop with 30 digitalization experts from all public sector levels at a meeting of public sector experts and a final interview. Table 1 gives an overview over the data sources types, quantity, duration, participants and outcomes.

As for the outcomes, the first round of interviews investigated the user-government interactions and their purpose for three specific services (dog licence fee, registration card, school transport). The services were chosen because they cover different domains of government (tax, registration office, welfare policy). The second round of interviews have been semi-structured interviews with digitalization and service design experts. Their purpose was to generalize from the three specific services to all public services and to investigate the interplay with service quality. The following workshop served as evaluation of the framework by applying it to a variety of services from different public sector levels. The final interview had the purpose of applying the improved framework again to one of the initial services (school transport). The two domain experts were interviewed together because they work on the same public services. One of the two was already interviewed in the first round, the second one was added to ensure a comprehensive perspective.

Table 1. List of data sources

Data type	Quantity	Duration	Participants	Outcome
First round of interviews	3	90–120 min	5 domain experts from the case municipality	Purposes of service interactions
Second round of interviews	6	40–75 min	2 digitalization experts from case municipality + 4 digitalization experts from 4 other municipalities	Generalization of interaction purposes and first draft framework
Workshop	1	45 min	30 digitalization experts from all public sector levels	Consolidated framework
Final interview	1	120 min	2 domain experts from the case municipality	Exemplary application of the framework

4   The Analysis Framework

4.1   Categorization of Interaction Purposes

We used the comparison of traditional versus digital public service characteristics by Lindgren et al. [8] as a starting point. The authors build on a classification of interaction aspects by Goodsell [31] to illustrate the effect of digitalization on the nature and purpose, the communication form and setting, the central actors involved, and the initiation, duration, and scope of an interaction. These aspects serve well for the investigation of a change in interactions, e.g. when service are digitalized. Yet, when services become more and more proactive, interactions will be reduced. The investigation of proactive, non-interactive services using interaction aspects therefore becomes less apparent. Hypothetically, for a government with fully non-interactive services only, the analysis by Lindgren et al. cannot be applied properly. However, in order to move from current interactive towards non-interactive services, the current purpose of interactions has still to be fulfilled somehow - except this time without the user. This allows for investigating the quality of a service through understanding the non-interactive fulfilment of typical interaction purposes in proactive services. For instance, most services are triggered by submission of a form. This interaction purpose now has to happen without a user, which effects service quality. While reducing the application effort, this change requires the user to trust the administration to trigger the service when needed. Depending on how the purpose of service triggering is implemented in a non-interactive service, the users trust in government will be affected positively or negatively. Consequently, the implementation of purpose fulfilment influences service quality and, thus, this lens might be of value for understanding the interplay of non-interaction and service quality.

Investigating three services from the case municipality and based on two rounds of interviews we found seven interaction purposes grouped into data provision and support functions (cf. Table 2).

Table 2. List of user-government interaction purposes and their descriptions.

Interaction purpose	Description
Data provisions	
Specification	Provision of data that specify the requested service, e.g. type of license
Eligibility	Provision of data that prove the qualification of the user to receive the service in question, e.g. physical handicap
Identification	Provision of data to identify a potentially eligible person, e.g. name and address of resident
Support functions	
Trigger	Initiates the service, e.g. via application form
Authentication	Proves the identity of a person to the authorities, e.g. authentication by eID
Payment	Payment of fees, taxes or other, e.g. by direct debit
Logistics	Move physical object from one place to another, e.g. pick up a public transport ticket

The group "data provisions" includes three types of purposes. Data for *specification* is used by the government in order to identify the exact service the user needs. An example from the investigated services is the race of a dog in the dog licence fee service. This information is provided in the application form and determines whether the owner has to pay the fee for fighting dogs, which is higher, or normal dogs. Data for *eligibility* includes all data necessary to determine whether the user fulfils the requirements for the service. An example requirement from the school transport service is a physical handicap that prevents a pupil to walk to school. The applicant has to provide a document to prove that the pupil fulfils this requirement. Data for *identification* is a common data provision required in many government forms. An example is the application for the registration card. In order to get this document the user has to identify him or herself by providing name and address. Based on the identification the government understand which registration card to issue.

The group "support functions" include four types of purposes. The *trigger* of a service is the initiation of the according process that leads to service provision. All three mentioned services have this requirement. For the dog licence, the school transport as well as the registration card the user has to indicate to the government his or her need for the service. In cases of all three services that happens via submission of the according form. *Authentication* is another interaction purpose of government services. An example is authentication by ID card. In case of the registration card, authentication can be done via use of the online function of the ID card. By electronically proving the possession of the card and a second factor (PIN) the user can authenticate for the service. The third provision type is *payments*. Payments can be necessary interactions in order to settle fees or taxes. In case of the dog fee the user has to allow the authorities to retrieve the fee from the user's bank account via direct debit. Finally, *logistics* are required to move physical objects such as documents from one place to another. For instance, government requires that pupils pick up the ticket for school transport in school.

4.2   A Framework for the Analysis of Services Towards Increased Service Quality

We present a framework for the analysis of services with two dimensions. The first dimension uses the lens of the interaction purposes and the second consists of service quality dimension. For the quality dimensions we use the ones proposed by Papadomichelaki and Mentzas [18] under the label e-GovQual. We chose these dimensions – efficiency, trust, reliability, and citizen support – for their orthogonality to the interaction perspective which avoids interdependencies of the framework dimensions. To include all users of public services – also companies and organizations – we renamed the latter dimension "user support". The resulting framework is shown in Table 3.

For each interaction the framework allows to evaluate how a proactive, non-interactive fulfilment of its purpose interplays with service quality via its dimensions. This allows to break down the interplay of non-interaction and service quality into aspects by interaction purpose and to consider it for different dimensions. We filled the cells of the table with aspects that arise for each intersection. The questions are intended to provide an example of an aspect of non-interaction that might affect a service quality dimension. This aspect can be used as a first impulse to evaluate the effects of reducing interactions that serve a specific purpose.

For the *trust* dimension we find aspects that can be attributed to the loss of control by the user, resulting from the non-interaction. For instance, in case of a non-interactive service specification by the government, the user might wonder whether that specification is best for his or her circumstances. Given the lack of interaction, the user has to trust government with this decision. Another example is the interaction purpose of authentication. Its non-interactive fulfilment might require the government to access private user data. This access and potential exploitation interplays with the perceived service quality via the trust dimension.

For the *efficiency* dimension we find aspects that consider side-effects of non-interaction. A non-interactive fulfilment of an interaction purpose might require some change in behaviour by the citizen to enable or control the alternative fulfilment. The immediate, non-interactive triggering of garbage collection, for example, might only be possible if a user notifies the registry office about moving in advance and not only within the legal deadline of two weeks after. As for the control, non-interactive payments want to be checked by the user for correctness which causes extra effort. Both necessary change in behaviour and controlling government actions interplay with service quality via efficiency.

For the *reliability* dimension we find aspects that address the correctness and timing of non-interactive purpose fulfilment. E.g. the non-interactive eligibility assessment has to be done without any direct input from the user. The correctness of this assessment interplays with the quality of the service via the reliability dimension. Similarly the

Table 3. Framework for the analysis of services and their quality in the continuum towards non-interaction

Non-interaction	Service quality dimensions			
	Trust	Efficiency	Reliability	User Support
Data provisions				
Non-interactive Specification	Best specification for user?	Effort for corrections necessary?	Specification correct?	What if specification wrong?
Non-interactive eligibility	Benevolent or strict?	Can be automated?	Assessment correct?	How to object?
Non-interactive identification	Privacy protection met?	Minimal possible amount of ID data?	Identification immediate?	What if not considered?
Support functions				
Non-interactive trigger	False trigger possible?	Extra effort to enable proactive trigger?	Trigger immediate?	How to manually trigger?
Non-interactive authentication	Privacy protection met?	New technology necessary?	Authentication correct?	How to object?
Non-interactive payment	Unexpected costs possible?	How big is verification effort?	Payment immediate?	Possibility to know payments in advance?
Non-interactive logistics	Confidentiality?	Lost resources due to erroneous service delivery?	Address correct?	Support information available from logistic 3rd parties?

immediacy of a purpose fulfilment, e.g. the identification of a user for a service, interplays with reliability and, thus, service quality.

Finally, for the *user service* dimension we find aspects that concern the situation in which – even though designed to be non-interactive – the user has to act. E.g. if a service is not triggered although needed or if a service is not specified in the best interest of the user this requires some form of user-government interaction. In this case, the quality of the service is affected through the user support dimension, i.e. the support of the government to these situations.

5   Discussion

5.1   Implications for Theory

The findings of this paper show that non-interaction interplays with service quality in a non-trivial way. While less interaction effort can have benefits for the user, the reduction of interactions might also have downsides such as trust or reliability aspects. Consequently, simply understanding non-interactivity as reducing interaction efforts for the user might not allow for a comprehensive understanding. In this line of argument, proactive government also not necessarily has to have the highest maturity as has been suggested [6]. The precise effects of proactive government on service quality should be considered is these considerations.

For the non-trivial nature of this interplay with service quality, we find that the lens of interaction purposes can help exploring its qualitative connections and correlations on a service level. The consideration of interactions by purpose allows to break down this interplay into different aspects, i.e. different purposes and their non-interactive fulfilment have different interrelations with different quality dimensions. We find that grouping purposes by information exchange, service provision and control or constraint as proposed by literature [8] is a useful starting point and can be operationalized by distinguishing seven purposes grouped into data provisions and support functions.

Finally, the existing conceptualizations of service quality can help understanding non-interactive services - even though the concepts were designed for interactive services. This reflects well on the assumption by literature that the evaluation of service quality is not changing from no-proactive to proactive government since it is still the users perception that counts [6]. However, this is only the case for a qualitative evaluation. As for quantitative assessment the questions proposed to quantify the used dimensions consider the interaction environment [18] and, hence, are not applicable to non-interactive services.

5.2 Implications for Practice

Practice can use the presented lens to analyse interactions of existing services towards non-interaction. The framework then can help design a version of the service that is non-interactive *and* has high service quality. This can foster the spread of proactive government. We demonstrate these implications by applying the framework to the exemplary service of free school transport. In Bavaria, the transport of pupils to and from school is free of charge by law [32]. The city of Munich puts that into practice by - upon application - providing tickets to pupils for their daily commute to school. The application is operationalized via form in the online portal of the city. The city checks the eligibility depending on a minimum distance to school, physical handicaps and potential danger zones on the way to school. All approved applicants can pick up the ticket at school.

The domain experts from the city consider the service to be suitable for a fully non-interactive implementation. The non-interactive implementation would use data from the public school data base and automatically check the eligibility for all students before the beginning of the school year. However, despite the assumption that saving the application effort for the user will increase service quality, the exact interplay of reducing interactions and service quality remains unclear.

Using the presented distinction of interaction purposes the experts can investigate the current interactions of the service and consider the potential non-interactive fulfilment of the purpose. For the service of free school transport three interactions can be distinguished. Organizing documents to prove eligibility in case of physical handicaps, the online application and the pick-up of the ticket in school. While the first interaction serves only the purpose of providing data on eligibility, the online application has multiple purposes. The corresponding form requires all types of data provision (specification, eligibility and identification) and acts as a trigger of the service. The pick-up in school fulfils the authentication and the logistics support functions. There is no interaction that fulfils the purpose of payment because for the service in question no payment is necessary.

Table 4. Application of the framework to the free school transportation service

Non-interaction	Service Quality Dimensions			
	Trust	Efficiency	Reliability	User support
Data provisions				
Non-interactive Specification	Same ticket for all pupils	–	Same ticket for all pupils	–
Non-interactive eligibility	–	Communication of danger zones among authorities might take time	Immediacy has to be ensured	Fast help in case of wrong refusal necessary
Non-interactive identification	Access to state school data base necessary	–	–	–
Support functions				
Non-interactive trigger	–	No application necessary	Provision at first day of school	–
Non-interactive authentication	–	No authentication necessary	–	
Non-interactive payment	–	–	–	–
Non-interactive logistics		No pick up in school	Need to send tickets to right parent	

Based on these interaction purposes and their potential non-interactive fulfilment, we evaluated versions of the service towards their interplay with the service quality dimensions of the framework. For instance, a non-interactive *eligibility* check, interplays with efficiency in two ways. On the one hand, not having to provide respective documents and evidence saves time and effort for the user. On the other hand an eligibility check without those documents might need more time. This also affects the reliability of proactive eligibility checks. If inefficient processes inside government take time, the immediacy of the service is not guaranteed and, thus, effecting its reliability. An important aspect of proactive eligibility checks is its reliability in terms of accuracy. If the ticket is refused wrongfully, the support of affected users can make a difference in the perceived quality of the service. A negative aspect of non-interactive tickets can occur from a data privacy point of view. The reduction of interactions is partly enabled by sharing data between schools and other administrations. The exact implementation of this sharing might affect the trust dimension of the service.

All considerations made are present in Table 4. Based on these considerations we developed a version of the service that is non-interactive and has a high service quality. In this version the ticket is automatically sent to all pupils before the first day of school every year. The eligibility check is realized by inter-organisational cooperation and economic data use. User support is established to help in case of wrongful refusal within 24 h.

6 Conclusion and Outlook

In this paper, we present the interaction purpose as a lens to study the interplay between non-interaction and service quality. To this end, we build a framework for analyzing public services towards their quality in a non-interactive version. The framework uses the lens of interaction purposes and four dimensions of service quality. We discuss implications for theory and practice. The latter is done by means of applying the framework to an exemplary service.

The findings of this paper have limitations that restrain their general applicability and should be met with further research. Interaction purposes are not the only lens on services that might be helpful in investigating the interplay of non-interaction and service quality. Other lenses and perspectives should be evaluated towards their contribution to this discussion. Also, the results of this paper were developed with experts from government. The user perspective mainly relies on insights of service quality literature. This literature was mostly established based on interaction-based services. Further research should reiterate on the suitability of service quality models and dimensions for evaluation of proactive, non-interactive service quality and include users directly. Moreover, the current framework allows only for qualitative assessment of services. Further works should aim at making these assessments quantifiable, also to enable assessing the suitability of services for proactive delivery which would help decision makers in practice. For theory as well as practice, it would be especially interesting to investigate the relationships between individual interaction types and the service quality dimensions. Finally, broader aspects such as the technical implementation of non-interactive services – e.g. elevated security threats because of centralized data storage and data privacy – are important and should be addressed as well.

Although limitations exist, we believe that our research is valuable to both theory and practice. In particular, we hope that the application of our framework will streamline the transformation of digital government services towards more high-quality proactivity.

Acknowledgments. This research was made possible by funding from the city of Munich. We thank the city's e- and open government team for the cooperation and valuable feedback.

References

1. Lindgren, I., Jansson, G.: Electronic services in the public sector: a conceptual framework. Govern. Inf. Q. **30**, 163–172 (2013). https://doi.org/10.1016/j.giq.2012.10.005
2. IT-Planungsrat: Digitalisierungsprogramm des IT-Planungsrats (Phase II): Start in die Verwaltungsdigitalisierung. https://www.it-planungsrat.de/DE/ITPlanungsrat/OZG-Umsetzung/Digitalisierungsprogramm/DigPro_node.html. Accessed 19 Nov 2019
3. e-Estonia Briefing Centre: All Estonian public e-services to function "invisibly". https://e-estonia.com/all-estonian-public-e-services-to-function-invisibly/. Accessed 16 Mar 2020
4. Scholta, H., Mertens, W., Kowalkiewicz, M., Becker, J.: From one-stop shop to no-stop shop: An e-government stage model. Govern. Inf. Q. **36**, 11–26 (2019). https://doi.org/10.1016/j.giq.2018.11.010
5. Linders, D., Liao, C.Z.-P., Wang, C.-M.: Proactive e-Governance: Flipping the service delivery model from pull to push in Taiwan. Govern. Inf. Q. **35**, 68–76 (2018). https://doi.org/10.1016/j.giq.2015.08.004
6. Scholta, H., Lindgren, I.: The long and winding road of digital public services—one next step: proactivity. In: ICIS 2019 Proceedings (2019)
7. Brüggemeier, M.: Auf dem weg zur no-stop-verwaltung. Verwaltung Management **16**, 93–101 (2010). https://doi.org/10.5771/0947-9856-2010-2-93
8. Lindgren, I., Madsen, C.Ø., Hofmann, S., Melin, U.: Close encounters of the digital kind: a research agenda for the digitalization of public services. Govern. Inf. Q. **36**, 427–436 (2019). https://doi.org/10.1016/j.giq.2019.03.002
9. Sirendi, R., Taveter, K.: Bringing service design thinking into the public sector to create proactive and user-friendly public services. In: Nah, F.F.H., Tan, C.H. (eds.) HCIBGO 2016. LNCS, vol. 9752, pp. 221–230. Springer, Cham (2016). https://doi.org/10.1007/978-3-319-39399-5_21
10. Schuppan, T., Koehl, S.: One stop government: stalled vision or a matter of design? – empirical findings from social services in Germany. In: Hawaii International Conference on System Sciences 2017 (HICSS-50) (2017)
11. Kuhn, P., Balta, D., Krcmar, H.: Was sind Herausforderungen proaktiver Verwaltungsleistungen in Deutschland? In: Wirtschaftsinformatik 2020 Proceedings (2020)
12. Jansen, A., Ølnes, S.: The nature of public e-services and their quality dimensions. Govern. Inf. Q. **33**, 647–657 (2016). https://doi.org/10.1016/j.giq.2016.08.005
13. Lindgren, I., Melin, U.: Time to refuel the conceptual discussion on public e-services – revisiting how e-services are manifested in practice. In: Janssen, M., et al. (eds.) EGOV 2017. LNCS, vol. 10428, pp. 92–101. Springer, Cham (2017). https://doi.org/10.1007/978-3-319-64677-0_8
14. Arias, M.I., Maçada, A.C.G.: Digital government for E-government service quality: a literature review. In: 11th International Conference on Theory and Practice of Electronic Governance (ICEGOV 2018), pp. 7–17 (2018). https://doi.org/10.1145/3209415.3209422
15. Parasuraman, A., Zeithaml, V.A., Berry, L.L.: A conceptual model of service quality and its implications for future research. J. Market. **49**, 41–50 (1985). https://doi.org/10.1177/002224298504900403
16. Tan, C.-W., Benbasat, I., Cenfetelli, R.T.: IT-mediated customer service content and delivery in electronic governments: an empirical investigation of the antecedents of service quality. MIS Q. **37**, 77–109 (2013)
17. Hien, N.M.: A Study On Evaluation Of E-Government Service Quality (2014). https://doi.org/10.5281/zenodo.1336168
18. Papadomichelaki, X., Mentzas, G.: e-GovQual: A multiple-item scale for assessing e-government service quality. Govern. Inf. Q. **29**, 98–109 (2012). https://doi.org/10.1016/j.giq.2011.08.011

19. Sá, F., Rocha, Á., Gonçalves, J., Cota, M.P.: Model for the quality of local government online services. Telemat. Inform. **34**, 413–421 (2017). https://doi.org/10.1016/j.tele.2016.09.002
20. Parasuraman, A., Zeithaml, V.A., Malhotra, A.: E-S-QUAL: a multiple-item scale for assessing electronic service quality. J. Serv. Res. (2005). https://doi.org/10.1177/109467050427 1156
21. Jansen, A., Ølnes, S.: The muddy waters of public e-services - The use and misuse of the concept and how to get out of the maze (2014)
22. Rhee, S.-K., Rha, J.-Y.: Public service quality and customer satisfaction: exploring the attributes of service quality in the public sector. Serv. Ind. J. **29**, 1491–1512 (2009). https://doi.org/10.1080/02642060902793441
23. Li, H., Suomi, R.: A proposed scale for measuring e-service quality. Int. J. u-and eService, Sci. Technol. **1–10** (2009)
24. Tambouris, E., Loutas, N., Peristeras, V., Tarabanis, K.: The role of interoperability in egovernment applications: an investigation of critical factors. J. Dig. Inf. Manage. **7**, 235–243 (2009)
25. Dawes, S.S.: Interagency information sharing: expected benefits, manageable risks. J. Pol. Anal. Manage. **15**, 377–394 (1996)
26. Scholta, H., Balta, D., Räckers, M., Becker, J., Krcmar, H.: Standardization of forms in governments. Bus. Inf. Syst. Eng. (2020). https://doi.org/10.1007/s12599-019-00623-1
27. Wimmer, M.A.: Integrated service modelling for online one-stop government. Electron. Markets **12**, 149–156 (2002). https://doi.org/10.1080/101967802320245910
28. Myers, M.: Qualitative research in information systems. Manage. Inf. Syst. Q. **21** (1997)
29. Wilde, T., Hess, T.: Forschungsmethoden der wirtschaftsinformatik. Wirtsch. Inform. **49**, 280–287 (2007). https://doi.org/10.1007/s11576-007-0064-z
30. Boell, S., Cecez-Kecmanovic, D.: A hermeneutic approach for conducting literature reviews and literature searches. Commun. Assoc. Inf. Syst. **34** (2014). https://doi.org/10.17705/1CAIS.03412
31. Goodsell, C.T.: The public encounter and its study. The Public Encounter: Where State and Citizen Meet, pp. 3–20 (1981)
32. Bayerische, S.: SchKfrG: Gesetz über die Kostenfreiheit des Schulwegs (Schulwegkostenfreiheitsgesetz – SchKfrG) in der Fassung der Bekanntmachung vol. 31. Mai 2000 (GVBl. S. 452) BayRS 2230-5-1-K (Art. 1–7). https://www.gesetze-bayern.de/Content/Document/BaySchulKostG/true. Accessed 25 May 2020

Automatization of Cross-Border Customs Declaration: Potential and Challenges
A Case Study of the Estonian Customs Authority

Markko Liutkevičius[(✉)], Karl Ivory Pappel, Sidra Azmat Butt,
and Ingrid Pappel[ⓘ]

Information Systems Group, Tallinn University of Technology, Akadeemia tee 15a,
12618 Tallinn, Estonia
{markko.Liutkevicius,karl.pappel,sidra.butt,ingrid.pappel}@taltech.ee

Abstract. This paper discusses challenges and obstacles of the Estonian customs authority while implementing the new EU VAT directive aiming to raise efficiency in the VAT declaration life-cycle. The general goal of the directive is to reduce cross-border fraud, gain revenue and modernize the system for governments and businesses. Due to the fact that the impact of the new VAT directive is tremendous, it also changes radically AS-IS work routines of customs authorities. The current paper presents the Estonian experience regarding the implementation of the new work procedures through providing data of the new technology developments and bringing out main concerns in terms of ongoing development activities. Transforming old ICT systems to newer platforms with regards to the new directive also changes current work procedures, which means that adjustments in the organization are also required. The central reason to move towards automatization is the dramatically increasing volumes of shipments requiring customs clearance. However, it is a complex process to achieve this task because of different or non-agreed data sets shared in the existing systems by various stakeholders as well as low quality of data. Consequently, the results of the paper are aimed to aid implementing the changes in various other customs authorities in the EU.

Keywords: Automatization · VAT · Customs declaration · Import one stop shop · IOSS

1 Introduction

In 2021, the new VAT directive and legislation will come into effect in the European Union (EU). Already now, the EU member states systematically prepare for adherence with the law. In these endeavours, the expected level of readiness of new customs declaration systems varies greatly between the EU member states. A major shift is caused by difficulties to handle the growing influx of new customs controls and declarations. Today, consignments with intrinsic value under

© IFIP International Federation for Information Processing 2020
Published by Springer Nature Switzerland AG 2020
G. Viale Pereira et al. (Eds.): EGOV 2020, LNCS 12219, pp. 96–109, 2020.
https://doi.org/10.1007/978-3-030-57599-1_8

EU member state's specific VAT *de minimis threshold* (DMT)[1] get a free pass into free circulation. From the beginning of 2021, all goods purchased from outside the EU (third country online marketplaces) by a customer situated in the EU will be declared for VAT collection purposes. Based on 2018 statistics of the Estonian customs authority, the abolishment of VAT DMT will increase the total amount of customs declarations for postal consignments from 23k to 3M, which is roughly 130 times[2]. As maintaining the seamless flow of goods is crucial, EU customs authorities including Estonia are working hard to adapt national customs declaration systems – customs declaration systems are national, i.e., each member state has developed its own implementation [1]. With the increasing amount of declarations, even small delays in the declaring process would have negative consequences for EU citizens when ordering goods outside the EU.

The aim of this paper is to analyse a case of the Estonian customs authority where automatization of customs declarations is under development, focuses on caseworkers' interpretations of the upcoming challenges, and analyses how changes affect the new work procedures. In order to understand to what extent automatization is applicable in the customs declaration process, we first analyse the current situation and developments of our chosen case country. As Estonia is also member of the EU Commission's Customs Expert Group (CEG), we are focusing on current challenges faced by customs authorities both locally in Estonia and in the EU. In addition, Estonia is known as tech-savvy country where digital signing is widely used [2], digitalization has been reached into invoice workflows [3] and local governments have received a very high level of digital document exchange as a basis for the e-service transformation [4–7]. Therefore, we highlight related issues and open ends that should be resolved for the upcoming changes to take place. Furthermore, as interoperability is essential to make different information systems and organizations work together [8] and establish automatization, we elaborate the related data requirements set by the European Commission. Hence, we have formed the following research questions:

- RQ1 What procedures are currently performed for customs declarations in the Estonian customs authority?
- RQ2 How can automatization of customs declarations aid to cope with challenges of the new VAT directive?
- RQ3 What concerns are raised in relation to the upcoming changes?
- RQ4 What data quality is required to meet the new requirements with respect to automatization?

In Sect. 2, we provide a brief description of the background of changing legislation in the EU. In Sect. 3, we describe the research methodology. In Sect. 4, we provide the results. We proceed with a discussion of possible future directions in Sect. 5 and we finish the paper with a conclusion in Sect. 6.

---

[1] The VAT *de minimis threshold* in the EU member states is between 10 EUR to 22 EUR and varies across EU member states.

[2] Based on meetings with Estonian customs authorities.

2   Theoretical Background

2.1   Changing Legislation in the EU

E-commerce marketplaces enable thousands of different merchants to sell goods from non-EU countries to EU countries. A recent report conducted in 11 EU countries summarized that in 2019 more than 60% of European consumers who shopped online from a foreign country bought products from China [9]. A 2016 study reports that roughly 70% of e-commerce consignments flow through public postal channels, where VAT is unpaid on 65% of consignments, amounting to a loss of VAT income of around 1 billion EUR [10]. Additionally, by current VAT rules, consignments imported into the EU are completely exempted from VAT if they have an intrinsic value of less than the DMT, which opens up an opportunity for fraud, e.g., through undervaluing expensive items in importation paperwork [11].

New EU regulations will be in force from 1 July 2021 in order to combat these problems. Firstly, Council Directive (EU) 2017/2455 [12] will abolish the VAT DMT (Table 1). Specifically, the VAT rate due has to be in accordance to the EU member state in which the consignment receiving customer is located. Secondly, the EU will introduce liability to marketplaces regarding VAT collection on packages sent by merchants on their platform. Finally, the EU will set up a new Import One Stop Shop (IOSS) and *special arrangements schemes* for online marketplaces. These schemes will not only help to ensure the collection of VAT, but will also introduce much-needed simplifications that make fulfilling VAT obligations easier for businesses [13].

Table 1. VAT and customs duties of consignments imported to the EU before and after 2021.

Value of consignment	Before 2021		After 2021	
	VAT	Customs duty	VAT	Customs duty
Under DMT	Exempt from VAT	Exempt from duty	VAT due	Exempt from duty
Over DMT, under 150€	VAT due	Exempt from duty	VAT due	Exempt from duty
Over 150€	VAT due	Customs duty due	VAT due	Customs duty due

A new legislation in the EU Customs Code (UCC) brings forth significant changes in how low value customs declarations can be handled [14]. Specifically, a new article (Article 143a UCC-DA "Customs declaration for consignments of low value") is radically changing EU customs and tax legislation for low value consignments. In general terms, this means that it will be possible to pre-lodge Super Reduced Data Sets (SRDS) of low value consignments prior to the UCC Article 5 (33) "presentation of the goods to customs" [15]. The SRDS technical details together with other declaration types are specified in the European Customs Data Model (EUCDM), which is part of UCC delegated regulations and the UCC implementing regulations. This separation of physical and fiscal flows of consignments helps to speed up the process of customs clearance and enables the potential of automatization.

2.2 Good Governance, Accountability and Transparency

Automatization of customs procedures plays an important role in the modernization of VAT collection. Through facilitating the VAT audits, collection of VAT and automatization of the customs processes, the opportunity to exercise fraud or inappropriate transactions can be minimized, particularly in the field of tax collection. Good governance remains one of the main reasons why a government or administration of a country works hard to provide services that are of quality and free of prejudice or corruption. According to Chan, "a mismanaged enterprise cannot flourish" [16]. Therefore, a government in its modern form, particularly in the developed countries, does not only depend on efficiency but also on the principles of accountability. The essence of the theory is to ensure that the citizens of the state are treated as the rightful citizens of the state and not just as the customers.

The research and analysis on good governance is usually limited to the issues related to development; taxation and VAT systems – as mentioned earlier – are an important part of development and require the application of practices related to good governance. The most essential factor utilized in order to ensure accountability in the area of public services, in particular, is transparency. Transparency is an important factor as it helps to hold accountable the personnel involved in the complete process. It remains as one of the main pillars on which the strategy to apply and implement an integrity system is built. According to Grindle "The principle of accountability in the real sense, emphasizes answerability for the use of state resources and assets earmarked for specific purposes, subject to the laws and their requirements" [17]. Accountability is a factor that is guaranteed through the element of transparency. It is one of the features that are important for decision making. The reason behind it is the fact that decisions that are made, need to conform to the set rules and regulations. A government that depends mostly on the tax revenues as compared to the natural resources or foreign aids is more likely to be held accountable by its citizens; as proper taxation serves as one of the main catalysts for the greater accountability of a government [18].

2.3 Related Work

The introduction and boom of e-commerce has allowed the EU countries to receive goods from the non-EU countries which has increased the number of stores and merchants sending products to EU consumers. Until now, as discussed earlier, VAT was not applied to a large proportion of these trades and purchases. However, with the growing number of e-commerce purchases, it has become essential to make sure that the necessary compliance strategies and procedures are in place [19]. Much research has been previously carried out in order to understand and recommend the necessary course of action to make e-commerce markets VAT compliant. In a research conducted by Papis, it is discussed that the VAT rules for e-commerce across different borders have gone through extensive modernization [20].

The emerging trend of e-commerce has also created several different issues related to the legality of the trade as well as the transactions being made online. The question here is to understand how VAT can be collected for these online purchases efficiently and effectively. There are certain compliance rules introduced and applied for the delivering of e-commerce products to customers in Europe. It is now a requirement for the business to establish where the customer is located in case the customer falls in the non-taxable category [21]. There are various different steps introduced that need to be followed to make sure that the businesses are VAT compliant. This includes determining the physical location of the customer in order to calculate the tax to be applied, keeping a record of all of the transactions as well as reports related to the VAT. This suggests that there is still a lot of work that needs to be done in order to make sure that VAT for the emerging e-commerce market and the policies related to it are up to date [22].

According to our previous research [23], the analysis of the European standards in today's system of VAT declaration is not enough by stating that the current system is "complex, burdensome, time-demanding, inconvenient, and not integrated". Thus, much needs to be done to achieve the required goals. An automated VAT system for this purpose can serve as a corner stone for a system that is agile as well as functional. Although, for the Estonian Government it can be beneficial but much more research is still required.

3   Research Methodology

The main author is currently involved in the Archimedes[3] research and development project 'e-Commerce EU VAT and Duty Declaration Digitalization 2021' as a leading analyst. The aim of the project is to develop an independent platform to exchange customs declaration data between various marketplaces and EU customs authorities. For the whole project and its research, the elements of action design research (ADR) [24] along with qualitative methods are applied to address the subject of automatization of customs declarations.

For this research, interviews are chosen as a source of primary data. The interviews are conducted with open ended questions with the purpose to get insight to actual concerns and open ends. In total, five focus group interviews were conducted with eight different people working at the Estonian Tax and Customs Board. Most interviewees were in the leading positions that are related to the changes influenced by VAT directive such as leading specialist, team lead, service manager, development analyst, development specialist from various departments etc. All discussion topics were sent prior to the meetings, so the Estonian customs authority representatives had enough time to prepare and gather relevant people to the focus group interviews. Table 2 provides an overview of the topics and the organizational origin of the participants.

Furthermore, a document analysis was used to serve as the secondary data which contains data gathered from various sources that focuses on the current

---

[3] https://archimedes.ee/en/archimedes-foundation/.

Table 2. Topics and the origin of participants in focus group interviews.

Interview	Topics	Origin of case worker
1	The existing roles and procedures and data needed for declaring goods. Existing taxation principles.	Customs Law Team (Case worker 1), Customs Services Management Team (Case worker 2), Office for Direct and Indirect Taxation (Case worker 3), Customs application team (Case worker 4).
2	The future roles and procedures for declaring goods.	Customs Law Team (Case worker 1), Customs Services Management Team (Case worker 2)
3	Data requirements for low value consignments. Roles and responsibilities in IOSS scheme.	Customs Law Team (Case worker 1), Customs Services Management Team (Case worker 2), Accounting Office (Case worker 5).
4	New updates on data requirements by EUCDM. Quotas management. Banned and dangerous commodity groups in Estonia.	Customs Law Team (Case worker 1), Customs Services Management Team (Case worker 2), Customs Supervision Development Team (Case worker 6).
5	The latest developments of the new customs declaration system. Integration and automatization opportunities.	Customs Law Team (Case worker 1), Customs Services Management Team (Case worker 2), Customs application team (Case worker 7 and Case worker 8).

situation of e-commerce and EU customs authorities. This also involves various standards and legal acts regulating the field.

4   Results

Answering RQ1: What procedures are currently performed for customs declarations in the Estonian customs authority?

Based on the interviews with Estonian Tax and Customs Board, the main declaration process of goods goes through the following stages: Entry Summary Declaration (ENS), Arrival Notification (NA), Presentation Notification (PN), Temporary Storage Declaration (TSD) and finally, Customs Declaration (CD). In every step, a consignment might be taken under closer inspection (Green, Yellow, Red corridor) in case any irregularities or suspicions occur. The following scheme shows the customs procedural flow in the case where a consignment undergoes customs clearance at the point of import, e.g. the (rare) case where a China post or DHL airplane lands in Estonia and declares goods at Estonian customs.

Although the cases where third countries fly their cargo directly to Estonia almost never happen, the scheme above illustrates procedures that are followed by any EU member state customs authority until the 2021 changes are in effect. It is important to note that to date the national customs ICT systems (such as in the Estonian case: ICS1, IMF, TERM, Complex and PL) are EU member state specific national systems developed by each EU member state customs authority

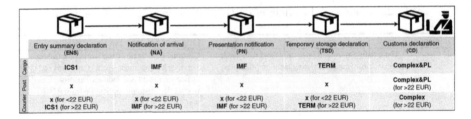

Fig. 1. Customs declaration stages and ICT systems used in case goods are imported to Estonia (until 31 December 2020).

separately. Together with differences in the ICT systems, there are some variations in country specific procedures. An example given by Case worker 1: "Temporary Storage Declaration process has been individual for each EU country, e.g. until 2016 in Germany warranty was not required but in Estonia, warranty was required. There were very diverse approaches. The new EU Customs Code regulates this procedure via establishment of harmonized EU wide data set as well as this process will be unified." (Case worker 1) From the perspective of different logistics operators, many procedural variations exist, e.g. the ENS, NA, PN and TSD procedures have not been required for postal operators. However, for logistics companies (couriers) this exception is valid only for consignments with intrinsic value under the DMT. In 2021, the distinction between different types of operators and other procedural differences will incrementally be harmonized.

Answering RQ2: How can automatization of customs declarations aid to cope with challenges of the new VAT directive?

In order to cope with the changes starting from 2021, the main focus of Estonian Tax and Customs Board is to incrementally implement three new ICT systems: ICS2, NES and IMPULSS. The transition from ICS1 to ICS2 will not happen all at once, but will be the final goal. "ICS1 made separation between consignment view and shipment view, this was a real problem between different stakeholders in the process. ICS2 will use an option called multiple filing, which means that logistics operator can insert data from its part, then goods expediter can add data from its shipment, so the main benefit of ICS2 is that information shared by multiple stakeholders will be used for example to generate common ENS. Initially only 7+1 data elements will be used and later all data elements will be gradually expanded until middle of 2020's." (Case worker 1) The Estonian customs procedures are expected to change as shown in Fig. 2.

Adding consignments to EU-wide common repository (ICS2) will ensure security and safety in the Union customs territory, bring consistency of customs clearance, and automatization of risk analysis of a consignment based on specific criteria [25]. The main reasons Estonia is implementing the new customs declaration ICT system (IMPULSS) to replace the existing ICT system (Complex) is because of the outdated technology, non-compliance with the new customs regulations and inability to handle the growing amount of declarations. To handle

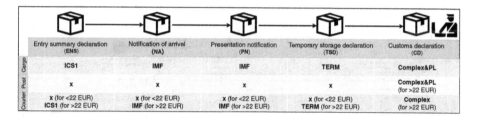

Entry summary declaration (ENS)	Notification of arrival (NA)	Presentation notification (PN)	Temporary storage declaration (TSD)	Customs declaration (CD)
ICS1	IMF	IMF	TERM	Complex&PL
x	x	x	x	Complex&PL (for >22 EUR)
x (for <22 EUR) ICS1 (for >22 EUR)	x (for <22 EUR) IMF (for >22 EUR)	x (for <22 EUR) IMF (for >22 EUR)	x (for <22 EUR) TERM (for >22 EUR)	Complex (for >22 EUR)

Fig. 2. Customs declaration stages and ICT systems used in case goods are imported to Estonia (after ICS2 implementation period).

the growing amount of declarations for consignments of low value (under EUR 150), the separate types of data sets are formulated, called super-reduced data sets (SRDS).

"The main difference between SRDS and regular declaration is that there are some types of goods defined that are not allowed to declare and there are specific value limit to what level goods can be ordered. What Estonia today is using is also reduced data set, but it is our specific solution in regards to private customers in Estonia. We decided to ask only 10 data elements, when we could ask for 40. So it has been really simplified." (Case worker 1) "The new regulation requires 22 data elements, so in reality the requirements declaring goods will not get simpler. However the data sets will be harmonized across the EU and there will be some flexibility for some data elements". (Case worker 1) "IMPULSS will be the system where VAT related information will be managed. The IOSS scheme and special arrangements will be dealt in IMPULSS. The IOSS scheme is efficient because goods will be released from VAT at the moment of entry to the EU. As time is a critical factor, goods flow and fiscal flow will be separated so that flow of physical goods would not be delayed because of declaration procedures." (Case worker 2).

Figure 3, which is based on our analysis, illustrates the expected future simplified process of physical consignment and data flow in case a low value consignment is purchased from a third country marketplace.

The process model explains the simplicity of declaring goods using the IOSS scheme (delivered duty paid - DDP). In reality, a logistics operator and declarant might not be in the same roles and a marketplace might not directly send the pre-lodged customs declaration to the EU customs authority (intermediate stakeholder could handle this type of task).

In 2021, if a marketplace facilitates a Delivered Duty Paid (DDP) sale from a third country to an EU member state, it will be responsible for paying VAT because it will be deemed to have purchased and then sold the goods. Hence, the marketplace is assigned to an IOSS scheme and has a VAT IOSS identification number registered in one of the EU member states. After checkout, the marketplace knows the assumed destination member state of the customer, either from IP address or from a destination address that the customer has specified. In our analysis, we assume the DDP model, i.e., the customer pays VAT

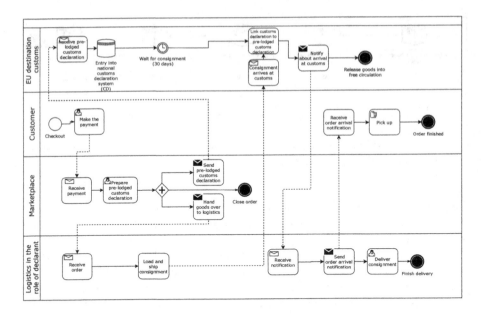

Fig. 3. Expected IOSS scheme process in case DDP (VAT is paid at checkout).

to marketplace at the point of checkout. After checkout, the marketplace will send the pre-lodged customs declaration (with SRDS) to the destination customs authority's ICT system. The SRDS can be sent to customs up to 30 days before the physical consignment arrives to customs. In that case, if the consignment is declared in another EU member state customs, the data set will be erased automatically.

In terms of the fiscal process, since the EU customs have periodical reporting procedures to tax authorities about in which country the goods were declared according to where the actual customer resided, the overview of expected VAT is still received through the collaboration of tax authorities. For example, if the customer lived in Estonia but goods were declared in Germany, then the VAT collected after checkout will be registered in the German customs and the reporting will go to the German tax authority who then periodically notifies the Estonian tax authority regarding how much tax is to be received from the marketplace's EU IOSS representative. Using such a separation of processes, automatization of declarations can be developed as well as transparency will be enabled, because tax authorities will be able to audit data sets and compare them with taxes received from third country marketplace IOSS representatives.

Answering RQ3: What concerns are raised in relation to the upcoming changes?

Multiple concerns were expressed throughout multiple interviews (see Table 3): IOSS VAT ID abuse, readiness, shifting the responsibility, localization and basis for developing the new CD system.

Table 3. Topics and quotations from meetings.

Topic	Case worker	Quotation
IOSS VAT ID abuse	Case worker 2	"Marketplaces will likely be trustworthy, they will likely not commit IOSS number fraud, but someone else could fraudulently use the IOSS number of a Marketplace."
Readiness	Case worker 1	"The IMPULSS technical specification will come in the first half of next year (2020). Were promised in the beginning of next year, but…"
Shifting the responsibility	Case worker 1	"This pressure stems from the fact that currently those who present data are exactly the ones responsible. This is one of the reasons why there is a desire to shift this responsibility from parties like Omniva, who have not even seen inside the consignment, to those who have actually produced the data. But this change has not been made. For us, the responsible party is still Omniva."
Localization	Case worker 3	"Customs declarations presented to us have to be in Estonian."
Basis for developing the new CD system	Case worker 1	"Currently, the plan is to proceed with the knowledge that we will be implementing the newest version; up until we receive the very final decision on this. As long as we see any possibility, we will implement the newest version."

Based on the new VAT directive, the IOSS VAT ID number of a marketplace will be the unique number filled under one specific customs declaration data element in the SRDS. The customs authorities will not check correct ownership of the IOSS number, only the validity of it. There are strict rules for marketplaces; if someone fraudulently uses another's IOSS number, then the IOSS number itself may be declared invalid. There are ongoing discussions on how to protect these numbers. Regarding the success of implementing the new CD ICT system IMPULSS, the Estonian tax authority heavily relies on what business decisions will be made by the different stakeholders; how will the postal operators contribute and how much will the couriers (e.g. DHL) contribute. During our research, the collaboration was thoroughly not initiated. Additionally, a concern was expressed regarding a mismatch between who is responsible for the content of a consignment versus who presents the customs declaration. Currently, the ones who are responsible (e.g. postal operators) have not seen the inside of a consignment. In the future, the responsible one should be the marketplace who presents the data for customs declaration. With the new changes ahead, a localisation issue seems to become a complication because so far, all declarations presented to the Estonian customs authorities are required to be in the local language (Estonian). However, the SRDS coming from third country marketplace is expected to be in English. Finally, it is still undecided whether the newest draft version or the current version of EUCDM will be required by the EU Commission. It could still be that different EU member states will implement different versions. For now, it is clear that from 2023, all member states will have to implement the newest version. However, before that there will be a period of confusion as evidenced by the Estonian example and how difficulties can occur for the implementation of the new CD system.

Answering RQ4: What data quality is required to meet the new requirements with respect to automatization?

During our research on the EU Customs Data Model (EUCDM), we noticed a crucial change in the data set. While consulting with the Estonian customs authority, the feedback suggested that there is no clear understanding of which version of EUCDM will be required as the basis of data sets for low value consignments in 1 July 2021. The data requirements are in Annex B of UCC-DA [26], and their formats and codes are in Annex B of UCC-IA [27]. By analyzing the UCC Annex B, we found that for some data elements there is no clear understanding of the required format (e.g. length, clarity). For example, the goods description field, which describes the goods in a consignment, does not have a length or material description requirement despite the field being strictly related to a specific nomenclature code called a Harmonized System (HS) code. Based on our interviews with the Estonian customs authority, if such requirements were in place, validation of consignments could be automated to a large extent. The quality of data-based customs clearance depends on the quality of data sent in advance. Historically, this data has been non-existent for low value consignments and very poor overall. Poor data quality within the logistics chain leads to obscure or missing details in import declarations and makes the risk analysis and fiscal assessment of consignments more difficult for the customs authorities. In 2021, the volume of consignments requiring customs clearance will increase dramatically, thus the workload on customs authorities across the EU will increase. Anecdotally, based on our interviews, we know that European customs declarations will increase to approximately 4 billion per year. For example, for the Estonian customs authorities, the total volume of customs declarations for postal consignments would increase by roughly 130 times.

5   Limitations and Future Work

In the current research, we mainly concentrated on the changes in the customs authority and customs declaration process. The actual impact will be influencing the wider stakeholder ecosystem of e-commerce (marketplaces, declarants, IOSS intermediaries and postal and logistics operators) and many additional digitalization attempts to various data sets and procedures such as ENS, NA, PN and TSD. We suggest that there should be further analysis and research done in these specific fields.

6   Conclusion

This research shows that, by the example of the Estonian customs authority, automatization of customs declarations requires joint efforts by various stakeholders. The main concerns are not only related to technological developments but also to the clear guidelines that are being developed by the EU Commission, and also to the affected stakeholders such as postal operators and couriers. We also identified various difficulties and complications that the Estonian customs authority may face in the process of implementing the new requirements by 1 July 2021. Based on the interview results, the main improvements and concerns were presented as well as the description of the current procedures. The current procedures were analyzed through an overview of ICT systems that are currently being used in relation to customs declaration procedures. The new data quality requirements are presented in connection to the newly planned information systems. The results of this research serve as a good stepping stone to the goal of the Archimedes project which is to develop an independent platform to exchange customs declaration data between various marketplaces and the EU customs authorities. We have conducted this research to set an example and help the other EU member state customs authorities to rapidly develop and scale their systems.

References

1. World Customs Organization: Annual Report 2018–2019. WCO (2019)
2. Pappel, I., Pappel, I., Tepandi, J., Draheim, D.: Systematic digital signing in Estonian e-government processes: influencing factors, technologies, change management. Trans. Large-Scale Data Knowl. Centered Syst. **16**, 31–51 (2017)
3. Pappel, I., Pappel, I., Tampere, T., Draheim, D.: Implementation of e-invoicing principles in Estonian local governments. In: Proceedings of ECDG 2017 - the 17th European Conference on Digital Government, Academic Conferences and Publishing, pp. 127–136 (2017)
4. Pappel, I., Pappel, I., Saarmann, M.: Conception and activity directions for training and science centre supporting development of Estonian e-state technologies. In: Proceedings of ICEGOV 2011 - the 5th International Conference on Theory and Practice of Electronic Governance, ACM, pp. 219–224 (2011)
5. Pappel, I., Pappel, I., Saarmann, M.: Digital records keeping to information governance in Estonian local governments. In: Proceedings of i-Society 2012, IEEE, pp. 199–204 (2012)
6. Draheim, Dirk., Koosapoeg, Kaarel., Lauk, Mihkel., Pappel, Ingrid., Pappel, Ingmar, Tepandi, Jaak: The design of the Estonian governmental document exchange classification framework. In: Kő, Andrea, Francesconi, Enrico (eds.) EGOVIS 2016. LNCS, vol. 9831, pp. 33–47. Springer, Cham (2016). https://doi.org/10.1007/978-3-319-44159-7_3

7. Pappel, I., Tsap, V., Draheim, D.: The e-LocGov model for introducing e-Governance into local governments: an Estonian case study. IEEE Transactions on Emerging Topics in Computing (2020)
8. Paide, K., Pappel, I., Vainsalu, H., Draheim, D.: On the systematic exploitation of the estonian data exchange layer X-Road for strengthening public-private partnerships. In: Proceedings of ICEGOV 2018 - the 11th International Conference on Theory and Practice of Electronic Governance, ACM, pp. 34–41 (2018)
9. PostNord AB: e-Commerce in Europe 2019. PostNord AB (2020)
10. Basalisco, D.B., Wahl, J., Okholm, D.H.: e-Commerce imports into Europe: VAT and customs treatment. Copenhagen Economics, May 2016
11. Lamensch, M., Ceci, E.: VAT Fraud: Economic Impact. Challenges and Policy Issues. European Parliament, Policy Department for Economic, Scientific and Quality of Life Policies (2018)
12. The Council of the European Union: COUNCIL DIRECTIVE (EU) 2017/2455. Official Journal of the European Union L 348/7 (2017)
13. The European Commission: COMMISSION IMPLEMENTING REGULATION (EU) 2020/194. Official Journal of the European Union L 40/114 (2020)
14. The European Commission: COMMISSION DELEGATED REGULATION (EU) 2019/1143. Official Journal of the European Union L 181/2 (2019)
15. The European Commission: Regulation (EU) No 952/2013 of the European Parliament and of the Council of 9 October 2013 laying down the Union Customs Code. Official Journal of the European Union L 269/1 (2013)
16. Chan, S., Ramly, Z.: The role of country governance on value-added tax and inequality. E+M Ekonomie a Management 21, 79–93 (2018)
17. Grindle, M.: Good governance, RIP: a critique and an alternative. Governance 30, 17–22 (2017)
18. Sok-Gee, C., Zulkufly, R., Mohd, Z.M.: Value-added Tax and Economic Efficiency: Role of Country Governance. Panoeconomicus, p. 20 (2018)
19. Dale, S., Vincent, V.: The European Union's approach to VAT and e-Commerce. World J. VAT/GST Law 6(1), 55–61 (2017)
20. Papis-Almansa, Marta: VAT and insurance: the European union. In: van Brederode, Robert F., Krever, Richard (eds.) VAT and Financial Services, pp. 337–364. Springer, Singapore (2017). https://doi.org/10.1007/978-981-10-3465-7_18
21. Hansen, P., Annovazzi-Jakab, L.: Facilitating cross-border movement of goods: a sustainable approach. In: The Global Enabling Trade Report 2008. World Economic Forum, pp. 1–741 (2008)
22. Sousa, L.D.: Understanding European cross-border cooperation: a framework for analysis. J. Euro. Integrat. 35(6), 669–687 (2013)
23. Kreos, K., Täks, E., Tsap, V., Pappel, I., Draheim, D.: On facilitating cross-border E-commerce through an automated VAT declaration system. In: Proceedings of ICEDEG 2019 - 6th International Conference on eDemocracy eGovernment, pp. 56–63 (2019)
24. Sein, M., Henfridsson, O., Purao, S., Rossi, M., Lindgren, R.: Action design research. MIS Q. 35, 37–56 (2011)
25. European Commission Directorate General: ICS2 Shared Trader Interface - Vision. European Commission (2017)

26. The European Commission: COMMISSION DELEGATED REGULATION (EU) 2015/2446 of 28 July 2015 supplementing Regulation (EU) No 952/2013 of the European Parliament and of the Council as regards detailed rules concerning certain provisions of the Union Customs Code. Official Journal of the European Union (2015)
27. The European Commission: COMMISSION IMPLEMENTING REGULATION (EU) 2015/2447 of 24 November 2015 laying down detailed rules for implementing certain provisions of Regulation (EU) No 952/2013 of the European Parliament and of the Council laying down the Union Customs Code. Official Journal of the European Union (2015)

AI-Enabled Innovation in the Public Sector: A Framework for Digital Governance and Resilience

Gianluca Misuraca[1]([envelope]) [iD] and Gianluigi Viscusi[2] [iD]

[1] European Commission's Joint Research Centre Edificio EXPO, Calle Inca Garcilaso 3, 41092 Seville, Spain
Gianluca.misuraca@ec.europa.eu
[2] Imperial College Business School Building, South Kensington Campus, SW7 2AZ, London, UK
g.viscusi@imperial.ac.uk

Abstract. This article aims to contribute to the theoretical debate on the relationships between digital governance and social innovation, and their impact on policy making for creating and capturing value from effective solutions addressing societal challenges. In particular, we question the drivers and challenges specifically considering the growing number of national strategies for innovation driven by artificial intelligence (AI) and the consequent wave of investments. To this end, a framework is presented aiming, on the one hand, to connect key dimensions and value drivers of digital governance for social innovation and complex systems methods for policy making; on the other hand, to position AI national initiatives with regard to welfare state initiatives. The framework is then applied to the analysis of cases of AI-driven innovation initiatives in Europe to assess their impact on social innovation.

Keywords: Digital governance · Social innovation · Social value · Crowdsourcing · Complex systems · Artificial intelligence

1 Introduction

Digitalization is not anymore an emergent phenomenon but the actual shape of everyday life interactions and transactions [1–3]. Compared to the private sector, where businesses have deployed initiatives to change their infrastructure, governance, and business models to create and exploit value from their digital assets, the public sector is still tied up to a consideration of technology as something separated from public sector reform and policy making. Accordingly, it is still preeminent in the public sector the focus on what can be considered the e-government rhetoric legacy, namely the provision of information and communication technology (ICT) enabled services mainly involving the public administration alone and the translation of administrative procedures in digital

---

G. Viscusi—Independent Researcher.

© IFIP International Federation for Information Processing 2020
Published by Springer Nature Switzerland AG 2020
G. Viale Pereira et al. (Eds.): EGOV 2020, LNCS 12219, pp. 110–120, 2020.
https://doi.org/10.1007/978-3-030-57599-1_9

format. This view is still present in most countries having officially claimed the adoption of an open government stance towards their initiatives: the result is, in the best case, an efficient public administration, yet still neither inclusive nor fully open, in terms of transparency and accountability [4].

Taking these issues into account, this article aims to contribute to the theoretical debate on the relationships between digital governance and social innovation, and their impact on policy making for creating and capturing value [5] from effective solutions addressing societal challenges. In particular, we question the drivers and challenges specifically considering the growing number of national strategies for innovation driven by artificial intelligence (AI) and the consequent wave of investments. To this end, a framework is presented aiming, on the one hand, to connect key dimensions and value drivers of digital governance for social innovation [6, 7] and complex systems methods for policy making, formerly introduced in another framework called i-Frame [8]; on the other hand, the framework aims to position AI national initiatives with regard to welfare state initiatives for an appropriate analysis of their premises and effects. The framework is then applied to the analysis of cases of AI-driven innovation initiatives in Europe.

The article is structured as follows. First, we discuss the related work positioning the proposal and its contribution, also considering the state-of-the-art frameworks and clarifying the difference with regard to, e.g., maturity models. Then, we present the framework starting with the conceptual model that is at its basis. Subsequently, we apply the model to a sample of four AI initiatives associated with welfare state actions or services from one national agency in continental Europe and three municipalities in different Nordic countries. Finally, the paper concludes outlining future research directions and policy implications.

2 Related Work

The rhetoric on the benefits of information and communication technologies (ICTs) for governments action is now encompassing the debate on the use of artificial intelligence (AI) solutions for innovating public sector services and decision-making [9–11] with a new emphasis on the need for governance of AI and not by AI [9] that resonates the former claims about the governance of ICTs vs. governance by ICTs [7]. Furthermore, although some kind of public value can be gained [12], the switch to social value from co-production [13, 14], by involving citizens and external actors, is still an ongoing challenge for public administrations willing to have a role in social innovation through the appropriate exploitation of the unprecedented amount of data available from information production, inside and outside public sector information systems [15]. This is particularly relevant when thinking about the use of crowdsourcing for deliberation, regulatory reviews, and policy initiatives [16–18], the development of open innovation in the public sector [19] as well as the emergent challenges of using, e.g., machine learning for deciding on welfare issues [20, 21]. Taking these issues into account, especially in the research area of e-government [22] quite a few scholars have commonly engaged in identifying key themes in the state of the art literature to outline research agendas emphasizing both challenges and opportunities of AI. In particular, Medaglia [22] has pointed out those related to decision-making in the public sector "where environmental variables are constantly changing, and pre-programming cannot account for all possible cases", further questioning the way "policy makers frame and legitimize AI-supported solutions". Accordingly, the framework proposed in this paper aims to provide an instrument to support policy-makers facing that question together with a deeper and situated understanding of the impacts of the initiatives that their actions may eventually enforce. However, it is worth noting that for our framework is not a matter of forecasting or predicting what are the future paths traced as maturity or stage models, like the ones that the e-government literature [23–25] have eventually tried to do for the various technology waves in the past, with different outcomes, likewise [26]. On the contrary, with this framework, we aim to consider deeply the intertwining of contextual and individual factors required and often implied by the AI applications in public sector services and initiatives, including the areas suggested by [26] (*technology, public organizations and society, human psychology, politics and public administration*, exception made for history that could be eventually part of future work). Thus, we follow what [26] points out as "the way of the hedgehog" (p. 12), resonating the insights by [27], aiming to provide a tool for public managers and policy makers that would prevent the "digital sclerosis" [28] that may be associated with the uptake of AI in the public sector.

3 The Interpretive Framework

In this paper, we propose a framework that extends to the AI the arguments at the basis of other state of the art proposals [6] used to analyze cases of ICT-enabled innovation of Social Protection Systems. At its basis we have defined a conceptual model that, on the one hand, moves to a general perspective on *social value*; on the other hand, it aims to link government initiatives to the micro level of individuals everyday life and

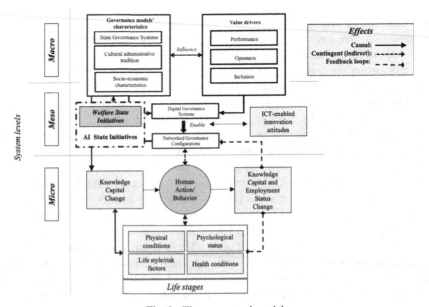

Fig. 1. The conceptual model

the environment that contain it, eventually also co-created by the interactions with the Internet of things (IoT) and the technology making up the infrastructure of the so-called "smart cities" [29]. In this Section, we first provide a summary of the main constructs and components making up the model shown in Fig. 1.

The macro and meso components include i) the digital governance model and the ii) typology of ICT-enabled innovation attitudes presented and discussed by [4, 7], to which we refer the reader for the full details about them. As shown in Fig. 1 the conceptual model comprises three key value drivers (*Performance*, *Openness*, and *Inclusion*) as well as their connection with a set of governance model characteristics, i.e., *State governance system*, *Cultural administrative tradition* and *Socio-economic characteristics* of the context of intervention. These elements influence each other and constitute the political, administrative, and socio-economic context embedding the enacted digital systems for e-government and e-governance [30, 31]. Furthermore, these systems mediate the interaction of public administrations with constituencies and the consequent potential outcome of the use of ICTs for their innovation.

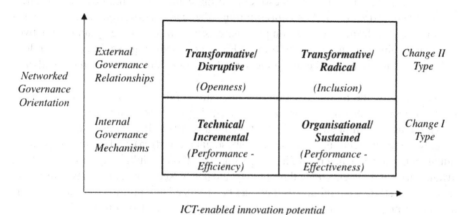

Fig. 2. Typology of changes for exploiting ICT-enabled innovation potential

It is worth noting that the degree of maturity of those systems (both at IT and government levels [24, 32]) is an input to the AI-and welfare state initiatives and may consequently enable different networked governance configurations related to their characteristics and impact on the micro-level. Those configurations also correspond to the various degrees of *openness* or *inclusion* reached by the public sector as well as the participation of the citizens. Consequently, the different digital governance systems have different impacts on the governance configuration of the stakeholders' networks, which may require or enforce innovation to a given context for certain governance models characteristics. Moreover, those systems and platforms represent the point where *openness, generativity,* and specific *affordances* [33] involved in the interactions with citizens lead to a change in the use of ICTs from e-government to "digital" government. As pointed out by [34] "these new digital technologies embrace ICT systems such as virtualization, mobility, and analytical systems and are integrated with back-office ICT", thus moving from a focus on the management of ICT infrastructure to "the interface with or fully on the side of customers" [35] or citizens in the case of public administration. Thus, in what follows we consider AI as another kind of ICT-enabled innovation, having its own characteristics, yet not independent from the ICT capabilities eventually developed for previous configurations of digital governance.

Taking those issues into account, each digital governance configuration corresponds to a type of innovation attitude within the public administration that can be identified for the considered domain of intervention, required to enable that governance configuration and/or enabled by that specific innovation (see Fig. 2).

According to the typology, ICT-enabled innovation can produce changes in governance processes in four ways (and a consequent set of innovation types or attitudes): *Technical/Incremental* change; *Organizational/Sustained* change; *Transformative/Disruptive* change; *Transformative/Radical* change. As a consequence of the above discussion, it is worth emphasizing here that the framework assumes as a key argument that ICT-enabled innovation cannot be decoupled from a public administration reform [4, 7, 36], thus encompassing public services and their impact on welfare [see also, 37]. The same can be applied at the meso level to the evolution of the government interests toward the adoption of AI solutions through dedicated innovation initiatives, which eventually move from simply accompanying or supporting welfare systems initiatives to actually substitute them (dotted lines in Fig. 1) or to leverage smart cities and digital initiatives to control and contain the spreading of epidemics among the population [38, 39].

Accordingly, the model also considers the structural connection [40] between the above-discussed elements (*governance models, digital systems, networked configurations*), the agency implied by welfare state initiatives (see Fig. 1) as discussed by [6] (namely: social protection, social investment, social innovation), and the impact on individuals classified here in terms of life stage (e.g., childhood, adulthood, etc.). Innovation, advance in digital systems (e.g., through AI), and networked governance may also enable bottom-up welfare state initiatives that may be produced and promoted by social enterprises/entrepreneurs, non-governmental organizations, etc. Also, it is worth noting that the described dynamics can lead to a change, e.g., in the government model's characteristics (see Fig. 1) that, on the one hand, enable or constraint the AI-welfare initiatives; on the other hand, they may require further reforms due to the emerging alignment or misalignment related to their current impact on each life stage. The same can be said for "value drivers" (see Fig. 1), which require to fit both the AI – welfare state initiatives and the current politics in place at micro-level, eventually leading to a tension between values that should be recursively solved by the government (either a central or local one).

Moreover, Table 1 provides an analytic view on the connection between the above elements, the types of resilience (*absorptive, adaptive, transformative* [6]), and value drivers per type of ICT-enabled innovation. Notwithstanding the effort by governments and institutions acting, e.g., at the European Union level [41], current initiatives are still mainly focused on performance as a value driver and a type of innovation that can be associated with social protection and early social innovation initiatives. These latter are not aligned with the need for knowledge capital change required to fully exploit the effects of digitalization and AI, thus, risking to exclude people without personal means and capabilities, such as, e.g., workers raised within the framework of social protection typical of the industrial production model of the second half of the 20th century, and currently facing the challenges of digitalized social services often without adequate skills and digital literacy [42–44].

Table 1. Welfare state initiatives, type of resilience and value driver per type of ICT-enabled innovation

Welfare State initiative	Type of resilience	Value driver	Networked governance orientation	ICT-enabled innovation
Social protection	Absorptive	Performance (Efficiency)	Internal governance relationship	Technical/ Incremental
Social investment	Adaptive	Performance (Effectiveness)		Organizational/ Sustained
Social innovation	Transformative	Openness	External governance relationship	Transformative/ Disruptive
		Inclusion		Transformative/ Radical

4 Cases

In this Section, we are going to apply the framework that we have above discussed to a sample of cases of AI initiatives associated with welfare state actions or services, some of them especially considering their administrative processes. To this end, we have considered one national agency in continental Europe and three municipalities in different Nordic countries. We briefly present them on the basis of the secondary data and discussion by [45].

In 2014, Kind and Gezin (Child and Family) [46], a Flemish public agency in Belgium for support and advice on children's well-being has developed a predictive AI system to identify day-care services in need of further inspection to keep their quality high to improve the wellbeing of children. It is worth noting here that the agency does the inspections in collaboration with the regional Health Care Inspection of the Department of Welfare, Public Health and Family.

Looking now at the Nordic countries, since 2016 the municipality of Trelleborg has used AI for automated-decision making in various social assistance pronouncements [see also 47]. In particular, it was an early adopter of Robotic Process Automation (RPA) for the management of applications for homecare, sickness benefits, unemployment benefits, and taxes. In the current diffused landscape of practices for testing future societies [48], the municipality of Espoo started in 2015 an AI experiment, funded also by the Six City Strategy, on the social and health data from all the Espoo residents to carry out a data-based segmentation aiming to predict the service paths of each individual. As for the future development of the experiment, the plans include the use of data of private

Table 2. AI and welfare state initiatives, drivers, type of resilience, governance, innovation and changes for impact at individual level

AI Initiative	Organization	Welfare State initiative	Type of resilience	Value driver	Networked governance orientation	ICT-enabled innovation	Type of Change	Individual conditions/life stage
AI to predict day-care services inspection	Flemish Agency for Child and Family (Belgium)	Social protection	Absorptive	Performance (Effectiveness)	Internal governance relationship	Organizational/ Sustained	Knowledge capital	Health (Childhood)
Robotic Process Automation (RPA) to handle welfare services applications and payments	Trelleborg, (Sweden)	Social protection	Absorptive	Performance (Effectiveness)	Internal governance relationship	Technical/ Incremental	Knowledge capital and employment status	Physical/Psychological (Adulthood)
AI prediction and clustering for service paths	Municipality of Espoo (Finland)	Social investment	Adaptive	Performance (Effectiveness)	Internal governance relationship	Organizational/ Sustained	Knowledge capital and employment status	Health/ Physical/Psychological (Adulthood)
AI for 'parallel societies'	Municipality of Gladsaxe (Denmark)	Social innovation	Transformative	Inclusion	External governance relationship	Transformative/ Radical	Knowledge capital	Life style/Risk factors (Childhood)

health care services and the Kela database [49] with statistics on basic social protection in Finland.

Finally, the municipality of Gladsaxe in Denmark has developed an AI system in 2018 to tackle 'parallel societies' in less developed and vulnerable areas. The project was part of a preventive risk assessment program for the automatic recognition of children in situations that eventually may lead to a disadvantaged condition. The system employed ~200 risk indicators from several data sources on health, social, employment, and education to assess the families' risk of social vulnerability. Then, children identified as at risk of abuse could be subject to intervention, eventually resulting in the forced removal from their original family.

Looking now at Table 2, what we observe is that most of the AI initiatives considered in our sample are oriented toward the better performance of public services mainly focused on social protection and social investment. At first, only the case of Denmark could be classified as somewhat related to social innovation with a kind of "inclusion" as value driver; although here and in the other cases there is a potential risk of enforcement of "algocracy", not in line with democratic values [50]. Also, most of the initiatives are guided by internal governance needs, involving mainly administrations or agencies, thus raising the ethical concerns AI such as trust by citizens (rather better considered by an external governance perspective), data security and privacy, not mentioning the bias potentially related to social protection and investment decisions [20]. It is worth noting, that from the initiatives seem also to emerge a specific attention to individual health and childhood as a life stage. Considering now the type of innovation paths, it emerges a general orientation toward an "organizational/sustained" type, also in cases such as the one of Trelleborg where the priority seems for a "technical/incremental" one, requiring a change in knowledge capital and employment status for public employees. Finally, the Danish experience results in a "transformative/radical" path toward social innovation, although with the above-mentioned risks of "algocracy" and a consequent normative perspective on the meaning of "inclusion".

5 Conclusion and Future Work

In this paper we have proposed a framework to connect, on the one hand, macro and meso elements enacting digital systems (in our case AI initiatives) and their related networked governance configurations; on the other hand, the framework aims to provide a view on how the choices made at macro and meso levels (instantiated in the welfare state and AI initiatives) impact (constraints/enable) knowledge capital and employment status change. Those choices frame the action/behavior of individuals (citizens) at micro level as well as their physical/health conditions, psychological status, and lifestyle/risk factors along the different stages of their life (see the bottom part of Fig. 1). Then, it is worth noting that the action/behavior of individuals (citizens) in terms of participation is both bounded and enacted by the changes to networked governance configurations and digital governance systems. As a consequence, different scenarios may require or enforce a specific innovation type of change in a given context as well as certain governance models characteristics (see left-hand side of Fig. 1). Thus, the framework discussed in this article may provide a richer and holistic/systemic representation for understanding which policies can be designed for appropriate governance of (AI as part of) digital innovation initiatives and reforms in the public sector suitable to enable a sustainable and resilient social innovation. In future work we are going to empirically apply the framework to further ongoing initiatives of AI innovation in Europe, thus complementing the limited testing set of cases discussed in this article; the goal is to deeply understand their implication for the welfare state and social innovation as well as to have a larger map of the current state of the art initiatives, including their potential effects and impact.

Acknowledgments. Work on this paper has benefited in part of the research activities on AI for the public sector conducted within the framework of the AI Watch, a joint initiative of DG CONNECT and the European Commission's Joint Research Centre.

Disclaimer. The views expressed in this paper are purely those of the authors and may not in any circumstances be regarded as stating an official position of the European Commission.

References

1. Tilson, D., Lyytinen, K., Sørensen, C.: Digital infrastructures: the missing is research agenda. Inf. Syst. Res. **21**, 748–759 (2010)
2. Degryse, C.: Digitalisation of the economy and its impact on labour markets. Work. Pap. Eur. trade union Inst. 02 (2016)
3. Yoo, Y.: The tables have turned: how can the information systems field contribute to technology and innovation management research? J. Assoc. Inf. Syst. **14**, 227–236 (2013)
4. Misuraca, G., Viscusi, G.: Is open data enough? E-governance challenges for open government. Int. J. Electron. Gov. Res. **10**, 19–36 (2014)
5. Lepak, D.P., Smith, K.G., Taylor, M.S.: Value creation and value capture: a multilevel perspective. Acad. Manag. Rev. **32**, 180–194 (2007)
6. Misuraca, G., Pasi, G., Viscusi, G.: Social Innovation and Resilience: exploring the dynamics and impacts on the digital transformation of governance & society. In: Kankanhalli, A., Ojo, A., Soares, D. (eds.) ICEGOV 2018 (11th International Conference on Theory and Practice of Electronic Governance). pp. 91–100. ACM, New York, NY, USA, Galway, Ireland — April 04–06 2018 (2018)
7. Misuraca, G., Viscusi, G.: Shaping public sector innovation theory: an interpretative framework for ICT-enabled governance innovation. Electron. Commerce Res. **15**(3), 303–322 (2015). https://doi.org/10.1007/s10660-015-9184-5
8. Misuraca, G., Geppert, L., Kucsera, C.: Deconstructing social policy innovation through the use of complex systems theory: a methodology for modelling and simulation of the impact of ICT-enabled social innovation. In: Gil-Garcia, J.R., Pardo, T.A., Luna-Reyes, L.F. (eds.) Policy Analytics, Modelling, and Informatics. PAIT, vol. 24, pp. 151–175. Springer, Cham (2018). https://doi.org/10.1007/978-3-319-61762-6_7
9. Sun, T.Q., Medaglia, R.: Mapping the challenges of Artificial Intelligence in the public sector: Evidence from public healthcare. Gov. Inf. Q. **36**, 368–383 (2019)
10. van Noordt, C., Misuraca, G.: New Wine in Old Bottles: Chatbots in Government BT - Electronic Participation (2019)
11. Androutsopoulou, A., Karacapilidis, N., Loukis, E., Charalabidis, Y.: Transforming the communication between citizens and government through AI-guided chatbots. Gov. Inf. Q. **36**, 358–367 (2019)

12. Cordella, A., Bonina, C.M.: A public value perspective for ICT enabled public sector reforms: a theoretical reflection. Gov. Inf. Q. **29**, 512–520 (2012)
13. Cordella, A., Paletti, A., Maha, S.: Renegotiating public value with co-production. In: Tucci, C., Afuah, A., Viscusi, G. (eds.) Creating and Capturing Value through Crowdsourcing, pp. 181–203. Oxford University Press, Oxford (2018)
14. Alford, J.: Public Value from Co-production by Clients. In: Benington, J., Moore, M.H. (eds.) Public Value - Theory and Practice. Palgrave Macmillan (2011)
15. Viscusi, G., Batini, C.: Information production and social value for public policy: a conceptual modeling perspective. Policy Internet **8**, 334–353 (2016)
16. Aitamurto, T., Landemore, H.: Crowdsourced deliberation: the case of the law on off-road traffic in finland. Policy Internet **8**, 174–196 (2016)
17. Lodge, M., Wegrich, K.: Crowdsourcing and regulatory reviews: A new way of challenging red tape in British government? Regul. Gov. **9**, 30–46 (2015)
18. Brabham, D.C.: Crowd sourcing the public participation process for planning projects. Plan. Theory. **8**, 242–262 (2009)
19. Viscusi, G., Poulin, D., Tucci, C.: Open innovation research and e-government: clarifying the connections between two fields. In: XII Conference of the Italian Chapter of AIS (itAIS2015). Luiss University Press, Roma, Italy (2015)
20. West, S.M., Whittaker, M., Crawford, K.: Discriminating Systems - Gender, Race, and Power in AI. https://ainowinstitute.org/discriminatingsystems.pdf
21. Reisman, D., Schultz, J., Crawford, K., Whittaker, M.: Algorithmic impact assessments: A practical framework for public agency accountability. https://ainowinstitute.org/aiareport 2018.pdf
22. Dwivedi, Y.K., et al.: Artificial intelligence (AI): multidisciplinary perspectives on emerging challenges, opportunities, and agenda for research, practice and policy. Int. J. Inf. Manage. 101994 (2019). https://doi.org/10.1016/j.ijinfomgt.2019.08.002
23. Lee, G., Kwak, Y.H.: An open government maturity model for social media-based public engagement. Gov. Inf. Q. **29**, 492–503 (2012)
24. Andersen, K.N., Henriksen, H.Z., Medaglia, R., Anderson, K.N., Henriksen, H.Z., Medaglia, R.: Maturity models in the age of digital diversity: beyond the layne & lee legacy. In: Snellen, I., Thaens, M., van de Donk, W. (eds.) Public Administration in the Information Age: Revisited, pp. 205–220. IOS Press, Amsterdam (2012)
25. Andersen, K.V., Henriksen, H.Z.: E-government maturity models: extension of the layne and lee model. Gov. Inf. Q. **23**, 236–248 (2006)
26. Bannister, F., Connolly, R.: The future ain't what it used to be: Forecasting the impact of ICT on the public sphere. Gov. Inf. Q. **37**, 101410 (2020)
27. Berlin, I.: The hedgehog and the fox: An essay on Tolstoy's view of history. Weidenfield and Nicholson, London (1953)
28. Andersen, K.N., Lee, J., Henriksen, H.Z.: Digital sclerosis? wind of change for government and the employees. Digit. Gov. Res. Pr. **1**(1), 14 (2020). https://doi.org/10.1145/3360000. Article 9
29. Kankanhalli, A., Charalabidis, Y., Mellouli, S.: IoT and AI for smart government: a research agenda. Gov. Inf. Q. **36**, 304–309 (2019)
30. Fountain, J.E.: Building the virtual state: information technology and institutional change. Brookings Institution Press (2001)
31. Cordella, A., Iannacci, F.: Information systems in the public sector: The e-Government enactment framework. J. Strateg. Inf. Syst. **19**, 52–66 (2010)
32. Pereira, R., Serrano, J.: A review of methods used on IT maturity models development: a systematic literature review and a critical analysis. J. Inf. Technol. **35**(2), 161–178 (2020). https://doi.org/10.1177/0268396219886874

33. Nambisan, S., Wright, M., Feldman, M.: The digital transformation of innovation and entrepreneurship: progress, challenges and key themes. Res. Policy 48(8) (2019). https://doi.org/10.1016/j.respol.2019.03.018
34. Loonam, J., Eaves, S., Kumar, V., Parry, G.: Towards digital transformation: lessons learned from traditional organizations. Strateg. Chang. 27, 101–109 (2018)
35. Matt, C., Hess, T., Benlian, A.: Digital transformation strategies. Bus. Inf. Syst. Eng. 57(5), 339–343 (2015). https://doi.org/10.1007/s12599-015-0401-5
36. Misuraca, G., Alfano, G., Viscusi, G.: A multi-level framework for ICT-enabled governance: assessing the non-technical dimensions of 'government openness'. Electron. J. e-Govern. 9, 152–165 (2011)
37. Larsson, H., Grönlund, A.: Future-oriented eGovernance: the sustainability concept in eGov research, and ways forward. Gov. Inf. Q. 31, 137–149 (2014)
38. Normile, D.: Coronavirus cases have dropped sharply in South Korea. What's the secret to its success?, https://www.sciencemag.org/news/2020/03/coronavirus-cases-have-dropped-sharply-south-korea-whats-secret-its-success#
39. Strickland, E.: An Official WHO Coronavirus App Will Be a "Waze for COVID-19." IEEE Spectr (2020)
40. Giddens, A.: The Constitution of Society - Outline of the Theory of Structuration. University of California Press, Berkeley and Los Angeles (1984)
41. Misuraca, G., Viscusi, G., Pasi, G.: Digital governance challenges for ICT-enabled innovation of social protection systems in the EU. In: Scholl, H.J., et al. (eds.) IFIP EGOV and ePart 2016. IOS Press, Guimarães (2016)
42. Helsper, E.J.: The social relativity of digital exclusion: applying relative deprivation theory to digital inequalities. Commun. Theory. 27, 223–242 (2016)
43. Hargittai, E., Piper, A.M., Morris, M.R.: From internet access to internet skills: digital inequality among older adults. University Access Information Society (2018)
44. Hargittai, E., Hinnant, A.: Digital inequality: differences in young adults' use of the internet. Communic. Res. 35, 602–621 (2008)
45. Misuraca, G., van Noordt, C.: Overview of the use and impact of AI in public services in the EU, EUR 30255 EN. Publications Office of the European Union, Luxembourg (2020). https://doi.org/10.2760/039619. https://ec.europa.eu/jrc/en/publication/eur-scientific-and-technical-research-reports/ai-watch-artificial-intelligence-public-services. ISBN 978-92-76-19540-5. JRC120399
46. vbjk: Kind & Gezin (Child & Family). https://vbjk.be/en/partners/kind-gezin
47. Ranerup, A., Henriksen, H.Z.: Value positions viewed through the lens of automated decision-making: the case of social services. Gov. Inf. Q. 36, 101377 (2019)
48. Engels, F., Wentland, A., Pfotenhauer, S.M.: Testing future societies? Developing a framework for test beds and living labs as instruments of innovation governance. Res. Policy 48, 103826 (2019)
49. Kela: About Kela. https://www.kela.fi/web/en/about-kela
50. Mchangama, J., Liu, H.-Y.: The Welfare State Is Committing Suicide by Artificial Intelligence. https://foreignpolicy.com/2018/12/25/the-welfare-state-is-committing-suicide-by-artificial-intelligence/

Technical Debt Management: A Systematic Literature Review and Research Agenda for Digital Government

Mille Edith Nielsen[1,2]([⊠]), Christian Østergaard Madsen[1,2], and Mircea Filip Lungu[1]

[1] The IT University of Copenhagen, Copenhagen, Denmark
{miln,chrm,mlun}@itu.dk
[2] Research Centre for Government IT, Copenhagen, Denmark

Abstract. Technical debt is created when software engineers knowingly or unknowingly introduce shortcuts or unsuitable choices in the development or maintenance of the software system, that will have a negative impact on the future evolution of the system until corrected. Therefore, it is crucial to manage established debt particular in the public sector. The aim of this study is to introduce Technical debt to the field of Digital Government. We create an overview of the state of the art of the knowledge on technical debt management, the methods applied to gain this knowledge, and propose a research agenda to Digital Government scholars. We conduct a systematic literature review, which focuses on the concept of technical debt management. Forty-nine papers published within 2017–2020 are selected and analyzed. We identify several gaps in the existing literature: 1) an absence of theory explaining the relation of events, 2) a shortage of studies conducted in the public sector, 3) and an absence of specific techniques such as observation to study actual technical debt management behavior.

Keywords: Technical Debt Management · Managing legacy systems · Systematic literature review · Technical debt

1 Introduction

Public and private organizations use information technology (IT) to improve their efficiency and service offerings [1]. During the development of IT-projects and the subsequent operation/maintenance, temporary suboptimal solutions are sometimes introduced to profit from the solutions faster. To capture this reality, Cunningham [2] coined the term technical debt (TD) to explain the process and pitfalls of programming to the management in the banking sector in 1992. Rios et al. [3, p. 117] describe TD as a conceptualization of *"problems faced during software evolution considering the tasks that are not carried out adequately during software development."* They conducted a tertiary literature review and found a variation in the application of the term. TD is often associated with any impediment related to the software product and the development process [3]. Griffith et al. describe technical debt management (TDM) as comprising

© IFIP International Federation for Information Processing 2020
Published by Springer Nature Switzerland AG 2020
G. Viale Pereira et al. (Eds.): EGOV 2020, LNCS 12219, pp. 121–137, 2020.
https://doi.org/10.1007/978-3-030-57599-1_10

"the actions of identification, assessment, and remediation of technical debt throughout a software system" [4, p. 1016].

TDM is important because it enables an organization a more optimal use of its resources [5]. For instance: An organization's IT-system breaks down, which leads to reduced production. For management, the possible solutions are to 1) accept the reduced production, 2) conduct a root cause analysis and fix the actual problem, 3) create a work-around that increases momentarily production speed, but does not solve the actual problem and will make the maintenance of the solution harder in the future. Solution 3 may be a viable course of action under certain circumstances, but it will result in the creation of technical debt. Moreover, since the consequences are no longer visible to management, this debt may be forgotten. If proper TDM methods were applied, management could identify the debt and repay it in a timely fashion.

We will claim, TD is important for the field of Digital Government, because TD can hinder the public sector in fully reaping the benefits of digitalization. Scholl encourages the field of Digital Government to engage with other disciplines *"which overlap with Digital Government as a practice area, but which might lack the forward-looking capabilities that Digital Government Research at least can provide in part"* [6, p. 11]. Moreover, Digital Government scholars can contribute to TD research, because they have both domain specific knowledge of the public sector's use of IT and methodological experience in studying IT and operation in this context [7].

In 2017, The Danish Ministry of Finance published an analysis of Danish public IT-systems. The report concluded that 157 of 428 society or business-critical IT systems' technical components (applications and IT-infrastructure) were not fully maintained [8]. Outdated software or hardware components can increase the risk of breakdowns, security breaches, and trouble the maintenance and the future development of the IT-systems maintained [8]. The Swedish National Audit Office conducted a similar analysis and found 70% of their IT-systems were outdated [9].

TD and the concept of legacy systems *"discuss a state of software that is sub-optimal, time constrained, and explain how this state can decrease an organization's development efficiency"* [7, p. 80]. A considerable source of TD originates from software legacy [10], e.g. during continuous development of a system in an outdated environment. In this review, we focus solely on TDM.

TD studies are primarily published in Software Engineering, especially after Cunningham's [2] introduction of the metaphor [3, 5, 11, 12]. However, Information Systems researchers have also published studies on TD [13, 14].

We found nine literature reviews and one tertiary review on TD and TDM (Appendix A). While these reviews offer important contributions, they only cover the literature up until 2017 and do not focus on examining methodology, use of theory or unit of analysis. In this study we aim to address these gaps.

We identify 49 TDM papers published within 2017–2020. We find the focus of the TD research fragmented: TD decreases morale, TD is difficult to measure, and numerous tools. The MTD workshops and a tertiary study encourage more research on strategies and management [P13, 3]. The papers primarily present data from open source projects and the private sector. This leaves a gap for research in the public sector. Finally, we offer a research agenda for Digital Government scholars on TDM.

1.1 Aim of the Study and Research Questions

This study reviews the latest published TDM papers (2017–2020). To the best of our knowledge, these papers have not been studied by other secondary studies. The TD field is rapidly evolving with nine secondary studies being published in the past six years. Our study indicates that the publishing rate has not decreased. In a four-year period, TD papers were published in 30 different outlets. This study introduces TD research and a research agenda to the Digital Government scholars. Therefore, we follow established guidelines for conducting systematic literature reviews within the Digital Government field [15, 16]. Our research questions are:

- RQ1. How is TDM studied and in which fields? RQ1a: Which authors and fields have contributed to technical studies debt management since 2017? RQ1b: What are the methods, context, level of analysis and data level used? RQ1c: Which theories and theoretical concepts are applied?
- RQ2. What does the TDM literature focus on? RQ2a Which topics are studied? RQ2b What do the findings show?
- RQ3. What research agenda should the Digital Government scholars investigate in the context of TDM? RQ3a What suggestions does the literature have for future studies? RQ3b What are the identified knowledge gaps in the literature?

The following sections are organized as follows: 2) search process, 3) brief mapping of previous TD literature reviews, 4) analysis, 5) results and suggestions for future study, 6) discussion, limitations, and finally, 7) conclusion. The previous literature reviews, and the pool of papers are listed in Appendix A and B.

2 Search Process

The initial search for papers occurred from January to April 2019, with an updated search conducted in March 2020. We applied Webster and Watson's [16] method for conducting systematic literature reviews (Fig. 1). Webster and Watson present a three-step process to search for papers [16].

Webster and Watson recommend, that scholars begin a review by searching for papers in known key outlets. The second step is a database search, as it enables the researcher to discover other fields. The third step is a backward-forward search, where papers citing or cited by the pool of papers are identified. The following sections explain each search step in detail.

1. Exploratory search: Using the software tool 'Publish or Perish' (Google Scholar)
2. Database search: Web of Science, DGRL and Scopus
3. Backwards and forward search (Google Scholar citations).

2.1 Explorative Search (Step 1)

Webster and Watson [16] recommend starting a review by searching key outlets. They assume that the researcher is familiar with the literature and key outlets. However, we

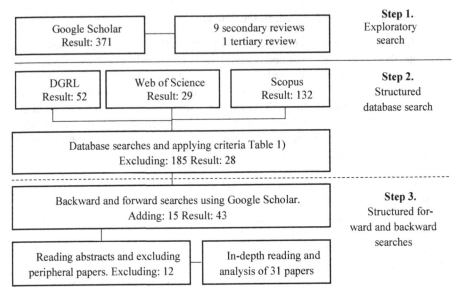

Fig. 1. Illustrates the initial process.

were not familiar with these at the time. Therefore, we chose to deviate from their method in the first step. In January 2019, we conducted an explorative search through Google Scholar to become familiar with the topic and academic literature [17]. We used the software "Publish or Perish" and Google Scholar as an underlying search engine [18]. This search created a foundation for the second step: the structured literature database search. The search informed: the selected search term, the selection criteria, and the temporal limitation. In this search process, we discovered nine secondary literature reviews and a tertiary review (Sect. 3 & Appendix A). The secondary and tertiary reviews informed our inclusion and exclusions criteria (Table 1).

2.2 Structured Database Search (Step 2)

In February 2019, we searched in the three databases: Digital Government Reference Library (DGRL), Scopus and Web of Science. DGRL version 15.5 contains references to approximately 12.500 peer-reviewed papers within the digital government field.

Webster and Watson [16] suggest using keywords when searching in databases, However, not all papers are presented with keywords in these databases. Therefore, we searched the databases for papers including the expression 'Technical Debt Management' anywhere in the text. We identified 213 primary research papers on TD.

Due to a large number of identified papers, and the existence of secondary and tertiary studies, we decided to introduce two additional selection criteria in our study (Table 1). This was done to position our review in relation to the previous secondary and tertiary studies. The secondary studies cover all papers on TD published until early 2017 (see Fig. 2). Thus, we focused the review on 1) papers studying TDM specifically,

Table 1. Selection criteria (+included/− excluded)

+/-	Assessment criterion	Argument
+	Topic should be TDM	Only papers focusing on TDM were included
+	Published within the period 2017-2020	The papers posted up until 2017 have been covered by other literature studies [21, 22]
+	Published conference or journal papers only	To ensure high quality, only papers that had undergone a peer-reviewed process were included
+	Only papers written in English	Due to the authors' language skill, we included papers in English only.
-	Books, chapters, blog posts, citations, thesis, presentations, reports, editorials & summaries	The scope of this literature review is to analyze the peer-reviewed papers. To avoid research duplicates books and books chapters were excluded [17].
-	Inaccessible papers	Papers, which appeared in the search but could not be accessed were excluded
-	Duplicates	Only the newest version of the paper was included (typically journal paper). Journal papers are generally more in-depth than conference papers [17].

this brought the number of papers to 130, 2) papers published from 2017 and onwards, which reduced the number to 28 papers.

2.3 Forward/Backward Search (Step 3)

In April 2019, we conducted backward and forward searches [16]. First, we reviewed the references in the previously identified papers (backward search) adding two papers. Second, we used Google Scholar to conduct a forward search for papers citing the identified papers, adding 13 papers. This brought the pool of papers to 31.

In March 2020 we updated the search and repeated step 2 and 3, we identified 18 new papers, bringing the total pool of papers in this review to 49 (Appendix B).

3 Previous Secondary Studies on TD

In the explorative search, we found nine secondary and one tertiary study. The nine studies cover literature published from 1992–2017 (Fig. 2). Benldris et al. [20] and Becker et al. [19] cover the year 2016 completely with a broad view of TD. We position our literature review to these existing secondary studies in the discussion section. Rios et al. published a tertiary study in 2018, which explores the state of TD research [3]. They evaluate 13 secondary studies from 2012 to March 2018. They identify three research directions and concepts studied in the secondary studies: TD identification, TD concepts, and TDM. They develop a taxonomy of 15 TD types and generate a TD landscape mapping out the TDM activities, strategies and tools. The period from 2017 does not appear to be covered and none of the literature reviews examine the context of the data.

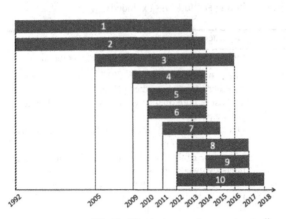

	Meta-studies
1	Li et al.
2	Behutiye et al.
3	Besker et al.
4	Ampatzoglou et al.
5	Ribeiro et al.
6	Alves et al.
7	Fernández-Sánchez et al.
8	Becker et al.
9	Benldris et al.
10	Rios et al. (tertiary)

Fig. 2. Illustrates previous meta-studies research on TD

4   Method for Analysis

The total pool of papers in our review includes 49 papers. Next, we explain the overall coding process, then we go more into detail in the following section.

The coding process was conducted iteratively. We developed a coding sheet (a template) containing: origin of data, theory and method, and unit of analysis [21]. We applied the template on 10 papers and discussed and adjusted the categories. The first author conducted the coding, while coding issues were discussed among all authors.

4.1   Detailed Description of Coding Elements

This section describes additional categories besides author and journal. We explain the reason for our coding, and the coding process in detail.

The Origin of the Data. We coded for country and sector (private or public) to uncover where the data originates from. We expanded the categorization to include open source projects. Open source projects allow for anyone, anywhere to contribute to the code without stating who they are or where they are from. In the papers, the authors describe where they extracted the data, e.g. by state the type of organization, from which we could interpret the sector.

Theory and Technique. We made an open coding for the technique; thus, we included a description of how the data was extracted. We coded for theory, focusing on explanations of the relation between concepts, observed phenomenon and why these relationships exist [22–24].

Findings and Future Studies. We coded the papers' main findings, typically from the results, discussion, and conclusion sections to identify the latest findings within TDM studies. Additionally, we coded for the authors' suggestions for future studies.

Unit of Analysis and Concepts. Webster and Watson [16] suggest creating a concept matrix and adding another dimension: the level of analysis. This dimension analyzes the abstraction level of the paper. This allows for more accurate identification of the existing literature. They suggest three levels of analysis: individual, group and organization. We discovered several papers that analyzed at the IT-system level and added this to the existing three levels of analysis. We coded for the overall concept within the paper, besides TDM. We began with a careful read-through of the first 10 papers. Here, a pattern emerged, and we identified four concepts. They were confirmed after going through the remainder of the pool of papers.

5 Results

Next, we present the findings of our study according to our research questions.

5.1 RQ1 How Is TDM Studied and in Which Fields?

RQ1a: Which Authors and Disciplines Have Contributed to TDM Research Since 2017? Papers concerning TDM have been published in 30 different journals and conferences since 2017. The eight outlets containing more than one paper are listed in Table 2, the remaining 23 papers are published in 26 different outlets.

Table 2. The most frequent publishing outlets for TDM research

Outlet	No. of papers
International Conference on Technical Debt	7
Journal of Systems and Software	4
ACM SIGSOFT Software Engineering Notes	2
ACM SIGSOFT Software Engineering	2
IEEE Transactions on Software Engineering	2
International Conference on Software Engineering	2
Euromicro Conference on Software Engineering and Advanced Applications	2
International Conference on Software Maintenance and Evolution	2

The International Conference on TD contains the most papers regarding TDM followed by the Journal of Systems and software. The mapping shows that TDM appears in a variety of outlets within the field of Software Engineering. The 65% of the papers do not specify the countries where the study was conducted. The papers which do specify this, primarily come from the Nordic countries - particularly Sweden [P2, P4, P11, P18, P21, P45]. The papers not specifying the country mainly use open source projects.

124 different authors have contributed to the literature of TDM, 15 of them contributed to two papers. Figure 3 presents the top contributors, note that many papers have several authors.

RQ1b: What are the Methods, Context, Level of Analysis and Data Level Used?
Only half of the papers specify the organizational context, which the data originates

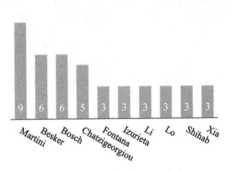

Fig. 3. The most active authors   **Fig. 4.** The most frequently used techniques

from. One paper use data from the public sector, 12 papers present open source data, and 12 papers present data from the private sector. The papers use different techniques during their research. The most frequently used techniques are survey, interviews and literature studies (Fig. 4). Note that some studies use more than one technique.

RQ1c: Which Theories and Theoretical Concepts are Applied? The authors introduced different concepts and frameworks to explain TD and the underlying interrelations. This was done from different perspectives; assessment, working environment or awareness. The papers seldomly use theory and the word 'theory' rarely occurs in the text of the papers. Two papers are presented as foundation for future theory [P39, P45]. The papers offer indicators and methods on how to reduce TD.

5.2 RQ2: What Does the TDM Literature Focus on?

RQ2a: Which Topics are Studied? Inspired by Webster and Watson [16], we have identified four main concepts and mapped the papers' level of analysis into a concept matrix Table 3). This gives an overview of how the concepts have been studied and which levels or concepts have not received attention in recent studies.

The concept *TD Assessment* entails research which assesses the effect of TD or as it is called, *interest rate*. This concept is the most analyzed and it has been analyzed at four different levels. Ten of the papers use the concept *Self-admitted technical debt*, which covers TD that is consciously admitted and is visible in code comments. This has been analyzed at the IT-System and Project level. The third concept of *TD awareness* covers the research creating awareness of TD. This can be achieved by visualizing the assessed TD; it is analyzed at the IT-system and the project level. The last concept *Working environment* focuses on morale and organizational culture. This is analyzed at both an individual and an organizational level.

A third of the papers analyze TD at the IT-System level, the most frequent analyzed level. The primary focus is TD assessment, which is explored in 21 papers. The organizational level is the least used level of analysis; one explanation is that organizational data is more challenging to access than surveys and on open source projects.

Table 3. Concept matrix illustrating the studied topics

Level of analysis	Individual employee	IT-system	Project	Organization
Self-admitted TD		P28, P19, P31, P17, P30, P27	P12, P23, P8, P41	
TD assessment	P4, P10, P33, P44	P20, P26, P5, P14, P31, P27, P37	P16, P22, P6, P14, P34, P38	P5, P15, P9, P21, P35, P39
TD awareness	P45, P46, P49	P24, P26, P19, P28, P17, P42, P43, P48, P37	P16, P22, P6, P47	
Working environment	P1, P2, P3, P11			P1, P18, P46

RQ2b: What do the Findings Show? Almost a third of the papers propose a tool, method, model or technique to aid TDM [P8, P16–20, P29–31, P34, P35, P41, P42, P47, P48]. Their findings focus on the results of evaluating their presented tools. The tools generally aid in TDM e.g. through TD identification or visualization. Increased TD visibility can benefit communication between stakeholders [P37].

The papers vary in approach and focus; thus, the findings of the papers are fragmented. We list seven general findings from the pool of papers: **1)** TD harms software development work [P2–4, P11]. **2)** All roles related to the system are affected [P4], and community-related factors contribute to TD's intensity [P46], however, **3)** the developer morale can be increased by proper management [P11]. **4)** Organizational factors can influence TD [P1], the number of collaborators and the size of the project correlate significant with the amount of TD [P14], and the breadth of the developers' experience lower the amount of TD [P1, P33]. **5)** TD is time consuming: practitioners estimate 36% of development time is wasted due to TD [P4], and TD increases the need to perform additional time-consuming activities [P3]. However, TD is not visible in the backlog [P45] and lack of development processes increase TD [P1] **6)** Architectural debt should be managed early in the process because the early introduction of architectural debt shows it persists during the whole software lifecycle [P2]. **7)** The estimation difficulties are proposed to be solved by a workflow, which "*provide more actual information including TD concepts to the stakeholders*" [P7, pp. 600–601].

5.3 RQ3: What Research Agenda Should the Digital Government Scholars Investigate in the Context of TDM?

RQ3a What Suggestions does the Literature have for Future Studies? The papers proposing a model, tool, method, approach or technique for TD aim to continue expanding and validating their model against new datasets [P1, P5, P8, P12, P14–15, P18–19, P23, P27, P29–31, P34–35, P41–42, P47–48]. Suggestions for future research for other researchers are scarce. However, both MTD workshops encourage a slight change in direction and provide several suggestions for future studies [P10, P13].

Quantifying the Value of TD. The report of MTD workshop of 2016 [P13] suggests the research agenda is on defining, understanding and operationalizing the value of TD. They urge researchers to understand the value that falls outside the core definition of TD, which is essential to how TD plays out in practice. Digital Government scholars can contribute to this with their experience. The 2017 report of MTD workshop [P10] recommends elevating the quantification of TD from low-level code to architectural opportunities. They identify a need to educate stakeholders to raise awareness level.

A Better Understanding of the Metrics. Three papers contain the following suggestions for future work: 1) to research more important metrics in the future [P16], 2) to understand the factors leading to TD [P14], 3) to study more change features that can introduce TD [P31]. Other research should be undertaken to investigate if other types of TD (besides Architectural Debt) have a significant correlation to the estimated wasted time. Thus, it creates a better understanding of the negative impact different TD has on wasted software development time [P2–3]. Lastly, the organization's maneuverability can be increased by determining the types of debt incurred [P18].

Strategies. Specific suggestions are to investigate concrete architecture problems: how they contribute to file bug-proneness, and possible ways of refactoring [P6]. Vadja et al. encourage future studies to develop methods to assist the stakeholders to estimate their TD [P22] or increase the breadth of the experience [P33]. Additionally, Dong et al. suggest exploration of TD recovery strategies due to a lack of discussed actual cases – particularly in the cross-disciplinary environment [P9]. Further research should focus on providing an in-depth understanding of the relationship between TD and developers' morale [P11]. Two papers aim to build a TD theory [P39, P45].

RQ3b What are the Identified Knowledge Gaps in the Literature? We identify five gaps which are presented in Table 4. 1) The papers suffer from a lack of theory and therefore cannot explain the relationship between events and concepts [24]. The debt metaphor contains some explanatory power; however, a metaphor cannot substitute for a theory [25]. Two papers present research as possible foundation for theory [P39, P45]. 2) The level of analysis is primarily focused on a project or system level, which leaves a gap in researching the organizational and individual levels. 3) Half of the papers have not specified the organizational context of the data, and the other half investigate open source projects or private companies. Only one paper use data from the public sector, this leaves a gap in research in this sector [P41]. 4) TD is explored through 16 different approaches and techniques - both quantitative and qualitative. Eight papers use more than one technique and combine both quantitative and qualitative methods. However, observation is not used actively as a data gathering technique.

This may be a problem, because what people say during interviews, may differ from what they do [26]. 5) All the papers are published within the field of software engineering leaving a gap for venue diversity. Table 4 summarizes the identified gaps in the papers and suggests why and how these gaps could be addressed.

When we compare the TD literature's suggested research RQ3a and the gaps we identify, we find that they can easily be combined. Our gaps contain a high abstraction level, whereas the suggested future research provides very specific suggestions.

Table 4. Identified gaps, their importance, and suggestions to how they can be addressed

Gap	Why is this a problem	Suggestion to how the gaps can be addressed
1. Lack of research from the public sector	The public sector has other restrictions than open source and the private sector. The TD challenges and management might differ	Study TD in the public sector
2. Lack of theory	Understand the connection of events and why they occur will help in determining how to prevent them from happening [27]	Develop a new theory or import theory from other fields
3. Lack of venue diversity	TD is relevant to other fields. Different disciplines may offer different perspectives and approaches to TD	Introduce TD to other fields than Software Engineering
4. Limited abstraction level of analysis	Examining TD from different levels generates a fuller picture. TD's impact goes beyond the IT-system	Examine TD from an organizational or individual level
5. Lack of technique diversity	Observations may inform us about people's actual behaviour, rather than how people claim they act [3]	Use observation to address people's behaviour

6   Discussion

First, we compare the findings of this review to comparable secondary studies. Second, we identify and discuss five findings further, 1) lack of research in the public sector, 2) empirical confirmation of negative effects of TD, 3) a tendency of reinventing the wheel, 4) gaps in diversity of approaches, and 5) the absence of theory.

Comparison to Related Work. Becker et al. [19] focus on decision-making and criticize the method and objective of the research. They find that the actual decision making was not studied. Ampatzoglou et al. [11] explore how financial aspects are defined and applied when studying TD. They encourage a balance between economic theories and software engineering. Li et al. [12] find that code-related TD and its management gain the most attention and encourage future studies to explore the whole TDM process. This corresponds to our findings in the concept matrix, as research on the organizational level or the working environment is limited. The tertiary review by Rios et al. [3] underline several gaps, which are in line with the MTD reports [P13, 3]: more research on strategies and management.

This literature review includes management of all types of TD, in line with several of the secondary studies [5, 11, 12, 19, 28]. However, none of the secondary studies analyze theory nor the organization type the data was extracted from. Furthermore, this review offers insights into the recent literature and present the concept and a research agenda to Digital Government scholars.

Lack of Research in the Public Sector. Half of the papers do not state the organizational context where data was collected. Only one paper appears to have conducted its data collection within the public sector [P41]. This is important, because the public sector is different from open source projects and the private sector. While some challenges may be similar, public organizations are subjected to specific requirements [29]. We suggest future Digital Government studies focus on studying TDM, both in terms of strategies, management and indicators.

A Tendency to Reinvent the Wheel. About a third of the papers propose a tool to support technical debt management [P8, P16–20, P29–31, P34, P35, P41, P42, P47, P48]. They evaluate their presented tool and plan to apply it within a different context. They rarely apply other researchers' tools or methods, instead, they develop their own. This is problematic as it does not advance the field through joint effort; instead of providing and testing a few select tools for practitioners, the number of tools becomes overwhelming.

Empirical Confirmations of the Negative Effects of TD. Technical debt harms software development work, both in terms of morale and wasted time [P2, P3, P4, P11]. However, community factors can also intensify TD [P46]. The size of the project correlates with the amount of TD [P14]. TD can be minimized by following some simple guidelines. However, if TD is addressed early it is less time consuming and the morale can be increased [P2, P3, P4, P11]. Thus, we need future studies to explore indicators of TD.

Gaps in the Diversity of Approaches. TDM is primarily studied from a quantitative approach, 30% of the papers used a qualitative approach. Six of the 31 papers use more than one method. This leaves a gap which can be addressed with the mixed method approach. Mixed methods may provide more comprehensive evidence [22]. None of the papers apply observation, this leaves people's actual behavior concerning TDM unstudied.

Absence of Theory. Concerning results, we see an absence of the use of theory, a few papers import theory and approaches from other fields, e.g. portfolio finance and games. We need theories to explain the relationship between the concepts and why these exist [22–24]. The absence of native theory is natural for a young field, where researchers are prone to import theory from a different field instead [30, 31].

7 Conclusion, Limitations and Future Studies

We have introduced TDM to the field of Digital Government and proposed a research agenda for Digital Government scholars. We conducted a systematic literature review to explore: 1) how and where technical debt management is studied, 2) what we know about technical debt and its management and lastly 3) a research agenda for scholars within Digital Government. Our findings are based on papers published from 2017–2020. We have discovered that 1) researchers focus on a specific type of technical debt and how it can be reduced. 2) TDM is still strongly rooted within the field of Software Engineering and 3) is primarily examined in open software projects or the private sector. 4) TDM is studied using primarily quantitative methods, finally, 5) there is a lack of theory to guide the studies and explain findings.

Limitations. We decided to only use the term "Technical debt management" in our literature search which can decrease the external validity, however the backward/forward searches strengthen the external validity. The papers were coded by the first author only which decrease the internal validity, in order to strengthen the internal validity, issues were discussed among all authors.

Research Agenda. We suggest Digital Government scholars research technical debt management, TD strategies and TD indicators, so the field is advanced further.

Acknowledgement. This study is funded by the Research Centre for Government IT, which is a collaboration between the IT University of Copenhagen, the Danish Digitization Agency and the self-owned institution ATP. The Research Centre's external funding partners were not involved in the research presented herein, or its dissemination.

Appendix A: Previous TD Literature Reviews

Authors	Title	Year	No. of papers	Period covered
Alves, Mendes, De Mendonça, Spinola, Shull, Seaman	Identification and management of technical debt: A systematic mapping study	2016	100	2010-2014
Ampatzoglou, Ampatzoglou, Chatzigeorgiou, Avgeriou	The financial aspect of managing technical debt: A systematic literature review	2015	69	2009-2014
Behutiye, Rodríguez, Oivo, Tosun	Analyzing the concept of technical debt in the context of agile software development: A systematic literature review	2017	38	1992-2014
Ribeiro, de F. Farias, Mendonça, Spínola	Decision Criteria for the Payment of Technical Debt in Software Projects: A Systematic Mapping Study.	2016	38	2010-2014
Becker, Chitchyan, Betz, McCord	Trade-off decisions across time in Technical Debt Management: a systematic literature review	2018	240	2012-2016
Li, Avgeriou, Liang	A systematic mapping study on technical debt and its management	2015	94	1992-2013
Fernández-Sánchez, Garbajosa, Yagüe	A framework to aid in decision making for Technical Debt Management	2015	51	2011-2015
Besker, Martini, Bosch	Managing architectural technical debt: A unified model and systematic literature review	2018	42	2005-2016
BenIdris, Ammar, Dzielski	Investigate, identify and estimate the technical debt: A systematic mapping study	2018	43	2014-2017

Appendix B: The Pool of Papers Analyzed in the Literature Review

ID	Author	Title	Year
P1	Besker & Martini	Embracing Technical Debt, from a Startup Company Perspective	2018
P2	Besker, Martini & Bosch	Impact of Architectural Technical Debt on Daily Software Development Work — A Survey of Software Practitioners	2017
P3	Besker, Martini & Bosch	Technical debt cripples software developer productivity: a longitudinal study on developers' daily software development work	2018
P4	Besker, Martini &Bosch	The Pricey Bill of Technical Debt: When and by Whom will it be Paid?	2017
P5	Bowlds, Fossaceca & Iammartino	Software obsolescence risk assessment approach using multicriteria decision-making	2018
P6	Cai, Xiao, Kazman, Mo, Feng,	Design Rule Spaces: A New Model for Representing and Analyzing Software Architecture	2018
P7	Cha, Dong & Vogel-Heuser	Preventing Technical Debt For Automated Production System Maintenance Using Systematic Change Effort Estimation With Considering Contingent Cost	2018
P8	Chicote	Startups and Technical Debt: managing technical debt with visual thinking	2017
P9	Dong, Ocker & Vogel-Heuser	Technical Debt as indicator for weaknesses in engineering of automated production systems	2019
P10	Fontana, Chatzigeorgiou, Trumler, Izurieta, Avgeriou & Nord	Technical Debt in Agile Development: Report on the Ninth Workshop on Managing Technical Debt (MTD 2017)	2017
P11	Ghanbari, Besker, Martini, & Bosch	Looking for peace of mind?: manage your (technical) debt: an exploratory field study	2017
P12	Huang, Shihab, Xia, Lo & Li	Identifying self-admitted technical debt in open source projects using text mining	2018
P13	Izurieta, Ozkaya, Seaman & Snipes	Technical Debt: A Research Roadmap Report on the Eighth Workshop on Managing Technical Debt (MTD 2016)	2017
P14	Jesus & Melo	Technical Debt and the Software Project Characteristics. A Repository-Based Exploratory Analysis	2017
P15	Klotins, Unterkalmsteiner, Chatzipetrou, Gorschek, Prikladnicki & Tripathi	Exploration of technical debt in start-ups	2018
P16	Kosti, Ampatzoglou, Chatzigeorgiou, Pallas, Stamelos & Angelis	Technical Debt Principal Assessment Through Structural Metrics	2017
P17	Liu, Huang, Xia, Shibab, Lo & Li	SATD detector: a text-mining-based self-admitted technical debt detection tool	2018
P18	Magnusson, Juiz, Gómez & Bermejo	Governing technology debt: beyond technical debt	2018
P19	Maldonado, Shibab & Tsantalis	Using Natural Language Processing to Automatically Detect Self-Admitted Technical Debt	2017
P20	Martini	Anacondebt: a tool to assess and track technical debt	2018
P21	Martini, Fontana, Biaggi & Roveda	Identifying and Prioritizing Architectural Debt Through Architectural Smells: A Case Study in a Large Software Company	2018
P22	Martini, Vajda, Vasa, Jones, Abdelrazek & Grundy	Technical debt interest assessment: from issues to project	2017
P23	Mensah, Keung, Svajlenko, Bennin & Mi	On the value of a prioritization scheme for resolving Self-admitted technical debt	2018
P24	Mera-Gómez, Ramírez, Bahsoon & Buyya	A Debt-Aware Learning Approach for Resource Adaptations in Cloud Elasticity Management	2017
P25	Mera-Gómez, Ramírez, Bahsoon & Buyya	A Multi-Agent Elasticity Management Based on Multi-Tenant Debt Exchanges	2018
P26	Rojas, Izurieta & Griffith	Toward Technical Debt Aware Software Modeling	2017

P27	Sierra	Is Self-Admitted Technical Debt a Good Indicator of Architectural Divergences?	2019
P28	Sierra, Shihab, Yasutake & Kamei	A survey of self-admitted technical debt	2019
P29	Skourletopoulos, Mavromoustakis, Mastorakis, Sahalos, Batalla & Dobre	A game theoretic formulation of the technical debt management problem in cloud systems	2017
P30	Wattanakriengkrai, Maipradit, Hata, Choetkiertikul, Sunetnanta & Matsumoto	Identifying Design and Requirement Self-Admitted Technical Debt Using N-gram IDF	2018
P31	Yan, Xia, Shihab, Lo, Yin & Yang	Automating Change-level Self-admitted Technical Debt Determination	2018
P32	Hacks, Hofert, Salentin, Yeong, Lichter.	Towards the definition of enterprise architecture debts	2019
P33	Fagerholm, Becker, Chatzigeorgiou, Betz, Duboc, Penzenstadler, Mohanani Venters	Temporal Discounting in Software Engineering: A Replication Study	2019
P34	Reboucas De Almeida, Treude, Kulesza	Tracy: A Business-Driven Technical Debt Prioritization Framework	2019
P35	Reboucas De Almeida	Business-Driven Technical Debt Prioritization	2019
P36	Njima, Demeyer	Value-based technical debt management: An exploratory case study in start-ups and scale-ups	2019
P37	Rindell, Bernsmed, Jaatun	Managing security in software or: How I learned to stop worrying and manage the security technical debt	2019
P38	Rindell, Holvitie	Security risk assessment and management as technical debt	2019
P39	Becker, Fagerholm, Mohanani, Chatzigeorgiou	Temporal discounting in technical debt: How do software practitioners discount the future?	2019
P40	Brenner R.	Balancing resources and load: Eleven nontechnical phenomena that contribute to formation or persistence of technical debt	2019
P41	Perez, Correal, Astudillo	A proposed model-driven approach to manage architectural technical debt life cycle	2019
P42	Pavlič, Hliš	The technical debt management tools comparison	2019
P43	Aragão, Andrade, Santos, Castro, Lelli, Darin	TestDCat: Catalog of Test Debt Subtypes and Management Activities	2019
P44	Amanatidis, Mittas, Chatzigeorgiou, Ampatzoglou, Angelis	The Developer's Dilemma: Factors affecting the Decision to Repay Code Debt	2018
P45	Besker, Martini, Bosch	Technical Debt Triage in Backlog Management	2019
P46	Palomba, Tamburri, Fontana, Oliveto, Zaidman, Serebrenik,	Beyond Technical Aspects: How Do Community Smells Influence the Intensity of Code Smells?	2018
P47	Li, Liang, Avgeriou	Architectural Technical Debt Identification Based on Architecture Decisions and Change Scenarios	2018
P48	Dai, Kruchten	Detecting Technical Debt through Issue Trackers	2017
P49	Rios, Spínola, Mendonça Seaman	Supporting Analysis of Technical Debt Causes and Effects with Cross-Company Probabilistic Cause-Effect Diagrams	2019

References

1. Cordella, A., Iannacci, F.: Information systems in the public sector: the e-Government enactment framework. J. Strateg. Inf. Syst. **19**, 52–66 (2010)
2. Cunningham, W.: The WyCash portfolio management system. ACM SIGPLAN OOPS Messenger **4**, 29–30 (1992)
3. Rios, N., de Mendonça Neto, M.G., Spínola, R.O.: A tertiary study on technical debt: types, management strategies, research trends, and base information for practitioners. Inf. Softw. Technol. **102**, 117–145 (2018)

4. Griffith, I., Taffahi, H., Izurieta, C., Claudio, D.: A simulation study of practical methods for technical debt management in agile software development. In: Proceedings - Winter Simulation Conference (2015)

5. Alves, N.S.R., Mendes, T.S., De Mendonça, M.G., Spínola, R.O., Shull, F., Seaman, C.: Identification and management of technical debt: a systematic mapping study. Inf. Softw. Technol. **70**, 100–121 (2016)

6. Scholl, H.J.: Digital government: looking back and ahead on a fascinating domain of research and practice. Digit. Gov. Res. Pract. **1**, 1–12 (2020)

7. Dečman, M., Jukić, T.: Editorial for EJEG **15**(1), 57 (2017)

8. Danish Ministry of Finance: Regeringens kasseeftersyn på it-området. Denmark, Copenhagen (2017)

9. The Swedish National Audit: Föråldrade it-system – Hinder för en effektiv digitalisering, Stockholm (2019)

10. Holvitie, J., et al.: Technical debt and agile software development practices and processes: an industry practitioner survey. Inf. Softw. Technol. **96**, 141–160 (2018)

11. Ampatzoglou, A., Ampatzoglou, A., Chatzigeorgiou, A., Avgeriou, P.: The financial aspect of managing technical debt: a systematic literature review. Inf. Softw. Technol. **64**, 52–73 (2015)

12. Li, Z., Avgeriou, P., Liang, P.: A systematic mapping study on technical debt and its management. J. Syst. Softw. **101**, 193–220 (2015)

13. Jeffery, M., Leliveld, I.: Best practices in IT portfolio management. MIT Sloan Manag. Rev. **45**, 41 (2004)

14. Magnusson, J., Juiz, C., Gómez, B., Bermejo, B.: Governing technology debt. In: Proceedings of 2018 International Conference Technical Debt - TechDebt 2018, pp. 76–84 (2018)

15. Schlichter, B.R., Kraemmergaard, P.: A comprehensive literature review of the ERP research field over a decade. J. Enterp. Inf. Manag. **23**(4), 486–520 (2010)

16. Webster, J., Watson, R.T.: Analyzing the past for prepare for the future: writing a literature review. MIS Q. **26**(2), xiii–xxiii (2002)

17. Boell, S.K., Cecez-Kecmanovic, D.: A hermeneutic approach for conducting literature reviews and literature searches. Commun. Assoc. Inf. Syst. **34**, 12 (2014)

18. Harzing, A.W.: Publish or Perish (2007). https://harzing.com/resources/publish-or-perish

19. Becker, C., Chitchyan, R., Betz, S., McCord, C.: Trade-off decisions across time in technical debt management. In: Proceedings of the 2018 International Conference on Technical Debt - TechDebt 2018, pp. 85–94 (2018)

20. BenIdris, M., Ammar, H., Dzielski, D.: Investigate, identify and estimate the technical debt: a systematic mapping study. Int. J. Softw. Eng. Appl. **9**, 01–14 (2018)

21. King, N.: Doing template analysis. In: Symon, G., Cassell, C. (eds.) Qualitative Organizational Research: Core Methods and Current Challenges. SAGE, Thousand Oaks (2012)

22. Blaikie, N., Priest, J.: Designing Social Research: The logic of anticipation. Cambridge Polity, Cambridge (2019)

23. Gregor, S.: The nature of theory in information systems. MIS Q. Manag. Inf. Syst. **30**, 611–642 (2006)

24. Whetten, D.: What constitutes a theoretical contribution. Acad. Manag. Rev. **14**, 490–495 (1989)

25. Derman, E.: Metaphors, models & theories. Q. J. Financ. **1**, 109–126 (2011)

26. Blomberg, J., Burrell, M.: An ethnographic approach to design. In: Jacko, J.A. (ed.) Human-Computer Interaction Handbook: Fundamentals, Evolving Technologies, and Emerging Applications. Lawrence Erbaum Associates, New York (2012)

27. Sutton, R.I., Staw, B.M.: What theory is not. Adm. Sci. Q. **40**, 371–384 (1995)

28. Fernandez-Sanchez, C., Garbajosa, J., Yague, A.: A framework to aid in decision making for technical debt management. In: Proceedings of the 2015 IEEE 7th International Workshop Managing Technical Debt, MTD 2015, pp. 69–76 (2015)
29. Danish Competition and Consumer Authority: Hvor lang løbetid må en rammeaftale have? https://www.kfst.dk/faq/udbud/nyt-udbud/fase-1/hvor-lang-loebetid-maa-en-rammeaftale-have/. Accessed 19 May 2020
30. Bannister, F., Connolly, R.: The great theory hunt: does e-government really have a problem? Gov. Inf. Q. **32**, 1–11 (2015)
31. Mathiassen, L.: Designing engaged scholarship: from real-world problems to research publications. Engag. Manag. Rev. **1**(1), 17–28 (2017). Article 2

Measure What Matters: A Dual Outcome Service Quality Model for Government Service Delivery

Willem Pieterson[1(✉)] and Cindy Weng[2]

[1] Center for eGovernment Studies/Pieterson Strategic, London, UK
willem@pieterson.com
[2] Microsoft Cloud Solutions, London, UK
cindy.weng@microsoft.com

Abstract. Measuring customer service quality evaluations has been important since the rise of the service industry and many models in this area have been published. Most models focus on one outcome with a set of predictors. These outcomes are often ill defined and concepts are used interchangeably causing issues in creating good and consistent measures of quality. In this study we develop a new model combining multiple outcome variables and a series of predictors to show the interdependent nature of service outcomes. We test the model using machine learning based on survey responses from 3702 Dutch people. The results indicate that two types of outcome variables are important; quality of the outcome and satisfaction with the process. Each is predicted in different ways by four dimensions. This means governments could benefit from a better specification of the desired outcomes of service delivery and targeted measurement approaches.

Keywords: Service quality · Service delivery · Machine learning · Gradient boosted decision trees

1 Introduction

Service delivery lies at the heart of the missions of many government agencies around the world and naturally governments have an interest in ensuring high quality service delivery. Finding an answer to what variables influence the quality of service delivery has been a prominent question in the services literature since the 1980s. During this time the first models defining outcomes of service delivery and possible determinants were published. SERVQUAL [1] is a prominent example. Soon different models appeared (e.g. SERVPERF [2]) arguing for the importance of other outcome variables.

Technological advancements (e.g. diffusion of the Internet) led to new types of models often used in this context, such as the technology acceptance model [3]. This focus on technology spawned new models geared towards electronic (government) service delivery, such as 'eGovQual' [4] and the model for evaluation of eGov services [5].

© IFIP International Federation for Information Processing 2020
Published by Springer Nature Switzerland AG 2020
G. Viale Pereira et al. (Eds.): EGOV 2020, LNCS 12219, pp. 138–150, 2020.
https://doi.org/10.1007/978-3-030-57599-1_11

The majority of these models have in common that they use one outcome variable plus a series of determining variables. However, they vary in their choice of outcome variable and often similar outcome variables are explained and/or measured slightly different. This trickles down to more practical research. For example, the bi-annual 'Citizen First' studies in Canada focus on 'satisfaction' as an outcome measure [6], while similar (annual) studies in the Netherlands used 'appreciation' [7]. This creates confusion about what outcomes are most important, as well as how to define and measure them. This creates challenges for researchers as it is ambiguous how measures should be defined and operationalized as well as practitioners who lack clear guidance on how measure their service quality and create actionable outcomes. Furthermore, despite the creation of newer models, some of the older models are still often used raising questions about their usefulness (given their age) as well as the usefulness of newer models, given the enduring popularity of models such as SERVQUAL.

In this paper we investigate the status quo of service quality research and rather than testing existing models or creating a new theoretical model based on the existing literature, we decided to adopt the users' perspective and create and test a new model focused on service delivery outcomes and the main factors determining these outcomes.

1.1 Overview of the Paper

The remainder of the paper is organized as follows. We first discuss the existing models and research on service quality in more detail. Subsequently, in Sect. 3, we present the method of our study, followed by de results of our empirical work (Sect. 4). We close the paper with our conclusions and points of discussion and recommendations.

2 Service Quality in the Literature

The topic of 'service quality' and how to measure it rose to prominence during the 1980s [1]. During this time, when the services industry came to maturity, the first models were developed that would describe certain outcomes of the service delivery process, as well as variables determining or predicting these outcomes. The most prominent example of these is SERVQUAL [1] which was published in 1988. This model suggests that the (perceived) quality of service delivery depends on five independent variables: reliability, assurance, tangibles, empathy, and responsiveness. Soon after, critiques on the model developed. A key argument is that 'quality' is not the dominant outcome of service delivery processes, but rather other variables, such as 'performance'. This led to models such as SERVPERF [2]. While developed in the context of private sector service delivery, these models were soon also used to study the quality of public sector service delivery [8, 9]. Many of these older (competing) models are still used and cited in the literature on governmental service delivery [e.g. 10–12].

As these models were being adopted in the public sector, the services landscape itself started changing. The arrival of new service channels, fueled by the diffusion of the internet, led to new opportunities of both private and public sector agencies to improve the quality of their service delivery [13]. This led to two developments in studying the quality of service delivery in the public sector. The first is the study of the adoption of these new service channels and the link between adoption models, such as the Technology Acceptance Model [3] and service quality, for example by correlating variables such as 'ease of use' of new channels with service quality [14, 15].

The second development is the creation of new, dedicated models that are targeted towards the quality of online service delivery online. An example of a generic model of this type is the E-S-Qual model [16], presented as an 'electronic' alternative to the 'traditional' SERVQUAL model. However, a breed of specific models for the government and/or public sector arrived quickly. Examples are 'eGovQual' [4] and the model for evaluation of eGov services [5], which, while both mentioning quality present different outcome variables of service delivery (in the context of service quality).

This, in sum, leads to a situation in which we can identify service shortcomings of the existing models that focus on service quality. The first is that many models exist that focus on different aspects of service delivery and these models all use different predictor variables that are often derived from other types of models, such as those focusing on adoption or acceptance of technology. Second, by creating the split between quality of online or electronic services versus quality of traditional services, these models ignore the fact that on- and offline service channels are often used in 'multiplex' processes of services delivery, i.e. those situations in which citizens use multiple channels either in parallel or sequentially [17]. Third, many of the 'older' models, while being critiqued, are still being used frequently, despite these shortcomings. Most models are never updated to reflect changing times. Fourth, while a multitude of models exist and are often cited, many exist only in theoretical form and lack (repeated) empirical testing (eGovQual is one example). Fourth, many models exist that focus on 'quality' of service delivery, definitions of quality vary and wildly varying measures for quality exist. Fifth, and more generally, the world of government service delivery is evolving rapidly. Many new service channels arrive on the scene frequently [18] and focal points of government service delivery shift rapidly. Variables such as privacy protection that feature heavily in many government service strategies nowadays (e.g. the EU's Talinn declaration) played hardly any role when most models were developed.

2.1 Research Questions

The goal of our study is to develop a new service 'quality' model that links the key outcomes of government service delivery to (predictor) variables that are relevant from the perspective of the recipients of governmental service delivery: citizens and businesses (clients) in the Netherlands. The following research questions guide the study:

RQ1. What are the main outcome variables of government service delivery that capture the quality of service delivery from the perspective of clients?
RQ2. What are the main variables influencing or predicting these outcomes?
RQ3. How well does this model perform empirically?

3 Method

In order to answer our research questions, we followed an inductive two-step research approach [19], using mixed methods. In our case this approach combines qualitative and quantitative techniques. A benefit of this combination is that it leads to a more complete understanding of a research problem [20]. We collected data for our study through an exploratory sequential mixed method approach in which we first conducted a qualitative study and based on the outcomes of that study developed our research model and instrument. These were subsequently used in the quantitative study.

3.1 Research Approach and Setting

The study took place in the Netherlands, a country with both high levels of internet adoption and online service maturity (13th in the 2018 UN eGovernment ranking [21]). The country launched a digital strategy in 2018 ("NL DIGIBeter") which focuses on the role of technology in the Dutch society as a whole. It contains specific aims towards service delivery, such as improving accessibility, understandability of information and personalization of service delivery. The government body coordinating the program is the Ministry of the Interior. This organization asked for this study to be conducted in the context of monitoring success of the digital strategy. The study focused on governmental service delivery in general and was aimed at the entire population using government services (anyone aged 16 or higher), including citizens and businesses.

A research agency was involved in the study and they recruited participants, facilitated the qualitative study and collected data for the quantitative study. The authors were in charge of instrument development, supervision of data collection, and analyses. Both parts of the study included other topics as well.

3.2 Qualitative Study

To gather insights in what clients perceive to be important variables and elements of public service quality, we decided to hold a series of focus groups. These focus groups are not merely a convenient way to gather insights from individual participants, but they "give rise synergistically to insights and solutions that would not come about without them" [22, p. 40]. A number between three and six groups is normally considered sufficient and groups should have between 7–10 participants [23].

We held five focus groups with a total number of 38 participants. Four of these focus groups consisted of citizens and one of representatives of small and medium businesses. The four citizen groups were split in two based on level of education (low/high). Within the groups we controlled for gender and age. The focus groups were held in April/May 2019 at various locations in the Netherlands to allow for geographical spread.

All focus groups were recorded (both audio and video) and notes were taken during the focus groups. The notes served as main source for the outcomes and the recordings served as reference material. As mentioned above, the interviews focused on many topics and in this paper the results of two interview questions are presented: a) what, in your eyes, determines whether or not service delivery is good (what are key results, what is important in your eyes, when are you satisfied and is satisfaction the only important outcome)? And b) what are key elements that impact these outcomes (what is important to you, what aspects related to the results or the process of service delivery can you think of and how important are these)? A list of potential variables derived from models discussed were used as examples of variables to stimulate the discussion.

3.3 Quantitative Study

Based on the outcomes of the qualitative study, a model and survey instrument were developed to test the relationships between outcomes of service delivery and relevant predictor variables. The instrument contained more questions and focused on several aspects of service delivery. For the purposes of this study, we focus on those questions targeting outcomes and predictors of service delivery. The instrument was pre-tested with 9 people to check for errors and interpretation issues and subsequently finalized.

Subsequently, the questionnaire was programmed and distributed among members of the research agency's online panel. The structure of the questionnaire was such that respondents were asked to indicate a) whether they had used government services in the past 12 months and b) which type of services they had used. Respondents were filtered based on these experiences to create a sample with relatively even distribution of users across the spectrum of government services (and types of agencies). Thus, the goal was not to get full and even representation across the (demographic groups in the) population, but rather to reflect use of government services. After three weeks of data collection, a total number of N = 3702 complete responses were recorded, of which n = 3120 were citizens and n = 582 were representatives of businesses.

The data were analyzed in SPSS and Python (using PyCharm), and a number of analyses were done. First, we clustered the predictor variables into a number of dimensions using factor analysis and reliability analyses of the derived constructs. Second, we created a number of linear regression models that were tested in SPSS. While such regression models are a good way to gain insights into linear causal relationships between variables, there are a number of issues with this approach in this context. The first is that is assumes (relative) independence of the variables involved and collinearity can cause issues [24]. In this case, it is likely that the different predictors (and outcomes) of service quality co-vary and could be dependent. Furthermore, it assumes linearity of the variables [25], which may not always be the case. Lastly, it is sensitive for sample size (e.g. on producing biased R-squares) and the effects of error on the model, as well as assuming exactly what (theoretical) relationships to expect in the model.

New types of analytics based on machine learning offer benefits over regression models. These data-driven approaches infer relationships by finding the intrinsic splits in the data, without relying on imposed relationships from theory. They use training approaches to assess the relevance of these relationships [26]. In our situation, we chose to apply gradient boosting to a decision tree model. The main reason is the relative simplicity of the approach, coupled with the success of this approach in yielding robust outcomes [26]. Furthermore, they are fast, input-agnostic, and work well in regression situations [27]. We trained the model with a subsample of 1200 cases, keeping the remaining number of cases to validate the model. Model (split) scores were converted to percentages of contribution to show their relative weight and the random mean square errors, and accuracy of the models was calculated to assess model fit.

4   Results

The results section consists of two parts. The first discusses the key outcomes from the qualitative focus groups. The second presents outcomes from the quantitative part.

4.1 Qualitative Study

The qualitative study, as mentioned above focused on two key questions: 1) the question of what important outcomes of service delivery are and 2) what influences these outcomes. The first question yielded a lively discussion with an inconclusive outcome in terms of whether 'quality' is the most important outcome and what this quality exactly is supposed to mean. The discussion did suggest that two components are relevant to the final result, these are:

- The experience with the process of service delivery. This points to the way in which the process is designed and handled by the government agency and includes such variables such as *the friendliness of customer service agents, the ease with which information can be found and forms can be completed*, the *design of websites*. This has very little to do with the outcomes of the process. Several participants mention that this 'experience' could still lead to a positive service evaluation, even if the outcome is not the desired outcome (e.g. not getting a permit or benefit). We label this **"Satisfaction with the Process"** (Satisfaction Process).
- Besides the experience with the process, the final evaluation is tied to the actual outcome of the service delivery process. That has less to do with whether the result is what clients desire, but more with whether the results is correct, just, and fair. This includes such aspects as the *correctness of information, getting a response within (legal) limits* and *getting an answer to a question*. We label this variable the **"Quality of the Outcome"** (Quality Outcome).

Subsequently we asked about variables that influence these outcomes. The initial discussions (in which participants were asked to write down what they feel is important and then these were discussed in the group) yielded a list of 20 different aspects. We then asked participants in the different sessions to rate the importance of these aspects and discuss the outcomes. This resulted in a total of 18 different variables that were used in the questionnaire. The Table 1 below gives an overview of these variables.

Table 1. Variable overview

#	Name	Description	#	Name	Description
1	Privacy	Whether privacy is well protected	10	Comprehension	Whether information is easy to comprehend
2	Security	Degree to which services are secure	11	Accessibility	Whether services are accessible to the user
3	Data control	Whether people have control over their own data when using government services	12	User Friendly	Whether services are designed to fit user needs

(continued)

Table 1. (*continued*)

#	Name	Description	#	Name	Description
4	Trust	Trust levels in government and government services	13	Simplicity	Language and design are simple
5	Transparency	Degree to which there is transparency in the service delivery process	14	Pro-active	Government service delivery is pro-active
6	Supportive	Whether people can get (customer) support from governments when needed	15	Personal	Service delivery is personalized
7	Responsibility	Degree to which governments take responsibility over delivering high quality services	16	Speed	Service delivery is fast
8	Solution	Whether governments provide solutions when problems occur	17	Ease of use	Government services are easy to use
9	Findability	Degree to which information and services can be found easily	18	Freedom of choice	Users can choose how to obtain services

In addition, the discussions suggested that *citizens* have different expectations of service delivery than *businesses*, suggesting clients' *role* influences outcomes. Furthermore, we observed possible differences between those users with much online experiences and use of technology in general (*media use*) and lastly, participants with different demographic characteristics (most notably *age*) appeared to value different aspects. Leading to the inclusion of *demography*, *media use* and *role* in the quantitative study.

4.2 Quantitative Study

The first step in the quantitative analysis was to run a factor analysis to see whether the 18 variables can be grouped in fewer dimensions. A varimax rotated factor analysis suggests a four-factor solution that explains 72.30% of the variance in the data. Subsequently, we ran a reliability test on these four dimensions to test for their internal cohesion. Cronbach alpha scores for each dimension range from $\alpha = 0.83$ to $\alpha = 0.92$, which is (much) higher than the commonly accepted threshold of $\alpha = 0.65$. Table 2 gives an overview of the dimensions and scores.

Based on the content of the dimensions, we created appropriate labels for these dimensions: 1) Security & Trust: this comprises those variables that relate to security, privacy, trust and control; 2) Help & Support: this entails those variables that focus on how governments support users; 3) Accessibility: this covers those variables that determine whether or not people can successfully use government services; 4) Service Design: this includes all variables that impact the user experience of service delivery.

Table 2. Relability of dimensions

Dimensions							
Security & trust		Help & support		Accessibility		Service design	
Variable	Scale if deleted	Variable	Scale if deleted	Variable	Scale if deleted	Variable	Scale if deleted
Privacy	0.83	Supportive	0.76	Findability	0.77	Pro-Active	0.66
Security	0.84	Responsibility	0.67	Comprehension	0.79	Personal	0.56
Data control	0.83	Solution	0.76	Accessibility	0.83	Speed	0.62
Trust	0.84			User Friendly	0.80	Ease of Use	0.64
Transparency	0.84			Simplicity	0.77	Freedom of Choice	0.66
Cronbach's alpha for dimensions							
$\alpha = 0.86$		$\alpha = 0.86$		$\alpha = 0.92$		$\alpha = 0.83$	

The reduction of the number of variables into four dimensions allows us to create the research model to be tested (Fig. 1). The first step of these tests was to run a series of two linear regression models. In the first model we used Quality of Outcomes as the dependent variable and Satisfaction with the Process, the four dimensions, and the personal characteristics as independent variables. In the second model, we swap Quality of Outcomes (now independent) and Satisfaction with the Process (now dependent). For both models we

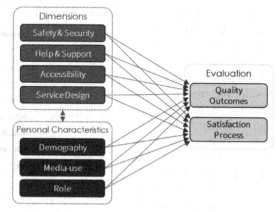

Fig. 1. Research model

calculate the R-Square, F-score and P value as main parameters and subsequently the regression coefficients as estimates. Both models show high R-squares and have significant fit (Table 3), suggesting that the independent variables explain the dependent variables well.

Table 3. Regression model parameters

	Quality outcomes	Satisfaction process
R square	0.72	0.73
F	907.78	954.14
Sig	.000	.000

Subsequently, the model estimates (Table 4) show that the Quality of Outcomes is predicted most strongly by the Satisfaction with the Process ($\beta = 0.74$, $p < .000$) and the other way around ($\beta = 0.72$, $p < .000$) suggesting a strong relationship between the two outcome variables. Furthermore, in both models do we find significant effects of the four dimensions on the dependent variables, but the strength of the coefficients varies between the two models. The role of personal characteristics is small (that of role is so small that it has been omitted from the table and subsequent analyses). We only find a small effect of media use on Satisfaction with the Process ($\beta = -0.02$, $p = .017$) and Age on the same dependent ($\beta = 0.03$, $p < .008$).

The last step in the analyses was the calculation of the parameters for the Gradient Boosted Decision Tree (GBDT) model as well as the model contributions. For both models, we yield similar RMSEs between the training and the testing models and for both models the testing RMSEs (shown in Table 5) are close to 1, indicating a good model fit. Furthermore, the accuracy of both models is fairly high (62.5% for Quality of Outcomes and 64.34% for Satisfaction with the Process). In line with the regression models, this confirms that the independent variables predict the dependents well.

The model contributions (Fig. 2) follow that line. We see that the largest model contributions are those of the other outcome variables, confirming that high quality outcomes lead to more satisfaction with the process and vice versa. However, the GBDT results show much bigger model contributions of the four dimensions and it highlights the differences between the two models.

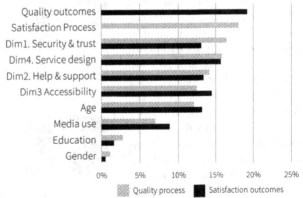

Fig. 2. Relative model contributions

Table 4. Regression model estimates

Variables	Quality outcomes		Satisfaction process	
	Bèta	Sig	Beta	Sig
(Constant)	.000	.022*	0.00	0.175
Quality outcomes	–	–	0.72	0.000**
Satisfaction process	0.74	0.000**	–	–
Dim 1. security & trust	0.07	0.000**	0.04	0.001**
Dim 2. help & support	0.04	0.001**	0.06	0.000**
Dim 3. accessibility	0.04	0.001**	0.09	0.000**
Dim 4. service design	0.03	0.008**	0.06	0.000**
Media use	−0.01	0.206	−0.02	0.017*
Age	0.01	0.565	0.03	0.008*
Education	−0.01	0.339	0.00	0.894
Gender	−0.02	0.071	0.01	0.164

*Significant at p = 0.05, **Significant at p = 0.01

Table 5. Gradient boosted decision tree model parameters

	Quality outcomes	Satisfaction process
Accuracy	62,52%	64.34%
Root Mean Squared Error (RMSE)	0.994667	0.977235

It appears that Quality of Outcomes is determined (in ascending order) by variables related to Security & Trust (Dim1), Service Design (Dim4), Help & Support (Dim2) and Accessibility (Dim3). That order is different for Satisfaction with the Process (Dim4, Dim3, Dim2, Dim1, respectively). In both models we find a moderate effect of Age and a smaller effect of Media Use. The other variables play a much smaller role.

5   Conclusions and Discussion

This empirical study among 3,702 citizens and businesses in the Netherlands was aimed at the development and test of a new service quality model for governmental service delivery. Three research questions guided this aim. The first research question (RQ1) asked about the main outcome variables that capture the quality of service delivery from clients' perspectives. Our research suggests two main variables are important:

- Quality of Outcomes. This refers to the degree to which clients receive an outcomes that is of high quality, i.e. free of errors, according to the norms, fair and just.

- Satisfaction with the Process. Whether clients are satisfied with the service delivery process, i.e. friendly staff, user friendly forms, well-designed websites.

These variables are not independent: a high level of satisfaction with the process will lead to a more positive evaluation of the quality of outcomes and vice versa. This highlights the importance of designing processes and the effect of the 'customer experience' on the outcomes of the process. Furthermore, it highlights how a focus on *quality* of outcomes can have a positive effect on the evaluation of the process as a whole.

RQ2 focused on the variables influencing these outcomes. We identified a total of 18 different variables that clustered in four different dimensions. All of these dimensions have a significant impact on the outcome variables across the different types of models we tested. However, we do find in our GBDT that the impact of the dimensions on the outcomes varies. For example we see a strong effect of 'security & trust' on the quality of outcomes and we find the strongest effect of 'service design' on the satisfaction with the outcomes. Security and trust is the least important dimension for satisfaction with the outcomes. This suggests clear differences between how different variables and dimensions contribute to certain outcomes of service delivery.

In general, the role of personal characteristics is less important. Age has some impact as well as the degree to which (online) media are used. This probably relates to peoples' digital skills and experiences in using (online) channels for service delivery [28].

The last research question (RQ3) concerns the performance of our model(s). In both tests they perform well. We find good model fit measures, as well as good r-squares and accuracies. These measures are by no means perfect, but do provide an excellent starting point for future iterations of the model.

In sum, in tying these back to our aim, we have created a new series of models to measure the outcomes of government service delivery based on the inputs of citizens and businesses in the Netherlands, and have tested this model empirically using a large sample in the Netherlands using several analytical approaches. The models yield significant results. This results in several implications for practitioners and researchers.

From a practical standpoint, our research shows that clients typically discriminate between two types of outcomes or measures of 'quality'. This is in contrast to more common approaches in which one outcomes variable is specified and often measured using wildly differing measures. Our research shows, these outcome measures are different *and* are determined by different variables. The implication is that practitioners need to be aware of the outcomes they want to measure and ensure the questions they ask match these outcomes. Second, our research shows that different types of variables influence different outcomes. For example, service design has a strong influence on the satisfaction with the process. Security and trust related variables influence the quality of the outcome. This means that governments need to be aware of the variables their policies influence and how these relate to outcomes. In other words: we give input in the types of levers governments have to improve certain types of outcomes. Lastly, while our research shows that the role of personal characteristics is relatively small, age and media use do have a role, suggesting that digital divide related variables remain important when considering the quality of service delivery as a whole.

For researchers and as points of discussion, we hope that our study gives further impetus to the development of new service quality models that combine different types of outcomes with multiple input variables. We find the determining variables to be quite different from those used in previous models and this suggests not only that a) the older, still often used, models have an 'expiration date', but b) moreover that newer models need to evolve and constantly be updated to reflect the evolving service delivery landscape. Second, while our model uses a large number of variables, the results show that we are not able to explain all variance in the data or accurately predict all outcomes. Thus, more or different variables could be included to improve these outcomes. Third, we tested the model once, in one country. Replication and validation in other settings could help strengthening this work. Lastly, we used an online research panel, inevitably meaning that people without online access were not included, thus we miss out on an important part of the population. This needs to be rectified in future work.

Acknowledgement. We would like to thank the Ministry of the Interior for funding this work. The Ministry of the Interior had no role in the preparation of this publication.

References

1. Parasuraman, A., Zeithaml, V.A., Berry, L.L.: SERQUAL a multiple-item scale for measuring consumer perceptions of service quality. J. Retail. **64**, 12 (1988). https://doi.org/10.1016/S0148-2963(99)00084-3
2. Cronin, J.J., Taylor, S.A.: Measuring service quality: a reexamination and extension. J. Mark. (1992). https://doi.org/10.2307/1252296
3. Davis, F.D.: Perceived usefulness, perceived ease of use, and user acceptance of information technology. MIS Q. Manag. Inf. Syst. (1989). https://doi.org/10.2307/249008
4. Papadomichelaki, X., Mentzas, G.: e-GovQual: a multiple-item scale for assessing e-government service quality. Gov. Inf. Q. **29**, 98–109 (2012). https://doi.org/10.1016/j.giq.2011.08.011
5. Alanezi, M., Kamil, A., Basri, S.: A proposed instrument dimensions for measuring e-government service quality. Int. J. u-and e-Serv. Sci. Technol. **3**, 1–18 (2010)
6. Institute for Citizen-Centered Service: Citizen First 2018, Ontario (2018)
7. Research, I.: De kwaliteit van de overheidsdienstverlening 2015 (2016)
8. Donnelly, M., Dalrymple, J.F., Wisniewski, M., Curry, A.C.: The portability of the SERVQUAL scale to the public sector. In: Kanji, G.K. (ed.) Total Quality Management, pp. 271–274. Springer, Dordrecht (1995). https://doi.org/10.1007/978-94-011-0539-2_39
9. Shieff, D.: Service quality components and group criteria in local government. Int. J. Serv. Ind. Manag. (1993). https://doi.org/10.1108/09564239310044280
10. Melo, A.I., Goncalo, S., Lima, R.: Measuring the quality of health services using SERVQUAL: evidence from Portugal. In: Handbook of Research on Modernization and Accountability in Public Sector Management, pp. 300–3187. IGI Global (2018)
11. Setiajit, D.G., Utomo, A.: A servqual measurement of public service from motor vehicle taxation office (SAMSAT) in Indonesia. J. Karya Dosen ITN Malang, 76–82 (2017)
12. Ocampo, L., et al.: Public service quality evaluation with SERVQUAL and AHP-TOPSIS: a case of Philippine government agencies. Socioecon. Plann. Sci. **68**, 10064 (2019)
13. van Deursen, A.J.A.M., Pieterson, W.: The Internet as a service channel in the public sector. In: ICA Conference, Dresden, Germany (2006)

14. Nguyen, M.H.: A study on evaluation of e-government service quality. Int. J. Soc. Manag. Econ. Bus. Eng. **8**, 16–19 (2014)
15. Sang, S., Lee, J.D.: A conceptual model of e-Government acceptance in public sector. In: Proceedings of the 3rd International Conference on Digital Society, ICDS 2009 (2009). https://doi.org/10.1109/ICDS.2009.30
16. Parasuraman, A., Zeithaml, V.A., Malhotra, A.: E-S-QUAL a multiple-item scale for assessing electronic service quality. J. Serv. Res. (2005). https://doi.org/10.1177/1094670504271156
17. Madsen, C.Ø., Hofmann, S., Pieterson, W.: Channel choice complications. In: Lindgren, I., Janssen, M., Lee, H., Polini, A., Rodríguez Bolívar, M.P., Scholl, H.J., Tambouris, E. (eds.) EGOV 2019. LNCS, vol. 11685, pp. 139–151. Springer, Cham (2019). https://doi.org/10.1007/978-3-030-27325-5_11
18. Pieterson, W., Ebbers, W., Madsen, C.Ø.: New channels, new possibilities: a typology and classification of social robots and their role in multi-channel public service delivery. In: Janssen, M., et al. (eds.) EGOV 2017. LNCS, vol. 10428, pp. 47–59. Springer, Cham (2017). https://doi.org/10.1007/978-3-319-64677-0_5
19. Blaikie, N.: Approaches to Social Inquiry. Polity, Cambridge (2010)
20. Creswell, J.W.: Research Design. Qualitative, Quantitative, and Mixed Methods Approaches. SAGE, London (2014)
21. United Nations: E-Government Survey 2018 (2018). https://doi.org/10.18356/d54b9179-en. ISBN:978-92-1-055353-7
22. Brown, J.S., Collins, A., Duguid, P.: Situated cognition and the culture of learning. Educ. Res. (1989). https://doi.org/10.3102/0013189X018001032
23. Krueger, R.A., Casey, M.A.: Planning the Focus Group Study. In: Focus Groups a Practical Guide for Applied Research (2015)
24. Wold, S., Ruhe, A., Wold, H., Dunn III, W.J.: The collinearity problem in linear regression. The Partial Least Squares (PLS) approach to generalized inverses. SIAM J. Sci. Stat. Comput. (1984). https://doi.org/10.1137/0905052
25. Wetherill, G.B., Seber, G.A.F.: Linear regression analysis. J. R. Stat. Soc. Ser. A. (1977). https://doi.org/10.2307/2345290
26. Natekin, A., Knoll, A.: Gradient boosting machines, a tutorial. Front. Neurorobot. (2013). https://doi.org/10.3389/fnbot.2013.00021
27. Hastie, T., Tibshirani, R., Friedman, J.: Springer Series in Statistics (2009). https://doi.org/10.1007/b94608
28. Ebbers, W.E., Jansen, M.G.M., Pieterson, W.J., van de Wijngaert, L.A.L.: Facts and feelings: the role of rational and irrational factors in citizens' channel choices. Gov. Inf. Q. **33**, 506–515 (2016). https://doi.org/10.1016/j.giq.2016.06.001

Digital Inclusion Competences for Senior Citizens: The Survival Basics

Jeremy Rose, Jesper Holgersson[✉], and Eva Söderström

School of Informatics, University of Skövde, 541 28 Skövde, Sweden
{jeremy.rose,jesper.holgersson,eva.soderstrom}@his.se

Abstract. The rapid pace of digitalisation provides many smarter and more efficient ways of interacting with the world, but may also lead to the exclusion of some groups. Senior citizens are one of these groups at risk. Taking the European Digital Competence Framework for Citizens as a starting point, we investigate digital survival skills for the elderly. Data was collected from digital education workshops for senior citizens organized jointly between Telia, Swedish municipalities, and the researchers. We use content analysis to understand seniors' perceptions of which competences they need to survive in an increasingly digital environment and provide a version of the Competence Framework targeted at senior citizen inclusion. Lessons for inclusion initiatives are drawn from the results.

Keywords: E-government · Digital inclusion · Digital competence · Senior citizens

1 Introduction

Digital exclusion may refer to limited access to the internet and digital equipment [1], but in developed countries with extensive digital infrastructure digital inclusion commonly addresses citizens' abilities to use the internet and digital equipment in order to access digital information services provided by government authorities [2] or commercial actors. Senior citizens constitute a large demographic in many advanced countries, though their requirements for digital information and services may be different – for instance the need for health care information and service often increases with age [3]. However the elderly are not prolific users of digital services [4], even where they have access to both internet and digital equipment in their homes [5]. Seniors are often therefore at risk of digital exclusion. At the same time, government authorities struggle with poor uptake of digital services. Citizens often view digital information, service and communication as unattractive options compared with existing channels such as phone, mail or physical meetings, not at least by digitally excluded elderly people [3]. Research initiatives concerned with promoting digital inclusion for senior citizens often focus on education [see e.g. 6, 7]. Such initiatives rely on underlying assumptions about ways of improving the digital competences of seniors. Digital technology competences are increasingly understood as life skills comparable to literacy and numeracy - both a

G. Viale Pereira et al. (Eds.): EGOV 2020, LNCS 12219, pp. 151–163, 2020.
https://doi.org/10.1007/978-3-030-57599-1_12

requirement and a right – and further as a basic underpinning for citizens to function in society, as an essential requirement for life, or even as a survival skill [8]. Thus an understanding of which competences the elderly require to function well in an increasingly digitalised society is fundamental to targeted educational programmes. We investigate basic survival competences for the elderly as expressed by Swedish seniors participating in the Mer Digital (More Digital) program[1] run by the Nordic telecommunications company Telia Sonera AB, in collaboration with Swedish municipalities. We use the European Digital Competence Framework for Citizens [9] as a starting point, framing the research question 'what competencies do Swedish seniors understand as necessary for digital inclusion?' We collected qualitative data at a series of Mer Digital workshops conducted in 2019 in municipalities around Sweden, and employed content analysis with Dedoose as the primary analysis method. The theoretical result is a version of the digital competence framework specialised for basic inclusion necessities for the elderly.

The paper is structured as follows: the next section introduces the concept of inclusion, which is followed by a presentation of DigComp, the European Digital Competences Framework. Explanation of the data collection and analysis approach is followed by a report of the data analysis results - explaining how the seniors we interacted with understand inclusion, and the competences they require to address digitalisation. This leads to a revise version of the framework which is focused on inclusions skills for the elderly. Conclusions discuss the implications and limitations of the research.

2 Digital Inclusion

The digital divide (also referred to as digital inclusion/exclusion) refers to *'the gap between those who do and those who do not have access to new forms of information technology'* [10, p. 221–222]. The original use of the term concerned access to the Internet and availability of digital equipment [1]; however recent commentators tend to understand digital inclusion as a ladder of participation, a continuum of different gradations of access and use rather than a binary divide between haves and have-nots [11]. Concerns about citizens ability to keep up with the changing nature of society are also condensed in the 'digital natives/digital immigrants' discussion [12] and in the various literacy research streams. Research focusing on computer literacy has in recent times been supplemented by ICT literacy studies (the ability to use computer hardware and software and related technologies effectively), Internet literacy (adding the ability to understand information, media, and to communicate through the Internet) and media literacy (the ability to analyse media messages and the media environment and the consumption and creation of digital media products) [13]. In developed countries like Sweden with extensive digital infrastructure and a relatively high standard of living, the digital divide is more likely to focus on skills inequality – competence and knowledge for how to use the internet and digital devices – rather than access. Sourbati [3] argues that skills inequalities for elderly citizens is problematic since: 1) the need for service increases with age (not least true for health care services), and 2) elderly citizens are rarely engaged and interested in digital technologies. They may have access to the

---

[1] https://www.telia.se/foretag/bransch/kommun/mer-digital.

Internet in their homes, but choose not to use for it personal reasons. Lack of engagement can be a result of either involuntary exclusion or personal choice [14]. Existing research focuses on the nature of the digital divide, its extent in different countries, and its causes. Complementary research concerns social inequalities, e-service provision [3], and the uptake of specific technologies like tablets and smartphones. There is, however, little research focusing on the inclusion of the elderly [15], though there is some agreement that 'the learning curve for many older digital entrants is very demanding and difficult' [16, p. 2]. Nevertheless, the potential benefits of including the elderly in digital society may be extensive, including reduction of social isolation, IT-supported communication with friends and family, active participation in an increasingly computerized healthcare system [17], prolonged independence, and improved cognitive abilities. Given demographic changes in Western societies, elderly are expected to be one of the largest groups of information and service consumers. They are nevertheless the group that exploits new digital capabilities the least - exhibiting both a general disinterest in digitalisation and a general discomfort with it [18]. The most commonly proposed actions for increasing digital inclusion are education and training. Fortes, Martins and Castro [6] conclude that different forms of training increase motivation as well as making the elderly more receptive towards mobile technologies. Loureiro and Barbas [19] run a set of workshops with the purpose of providing skills needed to take part in a networked society. Tsai, Shillair, Cotten, Winstead and Yost [7] show that working with other seniors with similar life situations enhances motivation for experimenting with new technology.

3   Digital Competence Framework

Digital competence can be understood as 'the set of knowledge, skills, attitudes, abilities, strategies and awareness that is required when using ICT and digital media to perform tasks; solve problems; communicate; manage information; behave in an ethical and responsible way; collaborate; create and share content and knowledge for work, leisure, participation, learning, socialising, empowerment and consumerism' [8, 9]. Table 1 shows The European Digital Competence Framework for Citizens [9], developed for the European Commission's Directorate-General for Employment, Social Affairs and Inclusion. The framework is based upon an overview literature study and analysis of 15 existing competence frameworks [8] and an online expert consultation exercise with 95 experts using the Delphi method [20]. The framework consists of five competence areas broken down into 21 competences. There are in addition eight proficiency levels, from foundational to highly specialised, (which are not shown here or used in our analysis) and examples of uses from different contexts.

The European Joint Research Council maintains a gallery of implementations[2] recording the framework's use in fifteen European countries for purposes including the professional development of teachers, content and student assessment for technology education, employability assessment and policy support [21]. The framework represents a picture of digital competences for European citizens in general, and is not targeted at elderly people.

---

[2] https://ec.europa.eu/jrc/en/digcomp/implementation.

Table 1. DigComp 2.1: the digital competence framework for citizens [9]

Competence area	Description	Competence
Information and data literacy	Identify, locate, retrieve, store, organise and analyse digital information, judging its relevance and purpose	Browsing, searching, filtering data, information and digital content
		Evaluating data, information and digital content
		Managing data, information and digital content
Communication and collaboration	Communicate in digital environments, share resources through online tools, link with others and collaborate through digital tools, interact with and participate in communities and networks, cross-cultural awareness	Interacting through digital technologies
		Sharing through digital technologies
		Engaging in citizenship through digital technologies
		Collaborating through digital technologies
		Netiquette
		Managing digital identity
Digital content creation	Create and edit new content (from word processing to images and video); integrate and re-elaborate previous knowledge and content; produce creative expressions, media outputs and programming; deal with and apply intellectual property rights and licences	Developing digital content
		Integrating and re-elaborating digital content
		Copyright and licences
		Programming
Safety	Personal protection, data protection, digital identity protection, security measures, safe and sustainable use	Protecting devices
		Protecting personal data and privacy
		Protecting health and well-being
		Protecting the environment
Problem solving	Identify digital needs and resources, make informed decisions on most appropriate digital tools according to the purpose or need, solve conceptual problems through digital means, creatively use technologies, solve technical problems, update own and other's competence	Identifying needs and technological responses
		Solving technical problems
		Creatively using digital technologies
		Identifying digital competence gaps

4   Research Approach

The research is conducted in Sweden - one of the world's most heavily digitalized countries. 98% of Swedish citizens have access to a mobile phone and internet, and 93% have a computer at home [22]. However, a large group of 430 000 citizens, mostly elderly, do not use the internet at all [22], indicating that Sweden, in common with other countries has a problem with digital exclusion of elderly citizens. Data was collected as part of a series of workshops organised by Telia Sonera in collaboration with Sweden's local authorities as part of the Mer Digital (More Digital) program. In short, each workshop was lasting for three hours, and had approximately 60–100 elderly participants. All the locality's elderly (65+) were invited without pre-conditions, and invited to formulate their own questions and problems, and bring their own devices. Participants were seated around tables with internet-connected computers, and help was offered by high school students recruited from local schools, who received a small financial compensation. The intention, as a follow up to an earlier successful pre-study was to enable the younger generation to teach the elderly about digitalization. The workshops were user-directed, in response to the elderly's request for help, without a specific programme of instruction that should be followed. Interactions between the generations both supports the learning curve of the elderly, and enables a sense of contribution for the high school students. It means overcoming existing prejudices about each other's generations. Typical enquiries ranged from how to use Google to specific needs such as starting an e-mail account, getting access to social media, or selling a rug on consumer-to-consumer sites. The high school students and the elderly did not know each other beforehand.

Data collection aimed at exploring the participants' attitudes and behaviour towards digitalization, their current digital knowledge base, and how their knowledge and attitudes were affected by the training session. Data was collected using qualitative inquiry [23], based on free text questions handed out as a short open-question questionnaire, and collected on site. In total, 633 inquires were analysed, collected from workshops distributed over four regionally distributed municipalities.

Data analysis was conducted using content analysis [24–26]. Content analysis yields 'a relatively systematic and comprehensive summary or overview of the data set as a whole' [26, p. 182], by observing repeating themes and categorizing them using a coding system. Dedoose was used as the coding tool. Inter-coder reliability was achieved by using a total of three coders. A hierarchical coding scheme was developed using the competence areas and individual competences given in Table 2. Two coders spent an afternoon working together to synchronise their understandings of the codes, before coding the rest of the text independently. Additional codes were developed to represent competences not covered by the original framework, with further discussion between coders. A third coder sampled the coding retrospectively to ensure coding consistency and inter-coder reliability.

5 Seniors' Understanding of Digital Inclusion and Necessary Digital Competences

Figure 1 shows the frequency of coding for the major competence areas of the European digital competence framework. The information and data literacy, communication and collaboration, and safety areas of the framework, were well represented in the responses of the elderly, whereas the digital content creation and problem solving areas hardly figured.

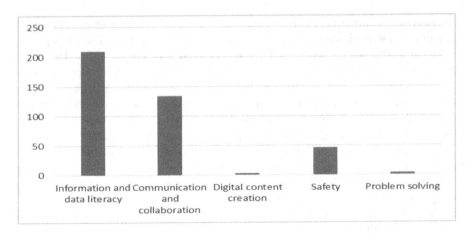

Fig. 1. Frequency of coding for the major competence areas

Figure 2 shows the competence areas and individual competences from the analysis with 10 or more codings. This was chosen as an (arbitrary) threshold for significance, representing roughly five percent of the most coded categories. The competences are a mixture of competences from the original framework and competencies developed during the analysis. Competences related to digital content creation drop out of the picture, whereas new competences particularly represent service transactions (local government and financial services), and safety fears.

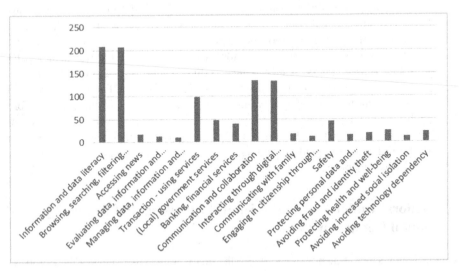

Fig. 2. Competence areas and individual competences with at least 10 codings.

5.1   Senior Citizens Fear of Exclusion

It is clear that the respondents realize that digitalisation is here to stay – *'most informa- tion and communication is digital today,' 'society takes it as given that everyone has a computer' 'That's the way today's society works'* and that it is essentially a step forward – *'the world gets closer', 'faster access to the channels of society.'* This means they have to get used to it, whether they like it or not: *'you're excluded from everything if you don't have a seat on the train,' 'if you know the new stuff you are less excluded from society'.* They often express that they don't have any choice in this matter - society forces them to go digital no matter what they think about it – *'the situation as it is today leaves you with no choice.'* However they feel that this is not a trivial task - its *'horror mixed with delight'* and *'something new when you are 80 years old.'* Seniors' view of digitalisation is characterized by a general sense of fear, of different kinds. Not being able to use digital equipment and services is commonly mentioned: *'I'm afraid that I cannot handle the digital society'* and *'I don't know when I do the right thing and when I don't'.* Various fears for their safety and personal development are described later. When asked to elaborate on how they thought digital inclusion could be increased, they often responded that knowledge and skill was the best way to reduce technology fear. This could be promoted in different ways for instance education and training (*'get the oppor- tunity to dare to use these things,' 'wake up and open your eyes'*), reducing fear (*'we are afraid and believe that something will collapse,' 'many are afraid to make mistakes … then you don't know what to do and that is scary'*), knowledge of better and newer technologies (*'it's not just to know what buttons to push but also to understand why you push that button'*), and assistance (*'I have my son here and I can use him whenever I can't do something by myself'*).

5.2   Information and Data Literacy

The elderly very frequently express the need to keep up with the world, expressed in Swedish as 'att hänga med', which also carries implications of some difficulty in the task and a disadvantage if it is not accomplished - in English 'to hang on': *'to keep up with the digital world,' 'its necessary to keep up, find information since it's getting hard to make contact by telephone, or get to some places to collect tickets, etc.'* As society is progressively digitalised, old forms of information seeking (finding out by making a telephone call) disappear, physical distribution points become further apart – and older people have more difficulties with mobility, so its easier to stay home. Keeping up is usually accomplished through the competence browsing and searching in the DigComp model. Some have more practical purposes in mind (*'compare prices at different businesses'*), others are driven by curiosity (*'to gather as much knowledge as possible'*). Keeping up includes both keeping up with digitalisation, and keeping up with events in the world (accessing news), since seniors recognised that much of the news media has relocated online: *'look at what's happening in the world', 'information on FaceBook on what's happening in our country – follow SVT's (Swedish Television) site a lot amongst others.'* Keeping up implies the need to sort and evaluate data (*'drowning in information – can be too much that is irrelevant'*) but also the need to evaluate the truth content of digital news (*'all the rubbish that gets spread' 'too much fake news'*).

Some requirement for managing digital data is also recognised, with organising photos mentioned several times.

5.3 Communication and Collaboration

Communication competences are much valued by seniors, in which a frequent phrasing is 'to be connected' (Swedish: uppkopplad) – *'with my surroundings', 'with the world',* coupled with the recognition that much of communication had moved online: *'get in touch with what I cannot get in touch with otherwise.'* They need to communicate digitally with friends (*'quick communication with Facebook friends'*), but particularly to keep in touch with distant family members and friends - children, grandchildren, and relatives, who don't always live close by, as they once tended to. Grandchildren are digital natives, and seniors feel disconnected if they cannot communicate with them with their own technologies. Some have noticed that there can be an economic advantage (*'the possibility of a simple conversation which is free of cost'*), whereas many have noticed that the various authorities (health, pension) expect them to be able to communicate through digital media. Several felt a sense of civic engagement (*'to participate in society'*) which could also be carried out online. However they show little sense of having a specialised digital identity (which might not coincide with their physical identity) which needs to be managed, except in the sense that they are worried that their digital identity could be stolen (see below).

5.4 Transaction – Using Services

A form of competence not much recognised or prioritised by the European DigComp framework is transactional competence. This was understood as a necessary survival skill by the elderly in our survey. They needed to *'be able to use the existing digital services'* and recognised that *'many services will be digitalised'* in the future. Therefore they need to take advantage of *'everything that can be done digitally where you don't have to go into town'*. Seniors repeatedly mentioned paying their bills online; the Swedish monetary system is increasingly digital, with many shops refusing to accept cash any longer. Payment through mobile phone services in increasingly common, with the most common service (Swish) often mentioned. Sweden contains remote, sparsely populated and inaccessible areas, in which banks increasingly rationalise their physical presence, so that *'being able to manage your economy'* is increasingly an online competence. Seniors need to be able to use digital services provided by government authorities, for example booking appointments to the healthcare, filling in a tax form. They are also increasingly aware of online retail *'buying things on the net, for example eBay'*.

5.5 Digital Content Creation and Problem Solving

DigComp has a competence area called digital content creation, but this was scarcely recognised by the elderly. They understood of course that they should write emails and take photos on their phones – these were understood as extensions of pre-digital competences like writing a letter. They showed no general inclination to write their own web-sites, shoot videos on their phones and post them, blog or vlog, become extensive Facebook posters or Tweeters, let alone develop careers as internet influencers, as far as we could discern from analysing their data.

DigComp includes a problem-solving competence, described as identifying digital needs and resources, making informed decisions on the most appropriate digital tools according to purpose or need, solving conceptual problems through digital means, creatively using technologies, solving technical problems, updating one's own and other's competence. Beyond a general irritation/despair at the number of low-level technical problems (*'how to change my password,' 'the printer suddenly stops working'*) sometimes at a rather extreme level (*'mental illness due to malfunctioning computer'*), our sample of the elderly showed little awareness of, or interest in higher-order problem-solving skills.

5.6 Safety

The participants exhibit a great concern regarding security and privacy issues, including having their personal information stolen (*'personal information can easily leak'*) and their computing devices infected by viruses. They fear fraud (*'being conned on the net,' 'you can conn a person on the net'*) and identity theft (*'danger of getting your ID hijacked'*), and feel (and may actually be) vulnerable to many new and difficult-to-understand digital fraud threats – *'there's a lot of fraud on that shitty net and intrusive selling ploys.'* They are generally nervous about their money and the net (*'worried about hackers in my internet bank and internet card payments,' 'don't want to pay on the net because it doesn't feel safe'*). Also commonly mentioned is an anxiety for spending too much time in the digital world. Seniors worry that moving online will increase their social isolation, since it takes time and reduces their face-to-face interaction with society around them – *'you lose human contact'*. There is a fear of being trapped behind a computer, or being dependent on it: *'it can be too much fun and take up a little bit too much time,' 'it can be an addiction'*, as well as a more general fear of the amount of time needed to keep up with advances in the digital world. Seniors worry about acquiring the screen addictions that they see in younger people.

6 Digital Competences for Senior Citizen Inclusion

Table 2 shows the Digital Competence model revised to focus on basic inclusion competences for senior citizens. The new digital competences identified are displayed in italics in Table 2.

Table 2. The revised digital competence model

Competence area	Description	Competence	Senior citizen's particular needs
Information and data literacy	Identify, locate, retrieve, store, organise and analyse digital information, judging its relevance and purpose	Browsing, searching, filtering data, information and digital content	
		Accessing news	*Frequently expressed need to keep up with the external world where news sources are diverse and often on-line*
		Evaluating data, information and digital content	
		Managing data, information and digital content	
Communication and collaboration	Communicate in digital environments, share resources through online tools, link with others and collaborate through digital tools, interact with and participate in communities and networks, cross-cultural awareness	Interacting through digital technologies	
		Communicating with family	*Senior citizens' immediate families (children, grandchildren) are often geographically separated in contemporary society and grandchildren in particular are digital natives*
		Engaging in citizenship through digital technologies	
Transaction - using services	*Perform, transactions on-line with a range of important service providers*	*(Local) government services*	*Service providers move on-line (often as a cost saving measure), and withdraw traditional service offers (over-the- counter, face-to-face, personal service)*

(continued)

Table 2. (*continued*)

Competence area	Description	Competence	Senior citizen's particular needs
		Banking, financial services	*As above compounded by the gradual withdrawal of physical money and the development of secure on line payment services, especially mobile*
Safety	Personal protection, data protection, digital identity protection, security measures, safe and sustainable use	Protecting personal data and privacy	
		Avoiding fraud and identity theft	*The elderly feel (and may be) vulnerable to many new and difficult-to-understand digital fraud threats*
		Protecting health and well-being	
		Avoiding increased social isolation	*Seniors worry that moving online will increase their isolation since it takes time and reduces their face-to-face interaction with society around them*
		Avoiding technology dependency	*Seniors worry about acquiring the screen addictions that they see in younger people*

7 Conclusions

In this article we focused on basic digital competences for the elderly, with a background in the European DigComp framework, using data collected from participants at series of educational workshops in the Swedish Mer Digital programme. We focused the model to reflect the views of senior citizens, excluding elements not prioritised by them, and introducing new elements (particularly transactional skills) where they were sufficiently prioritised or focused in the original framework. Thus the primary contribution of the article is the Digital Competences for Senior Citizen Inclusion framework. We expect this to be particularly useful to educators in the field, who can arrange digital inclusion programmes to reflect the needs that the elderly themselves recognise as important. We, in the same way, continue to inform the Swedish Mer Digital programme as it develops. We recognise limitations with the research. Its not certain that elderly are necessarily the only authorities in specifying their own digital competence needs, since they (with some exceptions) may not focus on the trajectory of digital development, and therefore may miss important competences which may be need in the near future. On the other hand, educators should expect more commitment to learning those competences which the elderly themselves recognise as essential. Nor is it certain that other countries follow the same digitalisation curve as Sweden – many western countries follow a similar trajectory, though they may be at different points in their development. Senior citizens from other regions of the world may have entirely different needs. Since digitalisation is a change process, its clear that the framework will in any case need updating in only a few years.

References

1. Bélanger, F., Carter, L.: Trust and risk in e-government adoption. J. Strateg. Inf. Syst. **17**, 165–176 (2008)
2. Ebbers, W.E., Jansen, M.G.M., van Deursen, A.J.A.M.: Impact of the digital divide on e-government: expanding from channel choice to channel usage. Gov. Inf. Q. **33**, 685–692 (2016)
3. Sourbati, M.: 'It could be useful, but not for me at the moment': older people, internet access and e-public service provision. New Media Soc. **11**, 1083–1100 (2009)
4. Nishijima, M., Ivanauskas, T.M., Sarti, F.M.: Evolution and determinants of digital divide in Brazil (2005–2013). Telecommun. Policy **41**, 12–24 (2017)
5. Hill, R., Beynon-Davies, P., Williams, M.: Older people and internet engagement: acknowledging social moderators of internet adoption, access and use. Inf. Technol. People **21**, 244–266 (2008)
6. Fortes, R.P.M., Martins, G.A., Castro, P.C.: A review of senescent's motivation in the use of tactile devices. Procedia Comput. Sci. **67**, 376–387 (2015)
7. Tsai, H.-Y.S., Shillair, R., Cotten, S.R., Winstead, V., Yost, E.: Getting grandma online: are tablets the answer for increasing digital inclusion for older adults in the U.S. Educ. Gerontol. **41**, 695–709 (2015)
8. Ferrari, A., Punie, Y., Redecker, C.: Understanding digital competence in the 21st century: an analysis of current frameworks. In: Ravenscroft, A., Lindstaedt, S., Kloos, C.D., Hernández-Leo, D. (eds.) EC-TEL 2012. LNCS, vol. 7563, pp. 79–92. Springer, Heidelberg (2012). https://doi.org/10.1007/978-3-642-33263-0_7
9. Carreteo, S., Vuorikari, R., Punie, Y.: DigComp 2.1: the digital competence framework for citizens. With eight proficiency levels and examples of use. In: Publications Office of the European Union, B. (ed.) (2017)
10. van Dijk, J.: Digital divide research, achievements and shortcomings. Poetics **34**, 221–235 (2006)
11. Livingstone, S., Helsper, E.: Gradations in digital inclusion: children, young people and the digital divide. New Media Soc. **9**, 671–696 (2007)
12. Prensky, M.: Digital natives, digital immigrants part 1. Horizon **9**, 1–6 (2001)
13. Christ, W., Potter, W.: Media literacy, media education, and the academy. J. Commun. **48**, 5–15 (1998)
14. Eynon, R., Helsper, E.J.: Adults learning online: digital choice and/or digital exclusion? New Media Soc. **13**, 534–551 (2011)
15. Silva, M., Correia, S.: ActiveBrain: online social platform for active and healthy ageing. Procedia Comput. Sci. **27**, 38–45 (2013)

16. Damodaran, L., Olphert, W.: Sustaining digital engagement: some emerging issues. Digit. Futur. 11–12 (2010)
17. Niehaves, B., Plattfaut, R.: Internet adoption by the elderly: employing IS technology acceptance theories for understanding the age-related digital divide. Eur. J. Inf. Syst. **23**, 708–726 (2014)
18. Kurniavan, S.: Older people and mobile phones: a multi-method investigation. Int. J. Hum Comput Stud. **66**, 889–901 (2008)
19. Loureiro, A., Barbas, M.: Active ageing – enhancing digital literacies in elderly citizens. In: Zaphiris, P., Ioannou, A. (eds.) LCT 2014. LNCS, vol. 8524, pp. 450–459. Springer, Cham (2014). https://doi.org/10.1007/978-3-319-07485-6_44
20. Janssen, J., Stoyanov, S., Ferrari, A., Punie, Y., Pannekeet, K., Sloep, P.: Experts' views on digital competence: commonalities and differences. Comput. Educ. **68**, 473–481 (2013)
21. Kluzer, S., Rissola, G.: Guidelines on the adoption of DigComp (Technical report) (2015)
22. Davidsson, P., Thoresson, A.: Svenskarna och internet 2017: undersökning om svenskarnas internetvanor (2017)
23. Patton, M.Q.: Qualitative Research & Evaluation Methods. Sage, London (2002)
24. Berelson, B.: Content Analysis in Communication Research. Free Press, New York (1952)
25. Krippendorff, K.: Reliability in content analysis: some common misconceptions and recommendations. Hum. Commun. Res. **30**, 411–433 (2006)
26. Silverman, D.: Interpreting Qualitative Data: Methods for Analysing Talk, Text and Interaction. Sage, London (2001)

Walking a Mile in Their Shoes—A Citizen Journey to Explore Public Service Delivery from the Citizen Perspective

Hendrik Scholta(✉), Sebastian Halsbenning, Bettina Distel, and Jörg Becker

ERCIS, University of Münster, Leonardo-Campus 3, 48149 Münster, Germany
{hendrik.scholta,sebastian.halsbenning,bettina.distel,
joerg.becker}@ercis.uni-muenster.de

Abstract. Up to now, public administrations have taken a supply-oriented approach to the design of electronic services for citizens resulting in low usage rates. In contrast, companies in the private sector have been relying on demand-oriented service design for many years. They make use of so-called 'customer journeys' to better understand the perception of services by customers and to tailor the design of electronic services to that perception. Although also governments and public administrations have been increasingly recognizing the benefits of customer journeys, there is still a lack of research on the application of customer journeys in the public sector. Especially, there is no customer journey that is applicable to a wide range of public services and serves as a general blueprint for public services. Therefore, in this paper, we present a generic citizen journey that depicts the delivery process for transactional public services from a citizen perspective. The citizen journey depicts the points of interaction that citizens have with public services. We evaluated the citizen journey in a focus group with public servants and a survey with citizens. The evaluation reveals the citizen journey's general usefulness. Researchers benefit from our citizen journey through a better understanding of the service delivery process and the different steps that could impact citizen experience. Practitioners can use the citizen journey in the design of citizen-centric services and during the actual service delivery to guide citizens through the delivery process.

Keywords: Customer journey · User journey · Service design · Digital government · Citizen journey

1 Introduction

The digitalization of the public sector progresses and public administrations have been increasingly offering more of their services to citizens electronically. While e-services in the private sector have been used by customers for many years (e.g. online banking), the usage rates for public e-services are still at a low level [1–4]. One reason for this discrepancy between the use of private and public e-services is, among other things, the

© IFIP International Federation for Information Processing 2020
Published by Springer Nature Switzerland AG 2020
G. Viale Pereira et al. (Eds.): EGOV 2020, LNCS 12219, pp. 164–178, 2020.
https://doi.org/10.1007/978-3-030-57599-1_13

different role of customers and citizens. In contrast to the private sector, where service designers focus on the customer perspective, researchers repeatedly point out that a more demand-driven perspective is needed in the public sector and that public administrations must design their (electronic) services according to the needs of citizens [5].

In service design, an established and widely used instrument to achieve a high level of customer orientation and customer satisfaction is the customer journey [6, 7]. A customer journey consists of the sequence of all points of contact, so-called touchpoints, between the customer and the company, brand or product in the course of a purchase, for example when placing an order [8]. Customer journeys are used to visualize, analyze and ultimately improve these points of contact [8]. The points of interaction are viewed from the customer's perspective. Customer journeys create an understanding of the ideal steps that customers ideally go through in order to purchase a product. This reveals artefacts and activities that are of high importance in the interaction between customers and companies and which should, therefore, be given high priority in service design, such as relevant websites. Customer journeys enable the identification of weaknesses and potential for improvement in these artifacts and activities. Thus, their application is particularly valuable as customers are involved in the creation process of a customer journey and complement the company's internal evaluation of the points of contact [9].

Meanwhile, also public administrations recognize this trend and move from a more supplier- and service-oriented perspective to more user-centric and demand-oriented approaches [10]. For example, the Danish Digital Strategy 2016–2020 explicitly refers to the development of customer journeys as a means of increasing transparency for citizens' rights and obligations [11]. Also, the promotion of demand-driven services with a high degree of personalization is an important trend, as citizens want services to be more closely tailored to individual needs and want to be more involved in the design and delivery of services [12]. Therefore, customer journeys have been increasingly used by public administrations and governments to ultimately improve the quality and use of public e-services e.g. [13–17]. Particularly with the increasing complexity of digital technology and the growing importance of e-services, it becomes increasingly important to understand and address the needs of citizens [18].

Although there are various examples of public administrations that apply citizen journeys in practice, there is scarce research on the use of the customer journey concept in the public sector [19–21]. Especially, researchers have not created a generic citizen journey that is applicable to a wide range of government services. To become more citizen-centric and understand the needs and desires of citizens, public administrations should create and analyze citizen journeys in public service design. To release public administrations from the necessity to design each journey and service from scratch, a blueprint for citizen journeys is deemed useful. Thus, we aim to support the application of the customer journey concept in the public sector by addressing the following research goal: *Design of a generic citizen journey that depicts the delivery process for transactional public services from a citizen perspective.* We focus on transactional services such as applying for child benefit. Other types of services such as informational (e.g. information on public events on websites), communicative (e.g. e-mail interaction) or participatory (e.g. participatory budgeting) services are not covered.

Despite their usefulness, the transfer of strategies from the private to the public sector is repeatedly criticized because of the sectors' fundamental differences. Several aspects need to be considered before implementing approaches that have been proven to be useful in the private sector. For example, customers and citizens cannot be treated equally, as they have different roles in the service process. In Sect. 2, we briefly review central differences between the public and the private sector. Thus, during the design of our citizen journey, which is presented in Sects. 3 (method) and 4 (results), we put specific emphasis on the differences between the public and private sectors. The citizen journey is intended to support service design in public administrations. It enables administrations to incorporate not only internal considerations in the service design but to consider also the citizens' needs and desires. Additionally, administrations can use the journey during service delivery to guide citizens through the process. Further implications for research and practice are discussed in Sect. 5.

2   Research Background

In the following section, the central concepts used in this study are delineated. Furthermore, we discuss their general applicability to the public sector context and shortly introduce the scarce extant public sector literature.

Customer Journeys and the Public Sector. The idea of customer journeys originates in the field of marketing research [22]. Hence, the majority of research and established design principles of such a journey are tailored to customer-company relationships. A customer journey describes how customers experience the totality of touchpoints between a customer and company. The fact that greater attention is now being paid to the customer's perspective is due to a paradigm shift in recent years, leading companies to increasingly focus on creating value for their customers that goes beyond the mere product [23]. Whereas in the past, customer management was mainly concentrated on generating maximum monetary success from customer relationships, the focus is now more on conveying a positive customer experience.

Similarly, the public sector has witnessed paradigm shifts in the past decades, first moving from traditional public administration to New Public Management (NPM) and, more recently, moving from the NPM paradigm to what Bryson et al. call the 'emerging approach to public administration' [24]. Under NPM, public administrations are viewed from an economic and managerial perspective and, as a consequence, citizens are treated as customers [24]. However, lately, this approach has been criticized for being short-sighted and reducing the citizens' role in the public sector too much. Instead, researchers point to the importance of appreciating the citizen as being multifaceted and considering the different roles the citizenry can take during the service process [25], from being a passive receiver of services to being involved in the policy process [26]. Thus, it is important to not only change the term 'customer journey' to *citizen journey* but to take into consideration the different notions this term encompasses.

Marketing research uses the concept of customer experience which describes "a multidimensional construct focusing on a customer's cognitive, emotional, behavioral, sensorial, and social responses to a firm's offerings during the customer's entire purchase journey" [23]. Companies are eager to understand the customer experience because "[t]he key objective of tracking the experience at customer touchpoints is to develop an understanding of how an experience can be enriched for the customer throughout what marketers call the 'customer decision-making process'" [7]. Companies use customer journeys to document and understand the experience a customer makes while interacting with a product [6]. Ostensibly, the same rationale might drive the use of citizen journeys in the public sector. Citizen-centricity is often claimed as desirable, both by practitioners and researchers, but the application of citizen journeys is more complex than that. Improving the perceived quality of public services impacts the efficiency with which public policy is put in practice [27]. Public administrations are accountable to the citizenry and the administration's overall goal is to "[c]reate public value in such a way that what the public most cares about is addressed effectively and what is good for the public is put in place" [24]. In this sense, citizen-centricity is about more than just satisfaction with the services provided; it is about the assurance of public values.

As mentioned in the introduction, only few examples of citizen journeys can be found in academic literature. One of the earliest applications of the customer journey concept to the public sector is provided by Parker and Heapy [20] who provide insights into service design from the public and private sector. Although they provide extant cases of customer and citizen integration, neither do they provide a template for a user journey nor do they focus on digitized services. Another example is given by Crosier and Handford [21] who provide a customer journey for the blind and partially sighted people. However, the journey they present is less tied to a specific good or service and more focused on the on-site shopping experience of disabled people. A recent example of an application of the concept is given by Trischler and Scott [19] who propose new methods for public service design, among which are customer journeys and visualization and mapping techniques.

Design and Visualization of Customer and Citizen Journeys. Customer journeys are typically divided into different subsequent phases. However, there is no consensus in literature on how broad or narrow these phases are. While Nenonen et al. [28] differentiate between orientation, approach, action, depart, and evaluation, the most basic definition of customer journey phases can be found in the work by Lemon and Verhoef [23] who distinguish a pre-purchase, a purchase and a post-purchase phase. The pre-purchase phase includes a customer's touchpoints before purchasing a service. This refers to all activities that fall in the period from the point where a customer recognizes a need to search for a solution to the point of his or her consideration to satisfy this need by purchasing the service. Subsequently, in the purchase phase she or he makes the choice to order a service, and finally pays for it. The purchase phase is generally seen as the heart of the customer journey with companies concentrating their efforts to improve customers' shopping experience. Finally, the post-purchase phase encompasses a customer's experience after buying a service. This includes consumption, usage, customer engagements, and service requests. A customer journey is not an isolated process as previous experiences are included as well, which influence future customer journeys. Furthermore, customers can quit their journey in any phase.

To enhance the understandability of a customer journey its visual representation has become increasingly important, for instance, in a diagram or a storyboard with pictures, sketches, and photos [6, 20, 22]. Although no standard for modelling a customer journey exists, visual representations allow a company to compare different service experiences and to compare the offered services to those of competitors [8]. Since these journeys represent experiences from a customer or citizen perspective, users are actively involved in their creation [9, 20, 29]. This helps in identifying factors that influence user satisfaction, including problem areas and opportunities for future innovation.

3   Research Design

This paper follows the design science research (DRS) paradigm which aims at the development of IT artifacts, namely constructs, methods, models and instantiations [30]. This paradigm is suitable for our paper since we propose a generic citizen journey which is a model and abstract representation of the public service delivery process from the citizens' perspective.

In order to conduct DSR to design our citizen journey, we follow the research process proposed by Österle et al. [31] that consists of the steps analysis, design, evaluation and diffusion. In the *analysis* step, we identified and investigated our research problem. We found the need and anchors for our research in practice-oriented and academic literature as presented in Sects. 1 and 2. This literature provided us with insights on current practices in government agencies and what knowledge we can build on from academic literature, especially on customer journeys applied in the private sector.

Subsequently, we developed the citizen journey in the *design* step. We built our citizen journey based on a well-established customer journey [23]. This is appropriate since the concept of customer journeys has been widely researched in academic literature on the private sector. Despite commonalities between the private and public sector, there are substantial differences so academic results cannot be transferred unreflectingly between them. Therefore, based on differences between the sectors and during discussions within our research group, we developed a first version of our citizen journey.

The *evaluation* step is essential to provide evidence for the usefulness of the developed artifact. We conducted two evaluations to redesign and develop further our version of the citizen journey. These evaluations were not focused on one specific service but on public services for citizens in general. In both evaluations, we asked our respondents to report on their experiences across situations and different public services. The *first evaluation* was conducted by means of a focus group. We aimed at interviewing public servants from different departments who do not hold a management position to get insights from different administrative perspectives and to ensure that the participants are in contact with citizens in their daily routine. This group of employees has the best insights into the processes and contact points of the citizens with the public administration. We structured the focus group interview along with six key questions with an evaluation of the first version of the citizen journey being the core of the discussion. A total of six employees from three different departments (social welfare, citizens' office and registry office) took part in the discussion, which lasted 105 min, was recorded and then transcribed. We conducted the analysis with a focus on the completeness and correctness of the citizen journey's phases, the sequence representing the delivery processes and the appropriateness of presentation and visual design. The results from the first evaluation were transferred to an additional *design* step in order to iteratively revise our citizen journey. Based on the insights gained through the focus group, the citizen journey was refined. Specific suggestions of the focus group participants but also statements on the general use of citizen journeys were evaluated and translated into a refined version of the citizen journey.

This step was followed by a *second evaluation*. As highlighted in Sects. 1 and 2, it is of utmost importance to include citizens into the development of citizen journeys in order to adequately capture their experiences with public service delivery. Thus, following the focus group and the re-design of the citizen journey, we carried out a survey to identify the steps and critical points of contact that are relevant from the citizens' perspective. The survey was conducted in person at the citizens' office of a small town in Germany. In order to reach as many different citizens as possible, we opted for a paper-based survey. The questionnaire consisted of several questions that revolved around the requested service, the citizens' preparation for this service request, and reasons for showing up in person. The respondents were also shown the refined citizen journey and were asked to evaluate the phases, their sequence, and their particular steps and order of steps. In total, 44 citizens took part in this non-representative survey. Similar to the analysis of the focus group discussion, the answers from the survey were evaluated qualitatively and with regard to the phases and steps of the citizen journey, their form of presentation and critical points of contact. After the analysis of the survey results, the citizen journey was re-*designed* a second time to adequately account for the citizens' experience with public service delivery.

Finally, the *diffusion* step will be conducted through dissemination activities such as scientific conferences and articles as well as workshops with practitioners.

4 Citizen Journey

4.1 Design

A customer journey can be divided into three phases [23]: prepurchase, purchase and postpurchase. This subdivision is also suitable for a transactional citizen journey (cf. Fig. 1). We renamed the three phases to *preparation, application* and *result* since a transactional service in the public sector—in contrast to the use of a service in the private sector—is typically characterized by the processing of an application [32–34]. In contrast to a customer journey, where the customer usually completes the journey successfully, i.e. receives a product after the necessary steps have been taken, the outcome for a citizen in the public sector is more uncertain, as there may be no entitlement to a service. In the following paragraphs, we describe the three phases in detail.

Preparation Phase. The subdivision of this phase from a customer journey [23] in need recognition, consideration and search is adopted here with minor changes. Most citizen journeys start with a *need recognition*, which is either triggered by the citizen or by law [18]. Most of the interactions between a citizen and the public administration are prescribed by legal regulations and are therefore mandatory [9, 35]. Needs triggered by law include, for example, the extension of a passport or driver's license, which becomes necessary due to reaching an expiry date. In such cases, a public administration may also inform a citizen of the need to apply for a renewal. In addition to the needs enforced by law, there are voluntary needs that are triggered by citizens themselves, such as marriage, business registration or parental allowance. Such needs are not triggered by law. There may also be needs for which no public services are available, for example, for a permission to open a shop on Sundays, as this may be prohibited for most businesses in some countries. Citizens can become aware of a situation both online (e.g. through information on a web portal) and offline (e.g. through conversations with other people), which can create a need.

Once the need has been detected, the citizen makes the *channel choice* for the subsequent activities of this phase, and various online (e.g. app) and offline options (e.g. city hall) are available. Here, a substantial difference to a customer journey becomes apparent: The citizen journey does not include the identification of different potential providers, since there is mostly only one provider for a service, usually the local government. For example, a parking permit may only be applied for at the respective municipal administration of the place of residence. Exceptions are, for example, the selection of a public school or kindergarten. As these are exceptions to the rule, the focus is on the choice of channel and not on other choices. The discussion on the online and offline use of public services and according usage rates indicate the importance of the channel choice for the public sector.

Afterwards, the citizen starts to *search for information* about a service to address the need, which can take place online and offline. This search can be different depending on the need. For example, a citizen can conduct a general search to gain more insights into the topic. This kind of search focuses exclusively on general information and does not address a specific service or public administration (general search). In some cases, citizens already know which service they are looking for and collect information about this service independently of the responsible public administration (service-specific search). An example is searching for the amount of child benefit to which a family is entitled according to the number of children. As the use of public services is usually accompanied by the submission of documents and forms, this search also includes searching for forms (e.g. online forms and PDFs) and information on what additional documents are generally required to be submitted—regardless of the responsible administration. While the search for information in e-commerce also includes the comparison of different services and providers (e.g. with regard to price and quality), these aspects are rare when searching for information on public services, as the responsible administration is often determined by the place of residence of the citizen or other properties such as his or her employer. It may also happen that citizens know the service and responsible administration and search the administration's website to find the opening hours, contact persons or online forms of this administration (administration-specific search). Finally, it can happen that all the necessary details of the service in question are known and therefore no search for information is necessary (no search). It is possible that citizens want to use electronic services, but are forced to use services on-site because the requested service is not offered electronically.

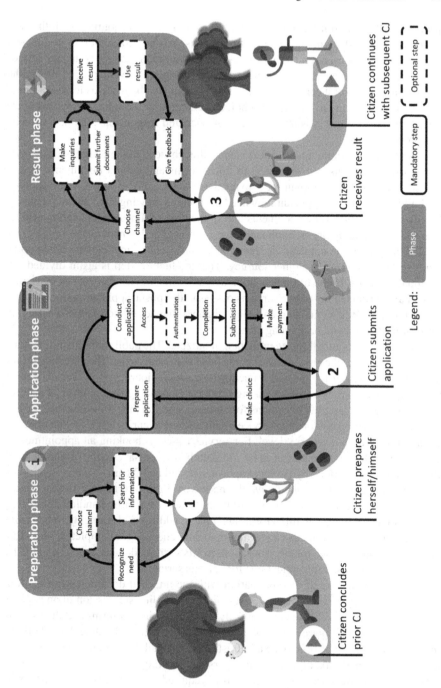

Fig. 1. Citizen journey

Application Phase. Similar to the second phase of a customer journey with the steps choice, ordering and payment [23], the second phase of our citizen journey begins with a *choice*. This includes, among other things, the decision to receive a voluntary service, such as parental allowance, or the choice of when to apply. If several people are entitled to receive a service for a certain case, the decision can also be made as to which one of them will receive it. In most cases, the choice of channel for the subsequent steps of this phase is the only choice citizens have since service and responsible administration are often predetermined.

In contrast to e-commerce, the next step of this phase is not ordering but *preparing the application*, because citizens have to fill in forms and submit documents that are checked by the administration in order to receive a service. For example, when applying for a building permit, an applicant may need to submit a drawing from an architect [34]. The citizen must collect the documents and in the case of a postal application also the forms to be filled in before an application for a service can be made.

After preparing the application, the citizen *conducts the application*, which corresponds to the order in a customer journey. The conduction step is again divided into individual substeps. In the offline channel, *access* to the service can consist of visiting the city hall and contacting public servants or—as with a postal application from home— sitting at a desk. When choosing an online channel, the access consists of visiting the administration's website or opening an app.

Some services require the *authentication* of citizens. The public administration must, therefore, ensure that the citizen is the person he or she claims to be. The authentication is specific to a citizen journey and barely occurs in a customer journey. However, exceptions are, for instance, purchases of a banking product. Depending on the level of security required, there are a number of options for authentication in the online channel, such as a user account with password for services with a lower security level, or identification with an eID for a high security level. For services such as booking an appointment at the city hall, authentication may even be completely unnecessary. In the offline channel, authentication can be done by personal appearance and an ID card.

During the subsequent *completion*, the necessary forms are filled in and necessary documents are attached. In electronic solutions, a service can be handled completely online, so that the citizen can fill in forms and upload additional documents. When using an online portal, the documents can be automatically checked for completeness. Portals can serve as online storage for electronic documents so that a document can be uploaded only once and then used in applications for various services.

The final *submission* of the application with the attached documents can be done online or offline. Digitalized service offers enable the online submission of an application. It may also be possible to electronically fill in and print out forms and then submit them by mail. Another possibility is that forms can be submitted online, but additional paper documents must be sent to the administration via mail. Essentially, the submission can be made by mail, fax, digitally or in a personal meeting.

Depending on the service, a *payment* may be required, either at the time of submission or at an earlier or later stage in the process. While this step is mandatory in e-commerce, citizens do not have to pay for every public service.

Result Phase. The result phase of our citizen journey has commonalities but also differences to the according phase of a customer journey which contains the steps consumption, usage, engagement and service requests [23]. In our case, first the *channel choice* for the next steps of this phase takes place. Here too, various online and offline options are available, such as contact by e-mail, telephone and mail. This step is optional, as in this phase only the receipt of the result is mandatory and the channel for this notification is often specified by the public administration.

Afterwards, citizens have the opportunity to *make inquiries*. For example, the current status of the procedure can be inquired by telephone or via an online portal, or questions can be asked about the understanding of information and documents requested by the administration.

While questions from citizens are directed to the administration, the administration can also contact citizens. This happens if the documents submitted by the applicant are unclear or incomplete and therefore missing documents or information must be submitted. In such cases, the administration informs the applicant of the need to *submit further documents*. The citizen then provides the necessary documents via the previously chosen channel. This step differs from a customer journey as there are usually no missing documents to be submitted after the purchase. An exception can be, for example, the submission of a direct debit mandate after the online acquisition of an insurance.

Irrespective of whether inquiries have been made and further documents have been submitted, the next step is to *receive a result*. One difference to e-commerce is this result of a service, that is, the notification. The public administration has made a decision based on the information provided and the citizen now receives this decision. In the positive case, the applicant receives the requested service. This can be a unique action such as issuing a certificate of good conduct or regular actions such as paying housing benefits. In contrast to e-commerce, where the purchase of a product is less frequently refused, the negative case of an application not being granted can occur more frequently in e-government. Of course, purchases can also be refused in the private sector, for example in insurance companies. However, these are exceptions when considering the entire private sector. In addition, customers in e-commerce often receive the product immediately after purchase; in the case of public services, the notification is issued only after the application has been examined in detail. Here, too, there are exceptions in the private sector, such as online shopping, and administrations can also transmit documents automatically and immediately online after the application was submitted such as resident parking permits. The result is received in person, by mail or by electronic means.

The next step is the *use of the result*. Citizens can use a notification and the according permissions, for example, to travel (passport), send a child to school (school registration) or invest the payments received (child benefit). Although this step is similar to the corresponding step in a customer journey [23], the use in a citizen journey is different. Public services often refer to a special entitlement and citizens cannot choose between different service providers and, therefore, the relevance for future 'buying' decisions is comparatively low. Since a service is not always granted, this step is optional in a citizen journey. Citizens might also decline to use the permissions granted. For instance, a citizen might receive a building permit but then he or she declines to construct a building.

Finally, the applicants can *give feedback* to the public administration, for example on the quality of the service or user satisfaction. Citizens can point out weaknesses in the process and provide ideas on improvements to the service. Additionally, inquiries regarding the individual notification, its understandability and use can be part of the feedback. In contrast to e-commerce, results of public services are more difficult to return and reverse. For example, it is more difficult to cancel a divorce than to return a product to an online retailer. Nevertheless, a citizen may wish to appeal against an administrative decision. This takes the form of a new citizen journey, i.e. an objection or appeal triggers a new citizen journey.

4.2 Evaluation

During the first evaluation with the focus group, the participants evaluated the citizen journey overall positively. They rated the general approach of a citizen journey as valuable and highly relevant as it facilitates a better understanding of administrative processes from the citizens' perspective. The participants argued on basis of their daily routine in which they often face citizens who have problems to understand the administrative processes. Here, a citizen journey would provide guidance for applicants to indicate in which sequence to receive a certain service. Moreover, the actual sequence of the initial citizen journey was rated as a good approximation to the real-world phenomenon as summarized by one interviewee: *"Well, I actually think, it all fits to get an understanding of [the process]."* Especially, the preparation phase offered little room for controversies as the participants commonly agreed on the three suggested steps.

The discussion also revealed some inaccuracies in the concrete sequence and completeness of steps in phases two and three. For the practitioners, the lack of an authentication step in the application phase was crucial and criticized. Here, the participants argued for the importance of authentication in public administration being mandatory in numerous service delivery processes. Consequently, we adopted this suggestion as an optional substep since not every service requires the citizen's authentication.

Additionally, it turned out that the steps of the result phase needed some redesign. The interviewees argued that in most cases the service delivery process is not finished with the result, i.e. the actual service delivery and its usage. After receiving the result and using it, two distinct kinds of feedback could arise depending on the legal quality: first, feedbacks could occur that are legally irrelevant acts such as claims, simple requests and other statements. This step was incorporated as a final step in the result phase after the first evaluation. Second, feedback can occur in terms of legal means to challenge a certain public service, such as legal objections or appeals. This underpins the relation to subsequent citizen journeys since concrete legal actions would trigger a new citizen journey as outlined in Sect. 4.1.

Furthermore, our first plain design of the citizen journey stimulated a discussion on the visual representation and possible embedding into websites. The participants suggested to design the journey comparably to a pathway that leads citizens through the process of consuming a public service. We did not follow suggestions to implement the citizen journey into a website or app as this suggestion is out of scope of our research.

After the first evaluation and re-design of the original journey, citizens were asked for their experiences with public service delivery and their evaluation of our re-designed citizen journey. Again, the overall feedback was positive. More than half of the respondents (26) stated that they would not change the citizen journey and overall experienced the service process as depicted.

Most of those who did experience the service delivery process differently reported differences for the preparation phase and the result phase. Thus, we applied changes to both phases in the second re-design of the citizen journey. Based on the insights gained through the survey, the step to choose a channel in the preparation phase was made optional as for some services citizens reported to have no choice after all because the requested services are simply not provided electronically. For the result phase, we added the channel choice to this phase, because citizens can decide how they want to make inquiries or give feedback irrespective of the channel used in the phases one and two.

However, the most obvious and profound change resulting from the survey was the visual depiction of our journey. Nearly all surveyed citizens stated that they perceived the original visualization as complex and not easy to understand. As this aspect was also raised in the focus group interview, the design of the citizen journey was changed to the pathway shown in Fig. 1.

5 Discussion and Conclusion

This paper contributes a generic citizen journey that depicts the steps of public service delivery from the citizens' perspective. We developed the citizen journey for transactional public services based on a customer journey from the private sector. The citizen journey was assessed in two subsequent evaluations with public servants and citizens. The results from the evaluations indicate the journey's general usefulness. Additionally, we used the feedback from the focus group and survey to improve the journey.

Our citizen journey provides implications for research and practice. Researchers benefit from our journey through a better understanding of the service delivery process and the different steps that could impact the citizens' experience. The journey can also be used to classify research endeavors and even trigger further research activities on those steps that are crucial for the citizen experience. For instance, the citizen journey can be used to identify how public administrations can design the service delivery process at the citizens' convenience. Additionally, through our citizen journey's derivation from a customer journey, researchers gain a better understanding of the differences between the private and public sectors and how they are reflected in citizen interactions.

Practitioners can use our citizen journey to design their services under specific consideration of their citizens' needs. It enables a more efficient co-design with citizens since a new citizen journey does not need to be developed from scratch for each service. Instead, our citizen journey can be reused for the various transactional services in a public administration. The journey serves as a basis for the design of artefacts that are relevant to its individual steps such as websites, apps and forms. The citizen journey is not only useful for service design but also during the actual service delivery. Citizens are often confused and do not know how public services work and what they need to do. Public administrations can use the citizen journey to explain how the delivery process for a certain service works. The citizen journey depicts the most relevant steps that need to be undertaken. Enriched with service-specific information, it could also yield information on which fees need to be paid, which documents need to be submitted, and who is responsible for the service. In consequence, we incorporated both stakeholder groups—public servants and citizens—into the evaluation of our citizen journey so it is constructed in a way that it becomes useful and understandable for public servants during service design and for citizens during service delivery.

Our work has also limitations and potential for future work. First, our citizen journey serves as a general blueprint for public services. We are aware that our journey might abstract from some details and specific cases, for instance when it comes to the differences between the public and private sector. However, we did not aim for covering all specifics since we intended to provide a citizen journey that is applicable to a wide range of transactional services. Therefore, slide adaptions might be necessary in exceptional cases if a public administration applies the journey to its services due to different kinds of administrations and services. Second, our journey focuses only on transactional services and the citizen journey might look different for other kinds of services such as participatory services. Future work could design citizen journeys for other kinds of services. Third, researchers can extend the citizen journey to more advanced models of public service delivery such as the no-stop shop [36, 37] where the citizen does not perform any action until she or he receives the notification. Fourth, researchers can undertake further evaluations with more citizens and public servants.

Despite these limitations and ideas for future work, we believe that our citizen journey constitutes a further step towards more citizen-centric operations in public administrations.

References

1. Akkaya, C., Wolf, P., Krcmar, H.: A comprehensive analysis of e-government adoption in the german household. In: Proceedings of the 11th International Conference on Wirtschaftsinformatik, Leipzig, pp. 1525–1539 (2013)
2. Anastasopoulou, K., Kokolakis, S.: Exploring citizens' intention to use e-government services: the role of cultural bias. Int. J. Electron. Gov. 6, 3–19 (2013)
3. Belanche, D., Casaló, L.V., Flavián, C.: Integrating trust and personal values into the technology acceptance model: the case of e-government services adoption. Cuad. Econ. y Dir. la Empres. 15, 192–204 (2012)
4. Rana, N.P., Dwivedi, Y.K.: Citizen's adoption of an e-government system: validating extended social cognitive theory (SCT). Gov. Inf. Q. 32, 172–181 (2015)
5. Klischewski, R., Lessa, L.: Sustainability of e-government success: an integrated research agenda. In: Gil-Garcia, J.R. (ed.) E-Government Success Factors and Measures: Theories, Concepts, and Methodologies, pp. 104–123. IGI Global (2013)
6. Richardson, A.: Using customer journey maps to improve customer experience. Harv. Bus. Rev. 15, 2–5 (2010)
7. Schmitt, B.H.: Customer Experience Management: A Revolutionary Approach to Connecting with Your Customers. Wiley, Hoboken (2003)
8. Stickdorn, M., Schneider, J.: This is Service Design Thinking. Basics - Tools - Cases. BIS Publishers, Amsterdam (2012)
9. Norton, D.W., Pine, B.J.: Using the customer journey to road test and refine the business model. Strateg. Leadersh. 41, 12–17 (2013)

10. Kaliontzoglou, A., Sklavos, P., Karantjias, T., Polemi, D.: A secure e-Government platform architecture for small to medium sized public organizations. Electron. Commer. Res. Appl. **4**, 174–186 (2005)

11. Danish Ministry of Finance. Local government Denmark and Danish regions: a stronger and more secure digital Denmark: Digital Strategy 2016–2020, Copenhagen (2016)

12. United Nations: United Nations e-government survey 2016 - e-government in support of sustainable development, New York (2016)

13. Cordes, C.: Mapping the user journey. https://www.digital.govt.nz/blog/mapping-the-user-journey/. Accessed 27 Mar 2020

14. Department of the Prime Minister and Cabinet New Zealand: journey mapping. https://dpmc.govt.nz/our-programmes/policy-project/policy-methods-toolbox/design-thinking/journey-mapping. Accessed 27 Mar 2020

15. State Government Victoria, bienalto, Huddle: Designing better government information and services: a service design toolkit for government. https://www.vic.gov.au/sites/default/files/2018-12/Designing_better_government_information_services_report.pdf. Accessed 27 Mar 2020

16. Ivey-Williams, K.: Why we use user journey maps in government. https://designnotes.blog.gov.uk/2016/03/30/why-we-use-user-journey-maps-in-government/. Accessed 27 Mar 2020

17. CX CAP Goal Team: Mapping the cross-agency customer experience journey. https://www.performance.gov/mapping-cx-journey/. Accessed 27 Mar 2020

18. Seufert, S., Meier, C.: From eLearning to digital transformation: a framework and implications for L&D. Int. J. Adv. Corp. Learn. **9**, 27–33 (2016)

19. Trischler, J., Scott, D.R.: Designing public services: the usefulness of three service design methods for identifying user experiences. Public Manag. Rev. **18**, 718–739 (2016)

20. Parker, S., Heapy, J.: The Journey to the Interface. How Public Service Design can Connect Users to Reform. Demos, London (2006)

21. Crosier, A., Handford, A.: Customer journey mapping as an advocacy tool for disabled people: a case study. Soc. Mar. Q. **18**, 67–76 (2012)

22. Følstad, A., Kvale, K.: Customer journeys: a systematic literature review. J. Serv. Theory Pract. **28**, 196–227 (2018)

23. Lemon, K.N., Verhoef, P.C.: Understanding customer experience throughout the customer journey. J. Mark. **80**, 69–96 (2016)

24. Bryson, J.M., Crosby, B.C., Bloomberg, L.: Public value governance: moving beyond traditional public administration and the new public management. Public Adm. Rev. **74**, 445–456 (2014)

25. Lehtonen, M., Tuominen, T.: Multiple voices of the user in public sector services. In: Sundbo, J., Toivonen, M. (eds.) User-Based Innovation in Services, pp. 227–250. Edward Elgar, Cheltenham and Northampton (2011)

26. Distel, B., Lindgren, I.: Who are the users of digital public services? In: Panagiotopoulos, P., et al. (eds.) ePart 2019. LNCS, vol. 11686, pp. 117–129. Springer, Cham (2019). https://doi.org/10.1007/978-3-030-27397-2_10

27. Araujo, R., Taher, Y., van den Heuvel, W.-J., Cappelli, C.: Evolving government-citizen ties in public service design and delivery. In: Electronic Government and Electronic Participation - Joint Proceedings of Ongoing Research of IFIP EGOV and IFIP ePart 2013, pp. 19–26. Gesellschaft für Informatik e.V., Bonn (2013)

28. Nenonen, S., Rasila, H., Junnonen, J.-M., Kärnä, S.: Customer journey – a method to investigate user experience. In: Proceedings of the Euro FM Conference, Manchester, pp. 54–63 (2008)

29. Jaakkola, E., Helkkula, A., Aarikka-Stenroos, L.: Service experience co-creation: conceptualization, implications, and future research directions. J. Serv. Manag. **26**, 182–205 (2015)

30. Hevner, A.R., March, S.T., Park, J., Ram, S.: Design science in information systems research. MIS Q. **28**, 75–105 (2004)
31. Österle, H., et al.: Memorandum on design-oriented information systems research. Eur. J. Inf. Syst. **20**, 7–10 (2011)
32. Goldkuhl, G.: What does it mean to serve the citizen in e-services? - towards a practical theory founded in socio-instrumental pragmatism. Int. J. Public Inf. Syst. **3**, 135–159 (2007)
33. Goldkuhl, G.: Generic regulation model: the evolution of a practical theory for e-government. Transform. Gov. People Process Policy **5**, 249–267 (2011)
34. Greunz, M., Schopp, B., Haes, J.: Integrating e-government infrastructures through secure xml document containers. In: Proceedings of the 34th Hawaii International Conference on System Sciences (HICSS 2001), Wailea (2001)
35. Bozeman, B.: All Organizations are Public: Bridging Public and Private Organizational Theories. Jossey-Bass, London (1987)
36. Scholta, H., Mertens, W., Kowalkiewicz, M., Becker, J.: From one-stop shop to no-stop shop: an e-government stage model. Gov. Inf. Q. **36**, 11–26 (2019)
37. Scholta, H., Lindgren, I.: The long and winding road of digital public services—one next step: proactivity. In: Proceedings of the 40th International Conference on Information Systems (ICIS 2019), Munich (2019)

The Role of Domain-Skills in Bureaucratic Service Encounters

Søren Skaarup[(✉)]

IT University of Copenhagen, Rued Langgaardsvej 7, 2300 Copenhagen, DK, Denmark
skaa@itu.dk

Abstract. Citizens are increasingly expected and even required to go online for much of their interaction with government, making the skills citizens bring to these encounters particularly important. Several skillsets for the use of online resources have been proposed in the general e-government literature. However, few empirical studies explore the experiences and strategies of citizens themselves related to the role of skills in their interaction with government. Consequently, there is a gap in the knowledge regarding which skills are specifically relevant when dealing with *government* online. To explore this gap, this paper presents a qualitative analysis of interviews with citizens in Danish municipal service centres. The analysis takes its departure in a review of the literature that addresses aspects of skills relevant for the (digital) citizen-government encounter. The paper contributes to the e-government literature, by introducing the concept of domain-skills as a central skill set for citizen self-service. Domain-skills constitute a scaffolding citizens can build on, when looking for and interpreting information and contextualizing it to their situation, making it easier for them to act on their own, with confidence.

Keywords: Citizen · e-government · Skills

1 Introduction

1.1 Background

Every year, millions of encounters take place between citizens and public authorities administering the services and benefits of the welfare state, be it face-to-face, by phone, e-mail, chat, video, or via self-service-systems. These "bureaucratic service encounters" [22] or "BSEs," are the primary context for contacts between citizens and authorities; it is here, authority comes to life.

In recent years, it has become mandatory for citizens in Denmark to conduct almost all text-based communication with authorities online. At the same time, access to other channels (phone and face-to-face) has been restricted in several areas, all putting a stronger emphasis on citizens' abilities to do things on their own online – to a certain extent having to become their own caseworkers [31]. Similar changes are taking place in other countries. In the face of these changes, the skills the citizens bring to the encounter acquire additional importance [27].

© IFIP International Federation for Information Processing 2020
Published by Springer Nature Switzerland AG 2020
G. Viale Pereira et al. (Eds.): EGOV 2020, LNCS 12219, pp. 179–196, 2020.
https://doi.org/10.1007/978-3-030-57599-1_14

The question of general ICT- or "internet" skills has been studied extensively in the e-government field [4, 19, 21, 45, 46]. However, little focus has been given to what skills might be specifically relevant to the situations where citizen encounter *government* online, and how these skills might affect citizens' strategies for these encounters. To address this gap, this paper analyses a large corpus of interviews with Danish citizens in the context of actual encounters with government.

The study offers an empirical contribution based on a detailed study of citizens' accounts of their experiences and strategies in relation to BSEs, as well as a theoretical contribution to the e-government literature by establishing a category of "Domain-skills" of specific relevance to the BSE.

1.2   Research Question

The overall research question guiding the study presented here is *how skills of particular relevance for the BSE, manifest themselves in citizens' experiences with and strategies for the encounter, above and beyond general skills related to the use of ICT.*

Exploring this question through an approach inspired by grounded theory [9, 10], this paper addresses the general call for research within the e-government field, that takes a clear citizen perspective and investigates how citizens perceive public sector digitalization and its effects [20, 24, 27, 39, 41].

This paper is structured as follows: Sect. 2 presents related research in order to further identify and describe the gap this paper aims to address. Section 3 presents the method for data creation and the analytical strategy. Section 4 presents the findings of the study, and Sect. 5 discusses these findings in relation to previous research. Finally, Sect. 6 presents concluding remarks, reflections on the limitations of the study, and suggestions for future research.

2   Related Research

The skill-gap has generally been addressed in the e-government literature as an aspect of a "digital divide" [12], construed as a matter of ICT skills [21, 45]. The skill-gap is usually linked to demographic factors such as age, education, employment, or disabilities [5, 13, 34, 37].

Empirical studies show that access and digital skills are not the only skills relevant to the BSE [28, 29]. A recent framework, suggested by Van Deursen, Helsper, and Eynon [46], based on a review of the literature, establish an Internet skills framework consisting of five types of skills. The basic technical skills to 1) use the internet and 2) use mobile technology, 3) Information navigation skills, related to searching, findings, selecting and evaluating sources of information, 4) Social skills, related to using online communication and social media, 4) Creative skills, related to content creation. The skills described in this framework are general-purpose skills applicable to the general use of digital devices, the internet, and social media. They do not address or purport to address, skills specifically relevant for the BSE.

Also, frameworks like this do not address the social and cognitive capacities involved in using technology for specific ends [8], the importance of having the understanding, and the capacity to "engage" and solve a problem [3, 4, 12]. Van Deursen and Van Dijk argue that such "cognitive resources …are largely responsible for differences in internet use and in the digital skills of different educational groups" [46:897] (they do not, however, elaborate on what these resources might entail). The Danish Technological Institute defines cognitive skills as reading/writing, problem-solving, spatial, visual, and mathematical skills. They concern "the ability to understand and interpret a given interaction or task in its context" [44] (my translation); this includes interpreting information, acting on it, and understanding the implications.

Two sets of skills then, apart from ICT-related skills, could be important for citizens successfully to engage in BSEs: 1) Skills of particular relevance for the BSE context and 2) social and cognitive skills. This paper focuses on the former.

2.1 Skills of Particular Relevance for the BSE Context

Gordon [18] suggests that "bureaucratic competence" is important for citizens' success with their BSEs. This entails knowing one's rights and mastering the formal aspects of bureaucracy (terminology, forms, documents), putting things in writing, the ability to handle the citizens part of the bureaucratic processes, and knowledge of how the system works. These skills are not explicitly tied to the use of technology but to the navigation of the bureaucratic context. Grönlund, Hatakka and Ask [19] use the term "administrative literacy," which they describe as the ability to understand and navigate bureaucracy, having a general idea how the institutions of society work, understanding the terminology applied by the authorities, knowing where to go for information and services, and understanding the information and being able to act on it. Bertot and Jaeger [6] use the term "Government literacy," which they describe as understanding the structure of government.

Bureaucratic competence/administrative literacy/government literacy (henceforth: "bureaucratic skills") are all described as general skills, in principle applicable to any citizen-government interaction. However, "government" covers many agencies delivering a wide range of services based on a comprehensive set of rules and regulations. Even more specific skills might be necessary for specific contexts.

Byström and Järvelin [7:195–196] divide the information needs for *professionals* in public administration when serving citizens into 1) Problem information: "describes the structure, properties, and requirements of the problem at hand." 2) Domain Information:" consists of known facts, concepts, laws, and theories in the domain of the problem," 3) Problem-solving information:" covers the methods of problem treatment." In a self-service context, citizens are expected to some extent to be their own caseworkers [28], and thus presumably to have and handle similar information needs. Seen from a citizen/skills perspective, this entails: 1) having a sufficient understanding of their problem and situation, 2) having a sufficient general understanding of government and bureaucracy (general bureaucratic skills) as well as a 3) a specific understanding of the particular rules and procedures relevant to the service in question (specific bureaucratic skills), and 4) knowing how to act in a relevant way in the situation, including searching for the right information in the first place.

Borrowing the meaning of the concept "domain" from cognitive linguistics, I propose to call these contextual and contextualizing skills, in a citizen context, "domain-skills."

In cognitive linguistics, words and concepts are understood with respect to domains of experience. A domain "represents a schematization of experience," which "relates elements and entities associated with a particular culturally-embedded scene, situation or event" [14:211]. It provides background information against which concepts can be understood and used. In cognitive linguistics, domains are interpretive contexts for words and phrases, I will here use the term in an expanded sense, as the interpretive frame for the information and tasks the citizens face in BSEs.

This set of skills, together with cognitive skills and ICT skills, arguably constitute the foundation for citizens to do things on their own online with government. However, the importance and meaning of such skills has not been studied in the context of citizens' choices and strategies in the face of actual bureaucratic service encounters.

The next section outlines the methods for exploring this issue, followed by a discussion of the findings.

3 Methods

The paper is based on an analysis of 332 interviews with citizens in citizens service centres, jobcentres, and benefits-centres in Denmark, conducted between 2010 and 2014. The data was generated as research for the author's Ph.D. thesis [42].

In order to explore citizens' experiences, perspectives, and strategies as close to actual encounters as possible, the study applied an" ethnographically informed" approach [11], drawing on key elements of ethnographical work: a long-term presence in the physical context where encounters take place, and a sensitivity to the life-world of the participants [47].

These experiences were explored through semi-structured interviews [25] with citizens onsite at municipal citizen service centres, benefit centres, and job centres, and by phone with citizens who had recently conducted a digital BSE. The interviews were supplemented by observations of face-to-face encounters, and of digital encounters in which citizens completed their online applications at the service centres.

Alvesson [2] expresses scepticism about the use of interviews to investigate the way participants create meaning. The risk is, he argues that their statements will be too much influenced by the interview situation and context, and by the cultural scripts about how one normally expresses oneself about specific topics. Participants in interviews may be expected to behave "appropriately" when confronted with someone with the special status of "researcher" [36]. They will try to cast themselves in a positive light. Also, participants may often be asked to discuss matters about which they may never have expressed any explicit thoughts or discussed previously. Here they draw not only on the discourse they immediately connect with the themes introduced by the interviewer but also on the "cues" given in the conversation – which frames the discourse in a specific way [15:72]. As a researcher, I attempted to counter this by being an attentive and appreciative conversation partner, to establish a rapport that allowed me also to ask questions that went beyond any" appropriate" answers, and by attempting to frame my inquiry as openly as possible and to be sensitive to and follow up on the framing the citizen herself applied.

Finally, I have attempted to counter possible framing effects by triangulating with other data sources [40]. One the one hand, knowledge from conversations with other participants in the study who had different backgrounds, were in different situations, and were reflecting on different experiences. On the other hand, my knowledge about the situation and the field based on five years as head of a citizen service centre. This enabled me, as Allina-Pisano puts it, to "distinguish ritual talk which captures the zeitgeist, from talk which deals with specific experiences" [1:70].

3.1 Selection of Participants and Sites

The aim has been to capture the difference in participants' backgrounds, attitudes, age, level of education, etc., as well as, as much variation as possible, in situations, experiences, motives, and strategies regarding the service-encounter [33, 43]. This aim has been achieved not by an elaborate sampling strategy, but by casting a wide net, basically through the selection of sites (municipalities and service-centres) for the fieldwork. The sites were strategically selected [16:475] to represent a broad range of services and citizens and to reflect different types of municipalities. Interviews were conducted in four municipalities, at citizen service centres with a broad range of services, as well as in benefits-centres and jobcentres. The sites were located in a large city, two municipalities in more rural areas, and a suburban municipality. Citizens with business in the service centres were approached when they left the centre or immediately after they had been served. Some had not had business relevant to this study, and of those who had, few declined to participate. There is no obvious pattern to those that declined.

The participants' business with the authority represented the whole range of services available at the sites in question with an overrepresentation of housing-benefit, pension, and taxes – all services that are often considered complex and are often consequential for the citizen. With a few notable exceptions, the participants reflect the general Danish population at the time, with regards to the distribution of age, level of education, general internet use, use of home banking, and experience with doing their taxes online (see appendix 1 for more details on the profile of the municipalities and the participants.

Younger participants (age 18–29), participants around the age of retirement (age 65–69), and participants with a high-school level education are overrepresented. Thus the study primarily represents the perspective of citizens with a shorter-level education, and in life-phases where context with authorities are more frequent and where most of the dealings with government are in situations, the citizen has never encountered before – the very situations where domain-skills may be most challenged. However, challenges with domain-skills are found in the study for citizens of all ages and all levels of education, indicating that domain-skills may be important to all citizens.

3.2 Analytical Strategy

The transcribed interviews in themselves constitute small "stories" about participants' experiences and attitudes, their motives, goals, and strategies. These stories are kept "alive" by exploiting and profiling what Gee [17] calls the "poetic" aspects of language; that is, drawing on the information that the spoken language contains, but which is often filtered out in transcriptions. This entails dividing the text into lines, which serve to emphasize the structure of the spoken account, its rhythm, intonation, and pauses. The text is used verbatim but sometimes abbreviated, with a minimum of contextual information (inserted in square brackets) where necessary to provide context. This reduction is not "innocent," even though it is based on "clues" in the spoken language. It is in itself an interpretation and frames the accounts in a particular way. The analysis itself has therefore been carried out on the reduced version with continuous consultation of the full transcript to ensure that this framing did not introduce problematic biases.

The coding was divided into three steps, roughly following Layder's [26] method of "adaptive coding," which again is inspired by the principles of coding espoused in grounded theory [9, 10]. The perspectives on domain-skills presented in the next section emerged from this analysis.

4 Results

This section presents the findings and answers to the research question. The findings are presented according to the five perspectives on domain-skills generated by the analysis (Table 1).

Table 1. Five perspectives on situation-related skills

1. Experience with the situation and context
2. The language used by government online
3. The basic understanding needed to search for and evaluate information
4. The role of other skills in handling things with government on your own
5. The effect of domain-skills on the citizen's sense of control and identity

4.1 Experience with the Situation and Context

When you have never been in a similar situation before and have no experience with a service or benefit or with the municipality in general, it may, as Anette, Naja, and Dan explains (all quotes in Table 2), be challenging to understand the information you find and what to do with it. Or you may, as Karen, have been in this situation before, but it is too long ago for you to remember how things went on (and rules and procedures may have changed since then). However, as Naja explains, when you do have the experience, it may be a lot easier to do things on your own. Anette emphasizes the importance of a sufficient understanding in the situation she is in. This is present in many of the participants' accounts: the nature of the situation and the importance of the information for handling the situation affects the importance of a perceived lack of skills.

Table 2. Insufficient experience with the situation and context (The quotes are presented in poetically reduced form. "/" indicates a line break, "//" indicates a stanza break, ... indicates passages that are left out. "[ ]" indicates contextual information from the rest of the interview. Participants are given fictitious names that reflects their gender and age. All quotes are translated form Danish by the author with an aim of preserving the tone and "spoken language" style of the participants).

Unfamiliar situation	"It is difficult for me to understand these things/because its all very new to me/there is so much I need to understand about tax/and how it works/I have very little knowledge about this .../and it was important for me to understand it" (Anette, 43, taxes)
No experience	"I know nothing about this subject/I have no experience/so ... it's more efficient/to have face-to-face contact/But if I know what to go for/and what to look for online/then I go online" (Naja, 46, supplementary social benefit)
Little contact with municipality	"I am very rarely in touch with the municipality/I don't know all them there rules and such/that's why sometimes/I find it easier to come here/because I'd be damned if I understand all those things/things I have never really tried before" (Dan, 42, housing benefit)
Recent experience important	"Even though I have tried to apply before/it's all so far away/that you really have no idea/what's actually going on/then it's out of your hands/you know" (Karen, 39, Social security)

4.2 The Language Used by Government Online

Bureaucratic language and vocabulary may add to the challenges of an unfamiliar situation. The authorities use, as Vibeke puts it, "mysterious words" (all quotes in Table 3), which make the exact meaning unclear and ambiguous. Frederikke, who studies communication at the university and should be reasonably adept at understating complex texts,

Table 3. Inaccessible language online

Paragraph-speak	"It's in paragraph-speak much of it/So you really have to concentrate/and I found it really hard to figure out" (Frederikke, 20, taxes)
Unknown terminology	"I am quite good with computers/but.. [online]/Often I find that they use mysterious words/and then you don't know exactly what they mean" (Vibeke, 31, social security)
Strange language	"I am pretty good at languages/but this language/The language that they use in the public sector/it's some kind of higher-level math/equations with three unknowns" (Valdemar, 71, tax, pension, housing benefit)

calls it "paragraph-speech." Valdemar, an elderly much read gentleman who prides himself of his knowledge of languages, likens government language to "equations with three unknowns."

4.3 The Basic Understanding Needed to Search for and Evaluate Information

As Rebecca describes it (quotes in Table 4), figuring things out online is a question of having sufficient knowledge and experience to provide a mental map or scaffolding you can build on when you encounter new information, having this, not only makes it easier for you to understand information but also to say the right things and ask the right questions. However, as Lærke explains, if you have no idea what it is about, you have no idea where to start. Ingelise's account shows how educational background and work experience may also contribute to situation-relevant skills, but also that this has its limits. She finds tasks that are heavily focused on financial information reasonably easy to do on her own, but tasks that she cannot build on her experiences are much more challenging to do. This indicates that the amount of transfer between different contexts may be limited. One thing is to understand the language and the rules in principle; another is to understand their relevance and applicability for the context – for the situation the individual citizen is in, right now, as Helle explains. What are my rights, obligations, and possibilities? A mapping from general rules to a specific situation is often challenging to do without sufficient situation-relevant skills. Without such skills, you have to guess – or as Lasse puts it – "read between the lines" to establish a sufficient understanding, and there is, as Lasse explains, no guarantee that you will succeed.

Table 4. No place to start/nothing to build on to search for and evaluate information

Knowledge to build on	"It's complicated, isn't it/You don't have the knowledge necessary to learn about it/and you don't know what you can say/if you are not used to it" (Rebecca, 19, housing benefit)
A place to start	"I can't figure taxes out/it's the only thing I can't figure out/everything else is under control/I have no idea what it's about/I have no idea where to start" (Lærke, 29, housing benefit)
Limited transfer-ability	"I find it hard to understand all that/what I may, and may not do/and how they do it/and what it means to me" (Ingelise, 65, housing benefit)
A basis for contextualization	"Often what they write is very technical/So you can't understand what they write/You would like a better explanation/and to understand in what context it [the different rules] is important/and things like that" (Helle, 64, Pension)
Reading between the lines	"And then [when face to face] you can look them in the eye/and get better guidance/rather than have having to read it/and what it says between the lines/and having to do it over and over/it's easier to be at the right place at the right time" (Lasse, housing benefit, deposit-loan, change of address)

4.4   The Volume and Complexity of Information Online

The sense of complexity as an issue in the BSE is already present in the accounts quoted above. In some accounts, complexity raises the bar on what skills are necessary to master the situation; in others, a lack of situation-relevant skills appears to induce a sense of complexity to the situation and the information. As Dan's account shows (all quotes in Table 5), when you lack situation-relevant-skills, it is difficult to filter the information you get into what is relevant and what is not, and this makes it difficult to manage the self-service process.

The situation itself may add to the complexity, when, as in Ronja's case (she just had a child), there are many things you have to take care of and what you should do and the order of doing things you should follow may be difficult to carve out of a large amount of information and possibilities. This theme is repeated in Charlotte's account, it is difficult for her to find out where to go, in the face of a multitude of options, because she has no situationally relevant "map" of who does what and where to go for what services, online.

Rikke's account outlines the strategy participants most frequently apply when they feel their skills are insufficient: establishing a framework or scaffolding through dialogue with someone with authoritative, professional knowledge of the matter. This was a frequent observation at the counters during my fieldwork: how citizens could start with very little information, even with a very vague idea of what they needed to know or wanted to do, and through a dialogue with the staff-member, gradually construct a (shared) and contextualized framework for understanding what was necessary to proceed. Such a dialogue is not merely an exchange of questions and answers, but a mutual construction

Table 5. Overwhelming amounts of information and complexity online

Lots of information	"I have tried to apply for housing-benefit online/There are so many, many things you have to know/And where to start/And lots and lots of information/And then I have to click on that/And then this thing pops up And how am I going to proceed from there?" (Dan, 42, housing-benefit)
Difficult to find your way online	"I have been to the website/but I found it a bit confusing/where to go and [what to do]/there is so much information there" (Ronja, 27, Housing benefit)
Public sector complicated	"The public sector is very complicated/You have to look under a lot of things Before you find what [you need]/And then/You often end up in the wrong place" (Charlotte, 45, taxes)
Dialogue a way to de-complicate	"It gets too complicated/when there is no one to ask/and get some guidance from/about the rules you have to know/if you want a benefit or help or something/To appear in person/and ask a lot of questions/has always worked for me" (Rikke, 20, medicine supplement)

of a shared understanding and the sharedness of this understanding contributes to making it safer for the citizen to proceed on her own afterward, at the same time being both empowering and assuring [42].

4.5   The Role of Other Skills in Handling Things with Government

Even when you consider yourself good at understanding things (like Valdemar) or good at using a computer (like Ellen) or have a strong educational background (like Frederikke and Charlotte), understanding government information and procedures online can be a challenge, indicating that situation-relevant skills are indeed something separate from cognitive skills and ICT skills.

Table 6. Other skills insufficient for handling things on your own

Computer skills not sufficient	"I need help with all these strange questions/interest, and dividends and all that stuff/it's all Greek to me/I sure as hell never did my tax-returns/or things like that/I really have no idea about things like that/I really don't" (Ellen, 65, pension)
Education not sufficient	"I am extremely bad at figuring out tax stuff/I have had a huge bill from the taxman before/And I don't want that again/I am well-educated and have a challenging job/I should be able to figure out my own taxes/But I can't/It's very opaque" (Charlotte, 41, Taxes)

4.6   The Effect of Domain-Skills on the Citizen's Sense of Control and Identity

Karen and Charlotte (quoted above in Table 2 and Table 6) describe another aspect of the effects of a lack of understanding: a sense of insufficiency, of diminished control and autonomy. For Vibeke (quoted above in Table 3), her lack of understanding is especially problematic because she has low trust in the authorities and lack of understanding may contribute to a lack of control and a lack of power vis a vis the authority[1].

The theme of lack of control is also prevalent in Anne's account (Table 7 below), where it is coupled with a sense of doing the right thing, being seen as a good citizen, and not a "social fraud." This is a strong theme in many interviews with participants who apply for social security, but also, as in Anne's case, for participants who are not under the stigma of being a "social benefit-recipient," but who feel intimidated by the discourse often connected with making mistakes in applications and filings, framing it as "cheating." Anne likes to be in control and project competence, and that is hard if you feel that you do not know what you are doing. She feels that she is being tested. She falls short when she does not understand what she is supposed to do and make mistakes. For Anne, it is a matter of identity, of being recognized as a good and worthy citizen, who follows the rules and does what is expected of her.

---

[1] This information is from the interview, but not part of the quote.

Table 7. Insufficient situation-relevant skills may affect a sense of control and identity

Control, identity	"I simply can't/when you read those descriptions/on the tax-website/I can read those rules five times/and I still don't understand.
	I like to be in control of things/I I don't feel that I am in control/If I don't understand what I am doing
	It's this feeling/that I understand completely which box to check/but if you feel that/no matter how many times you read it/you could still check all four boxes/checking the right box/is like passing an exam/proving that you have understood
	And you quickly gets to feel like some kind of fraud/when you cant explain what you are doing/and that's not a very nice feeling/So it's personal in a way/you want to be a law-abiding citizen/its a matter of honour to do things right/and its extremely important for me/no doubt about that"
	(Anne, 28, taxes)

5 Discussion

The analysis confirms previous findings that access and digital skills are not sufficient for handling the BSE [29, 31]. The skills the participants describe, include the basic bureaucratic competencies of knowing and understanding the rules and procedures, understanding bureaucratic language, and engaging in bureaucratic processes (as described by [6, 18, 19], but also the ability to draw on previous experiences to establish a frame for understanding information and procedures, and the skills required to grasp what is situationally important of this bureaucratic frame and to apply this in relation to the situation, needs, and resources at hand.

With no similar or sufficiently similar experiences to draw on, it can be hard to seek, interpret, and act on information with confidence. When looking for government information online, you have to know what you are looking for and, without sufficient skills, it may be difficult to identify and formulate the right questions, and you may easily end up using the "wrong" search terms.

Citizens need a basic scaffolding or frame for seeking, interpreting, contextualizing, and applying information. This scaffold creates a mental map that serves as a guide for how to proceed in the situation.

Based on this analysis, the following definition of "Domain-skills" is proposed:

Domain-skills are the ability to look for and, to the extent necessary, understand and meaningfully apply information (e.g., concepts, rules), procedures and roles, drawing on the contextual knowledge provided by relevant previous experiences (with the same or similar situations or authority or with the same or similar services), as well as by a general understanding of the workings and norms of bureaucracy and government, including basic knowledge of who does what and where to go for information and services.

The participants' accounts show how the nature of the situation may accentuate the importance of sufficient domain-skills. When something is at stake – substantially or identity-related, in situations of high uncertainty or high vulnerability, it becomes extra important to have a sufficient understanding and to do things correctly to be a "good citizen," project competence and gain recognition. A lack of domain-skills is then more than a merely practical issue, which may confound an application process, or a substantial issue which may determine whether you get a benefit or not, but also a matter of identity, recognition, and self-worth, and a sense of self-efficacy.

Another driver of the need for domain-skills, as well as a source of a sense of insufficient domain-skills, is the perceived complexity of the situation, information, and procedures, as discussed by Pieterson [38]. The sense of complexity is driven by the amount of information and complex language, as well as how many tasks and authorities are involved in the situation and how complex the whole task-journey is.

Several of the accounts show how dialogue can be important to establish the domain-framework. Dialogue creates a shared understanding which provides a safe platform from which to proceed, and this shared understanding assures the citizen in her understanding.

As Helbig et al. [21] argue, different skills should not be understood as discrete and independent, but as interacting and recursive. Domain-skills are closely related and can sometimes be hard to separate from cognitive and ICT skills. Difficulties in reading and writing may be the underlying causes of deficient domain-skills – or of difficulties in acquiring the necessary skills. What participants themselves may identify as lack of the necessary ICT skills may, in fact, often be the lack of domain-skills – as evidenced by them being otherwise digitally active and competent.

Domain-skills may be acquired through experience, education or work, or from family and friends. As demonstrated by previous studies for digital skills [5, 13, 34], domain-skills appear to be especially challenging for participants with less education, but also for quite a few with a higher education.

In many cases, it may not be the "absolute" skill as such that matters, but the skill relative to the citizen's perceptions of what skills are necessary to perform the task, solve the problem and fulfil her needs – the perceived skill gap – that matters [32].

The bar for what would be sufficient domain-skills may be raised by the bureaucratic artefacts citizens encounter, such as self-service systems, websites, or letters, or even the buttons on the queue system at the service centre or the menus phone system [42]. These artefacts may be organised according to principles that make sense internally in the organisation but not to the citizens and apply terminology with which citizens are not familiar. Difficulties in finding the right information, finding the right form, finding the self-service system, and navigating the information space, may have to do with some degree of mismatch between the organising principles of the site or DSS, and the initial frame of understanding with which the citizen approaches the issues. This may exacerbate any lack of skills or render otherwise reasonable skills insufficient.

Finally, the participants' accounts indicate that there may be a limited transferability between domains. The basic understanding of bureaucratic organizations, language, and procedures may be transferable. However, the specific understanding of the situation, the organisations involved, the specific rules and procedures, and how they apply to the specific individual and situation may be less transferable. Sufficient domain-skills for handling a change of address involving an application for housing benefit may, for example, be of little relevance to another situation involving loss of employment and application for social security.

6 Conclusion

This paper set out to investigate how skills relevant for the BSE manifest in citizens' experiences with and strategies for the encounter, above and beyond ICT skills. Through an analysis of a large corpus of interviews with citizens in the context of situations where they needed contact with government, I have identified a specific set of "domain-skills" of particular relevance for the bureaucratic service encounter. Domain-skills constitute the conceptual scaffolding, which assists citizens in finding, evaluating, and applying information on their own.

Citizens' perceptions of their mastery of these skills have a significant influence on their strategies towards the BSE. If domain-skills are insufficient, the situation will often be characterised by ambiguity, making it difficult for the citizens to do things on her own with a sufficient degree of certainty. This is especially problematic in situations where something is at stake for the citizen. Some domain-skills elements may be transferable between different domains, while others appear to be relevant only for specific domains. This arguably makes domain-skills less transferable than other types of skills (i.e., ICT skills and cognitive skills). Participants' primary strategy in the face of insufficient domain-skills is to seek a dialogue with an expert, with whom they can create a shared understanding and thus establish the necessary framework to proceed confidently on their own.

This has implications for the design of service-processes and self-service systems and for how much government can expect citizens to do on their own. In some cases, the most efficient solution may even be to frontload a process with communication/dialog to establish sufficient foundations for the citizen to proceed on her own.

As domain-skills are, to a large extent, context-specific, the concept may apply to other types of online-interaction outside the public sector.

The study is based on data which are 6–10 years old, generated in the years where mandatory self-service was being implemented. However, domain-skills do not appear to be dependent so much on citizens' experience with technology, as on their experience with government and with the life-situations where they need to interact with government. There is therefore no reason to believe that the nature and importance of domain-skills will have changed since the interviews were conducted. This also entails that the findings should be applicable in other countries with a different level of digitalization in the population and in the interaction between citizens and government.

The influence of domain-skills on citizen's choice and use of channels may change over time when and if changes in the channel's enactment increase or decrease the level of support given to the citizen to establish the level of domain-skills needed in the situation. To give two hypothetical examples: if self-service systems get better at contextualising and framing the service in question, this may increase the utility of self-service systems for citizens with insufficient domain-skills. Conversely, if staff at call centres and at the counter become less capable at providing the contextualization and framing that citizens seek in these channels (e.g. because of deskilling of staff), citizens may use these channels less frequently, or be less satisfied with the service they get.

Future studies could explore the influence of digitalization and centralisation on citizens' ability to build domain-skills when this increasingly has to be done through online interaction, as well as the influence of better design of websites and self-service-systems on the type and scope of domain-skills necessary and of the effect of "deskilling" and other types of limitations in the interpersonal channels on citizens choice of these channels to compensate for lack of domain-skills. Further studies could also investigate the relationship between domain-skills and other types of skills at play in the BSE – most notably ICT skills and cognitive skills, and they could investigate for what types of services, situations and citizens frontloading the process with in-person communication (phone or face-to-face) might increase effeciency, quality and satisfaction.

Appendix 1: Profile of Sites and Participants

The demographical profiles of the municipalities serve to show how typical they are for the Danish context in general, as well as to outline any specific issues that may affect the contact patterns of the authorities involved – specifically: a high unemployment rate, many young or elderly people, many with low education levels.

Demographical data on the municipalities involved show that apart from Copenhagen (on several parameters), and Ballerup – on public housing, the municipalities involved are fairly representative of Danish municipalities in general, on the selected paramters (all data from Danish Statistical Databank for 2013, unless otherwise stated) (Table 8).

Table 8. Demographical profile of the municipalities where fieldwork was conducted

Municipality	Ballerup	Næstved	Holbæk	Copenhagen	Denmark
Population	48.500	81.272	69.093	569.000	Median: 42.615
Unemployment %	6,3	5,8	4,8	7,2	5,6
18- to 66-year-olds on social security	5,5	4,9	5,1	6,4	4,9
Pct. of households receiving housing benefits	71,7	53,9	48,2	43,2	48,6
Average income (1000 Dkr/individual)[a]	294	279	288	283	292

[a] Data from Denmark's Statistic 2012

A1.2 Demographical Profile of Participants

All age groups are represented in the data, some more than others. Figure 1 shows the differences between the age-profile of the participants (whose age was registered) across all sites and the age profile of the general Danish population[2].

[2] The source of population data is the Danish Statistical Databank, except when otherwise stated.

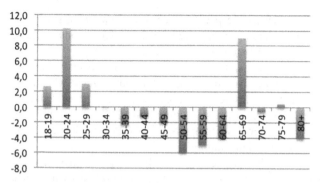

Fig. 1. Over-/underrepresentation of age groups in study, compared to DK population. (in %) n = 335

The age of the participants reflects the age of the Danish population [48] a deviation of 6% or less or all age groups, except for the age-group 20–24 which has a 10% overrepresentation and the age-group 65–69 with a 9% overrepresentation. This was to be expected as younger citizens and citizens around the age of retirement typically have more frequent interactions with authorities are more often in situations they have not been in before, which tends to lead to a greater need for face-to-face interaction [42] The level of education also represents the Danish population with a deviation of less than 5% except for those with only a high-school education.

Figure 2 shows the education profile of all participants of 20 years or over compared to the total Danish population (also 20+).

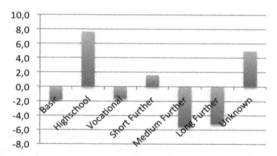

Fig. 2. Over-/underrepresentation of level of education in study, compared to DK population (in %) (further = further education, short = 2–3 years, medium = 3–5,5 years, long = 5–6 years) n = 335

The overrepresentation of high-school graduates can be explained by the overrepresentation of the younger age-group where many are still studying. The underrepresentation of citizens with a medium to longer education could be explained in part by the overrepresentation of elderly people – a group in which fewer people got a longer education than in the younger groups. But it may also be because the need and indeed eligibility for citizen services (especially the various benefits) is smaller among the well-educated, or because they have less need for face-to-face contact, being more able to take care of themselves through other channels.

For the variation of the perspectives represented in the study, this data would imply that we may lack perspectives from well-educated citizens, who may have different experiences with and find different meanings in digitisation and centralisation than citizens with less education. At the same time, this group of citizens could arguably be expected to have an easier time compensating for lack of domain-skills and thus less need of contextualization and framing.

Participants use of the internet, of home banking and their experience with doing tax online (representing a "service" all adults need to interact with at least once a year) – deviated 5% or less from that of the general population [48] (Fig. 3).

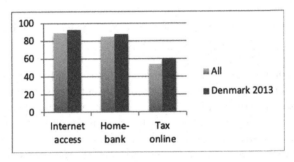

Fig. 3. Participants accesses to, home banking and Tax-self service. N = 335

References

1. Allina-Pisano, J.: How to Tell an Axe Murderer: an essay on ethnography, truths and lies. In: Schatz, E. (ed.) Political Ethnography: What Immersion Contributes to the Study of Power. University of Chicago Press, Chicago (2009)
2. Alvesson, M.: At home ethnography. In: Ybema, S., et al. (eds.) Organizational Ethnography. Sage, London (2009)
3. Andersson, A., Grönlund, Å.: e-Society accessibility: identifying research gaps. In: Traunmüller, R. (ed.) EGOV 2003. LNCS, vol. 2739, pp. 15–20. Springer, Heidelberg (2003). https://doi.org/10.1007/10929179_2
4. Barnard, E., Cloete, L., Patel, H.: Language and technology literacy barriers to accessing government services. In: Traunmüller, R. (ed.) EGOV 2003. LNCS, vol. 2739, pp. 37–42. Springer, Heidelberg (2003). https://doi.org/10.1007/10929179_6
5. Belanger, F., Carter, L.: The impact of the digital divide on e-government use. Commun. ACM **52**, 132–135 (2009)
6. Bertot, J.C., Jaeger, P.T.: The e-government paradox: better customer service does not necessarily cost less. Government Inf. Q. 25(2), 149–154 (2008)
7. Byström, K., Järvelin, K.: Task complexity affects information seeking and use. Inf. Process. Manage. 31(2), 191–213 (1995)
8. Casacuberta, D.: Informational literacy. In: Anttiroiko, A.-V., Malkia, M. (eds.) The Encyclopaedia of Digital Government, pp. 1083–1088. IGI, London (2007)

9. Charmaz, K.: Constructing Grounded Theory: A practical Guide Through Qualitative Analysis. Sage Publications, London (2006)
10. Corbin, J., Strauss, A.: Grounded theory research: procedures, canons, and evaluative criteria. Qual. Sociol. **13**(1), 3–21 (1990)
11. Czarniawska, B.: Exploring Complex Organizations: A Cultural Perspective. SAGE, London (1992)
12. DiMaggio, P., Hargittai, E.: From the "Digital Divide" to "Digital Inequality": studying internet use as penetration increases. In: Centre for Arts and Cultural Policy Studies, Princeton University. Working Paper Series 15 (2001)
13. Ebbers, W.E., Jansen, M.G., van Deursen, A.J.: Impact of the digital divide on e-government: expanding from channel choice to channel usage. Gov. Inf. Q. **33**(4), 685–692 (2016)
14. Evans, V., Green, M.: Cognitive Linguistics – An Introduction. Edinburgh University Press, Edinburgh (2006)
15. Fairclough, N.: Discourse and Social Change. Polity Press, Cambridge (1992)
16. Flybjerg, B.: Fem misforståelser om casestudiet. In: Brinkmann, Svend & Tanggaard, Lene (red.): Kvalitative metoder - en Grundbog. København, Hans Reitzels Forlag (2010)
17. Gee, J.P.: The narrativization of experience in the oral style. J. Educ. **167**(1), 9–35 (1985)
18. Gordon, L.K.: Bureaucratic competence and success in dealing with public bureaucracies. Soc. Probl. **23**(2), 197–208 (1975)
19. Grönlund, Å., Hatakka, M., Ask, A.: Inclusion in the e-service society – investigating administrative literacy requirements for using e-services. In: Wimmer, M.A., Scholl, J., Grönlund, Å. (eds.) EGOV 2007. LNCS, vol. 4656, pp. 216–227. Springer, Heidelberg (2007). https://doi.org/10.1007/978-3-540-74444-3_19
20. Heeks, R., Bailur, S.: Analysing eGoverment research: perspectives, philosophies, theories, methods and practices. In: E-government Working paper Series. Manchester, Institute for Development Policy and Management (2006)
21. Helbig, N., Gil-Garcia, R.J., Ferro, E.: Understanding the complexity of electronic government: implications from the digital divide literature. Gov. Inf. Q. **26**, 89–97 (2009)
22. Katz, D., Gutek, B., Kahn, R.L. Barton, E.: Bureaucratic Encounters. University of Michigan Survey Research Centre, Ann Arbor (1975)
23. Klaassen, R., Karreman, J., van der Geest, T.: Designing government portal navigation around citizens' needs. In: Wimmer, M.A., Scholl, H.J., Grönlund, Å., Andersen, K.V. (eds.) EGOV 2006. LNCS, vol. 4084, pp. 162–173. Springer, Heidelberg (2006). https://doi.org/10.1007/11823100_15
24. Kolsaker, A., Lee-Kelley, L.: Citizen-centric e-government: a critique of the UK model. Electron. Gov. **3**(2), 127–138 (2006)
25. Kvale, S.: Interview. En introduktion til det kvalitative forskningsinterview. København, Hans Reitzels Forlag (1997)
26. Layder, D.: Sociological Practice - Linking Theory and Social Research. Sage Publications, London (1998)
27. Lindgren, I., Madsen, C.Ø., Hofmann, S., Melin, U.: Close encounters of the digital kind: a research agenda for the digitalization of public services. Gov. Inf. Q. **36**(3), 427–436 (2019)
28. Madsen, C.Ø., Christensen, L.R.: Integrated and seamless? Single Parents' experiences of cross-organizational interaction. In: Selected Papers of the IRIS, Issue Nr 9 (2019)
29. Madsen, C.Ø., Kræmmergaard, P.: The efficiency of freedom. Single parents' domestication of mandatory e-government. Gov. Inf. Q. **32**(4), 380–388 (2015)
30. Madsen, C.Ø., Kræmmergaard, P.: Warm experts in the age of mandatory e-application for public benefits. Electron. J. e-Gov. **14**(1), 87–98 (2016)

31. Madsen, C.Ø., Hofmann, S., Pieterson, W.: Channel choice complications. In: Lindgren, I., Janssen, M., Lee, H., Polini, A., Rodríguez Bolívar, M.P., Scholl, H.J., Tambouris, E. (eds.) EGOV 2019. LNCS, vol. 11685, pp. 139–151. Springer, Cham (2019). https://doi.org/10.1007/978-3-030-27325-5_11

32. Mathieson, K., Peacock, E., Chin, W.: Extending the technology acceptance model: the influence of perceived user resources. Data Base **32**, 86–112 (2001)

33. Maynard-Moddi, S., Musheno, M.: Cops, Teachers, Counsellors - Stories from the Front Lines of Public Service. University of Michigan Press (2003)

34. Morgenson, F.V., Van Maburg, D., Mithas, S.: Misplaced trust? Exploring the structure of the e-government-citizen trust relationship. J. Admin. Res. Theory Adv. Access (2010)

35. Mossberger, K., Tolbert, C.J., Stansbury, M.: Virtual Inequality - Beyond the Digital Divide. Georgetown University Press, Washington D.C. (2003)

36. Münscher, R., Kühlmann, T.M.: Using critical incident technique in trust research. In: Lyon, F., Mollering, G., Saunders, M.N.K. (eds.) Handbook of Research Methods on Trust. Edward Elgar, Cheltenham (2012)

37. Norris, P.: Digital divide: civic engagement, information poverty, and the internet worldwide. Cambridge University Press, New York (2001)

38. Pieterson, W.: Channel Choice – Citizens Channel Behaviour and Public Service Channel Strategy. Ph.D. thesis, University of Twente (2009)

39. Reddick, C.G.: Citizen initiated contacts with government comparing phones and websites. J. E-Gov. **2**(1), 27–53 (2005)

40. Schwartz-Shea, P.: Judging quality – evaluative criteria and epistemic communities. In: Yanow, D., Schwartz-Shea, P. (eds.) Interpretation and Method, pp 91–109. M.E. Sharp, New York (2006)

41. Scott, M., DeLone, W.H. Golden, W.: IT quality and eGovernment Net benefits: a citizen's perspective. In: 31st International Conference on Information Systems, St. Louis (2010)

42. Skaarup, S.: The Mediation of Authority - How citizens perceive and engage the mediations of the Bureaucratic Service Encounter and changes in its mediation matrix. Ph.D. Dissertation. University of Southern Denmark (2016)

43. Small, M.L.: "How many cases do I need?": on science and the logic of case selection in field-based research. Ethnography **10**(1), 5–38 (2009)

44. Technological Institute: Analyse af Danskernes IKT færdigheder. Taastrup, Teknologisk Institut (2005)

45. Van Deursen, A.J.A.M., van Dijk, J.A.G.M.: Internet skills and the digital divide. New Media Soc. **13**(6), 893–911 (2010)

46. Van Deursen, A.J.A.M., Helsper, E.J., Eynon, R.: Development and validation of the Internet Skills Scale (ISS). Inf. Commun. Soc. **19**(6), 804–823 (2016)

47. Wedeen, L.: Ethnography as interpretive enterprise. In: Schatz, E. (ed.) political Ethnography: What Immersion Contributes to the Study of Power. University of Chicago Press, Chicago (2009)

48. Danmarks Statistik 2013

Aligning Stakeholder Interests, Governance Requirements and Blockchain Design in Business and Government Information Sharing

Sélinde van Engelenburg[1]([⊠]) ⓘ, Boriana Rukanova[1] ⓘ, Wout Hofman[2] ⓘ,
Jolien Ubacht[1] ⓘ, Yao-Hua Tan[1] ⓘ, and Marijn Janssen[1] ⓘ

[1] Delft University of Technology, Delft, The Netherlands
{S.H.vanEngelenburg,B.D.Rukanova,J.Ubacht,Y.Tan,
M.F.W.H.A.Janssen}@tudelft.nl
[2] TNO, The Hague, The Netherlands
wout.hofman@tno.nl

Abstract. Governance requirements for systems supporting information sharing between businesses and government organisations (B&G) are determined by a high variety of stakeholders with often conflicting interests. These conflicting interests can hamper the introduction and scaling-up of ICT-innovations that change their roles and authorities. We address one such innovation: the introduction of blockchain technologies in the B&G context. Who can govern data and the system depends on several elements of the design of a blockchain-based system, particularly the data structure, consensus mechanism and network topology. Design choices regarding these elements affect who can make decisions and hence we call them blockchain control points. These control points require an explicit and well-understood relationship between the design decisions and the interests of stakeholders. Yet, the literature on blockchain technology and governance does not offer such insight. Therefore, we developed a framework to assess the alignment between stakeholders interest and blockchain design choices. This framework consists of three views and their interrelationships, 1) a stakeholder view providing insight into the tensions between stakeholder's interests and governance requirements, 2), a governance view on the rights concerning the data and the system, and 3) a blockchain control view describing how design decisions on the control points affect whether governance requirements are met and how parties can exercise their rights. Making these links explicit enables an understanding of how technical design choices can trigger organizational dynamics from the stakeholder view and vice versa. Based on the framework we formulate a research agenda concerning blockchain design choices and governance.

Keywords: Blockchain technology · Distributed ledger technology · Governance · Business · Government · Information sharing · Access control · Consensus mechanism

G. Viale Pereira et al. (Eds.): EGOV 2020, LNCS 12219, pp. 197–209, 2020.
https://doi.org/10.1007/978-3-030-57599-1_15

1 Introduction

The literature on information sharing between businesses and/or government organisations (B&G information sharing) describes various blockchain-based systems, ranging from supply chain management to information sharing to improve safety and security, and to e-government (e.g., [1–5]). In these domains, various stakeholders are involved, with often conflicting interests. For example, it might be in the interest of businesses in a supply chain to share information to reduce the bullwhip effect and reduce costs [6, 7]. Furthermore, the government might want to reuse the same data for risk assessment [8]. However, businesses might only want to share data if it is secure and can only be controlled and accessed by the appropriate and identifiable parties [9–11]. Parties like IT providers also have their interests. Hence, we view blockchain-based systems as complex socio-technical systems in which many stakeholders with divergent interests are involved.

In 2009, Satoshi Nakamoto [12] combined several existing technologies to solve the double-spending problem for the cryptocurrency Bitcoin without an intermediary. He created the first example of what was later called blockchain or distributed ledger technology. Later on, blockchain technology was generalised to other application domains. Blockchain technology (BCT) has several features that can make it also useful for B&G information sharing: a high level of transparency, immutability and reliability.

In contrast to the more simple case of cryptocurrencies in which a transaction takes place between two parties that send and receive the currency, in the case of B&G information sharing, a diversity of types of transactions can occur in which multiple stakeholders are involved. Stakeholders that can play a diversity of roles and have different types of relationships. This leads to a complicated context that requires different technological design choices. For example, if BCT is used to support cryptocurrencies, usually all nodes can view and verify transactions and are anonymous [12]. But when businesses want to reduce the bullwhip effect in supply chains, the data needs to be accessible only to a select number of identifiable parties to avoid disclosure of sensitive business data.

In the literature, some solutions in the domain of blockchain technology are provided that can help to deal with the different governance needs for B&G information sharing, e.g. the use of private networks or proof of authority as a consensus mechanism [1]. However, no framework exists that helps to assess the relationship between the design of the blockchain-based system on the needs for governance in the B&G information sharing domain and vice versa. Simultaneously, it requires looking at the entire technical design of the system to assess whether these needs are met and aligned with stakeholder interests. In this paper, we present a framework to provide insight into the relationship between blockchain design choices and governance for B&G information sharing. This insight can enable adaptive government and contribute to an agile government [13, 14].

First, we provide an overview of the framework in Sect. 2. Next, in Sect. 3, we present the stakeholder view of the framework which provides insight into the complexities and dynamics of B&G information sharing. We illustrate this by a case of B&G information sharing in international trade. In Sect. 4, we introduce the concept of governance requirements to make the rights of stakeholders explicit. In Sect. 5, we present the blockchain control points and how different design choices affect which rights parties can exercise. In Sect. 6, we show the use of the framework based on the case of TradeLens. Based on this, in Sect. 7, we outline our research agenda for further research into the relationship between blockchain design choices and governance.

2 A Governance Framework for Blockchain-Based B&G Information Sharing

In this section, we present an overview of the proposed framework. The framework allows for systematically analysing the relationships between the stakeholder context of parties involved in B&G information sharing, the governance requirements stemming from this context and the blockchain design choices (see Fig. 1). Here, we present the relationships between the views of the framework.

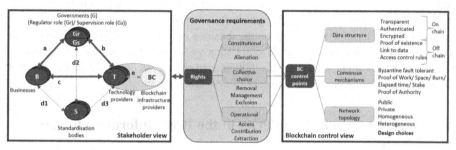

Fig. 1. Overview of the proposed framework for systematically analyzing the relationship between governance in B&G information sharing and design choices in blockchain technology.

Governance as an abstract concept can be seen as all processes of social organization and social coordination [15]. We use the term governance in the broad sense as processes of social organization and coordination that relate to blockchain-based B&G information sharing. We use the term governance requirements, as discussed later in this paper, in a more narrow sense as decision rights that parties should be able to exercise based on stakeholder dynamics and the design choices.

The first view of our framework is the stakeholder view where we classify the stakeholders in B&G information sharing and discuss their interests and potential tensions between them. The blockchain control view refers to blockchain control points. Control points enable parties to exercise power over other actors in a sociotechnical system and are often domain-specific [16, 17]. We identified several control points for blockchain-based systems that are subject to design choices. By making design choices, different ways of governing the data and the system are enabled. Therefore, changes in configurations of design choices for these blockchain control points can also lead to a change in the power dependencies among the stakeholders involved.

It is difficult to systematically translate high-level dynamics between stakeholders into blockchain design choices, and vice versa. The needs for governance in B&G information sharing of the stakeholder view are complicated and often described based on high-level concepts. While considering governance in this way helps to reveal the high-level dynamics at play, it is difficult to translate to and from more low-level design choices for the information-sharing system.

Therefore, to allow for a systematic analysis of the interaction between design choices at blockchain control points and the stakeholder interests, we introduce another view of the framework, which relies on the concept of governance requirements. The governance requirements act as an intermediary between high-level governance considerations and low-level technical design choices. Governance requirements describe decision rights that parties should be able to exercise explicitly. The determination of the rights for the stakeholders involved starts in the stakeholder view and leads to agreements (e.g., specified in contracts). On the other hand, what rights parties can exercise depends on the technological design choices made. The framework shows this relationship by placing the governance requirements between the stakeholder and the blockchain control view.

The framework can be used in two ways: 1) a. analyze the stakeholder dynamics to come to an agreement and determine what governance requirements should be met and then b. identify the design choices that allow for meeting these requirements, and 2) a. determine the effect of certain design choices on the meeting of governance requirements, and b. determine the effects on the tensions between the stakeholders involved. The framework could be used at different stages of the design process. For example, relationships and interests among stakeholders can change, or external factors can force different design choices, e.g., in the case of new laws or regulations.

3   Stakeholders and Complexity in the B&G Information Sharing Domain

The B&G domain is fundamentally different from the cryptocurrency domain. To develop blockchain-based systems, the complexities and specificities of the B&G domain are key for understanding the design options. As indicated in Fig. 1, we identify four main stakeholder groups on a high level of abstraction (labelled by multiple ovals) that are relevant in the context of B&G information sharing:

1. *Businesses* (B), such as supply chain partners, are in the business stakeholder group. Their motivation to use blockchain technology is usually driven by a strive for competitive gains and economic benefits, and increasingly by social responsibility.
2. *Government agencies* (G) can act in different roles, e.g. as a regulator (Gr) or as a body supervising the activities of businesses (Gs). In their regulatory role, government agencies can issue laws and regulations or can adopt policies to stimulate developments by e.g. providing public funding. In their role of government supervision, governments are interested in receiving additional information from businesses to perform their supervision processes, such as customs risk assessment or compliance management.
3. *Technology providers* (T) refer to infrastructure and platform providers. These are providers of technical solutions to businesses and government and they are driven by their business model. Recently, this group also includes new actors (BC) that specifically provide blockchain infrastructures such as Hyperledger.
4. *Standardization bodies* (S) also play a role in the B&G domain. The growth in multiple blockchain-enabled solutions requires standardization for interoperability of blockchain-based systems and services.

Figure 1 shows that these actors are interrelated. We show the primary relationship between government, business and technology providers as solid arrows labelled with *a*, *b*, and *c* respectively. The dotted arrows labelled *d* denote the secondary link of each of these stakeholders with standardization organizations. We also explicitly depict the link between technology providers and blockchain providers (arrow labelled *e*) as there can be conflicting and mutual interests between these parties as well. All of these links can be used to identify potential tensions.

While the model is quite general and would apply to other cases as well, we illustrate it by using the example of international trade. Here, we see the complexity of the international supply chains that link many business actors. When goods are moved on a global scale, a diversity of governing authorities (e.g., customs) are involved when the goods cross national borders. Especially in a global setting, multiple levels of government, ranging from national, supranational (e.g., EU) to global (e.g., World Customs Organization) are involved. These governmental organisations exchange information with other governments and businesses.

In B&G information sharing, standardization plays a key role. International standardization bodies such as UN CEFACT play a crucial role in standardizing business documents and data sets. The World Customs Organization developed the World Customs Data Model. Currently, these standards focus on older means of information sharing, such as messaging and declarations. This means that innovative implementations take a lot of time before actual adoption.

The B&G information-sharing world is quite fragmented. Over the last decades, efforts have been made on the side of both businesses and governments to overcome such fragmentation and to allow for better information sharing. Recently, global digital trade infrastructures enabled by blockchain have emerged that allow government agencies to access (additional) business information from the supply chains, which is provided voluntarily [18]. While technically it is becoming increasingly easy to share information in the B&G domain, information sharing remains a complex issue [19]. Businesses and governments are extremely careful that key information is not accessible to parties that are not authorized to see it. In the B&G domain, parties are rarely anonymous, as is often the case with cryptocurrencies. For example, in purchasing contracts and subcontracting contracts, different parties will need to be named. Government agencies need to know which parties are filing import and export declarations, so these parties need to be registered to perform these operations. Linking these stakeholder dynamics to blockchain design choices directly is difficult. In the next section, we introduce the governance requirements as a way to link the two.

4   Governance Requirements

We now turn to the governance requirements in our framework. These have two dimensions: 1) which parties should have control, and 2) the extent to which parties should have control. For the first, we turn to the work of Constantinides [20]. He relies on work from the field of natural resource commons arrangements. This viewpoint is relevant, as the distributed nature of blockchain with the complexities of B&G information sharing will rarely lead to simple centralised governance arrangements. Constantinides [20] views infrastructure resources, such as a database containing data, in a way analogous to natural resources, such as a forest containing trees. In our case, the main resource is the blockchain on which different types of data are stored. These can include transactions, smart contracts, events or documentation.

In some cases, the data in B&G information sharing is not stored in the blockchain itself, but the blockchain stores only hashes of the data, links to the data, or rules for controlling access to the data. This turns the databases that store the actual data into resources as well. Furthermore, if the data on the blockchain is encrypted, then the system for generating and sharing keys is also a resource, for example.

Table 1. Different types of rights in blockchain-based B&G information sharing systems (adapted from [20, 21])

Rights		Rights in a blockchain-based system for B&G information sharing
Constitutional rights	Alienation	Right to determine who has what collective rights
Collective choice rights	Removal	Right to remove parts of the blockchain-based system
	Management	Right to determine how, when, and where parts of the blockchain-based system can be used and choices on control points may be changed
	Exclusion	Right to determine who has what operational and removal rights and how these can be transferred
Operational rights	Access	Right to access parts of the blockchain-based system (i.e., nodes, external databases or key management system)
	Contribution	Right to store, revise or delete data shared using blockchain.
	Extraction	Right to obtain access to data shared using blockchain

Constantinides [20], based on the work of Ostrom [21], describes three types of rights, namely constitutional, collective choice and operational rights. Constitutional rights refer to who may or may not participate in making collective choices for the system [20]. Collective choice refers to rights concerning users and components within the information system, and operational rights refer to those related to access to the information system and the data [20]. In Table 1, we describe how these types of rights can be applied in the case of a blockchain-based B&G information sharing system. It is important to note here that 'data shared using blockchain' can refer to data that is directly stored in the blockchain, as well as data that is stored elsewhere.

A governance requirement is a description of to what extent certain parties should have what rights. As the domain of B&G information sharing is complex due to multiple stakeholders with various interests, parties will often need to share rights and there will not be a single party that can make all decisions by themselves. For example, a consortium of parties might need to share the right to decide who can be a node in the network. The consortium in that case then shares exclusion rights concerning access to the system. The consortium might also decide that a carrier should have extraction rights, which is a governance requirement. To fulfil this requirement, the system needs to be designed such that the carrier can prevent or permit others to extract data. Whether this is the case, depends on the design choices described in the next section.

5 The Blockchain Control View

The blockchain control view connects design choices and governance requirements. First, we identify control points that can be used to control who can exercise what rights in the system. Then, we identify possible design choices for those control points. Next, we relate the effects of the design choices to the rights presented in Table 1. Table 2 shows the control points and each design choice we identified.

Table 2. Overview of control points and design choices in the framework

Control point	Design choice	Description
Data structure	Transparent	The data to be shared is stored on the blockchain without encryption
	Authenticated	The data to be shared is stored on the blockchain. The party that adds the data encrypts it to authenticate it. Others can decrypt and verify their identity.
	Encrypted	The data to be shared is stored on the blockchain. The party that adds the data encrypts it to keep it confidential from others. Only parties provided with a key can view the data.
	Proof of Existence	A hash of the data to be shared is stored on the blockchain to prove it existed when it was added and make it possible to determine whether the data changed afterwards. The data itself is stored elsewhere.
	Link to data	A link to the data to be shared is stored on the blockchain. The link can be used to find the data stored elsewhere.
	Access control rules	Rules for controlling access to the data that needs to be shared is stored on the blockchain. Parties are allowed to extract the data stored elsewhere based on these rules.
Blockchain network topology	Public	Anyone can be a node in the network.
	Private	Only some parties can be a node in the network and have certain rights.
	Homogeneous	All nodes store the same data and link in the same way to other nodes.
	Heterogeneous	Nodes differ in the data that they store and/or the links they have to other nodes.
Consensus mechanism	Byzantine fault-tolerant	Relies on 'good' nodes not forwarding malicious messages to the rest of the network. Requires the network not to be public to avoid Sybil attacks.
	Proof of work/ space/ stake/ ...	Relies on nodes performing a certain task or having a certain property and the rest of the network checking this before accepting the blocks they add.
	Proof of Authority	Only authorized nodes control who can add blocks to the blockchain.

Some design choices can be combined, such as authenticated and encrypted data. The data structure control point refers to the form of the data stored in the blocks and whether the data that is to be shared is stored in the blockchain itself, or whether the blockchain is only used to share data stored elsewhere. An important effect of the choice of encrypting data is that someone with extraction rights requires a key to be able to exercise their rights. When only proofs of existence, links, or access control rules are stored for the data, then not only the rights over the blockchain components and the data in the blockchain will need to be considered, but also over the additional databases and the data that is stored there. Storing the actual data elsewhere, however, does provide new opportunities, for example, to remove the data.

The blockchain network topology control point refers to the arrangements concerning who can be a node in the blockchain network and how nodes are linked. Public and private refers to whether the network is publicly accessible or not. Of course, the main effect of design choices for the blockchain network topology is in the access rights to nodes. Whether a party can be a node, in turn, determines whether they can exercise other rights, such as contribution rights. Whether the network is homogeneous or heterogeneous can play a role in who has extraction rights as it affects what data they can store or receive.

The consensus mechanism also affects different rights. The consensus mechanism determines how a consensus is reached between parties about what blocks should be in the chain and who can add them and under which conditions. The choice for consensus mechanism thus directly affects contribution rights. For example, the parties that provide Proof of Work (PoW) can exercise contribution rights, while for Byzantine Fault Tolerance (BFT) all nodes that do not send messages that are considered malicious by the other nodes can do so. Furthermore, the consensus mechanism determines who can decide who should be able to exercise contribution rights. In the case of BFT, this is 2/3 of the nodes and for PoW this is the nodes with 51% of CPU power [12, 22].

6   Demonstration of the Framework: The TradeLens Case

We use an empirical case to demonstrate the use of the framework. In-depth knowledge of the development of TradeLens was gained by participatory research as part of the PROFILE[1] Horizon 2020 EU project. TradeLens[2] is a global blockchain-enabled infrastructure driven by IBM and Maersk, that allows for sharing events and documents in international trade. Initial development and piloting started in 2015. In 2018, it was rolled out as a global commercial infrastructure. The goal of TradeLens is digitizing global trade [18]. Digitization and development of digital trade infrastructures such as data pipelines are aimed at overcoming fragmentation of the information passed through systems of supply chain partners and authorities, and overcoming inefficiencies in the exchange of paper documents [8, 23, 24].

Stakeholder View: The stakeholder group for TradeLens includes various network partners and client groups, such as carriers, government authorities, shippers, and providers of financial services. TradeLens is intended to be open to other industry parties. But,

---

[1] https://www.profile-project.eu/.
[2] https://www.tradelens.com/.

carriers are competitors and therefore they do not want to provide their data to each other. Authorities are interested in access to business data to perform their customs risk assessment and to cross-validate the customs declaration data against business data.

Governance Requirements: Considering the governance requirements, TradeLens is owned by IBM and MAERSK and, therefore, they hold the constitutional rights. As TradeLens is intended to be open to other industry parties, the collective choices are made by the TradeLens board, which includes IBM, Maersk and additional carriers. Businesses and government authorities who interact with TradeLens are granted operational rights. The operational rights are defined in data sharing specifications agreed upon by stakeholders. For example, TradeLens has access rights to be a node to provide its services, but by default does not have extraction rights to the data. Authorities only have extraction rights to relevant data. Also, it is required that carriers cannot extract each other's data.

Blockchain Control View: For TradeLens, design choices were made to provide the parties involved with the ability to exercise their rights and to allow for scaling up the system. Regarding the network topology, the choice was made to rely on Hyperledger. The network consists of several private networks called channels. As a carrier can be a node, they can exercise their access right. Other parties that have access rights can become one as well. To meet the governance requirement that carriers cannot extract each other's data, the channels are reserved for single carriers in a private network. TradeLens has a node in each of these private networks, and the network is thus heterogeneous.

Regarding the data structure, initially, the design choice was to store documents on the blockchain and encrypt them to ensure that only the appropriate parties can extract them. Later, to enhance scalability, documents were stored off-chain and a link to the document plus a hash of the content of the document is stored on the chain. Authorities can use the link to determine where the data is stored and the hash of the retrieved document will be compared with the hash stored on the chain, to prove the document's content has not changed.

Several issues propagate from the stakeholder view through the governance requirements to the blockchain control view and vice-versa. We illustrate the interdependency between the views with two examples. The government has extraction rights to some documents. When the data was stored on-chain, they exercised that right by obtaining data from the blockchain and by obtaining a decryption key. However, when the data was stored off-chain, the documents need to be stored in an external document storage where they need to obtain them from. This triggers additional complexity in the stakeholder view. In particular, the question becomes who will provide the document store and how to ensure that the documents will not be deleted. In principle, TradeLens, other technology providers or the businesses themselves can host a document store. Momentarily, complexity is reduced by TradeLens offering the document storage themselves, with the agreement of the other parties. If in the future parties prefer to arrange their own document storage, this will trigger additional stakeholder dynamics, as additional negotiations and agreements on how the data storage would be handled would need to be made between TradeLens and these other actors.

One more example is related to illustrating the dynamics among different technology providers (represented with multiple (T) ovals in our framework in Fig. 1). In this case, we take a specific example of the creation of value-added services by other technology providers. TradeLens is a node but only has access rights and no extraction rights. This is similar to the role of a Port Community Systems (PCSs) for its members in the Netherlands (i.e. facilitating data sharing without extraction rights). TradeLens collaborates with the PCS in Rotterdam. The PCS has information about the container when the container arrives at the Port of Rotterdam. TradeLens has information about the route of the container and possible rerouting before it arrives at the port of Rotterdam. TradeLens and PortBase are collaborating to link their systems. An independent company which provides services for the planning of pick-up slots for barges arriving at the port of Rotterdam was able to arrange extraction rights to the data of the PCS and TradeLens to offer value-added services. They approached the relevant businesses that own the data that is held in TradeLens and the PCS and requested permission to see their data. Once the businesses gave permission, the independent company could access the data and provide the value-added services. This example shows how technology providers like third-party app providers can make use of platforms like TradeLens to create value-added services on top of the blockchain-based system. Therefore by detailing the technology (T) stakeholder group from the stakeholder view we can reason about the dynamics of actors involved in this group and how this relates to the blockchain design choices.

7   Directions for Further Research

The examples in Sect. 6 illustrate how our framework enables manoeuvering back and forth from an abstract understanding of the domain and stakeholders to a detailed understanding of the dependencies between governance requirements, blockchain control points and design choices. This interplay allows us to gain insight into the dependencies within complex socio-technical systems based on a blockchain-based system.

We demonstrated the framework in a case from the global trade logistics domain. We identified examples of interdependencies between the components of the framework. As the relationship between the stakeholder interests, the governance requirements and the control points in the blockchain architecture were not addressed in the extant literature, we consider the framework as a starting point for future research. The framework provides a structured approach to identify interdependencies in other complex sociotechnical blockchain-based systems. Table 3 provides an initial overview of future research topics based on the interactions that we identified in the framework.

Table 3. Future research topics based on interactions between views in the framework

Interactions	Topics for further research
Stakeholders → governance requirements → blockchain control points	Detailing the technology stakeholders into blockchain infrastructure, blockchain solution and app providers and investigating: - possible scenarios regarding the distribution of rights among the technology providers and how they impact their business models; - the effects of the scenarios on user rights; - what the different scenarios are for adding value-added services (e.g. smart contracts or off-chain apps relying on blockchain data) and how these can affect the business models of technology providers and the user stakeholder group; - what are complexities for determining the true ownership of data in the stakeholder view and how does it affect the distribution of rights.
Design choices → governance requirements	Investigating the effects of design choices on management and alienation rights; The effect of combinations of design choices on governance requirements (i.e. encrypted data and BFT); For what governance requirements do we need to develop different architectures, because they cannot be met?
Blockchain control points → design choices	Which are additional control points and design choices? Which are additional effects of the current design choices?

8   Conclusions

This paper presents a novel framework that provides a broad understanding of the link between governance and blockchain design choices. The key elements of this framework are considering various stakeholders and their conflicting and mutual interests in B&G information sharing, governance requirements and blockchain control points. Control points are important, but often not considered in the information system's design, whereas blockchain often is used to improve control and thereby creating trust.

The framework can be used to analyse the effect of design decisions. We demonstrate how technical design choices can trigger organizational dynamics at the stakeholder level and vice versa. The tensions and opposing interests of stakeholders result in blockchain design choices that influence how data is shared and rights can be exercised. The framework draws attention to relevant elements to analyse this interaction. Although requirements like transparency and access control are clear, they can be realized in different ways, which influences design and governance. We demonstrate how they can be accounted for simultaneously when designing blockchain applications.

Our intention is not to present a complete framework. New control points and design choices that affect governance requirements might be found or developed and a lot of research still needs to be performed to get full insight into the relationship between the control points and governance. Rather, we present a framework that links control points and design choices to rights. This also can help to identify gaps in knowledge, for example by looking at what relationships are unknown or what governance requirements stakeholders have that cannot be met with the current design choices. Additionally, embedding new knowledge in the framework systemizes it and helps to translate it into a form that can be applied directly in B&G information sharing. Evaluation of the framework using empirical cases in other B&G domains is part of future research. This will lead towards the development of a robust conceptual framework that supports the design of blockchain architectures that align the stakeholder interests, the governance requirements and the blockchain control points.

Acknowledgements. This research was partially funded by the PROFILE Project (nr. 786748), which is funded by the European Union's Horizon 2020 research and innovation program. Ideas and opinions expressed by the authors do not necessarily represent those of all partners.

The authors would like to also thank Norbert Kouwenhoven for his contribution to demonstrating the framework in the TradeLens examples.

References

1. Ølnes, S., Ubacht, J., Janssen, M.: Blockchain in government: benefits and implications of distributed ledger technology for information sharing. Gov. Inf. Q. **34**, 355–364 (2017). https://doi.org/10.1016/j.giq.2017.09.007
2. Korpela, K., Hallikas, J., Dahlberg, T.: Digital supply chain transformation toward blockchain integration. In: Proceedings of the 50th Hawaii International Conference on System Sciences, pp. 4182–4191 (2017). https://doi.org/10.24251/HICSS.2017.506
3. van Engelenburg, S.: Designing context-aware architectures for business-to-government information sharing (2019). https://doi.org/10.4233/uuid:d25fd4fd-02d7-4811-b675-615badbb3c05
4. Segers, L., Ubacht, J., Rukanova, B., Tan, Y.H.: The use of a blockchain-based smart import declaration to reduce the need for manual cross-validation by customs authorities. In: ACM International Conference Proceeding Series, pp. 196–203 (2019). https://doi.org/10.1145/3325112.3325264
5. Tian, F.: An agri-food supply chain traceability system for China based on RFID & blockchain technology. In: 13th International Conference on Service Systems and Service Management (ICSSSM), pp. 1–6 (2016). https://doi.org/10.1109/ICSSSM.2016.7538424
6. Lee, H.L., Padmanabhan, V., Whang, S.: Information distortion in a supply chain: the bullwhip effect. Manag. Sci. **43**, 546–558 (1997). https://doi.org/10.1287/mnsc.43.4.546
7. Bray, R.L., Mendelson, H.: Information transmission and the bullwhip effect: an empirical investigation. Manag. Sci. **58**, 860–875 (2012). https://doi.org/10.1287/mnsc.1110.1467
8. Hesketh, D.: Weaknesses in the supply chain: who packed the box. World Cust. J. **4**, 3–20 (2010)
9. Fawcett, S.E., Osterhaus, P., Magnan, G.M., Brau, J.C., McCarter, M.W.: Information sharing and supply chain performance: the role of connectivity and willingness. Supply Chain Manag. Int. J. **12**, 358–368 (2007). https://doi.org/10.1108/13598540710776935
10. Lee, H.L., Whang, S.: Information sharing in a supply chain. Int. J. Manuf. Technol. **1**, 79–93 (2000). https://doi.org/10.1504/IJMTM.2000.001329
11. Hart, P., Saunders, C.: Power and trust: critical factors in the adoption and use of electronic data interchange. Organ. Sci. **8**, 23–42 (1997). https://doi.org/10.1287/orsc.8.1.23
12. Nakamoto, S.: bitcoin: a peer-to-peer electronic cash system (2008)
13. Janssen, M., van der Voort, H.: Adaptive governance: towards a stable, accountable and responsive government. Gov. Inf. Q. **33**, 1–5 (2016). https://doi.org/10.1016/j.giq.2016.02.003
14. Mergel, I., Gong, Y., Bertot, J.: Agile government: systematic literature review and future research. Gov. Inf. Q. **35**, 291–298 (2018). https://doi.org/10.1016/j.giq.2018.04.003

15. Bevir, M.: What is governance? In: Key Concepts in Governance, pp. 2–11. SAGE (2008)
16. Elaluf-Calderwood, S., Eaton, B., Herzhoff, J., Sorensen, C.: Mobile platforms as convergent systems – analysing control points and tussles with emergent socio-technical discourses. In: Maícas, J.P. (ed.) Recent Developments in Mobile Communications: A Multidisciplinary Approach, pp. 97–112 (2011). Books on Demand
17. Rukanova, B., de Reuver, M., Henningsson, S., Nikayin, F., Tan, Y.H.: Emergence of collective digital innovations through the process of control point driven network reconfiguration and reframing: the case of mobile payment. Electron. Mark. (2019). https://doi.org/10.1007/s12 525-019-00352-z
18. Tan, Y.-H., Rukanova, B., Engelenburg, S. van, Ubacht, J., Janssen, M.: Developing large scale B2B blockchain architectures for global trade lane. In: 6th Innovation in Information Infrastructures (III) Workshop, University of Surrey (2019)
19. Eckartz, S.M., Hofman, W.J., Van Veenstra, A.F.: A decision model for data sharing. In: Janssen, M., Scholl, H.J., Wimmer, M.A., Bannister, F. (eds.) EGOV 2014. LNCS, vol. 8653, pp. 253–264. Springer, Heidelberg (2014). https://doi.org/10.1007/978-3-662-44426-9_21
20. Constantinides, P.: Perspectives and implications for the development of information infrastructures. IGI Global (2012). https://doi.org/10.4018/978-1-4666-1622-6
21. Ostrom, E.: How types of goods and property rights jointly affect collective action. J. Theor. Polit. **15**, 239–270 (2003). https://doi.org/10.1177/0951692803015003002
22. Lamport, L., Shostak, R., Pease, M.: The byzantine generals problem. ACM Trans. Program. Lang. Syst. **4**, 382–401 (1982). https://doi.org/10.1145/357172.357176
23. Klievink, B., et al.: Enhancing visibility in international supply chains: the data pipeline concept. Int. J. Electron. Gov. Res. **8**, 14–33 (2012). https://doi.org/10.4018/jegr.2012100102
24. Rukanova, B., Henningsson, S., Henriksen, H.Z., Tan, Y.-H.: Digital trade infrastructures: a framework for analysis. Complex Syst. Inform. Model. Q., 1–21 (2018). https://doi.org/10.7250/csimq.2018-14.01

Approaches to Good Data Governance in Support of Public Sector Transformation Through Once-Only

Maria A. Wimmer[1]([⊠]) [iD], Alessia C. Neuroni[2], and Jan Thomas Frecè[3]

[1] Institute for IS Research, University of Koblenz-Landau, Koblenz, Germany
wimmer@uni-koblenz.de
[2] Institute Public Sector Transformation, Berne University of Applied Sciences, Berne, Switzerland
alessia.neuroni@bfh.ch
[3] Institute Sustainable Business, Berne University of Applied Sciences, Berne, Switzerland
jan.frece@bfh.ch

Abstract. The Once Only Principle (OOP) drives current public sector modernization through the reduction of administrative burdens. It requires public authorities not to ask citizens and companies to repeatedly provide information to the public authorities. Instead, public authorities shall share and re-use data among themselves in due respect of data protection regulation. The sharing and re-use of sensitive and non-sensitive data among public administrations demands for broad acceptance by all stakeholders. Trust and transparency are key success criteria in such data-driven public sector transformation. Establishing proper governance mechanisms for the data infrastructures that enable the sharing and re-use in public service provisioning, and that provide the necessary transparency and trust levels is expected to effectively improve public service. This research investigates approaches for establishing a good data governance in OOP settings tackling the sharing and re-use of sensitive or personal data. Geographical focus is on the European Union and Switzerland.

Keywords: Digital transformation · Once Only Principle · OOP · Sharing and re-use of sensitive data · Data infrastructure · Data governance · Good data governance

1 Introduction

In the eGovernment Action Plan 2016–2020, the European Union commits to seven principles of public sector transformation in order to modernize governments across Europe and therefore to contribute to economic growth, jobs as well as sustainable and resilient societies [1]. The Once Only Principle (OOP) is one of these principles, aiming at the reduction of administrative burdens by asking citizens and companies to provide certain (standard) information to the public authorities only once. Likewise, public authorities

© IFIP International Federation for Information Processing 2020
Published by Springer Nature Switzerland AG 2020
G. Viale Pereira et al. (Eds.): EGOV 2020, LNCS 12219, pp. 210–222, 2020.
https://doi.org/10.1007/978-3-030-57599-1_16

"take action if permitted to internally re-use this data, in due respect of data protection rules, so that no additional burden falls on citizens and businesses" [1]. The sharing and re-use of sensitive and non-sensitive data of citizens and companies – such data has to be differentiated from open and big open linked data (!) – among the actors in public service provisioning demands for broad acceptance by all stakeholders. Trust and transparency are key success criteria in such data-driven public sector transformation. Establishing proper collaborative governance mechanisms for data infrastructures that enable the sharing and re-use in public service provisioning is expected to effectively improve the success of digital transformation in governments.

Fostering data-driven innovation with a successful OOP realization requires coherent data governance to balance openness and public value, as well as privacy and data security [2]. Lending from the good governance principles [3], *good* data governance refers to data governance, which embodies the good governance principles (accountability, coherence, effectiveness, openness, participation, transparency [4], p. 8, 27) and caters for the necessary privacy and data security. Good data governance is particularly important when dealing with citizen data, since data access, security, ownership and privacy are more acute for such data [5, 6].

With the vision of the OOP creating value for society and economy through a data-driven transformation of the public sector, trust and transparency become crucial vehicles for success and acceptance. The motivation for this paper is therefore to elicit relevant approaches for a data-driven public sector transformation, which inform a comprehensive good data governance concept for OOP realization. The research question for this paper is: "What prerequisites for sharing and re-using sensitive or personal data in inter-agency collaboration in the public sector exist and how can good data governance mechanisms support a successful OOP implementation therewith nurturing trust and transparency?".

To answer this research question, we investigate scientific literature, strategic policies and case studies of data governance and OOP implementations with the aim to understand the crucial elements for a good data governance concept supporting OOP. The paper employs systematic literature analysis [7–9], gathering also insights from existing research on data infrastructures for open data. However, the focus of this paper is on sharing and re-use of sensitive or personal data (not open data). The selection of literature and of strategic documents for this study is based on the one hand on previous research, which the authors conducted in relevant studies (e.g. [10–15]). On the other hand, google scholar was scanned and the snowball principle was applied on identified literature to enrich the research with current findings from the literature and with recent strategic documents on public sectors' digital transformation from the EU and Switzerland. The findings from literature were complemented and refined along virtual and physical discussion sessions among the three authors and along asynchronous reviews.

The remainder of the paper is as follows: Sect. 2 investigates needs for data sharing and re-use concepts for OOP implementations by studying literature on data as an infrastructure and on data-driven transformation. Section 3 reviews digitalization concepts and trends in public sector transformation. It also elaborates challenges and needs of collaboration and stakeholder engagement in order to tackle trust and transparency in OOP settings. The synthesis elicits further needs for good data governance in OOP contexts. Section 4 synthesizes elements of good data governance for OOP realization in inter-agency collaboration. The paper concludes with a discussion and outlook into future research towards a comprehensive good data governance concept.

2 Foundations of Data Sharing and Re-use

The following subsections review academic literature and policy documents regarding data as infrastructure asset and data-driven transformation in the public sector. Each subsection concludes with a synthesis of needs for a comprehensive good data governance concept.

2.1 Data as an Infrastructure Asset in the Public Sector

According to OECD, data has become an essential driver of innovation, and it is considered as one of the society's central infrastructure resources [16]. Shin stresses that data infrastructure is a community-wide need [16] and even a public good.

Data meets typical characteristics of infrastructure resources [17–19]: First, data is a non-rival good and it may be consumed for an appreciable range of demands. Second, the social demand for data is driven primarily by downstream productive activities that require them as an input. Third, data may serve as input to a wide range of goods and services. OECD argues that data can serve as a transparent vehicle in the interaction with the sovereign, as an asset for policy making and in the provision of better public services, and/or – through data exchange – as a bond for strengthening collaboration among public agencies [2].

In the last few years, e-government researchers address infrastructure development in a digital environment, stressing that such infrastructures are to be flexible and evolve over time in accordance with the needs of their multiple users [20]. Zuiderwijk criticizes, though, that there is no common understanding of what an infrastructure comprises [21]. Interestingly, little research addresses data as infrastructure asset in the public sector.

Bekkers stresses that data infrastructures entail both technical and social elements [22]. This understanding is extended by Jetzek, who adds a regulatory infrastructure besides the IT infrastructure [23]. The regulatory infrastructure is crucial for trustworthiness, transparency and accountability in sharing sensitive or personal data. However, in a digitalized world, the operationalization of the regulatory or social elements need to be mapped to, and be holistically intertwined with the technical infrastructure.

Data-exchange infrastructures enabling inter-agency collaboration [24] in OOP contexts (i.e. sharing and re-using personal and sensitive data of citizens or business) provide the foundations for interoperable and re-usable solutions of seamless public service provisioning. They embody base registers and directories as key components that are legally controlled and maintained by public administrations and provide authentic sources of information on items such as persons or companies. Along these lines of digital transformation, authentic sources are a key enabler for enhanced service provision. Next, we therefore outline the political significance of data-driven transformation.

While the current research on data as infrastructure focuses mostly on public and open data (see e.g. [19, 21, 25]), the realization of the once-only principle demands for the sharing and re-use of data that is sensitive and that falls under the data protection regulations. We therefore resume that a comprehensive governance for data infrastructures (that enables the sharing and re-use of sensitive and personal data) requires mechanisms to address trustworthiness, transparency as well as data protection to ensure the acceptance by the users. Furthermore, such governance mechanisms must provide appropriate support of inter-agency collaboration. Accordingly, governance mechanisms therefore need to operate in two directions: towards the customer of public service and in the interplay among public agencies.

2.2 Political Significance of Data-Driven Transformation with the OOP

While, as mentioned before, the discussion in the area of data-driven transformation so far focuses on open data infrastructure, the once-only principle addresses sensitive and non-sensitive data. Subsequently, we review the discourse of data as an infrastructure asset with focus on the public sector, highlighting the political relevance of data-driven transformation in an international setting.

A customer-centric approach conveys the proposition of creating value for society and economy. The once-only principle demands that citizens and companies will only have to provide certain standard information to the public agencies once. The once-only principle therefore requires to re-use and exchange (sensitive and personal) data within public authorities to reduce administrative burden for citizens and businesses [1, 26–29]. However, sharing and re-use of such data must be done with due respect of data protection regulations [30], as otherwise trustworthiness of public service provisioning would be hampered tremendously. Hence, trust plays an essential role in inter-agency collaboration.

The implementation of the once-only principle in the European Union is a policy goal settled in the eGovernment Action Plan 2016–2020 [1] and one of the pillars of the strategy for the Digital Single Market [31]. It has been reinforced in the "Tallinn Declaration" signed by the European digital ministers [32] in 2017. The OOP principle is also the underlying vision for the Single Digital Gateway (SDG) Regulation [33], which requires European Member States to build up and connect to a single European portal and infrastructure, through which citizens, businesses and public administrations can execute public services across borders with the OOP as underlying principle.

While the overall implementation of the OOP and of the SDG are still fragmented across the EU, and cross-border applications are limited to a few cases and services, mature infrastructure exists for example in Belgium, Estonia or the Netherlands [12, 34, 35]. In Switzerland, data as infrastructure and data governance play a key role in national strategic papers such as the "Digital Switzerland Strategy" (cf. [19, 36]) and the renewed "E-Government Strategy 2020–2023". Even though Switzerland is not an early adopter regarding digital transformation of the public sector [37], data-centric public sector transformation is gaining political awareness and importance.

To realize the SDG or the Swiss E-Government Strategy, a successful implementation of the OOP requires transfer and re-use of sensitive or personal data between government agencies across borders involving actors on different levels of a political system. Significant effort for the development of a technical infrastructure as well as organizational frameworks are currently developed in several research projects. In an analysis of drivers and barriers for OOP implementation in the SCOOP4C project, trust is stressed as underlying condition [12, 38, 39]. In the TOOP project, trust is addressed with a technical approach by defining a trust architecture as part of the system design [40, 41]. In a broader perspective, TOOP also links the question of trust to the organizational culture of government agencies. However, a systematic and scientifically grounded rigorous analysis of the organizational challenges is currently lacking.

To investigate and elicit the requirements of interoperable data and information sharing along a structured approach, the European Interoperability Framework (EIF) provides a conceptual model for public services and considers data-related services as a basic component for service provision [42]. The SCOOP4C and TOOP projects rely on this EIF to structure their investigations of barriers, enablers and architecture for a comprehensive OOP implementation.

The investigation of the political significance of data-driven transformation with the OOP unveils, in addition to trust, the need for architectural features and interoperability to be addressed in a comprehensive good data governance concept.

3   Digitalization and Collaboration Concepts in the Public Sector

Research on public sector digitalization is continuously changing to reflect how governments react to social, economic, political and other pressures, and how they transform themselves in the process [43]. In this section, we review digitalization concepts and trends of the public sector, and introduce collaboration as a core asset and challenge in the digital transformation. Stakeholder engagement is the third concept, which we see highly relevant when implementing the OOP through data infrastructures in systems interacting across different borders (federal, cross-border in the EU, and similar).

3.1   Digitalization Concepts and Trends in Public Sector Transformation

In literature, scholars discuss the e-government evolution along different models (information, interaction, transaction, integration; e.g. [44–46]). Janowski [43] argues that the concept of electronic government evolves toward more complexity and greater contextualization and specialization. His evolution model comprises digitalization (i.e. technology in government), transformation, engagement and contextualization (i.e. policy-driven digital governance). While digital transformation in the private sector is mostly associated with the need to use new technologies to stay competitive, the goal in the public sector can be manifold: transforming service delivery, transforming organizational culture and relationships with citizens, or value creation as a transformation outcome [47]. These different aspects need integration into a comprehensive good data governance concept.

Recent annual OECD reports spot relevant digitalization trends. The 2017 report stresses new approaches to activating citizens as a partner to shape the future together [48]. In 2018, improving identity, systems approaches and enablers, and inclusiveness are identified as key trends [49]. The 2019 report argues trends such as more transparency, new technologies/open government data/new business models for new ways of public value creation, and transforming policy-making and legislation to be machine-readable and based on algorithms [50]. Exchange of sensitive or personal data between agencies touches upon all of these trends and needs thorough investigation of trustworthiness and data governance.

3.2 Collaboration as Core Asset for Transformation

Inter-agency information sharing is discussed in e-government literature as critical to helping solve complex challenges that are beyond the capacities and capabilities of a single agency. While hierarchical structures continue to have value for government, they do hinder efforts to respond to those policy problems and demands that require collaborative approaches. Clarity of roles and responsibilities nurtures the success of inter-organizational efforts by enabling other relevant determinants, such as building trust among members, increasing their willingness to participate, and mitigating concerns about security [51].

Even though cooperation and collaboration have been addressed in research in the context of digitalization of government, there are few validated results about the determinants of effective governance in inter-organizational settings, especially in the public sector [18]. Research in the field deals with the challenges for inter-organizational cooperation and/or formulates strategies on how to deal with identified key barriers. It often focuses on issues related to cross-agency information sharing in the context of service delivery [52]. Generally, there is a consent that inter-organizational cooperation is demanding: it often combines competition, questions of autonomy, and interdependence [53] and relates to issues associated with the notion of trust [54, 55]. Accordingly, governing and managing in inter-organizational arrangements is different from management within organizations. Enabling leadership is important, since there is no central authority [24]. To illustrate the specific requirements with regard to leading inter-organizational e-government projects, Thomson and Perry identify key dimensions of collaboration, focusing on concrete activities and processes from collaborative governing and administration over forging mutually beneficial relationships to establishing social norms [56].

Klievink and Janssen [57] elaborate on the need for a coordinated e-government service delivery and propose an analytical framework of coordination. They stress that coordination creates dependencies at various levels, including channels for contacting government agencies, business processes, information (systems) and infrastructural dependencies within and among governmental organizations. The most recent version of the European Interoperability Framework (EIF) embodies the concepts of interoperability governance and public service governance as key pillars to ensure interoperability in inter-agency collaboration [13, 42, 58, 59].

3.3 Stakeholder Engagement

The term 'stakeholder' stems from organizational theory and has become an integral concept of information systems research. Freeman defines stakeholder as "*any group or individual who is affected by or can affect the achievement of an organization's objectives*" ([60], p. 3). Bryson argues that stakeholders and their concerns "*must be taken into account by leaders, managers and front-line staff*" [61].

In particular along the transition to deliver online public services basing on the OOP, public services need to be designed 'customer-centric by default', encompassing simplification and seamless combinations of service building blocks from different government entities [62] and with the customer's needs at focus. Concepts like co-creation and co-production can help to engage citizens and other stakeholders in the innovation of public service routines [63].

The SCOOP4C project studied different stakeholder roles along the provision and consumption of data in public services as well as the supervision of compliance towards data protection and privacy [14]. The study comprises case studies to elicit stakeholders and their roles in four public service contexts with sharing and re-use of sensitive or personal data. Subsequently, Panopolou et al. developed a stakeholder engagement plan, which guides strategic decision-makers and project managers in how to involve relevant stakeholders with their different roles in the design and implementation of OOP-driven public services [15].

Stakeholder engagement is a core concept of architecture frameworks like The Open Group Architecture Framework [64]. Such architecture frameworks must provide methods and tools to identify and manage the stakeholder concerns and their interrelationships [61, 64] on the data sharing and re-use contexts.

4   Good Data Governance for OOP Realization

Wang investigates six driving forces or barriers in inter-agency government information [data] sharing: administrative pressure, legal power, department capacity, department interest, risk and accountability, and information demand [65]. The author puts these forces into a dynamic mechanism model of interagency government data sharing and argues that these cross-boundary views need to be properly addressed in an architectural framework supporting good data governance, which include effective mechanisms for incentives, empowerment, institutional enablement, accountability, pulling of data demands, and feedback. In view of implementing the OOP, fostering data-driven innovation therefore requires coherent good data governance to balance access to data and public value, as well as ownership, privacy and data security [2, 5]. Rosenbaum describes this as the process of conceptualizing and realizing data stewardship responsibilities [5], providing a set of governance policies, principles, functions and structures to steer data use and re-use in inter-agency collaborations. To create public and economic value, incentive systems for cooperation and collective action to realize the OOP are needed, covering the entire data life-cycle, as stressed e.g. in [22, 24, 66–68].

Implementing the sharing and re-use of data in inter-agency contexts demands for appropriate organization-wide and inter-agency data governance policies, principles, functions and structures that ensure data quality (through data quality governance) (see e.g. [69]), data availability (data access), adherence to the data principles, data life-cycle and proper use of semantics/metadata [70, 71]. In a literature review, Brous et al. spotted 25 core concepts and principles of data governance, which they clustered into four data governance principles: organization, alignment, compliance, and common understanding [72]. Similarly, Thomson et al. identified three pillars of effective data governance: people, standards and compliance [73].

IT governance research suggests three concepts for preparing, making and implementing decisions on strategic and tactical level, namely: structures, processes, and relational mechanisms [71]. These components are also relevant to data governance. While company-wide data governance frameworks (incl. data quality) have been a topic in information science for decades [69], the inter-organizational use of distributed data raises new challenges. Data governance therefore needs to focus on the key elements that are relevant for cross-boundary common views of reality [74]. In a case study, a set of governance roles and functions was identified [59] and different governance structures were depicted for the digitization of public service and interoperability along four levels of governance: policy (legislation), strategic, tactical and operational [13, 58]. Good data governance needs to provide respective organizational models (structures) for governance and the corresponding roles and functions assigned to the responsible actors to ensure effective and sustainable enablement of sharing and re-use of (sensitive or personal) data in public service provisioning [75]. A relevant framework guiding in the implementation of the OOP is the EIF [42]. The four layers serve as a structure to address open issues in the sharing and re-use of data in inter-agency collaboration.

5 Discussion and Future Research

This paper aimed at reviewing existing literature, policy documents and case studies of data governance and digital transformation in the public sector with a scope of implementing the once-only principle. The objective was to identify factors for a comprehensive good data governance concept, which tackles relevant aspects related to the sharing and reuse of sensitive or personal data in public service provisioning, where the once-only principle is applied.

In answering the research question posed in the introduction, the review of relevant literature identified the following factors, which a comprehensive good data governance concept should address when sharing and reusing sensitive or personal data in public service provisioning based on the OOP:

- To effectively realize digital transformation in the public sector, data is a central infrastructure asset. The different roles data play in public service require a differentiated approach to data infrastructures and to data governance:

  - Open data infrastructures require their peculiar data governance as is discussed largely in literature;
  - The sharing and reuse of sensitive or personal data in inter-agency collaboration demands for its own data infrastructures and good data governance mechanisms. In particular, trustworthiness, transparency and data protection are concepts that must be embodied in a comprehensive good data governance concept.
  - Furthermore, a comprehensive good data governance needs to encompass diversified mechanisms of granting access to data from base registers vs. data being collected from normal sources or form the users.

- The once-only principle builds on data sharing and re-use in inter-agency collaboration of public sector actors. To effectively enable inter-agency collaboration in OOP settings, governance mechanisms need to address stakeholder engagement and data governance in two directions: towards the customer of public service (citizens and business) and in the interplay among public agencies.

- Since the OOP is put forward and politically promoted at European Union level, interoperability is an asset that needs to ensure interoperability and common approaches to data infrastructures at EU and in Member States (and affiliated countries such as Switzerland) alike. The European Interoperability Framework provides a good basis for this. However, in the individual countries, interoperable implementations need to reach out also to the local level actors. A comprehensive good data governance concept needs to reflect this differentiating structural dimension. It needs to accommodate the application of available standards and it needs to ensure compliance of solutions with the political, legal and organizational foundations.
- To master the complexity resulting from the manifold views and viewpoints of sharing and reusing sensitive or personal data in public services, a comprehensive good data governance concept should be closely connected with a supportive architectural framework. Such an architectural framework can guide in the handling of different views and viewpoints, in particular in data sharing in inter-agency collaboration, to tackle the necessary trust, transparency and data protection needs.
- With the new trends in digital transformation as reported in Sect. 3.1, a good data governance concept becomes even more important to ensure trustworthiness and transparency, and ultimately user acceptance of new ways and models of delivering public services. Therefore, stakeholder engagement and co-creation mechanisms need to form integral components of such a governance concept.
- A comprehensive good data governance concept needs to embody clear roles, responsibilities and functions of the actors that interact in data sharing and reuse in OOP contexts and in inter-agency collaborations at different levels of government.
- Beyond individual considerations along the above needs, a good data governance concept has to tackle the interdependencies and mutual influences among these aspects, leading to a comprehensive framework that is actionable. This includes governance policies, principles, functions (or processes) and structures to steer data use and re-use in inter-agency collaboration (including data infrastructures) along the entire data life-cycle.

To sum up the findings in this paper, good data governance not only needs to clarify who can have access to what data for what purpose and under what conditions. It also needs to assign responsibilities and retribution mechanisms for data maintenance and enhancement to ensure the sustainability, trustworthiness and transparency of the common data infrastructure along with the implementation of the good governance principles. All these aspects need to be integrated into a comprehensive concept for a trustworthy and transparent data infrastructure enabling the sharing and re-use of (sensitive or personal) data. The development of such a comprehensive good data governance concept, which also embodies the relevant data and IT security mechanisms, is a next step of our research. The result is envisaged as a framework for good data governance, which addresses the good data governance principles and relevant implementation mechanisms. Along this next step of research, the differentiation of sensitive and non-sensitive data needs to be revisited and examined in more detail. The examination of the resulting good data governance concept is planned through case study research and qualitative empirical research.

References

1. European Commission: EU eGovernment Action Plan 2016–2020 - Accelerating the Digital Transformation of Government. COM/2016/0179 final, Brussels (2016)
2. OECD: Data-Driven Innovation: Big data for growth and well-being, Paris (2015)
3. Agere, S.: Promoting good governance: principles, practices and perspectives. management and training services division, commonwealth secretariat, London (2000)
4. European Commission: European Governance - A white paper. COM/2001/428, Brussels (2001). https://ec.europa.eu/commission/presscorner/api/files/document/print/en/doc_01_10/DOC_01_10_EN.pdf
5. Rosenbaum, S.: Data governance and stewardship: designing data stewardship entities and advancing data access. Health Serv. Res. **45**(5), 1442–1455 (2010)
6. Schintler, L.A., Kulkarni, R.: Big data for policy analysis: the good, the bad, and the ugly. Rev. Policy Res. **31**(4), 343–348 (2014)
7. Kitchenham, B., Brereton, O.P., Budgen, D., Turner, M., Bailey, J., Linkman, S.: Systematic literature reviews in software engineering – a systematic literature review. Inf. Softw. Technol. **51**(1), 7–15 (2009)
8. Webster, J., Watson, R.T.: Analyzing the past to prepare for the future: writing a literature review. MIS Q. **26**(2), iii–xiii (2002)
9. Müller-Bloch, C., Kranz, J.: A framework for rigorously identifying research gaps in qualitative literature reviews. In: Proceedings of 36th International Conference on Information Systems (2015)
10. Estermann, B., Fraefel, M., Neuroni, A.C., Vogel, J.: Conceptualizing a national data infrastructure for Switzerland. Inf. Polity **23**, 1–23 (2018)
11. Klievink, B., Neuroni, A., Fraefel, M., Zuiderwijk, A.: Digital strategies in action - a comparative analysis of national data infrastructure development. In: Proceedings of the 18th Annual International Conference on Digital Government Research (2017)
12. Roustaei, A., et al.: Gap analysis report of challenges, needs and benefits of the OOP4C analysis. In: SCOOP4C Consortium (2019). https://scoop4c.eu/sites/default/files/2019-06/SCOOP4C_D4.1_v1.1.pdf
13. Wimmer, M.A., Scanlon, M., Boneva, R., Rigole, C.: Interoperability governance models. Deliverable for ISA2 Action. European Commission (2017)
14. Kalampokis, E., et al.: Identification and mapping of stakeholders. In: SCOOP4C Consortium (2017). https://scoop4c.eu/sites/default/files/2018-01/SCOOP4C_D2.1.pdf
15. Panopoulou, E., et al.: Strategic stakeholder engagement plan. In: SCOOP4C Consortium (2019). https://scoop4c.eu/sites/default/files/2019-10/SCOOP4C_D22_v1.14_final_0.pdf
16. Shin, D.H.: A critique of Korean national information strategy: case of national information infrastructures. Gov. Inf. Q. **24**(3), 624–645 (2007). https://doi.org/10.1016/j.giq.2006.06.011
17. Frischmann, B.M.: An economic theory of infrastructure and commons management. Minnesota Law Rev. **89**(4), 917–1030 (2005)
18. Estermann, B., Riedl, R., Neuroni, A.C.: Integrated and transcendent e-government: keys for analyzing organizational structure and governance. In: Proceedings of DG.O, pp. 162–171 (2009)
19. Klievink, B., Neuroni, A.C., Fraefel, M., Zuiderwijk, A.: Digital strategies in action – a comparative analysis of national data infrastructure development. In: Proceedings of DG.O, pp. 129–138 (2017)

20. Janssen, M., Chun, S.A., Gil-Garcia, J.R.: Building the next generation of digital government infrastructures. Gov. Inf. Q. **26**(2), 233–237 (2009)
21. Zuiderwijk, A.: Open data infrastructures: The design of an infrastructure to enhance the coordination of open data use. Doctoral thesis, TU Delft, 's-Hertogenbosch (2015). https://doi.org/10.4233/uuid:9b9e60bc-1edd-449a-84c6-7485d9bde012
22. Bekkers, V.: Flexible information infrastructures in Dutch E-Government collaboration arrangements: experiences and policy implications. Gov. Inform. Q. **26**(1), 60–68 (2009)
23. Jetzek, T.: Managing complexity across multiple dimensions of liquid open data: the case of the danish basic data program. Gov. Inf. Q. **33**(1), 89–104 (2016)
24. Neuroni, A.C., Fraefel, M., Riedl, R.: Inter-organizational cooperation in Swiss eGovernment. In: Janssen, M., Scholl, H.J., Wimmer, M.A., Tan, Y.-h. (eds.) EGOV 2011. LNCS, vol. 6846, pp. 259–272. Springer, Heidelberg (2011). https://doi.org/10.1007/978-3-642-22878-0_22
25. Zuiderwijk, A., Janssen, M.: Open data policies, their implementation and impact: a framework for comparison. Gov. Inf. Q. **31**(1), 17–29 (2014)
26. Wimmer, M.A., Marinov, B.: SCOOP4C: Reducing administrative burden for citizens through once-only - vision & challenges. Jusletter IT (2017)
27. Stocksmeier, D., Wimmer, M.A., Führer, M., Essmeyer, K.: Once-only in Deutschland und Europa: Eine Roadmap grenzüberschreitender Vernetzung im Bereich Steuern. In: Digitalisierung von Staat und Verwaltung, pp. 87–98 (2019)
28. Kalvet, T., Toots, M., van Veenstra, A.F., Krimmer, R.: Cross-border e-government services in Europe: expected benefits, barriers and drivers of the once-only principle. In: Proceedings of the 11th International Conference on Theory and Practice of Electronic Governance (ICEGOV 2018), pp. 69–72 (2018)
29. Krimmer, R., Kalvet, T., Toots, M., Cepilovs, A., Tambouris, E.: Exploring and demonstrating the once-only principle: a european perspective. In: Proceedings of the 18th Annual International Conference on Digital Government Research, pp. 546–551 (2017)
30. European Union: Regulation 2016/679 of the European parliament and the council of the European Union. Off. J. Eur. Commun. (2016). https://eur-lex.europa.eu/eli/reg/2016/679/oj
31. European Commission: A digital single market strategy for Europe. COM 192 final (2015). https://eur-lex.europa.eu/legal-content/EN/TXT/?uri=celex%3A52015DC0192
32. Tallinn Declaration: Tallinn declaration on eGovernment at the ministerial meeting during Estonian Presidency of the council of the EU (2017). https://ec.europa.eu/newsroom/document.cfm?doc_id=47559
33. European Union: Regulation (EU) 2018/1724 of the European Parliament and of the council of 2 October 2018 establishing a single digital gateway to provide access to information, to procedures and to assistance and problem-solving services. Off. J. Eur. Commun. (2018). https://eur-lex.europa.eu/legal-content/EN/TXT/?uri=uriserv:OJ.L_2018.295.01.0001.01.ENG
34. Cave, J., Botterman, M., Cavallini, S., Volpe, M.: EU-wide digital once-only principle for citizens and businesses. Study for the European Commission (2017). https://ec.europa.eu/esf/transnationality/filedepot_download/1671/1692
35. Vallner, U., et al.: State of play report of best practices. In: SCOOP4C Consortium (2017). https://scoop4c.eu/sites/default/files/2018-01/SCOOP4C_D1.2_0.pdf
36. Schweizerische Eidgenossenschaft: Strategie "Digitale Schweiz". Bundesrat, Bern (2018). https://www.bakom.admin.ch/bakom/de/home/digital-und-internet/strategie-digitale-schweiz.html
37. Neuroni, A., Kissling-Näf, I., Riedl, R.: E-Government und smarter Staat: Die Schweiz auf halbem Weg. In: Stember, J., Eixelsberger, W., Spichiger, A., Neuroni, A., Habbel, F.-R., Wundara, M. (eds.) Handbuch E-Government, pp. 163–180. Springer, Wiesbaden (2019). https://doi.org/10.1007/978-3-658-21402-9_12

38. Wimmer, M.A., et al.: Roadmap for future areas of actions, and policy recommendations. In: SCOOP4C Consortium (2019). https://scoop4c.eu/sites/default/files/2019-11/SCO OP4C_D4.2_v1.2.pdf
39. Wimmer, M.A. et.al.: Vision of the once-only principle for citizens, including key enablers and major barriers. In: SCOOP4C Consortium (2017). https://scoop4c.eu/sites/default/files/2018-01/SCOOP4C_D1.1.pdf
40. Pavleska, T., Aranha, H., Masi, M., Grandry, E., Sellitto, G.P.: Cybersecurity evaluation of enterprise architectures: the e-SENS case. In: Gordijn, J., Guédria, W., Proper, H.A. (eds.) PoEM 2019. LNBIP, vol. 369, pp. 226–241. Springer, Cham (2019). https://doi.org/10.1007/978-3-030-35151-9_15
41. Grandy, E., et al.: Generic federated OOP architecture. In: TOOP Consortium (2018). http://www.toop.eu/sites/default/files/D22_Generic_Federated_OOP_Architecture_Final.pdf
42. Commission, E.: New European Interoperability Framework - Promoting Seamless Services and Data Flows for European Public Administrations. Publications Office of the European Union, Luxemburg (2017)
43. Janowski, T.: Digital government evolution: from transformation to contextualization. Gov. Inf. Q. **32**(3), 221–236 (2015)
44. Layne, K., Lee, J.: Developing fully functional E-government: a four stage model. Gov. Inf. Q. **18**(2), 122–136 (2001)
45. Andersen, K.V., Henriksen, H.Z.: E-government maturity models: extension of the Layne and Lee model. Gov. Inf. Q. **23**(2), 236–248 (2006)
46. Scholta, H., Mertens, W., Kowalkiewicz, M., Becker, J.: From one-stop shop to no-stop shop: an e-government stage model. Gov. Inf. Q. **36**(1), 11–26 (2019)
47. Mergel, I., Edelmann, N., Haug, N.: Defining digital transformation: results from expert interviews. Gov. Inf. Q. **36**(4), 101385 (2019)
48. OECD: Embracing innovation in government - global trends 2017 (2017)
49. OECD: Embracing innovation in government - global trends 2018 (2018)
50. OECD: Embracing innovation in government. Global trends 2019 (2019)
51. Gil-Garcia, J.R., Guler, A., Pardo, T.A., Burke, G.B.: Characterizing the importance of clarity of roles and responsibilities in government inter-organizational collaboration and information sharing initiatives. Gov. Inf. Q. **36**(4), 101393 (2019)
52. Karlsson, F., Frostenson, M., Prenkert, F., Kolkowska, E., Helin, S.: Inter-organisational information sharing in the public sector: a longitudinal case study on the reshaping of success factors. Gov. Inf. Q. **34**(4), 567–577 (2017)
53. McGuire, M.: Collaborative public management: assessing what we know and how we know it. Public Admin. Rev. **66**(s1), 33–43 (2006)
54. Agranoff, R., McGuire, M.: Big questions in public network management research. J. Public Admin. Res. Theory **11**(3), 295–326 (2001)
55. Gil-Garcia, R.J., Chengalur-Smith, I.S., Duchessi, P.: Collaborative e-Government: impediments and benefits of information-sharing projects in the public sector. Eur. J. Inf. Syst. **16**(2), 121–133 (2007)
56. Thomson, A.M., Perry, J.L.: Collaboration processes: inside the black box. Public Adm. Rev. **66**(s1), 20–32 (2006)
57. Klievink, B., Janssen, M.: Developing multi-layer information infrastructures: advancing social innovation through public-private governance. Inf. Syst. Manag. **31**(3), 240–249 (2014)
58. Wimmer, M.A., Boneva, R., di Giacomo, D.: Interoperability governance: a definition and insights from case studies in Europe. In: Proceedings of 19th Annual International Conference on Digital Government Research (2018)
59. Wimmer, M.A., Zamboni, A., Boneva, R.: Organisational interoperability guidelines. Deliverable for ISA2 action. European Commission (2016)

60. Freeman, E.R.: Strategic Management: A Stakeholder Approach. Pitman, New York (1984)
61. Bryson, J.M.: What to do when stakeholders matter: stakeholder identification and analysis techniques. Public Manag. Rev. **6**(1), 21–53 (2004)
62. Kavanaugh, A.L., et al.: Social media use by government: from the routine to the critical. Gov. Inf. Q. **29**(4), 480–491 (2012)
63. Wimmer, M.A., Scherer, S.: Supporting communities through social government in co-creation and co-production of public services: the SocialGov concept and platform architecture. Int. J. Public Adm. Digit. Age **5**(1), 18–35 (2018)
64. The Open Group: The TOGAF® Standard. Version 9.2, 11th edn. Van Haren Publishing, 's-Hertogenbosch (2018)
65. Wang, F.: Understanding the dynamic mechanism of interagency government data sharing. Gov. Inf. Q. **35**(4), 536–546 (2018)
66. Cordella, A., Bonina, C.M.: A public value perspective for ICT enabled public sector reforms: a theoretical reflection. Gov. Inf. Q. **29**(4), 512–520 (2012)
67. Millard, J.: Open governance systems: doing more with more. Gov. Inf. Q. **35**(4), 577–587 (2018)
68. Klievink, B., Bharosa, N., Tan, Y.-H.: The collaborative realization of public values and business goals: governance and infrastructure of public–private information platforms. Gov. Inf. Q. **33**(1), 67–79 (2016)
69. Weber, K., Otto, B., Österle, H.: One size does not fit all—a contingency approach to data governance. J. Data Inf. Qual. **1**(1) (2009). https://dl.acm.org/doi/10.1145/1515693.1515696. Article 4
70. Cheong, L.K., Chang, V.: The need for data governance: a case study. In: Proceedings of 18th Australasian Conference on Information Systems, pp. 999–1008 (2007)
71. Khatri, V., Brown, C.: Designing data governance. Commun. ACM **53**(1), 148–152 (2010)
72. Brous, P., Janssen, M., Vilminko-Heikkinen, R.: Coordinating decision-making in data management activities: a systematic review of data governance principles. In: Scholl, H.J., et al. (eds.) EGOVIS 2016. LNCS, vol. 9820, pp. 115–125. Springer, Cham (2016). https://doi.org/10.1007/978-3-319-44421-5_9
73. Thompson, N., Ravindran, R., Nicosia, S.: Government data does not mean data governance: lessons learned from a public sector application audit. Gov. Inf. Q. **32**(3), 316–322 (2015)
74. Soma, K., Termeer, C., Opdam, P.: Informational governance – a systematic literature review of governance for sustainability in the information age. Environ. Sci. Policy **56**, 89–99 (2016)
75. Spichiger, A., Rötzer, H.J., Neuroni, A.: Hoheitliches Handeln und Registerführung. In: Stember, J., Eixelsberger, W., Spichiger, A., Neuroni, A., Habbel, F.-R., Wundara, M. (eds.) Handbuch E-Government. LNCS, pp. 229–244. Springer, Wiesbaden (2019). https://doi.org/10.1007/978-3-658-21402-9_23

Governance Challenges of Inter-organizational Digital Public Services Provisioning: A Case Study on Digital Invoicing Services in Belgium

Stijn Wouters[1]([⊠]) [iD], Marijn Janssen[2] [iD], and Joep Crompvoets[1] [iD]

[1] KU Leuven, Louvain, Belgium
{Stijn.Wouters,Joep.Crompvoets}@kuleuven.be
[2] Delft University of Technology, Delft, The Netherlands

Abstract. Governments aim to digitalize public services. Whereas initially they worked in isolation, nowadays they increasingly link different building blocks together to realize integrated public services. This evolution poses challenges concerning the governance of public services. The purpose of this paper is to identify governance challenges in inter-organizational digital public service delivery. To do this, we investigated a case study that deals with the creation of digital invoicing services in Belgium. The findings show seven groups of governance challenges that incorporate technical, organizational and inter-organizational factors. Governance challenges can be external, related to the environment and the users, as well as internal, related to the digitalization objectives and governance dynamics. Moreover, as public services evolve over time, so do governance challenges, suggesting that governance regimes may have to evolve accordingly to maintain coordinated service delivery.

Keywords: Public service delivery · E-government · Inter-organizational collaboration · Governance challenges

1 Introduction

Public administrations are continuously undertaking efforts to digitalize and integrate public services. Numerous factors drive these efforts, including technological innovations, changing user expectations, more holistic views on how services can be delivered to citizens, but also persisting goals to realize efficiency gains and increase service delivery effectiveness [5, 7]. Many administrations are, however, still characterized by fragmentation. This is due to specialization, the legal context and the impact of administrative reforms [22]. In such a context, integration efforts transform the delivery of public services from organizational boundaries or governmental 'silos' to complex inter-organizational networks [4, 7].

Inter-organizational services can be conceptualized as service delivery chains consisting of several building blocks [23]. Building blocks are managed separately or jointly by different public sector organizations. They provide functionality that can be reused

© IFIP International Federation for Information Processing 2020
Published by Springer Nature Switzerland AG 2020
G. Viale Pereira et al. (Eds.): EGOV 2020, LNCS 12219, pp. 223–235, 2020.
https://doi.org/10.1007/978-3-030-57599-1_17

across multiple integrated and inter-organizational services. Examples include platforms to allow the exchange of information and building blocks for identification and authentication services. In general, service provisioning within the larger digital government infrastructure can be characterized as modular [25] and consists of delivery chains of loosely-coupled building blocks. Such services deal with for example life events or procurement services.

Developing and maintaining integrated public services also faces multiple challenges [26]. This is related to many factors, including how administrations function, what skills and capabilities are necessary and how building blocks, services and organizations can be managed [1]. Governance is necessary to navigate those challenges [25].

In the context of integrated service delivery, Klievink and Janssen [23] identified several challenges that deal with interdependencies regarding the coordination of business processes, information, standards, (legacy) information systems and infrastructures within and across organizations. Yang and Maxwell [34] reported challenges relating to outsourcing, differing technological capabilities between involved organizations, and ensuring information security. Other challenges are related to developing flexible architectures, maintaining the goals and objectives of the particular digital public service [33] and understanding the various stakeholders in the public, private and non-profit sectors [2].

A specific challenge has to do with improving and retaining interoperability. Interoperability is the ability of disparate systems to exchange and use information in such a way that allows them to work together [29, 34]. On a technical level this relates to building a flexible infrastructure and connecting building blocks at a low cost to deliver new services [32]. On an organizational level this concerns the ability to share resources effectively across stakeholders [29]. According to Pardo et al. [29], interoperability is a capability that alleviates interdependencies. For example, organizations that already use the same data standards and have compatible regulatory frameworks can more easily link together existing buildings blocks to deliver new or integrate existing services.

Although many challenges can be found in the literature, research on governance challenges concerning inter-organizational services in particular remains rather scarce [8]. Therefore, we pose the following research question: *What are governance challenges in developing and maintaining inter-organizational digital public services and how do they evolve over time?*

We investigated a single case study on inter-organizational digital public services provisioning in-depth that involves the digitalization of invoicing in Belgian public administrations. Traditionally, sending invoices relied on direct communication between the procuring public organization and the private supplier. Invoicing services were characterized by a high administrative burden with long processing times and fines for public administrations due to late payments. Digitalization efforts have led to the creation of a common building block with user-to-machine (U2M) communication and machine-to-machine (M2M) integration based on the receiving capabilities of both businesses and public sector organizations.

The paper proceeds as follows. In Sect. 2, we review the literature and the challenges that have been identified in inter-organizational digital public services. Section 3 details the research approach and provides the description of the case. In Sect. 4 we present and discuss our main findings, while Sect. 5 provides the conclusion.

2 Background: Governance Challenges

Research specifically focusing on governance challenges within an inter-organizational setting is rather limited [8]. To gain a first insight into governance challenges of inter-organizational digital public services, we also look at the general e-government literature on service delivery. In a study on challenges concerning the inter-organizational dimension of integrated service delivery, Christiansson et al. [8] classify challenges based on the development phases of a digital service (pre-conditions, design, and development and delivery). Klievink and Janssen [23] note that (inter)dependencies are a major challenge to realize coordinated public service delivery. Those (inter)dependencies can be affiliated with one or more factors. Factors that have been identified include technical, informational, (intra-)organizational, managerial, cultural, legal, political, institutional and strategic factors [7, 16, 23, 28, 34]. In the following, we consider technological, organizational and inter-organizational factors [7, 28] and corresponding challenges as a starting point to distinguish the governance challenges of inter-organizational digital public services in the case.

Technological factors (including factors due to information) relate to the integration of separate building blocks into functional services. Challenges in this regard have to do with finding agreement on semantic and technical standards to be able to integrate building blocks, to automate and exchange data in a meaningful way and to integrate and automate business processes and rules [6, 16, 23]. Christiansson et al. [8] add security issues. Elements identified by Chen et al. [7] also regard the quality of building blocks (e.g. ease of use, functionalities) and the quality of the overall service. Yang and Maxwell [34] also identify challenges related to the outsourcing of building blocks to the private sector, which have to do with the sharing of information concerning the specification of the building blocks or incorporating changes to the functionalities.

Organizational (also managerial) factors deal with management support towards inter-organizational collaboration, the creation of an organizational culture that incentivizes collaboration and holistic views on service delivery in relation to the user and the development of adequate organizational capabilities [7, 11]. They also include the development of adequate organizational capabilities [28]. One such organizational capability has to do with creating and sharing knowledge, both overall as well as for a specific service [8]. Lindgren and Melin [26] note challenges due to a lack of resources, which can be related to (inter alia) financial capacity [16, 33]. Organizations also need to possess the necessary technical capabilities to be able to adopt new technologies or integrate building blocks [6].

Inter-organizational (also institutional) factors contain challenges relating to how or why organizations collaborate in networks. Fan et al. [13] cite shared resource management, competing authority and the number of participants as specific inter-organizational challenges. Interdependencies are a main driver for collaboration [7]. Thus, knowledge about these interdependencies is a key element to foster and sustain collaboration. Axelsson et al. [2] note challenges regarding stakeholder management and the division of roles and responsibilities. Additionally, Christiansson et al. [8] found challenges relating to expectations management on service quality, finding partner matches, and leadership.

According to Klievink and Janssen [23], the conclusion of agreements and contracts may be necessary to coordinate roles and responsibilities. Such agreements can also alleviate challenges relating to data ownership, risks and accountability [10].

Interoperability also has an inter-organizational component [7]. Specifically, it requires shared goals and values between collaborating organizations to develop common standards and share information [6]. Pardo et al. [29] find that interoperability necessitates that diverging policies are aligned and regulatory frameworks are changed to enable the sharing of information and resources.

Many authors also denote creating and maintaining trust as a necessary element for successful collaboration [4, 7, 34]. Trust is enabled through shared objectives, a shared understanding of the problem and past collaboration [6, 34]. It does not only decrease the complexity of the inter-organizational network, but also enhances organizational learning and future collaboration [6].

Dawes et al. [11] mention cultural challenges related to the creation and embeddedness of knowledge within organizations (which can be entrenched within processes and data structures), but also risk-averseness (or even resistance) towards inter-organizational collaboration and potential innovation [7]. Dawes et al. [11] advocate incentives for information sharing, a supportive culture towards collaboration at the organizational level, but also more generally advocate legal and regulatory frameworks and appropriate legal authority to overcome such challenges (see also [28]).

Concerning environmental factors, Cordella and Bonina [10] distinguish challenges posed by the administrative, legal and political context. Together, these context factors might constitute constraints on the possibility to integrate different building blocks across organizations and across administrative levels, to develop and use shared building blocks, to exchange of information and to allow inter-organizational collaboration to form. For example, the administrative context has an impact on the horizontal and vertical fragmentation of the supply of public services. The legal context also delineates who can take responsibility to provide specific services. The political context is relevant, because it can uphold commitment through executive support [16]. This is manifested through authority, but also the passing of necessary legislation and the provision of resources. Executive support appears especially relevant in the early phases of collaboration, before the formalization of roles and financial resources [16].

3   Research Method

To examine the governance challenges in the case of e-invoicing, we take a research approach that can ontologically be considered as case-centric research. The interpretivist and pragmatic approach towards epistemology is aimed at identifying governance challenges that are constructive in relation to the research question, i.e. the former is instrumental to the latter [18]. Following the research question, an exploratory case study was chosen. It offers the advantage of studying complex phenomena with a limited number of actors into extensive detail and allows to take the context into account, which is key to identify governance challenges [16]. A qualitative methodological choice allows us to delineate governance challenges in the case [36].

The criteria for case selection were the following: the case had to entail multiple public administrations, the involved public sector organizations collaborated to create a new integrated inter-organizational service, and the service could be conceptualized as a service delivery chain, based on the integration of existing building blocks or the development of new (shared) building blocks to deliver required capabilities.

We used a case that aims to digitalize invoicing services in Belgium. Data collection rested on multiple data collection types. A document analysis was done with public and internal policy documents (that were made available), laws, regulations, government white papers and technical specifications at the regional, federal and European levels. From the document, we could derive (changes in the) infrastructure and (changing) strategic and operational goals. This was complemented with 14 interviews, conducted between 2016 and 2018, with project and product managers of public sector organizations at the Belgian federal and regional levels. The criterion for purposeful sampling of the respondents was their affiliation with the governance of the invoicing services and the management of the corresponding building blocks (i.e. the common invoicing building blocks, enterprise service busses and enterprise resource planning systems). Using a semi-structured format, the questions ranged from motivations relating to architecture, solutions and goals, as well as governance challenges between the different users, stakeholders and the political level from a strategic, legal, organizational, informational, technical and financial point of view. This allowed us to delimit the most important governance challenges, but also revealed the interdependencies between the challenges, changes over time and coping strategies. The analysis rested on an iterative process that used the literature as a starting point to guide the categorization of the responses into governance challenges [20, 34]. Two follow-up interviews were organized in 2019 with the two central actors regarding the phases in the evolution of the service and the governance challenges we distinguished.

As part of e-procurement, e-invoicing consists of the electronic transfer of billing and payment information between business partners. Typically, this includes a supplier of procured goods or services, a buyer and/or intermediaries [31]. The digitalization of invoicing can be described by four phases. First, an initiation phase took place. Multiple regional administrations and the federal administration separately investigated options to develop a shared infrastructure for their own administrative level. In the second phase, a pilot was commenced by the federal government and later joined by one of the regional governments to (1) test the shared infrastructure and (2) to extend it to multiple administrations. The third phase dealt with operationalizing the pilot. It saw the incorporation of the elements of its evaluation, adapting to European legislation, the extension of the interaction to various stakeholders, alignment with other regional governments and the implementation of (uncoordinated) adoption strategies.

We also discerned a fourth phase that is characterized by expansion and adaptation. The use of the shared infrastructure was expanded to new groups of users, especially local administrations and organizations within the broader public sector. Additional capabilities were also added to the infrastructure to cope with differing expectations. The scope was enlarged as well. While first focus was directed to business-to-government (B2G) and business-to-business (B2B) invoicing, later phases also included government-to-business (G2B) invoices and other services associated with e-procurement.

4 Findings

This section presents and discusses each of the governance challenges we discerned in the case. Based on the methodology described above, we were able to distinguish seven main groups of governance challenges in the case through a triangulation of the literature, documents and interviews. While they have been put forward in the literature separately to a greater or lesser extent, we found that (1) each of those challenges varied over time. Moreover, (2) the governance challenges do not correspond one to one regarding the categorization of challenges into technological, organizational and inter-organizational factors. Rather, most governance challenges incorporate multiple factors. (3) Governance challenges can be interrelated and require coordinated action.

Table 1 comprises the governance challenges prevalent in the case. First, it details the factors of which each challenge is composed of, i.e. technological (T), organizational (O) and inter-organizational (IO). Second, it shows how the governance challenges evolve over the four phases in the case. In what follows we analyze each governance challenge and its prevalence over time.

Table 1. Governance challenges in e-invoicing.

Governance Challenges (factors)	Phase 1: Initiation	Phase 2: Piloting and Evaluating	Phase 3: Operationalizing	Phase 4: Expansion and Adaptation
1. User approach (T, O, IO)	Examination of the scope and choice of an approach towards the user as part of the strategy		The evaluation (and expansion of the) scope and approach. The coordination of adoption strategies	
2. Functionalities, shared infrastructure and capabilities (T, O, IO)	The identification of the necessary functionalities and capabilities	The piloting and evaluation of the service, connecting building blocks	Redefinition of functionalities, building capacity. Coordination of demand and supply	Expansion of functionalities, phasing out of legacies. Development of additional shared building blocks
3. Dependencies & relation to the environment (T, O, IO)	Identification of relevant dependencies	Coordination of dependencies	Coordination of internal path dependencies and external relation to the environment	
4. Division of roles and responsibilities (O, IO)	Identification of leadership	Sustaining coordinated leadership. Make a division of the roles and responsibilities of leadership and stakeholders. Build and maintain governance dynamics		
5. Stakeholder management (IO)	Identification of stakeholders, in relation to the user approach	Identification stakeholders for pilot. Creation of a stakeholder community	Identification of new stakeholders in relation to the user scope and approach, as well as towards adoption strategies. Coordination with stakeholder community	
6. Expectations management (IO)	Exploration of expectations and finding mutual understanding		Maintaining and coordinating changing expectations in relation to the user approach	
7. Agreements and contracts (O, IO)	Identification of necessity of agreements	Mutual understanding on cost distribution	Agreement on cost distribution, formal agreements depending on inclusion of outside stakeholders	

The first governance challenge refers to establishing a coordinated **approach to interact with the user (1)**, whereas administrations are fragmented. In the initial phases, the user approach dealt with setting up a strategy about how to address user needs and incorporate user preferences. This first required the identification of the (possible) internal and external users. For invoicing, these were private suppliers and their intermediaries on the on hand, and public sector organizations at all administrative levels on the other hand. Second, the (prioritization of the) scope of the service had to be settled (i.e. B2G and B2B invoicing, followed by G2B invoicing). The integrated user approach had an impact on many factors. Concerning technological factors, a new building block for invoices had to be developed. Regarding organizational factors, procuring public sector organizations had to change the way they interacted with their suppliers. With respect to inter-organizational factors, adoption strategies needed to be coordinated. This especially became a challenge in the later phases. Political priorities were not aligned, which perpetuated a fragmented approach. Agreement on the architecture of the service in relation to the user approach could only partly alleviate this lack of political coordination.

Delineating an approach to interact with the user is not straightforward. Many different (groups of) users might exist, each with different roles and varying capabilities [2]. While ideal, it is difficult to fully understand user needs [7, 8]. This is especially so as they might shift over time in reaction to the new service.

The second governance challenge is the identification, creation, linking and prioritization of (i) the **functionalities** that are distributed over many organizations into a **shared infrastructure,** as well as (ii) the **(technological and organizational) capabilities** those organizations have to possess to provide integrated services **(2)**. It is preferable to assess whether existing building blocks have the required functionalities and can be incorporated into the service before setting up shared building blocks [14]. Elements of such as an assessment can include the functionalities of legacies and the financial capacity to develop new building blocks. In the initiation phase, it was not immediately clear what functionalities were necessary or reusable. Governments eventually settled on a new building block, Mercurius, that allowed the manual entering of invoices through a portal, but clearly favored M2M communication. Mercurius was also designed to mediate the different receiving capabilities of small and large businesses as well as those of public sector organizations. This allowed the gradual implementation of ICT-changes [6].

A flexible infrastructure has been favored to overcome challenges [22]. Together with an incremental approach towards the integration of user groups, this could allow focus to be directed first on essential functionalities [8] and an effective end-to-end service design. Also, a gradual adoption of the service may overcome limited financial resources the project receives. Based on the interaction of the proposed service design with users, shared building blocks might need to be redefined. Janssen and van der Voort [21] advocate agile development methods to alleviate this challenge.

As a third challenge, governance has to constantly take into account **dependencies and the environment (3)** to establish high quality services, incorporate opportunities and quickly deal with possible constraints [12, 21, 23]. In the case, legal barriers for formal intergovernmental collaboration were high due to the federal state structure. This paved the way to an informal collaboration and governance challenges relating to the division of roles and responsibilities and stakeholder management. Concerning technological factors an issue in the case related to the creation of a common identifier for each single public sector organization. Business rules had to be created on top of the standardized (European) invoice format, as well as additional functionalities to deal with the different syntaxes mandated by the European legislation.

Another challenge within the case was balancing the cost to alleviate path-dependencies in terms of time and effort with the overall progress in relation to the objectives. To deal with dependencies, interoperability is of vital concern [3]. Interoperability is especially relevant in the development of a service, for example concerning semantic interoperability or quickly connecting existing building blocks [32]. However, interoperability also needs to be maintained in later phases.

Other environmental factors that might be relevant are changing user preferences (both internal as an outcome of the changes in the service delivery and external from digital transformation outside of the public sector, [29]), and technological innovations [22] that might provide more suitable solutions regarding the needs of the users.

The fourth governance challenge refers to the **division of the roles and responsibilities across stakeholders (4)** to reduce role ambiguity and uncertainty among diverse actors [17]. In the case, authority resulted from multiple political decisions that gave a broad mandate to central government organizations within clearly defined strategic and operational goals [16]. For each administrative level, different public sector organizations were mandated to steer e-invoicing projects. Since the legal context did not allow hierarchical intergovernmental relations, those public sector organizations had to come to an agreement on a division of roles and responsibilities. This was found through the coordination of the approach towards the overall development of the service, the evaluation of the pilot, a distribution of financial resources, as well as measures to foster adoption and adapt to changes in the environment. Other roles were mainly tied to responsibilities concerning the management of the involved building blocks. Another challenge concerned the formation of leadership between stakeholders, and creating what Emerson et al. [12] describe as a collaborative dynamics. In the case, prior collaborations between the project managers created a functional partner match generated mutual trust [8, 34].

The distribution of roles and responsibilities is also likely to change over phases. In the initiation phase, for instance, an administrative simplification team was instrumental to bring together stakeholders in a more formal governance structure. Leadership in later phases was asserted by formally assigned lead organizations and project managers.

The fifth governance challenge deals with the **management of public and private stakeholders (5)** with different needs and interests. Good stakeholder management is key to building and maintaining commitment, since stakeholders are likely to give up part of their autonomy. Central questions are the identification of the internal and external stakeholders, the involvement of the users (in an active role as co-creators, or a more passive role as consumers), and the form of stakeholder management.

The governance regime in the case of e-invoicing can be characterized as a lead-government organization network [31]. To organize the diverse number of stakeholders (in addition to the building block owners, the representatives of businesses, intermediaries, and procuring public sector organizations), the lead-government organizations opted for a loose stakeholder community. On the one hand they organized different groups of public and private stakeholders based on the capabilities of the building blocks under their responsibility. On the other hand, they reused already existing coordination structures. Stakeholders were involved based on the specific governance challenges at hand. Participation of stakeholder groups also varied depending on the phase and the particular governance challenge (in particular the specific user scope).

Sixth, closely related to stakeholder management is the **management of expectations (6)** between the variety of stakeholders' needs, motivations and expectations [8]. This is necessary to create a capacity for joint action [4, 12] and to reduce the possibility of stakeholder resistance [2]. For the invoicing case, the impetus for collaboration initially was the potential increase in the internal efficiency of the involved public administrations. Later phases saw shifts toward user-orientation and external efficiency. This had a profound impact on the architecture of the service. The lead-government organizations also had to deal with possible resistance caused by the disruption of digital invoicing in the market of intermediaries (e.g. accounting offices), since many businesses rely on those intermediaries to process invoices. One strategy was to change the expectations of the businesses to favor digital invoicing over sending PDF's. Gil-Garcia et al. [17] advocate balancing the varying expectations between different groups of stakeholders to diminish the risk that stakeholder resistance threatens both development and adoption. If users value the new service, adopt it and change their expectations, existing dependencies between partnering public (and private) organizations will likely intensify and create strong incentives to continue delivering integrated services.

The seventh governance challenge deals with finding a balance between the extent that **agreements and contracts (7)** are necessary and facilitate collaboration and the extent that they pose barriers to integration. Differences exist between agreements and contracts among involved organizations on the one hand and those with external service providers on the other hand [34]. In the case of e-invoicing, it was opted not to negotiate formal agreements because of uncertainty regarding the effectiveness of the preferred architecture. Nevertheless, agreements still had to be found concerning the cost distribution and to allow adequate flexibility for different governments to speed up the rollout of the service and the addition of functionalities. An equitable cost distribution was mainly realized through the negotiation of an open framework contract with the external service provider of the shared building block. This created trust between the partners and alleviated earlier uncertainties about commitment. As the service matures, more formal agreements between partners might become necessary to give voice and exit options to stakeholders (if they want to end the collaboration without disrupting service delivery) and to agree to a more concrete cost distribution.

In addition to these seven governance challenges acting separately, they are also likely to be **interdependent**. This appears especially relevant regarding the incorporation of a holistic view in relation to the entire service ecosystem. It appears that service delivery is not static, but changes over time. The external service environment, the dynamics of the internal service environment and their interaction both shape and change the provisioning of a service. Many groups of users may exist at different ends of the service chain. This can create additional complexity. Ideally, a flexible infrastructure can provide coping mechanisms to alleviate the different technical capabilities.

As the service matures, governance challenges may shift. In early phases, dealing with challenges regarding the architecture and a coordinated user approach was paramount. Later phases saw attention directed to stakeholder management, expectations management and finding agreements and contracts.

The relative importance of governance challenges can also change over time. When designing and developing inter-organizational services, delineating mutual goals, building trust and coming to a mutual understanding on the eventual infrastructure is vital for success. Once the integrated service becomes stable and more mature, governance needs to become more mature as well. More formal agreements might be preferable, but it is also important that they remain sufficiently adaptable.

5   Conclusion

The aim of our study was to identify governance challenges of inter-organizational digital public services. From a single exploratory case study, our analysis revealed seven diverse groups of governance challenges that are themselves interdependent. They are related to (1) creating a coordinated approach to the groups of users by various organizations, (2) exploring the necessary functionalities offered by different organizations and building shared infrastructures, (3) managing path-dependencies and changes in the environment, (4) dividing roles over many organizations and coordinating leadership, (5) identifying and managing the different needs of stakeholders and (6) their expectations, and (7) the extent of clear agreements and contracts, the latter which includes the distribution of costs among the stakeholders.

The challenges do generally not fit clearly within the more typical classification of challenges into technological, organizational and inter-organizational factors in the literature. This suggests that governance strategies cannot deal with just one factor at the time, but that they have to address factors simultaneously to enable integrated service delivery. The case also revealed that public services are not static, but change over time and that accordingly governance challenges and their relative importance may change as well. To enact the transformation of service provisioning and foster adoption, attention might have to be paid to the different speeds at which users can integrate.

The inter-organizational context adds complexity and creates further dependencies. Challenges in this regard relate to maintaining (possibly changing) shared objectives among the actors and coordinating adoption at the political level, managing uncertainty, prioritization the development of functionalities, expanding the service delivery to different types of users, building a capacity to be adaptive and cope with legacies, and incorporating the time necessary to implement changes, develop capabilities.

The limitations of the single case study research include the generalizability of the governance challenges faced in different countries, in different contexts, within other types of services as well as governance challenges faced by other groups of stakeholders.

The findings point to practical insights that might also be relevant for similar contexts. Public administrators in charge of specific inter-organizational services or for the separate building blocks might benefit of a holistic view on digital services as well as long-term and step-by-step development and adaptation processes, where governance is aligned to the challenges.

While out of the scope of this research, it might be possible that to deal with these challenges, public organizations can take advantage of multiple and changing instruments for governance, that rely on different mechanisms. This is a path for future research, together with building on the identified challenges through the examination of different inter-organizational services.

Acknowledgements. This research has been supported by the Policy Research Centre on Governance Innovation in Flanders, Belgium.

References

1. Agranoff, R.: Collaborating to Manage: A Primer for the Public Sector. Georgetown University Press, Washington, D.C. (2012)
2. Ashaye, O.R., Irani, Z.: The role of stakeholders in the effective use of e-government resources in public services. Int. J. Inf. Manag. **49**, 253–270 (2019)
3. Axelsson, K., Melin, U., Lindgren, I.: Public e-services for agency efficiency and citizen benefit – findings from a stakeholder centered analysis. Gov. Inf. Q. **30**(1), 10–22 (2013)
4. Bekkers, V.: The governance of back-office integration. Public Manag. Rev. **9**(3), 377–400 (2007)
5. Chen, B.: Assessing interorganizational networks for public service delivery: a process-perceived effectiveness framework. Public Perform. Manag. Rev. **31**(3), 348–363 (2008)
6. Chen, Y.-C.: Citizen-centric e-government services: understanding integrated citizen service information systems. Soc. Sci. Comput. Rev. **28**(4), 427–442 (2010)
7. Chen, Y.-C., Lee, J.: Collaborative data networks for public service: governance, management, and performance. Public Manag. Rev. **20**(5), 672–690 (2018)
8. Chen, Y.-C., Hu, L.-T., Tseng, K.-C., Juang, W.-J., Chang, C.-K.: Cross-boundary e-government systems: determinants of performance. Gov. Inf. Q. **36**(3), 449–459 (2019)
9. Christiansson, M.-T., Axelsson, K., Melin, U.: Inter-organizational public e-service development: emerging lessons from an inside-out perspective. In: Tambouris, E., et al. (eds.) EGOV 2015. LNCS, vol. 9248, pp. 183–196. Springer, Cham (2015). https://doi.org/10.1007/978-3-319-22479-4_14
10. Cordella, A., Bonina, C.M.: A public value perspective for ICT enabled public sector reforms: a theoretical reflection. Gov. Inf. Q. **29**(4), 512–520 (2012)
11. Dawes, S.: Interagency information sharing: expected benefits, manageable risks. J. Policy Anal. Manag. **15**(3), 377–394 (1996)
12. Dawes, S., Cresswell, A., Pardo, T.: From "need to know" to "need to share": tangled problems, information boundaries, and the building of public sector knowledge networks. Public Adm. Rev. **69**(3), 392–402 (2009)
13. Emerson, K., Nabatchi, T., Balogh, S.: An integrative framework for collaborative governance. J. Public Adm. Res. **22**(1), 1–29 (2012)
14. Fan, B., Liu, R., Huang, K., Zhu, Y.: Embeddedness in cross-agency collaboration and emergency management capability: evidence from Shanghai's urban contingency plans. Gov. Inf. Q. **36**(4), 101395 (2019)
15. Fraefel, M., Selzam, T., Riedl, R.: Organization requirement for building up national e-government infrastructures in federal settings. In: Bui, T.X., Jr. Sprague, R.H. (eds.) Proceedings of the 46th Hawaii International Conference on System Sciences (HICSS-46), pp. 1642–1651. IEEE, Koloa (2013)

16. Gerring, J.: What is a case study and what is it good for? Am. Polit. Sci. Rev. **98**(2), 341–354 (2004)
17. Gil-Garcia, J.R., Sayogo, D.S.: Government inter-organizational information sharing initiatives: understanding the main determinants of success. Gov. Inf. Q. **33**(3), 572–582 (2016)
18. Gil-Garcia, J.R., Guler, A., Pardo, T.A., Burke, G.B.: Characterizing the importance of clarity of roles and responsibilities in government inter-organizational collaboration and information sharing initiatives. Gov. Inf. Q. **36**(4), 101393 (2019)
19. Goldkuhl, G.: Pragmatism vs interpretivism in qualitative information systems research. Eur. J. Inf. Syst. **21**(2), 135–146 (2012)
20. Hay, C.: Political Analysis. Macmillan, Basingstoke (2002)
21. Janssen, M., van der Voort, H.: Adaptive governance: towards a stable, accountable and responsive government (editorial). Gov. Inf. Q. **33**(1), 1–5 (2016)
22. Janssen, M., Chun, S.A., Gil-Garca, J.R.: Building the next generation of digital government infrastructures. Gov. Inf. Q. **26**(2), 233–237 (2009)
23. Klievink, B., Janssen, M.: Realizing joined-up government: dynamic capabilities and stage models for transformation. Gov. Inf. Q. **26**(2), 275–284 (2009)
24. Klievink, B., Janssen, M.: Coordinating e-government service delivery. In: Chun, S.A., Moses, J., Luna-Reyes, L. (eds.) Proceedings of the 11th Annual International Conference on Digital Government Research, pp. 209–216, Puebla, Mexico (2010)
25. Klievink, B., Bharosa, N., Tan, Y.-H.: The collaborative realization of public values and business goals: governance and infrastructure of public–private information platforms. Gov. Inf. Q. **33**(1), 67–79 (2016)
26. Kostakis, V.: How to reap the benefits of the "digital revolution"? Modularity and the commons. Halduskultuur: Estonian J. Adm. Cult. Digit. Gov. **20**(1), 4–19 (2019)
27. Lindgren, I., Melin, U.: Time to refuel the conceptual discussion on public e-services – revisiting how e-services are manifested in practice. In: Janssen, M., et al. (eds.) EGOV 2017. LNCS, vol. 10428, pp. 92–101. Springer, Cham (2017). https://doi.org/10.1007/978-3-319-64677-0_8
28. Luna-Reyes, L.F., Picazo-Vela, S., Luna, D.E., Gil-Garcia, J.R.: Creating public value through digital government: lessons on inter-organizational collaboration and information technologies. In: Bui, T.X., Jr. Sprague, R.H. (eds.) Proceedings of the 49th Hawaii International Conference on System Sciences (HICSS-49), pp. 2840–2849. IEEE, Koloa (2016)
29. Mergel, I.: Digital service teams in government. Gov. Inf. Q. **36**(4), 101389 (2019)
30. Pardo, T.A., Gil-Garcia, J.R., Luna-Reyes, L.F.: Collaborative governance and cross-boundary information sharing: envisioning a networked and IT-enabled public administration. In: O'Leary, R., Van Slyke, D.M., Kim, S. (eds.) The Future of Public Administration around the World: The Minnowbrook Perspective, pp. 129–139. Georgetown University Press, Washington, D.C. (2010)
31. Poel, K., Marneffe, W., Vanlaer, W.: Assessing the electronic invoicing potential for private sector firms in Belgium. Int. J. Digit. Account. Res. **16**, 1–34 (2016)
32. Provan, K.G., Kenis, P.: Modes of network governance: structure, management, and effectiveness. J. Public Adm. Res. Theory **18**(2), 229–252 (2008)
33. Scholl, H.J., Klischewski, R.: E-government integration and interoperability: framing the research agenda. Int. J. Public Adm. **30**(8–9), 889–920 (2007)
34. Sundberg, L.: Risk and decision in collaborative e-government: an objectives-oriented approach. Electron. J. e-Gov. **14**(1), 36–47 (2016)
35. Walsham, G.: Interpretive case studies in IS research: nature and method. Eur. J. Inf. Syst. **4**(2), 74–81 (1995)

36. Yang, T.-M., Maxwell, T.A.: Information-sharing in public organizations: a literature review of interpersonal, intra-organizational success factors. Gov. Inf. Q. **28**(2), 164–175 (2011)
37. Yin, R.K.: Case Study Research: Design and Methods. Sage, Thousand Oaks (2014)

Open Data: Social and Technical Aspects

A Methodology for Retrieving Datasets from Open Government Data Portals Using Information Retrieval and Question and Answering Techniques

Raissa Barcellos$^{(\boxtimes)}$, Flavia Bernardini, and Jose Viterbo

Institute of Computing, Fluminense Federal University, Rio de Janeiro, Brazil
raissabarcellos@id.uff.br, {fcbernardini,viterbo}@ic.uff.br

Abstract. Public administration is one of the largest producers and collectors of data in several domains. Bearing in mind that one of the main pillars of public transparency is the release of social value through government data, and that this right remains a challenge for citizens, in this work we implemented a methodology that uses techniques and Answers and Information Retrieval to retrieve data sets and respond to questions from citizens on a Brazilian open government data portal. Using metrics of information retrieval evaluation, such as accuracy and recall, we obtained satisfactory results in applying the proposed methodology.

Keywords: Open government data · Information Retrieval · Question and Answering

1 Introduction

Around the world, governments have already realized the importance of higher data openness and data transparency [3]. Currently, there are open data portals in whole world, which provide access to large volumes of them in increasing numbers around the globe. Nowadays, more than a million datasets have been made available by governments around the world [14]. This fact is a consequence of a large amount of public information generated continuously, which can refer to finance, health, human development, among other topics [9]. Open government data allows easy access to large amounts of data without the need for repeated data requests, transcription of data from printed formats to electronics, and other tasks that would limit the user's interest and usefulness of the data [22]. Through this openness, the government has the potential to promote transparency, increase citizen participation, and stimulate innovation. Also, open data initiatives can help citizens learn about government activities [22].

Government data geared to the citizen's objective is a useful contribution to decision making. However, open government data portals are complex and multi-functional, due to a large amount of data, usually fragmented and hidden within

© IFIP International Federation for Information Processing 2020
Published by Springer Nature Switzerland AG 2020
G. Viale Pereira et al. (Eds.): EGOV 2020, LNCS 12219, pp. 239–249, 2020.
https://doi.org/10.1007/978-3-030-57599-1_18

the portal. An earlier study, conducted by [15], with data professionals across a wide range of domains and skillsets states that, in most cases, data search shows characteristics of a complicated task, involving multiple queries, iterations and improvement of the need for original information, in addition to complex cognitive processing. It becomes a challenge for citizens to access, retrieve, and understand the data made available [14]. So, the goal of this work is to present a methodology that uses Question and Answering and Information Retrieval techniques to retrieve datasets and answer citizen' questions, using technologies like natural language processing and the CKAN API for data retrieving.

The work is organized as follows: In Sect. 2, we present a background on open government data, information retrieval, and Question-Answering. In Sect. 3, we present a literature review. In Sect. 4, we present our methodology. In Sect. 5, we present our experimental analysis. Finally, in Sect. 6, we present our conclusions and future work.

2   Background

Open Government Data: According to Jetzek *et al.* [11], the open data term refers primarily to data that has been created or collected by government agencies for one purpose, but which is now available to the public for other purposes. Opening government data leads to several different communities using it simultaneously for different and productive purposes, and can be used as a means to achieve many ends. According to Jetzek *et al.* [11], the following three criteria are arguments in favor of the potential benefit of opening government data: (i) the data can be shared and used by many at the same time at no additional cost; (ii) the data have productive value, often used as a resource for the production of something of interest and are rarely consumed directly; and (iii) the data is versatile and can be used as an input for a wide range of goods and services.

Also, according to Alzamil *et al.* [2], the availability of government data can play a crucial role in decision-making by government agencies. By making government data available to the public, citizens, professionals, and other interested groups can access the data to help monitor public spending and increase overall participation. In addition to better decision making, making data available can help prevent or minimize the abuse of government resources. When government officials know that their work is being monitored, they are less likely to make mistakes [2].

In this scenario, one important issue in Open Government Data is finding and recovering information from different sources. However, there is a lack of patterns for providing data in data portals, as well as data models interpretable by machines that could be useful for this task. In this work, we propose the use of Information Retrieval (IR) and Question and Answering (QA) techniques for this end.

Information Retrieval: According to [18], Information Retrieval (IR) is related to finding material (usually documents) of an unstructured nature (usually text) that satisfies an information need from within large collections (usually stored in computers). So, IR is frequently used for helping people to recovery documents, typically by librarians, paralegals, and similar professional searchers.

In order to assess the quality of IR systems, we should measure retrieved data sets as relevant and non-relevant, through formal and appropriate IR assessment metrics. Two metrics widely applied for evaluating IR systems are Precision and Recall. For calculating these metrics, for each search result, all retrievable items fit one and only one of the four cells in a confusion matrix, shown in Table 1: (i) Retrieved or Not Retrieved, and (ii) Relevant or Not Relevant [5]. In this same Table, N_{rec} is the number of retrieved data and N_{rel} is the number of relevant data sets.

Table 1. Confusion matrix

	Relevant	Not relevant	Total
Retrieved	$N_{rec \cap rel}$	$N_{rec \cap \overline{rel}}$	N_{ret}
Not retrieved	$N_{\overline{rec} \cap rel}$	$N_{\overline{rec} \cap \overline{rel}}$	$N_{\overline{ret}}$
Total	N_{rel}	$N_{\overline{rel}}$	N_{tot}

For a retrieved dataset, with each item labeled as relevant or irrelevant, and its respective constructed confusion matrix, Recall R is the proportion of the number of relevant retrieved items regarding to all relevant items, i.e., $R = N_{rec \cap rel} \div N_{rel}$. Precision P is the proportion of the number of relevant items regarding to all retrieved items, i.e., $P = N_{rel} \div N_{rec}$.

Question-Answering: Question-Answering Systems (QAS) are an extension of search engines using IR techniques, as they aim to automatically provide users accurate answers to questions asked in natural language, rather than only returning a list from relevant sources based on a set of keywords [6]. The architecture of this type of system depends on the type of explored sources. A common approach is to use traditional IR techniques combined with Machine Learning and Natural Language Processing methods to extract answers from simple questions [6].

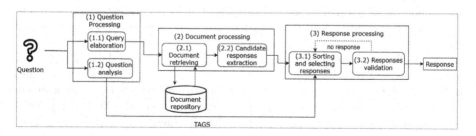

Fig. 1. Basic architecture of QA systems. Fonte: [1]

According to [10], the QA systems present an architecture composed of three basic modules: (i) processing of the question, (ii) processing of the document, and (iii) processing of the response, as shown in Fig. 1.

The first step "(1) Question Processing" consists of transforming the question asked by the user—from natural language to computational language—and understanding the question in order to extract information that supports the selection of answers. In the second stage, "(2) Document Processing", the query already generated is used to retrieve relevant documents or datasets, and to extract candidate responses. Finally, in the third step, "(3) Response Processing", the candidate responses are ordered based on the analysis of the similarity between the question and the candidate responses and, thus, presented to the user. QAS commonly present a single answer to the user's question. However, they can also present several answers ordered by relevance, whether these responses are in text or visual format [4].

3   Literature Review

There are some works in literature that tries to enrich user experience when leading to open government data, turning easier to manipulate the available data. Lahti et al. (2017) [17] introduce a package in R programming language, called Eurostat, for providing a rich collection of data through the open data service, including thousands of demographic datasets, economy, health, infrastructure, traffic, and other European topics. Statistics are generally available with optimal geographic resolution and include time-series that span several years or decades. The implemented package provides customized tools for accessing Eurostat's open data. The main features, such as cache, date formatting, organized data principles, and table data format, support seamless integration with other tools for data manipulation and analysis.

Kuo and Chou (2019) [16] propose an evaluation mechanism based on metadata for analysis of metadata quality, spatial similarity and temporal similarity between user requests and open data. When evaluating metadata for each dataset, the metadata score in the engine contributes two scores, mandatory and optional scores. From the required fields and a combination of recommended and optional metadata fields, they calculate two scores. By extracting keywords from the user's input or addressing the location on a map, they perform the spatial similarity analysis. Also, they conducted a temporal similarity analysis comparing a query and the open dataset. A developed platform presents data related to punctuation, similarity, and classification that help users to obtain the expected data.

A significant problem that Smart Cities' information and data management systems are currently facing is the heterogeneity, not only of data flow but also of external data sources, such as the Linked Data web, whose use is inevitable in making decision making on the scale of a city. Kettouch et al. (2017) [12] present a theoretical framework to manage data flow in Smart Cities and integrate it immediately with Linked Data for data retrieving and web semantics. The structure consists of a modular architecture that receives, as input, semi-structured, and heterogeneous linked data retrieved from various sensors and the data network, respectively. The general objective of the system is to offer an interface to facilitate automatic access to data from Smart Cities and publish it on Linked Datacloud to allow for future reuse.

Oliveira et al. (2016) [19] propose a platform capable of enriching police reports with public data available on the Web. The authors present an evaluation tool, which consumes the linked data provided by a Web API, expands it with data extracted from other sources, and provides an interface to assess the relevance of the expansions. The tool is capable of retrieving police reports to store data in a structured format. The main component of the proposed platform is a REST Web API that offers police report data extracted from the Public Security Secretariat of the state of São Paulo system website. The Web API provides report information in a structured and semantically annotated manner with vocabulary terms and ontologies used in linked open data.

As we can observe in these works, none of them present a general proposal that gather data in order to smartly responding open government data portal users. As far as we know, there is not any work in literature that explores IR and QA techniques in this scenario. In what follows, we present our methodology.

4   Methodology

Usually, open government data portals offer to users at maximum a basic search interface, similar to the basic internet search engines. The goal of our methodology is to allow smart data retrieval by users in open government data portals. It is basically divided into two steps: (i) Processing User Questions and (ii) Retrieving and Delivering Data. Figure 2 illustrates the methodology used in this work.

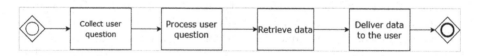

Fig. 2. Methodology illustration

Processing User Questions: Our methodology firstly identify the citizen's question. We used Natural Language Processing (NLP) techniques, like tokenization and removal of stopwords [18], for question processing, in order to point out the real purpose of the citizen when typing his search in the search bar of the application. For this, we used nlpnet library [8], a Python library for NLP tasks, based on neural networks. Currently, it performs identification of semantic functions. It can be used as a Python library or through its independent scripts. Most of the architecture is independent of the language, but some functions have been specially adapted to work with Portuguese. The nlpnet uses word vector representations as input resources for a conventional neural network architecture [7]. Based on the result of the semantic interpretation of the user's question, we retrieve the title and description of the datasets. In work [21], the authors also take a similar approach, implementing a semantic analysis based on open government data, but the analysis is performed to minimize misunderstandings with the semantics of the dataset categories used.

Retrieving and Delivering Data: From the results of the semantic interpretation of the user's question, a tool for collecting or harvesting data is necessary in this step. We use the CKAN API or Comprehensive Knowledge Archive Network for data retrieval task. CKAN[1] is a web-based management system, developed by Open Knowledge Foundation[2] and is being used by more than 192 governments, institutions, and other organizations worldwide to manage open government data. CKAN is written in Python and it is useful for developers who want to write code that interacts with CKAN sites and their data. The API is also extensively documented and provides a comprehensive way to retrieve the metadata from the [13] data catalog. For performing data retrieval, it is necessary to perform an API request, where the answer is a JSON file in a data dictionary format. In order to demonstrate the results, we developed two usage scenarios for the experiment.

5   Experimental Analysis

We implemented a tool that follows the steps of our methodology, available at https://github.com/RaissaBarcellos/openIR, using Python. For conducting our experiment, we retrieved data from a catalog of open government data in Brazil called *dados.gov*[3]. It aggregates data from the 26 Brazilian federal states and their municipalities. In order to evaluate the results obtained in both scenarios, we must label each answer for a question from the retrieved answers as relevant and not relevant, in order to calculate P and R metrics. For calculating Recall, it should be necessary to verify each of the 39269 datasets if they are relevant or not for each question. So, for calculating R (Recall), we used Gauss curve equation to sample data from the portal [20]. Equation 1 defines the number n of samples should be selected from the entire population. In this equation, n is the sample size to be calculated; N is the population size (in the case of the experiment, 39269 datasets); Z is the standard normalized variable associated with the confidence level (in this case, a confidence level of 95%); p is the proportion we want to find (in this case, p = 0.5); e is the sampling error (in this case, e = 0.05). Using this equation, we sampled 380 documents at random from the entire data.gov portal.

$$ n = \frac{N \cdot Z^2 \cdot p \cdot (n - p)}{Z^2 \cdot p \cdot (1 - p) + e^2 \cdot (N - 1)} \tag{1} $$

---

[1] https://ckan.org/.
[2] https://okfn.org/.
[3] https://dados.gov.br/.

Based on this, in order to validate our methodology, we conducted two experiments in two different usage scenarios.

Table 2. 10 first datasets retrieved in our platform for UC1

Retrieved dataset	Relevant/not relevant
UFMS sport projects 2019	Relevant
Number of projects that raised funds under the sports incentive law	Relevant
High performance sports equipment	Relevant
Number of municipalities involved in the sport and leisure program of the city	Relevant
Sport and recreational craft by DN	Relevant
Diagnosis of youth with sport and leisure theme - Year 2008	Relevant
Sport initiation center	Relevant
Total funds raised by sports projects linked to the sports incentive law	Relevant
Number of centers implemented by the sport and leisure program of the city	Relevant
High performance sports equipment in the INDE viewer	Relevant

Usage Scenario 1 (UC1): Maria wants to promote a debate about the sports context of Brazil, in her class of the 1st year of high school. With the platform, she can efficiently introduce students to the reality of the situation regarding initiatives to support sports in the country, using open government data. For this, using our methodology, she follows the following steps: (i) She connect to the platform; (ii) She writes "I want to know about sports in Brazil"; and (iii) She gets data related to the requested, shown in Table 2. The first column shows the title of the retrieved dataset, and the second column shows if the dataset is relevant or not for the question, labeled by a researcher in our university. We can observe that all of the datasets are relevant in this case. For matters of comparison, we asked the same question: "I want to know about sports in Brazil", in the search box on *dados.gov*, the results are shown in the Table 3. We can observe that none of the datasets returned by *dados.gov* are relevant to the question.

Usage Scenario 2 (UC2): Sebastiao wants to understand more about Science in Brazil. With the platform, he can get to know the real situation about the country's Science, using open government data. For this, he follows the following steps: (i) He connect to the platform; (ii) He writes "Science in Brazil"; (iii) He

Table 3. 10 first datasets retrieved in *dados.gov* for UC1

Retrieved dataset	Relevant/not relevant
[2013 to 2016] stricto sensu graduate teachers in Brazil	Not relevant
Methodological adjustment on internal debt - balances (R$)	Not relevant
Methodological adjustment on external debt - balances (R$)	Not relevant
Demographic census	Not relevant
Union properties	Not relevant
School-age distortion rates in basic education	Not relevant
Marcantonio vilaça plastic arts award	Not relevant
School census microdata	Not relevant
Primary income - monthly - expenditure	Not relevant
Primary income - monthly - revenue	Not relevant

gets data related to the requested, shown in Table 4. We can observe that all the datasets are relevant in this case. For matters of comparison, we asked the same question: "Science in Brazil", in the search box on *dados.gov*, the results

Table 4. 10 first datasets retrieved in our platform for UC2

Retrieved dataset	Relevant/not relevant
Number of selected in the research support notice of the women and science program	Relevant
Scholarships awarded in the Science Without Borders Program	Relevant
2.1.1 Brazil: national expenditure on science and technology (S&T) (1), in current values, by activity, 2000–2016	Relevant
Expenditure on science and technology	Relevant
2.1.2 Brazil: national expenditure on science and technology (S&T) (1), in current values, in relation to total S&T and gross domestic product (GDP), by institutional sector, 2000–2016	Relevant
Computer science - 2011	Relevant
2.2.1 Brazil: federal government expenditure on science and technology (S&T) (1) by activity, 2000–2016	Relevant
2.2.2 Brazil: federal government expenditures on science and technology (S&T) (1) (2) by agency, 2000–2016	Relevant
2.2.3 Brazil: federal government expenditure on science and technology (S&T) (1) (2), applied by the Ministry of Science, Technology and Innovation (MCTI), by budgetary unit and activity, 2000–2016	Relevant
Number of science and technology dissemination and popularization projects supported	Relevant

Table 5. 10 first datasets retrieved in *dados.gov* for UC2

Retrieved dataset	Relevant/not relevant
Innovation research	Relevant
National science, technology and innovation indicators	Relevant
Brazil-Argentina: a strategic relationship	Not relevant
Strategic alliances for Brazil: China and India	Not relevant
List of species of Flora do Brazil 2015 - Brazilian flora checklist	Not relevant
VII national meeting of strategic studies - volume II	Not relevant
VII national meeting of strategic studies - volume I - 2007	Not relevant
Perspectives for the boundary strip	Not relevant
Study meeting - indigenous question	Not relevant
Study meeting - climate change	Not relevant

are shown in the Table 5. We can observe that only one of the datasets returned by *dados.gov* are relevant to the question.

In addition to the natural language processing work, our approach performs a search engine where we thoroughly analyze all the titles and descriptions of the datasets, so that there is a more effective result for the user. For each usage scenarios, in our platform, we obtained the following P values (Table 6); R values (Table 7).

Table 6. Precision results

	Total retrieved items	Total relevant items	Precision
UC1	21	21	100%
UC2	77	74	96%

Table 7. Recall results

	Total relevant items in the sample	Total retrieved items	Recall
UC1	1	1	100%
UC2	3	3	100%

From these results, we observed high values of precision and recall. The high precision obtained means that our experimental platform returned substantially more relevant than irrelevant results. While the high recall value obtained means that the experimental platform returned most of the relevant results present on the portal.

6   Conclusions

We present in this work a methodology for retrieving data using Information Retrieval and Question and Answering techniques and methods. Our methodology involves using Natural Language Processing techniques to extract semantic meaning of the user's question and then perform the IR task. We implemented our methodology in a tool, available at https://github.com/RaissaBarcellos/openIR. We carried out an experiment performing two task of recovering open government data taking into consideration the user's question. We used the Brazilian open government data portal *dados.gov*. We compared ur mechanism for retrieving data with the simple mechanism available by *dados.gov*. The results were expressive, considering that high values of precision and recall indicate a high power of data recovery of the platform. As future work, we intend to conduct a discussion of how semantic information retrieval mechanisms are essential in open data portals As a limitation of this work, we experimented with just one open government data portal, we can still perform the integration with other portals.

References

1. Almansa, L.F.: Uma arquitetura de question-answering instanciada no domínio de doenças crônicas. Ph.D. thesis, Universidade de São Paulo (2016)
2. Alzamil, Z.S., Vasarhelyi, M.A.: A new model for effective and efficient open government data. Int. J. Discl. Gov. **16**, 1–14 (2019)
3. Anastasiu, I., Foth, M., Schroeter, R., Rittenbruch, M.: From repositories to switchboards: local governments as open data facilitators. In: Hawken, S., Han, H., Pettit, C. (eds.) Open Cities — Open Data, pp. 331–358. Springer, Singapore (2020). https://doi.org/10.1007/978-981-13-6605-5_15
4. Athenikos, S.J., Han, H.: Biomedical question answering: a survey. Comput. Methods Programs Biomed. **99**(1), 1–24 (2010)
5. Buckland, M., Gey, F.: The relationship between recall and precision. J. Am. Soc. Inf. Sci. **45**(1), 12–19 (1994)
6. Dimitrakis, E., Sgontzos, K., Tzitzikas, Y.: A survey on question answering systems over linked data and documents. J. Intell. Inf. Syst. 1–27 (2019)
7. Falci, D.H.M.: An automatic semantic role labeler for the Portuguese language. Ph.D. thesis, Mestrado em Sistemas de Informação e Gestão do Conhecimento (2018)
8. Fonseca, E.R., Rosa, J.L.G.: A two-step convolutional neural network approach for semantic role labeling. In: The 2013 International Joint Conference on Neural Networks (IJCNN), pp. 1–7. IEEE (2013)
9. Gascó-Hernández, M., Martin, E.G., Reggi, L., Pyo, S., Luna-Reyes, L.F.: Promoting the use of open government data: cases of training and engagement. Gov. Inf. Q. **35**(2), 233–242 (2018)
10. Hirschman, L., Gaizauskas, R.: Natural language question answering: the view from here. Nat. Lang. Eng. **7**(4), 275–300 (2001)
11. Jetzek, T., Avital, M., Bjorn-Andersen, N.: The sustainable value of open government data. J. Assoc. Inf. Syst. **20**(6), 6 (2019)

12. Kettouch, M., Luca, C., Khorief, O., Wu, R., Dascalu, S.: Semantic data management in smart cities. In: 2017 International Conference on Optimization of Electrical and Electronic Equipment (OPTIM) and 2017 Intl Aegean Conference on Electrical Machines and Power Electronics (ACEMP), pp. 1126–1131. IEEE (2017)
13. Kirstein, F., Dittwald, B., Dutkowski, S., Glikman, Y., Schimmler, S., Hauswirth, M.: Linked data in the European data portal: a comprehensive platform for applying DCAT-AP. In: Lindgren, I., et al. (eds.) EGOV 2019. LNCS, vol. 11685, pp. 192–204. Springer, Cham (2019). https://doi.org/10.1007/978-3-030-27325-5_15
14. Koesten, L., Singh, J.: Searching data portals-more complex than we thought? In: SCST@ CHIIR, pp. 25–28 (2017)
15. Koesten, L.M., Kacprzak, E., Tennison, J.F., Simperl, E.: The trials and tribulations of working with structured data: -a study on information seeking behaviour. In: Proceedings of the 2017 CHI Conference on Human Factors in Computing Systems, pp. 1277–1289 (2017)
16. Kuo, C.L., Chou, H.C.: Metadata assessment for efficient open data retrieval. In: Accepted Short Papers and Posters from the 22nd AGILE Conference on Geo-Information Science (AGILE 2019), Cyprus, Greece (2019)
17. Lahti, L., Huovari, J., Kainu, M., Biecek, P.: Retrieval and analysis of eurostat open data with the eurostat package. R J. **9**(1), 385–392 (2017)
18. Manning, C.D., Raghavan, P., Schütze, H.: Introduction to Information Retrieval. Cambridge University Press, Cambridge (2008)
19. Oliveira, B.C., Salvadori, I., Huf, A., Siqueira, F.: A platform to enrich, expand and publish linked data of police reports. In: Proceedings of the 15th International Conference WWW/Internet, pp. 111–118 (2016)
20. Pasquali, L.: A curva normal. Matemática Discreta. Rio de Janeiro (2006)
21. Pinto, H.D.S., Bernardini, F., Viterbo, J.: How cities categorize datasets in their open data portals: an exploratory analysis. In: Proceedings of the 19th Annual International Conference on Digital Government Research: Governance in the Data Age, pp. 1–9 (2018)
22. Whitmore, A.: Using open government data to predict war: a case study of data and systems challenges. Gov. Inf. Q. **31**(4), 622–630 (2014)

Open Government Data from the Perspective of Information Needs - A Tentative Conceptual Model

Jonathan Crusoe[1]([✉]) [ID], Elisabeth Gebka[2] [ID], and Karin Ahlin[3] [ID]

[1] Division of Information Systems, Linköping University, 581 83 Linköping, Sweden
jonathan.crusoe@liu.se
[2] Creativity and Innovation Research Center, University of Namur,
5000 Namur, Belgium
elisabeth.gebka@unamur.be
[3] Department of Computer and System Science,
Mid Sweden University, 831 36 Östersund, Sweden
karin.ahlin@miun.se

Abstract. Information seekers can use products and services based on open government data (OGD) to satisfy their information needs. These solutions are provided by data transformers reusing OGD shared by publishers. OGD is believed to lead to several benefits, such as transparency and innovation. However, there is a noted lack of OGD use, and little seems to be known about the need for OGD. Therefore, we developed a tentative conceptual model, from which data transformers and publishers can understand and consider the information needs of information seekers. We used design science research to develop the model based on previous research and empirical material from workshops. We conducted workshops in Belgium with nine researchers and eleven students and presented the model at a Scandinavian e-government workshop. The findings from the study show that information needs are complex and can be challenging to capture, but are one possible way to understand how the benefits of OGD could be realized. One practical implication is that publishers and data transformers should identify information needs in society, study existing solutions, and attempt to go beyond them with OGD. The synthesized theoretical implication is that information needs might help to guide on the role of OGD in society.

Keywords: Open government data · Information seeker · Information need · Conceptual model

1 Introduction

In previous open government data (OGD) research, little seems to be known about the relationships between information seekers, data transformers, and publishers. This gap leaves it unclear why OGD would be integrated into the rest

© IFIP International Federation for Information Processing 2020
Published by Springer Nature Switzerland AG 2020
G. Viale Pereira et al. (Eds.): EGOV 2020, LNCS 12219, pp. 250–261, 2020.
https://doi.org/10.1007/978-3-030-57599-1_19

of society. This article presents a tentative conceptual model from which data transformers and publishers can understand and consider the information needs of information seekers. Information needs arise when people experience a gap in their knowledge [3]. These needs can be satisfied when people make sense out of data [15]. One source of data is OGD which is shared by public organisations (publishers) for anyone to be freely reused [1]. OGD can be used directly or integrated into services and products (solutions) by data transformers for information seekers to satisfy their information needs [9]. Data transformers can, for example, be developers, journalists, or researchers [22], while information seekers are people that seek information to satisfy their information needs.

Publishers, data transformers, and information seekers can experience problems. Publishers may lose income or data transformers may be unable to find data [25], while information seekers can have unexpressed or unrecognised information needs [11]. Previous research tends to focus on the publisher and data transformer, while the information seeker is in the background or a type of data transformer [e.g., 10,16,26]. This placement needs to change since the public interest in the re-use of OGD has been declared a myth [14]. The myth may come from that current information needs are already satisfied by other solutions [20]. The satisfaction of information needs may be the event where data and information, through use, impact information seekers' lives to realize the promised benefits of OGD.

The purpose of this article is two-fold: (1) create an initial understanding of information needs in relation to OGD and (2) suggest possible considerations for data transformers and publishers, both presented in a conceptual model. A conceptual model is a set of assumptions that supports and informs the research and is a key part of the design [19]. The model can help data transformers and publishers understand how OGD and OGD solutions can be of value to information seekers. On the other hand, researchers can use the model as a basis for future research on how to increase the use of OGD or how OGD can have an impact on society. In this paper, we focus on everyday activity-based information needs, such as finding your way to work or keep up-to-date on your urban surroundings. The following research question guides the research: *what may data transformers and publishers need to consider about information needs of information seekers in an everyday context?*

This paper starts by presenting the background, then the research process, and the conceptual model followed by a discussion. This paper ends with a conclusion.

2   Background

This section explains the concept of information needs and information solutions.

2.1   Information Needs of Information Seeker

People experience information needs when they experience a gap in their knowledge [3], which can happen when they attempt to satisfy a primary need [24].

If the situation is unclear, confusing, or difficult to understand the information seeker might be unable to formulate questions (identify information needs) that can help them identify the right information [8]. Information needs are determined by individual's social role, environment, and previous knowledge [24] and satisfying them can help people work effectively, solve a problem satisfactorily, or pursue a hobby [20]. Information seekers' information needs can be complex. For example, in a modern city environment the urban system is a vast system of systems where information seekers can have different roles based on what functions of the city they are using, such as a citizen, professional, or commuter [12]. In each role, they have different information needs. OGD can be socially valuable when understandable and usable by the intended people or communities. OGD should fit the preferences, level of expertise, and personal needs of the information seekers [4]. Visualizations are one important tool to achieve these requirements [2].

People can use information for: (1) fact-finding – getting hold of answers to specific questions, (2) staying aware – keeping up to date on something, (3) researching – investigating a new field in depth, (4) briefing – obtaining background understanding of an issue or topic, (5) stimulus – procuring ideas or stimuli, and (6) recreation – looking for interesting tidbits of information just for the fun of it [20]. At the same time, individuals, experiences, and situations are sources of information and knowledge, and information can be found in unexpected ways and places [11]. In the digital world, information seekers are creative and able to choose from a large offer of information sources and even influence information solutions. The information providers have to consider them as clients to meet their needs properly, at the risk of seeing them choosing other solutions [20].

2.2   Information Solutions from Data Transformers and Publishers

An information solution is a product or service that supports the sense making of information from data or presents information or data to the information seeker. Here, we focus on digital solutions, which seem to be well-suited to satisfy information needs [17]. In the case of OGD, *a published dataset is considered an information solution*. The publisher is assumed to be a public organisation that releases data. On the abstract level, the release process for data starts with collecting data, then preparing data, publishing data, maintaining data, engaging data transformers, and ends with collecting feedback [1,5,26]. The result of the process is OGD that can be used by data transformers or information seekers. Data transformers can transform the data into facts, information, interfaces, new datasets, or services [9], which can cover a wide variety of roles and business models for the data transformers [16]. The solutions should be specifically fit to their intended purpose or function [20]. The products can, for example, be reports, visualisations, simulations, and news articles, while services can be a web service that notifies information seekers about interesting events [7]. On the other hand, information seekers can read some facts in a dataset and be satisfied [9].

3   Research Process

This research is using design science research (DSR) to build a tentative conceptual model that is a new artifact. The conceptual model is directed toward solving a practical problem. This research followed the steps of DSR [21]: (1) problem identification and motivation, (2) definition of the objectives for a solution, (3) design and development, (4) demonstration, (5) evaluation, and (6) communication. The steps 2 to 5 were done in iterations. A previous version of the model was communicated at the 17th Scandinavian Workshop on E-Government. Here, we want to note that this paper has a sibling paper also presented at the workshop and accepted as ongoing research to the EGOV-CeDEM-ePart 2020 conference, which developed the data collection workshop [see 13].

3.1   Problem Identification and Motivation

This research was initiated when reflecting on the possible sources of the noted lack of use [22] to then wonder about the need for OGD solutions. This reflection prompted a traditional literature review to identify previous research [6]. This literature review is presented in the background section. Google scholar was used as the search engine, as it has a good coverage and recall and we used simple keywords, which the search engine has a prevision above average with [23]. Examples of used keywords are "open data", "information needs", "open data information needs", and "citizens information needs".

The design problem of this research is how to conceptualise the connection between information seekers' information needs, data transformers' solutions, and publishers' OGD to gain insight into how OGD and OGD solutions could be valuable to information seekers. Also, to identify considerations to data transformers and publishers to ensure this value. The theoretical motivation of the problem continues on previous research on information needs and OGD by combining both. The practical motivation is a perceived need to increase the use of OGD, which is believed to lead to several benefits. An important aspect of the development of the model was to use an information seeker perspective, which takes into account the publisher's and data transformer's role for the solutions.

3.2   Iterations

The iterations consist of step 2 to 5 of DSR [21]. For the first iteration, the purpose was to explore information needs. Two of the three researchers observed an information-rich bus-hub in a medium-sized Swedish town, conducted six structured-interviews with available commuters, and one in-depth interview with a veteran commuter. They were asked about activities and needed information. The empirical material was discussed between the two researchers and the insights were then used to design a workshop method [13], as observations and interviews gave insufficient results or were too time-consuming.

The Workshop Method. The workshop method [13] was used one time in the second iteration and one time in the third iteration. For the participants of the workshops to recognise information needs, they needed to face a situation where they experience knowledge gaps but are not so unfamiliar they cannot formulate questions. To simulate this situation, a scenario was developed and used in a collaborative workshop, since participatory approach can help participants identify information needs [2]. The selected scenario was *"moved into a new city but not settled"* (which in the first iteration generated the richest data about activity-based information needs in an everyday context). The second iteration allowed the participants to freely suggest categories of activities and information needs in the scenario context. However, it slowed down the discussions and idea generation as their focus was on clarifying the situation. The third iteration consisted of pre-defined options of activity domains, selected from the occurrences of the second iteration based on perceived commonness. At both workshops, participants, alternately alone and in small teams of 2 to 4, wrote down activities with the needed information, possible existing solutions, and brainstormed new dream solutions on specific cards. Finally, the result was presented and discussed together. In total, two workshops were conducted: the first with nine Belgian researchers and the second with eleven Belgian students. The Belgian participants came from the University of Namur. The university is part of the city of Namur, which is the regional capital of Wallonia. The city has 110,939 inhabitants, a dominant service industry (e.g., commercial activities and the university), and publishes OGD. Table 1 presents a summary of the empirical material.

Analysis of the Results. Cards from the groups were grouped, skimmed, and prioritised based on their size and clearness on information needs (smallest and clearest first). This approach was chosen as it allowed the conceptual model to grow slowly and steadily. One at a time, the card groups were discussed and analysed by two of the researchers conducting this study based on the concepts presented in the background section. This process involved writing the data from the cards to a memo where analytical notes were added through discussion and analysis. The conceptual model was constructed through constant comparison between the current group and the model, which allowed for the identification of the theoretical concepts in the empirical material. This process helped to demonstrate and evaluate the model in small steps. Once the two workshop iterations had been executed, the memos and model were analysed by one of the researchers conducting this study and condensed to one memo, which was further refined to a new memo representing a new model. The process was then presented and discussed with one of the researchers of this study. Afterwards, the model was conceptualised and studied to identify gaps. The model was then reviewed by the remaining two researchers conducting this study based on [18]: fidelity with real-world phenomena, completeness, level of detail, robustness, and internal consistency. Finally, the model was submitted to a Scandinavian e-government workshop and received final touches based on feedback and recommended research. Previous research has supported the development of the

Table 1. Summary of the empirical material from the workshops

		Participant background	Primary needs	Information needs
Workshop 1 Activities (primary needs) open to suggestions	Group 1	Researchers in information management (1), computer science (2), and business informatics (1)	Move to the city Discover the city Make friends Find store	Public transport List: description and accessibility of events, and available products Points of interest Recommendations for finding friends
	Group 2	Researchers in education (1), management and creativity (1), management (1)	Find friends Find services (doctors, sport, shops) Environment	Descriptions: facilities, location, prices, timetables, soft skills, and atmosphere of the places Like-minded people Peer recommendations
	Group 3	Researchers in education and management (1), media industry (1)	Get dressed Leisure, shopping, services, and schools Local integration, safety, and health	Weather, fashion, streets Descriptions: facilities, location, prices, timetables, and attendees Local food, stereotypes Best schools, doctors, and service providers Peer recommendations and tacit rules Like-minded people
Workshop 2 Activities (primary needs) from suggested categories	Group 4	Students in management (3)	Eat and drink: restaurants, shops bars, and delivery services	Descriptions: facilities, location, prices and payment, timetables, delays, attendees, and occupation rate per hours Peer recommendations and trustful reviews
	Group 5	Students in Informatics (1) political sciences (1) project management (1) unspecified (1)	Socialize and make friends	Places to go out Like-minded people Associations and activities on the campus
	Group 6	Students in analytics and digital business (4)	Socialize and make friends	Services and activities, carpooling with friends, and accommodation with friends Descriptions: location, schedules, prices, accessibility, and conditions Attendees in working groups, travels, music bands, and parties

data collection, guided the analysis, and became a part of the conceptual model. The concepts and considerations were interpreted from previous research and the empirical material, where the first provided a skeleton, which the second added to.

4   A Tentative Conceptual Model

In this section, we present a tentative conceptual model (see Fig. 1). As the concepts are presented in the text below, examples from group 1, group 3, and group 4 are given. These groups were selected based on the perceived clearness of information needs and completeness and size of their descriptions. The presentation will follow information seeker, then data transformer, and, finally, publisher.

4.1 Information Seeker

The model starts with the information seekers trying to satisfy a **primary need**, which is the basic incentive to move and undertake any activity. However, they encounter a perceivable gap in their knowledge to perform the desired activity [3,8,24]. If the gap is filled, it can help them satisfy their primary need through the activity. The activity domain chosen by group 1 was to make new friends or socialise by participating in the local life (primary need of love and belonging), group 3 was to go to shops (physiological needs), and group 4 sought to eat and drink in the city (physiological needs and sense of belonging). However, in the given scenario (settling down in a new town), they lacked information.

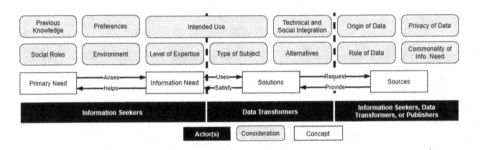

Fig. 1. The tentative model of information needs, solutions, and sources.

The information seekers recognize their knowledge gap and an information need arises. They start to search for solutions that they can use to satisfy their **information need**. This need takes the form of unformulated questions (gaps) with specific requests for data [3,8,20]. Group 1 explained that they wanted descriptions and accessibility of events and products, but also possible friends. The information should contain recommendations, a list of social activities and groups, points of interest, prices, profiles of people attending, and schedules. Group 3 sought information about the weather, fashion, street descriptions, and shops. Group 4 saw four ways to approach their primary needs. First, look for a bar. Second, food delivery services. Third, look for where to purchase groceries. Fourth, look for restaurants. They also wanted ratings with the four approaches. In common, the groups tended to omit important data, such as locations for weather and opening hours for businesses.

The expression of an information need coalesce (grow together to form one thing) with different factors, which should be **considered** by data transformers and publishers. The information seeker's previous knowledge about a topic, preferences, intended information use, social roles, environment, and level of expertise coalesce with the information need to become the expression of their information need [4,12,20,24]. These requirements should be met to enable good satisfaction of the primary need [20]. Group 1 explained that new friends should have similar interests or needs, while the activities should be similar to their interests, reoccurring, prioritised, and in a certain format (e.g., parties and pubs). Group 3 wanted to quickly reach their destination in fresh and comfortable condition. Group 4 wanted the services to be rated by other customers to gain more transparency and trust from the provided information.

As a result, it can be interpreted that the participants seek *reliable* and *useful* information. Both social groups (researchers and students) value the transparency carried by peer reviews and their community, since the information source is not always clearly identified in a final solution, whatever the data comes from (OGD or businesses). The usefulness perception of the information is constrained by the personal considerations (e.g. preferences, previous knowledge, social role). For instance, for the food and restaurants activities, both groups mentioned categories of information such as price, location, and available products or menus. However, what is really valued and will make the difference is the personal consideration about the information (what is "expensive" for the information seeker, what makes a restaurant "good"). This evaluation of the information is better supported by the community ratings than by the transparency feature of OGD.

4.2   Data Transformer

Data transformers develop solutions that they provide to information seekers. A **solution** provides information and data that can answer questions and fill knowledge gaps [7,9,20]. Group 1 saw two possible solutions to their information need. First, Tinder4Friends is an application that suggests activities where they can find friends based on the information seeker's profile. Second, Place2Be is a website that describes where to be every day and night based on the information seekers' profiles and interests. The locations can be shared on social media to organise the activity with their friends. Group 3 suggested two solutions: (1) Mode-Fashion is an online catalog that in real-time provides the latest fashion and (2) Streets is a pedestrian navigation application (using a routing algorithm) based on community contribution that helps the information seeker navigate to shops. The community adds data about the state of streets, parking, pollution, snow levels, and the number of steps on the way. Group 4 suggested that every bar or restaurant has a happy and a sad button that customers can press to rate the service. The ratings are then published on a website or in an open database.

The data transformers have some possible **considerations**. First, how the solutions are designed for its intended use [12,24]. Tinder4Friends and Place2Be help to brief the information seeker about people or events in an area. Mode-Fashion helps the information seeker to stay aware on a topic. Streets helps the information seeker to find facts (a route between two locations). On the other hand, the button with its website could allow the seeker to brief or find facts depending on the implementation. "Brief" if it allows the seeker to see all options together. "Find facts" if the seeker can only ask for one restaurant at a time. Second, the type of subject in the solution [20] can be based on topics (e.g., fashion), problems (e.g., navigation), or events (e.g., parties). Third, how the solution is integrated with other solutions (e.g., social media) and the information seeker communities (e.g., in the Streets, the community contributes with data, while in Place2Be users find each other through common events). Fourth, alternatives to the solution [20]. Tinder4Friends and Place2Be satisfy the same need with a slight variation which could make them compete if developed. On the other hand, Mode-Fashion and Streets together help to satisfy an information need, which means they collaborate.

In sum, the respondents expressed their demand for *efficient* information solutions that can satisfy several information needs at a time, in one place. They value the quality standards and functionalities they know from other solutions, but more than everything, they value the fact they can find all information at once, save time, energy, with trust.

4.3   Publisher

The conceptual model focuses on the information seeker, while giving some attention to the publisher, who provides data requested by solutions. Data **sources** can originate from information seekers, data transformers, publishers, or a mix of them. The data transformers and publishers have some possible **considerations**. First, the origin of the data [16,20]. The data transformer can provide data through the solution, or the information seeker can add data to the solution. The data provided can either be OGD from publishers or data from other sources, such as shops or restaurants. Second, the privacy of the data. Added data can range from private data (not shared) to public data (shared with other information seekers). Third, the role of the data. Provided data can act as a base or skeleton for other data, while added data can help to evaluate (e.g., ratings of restaurants). Origin, privacy, and role of data can be mixed in one solution. Streets could use locations from publishers, state and pollution of streets from information seekers, and private location data from an information seeker to calculate a route. Third, the commonality of the information needs of a group, community, or society [20]. The solutions and related data have a window of possible uses. The dream solution Streets is for traveling or planning to travel, Mode-Fashion is for when the information seeker wants to refresh their knowledge about fashion, and Place2Be when he seeks something to do with friends.

In sum, what matters for the information seekers is how a given solution meets their information needs. For that, many sources might be required to provide relevant data and offer a comprehensive solution. The real value proposition of the solution depends on the match between the solution and its user's information needs. In the activity-based scenario of this study, the solution never depends on one single publisher, regardless the quality of its data.

5   Discussion

Information needs are complex and not easy to capture. One described example of this is that there is a tendency to omit important data (e.g., geographical data for weather). This behaviour could be a form of unrecognised information need [11], but likely the data is perceived to be commonly understood by the participants. Following that the information seekers do not fully deal with the underlying datasets is that data transformers and publishers have to take care about information seekers' information needs. They have to match the information seekers and their information needs with their solutions and data [e.g., 7,9]. Therefore, OGD does not follow a one-directional flow. Rather, two sides of need and data meet in one solution. The data transformer has to ensure that the two sides mix properly, while he has little ability to control both.

5.1   Implications

We have also identified some implications for practice and future research. The **practical implications** are directed to publishers and data transformers of OGD. The model has taught us that before publishers provide OGD or data transformers develop solutions, they should identify information needs in their society, study existing solutions, and come up with ways to go beyond them. Data transformers should consider the content of their solution to ensure it can be used to answer questions that can come from several knowledge gaps. They are also recommended to think about how data is mixed from different sources and what data will be provided or added for the perceived value it adds to the solution for the information seeker (e.g., trust, reliability). On the other hand, publishers should consider how their data can be combined with other data of similar type (e.g., environmental or transportation) or relatedness (e.g., roads and weather). Identifying information needs and the possible answers could help reveal the relatedness. The **theoretical implications** are aimed towards OGD and e-government researchers. OGD tended to be painted as a supply or demand issue [e.g., 10]. Our model expands on this idea as it focuses on information needs that arise when there is a gap in the knowledge of the individual, while information demands are requests for information that are believed to be needed [20]. Based on the tentative model, there are some suggestions. The information seeker's role in OGD can be considered in relation to information needs in society. Previous research about information needs may be able to help, support, and guide future OGD research.

5.2   Limitations and Future Work

The above model can be generalised to primary needs and information needs that are activity-based in an everyday context where it is easy to formulate questions. The scenario was general enough to be experienced beyond researchers and students in Belgium, but focused on the "fact-find", "brief", and "stay aware" use of solutions. Future research is needed about situations with research-based, stimulation-based, and recreational-based information use. The literature review aimed at gaining insight into an issue, and the resulting background could be further developed with a systematic literature review, but we believe it has captured relevant research for this study. The current model is based on the perspective of the information seeker and should be extended with the perspective of publishers and data transformers. At the same time, it needs further testing in other contexts. Further research is needed about how to bridge the gap between publishers and information seekers through the development and use of solutions. The combination of information needs and benefits of OGD is one possible direction. The connection between providing and adding data in a solution is one interesting gap that can be explored further.

6   Conclusion

The contribution of this paper is two-fold: a tentative conceptual model and possible considerations (see Fig. 1). The model is one way to understand how OGD can be integrated into society by satisfying information needs. The use of data and information in solutions can impact information seekers' lives to realize the benefits of OGD. However, information needs come in many shapes and forms, are complex, and not always fully expressed, which can make them challenging to capture. Data transformers and publishers can view the information in a solution as a data concoction brought together from different sources rather than a one-way data flow. The model presents the complexity of connecting the needs of information seekers with data provided by publishers through a solution changeable by data transformers.

References

1. Attard, J., Orlandi, F., Scerri, S., Auer, S.: A systematic review of open government data initiatives. Gov. Inf. Q. **32**(4), 399–418 (2015)
2. Barbosa Tavares, R., Hepworth, M., De Souza Costa, S.M.: Investigating citizens' information needs through participative research: a pilot study in Candangolândia, Brazil. Inf. Dev. **27**(2), 125–138 (2011)
3. Belkin, N.J., Vickery, A.: Interaction in information systems: a review of research from document retrieval to knowledge-based systems, No. 025.04 BEL. CIMMYT (1985)
4. Cabitza, F., Locoro, A., Batini, C.: Making open data more personal through a social value perspective: a methodological approach. Inf. Syst. Front. **22**, 1–18 (2018)
5. Carrara, W., Oudkerk, F., Van Steenbergen, E., Tinholt, D.: Open data goldbook for data managers and data holders (2018)
6. Cronin, P., Ryan, F., Coughlan, M.: Undertaking a literature review: a step-by-step approach. Br. J. Nurs. **17**(1), 38–43 (2008)
7. Crusoe, J.R., Ahlin, K.: Users' activities for using open government data-a process framework. People, Process and Policy, Transforming Government (2019)

8. Daft, R.L., Lengel, R.H.: Organizational information requirements, media richness and structural design. Manag. Sci. **32**(5), 554–571 (1986)
9. Davies, T.: Open data, democracy and public sector reform. A look at open government data use from data.gov.uk, pp. 1–47 (2010)
10. Dawes, S.S., Vidiasova, L., Parkhimovich, O.: Planning and designing open government data programs: an ecosystem approach. Gov. Inf. Q. **33**(1), 15–27 (2016)
11. Erdelez, S.: Information encountering: it's more than just bumping into information. Bull. Am. Soc. Inf. Sci. Technol. **25**(3), 26–29 (1999)
12. Fernández-Güell, J.M., Collado-Lara, M., Guzmán-Araña, S., Fernández-Añez, V.: Incorporating a systemic and foresight approach into smart city initiatives: the case of Spanish cities. J. Urban Technol. **23**(3), 43–67 (2016)
13. Gebka, E., Crusoe, J., Ahlin, K.: Open data reuse and information needs satisfaction: a method to bridge the gap. In: Proceedings of CEUREGOV-CeDEM-ePart (2020). ongoing Research; Accepted; Not Published
14. Hellberg, A.S., Hedström, K.: The story of the sixth myth of open data and open government. Transform. Gov.: People Process Policy **9**(1), 35–51 (2015)
15. Hey, J.: The data, information, knowledge, wisdom chain: the metaphorical link. Intergov. Oceanogr. Comm. **26**, 1–18 (2004)
16. Lindman, J., Kinnari, T., Rossi, M.: Business roles in the emerging open-data ecosystem. IEEE Softw. **33**(5), 54–59 (2016)
17. Madsen, C.Ø., Hofmann, S., Pieterson, W.: Channel choice complications - exploring the multiplex nature of citizens' channel choices. In: Lindgren, I., et al. (eds.) EGOV 2019. LNCS, vol. 11685, pp. 139–151. Springer, Cham (2019). https://doi.org/10.1007/978-3-030-27325-5_11
18. March, S.T., Smith, G.F.: Design and natural science research on information technology. Decis. Support Syst. **15**(4), 251–266 (1995)
19. Maxwell, J.A.: Qualitative Research Design. SAGE Publications Inc., Thousand Oaks (2012)
20. Nicholas, D., Herman, E.: Assessing Information Needs in the Age of the Digital Consumer. Routledge, Abingdon (2010)
21. Peffers, K., Tuunanen, T., Rothenberger, M.A., Chatterjee, S.: A design science research methodology for information systems research. J. Manag. Inf. Syst. **24**(3), 45–77 (2007)
22. Safarov, I., Meijer, A., Grimmelikhuijsen, S.: Utilization of open government data: a systematic literature review of types, conditions, effects and users. Inf. Polity **22**(1), 1–24 (2017)
23. Walters, W.H.: Comparative recall and precision of simple and expert searches in google scholar and eight other databases. Portal: Libr. Acad. **11**(4), 971–1006 (2011)
24. Wilson, T.D.: On user studies and information needs. J. Doc. **37**(1), 3–15 (1981)
25. Zuiderwijk, A., Janssen, M.: Barriers and development directions for the publication and usage of open data: a socio-technical view. In: Gascó-Hernández, M. (ed.) Open Government. PAIT, vol. 4, pp. 115–135. Springer, New York (2014). https://doi.org/10.1007/978-1-4614-9563-5_8
26. Zuiderwijk, A., Janssen, M., Davis, C.: Innovation with open data: essential elements of open data ecosystems. Inf. Polity **19**(1–2), 17–33 (2014). https://doi.org/10.3233/IP-140329

Towards a Framework for Open Data Publishers: A Comparison Study Between Sweden and Belgium

Jonathan Crusoe[1]([⊠]) [iD], Anthony Simonofski[2,3] [iD], and Antoine Clarinval[2] [iD]

[1] Division of Information Systems and Digitalization,
Linköping University, 581 83 Linköping, Sweden
`jonathan.crusoe@liu.se`
[2] Namur Digital Institute, University of Namur, Namur, Belgium
{`anthony.simonofski,antoine.clarinval`}`@unamur.be`
[3] Faculty of Economics and Business,
Katholieke Universiteit Leuven, Leuven, Belgium
`anthony.simonofski@kuleuven.be`

Abstract. Public organizations in the role of publishers publish data for anyone to reuse, which can lead to benefits. However, the process descriptions for this publishing work focus on one or a few issues, which leaves out important areas and decisions. Little seems to be known about variations between publishers based on one common point of comparison. Therefore, this paper presents a comparison between two publishers: Namur (Belgium) and Linköping (Sweden). The comparison is based on a process framework, seven in-depth interviews, document studies, and a verification meeting with one respondent. We learned that the OGD manager is an agent of change who need to balance implementation and guidance, the orthodox method of e-mail registration can be used to engage users and monitor impact, the organizational unit for OGD is cross-organizational, and the publisher process framework could be used as ex-ante strategic guidelines and context-specific recommendations.

Keywords: Open Government Data · Publisher · Process framework · International comparison

1 Introduction

Open Government Data (OGD) refers to interoperable data that is freely shared by public organizations over the Internet for anyone to reuse without restriction [1,21]. The data can come from or be parliament minutes and weather reports [1,2,20]. The use of OGD could lead to benefits, such as increased governmental transparency and citizen participation [11,14,15,26], but there are also risks, such as privacy violations as well as misinterpretations of data [3,27].

This paper focuses on the key stakeholders who share data in public organizations: the publishers. A main challenge of OGD resides in the variation in

© IFIP International Federation for Information Processing 2020
Published by Springer Nature Switzerland AG 2020
G. Viale Pereira et al. (Eds.): EGOV 2020, LNCS 12219, pp. 262–274, 2020.
https://doi.org/10.1007/978-3-030-57599-1_20

how data is shared by publishers [1], which can come from differences in the publisher process that tends to be ad-hoc. Descriptions of this process vary from technical [13], lifecycle [10] to metadata and information management [18,22]. They often focus on one or a few issues, which leaves out important areas and decisions. However, little seems to be known about possible variations based on one common reference point. This lack of knowledge can impede the analysis and comparison of publishing processes by researchers or practitioners. Therefore, in this paper, we apply a publisher process framework to two international cases: Namur (Belgium) and Linköping (Sweden). The application of this framework reveals similarities and differences in a structured manner and we discuss lessons learned from the comparison for research and practice.

The rest of this paper is organized as follows. Section 2 presents the background related to the publishing of OGD. Section 3 presents the methodology followed to perform the international comparison. Section 4 presents publishing processes of both cities and their comparison. Section 5 discusses lessons learned, implications for both research and practice, the study's limitations, and leads for further research. Finally, Sect. 6 summarizes the contributions of this study.

2 Background

The publisher process of OGD has been studied by academic and practical authors. Two early examples are [13] that details the steps to publish linked OGD, and [10] which focuses on the general lifecycle. [5] presents a publisher process with a focus on strategies, technical publishing, and a lifecycle. However, in recent practical descriptions, there is an increased focus on information management and metadata [18,22], but publishers are still using ad-hoc processes. In general, the descriptions have gaps, variations, uneven details, and fragmented coverage of the publisher process, which indicate the publishing is more than releasing data. In this paper, the publisher process is viewed as groups of processes in a sequence with variations, decisions, and choices, and the final output is OGD. This approach follows the publisher process framework of Crusoe and Ahlin [6]. This framework is a recent attempt to synthesise previous research and empirical material on the publishers' processes and is based on the findings of [5,8,10,13,16–19,22,25]. The authors explain that publishing OGD is more than releasing data and, thus, the framework comprises six process groups detailed here. The groups cover the introduction of OGD to its withdrawal by the publisher. **Initiation** processes contribute to a long-term and sustainable work with OGD. For example, education, appointment of an OGD manager, and creation of strategies. **Inventory** processes contribute to the organization's information management with the purpose to enable and help the prioritization and preparation of publishing OGD. For example, find an information center and audits of the organization's information resources. **Publish** processes design and implement the data publishing that extracts data from inside the organization to share it with external users. For example, prepare the data, IT-systems, and maintenance of OGD. **Sustain** processes maintain the data provision and monitor the internal and external impact of OGD to guide and direct the work with

OGD. For example, evaluate and improve the data provision. **Withdrawal** processes stop the data provision or cut the connection between data production and OGD storage [19]. **User engagement** processes are red threads through the work with OGD and can broadly be divided into raising awareness and promote reuse, which can have the purpose to identify valuable datasets to publish or build trust [17]. Moreover, this framework is well theoretically grounded but still needs to be applied in practice. Also, it does not capture the variations between different publishing processes. We attempt to fill this gap in our study.

3 Methodology

We conducted two qualitative case studies to explore how the publisher process groups are followed in two cities. Here, we note that this research is part of verifying and further developing the framework proposed in [6]. From this framework, we selected the process groups presented in Sect. 2. First the research process is described and then the cases are introduced.

3.1 Data Collection and Data Analysis

Between November 2019 and January 2020, three researchers collected empirical data through a combination of seven in-depth interviews with key stakeholders (Table 1), and supplementary official documents, agendas, and internal documents provided to us by the interviewees and identified on their websites. The interviews were semi-structured [9]. We structured the interview guide around the main process groups of the publisher framework described in Sect. 2. The interviews were limited to three for Namur and four for Linköping as the interviewees stated that these were, for each case, the main functions involved in the OGD strategy and day-to-day implementation at the city level.

The interviews were analyzed with process and initial coding [23]. First, we transcribed the recorded interviews in memos, structured around the publisher framework's groups. Then, we skimmed the memos to grasp their themes and highlight important sentences based on the research objective. The codes were then inserted in a table to summarize the main insights. The official documentation helped us to outline the context of each city as it provided a frame of reference regarding local policies, agendas, and strategies. It also served as a resource for additional information regarding topics that were discussed during interviews. Thanks to the diversity and complementarity in the profiles and backgrounds of the interviewees, the analysis performed by multiple researchers, and the triangulation with the official documentation, we were able to limit the subjective perception in the data. The comparison and framework were discussed with the Swedish OGD manager and follow-up questions were asked.

3.2 Case Studies

The selected cities are Namur (Belgium) and Linköping (Sweden). Namur is the regional capital of Wallonia and has 110,939 inhabitants. The service industry is

Table 1. Interviewees

ID	City	Function	Relevance
N1	Namur	OGD manager	Overall view on the data process
N2	Namur	Head of data office	Strategic and historic view on OGD
N3	Namur	Technical agent	Technical view on the data cleaning and publishing process
L1	Linköping	OGD Manager at the IT-unit	Overall responsible for the OGD project
L2	Linköping	Ex-politician for the moderate party and municipal councilor	Political view on OGD
L3	Linköping	Digitalization director	Strategic view on OGD
L4	Linköping	System manager at the construction and environment committee	Responsible for the IT-system from which the data is extracted from

dominant (presence of a university, commercial activities, etc.). Namur has 127 datasets (e.g., mobility, thermography) published on its OGD portal. Linköping is the regional capital of Östergötland with a population of 161,499 people. The city focuses on ICT and knowledge development (with a university and several large IT- and technology-focused businesses), manufacturing, and a growing service sector. It has 18 datasets (e.g., air quality, open job positions) published on its OGD portal. The cities were selected based on accessibility for the researchers, history with OGD, and perceived closeness in context: both are regional capitals with a population above 100,000, similar industries, and presence of a university.

4 Findings

In this section, we describe the OGD publisher process groups for Namur and Linköping. For both, the insights of the interviewees were merged, for each group of the process framework. Their comparison is given in Table 2. In order to structure the comparison, each process group was refined into themes defined from the analysis of the transcript memos.

4.1 Publisher Process: The Case of Namur

Initialization. The emergence of OGD in Namur is the result of four factors. First, the possibility to technically monitor the administration. Second, the call from the political opposition for data openness and transparency. Third, the increasing interest and hype of the smart city theme. Finally, the PSI directive from the European level. It led to the creation of a dedicated data office, based on a former geographic department. Later, a person was hired to manage the cartographic data. The work on OGD was reorganized around this person, who is now the OGD manager. Namur has set its goal at the fourth level of Tim Berners Lee's model [4]. At the start of the OGD work, the OGD manager conducted numerous meetings, department by department, almost person by person, to discuss OGD. He organized trainings (first with external companies, then by himself) and found that most of the public agents were willing to learn and improve the functioning of the administration. As for the resources, there was no additional hiring of people for OGD. The data office's budget is part of the IT department's budget and is decreasing over the years. Overall, this merge causes resource issues for the OGD work.

Inventory. OGD in Namur is driven by the existing cartographic data. The publishing of data can be viewed as a migration of the cartographic data to the portal. The OGD manager is in charge of the prioritization of the datasets to publish, however, prioritization is rare. He started by publishing data "he was certain about", such as buildings or roads. The data had no potential sharing issues and personal details. The decision to publish data or not was in fact a balance between the necessity to publish it and its quality. This balance was weighted through meetings and discussions with the technical agent and the head of the concerned department. In addition to cartographic data, some datasets come from other departments, which are identified by the OGD manager and then published on the portal by the technical agent. These datasets are the most used or relevant for the entire administration (e.g. mobility data). One of the goals is to make the datasets available to the entire administration.

Publishing. The technical agent is in charge of uploading the datasets to the OGD portal. The most popular solution in Belgium (OpenDataSoft) was picked for the portal, without involving the technical agent. The data publishing is straightforward with the Opendatasoft back office. When the data is cleaned beforehand through the ETL software (SafeFME), publishing is done fast without impediments. When anomalies are spotted, the technical agent corrects them or asks other departments for corrections, which she can obtain easily. There were some issues with older data (30+ years), as their encoding had changed, or content was irrelevant or incorrect. This required a careful cleansing of the data. However, the most time consuming part of the process is to generate metadata. The technical agent manually sets column titles and descriptions of the datasets.

Sustain. The OGD portal in Namur serves both as an internal tool to allow all departments to access the data of other units and as an external tool to give citizens access to data from the administration. Some data is automatically updated (e.g. every minute for the location of bikes). On the other hand, some data still needs manual updates, which they do not have time for anymore. In order to reach the fourth level of Tim Berners Lee's model, the head of the data office is pushing towards dynamic data on the portal. The city of Namur has received no feedback on the impact of OGD (even though there is a feature on the portal where re-users can share their reuse), which the technical agent described as "pretty frustrating". The only identified reuse is a one-off collaboration with the University of Namur [7]. Data corrections are based on feedback received by e-mail from citizens or public agents. The feedback is often about the metadata.

Withdrawal. The city of Namur has not withdrawn any dataset from the OGD portal. The only negative feedback they received was on the thermographic data they represented on a 3D plan. However, they explained the relevance of having this data on the portal and the complaint was dropped. As a consequence, there is now the possibility for people to ask for the withdrawal of data.

User Engagement. The OGD manager used several participation methods to develop and improve the OGD portal, such as interviews and meetings for the requirements analysis and prototyping for the development. The technical agent views citizen participation as a great opportunity to foster OGD reuse. The head of data office indicated that monitoring the reuse of OGD was still at the stage of a project. Namur wants to make efforts in this direction, although the lack of available resources is a barrier to conduct OGD projects. A first step was made through the 3D representation of some open datasets on the portal.

4.2 Publisher Process: The Case of Linköping

Initialization. OGD in the municipality started for two reasons: (1) the ex-politician realized the potential of OGD when visiting a hackathon and (2) a citizen requested an OGD portal for the municipality. The ex-politician advocated for this proposal and a mission was given to an official (the first OGD manager) to create the portal in 2012. The ex-politician drove the issue forward to ensure it was prioritized. The first OGD manager left and was replaced by the OGD manager interviewed for this study. The two managers have worked together. The current OGD manager is a member of the IT-unit. Part of the OGD manager's work is to inform about OGD and implement APIs. In his daily work, he comes in contact with information resources that he can evaluate. The current objective is to release 3–4 datasets per year and continue to develop the OGD portal. He and the ex-politician are in favor of the open by default principle. Moreover, no OGD strategy has been created and there are no strategic goals. They have more resources than they can consume, but the OGD manager expressed a need for more people to work with OGD. The municipality has also developed information security policy and guidelines, but have none for OGD.

Inventory. The OGD manager explained that they identify data that is interesting to citizens, which is often already published on the municipality's website. He once looked at the statistics for the top 10 visited information pages and continued to investigate them. Business representatives often have a feeling for what data is demanded by the public. Once they have identified interesting data, they meet with the unit responsible to inform them about OGD and that they seek to supplement the municipality's OGD, what OGD can and cannot do, and possible effects. Sometimes users come with suggestions about new datasets to publish and these are taken into account. For example, a citizen asked if they could publish the road works dataset and so they did. Moreover, the system manager was introduced to OGD by the OGD manager when he wanted to publish their data. The system manager and his organizational unit accepted the idea of OGD as they understood the data to be interesting to the public. He views it as a form of public service. He helps the OGD manager select parameters to publish. When publishing data, they do risk and technical analyses. The risk analysis involves studying the data, its information classification, legal parts, and data quality and its possible consequences.

Publishing. The technical analysis can involve identifying the current IT-systems and the need for an intermediate storage. Intermediate storage is important for sensitive data and can help to protect the original IT-systems, which was emphasized by the system manager. The OGD manager puts together groups where they discuss the risk and technical issues. The organizational unit often has an idea about the potential of the data and of how the citizens want the data. They also write documentation for the data and have recently started to experiment with tools for it. They control what information they can share, publish it, and then communicate about it to the users.

Sustain. They aim to have all of their data automatically updated. They tried manual updating at the start, but it was too resource consuming. Their OGD portal is custom-built, but is slowly being replaced by a private-provided solution (Entryscape). On their portal, roughly 50% of the published OGD requires an API-key. To get the API-key the user has to register an e-mail address. This setup allowed the publishers to contact users and ask questions about what they are doing with their data. This setup was not planned from the start, but came from internal worries and is perceived as orthodox from an OGD perspective. They collect statistics about the number of API calls, but it is not something they monitor. Moreover, their OGD is used internally by their decision makers in different decision-support systems. However, there is currently limited monitoring of the Swedish development of OGD. They do not follow any maturity framework, rather they focus on users' needs and on API access.

Withdrawal. The OGD manager explained that GDPR started discussions on limiting the real estate designations dataset. However, they do not want to withdraw data and the risk analysis is supposed to avoid it. They do not want data to "end up in the wrong hands" or break the law. The food data is currently not accessible as a new law is stopping it from being published.

Table 2. Comparison between Namur and Linköping publisher processes.

Process groups	Themes	Namur Differences	Namur Similarities	Linköping Differences
Initialization	Drivers	Technological monitoring; Smart city theme; Call for openness from opposition; PSI directive	Overall top-down	Politicians saw potential; Citizen proposal; Hackathon; Public app development
	Organization	Geographic department	No OGD strategy	IT-unit; Release 3-4 datasets/year
	Resources	Decreasing budgets	Need more people	Have the resources
	Cultural Journey	External technical trainings	Numerous meetings	Open by default
Inventory	Data Discovery	Existing geographical data migration	Internal search	Look at the website; Citizen requests
	Prioritization	Rare; Migration list; Usefulness vs. data quality	Need-driven	Citizen interest; Business representatives
Publishing	Preparations	Strong focus on metadata	Technical analysis	Strong focus on risk analysis
	Publishing Portal	Private-owned (OpenDataSoft)		Custom-built, but moving towards private-provided
	Maturity Framework	Tim Berners Lee [4]		API access; Use focus
Sustain	Maintenance	Manual	Mix	Automated
	Monitor		Collect download statistics that are not used	Some e-mails collected; Internal use
Withdrawal	Occurrence of Withdrawal	—	Never withdrawn datasets but awareness exists	—
User engagement	Re-use Stimulation	One-off collaboration with university; 3D platform	Publish news	Participated in a hackathon (5 years); Know possible uses
	Feedback	Supplemented metadata	E-mail	Supplemented dataset parameters

User Engagement. The e-mails collected for their API-key registration have allowed the municipality to contact users. For example, a family uses the data in their digital home, while a developer has implemented a food inspection presenter app. The OGD manager said that the developer praised the municipality for their APIs as it was the easiest data retrieval of all municipalities. The municipality used to participate in the arrangement of a hackathon called East Sweden Hack, but it closed after five years due to a decision from the top. The municipality has since then arranged Innovations and Social impacts instead. Today, they publish news and information about their OGD, but do not actively work with the users since some instances, such as SKL (Sweden's municipalities and regions) and Vinnova (Sweden's innovation agency), focus on what data municipalities can publish instead of user engagement. The OGD manager explained that they only try to publish data and inform that it exists. They listen to users' feedback and have supplemented their dataset with new parameters based on requests.

5   Discussion

This section discusses the lessons learned from the similarities and differences of the cases, the theoretical and practical implications of the study, and limitations and future research leads.

5.1   Lessons Learned from the Comparison

We reflect on three key discrepancies between the case studies and previous research: the OGD manager role, user engagement, and re-use monitoring.

OGD Manager Role. In previous literature, the OGD manager is responsible for OGD and requirements and/or coordinating and managing activities [19,22]. The two cases nuance this description. They are close enough to the operations to get their hands into the manual publishing process, which they found resource consuming. They are not responsible for data production (unlike [5]) neither considered project managers (unlike [10]). Both OGD managers cause change in the organization and manage an OGD unit, which is an overlapping subunit of other organizational units (e.g., IT and Construction and Environment Committee). They are responsible for OGD and related requirements [22]. For example, when needed they can take help from developers, legal advisors, and data owners [5,10,19]. The managers also work with continual education and help to spread the idea of OGD in the organization. Education is a critical success factor for OGD initiatives [25]. However, the degree of education between the two cases differ. Namur had external technical training, while Linköping had not, which is likely a consequence of the commonness of digital skills in Sweden. In conclusion, the findings provides new insight into the work of OGD managers. Once basic OGD infrastructure is in place, such as OGD portals and curating tools (e.g., Opendatasoft), an OGD manager works to connect the data production processes with the OGD infrastructure while simultaneously changing peoples' minds and behaviors.

User Engagement. Previous research stresses the importance of user engagement [5,10,17,25]. The cases do not actively work with user engagement. Namur is impeded by the lack of resources, while Linköping focuses on publishing their data because of the focus of other organizations in their environment. At the same time, the cases do not currently monitor the impact of OGD. Linköping did engage the users through a hackathon, but then stopped. It seems that the cases lack resource-effective methods to engage users.

Re-use Monitoring. Previous literature also recommends to monitor OGD [5,10, 18,25]. However, it seems that a simple e-mail solution has provided Linköping with proofs of the value of their OGD in the wild, which their hackathon could not. The e-mails combine very light user engagement and anonymous monitoring. They could track API call statistics for individual users and then contact them and ask questions. This setup, while orthodox, could be a good way forward to get local proofs of valuable OGD for a publisher.

5.2 Theoretical Implications

The publisher process framework [6] is a good fit for the comparison of the two cases as it allowed us to structure the data collection and analysis. The overall structure was followed in the work of the publishers and interviews generated rich empirical material, allowed us to identify new roles, and brought some points of reflections to the participants (e.g., monitoring and user engagement). However, the framework is divided into different process groups, which created some dilemmas when analysing the data. For instance, the initiation group was revisited between inventory and publishing when OGD managers educated organizational units about OGD. The empirical material also showed a need for certain basic OGD infrastructure to be in place before any data could be published, which is not currently part of the framework. However, all mentioned activities of the publishers fit well within the framework.

5.3 Practical Implications

This study helped to provide empirical validation of the publisher process framework. This framework can be considered as a basic ex-ante strategic framework for OGD development. Practitioners within administrations could use the process groups as an actionable template for their strategies and use the diverse themes as key attention points to be taken into account.

Furthermore, the analysis of the OGD publisher processes of Namur and Linköping revealed similarities and also key differences in their process. Therefore, context-specific recommendations could be issued for each group depending on the variations of each city.

5.4   Limitations and Further Research

This study also presents some limitations. First, data collection was based on document studies, one in-depth interview with each of the participants, and a verification meeting with the Swedish OGD manager. The empirical material could be further enriched with meetings where the framework is presented and discussed between different participants.

Second, the analysis of the publishing process of the two cities did not follow a pure deductive approach, but the tentative OGD publishing process framework is based on several literature sources [6]. This approach allowed for structure in the data collection and analysis, but it is possible that more process groups, activities, and variations need to be identified.

Third, the publisher process has been applied to two comparable cities in terms of size and number of stakeholders involved. Even though they constitute a first validation step, the application of the framework to a more diverse set of cities would provide more extensive validation and would allow discovering more variations in the OGD publishing processes and help to suggest context-specific recommendations. The elicitation of the factors impacting the process such as national culture [12], city context [24], or degree of OGD institutionalization would constitute a promising step. Furthermore, the impact of these factors on the process and the variations they introduce would also be an interesting next step. In this study, we focused on key variations in the process but the analysis of the impediments that publishers face would also enable to issue better recommendations for practice.

6   Conclusion

In this paper, through the lens of a theoretical framework, we have compared the OGD publishing process groups of two cities: Namur (Belgium) and Linköping (Sweden). This study contributes at several levels. First, we provide a first empirical validation of the OGD publishing framework suggested by [6]. Second, we take an in-depth look at the processes followed by Namur and Linköping and clearly identify their similarities and differences. We identified that OGD managers are agents of change for the operations and business of the organization, while needing to balance implementation and guidance. Linköping used an orthodox method to engage and monitor users (account registration with e-mail only requirement), which allowed them to identify concrete value of their published data in the wild. Namur placed their OGD unit in a data office, while Linköping placed their OGD unit in an IT-unit. Finally, we suggest to use the process as ex-ante strategic guidelines and to open the discussion for context-specific recommendations.

References

1. Attard, J., Orlandi, F., Scerri, S., Auer, S.: A systematic review of open government data initiatives. Gov. Inf. Q. **32**(4), 399–418 (2015)
2. Ayre, L.B., Craner, J.: Open data: what it is and why you should care. Public Libr. Q. **36**(2), 173–184 (2017)
3. Barry, E., Bannister, F.: Barriers to open data release: a view from the top. Inf. Polity **19**(1–2), 129–152 (2014)
4. Berners-Lee, T.: 5-star open data (2015). http://5stardata.info/en
5. Carrara, W., Oudkerk, F., Van Steenbergen, E., Tinholt, D.: Open data goldbook for data managers and data holders (2018). https://www.europeandataportal.eu/sites/default/files/goldbook.pdf. Accessed 27 Aug 2019
6. Crusoe, J., Ahlin, K.: Publisher' activities for working with open government data - a process framework. In: Scandinavian Workshop of e-Government Scandinavian Workshop of e-Government SWEG 2020. The University of Gothenburg, Campus Lindholmen, 29–30 January (2020). [Work in progress; not published]
7. Crusoe, J., Simonofski, A., Clarinval, A., Gebka, E.: The impact of impediments on open government data use: insights from users. In: Proceedings of the 13th IEEE International Conference on Research Challenges in Information Science (2019)
8. Denis, J., Goëta, S.: Exploration, extraction and 'rawification'. the shaping of transparency in the back rooms of open data. The Shaping of Transparency in the Back Rooms of Open Data (2014)
9. Drever, E.: Using semi-structured interviews in small-scale research. A Teacher's Guide, ERIC (1995)
10. Folmer, E., Reuvers, M., Quak, W., van den Broek, T., van Veenstra, A.F.: Walking the extra byte: a lifecycle model for linked open data. In: Linked Open Data-Pilot Linked Open Data Nederland, pp. 95–111. Remwerk (2011)
11. Hartog, M., Mulder, B., Spée, B., Visser, E., Gribnau, A.: Open data within governmental organisations: effects, benefits and challenges of the implementation process. eJ. eDemocr. Open Gov. **6**(1), 49–61 (2014)
12. Hofstede, G.: Dimensionalizing cultures: the hofstede model in context. Online Read. Psychol. Cult. **2**(1), 2307 (2011)
13. Hyland, B., Wood, D.: The joy of data-a cookbook for publishing linked government data on the web. In: Wood, D. (ed.) Linking Government Data, pp. 3–26. Springer, New York (2011). https://doi.org/10.1007/978-1-4614-1767-5_1
14. Janssen, M., Charalabidis, Y., Zuiderwijk, A.: Benefits, adoption barriers and myths of open data and open government. Inf. Syst. Manag. **29**(4), 258–268 (2012)
15. Kucera, J., Chlapek, D.: Benefits and risks of open government data. J. Syst. Integr. **5**(1), 30–41 (2014)
16. Kucera, J., Chlapek, D., Klímek, J., Necaský, M.: Methodologies and best practices for open data publication. In: DATESO, pp. 52–64 (2015)
17. Lee, D.: Building an open data ecosystem: an Irish experience. In: Elsa, E., Marijn, J., Luís, B. (eds.) Proceedings of the 8th International Conference on Theory and Practice of Electronic Governance, pp. 351–360. ACM Press (2014)
18. Naturvårdsverket: Tillgängliggöra data och följa upp informationshantering (2018). https://www.naturvardsverket.se/Stod-i-miljoarbetet/Vagledningar/Oppna-data/. Accessed 10 Oct 2019
19. Nečaský, M., et al.: Deliverable d5.1: methodology for publishing datasets as open data. Master Spreadsheet (2014). https://docs.google.com/spreadsheets/d/1CLwsCm-yJuvZeEWfFYS1NwUfBlR4sQyycafyaG-3yYY/

20. Okamoto, K.: Introducing open government data. Ref. Libr. **58**(2), 111–123 (2017)
21. Open Knowledge: Open data handbook (2012). http://opendatahandbook.org/. Accessed 9 Feb 2020
22. ÖppnaData.SE: Skapa & publicera öppna data - den nationella portalen för öppna data och psi (2018). https://oppnadata.se/skapa-publicera-oppna-data/. Accessed 27 Aug 2019
23. Saldaña, J.: Thinking Qualitatively: Methods of Mind. Sage Publications, Thousand Oaks (2014)
24. Simonofski, A., Vallé, T., Serral, E., Wautelet, Y.: Investigating context factors in citizen participation strategies: a comparative analysis of Swedish and Belgian smart cities. Int. J. Inf. Manag. 102011 (2019)
25. Susha, I., Zuiderwijk, A., Charalabidis, Y., Parycek, P., Janssen, M.: Critical factors for open data publication and use: a comparison of city-level, regional, and transnational cases. eJ. eDemocr. Open Gov. **7**(2), 94–115 (2015)
26. Virkar, S., Viale Pereira, G.: Exploring open data state-of-the-art: a review of the social, economic and political impacts. In: Parycek, P., et al. (eds.) EGOV 2018. LNCS, vol. 11020, pp. 196–207. Springer, Cham (2018). https://doi.org/10.1007/978-3-319-98690-6_17
27. Zuiderwijk, A., Janssen, M.: The negative effects of open government data-investigating the dark side of open data. In: Proceedings of the 15th Annual International Conference on Digital Government Research, pp. 147–152. ACM Press (2014)

Open Government Data Systems: Learning from a Public Utility Perspective

Jonathan Crusoe[1]([✉]) [iD], Anneke Zuiderwijk[2] [iD], and Ulf Melin[1] [iD]

[1] Division of Information Systems and Digitalization,
Linköping University, 581 83 Linköping, Sweden
{jonathan.crusoe,ulf.melin}@liu.se
[2] Faculty of Technology, Policy and Management,
Delft University of Technology, 2628 BX Delft, The Netherlands
A.M.G.Zuiderwijk-vanEijk@tudelft.nl

Abstract. Previous research on Open Government Data (OGD) strug-
gles with synthesising a holistic perspective of OGD systems. A perspective that has dealt with vast, complex systems is public utility. Public
utilities are, for example, water supply networks and electric power grids.
This study explores what we can learn from a public utility perspective
when perceiving and organising OGD systems. We used a hermeneutic
literature review combined with a snowballing approach, resulting in a
selection of 39 studies. We compare public utilities and OGD systems to
derive five lessons: (1) an OGD system can be perceived from a node-flow
view, (2) the foundational data flow of an OGD system starts at data
collection and ends at data used by the public in an everyday context,
(3) the organisation of OGD systems needs to consider the combinability,
interpretability, and boundless reusability of data, (4) OGD systems need
governance organisations that cover the whole system, and (5) OGD systems could replace existing data provision systems and be made a public
utility if certain characteristic problems are overcome.

Keywords: Open data · Open Government Data · Public utility ·
System

1 Introduction

Public organisations openly share data over the Internet. Ideally, this data can be
reused by anyone without restrictions. Data providers and data users organise as
an Open Government Data (OGD) system by following the OGD principles (e.g.,
non-discriminatory data access and machine-readable data) [4,23,45]. The actors
(people and organisations) work together for a particular purpose or conduct
similar activities [44]. They believe that the OGD system will lead to benefits,
such as increased transparency and improved government services [33].

© IFIP International Federation for Information Processing 2020
Published by Springer Nature Switzerland AG 2020
G. Viale Pereira et al. (Eds.): EGOV 2020, LNCS 12219, pp. 275–289, 2020.
https://doi.org/10.1007/978-3-030-57599-1_21

An OGD system consists of interacting subsystems, such as an ecosystem of data providers or an ecosystem of data users [24,47]. These subsystems have their own rules, behaviours, and interactions [24,40]. Events or changes in one subsystem can impact other subsystems [24,25]. The OGD system is dependent on infrastructure [17]. The infrastructure help actors discover data through OGD portals [13,30] and enables the transfer of data between actors [29]. The OGD system is also limited and enabled by laws, regulations, and licenses [42].

While previous OGD research contains attempts to study OGD systems from a holistic perspective, such as ecosystem [e.g., 18], lifecycle [e.g., 21], and value network perspectives [e.g., 3], there are still three major issues related to the synthesis of a holistic perspective in OGD research. First, the OGD system is often treated as one system without subsystems and their interactions [e.g., 21,36,39], which may cause the rules and behaviours of the subsystem to be lost or merged with other subsystems. Second, the extensive infrastructure is often abated (to make something less serious) by not being fully integrated into holistic perspectives of OGD systems [e.g., 15,18,48]. Third, the legal system tends not to be incorporated into holistic perspectives of OGD systems [e.g., 1,3,15]. The legal system is one source of rules and impediments for the subsystems.

A holistic perspective that has dealt with vast, complex systems is the public utility perspective. Examples of public utilities include water supply and power supply [9]. A public utility is a large group of public service organisations that produce and manage a variety of products and services vital to modern life [38]. Their system is based on an extensive infrastructure that helps them to create products or services at one location and distribute them to several customers [22,38]. The government can be involved, oversee, or regulate this system that has to serve all customers without discrimination [38].

We argue that knowledge about public utilities could help OGD researchers synthesise a holistic perspective of OGD systems and be informative about how to organise OGD systems. The objective of this study is to explore what we can learn from a public utility perspective when perceiving and organising OGD systems.

This paper contains the following sections. First, the research approach used to identify literature about OGD systems and public utilities is described. Second, a synthesised description of public utilities with two examples is presented. Third, OGD systems and public utilities are compared. Then, five lessons are presented. Fourth, a conclusion with limitations and future work is given.

2   Research Approach

This paper is based on an exploration of the literature using a hermeneutic literature review method with citation tracking and citation analysis (snowballing) [8]. The review aimed to synthesise two bodies of literature and develop an understanding of OGD systems, drawing on literature concerning public utilities. The result also includes generic concepts (comparative categories) that were used as common points of reference for the comparison between OGD systems and public utilities [41]. Next, the two phases of the review are described.

The **first phase** focused on exploring literature about public utilities. We used the keyword "public utility" with Google Scholar and Google to identify literature about public utilities' organisation and development from a holistic perspective. Google Scholar was used since the search engine has a good coverage and recall speed with a precision above-average for simple keyword searches [49]. Google was used to identify sources that could contain relevant literature, such as online book shops or ResearchGate or synonyms to keywords. The keywords developed over time as new literature was identified. The keyword "public utility" was also combined with other keywords, such as "infrastructure" and "public administration". We identified literature by skimming their titles and abstracts, then, if needed, a quick internal search of the main text was done. In the case of books, if needed, reviews were read. In total, four books and two book chapters about public utilities were identified as relevant. Then, we mapped key ideas and insights about the topic by studying paragraphs and chapters to synthesise them, which resulted in a textual overview. Finally, we used the result to write this paper and as an input for the next phase.

The **second phase** focused on OGD systems, the comparative categories, and the comparison between public utilities and OGD systems. We used the keywords "open data" or "open government data" combined with "ecosystem", "lifecycle", and "value network". We skimmed the titles and abstracts to identify their relevance. If needed, their content was skimmed or quickly searched through to identify key ideas and insights about the topic. We considered studies to be relevant if they contributed to the understanding of OGD systems or the comparison between OGD systems and public utilities. In total, one book, one thesis, three reports, five empirical texts (e.g., OGD principles), four conference papers, and 19 journal articles about OGD were identified as relevant. We studied the relevant literature for key ideas and insights. We then compared the literature about OGD systems and public utilities to identify possible areas of comparison and create a list of the comparative categories. From this list, we selected the comparative categories "the system", "infrastructure", and "governance", as they relate to the problem described in the introduction. Also, the comparative category "the public" was included since the public (citizens) are important beneficiaries of both public utilities and OGD systems, while the comparative category "resource" was included because of its stressed and varied nature in the public utility literature. We then filled out each of the selected comparative categories for OGD systems and public utilities, which became the comparison. Lessons were drawn from each comparative category by identifying and analysing the comparison.

3   Public Utilities

This section presents the synthesis of the identified public utility literature, where two public utilities are described in detail. We define public utilities as *"[...] the large group of public service organisations that exist to locate, produce or collect, transmit, distribute and/or process and store, a variety of products and services that are vital to modern life. These products and services are ubiquitous."* [38, p. 5]. Public utilities are based on an extensive network structure that acts as a distribution system and is built from components with strong physical linkages. Organisations create products or services at one location and then distribute them over the network to several customers. The base infrastructure is often partly owned by the government, and, typically, there is a substantial sunk cost since the infrastructure is extensive [22,38]. The infrastructure is often shared with other actors, and if not managed properly, could lead to congestion [22].

The activities of public utilities can be divided into production, transmission, and distribution components (e.g., electricity: generating plants, high-voltage lines, and local power lines) [14,22]. The governance of public utilities is complex. Governments are involved, oversee, or regulate public utilities, and the utilities have to serve all customers without discrimination within their market area [38]. Regulations can help to enact standards to ensure reasonable service [46]. On the other hand, rigid standards can handicap utilities, such as when gas utilities went from illumination to cooking and heating [46]. The enforcement of standards is an important task for public organisations and can occupy a large portion of their time [46]. The income of public utilities can come from payments, stocks, bonds, and taxes [38]. In this paper, the public refers to the end-users who use and benefit from the services and products in an everyday context.

Public utilities provide essential services necessary for modern life. Without them, there can be no cities and nations [38]. They are often commonly found wherever people are living in villages, towns, and cities [46]. They are needed to support large populations, overcome the social consequences from the concentration of people, and allow cities to grow beyond their countryside [9,46]. In the past, when towns were generally small, public utilities were often simple, such as rivers and wells [9]. Over time, city development, urbanisation, industrialisation, and digitalisation have had a significant impact on public utilities' growth and development [38,46]. Public utilities can form monopolies, which occur when a single firm can supply a market at a cost and price far lower than would be possible if several firms served the market [38] or when there are natural limitations in supply or conditions of service [46].

Two common public utilities in any modern society are the water supply networks and electric power grids. We will present each public utility in detail to gain an in-depth understanding of their characteristics. **Water Supply Networks** are the most basic of public utilities. No town can survive long without a water supply for drinking, washing, and various industrial processes [9]. If the supply becomes polluted, disease and death can follow [38]. A water supply network consists of the water source, collection, transportation, raw water storage, treatment, finished water storage, distribution, and process monitoring components [38]. The monitoring could include identifying and fixing leaks [2]. To give an example of the public utility: aquifer pumps [9] or watersheds provide water to reservoirs. Aqueducts, culverts, or large pipes then move the water in large quantities to populated areas. The water is treated or filtered to ensure consistent quality (e.g., remove dirt or kill bacteria) [2,9]. The water is then distributed to households through local water supply networks where people can access the water with, for example, faucets, showers, or toilets [2]. Water supply utilities are also regulated. For example, the American Safe Drinking Water Act sought to protect public health by regulating the nation's public drinking water supply. The act requires the American Environmental Protection Agency (EPA) to set national health standards, which they do in a three-step process. The EPA also proposes treatment techniques and monitor the water supply networks [38].

The instant availability of electricity is assumed in the modern industry and domestic life. **Electric power grids** have become the largest public utility in modern societies. One of its greatest achievements is enabling lamps almost everywhere. Among the first power grids were pioneered as early as 1879 [9]. Electric power grids consist of four functional components: (1) power generation, (2) transmission of high voltage power, (3) distribution of low voltage power, and (4) marketing functions [38]. To give an example of the public utility: electricity is generated by power plants [2]. The electricity is sent to a substation where transformers increase its voltage, which allows it to travel long distances. The electricity travels over the high-voltage transmission grid to an area substation where it is stepped down to a lower voltage to be sent over the distribution grid. It is then distributed to homes and businesses [2]. People access the electric grid through plugging an electric device's cable into an electrical outlet. The device could be a computer or a dishwasher [2]. One major challenge with electricity is its behaviour (loop flow) to take all available routes to get from one point to another. If one line shuts down, the load is dispersed to all other lines, which can cause an overload that shuts down the entire grid [38]. Another major challenge is that electricity cannot be economically stored. It needs to be used as it is produced. Consequently, the grid has to be monitored to ensure that the grid is always met demand and does not overload [38]. Electrical power grids are also regulated. For example, Order 889 issued by the American Federal Energy Reliability Council (FERC) required all investor-owned utilities to participate in an open access same-time information system (OASIS) to make pricing and accessing processes more transparent [38].

4   Comparison Between OGD Systems and Public Utilities

This section first presents a summary of the comparison between public utilities and OGD systems (see Table 1). Then, each of the comparative categories is, in turn, presented with previous OGD research and their comparison and analysis to draw lessons learned. This section ends with an intermediate conclusion based on the comparison. The categories are the system, the public, infrastructure, resource, and governance.

4.1   The System

The system is concerned with how the system is holistically perceived as parts (e.g., elements and subsystems) and interactions. An OGD system has at least

Table 1. Comparison between OGD system and public utilities

Comparative categories	Public utilities	OGD system
The system	Objects or components with distribution and transmission [14,22,38]	Actors' interactions or elements with data flows [1,15,37,52]
The public	Served, costly products or services endowed by the public and limited access to the infrastructure [2,38]	Shared, free data, the public's interest in reusing the data is a myth, and open access to the data source [16,26,32]
Infrastructure	Distribution networks of social and technical parts over large areas [22,38]	Technical, functional artifacts (possibly on the Internet) for use by different actors [10,17,29,52]
Resource	A small set of homogeneous, standardised, public, physical, ubiquitous resources that are vital to modern life [9,38]	A large set of heterogeneous, standardized, public, intangible, recorded, interoperable data that needs interpretation [4,5,12,16]
Governance	Resource governance, regulated by law, governance organisations, and heavy involvement in the operations of actors and their interactions [38,46]	Suggested resource governance, regulated by law, international principles, more self-regulation, and unrestricted users [7,11,18,23, 32,36,42,45,47,48,51,52]

three ecosystems: data providers, (intermediate) data users, and end-users [47]. Data providers are public organisations who share their data [4,18]. They often have natural monopolies on their data because of high fixed costs, low variable costs, and a small number of potential data users [25]. Data users can be developers, journalists, and researchers [43]. They can take many different roles (e.g., data analyser or user experience provider [37]) and can use data to either provide new enhanced data back into the OGD system or products and services to the public [16,37]. End-users (the public) are any actor that uses the data directly by extracting facts or indirectly through using products and services provided by data users [16]. The data is often holistically perceived as a flow from data providers to data users and sometimes end-users [e.g., 16,37]. OGD systems can also be perceived as a collection of elements, such as data audit, data access, and data use [18,36,52].

OGD systems and public utilities follow the same basic pattern: (1) produce, (2) transmit and distribute, and (3) use products or services [e.g., 2,25]. Both holistic perspectives attempt to identify and order key activities in the system following the logic of a chain or flow. OGD systems use the terminology elements, while public utilities use components. We will continue to use 'component' for both. However, OGD research focuses on actors (e.g., data providers and data users) with data flows [e.g., 1,15,37,47,52], while public utilities focus on objects and their systematic purpose (e.g., generating plants or high-voltage lines [14,22,38]). Previous OGD research tends to focus on the interaction between data providers and users [e.g., 24, 52], while public utilities focus on a chain of objects and activities [14, 22, 38].

The idea of key activities, actors, and objects seem to be a promising way to holistically perceive vast, complex systems where they start at the origin of the product (e.g., data, water, or electricity) and then continue to its distribution and transmission. The activities, actors, and objects as components can roughly be divided into nodes (e.g., weather data collection, water treatment, or power generation) and infrastructure (e.g., the Internet, aqueducts, or high-voltage grids). However, if we stay at nodes and infrastructure as a chain of components, behaviours, such as monopolies or infrastructure congestion, or needs to monitor the infrastructure can be lost. We combine the idea of components with the insight that OGD systems are known to consist of subsystems [24, 47, 52] to get functional systems. This approach follows in McNabb's [38] components of the water supply networks and functional components of electric power systems. A functional system is a collection of nodes with a similar purpose and similar key activities in the OGD system. The system is connected to other functional systems to organise as a data flow. The nodes can have relationships and interactions that will impact functional systems later down the chain.

4.2   The Public

The public is concerned with the availability and access of products, services, or data (resources) of the systems to the public. In OGD systems, data is provided under an open license that allows anyone to acquire it for free and use and distribute it without restriction [11, 23, 32, 45]. OGD systems and public utilities both provide their resources to the public without discrimination (anyone has the right to access and use the resource). However, they differ on at least four points. First, OGD systems share data to anyone with an Internet connection [16], while public utilities serve the public in their market area [38]. Second, the public interest in reusing OGD has been declared a myth [26], while public utilities are endowed by public interest [38]. Third, the public has direct access to the data in OGD systems [32], while the public has limited access to the infrastructure of public utilities, such as high-voltage grids and aqueducts [2]. Fourth, in OGD systems, the data is free [32], while in public utilities, the products or services can need payment (e.g., via tax or direct fees) [38].

Some of the differences are likely a consequence of the rather immature age of OGD [5] in comparison to the ancient history of public utilities [9]. While the data might not be interesting, it is arguable that the products built with it are attractive [20]. The use of data requires certain technical skills and expertise [43], which limits the development of these products to specialists. It is perceivable that OGD systems could follow in the steps of water supply networks or electric power grids. For example, data users could sell products that the public uses by plugging them into the data infrastructure. This situation is similar to how the public buys electrical devices and plug them into an electrical outlet or the water supply network (e.g., dishwashers) [2]. However, in the case of OGD systems, the resource that powers the device would be free. This possibility would continue to build on the idea of data users as intermediaries [e.g., 25, 28], but stresses that the raw data might only be for specialists and that the products and services should be sought after by the public. Consequently, the foundational data flow of an OGD system can be perceived to start at data collection and end at the use of data-based products or services by the public in, for example, their homes and businesses.

4.3 Infrastructure

Infrastructure focuses on the use of infrastructure in the systems, but also how it is holistically perceived. OGD systems are dependent on an OGD infrastructure, where the Internet is one part [16, 17, 23]. However, there is no agreed definition of infrastructure for OGD systems [e.g., 10, 43], but it seems to be either specific artefacts and the Internet [e.g., 17, 52] or something that facilitates data exchange between actors or the use of the data [e.g., 29].

OGD systems and public utilities have in common that they holistically perceive infrastructure as a tool with a specific purpose or use. In OGD systems, infrastructure is heavy technical with a focus on its use by different actors [10, 17, 52], while in public utilities, infrastructure is a mixture of social and technical parts over a large area [2, 22, 38]. Previous OGD research perceives infrastructure as functional artefacts that can exist on the Internet [17, 29, 52], while public utilities perceive it as a distribution network [22, 38].

For the system category, we divided components into nodes and infrastructure. The idea to holistically perceive infrastructure as a distribution network seems to be promising for OGD systems, as the Internet can similarly be used to request and send data packages between locations [35]. However, public utilities differ from OGD systems in how resources are supplied. Electricity and water, once in their infrastructure, are accessible to anyone who can use the infrastructure. On the other hand, for OGD systems, the data is first published on the Internet, then must be found [13, 30], and, finally, it can be downloaded. Consequently, while the Internet is a clear psychical infrastructure (e.g., servers, routers, and fibre cables [35]), OGD systems have two complementary infrastructure networks: data distribution and data discovery. The networks help to connect the nodes and functional systems and ensure that data can be found, transmitted, and distributed between them.

4.4 Resource

Resource is concerned with the properties of the central products, services, or data provided by or in the systems. In OGD systems, data is a resource (e.g., weather data [5]) that is shared to be used [36], ideally, without direct cost. The data is a selection of facts people have paid attention to and collected and becomes information when people attribute meaning to the data [12]. Data has boundless uses, as it is not used-up in its process of being used. The data of OGD systems needs to be machine-readable, complete, primary, timely, accessible, non-proprietary, and interoperable [23, 32, 45]. At the same time, the data, while anonymous, could be combined with other data to re-identify individuals, which then threatens peoples' right to information privacy [34].

The resources of OGD systems and public utilities are placed under standards and provided to be used by the public. However, data of OGD systems are large sets of heterogeneous resources (e.g., weather reports, crime reports, or postal codes [5]) that are intangible, recorded, and supposed to be interoperable with other data (e.g., blog posts and interactive maps [16]). The data requires interpretation by users to be used or understood [12] and has boundless reuses, where visualisations and mash-ups can help in the process [4]. The data can be used alone or in combination, which leads to a large set of possible uses based on its heterogeneity. The possible uses of a single dataset (e.g., weather) have limited applications, but together the application is vast. On the other hand, resources of public utilities are small sets of homogeneous resources (e.g., water, electricity, gas, transportation, communication [9]) that are physical, consumable, ubiquitous, and vital to modern life [38]. These resources have a wide range of applications [2,9].

The properties of the resources in public utilities impact the organisation of the utilities. For example, water supply networks have to identify and repair leaks [2], while electric power grids have to monitor the grid to ensure that supply meets demand, and it does not overload [38]. Similarly, anonymous data can be combined to re-identify individuals [34], while there is also a fear of misinterpretation and fraud [6]. OGD systems need to be organised with consideration of the properties of data as a resource.

4.5   Governance

Governance covers both formal and informal processes and institutions that guide and restrain the collective activities of systems [31]. It is the internal and external exercise of direction, control, management, and policy-shaping of the components of the systems [38]. In OGD systems, data is a common, shared resource that should be governed by data providers to ensure it has sufficient quality for use [29]. For example, [19] suggest institutional cooperation, model frameworks, international agreement, and social certification to govern data ownership. The foundational flow of data from collection to use to function properly and realise the benefits of OGD needs to be coordinated [51], and so does the infrastructure [17]. For example, published data need to be usable and discoverable by users, responsibilities between data providers and users need to be clear, and the process should follow standards [51]. This type of governance involves feedback and discussions between data providers and users [18,51,52], licenses and principles [11,23,32,45], and legal and regulatory frameworks [47]. Laws, policies, standards, and agreements have a bearing on OGD systems [48], which can limit and enable actors [42]. Data protection laws must be followed by the actors, and the data cannot be linked back to individuals [36]. Important legislation for OGD can relate to freedom of information, public sector information, data protection, data sharing, and statistics [36].

OGD systems and public utilities are governing resources and regulated by laws. However, they differ on at least three points. First, OGD systems follow international principles and open licenses [7,11,23,32,45], while public utilities follow national regulations and standards from many levels (e.g., federal, state, and local in the USA) [38]. Second, OGD systems are more self-regulated with a focus on the interaction between data providers and data users (e.g., discussion and feedback) [18,51,52], while public utilities have governance frameworks or organisations that can monitor, regulate, or enforce standards to ensure reasonable service (e.g., EPA for water and FERC for electricity) [38,46]. Third, in OGD systems, data users are under no restrictions on their use or distribution [11,23,32,45], while in public utilities, the actors' operations and interactions can experience heavy involvement from governance organisations [38,46].

While there are similarities between OGD systems and public utilities, they are different in how they approach governance. OGD systems have a focus on governance of production and the interaction between a data provider and a data user [18,29,50,52], while public utilities cover production to consumption where every actor can be directly or indirectly governed [38,46]. The OGD system approach most likely leads to an increased perception of risks and need to build trust. However, when a system becomes vast and complex, reoccurring interactions between parties become difficult, which could be a reason for the governance organisational approach of public utilities. The use of governance organisations could help OGD systems be beneficial for the public, data providers, and data users, but can collide with OGD principles, such as unrestricted use and use by anyone. On the other hand, there are already organisations that seem to try to govern OGD systems, such as, the meeting that resulted in the eight OGD principles [45] and the Open Knowledge Foundation [32].

4.6   Are OGD Systems a Type of Public Utility?

OGD systems and public utilities are similar in their basic pattern, infrastructure, and relationship to the public. However, OGD systems provide a free, heterogeneous resource, ideally, to anyone, while not being endowed by the public. The OGD principles (e.g., unrestricted use and access to anyone), the properties of data (e.g., ability to combine and need for interpretation), and lack of interest are three characteristic problems that can be interpreted against viewing OGD systems as a type of public utility. On the other hand, public utilities vary a lot (e.g., airlines, trucking, telecoms, electricity, natural gas, and railroads [14,22]) and are still considered to belong to the same type. Public utilities are vital to modern life [38], while the benefits of OGD is more proclaimed than empirically tested [43]. On the other hand, not all public utilities started as vital for society. For example, the electric power grids were introduced in the 19th century and partly or fully replaced heating and lighting based on the gas supply networks [9]. Today, data is arguably everywhere in modern life and vital for a modern society. It can be found at many locations (e.g., parliament minutes and governmental budgets [4]). OGD systems could be a replacement of existing data provision systems. We argue that if OGD systems overcome the three characteristic problems, OGD systems could become a public utility. We conclude that public utilities can teach OGD researchers about large-scale organisation and governance, and how vast, complex systems can be perceived.

5   The Lessons Learned

In this section, we present five lessons learned from the comparison and their implications for OGD research and OGD practice. The two initial lessons came from synthesising the holistic perspectives of public utilities and OGD systems to supplement the latter, the following two lessons are what public utilities taught us about organising OGD systems, and the final lesson gave us a possible future for OGD systems based on public utilities.

The first lesson is that *an OGD system can be perceived as a collection of nodes (functional systems) connected by complementary infrastructure networks that together organise a foundational data flow.* This perspective shifts the actor-interactions view in previous OGD research [e.g., 24,48,52] to a node-flow view similar to [37]'s actor-flow view, but the focus is on infrastructure connecting nodes of activities, objects, and actors to enable the OGD system. This shift was enabled by the public utility perspective.

The second lesson is that *the foundational data flow of an OGD system starts at data collections and ends where the public uses the data in an everyday context by plugging it into the data distribution network.* This lesson adds to [e.g., 16,18,37] by empathizing data collection, the needs for the data to have utility for the public, and the role of data users as specialists (similar to the intermediary view [e.g., 25,28]). It also shifts the focus from the interaction between data providers and data users [e.g., 4,52] to how OGD systems work to provide benefits to the public and subsystems developing from and connecting to the foundational flow.

The third lesson is that *OGD systems need to be organised with consideration to data's properties: combinability, interpretability, and boundless reusability.* Water can leak from pipes, and electricity can overload grids [2], while data could be misunderstood or abused [6,34]. This lesson is based on the need to interpret data [12] and the data's heterogeneous nature and ability to be combined.

The fourth lesson is that *OGD systems need governance organisations that govern the whole system and not only the publishers and their interactions with users towards being beneficial for the public, data providers, and data users.* OGD systems are based on principles [e.g., 11,23,32,45], licenses [e.g., 32], laws [e.g., 36,42,47,48], and feedback loops [e.g., 18,52] that are currently dispersed over different actors. Governance organisations can centralise the responsibility to enforce principles, licenses, laws, and feedback and oversee actors too, for example, help with trust and mitigate risks.

The fifth lesson is that *OGD systems could be a replacement of existing data provision systems and become a public utility if it overcomes problems from the OGD principles, the properties of data, and the lack of public interest.* Previous OGD research has viewed OGD systems from many perspectives, such as ecosystem [e.g., 18], lifecycle [e.g., 21], and value network perspectives [e.g., 3]. If OGD systems are made into a public utility, it can include all of these perspectives. Ecosystem for the nodes and their interactions. Lifecycle for a node or two nodes and the interactions. Value network for the node-flow view. The public utility perspective also includes the notion of the public and empathise that the OGD systems exist to benefit the public. The public utility perspective is one approach that can help to synthesise a holistic perspective of OGD systems.

6 Conclusion

The objective of this study was to explore what we can learn from a public utility perspective when perceiving and organising OGD systems. The study used a hermeneutic literature review with a snowballing approach to identify 39 studies about the two topics. The topics were compared based on five comparative categories, which resulted in five lessons (see Sects. 4 and 5). The review covers key literature but recognises that there is more research about OGD systems, data properties, and public utilities to be included. Not every identified comparative category was used in the comparison, such as economics (income and costs) and system purpose. The economic side of public utilities [38,46] is a promising avenue of future research that could help solve issues with economic sustainability for OGD systems [27]. At the same time, governance was identified in the public utility literature, but sparse in the OGD literature.

This paper contributes by showing that OGD research can learn for public utilities and has three implications for OGD research and OGD practice. First, OGD systems can be perceived from a node-flow view. This view contributes to the development of a holistic perspective of OGD systems that can help OGD researchers with model building, analysis, and data collection. OGD practitioners should work to identify and organise nodes (e.g., data collection or data processing) and match the OGD system with the needs of the public.

Second, governance and the properties of data needs consideration in the organisation of OGD systems. OGD researchers can study how to govern OGD systems and the implications of the properties of data on the organisation of the OGD systems. OGD practitioners should consider the properties of data in their work and the establishment of national governance organisations.

Finally, OGD systems could replace existing data provision systems and be made into a public utility. OGD researchers and OGD practitioners should discuss the role of OGD in everyday life of the public, which may challenge the OGD principles and underlying assumptions. The governance of OGD systems is a promising avenue of future research that could help practitioners deliver value, mitigate risks, and work together. The comparison between OGD systems and public utilities has also opened for the discussion and research into if OGD systems should be made into or is a type of public utility.

References

1. Abella, A., Ortiz-de Urbina-Criado, M., De-Pablos-Heredero, C.: The process of open data publication and reuse. J. Assoc. Inf. Sci. Technol. **70**(3), 296–300 (2019)
2. Ascher, K., Marech, W.: The Works. The Penguin Group, New York (2005)
3. Attard, J., Orlandi, F., Auer, S.: Data value networks: enabling a new data ecosystem. In: 2016 IEEE/WIC/ACM International Conference on Web Intelligence (WI), pp. 453–456. IEEE (2016)
4. Attard, J., Orlandi, F., Scerri, S., Auer, S.: A systematic review of open government data initiatives. Gov. Inf. Q. **32**(4), 399–418 (2015)
5. Ayre, L.B., Craner, J.: Open data: what it is and why you should care. Public Libr. Q. **36**(2), 173–184 (2017)
6. Barry, E., Bannister, F.: Barriers to open data release: a view from the top. Inf. Polity **19**(1–2), 129–152 (2014)
7. Berners-Lee, T.: Star open data. 5 Star Data (5). https://5stardata.info/en/
8. Boell, S.K., Cecez-Kecmanovic, D.: A hermeneutic approach for conducting literature reviews and literature searches. CAIS **34**, 12 (2014)
9. Buchanan, R.A.: Public utilities. In: McNeil, I. (ed.) An encyclopedia of the History of Technology, Chapter 20, pp. 949–966. Routledge, London (1990)
10. Charalabidis, Y., Zuiderwijk, A., Alexopoulos, C., Janssen, M., Höchtl, J., Ferro, E.: The World of Open Data. Springer, Heidelberg (2018). https://doi.org/10.1007/978-3-319-90850-2
11. The Open Data Charter: International open data charter - principles (2015). https://opendatacharter.net/principles/
12. Checkland, P., Holwell, S.: Information, Systems and Information Systems: Making Sense of the Field, vol. 1. Wiley, Chichester (1998)
13. Colpaert, P., Joye, S., Mechant, P., Mannens, E., Van de Walle, R.: The 5 stars of open data portals. In: 7th International Conference on Methodologies, Technologies and Tools enabling e-Government (MeTTeG) (2013)
14. Crandall, R.W., Ellig, J.: Economic deregulation and customer choice: lessons for the electric industry. George Mason University, Center for Market Processes (4084 University Dr.) (1997)
15. Crusoe, J.: Why is it so challenging to cultivate open government data? - Understanding impediments from an ecosystem perspective. Ph.D. thesis, Linköping University, LiU-Tryck, Linköping, Sweden (April 2019). compilation licentiate thesis
16. Davies, T.: Open data, democracy and public sector reform. A look at open government data use from data. gov.uk (2010)
17. Davies, T.: Open data: infrastructures and ecosystems. Open Data Research, pp. 1–6 (2011)
18. Dawes, S.S., Vidiasova, L., Parkhimovich, O.: Planning and designing open government data programs: an ecosystem approach. Gov. Inf. Q. **33**(1), 15–27 (2016)
19. De Beer, J.: Ownership of Open Data: Governance Options for Agriculture and Nutrition. Global Open Data for Agriculture and Nutrition, Wallingford (2016)
20. Serra, L.E.C.: The mapping, selecting and opening of data. Rec. Manag. J. **24**(2), 87–98 (2014)
21. Folmer, E., Reuvers, M., Quak, W., van den Broek, T., van Veenstra, A.F.: Walking the extra byte: a lifecycle model for linked open data. In: Folmer, E., Reuvers, M., Quak, W. (eds.) Linked Open Data-Pilot Linked Open Data Nederland, pp. 95–111, Remwerk (2011)
22. Geddes, R.: Public utilities. The Encyclopedia of Law and Economics (1998)

23. Handbook, O.D.: What is open data? (2015). http://opendatahandbook.org/guide/en/what-is-open-data/
24. Harrison, T.M., Pardo, T.A., Cook, M.: Creating open government ecosystems: a research and development agenda. Future Internet 4(4), 900–928 (2012)
25. Heimstädt, M., Saunderson, F., Heath, T.: Conceptualizing open data ecosystems: a timeline analysis of open data development in the UK. In: CeDEM14: Conference for E-Democracy an Open Government, p. 245. MV-Verlag (2014)
26. Hellberg, A.S., Hedström, K.: The story of the sixth myth of open data and open government. Transform. Gov.: People Process Policy 9(1), 35–51 (2015)
27. Hossain, M.A., Dwivedi, Y.K., Rana, N.P.: State-of-the-art in open data research: insights from existing literature and a research agenda. J. Organ. Comput. Electron. Commer. 26(1–2), 14–40 (2016)
28. Janssen, M., Zuiderwijk, A.: Infomediary business models for connecting open data providers and users. Soc. Sci. Comput. Rev. 32(5), 694–711 (2014)
29. Jetzek, T., Avital, M., Bjorn-Andersen, N.: Data-driven innovation through open government data. J. Theor. Appl. Electron. Commer. Res. 9(2), 100–120 (2014)
30. Kalampokis, E., Tambouris, E., Tarabanis, K.: A classification scheme for open government data: towards linking decentralised data. Int. J. Web Eng. Technol. 6(3), 266 (2011)
31. Keohane, R.O., Nye, J.S., Donahue, J.D.: Governance in a globalizing world. Power and Governance in a Partially Globalized World, pp. 193–218 (2002)
32. Knowledge, O.: The open definition (2015). https://opendefinition.org/
33. Kucera, J., Chlapek, D.: Benefits and risks of open government data. J. Syst. Integr. 5(1), 30–41 (2014)
34. Kulk, S., Van Loenen, B.: Brave new open data world? Int. J. Spat. Data Infrastruct. Res. 7, 196–206 (2012)
35. Kurose, J.F., Ross, K.W.: Computer Networking: A Top-Down Approach. Pearson International Edition, 5th edn. Addison Wesley, Boston (2009)
36. Lee, D.: Building an open data ecosystem: an Irish experience. In: Proceedings of the 8th International Conference on Theory and Practice of Electronic Governance, pp. 351–360 (2014)
37. Lindman, J., Kinnari, T., Rossi, M.: Business roles in the emerging open-data ecosystem. IEEE Softw. 33(5), 54–59 (2015)
38. McNabb, D.E.: Public Utilities: Old Problems, New Challenges. Edward Elgar Publishing, Cheltenham (2016)
39. Oliveira, M.I.S., Lóscio, B.F.: What is a data ecosystem? In: Proceedings of the 19th Annual International Conference on Digital Government Research: Governance in the Data Age, pp. 1–9 (2018)
40. Pickett, S.T., Cadenasso, M.L.: The ecosystem as a multidimensional concept: meaning, model, and metaphor. Ecosystems 5(1), 1–10 (2002)
41. Rose, R., Mackenzie, W.J.M.: Comparing forms of comparative analysis. Polit. Stud. 39(3), 446–462 (1991)
42. de Rosnay, M.D., Janssen, K.: Legal and institutional challenges for opening data across public sectors: towards common policy solutions. J. Theor. Appl. Electron. Commer. Res. 9(3), 1–14 (2014)
43. Safarov, I., Meijer, A., Grimmelikhuijsen, S.: Utilization of open government data: a systematic literature review of types, conditions, effects and users. Inf. Polity 22(1), 1–24 (2017)
44. System: The Cambridge Dictionary. Cambridge University Press (2020). https://dictionary.cambridge.org/dictionary/english/system. Accessed 26 Feb 2019

45. Tauberer, J.: The 8 principles of open government data (2007). https:// opengovdata.org/
46. Thompson, C., Smith, W.R.: Public Utility Economics. McGraw-Hill Book Company, New York (1941)
47. Ubaldi, B.: Open government data - towards empirical analysis of open government data initiatives. Tech. rep. 22, OECD Working Papers on Public Governance (2013)
48. Van Schalkwyk, F., Willmers, M., McNaughton, M.: Viscous open data: the roles of intermediaries in an open data ecosystem. J. Inf. Technol. Dev. **1102**(Special Issue), 68–83 (2015)
49. Walters, W.H.: Comparative recall and precision of simple and expert searches in google scholar and eight other databases. Portal: Libr. Acad. **11**(4), 971–1006 (2011)
50. Welle Donker, F., van Loenen, B.: How to assess the success of the open data ecosystem? Int. J. Digit. Earth **10**(3), 284–306 (2017)
51. Zuiderwijk, A., Janssen, M.: A coordination theory perspective to improve the use of open data in policy-making. In: Wimmer, M.A., Janssen, M., Scholl, H.J. (eds.) EGOV 2013. LNCS, vol. 8074, pp. 38–49. Springer, Heidelberg (2013). https://doi.org/10.1007/978-3-642-40358-3_4
52. Zuiderwijk, A., Janssen, M., Davis, C.: Innovation with open data: essential elements of open data ecosystems. Inf. Polity **19**(1–2), 17–33 (2014)

Collaboration in Open Government Data Ecosystems: Open Cross-sector Sharing and Co-development of Data and Software

Johan Linåker[✉] and Per Runeson

Lund University, Ole Römers väg 3, Lund, Sweden
{johan.linaker,per.runeson}@cs.lth.se

Abstract. *Background*: Open innovation highlights the potential benefits of external collaboration and knowledge-sharing, often exemplified through Open Source Software (OSS). The public sector has thus far mainly focused on the sharing of Open Government Data (OGD), often with a supply-driven approach with limited feedback-loops. We hypothesize that public sector organizations can extend the open innovation benefits by also creating platforms, where OGD, related OSS, and open standards are collaboratively developed and shared. *Objective*: The objective of this study is to explore how public sector organizations in the role of platform providers facilitate such collaboration in the form of OGD ecosystems and how the ecosystem's governance may be structured to support the collaboration. *Method*: We conduct an exploratory multiple-case study of two such ecosystems, focused on OGD related to the Swedish labor market and public transport sector, respectively. Data is gathered through interviews, document studies, and prolonged engagement at one of the platform providers. *Results*: The study presents governance structure and collaboration practices of the two ecosystems and discusses how these contribute to the platform providers' goals. The case studies highlight the need for platform providers to take an active and multi-functional role in enabling the sharing of data and software from and between the members of the ecosystem. *Conclusions*: We conclude that OGD ecosystems offer public sector organizations a possibility to catalyze the potential innovation output of OGD, but that it requires investment and adoption of an open and collaborative mindset.

Keywords: Open Government Data · Open Source Software · Open standard · Ecosystem · Public sector

1 Introduction

Open Innovation has been widely adopted among software companies through the use of Open Source Software (OSS) as a means to share costs and accelerate innovation [14]. In the public sector, however, the focus has been more on sharing of Open Government Data (OGD) as a way to drive innovation [2] and less on OSS [3]. To

© IFIP International Federation for Information Processing 2020
Published by Springer Nature Switzerland AG 2020
G. Viale Pereira et al. (Eds.): EGOV 2020, LNCS 12219, pp. 290–303, 2020.
https://doi.org/10.1007/978-3-030-57599-1_22

catalyze the potential innovation output [2], data providers and data users may form a business ecosystem around the OGD [25]. Actors within an OGD ecosystem together create a value network, where the OGD is enriched from raw data into valuable content to be used in new products and services [12]. Interaction is usually limited to feedback on the quality and what data-sets to release next [4,8,15], although the need for more collaboration is highlighted [20,23].

Looking at Open Source Software (OSS) ecosystems (also commonly referred to as communities) [6], actors collaborate to a much a higher degree through the co-development of the OSS. Together they evolve the OSS in an open setting where new functionality is continuously asserted, discussed, and implemented and thereby they accelerate the innovation and development beyond what any single member of the ecosystem could perform alone [14].

We hypothesize that by adopting the collaborative practices, OGD ecosystems would be able to elicit similar benefits [21,23]. Further, we hypothesize that both the sharing and adoption of OGD would be catalyzed by extending collaboration to include the development of related standards, APIs, and supporting tools, frameworks, and example applications as OSS [8,20,25]. With these characteristics, we define an OGD ecosystem as *a networked community of organizations, which base their relations to each other on a common interest in an underpinning technological platform consisting of OGD and related OSS and open standards, and collaborate through the exchange of information, resources and artifacts*, adapted from [10,25].

Existing research has mainly focused on the collaborative practices used in OSS ecosystems [1,10], and has in terms of OGD ecosystems [2] been limited, both regarding collaboration on OGD or any related software or standard, even though identified as a need [17,20,23]. The **research goal** of this study is to therefore to *explore how collaboration in OGD ecosystems may be facilitated from the platform providers' point of view and how the ecosystems' governance may be structured to support the collaboration.* We find this as an interesting perspective as trust towards the platform provider is pivotal in order to enable collaboration and growth of an ecosystem [9,12].

This paper presents a multiple-case study [22] of two OGD ecosystems in which OSS, open standards, and related collaborative practices are adopted, aiming to foster collaboration and increase the adoption of OGD. The two ecosystems are initiated and governed by public sector organizations in the role of platform providers and focus on OGD related to the Swedish labor market and public transport sector. We present the governance structure and collaboration practices of these ecosystems and discuss how these contribute to the platform providers' goals.

2   Background

Below we provide an overview of OGD and software (including OSS) ecosystems and present a governance model used in the analysis of the two case studies.

2.1 Ecosystems for Open Source Software and Government Data

Software ecosystems is a rather mature [1,10] but yet expanding field of research. Originating from the field of business ecosystems (and in turn its biological ancestor) [7], it offers a lens for analyzing how networked communities of organizations collaborate around their common interest in a central software technology [13]. Other definitions refer to technological platforms underpinning the ecosystem [10], which in a wider sense may consist of either technologies, products, or services, serving in the common interest of the ecosystem.

For OSS ecosystems, the OSS project makes up the technological platform underpinning its community which we refer to as the ecosystem [6]. Similarly, OGD and its related APIs can also be viewed as a platform, underpinning the surrounding ecosystem of actors [25]. OGD ecosystems and similar concepts [23,24] are however not as well explored as software and OSS ecosystems.

Oliveira et al. [17] define a data ecosystem as *"socio-technical complex network in which actors interact and collaborate with each other to find, archive, publish, consume, or reuse data as well as to foster innovation, create value, and support new businesses"*. OGD ecosystems, or Government Data Ecosystems as referred to by Oliveira et al. [17], are based on OGD initiatives and focused on promoting the use and publication of OGD.

In terms of roles in these ecosystems, a general distinction can be made between data providers and data users [25]. The roles can be further refined into data providers, service providers, data brokers, application developers, application users, and infrastructure and tool providers [8,11]. The data provider is usually constituted by a public-sector organization [17]. Services or functions needed include an infrastructure to share the data (preferably from multiple providers), documentation, tools for application developers, help in finding use-cases, as well as the possibility to discuss, provide feedback and make requests [4,8,25]. A general observation regards the need for improved feedback-loops, collaboration and a more demand-driven publication of OGD [4,15,20,25].

This study aims to investigate how such collaboration may be facilitated, both in terms of sharing and co-developing OGD, related OSS, and open standards. We hypothesize that this will provide further opportunities and benefits of what open innovation has to offer to the platform providers and their ecosystems [14,21].

2.2 Ecosystem Roles and Governance Structure

Existing research is limited in regard to governance in OGD ecosystems [17]. Governance has received more attention for software ecosystems [1]. Three types of roles are commonly referred to [7,10]. The first role is that of the *platform provider* who is the owner and supplier of the platform and thereby also usually the orchestrator of the ecosystem. As an orchestrator, the platform provider also decides on the governance model for the ecosystem, meaning the ways in which it maintains control and decides on the direction, but also on the governance structure, meaning "the distribution of rights and responsibilities among the

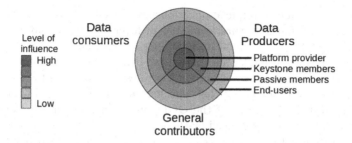

Fig. 1. Overview of the proposed governance model adapted from Nakakoji et al. [16].

[ecosystem's members], and the rules and protocols that need to be followed in order to make decisions regarding the [ecosystem]" [1].

Keystone and *Niche players* are two other roles within an ecosystem. A keystone is an actor who nurtures a symbiotic relationship with the ecosystem and its other actors, looking to actively improve its health [9]. Usually, they have a close connection with the platform provider, who also may be referred to as a keystone if it has similar symbiotic intents. Niche players are actors focused more on a specific niche of the market, or use-case, and is primarily a user of the resources provided by the ecosystem [7].

For OSS ecosystems, the platform provider can be the owner of the OSS project, usually either a software vendor or the ecosystem of actors directly or via a proxy organization (e.g., a foundation) [18]. Governance, however, does not have to be aligned with the ownership. In more autocratic ecosystems, it can be centered around a vendor or individual, while more democratic ecosystems it is distributed [5]. In the latter case, control of the OSS project is usually maintained by a central group of actors who have gained a level of influence by proving merit, building trust, and social capital through contributions to the OSS project.

2.3 Governance Model for Open Government Data Ecosystems

A popular way of illustrating the governance structure of an OSS ecosystem is the Onion model [16], where the center is those in control (see Fig. 1). The closest layers may be those who contribute actively to the project and thereby maintain an influence although not in direct control. For each outer layer, actors become less active in terms of contributions and thereby decrease in influence on the OSS project. Robles et al. [19] recently applied the model in a case study on the X-Road OSS project, an originally Estonian eGovernment project for creating a data-sharing infrastructure, which now is governed jointly by Estonian and Finnish government agencies. The project is centrally controlled, and contributions are primarily made by companies on behalf of, and paid by, the government agencies.

For OGD ecosystems, we consider the core to be occupied by the *platform provider* (see Fig. 1), which is either the government entity (or entities in collaboration) which provide OGD via a software platform where APIs and supporting tools, frameworks, and example applications are available as OSS. Depending on the specific ecosystem structure a number of layers follow. In layers closest to the core are the *Keystone members* including actors that are of special importance to the platform provider and the overall health of the ecosystem [9]. In the following layer, *Passive members* of similar roles may be found although these are more focused on addressing their specific niche or use-case. In the last and outer layer are the *End-users* of the OGD, either directly or via the proxy of applications and services produced by the actors in the inner layers of the model.

As illustrated in Fig. 1, actors can in general also be divided between three groups in terms of their usage of and contribution to the platform:

- A *Data consumer* uses the data available via the platform.
- A *Data producer* contributes data, either actively via a donation to the platform, or passively by letting the platform provider collect data from them, which is then made available via the platform.
- A *General contributor* is not necessarily a consumer or producer of data, but in some other way contributes to the platform and health of the ecosystem, e.g., through knowledge sharing or contributing new or to existing OSS projects related to the platform.

Actors can be further categorized based on their type of operations, including e.g., service providers, application developers, data brokers, infrastructure and tool providers, and potentially additional data providers [8,12]. We expect this type of categorization to be dependent on each ecosystem.

3   Research Design

An exploratory multiple-case study [22] was conducted to investigate two instances of OGD ecosystems. Case 1 is the JobTech Dev ecosystem, initiated and facilitated by The Swedish Public Employment Service. Case 2 is the Trafiklab ecosystem, initiated and facilitated by Samtrafiken. The unit of analysis is the ecosystems' governance [1].

We use an adapted version of the Onion model (see Sect. 2.3) to structure and analyze the findings of the two ecosystems' governance. The model is commonly used for describing the governance in OSS ecosystems [16] and was recently applied to a government-initiated OSS ecosystem [19].

The research effort was initiated with Case 1, where the first author of this study is embedded as an action researcher, as a part of a long-term research project. The researcher was hence able to generate in-depth knowledge through prolonged engagement along with access to extensive documentation. The documentation along with field notes could be used to triangulate findings along with three semi-structured interviews. To ensure construct validity [22], we based the questionnaire on earlier work on assessing the governance structure of software ecosystems [1,10]. The interviewees were the platform's product owner, community manager, and policy strategist.

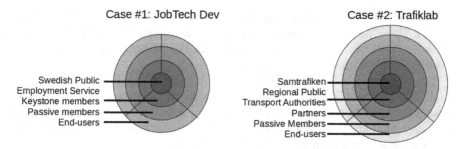

Fig. 2. Overview of the governance structure of the two cases in this study, JobTech Dev (left) and Trafiklab (right), based on the governance model presented in Sect. 2.3.

Data gathering from Case 1 was performed before any intervention had been introduced from the action research. To avoid researcher bias, peer-debriefing between the first and second authors was performed [22].

For Case 2, data were gathered in a similar manner through a semi-structured interview with the platform's product manager, using the same questionnaire. All interviews were audio-recorded with additional notes taken. A threat regarding the reliability concerns that only the first author conducted the interviews [22]. To mitigate the threat, member-checking was performed in both cases where synthesized findings were presented to all interviewees who were asked for correctness, misinterpretations, and redundancy.

4   Results

Below we present the results from our two studied cases, JobTech Dev and Trafiklab.

4.1   Case 1: JobTech Dev

JobTech Dev is an ecosystem, initiated in 2018, bringing actors together, operating within or in relation to the Swedish labor market to collaborate on a common platform of OGD, connected APIs, and complementary OSS projects. The ecosystem and its platform are developed and orchestrated by the Swedish Public Employment Service (SPES), a Swedish national government agency responsible for enabling the match-making between job-seekers and employers on the labor market. JobTech Dev was created as a part of this mission with the intention to enable the actors in the ecosystem to accelerate their innovation process, improve their services, and thereby improving the digital match-making on the labor market.

Platform Content. The platform consists of four parts: *Jobs, Taxonomy, Career*, and *Search*.

Jobs is a service intended to collect all available job advertisements on the Swedish labor market and make these available through an API. The online ads are collected from the ten organizations in the labor market, providing the majority of the available advertisements.

Taxonomy is a collection of skills and job titles and relationships between them. The data set is developed and maintained within SPES. By opening up the data through APIs, the actors in the ecosystem are enabled to "speak the same language" enabling e.g., improved reporting and statistics and match-making between job advertisements and job-seekers' resumes.

Career is (unlike Taxonomy and Jobs) not OGD. It is a service where job-seekers can store their resumes on a central location in an encrypted format. The job-seekers can grant and withdraw permission to organizations, e.g., recruitment firms, social networks, and insurance firms to access their information. The service is based on the MyData principles[1] and enables job-seekers to only have to maintain one copy of their resume and to distribute and manage their data with kept control over their integrity and privacy.

Search is an OSS search engine that enables actors to search among available job advertisements. Search is available both through an API and as an OSS project which can be adopted and integrated by the ecosystem's actors.

Ecosystem Governance Structure. In terms of operations, the members of the ecosystem can generally be categorized within one of the areas: 1) recruiting and staffing firms, 2) education and guidance providers, 3) national, regional or local governments, 4) workers' unions, 5) employers' associations, 6) job advertisers, and 7) job seekers. Depending on the category, a member's interest in the platform may be limited to certain parts of the platform.

Considering the governance structure, SPES is positioned in the center as the platform provider orchestrating and governing the ecosystem (see Fig. 2, left). SPES ultimately decides on requirements and road-map for the platform, including what data to make available, when, and how. They perform the necessary development and maintenance and provide the infrastructure needed to access and use the data.

Outside of SPES are the members whose opinions may be considered as extra important for SPES in terms of developing the platform and growing the ecosystem. These members may, e.g., have a large user base, or valuable competencies and resources, and thereby contribute to the health of the ecosystem. In the second layer are the general members and in layer three the end-users. Each layer is viewed to potentially consist of members from all types of operations.

Orchestration and Collaboration. Due to the limited internal resources, SPES does not have the capacity to maintain formal and direct relationships with all ecosystem members. Teams carrying out development inside SPES therefore primarily work and communicate through close relationships with the key

---

[1] https://mydata.org/guiding-principles/.

members to optimize the impact. However, SPES is striving to adopt an open development model and maintain an open dialogue where the whole ecosystem (including all layers in Fig. 1) can influence the direction of the platform.

Anyone can, for example, request and discuss a new feature, an API, or data-set through a synchronous open communication platform or by attending occasional meetups arranged by SPES. It is also possible to contribute to the development, as all source code for the APIs is available as OSS. To lower adoption barriers of the data provided via the platform, example applications are developed and released as OSS. Members consuming the data, specifically startups, have expressed the value provided by these examples as it helps them understand use-cases and accelerate their development. Contributions to the OSS have been limited to bug reports and feature requests, while the intention is to encourage and enable members to contribute both new projects and to exist.

In terms of data, there are examples – although limited – of members producing and contributing directly to the platform. One example is a set of soft skills and their relationship to different job titles, which was contributed to the Taxonomy part of the platform. Processes are not yet established for how these types of contributions should be managed; a process more simpler if considering OSS. In this case, a formal contract was established between the two parties.

Close collaborations and direct dialogues with key members have been important to establish the ecosystem and gain general acceptance. For example, the collection of all job-ads on the market and making these freely available, made incumbents offering recruiting and staffing services initially question the intent from SPES as well as the suggested benefits. SPES views the commoditization of job-advertisement data, as with the ecosystem at large, as a way to push the actors working with digital match-making and guidance services forward, nurturing innovation and lowering barriers to entry for new actors.

After a more than two-year process, even the more conservative incumbents started to accept the ecosystem and see potential benefits with it. A formal collaboration was initiated between SPES and the ten largest job advertisement providers where they agreed to allow job-advertisements to be collected. Once collected, the ads are converted to an industry-specific open standard, and then enriched with metadata such as date of publishing and deadline for applications. A compromise was reached to only provide a "stub" of the advertisements, meaning that only that job title, metadata, and a link to the original advertisement would be provided through the platform's API.

4.2   Case 2: Trafiklab

Trafiklab is an ecosystem, initiated in 2011, that brings actors within the Swedish public transport sector together to collaborate on a platform with open traffic data, connected APIs, and complementary OSS projects. The ecosystem's vision is to facilitate the creation of new services that makes it easier and more attractive to travel with public transport. The ecosystem and its platform are developed and orchestrated by Samtrafiken, a corporate entity co-owned by all the regional public transport authorities and most of the commercial transport operators in Sweden. The commercial transport operators also have the option of being a partner to Samtrafiken.

Platform Content. The platform consists of data-sets and APIs, either maintained by Samtrafiken or independently by members of the ecosystem. All data hosted on the Trafiklab-platform is released with a custom license based on the principles of the Creative Commons Attribution-license.

Four APIs provide static and real-time data on public transport, related to, for example, time-tables and interruptions. This data is currently made available in two types of standard formats, maintained by Samtrafiken and gathered from the regional public transport authorities and private operators in accordance with a government directive. Two further APIs provide time-table data for a trip-planner, an externally procured product that is offered for free to the ecosystem.

Certain APIs are maintained by other organizations, both public and private, and made available on the Trafiklab-platform. Data includes time-table and service data from Stockholm Public Transport and traffic information from the Swedish Transport Administration. The platform also links to related APIs that are maintained and hosted by other organizations. These include data from regional public transport authorities, local counties, and private entities.

Ecosystem Governance Structure. In terms of operations, the members of the ecosystem can generally be categorized within one of the areas: 1) regional public transport authorities, 2) private and publicly owned train operators, 3) national, regional, and local governments, 4) private bus operators, and 5) private product and service providers. Future plans include integration with related actors, such as taxi operators and rental-service providers of e.g., cars and bikes.

In terms of the governance structure, Samtrafiken is positioned in the center as the platform provider orchestrating and governing the ecosystem (see Fig. 2, right). Outside of Samtrafiken in the first layer are regional public transport authorities. As these are formal owners of the platform, they have a strong influence on the direction of Trafiklab. In the second layer are the formal partners to Samtrafiken which may include actors with different types of operation. The third layer primarily consists of private product and service providers, while end-users are positioned in the fourth layer.

Orchestration and Collaboration. Close relationships are maintained to regional public transport authorities and partners as these are the primary data producers but also consumers. The ecosystem at large has the possibility to report bugs, ask for help, and request and discuss new features, APIs, or data-sets through an asynchronous, open communication platform. Physical meetings can also serve a similar purpose as Samtrafiken frequently hosts hackathons and meetups related to Trafiklab.

As with SPES, Samtrafiken is transitioning to a more open and collaborative way of engaging with its ecosystem, a need identified in earlier research [20].

Table 1. General characteristics of the two ecosystems investigated, JobTech Dev and Trafiklab, in terms of their platform provider and keystones, but also in regards to the data and software provided on their underpinning platforms.

	JobTech Dev	Trafiklab
Platform provider	A single government agency	A public entity co-owned by multiple public sector organizations
Keystones	Organizations with large user bases, or valuable assets (e.g., data)	Owners and partners
Data sources	Produced internally Collected externally Contributed from third party	Collected externally Contributed by third party
OSS	APIs, example applications	Example applications, toolkits, libraries, frameworks

As an example, they are discussing a more formal approach where users can request and vote on what data sets should be prioritized. In regards to OSS, they currently have a number of software development kits and example applications available. Their intention is to develop a new OSS trip planner and share their APIs as OSS along with their internal road-maps for the different parts of the platform. Contributions have been limited to bug reports and feature requests.

Regarding the data, all of the provided data sets originate from data producers within the ecosystem. Depending on the case, Samtrafiken may transform the data to certain standard formats, develop and maintain the necessary APIs, and provide the necessary infrastructure for data consumers. A challenge with growing the ecosystem and gaining new data producers is related to standard formats of the data. For smaller actors, it is an expensive process to transform the data, and for Samtrafiken a recognized risk is that data may be destroyed when transformed between standards. Samtrafiken is, therefore, developing an input-portal to enable further actors to share their data on Trafiklab and to automate the transformation process. The portal is specifically intended for actors in areas related to public transport, such as taxi operators and rental-service providers.

The input-portal is a result of a long-term investigation conducted by Samtrafiken and its partners into the future potential and needs for public transport-related OGD. The investigation also rendered in a plan to introduce 12 new data sets by 2021. Other than helping data producers to transform their data into different standards, Samtrafiken and its partners within the Trafiklab ecosystem also collaborate on the development of new standards when needed. A standard for tickets and payment transactions was developed in response to difficulties with different proprietary solutions not being able to interface with each other.

5   Discussion

JobTech Dev and Trafiklab present both similar and differentiating attributes as OGD ecosystems (see Table 1). Considering the type of governance structure, we observe that JobTech Dev is governed by SPES, a single government agency, while Trafiklab is governed by Samtrafiken, an organization co-owned by all the Swedish public transport authorities, whom all are situated in the inner layer of the governance structure (cf. [5]). SPES has the advantage that it potentially can move quickly but also has the risk that its directive can easily change due to change in the national government. The latter could be a concern for existing and new members whether they can trust the direction and stability of the platform and ecosystem, and thereby if they should invest in platform integrations.

Samtrafiken, on the other hand, is an investment by several authorities and provides a somewhat neutral body with which commercial traffic operators can become co-owners or create formal partnerships with. This may be a way to ensure trust in the platform provider's commitment and a guarantee for the long-term stability of the ecosystem. Similarities may be drawn to the role of foundations as a proxy-organization and neutral home for OSS projects where actors can collaborate and invest together in a way that benefits them all and with clear charters stating how the project will be technically governed [5].

X-roads, a governmental OSS project [19], has a centralized governance model, which can be used for reference. It is clear that they are in control of the ecosystem but at the price of limited contributions from other members. The central governance actors paid the members for their contributions to evolve the OSS. Clearly, there is a trade-off between control and inclination to contribute.

In regards to data sharing, there is also some level of distinction between the two ecosystems. In JobTech Dev, taxonomy data originate from and is provided by SPES, job-advertisement originates from a number of organizations and is collected by SPES, while resume-data is provided on an individual level by the job-seekers. In Trafiklab, all data originate from a third party. Samtrafiken collects, (in some cases transforms) and provides the data on the Trafiklab-platform. The platform's roadmap includes the development of an input-portal to enable further third-parties to contribute their data. Both SPES and Samtrafiken thereby show an active role in enabling and incentivizing the members of the respective ecosystems to share their data, either by collecting the data or by enabling a self-service function where the member can provide the data themselves.

Concerning OSS both SPES and Samtrafiken see the value in developing complementary and supporting software as OSS, even though outside contributions thus far have been limited for both. This may, however, be subject to change as both are striving towards adopting a more open and collaborative way of working and collaborating with their ecosystems (cf. [20,23]). Observations of the X-roads project may generalize to these contexts as well [19].

Looking at the responsibilities taken on by the platform providers in the investigated ecosystems, they cover many of the roles as reported in literature [8,12]. Besides being *data providers*, both SPES and Samtrafiken may be described as *data brokers* as they gather, promote, and distribute data from third-party [8], but also data transformers as the transform data between different standards based on ecosystem needs [12]. Another important role is that of *tool providers* as they both develop supporting tools, frameworks, and example applications for their ecosystems [8]. Hence, for the collaboration in OGD ecosystems to function the platform provider is required to perform multiple functions compared to traditional OGD ecosystems where tasks are more divided among the actors [8,12]. In contrast, when entering an existing ecosystem, an organization may consider taking a peripheral less complex role [20]. This is, however, a trade-off between influence on the platform development and value capture, i.e., if the organization's goals can still be achieved.

As Samtrafiken started their ecosystem in 2011, and SPES in 2018, the former is more mature in its role as a platform provider. For example, it has an existing and active ecosystem with several successful applications and use cases, mechanisms for collecting and enabling actors to share their data, and also practices for enabling and collaboratively designing open standards for the data. SPES has been able to catch up rather rapidly however in terms of platform content due to the dedicated resources, and the existence of both data and software that could be opened up.

6   Conclusions

This paper explores the collaboration in OGD ecosystems between actors in terms of sharing and co-development of both OGD, related OSS, and open standards. We focus on the platform provider's point of view and explore how these ecosystems may function in terms of collaboration and governance.

The case studies contrast how the governance structure may differ when the platform provider represents a single or multiple public sector organizations. The case studies further highlight the need for the platform provider to take on an active and multi-functional role in enabling the sharing of data and software from and between the members of the ecosystem. Responsibilities include the creation of processes and technical infrastructure, facilitating standard development and enabling automated transformation between the formats, and co-developing APIs, complementary tools, frameworks, and example applications as OSS.

We hypothesize that this type of collaboration can extend the potential benefits for the platform provider and the ecosystem, including reduced cost and accelerated innovation, but also increased adoption and sharing of data. As this study is limited to exploring the collaboration in two instances of OGD ecosystems, further research is required to validate these hypotheses, create a deeper understanding, and improve the external validity [22]. Readers should consider the context of the platform providers and their ecosystems as reported and adopt an analytical generalization to cases with similar characteristics [22].

Several avenues for future research exist. From a platform provider's perspective, for example, *i)* what challenges they experience when "opening up" the development of the platform towards the surrounding ecosystem, and *ii)* how the governance and processes for collaborative development should be designed accordingly. From the ecosystem's perspective, including both keystones and niche players, *iii)* what motivates their usage of the platform, sharing of resources and knowledge, as well as active collaboration on the platform's development, *iv)* what challenges do they perceive in these regards, and *v)* how the collaborative development and governance should be designed to best support their participation. Further, *vi)* how do these aspects, as well as dynamics and inter-relationships between the different roles, vary with the up-scaling of the ecosystems, and also between contexts, as with the two cases in this study.

References

1. Alves, C., Oliveira, J., Jansen, S.: Understanding governance mechanisms and health in software ecosystems: a systematic literature review. In: Hammoudi, S., Śmiałek, M., Camp, O., Filipe, J. (eds.) ICEIS 2017. LNBIP, vol. 321, pp. 517–542. Springer, Cham (2018). https://doi.org/10.1007/978-3-319-93375-7_24
2. Attard, J., Orlandi, F., Scerri, S., Auer, S.: A systematic review of open government data initiatives. Gov. Inf. Q. **32**(4), 399–418 (2015)
3. Borg, M., Olsson, T., Franke, U., Assar, S.: Digitalization of Swedish government agencies-a perspective through the lens of a software development census. In: 40th International Conference on Software Engineering, pp. 37–46. IEEE (2018)
4. Dawes, S.S., Vidiasova, L., Parkhimovich, O.: Planning and designing open government data programs: an ecosystem approach. GIQ **33**(1), 15–27 (2016)
5. De Noni, I., Ganzaroli, A., Orsi, L.: The evolution of OSS governance: a dimensional comparative analysis. SJM **29**(3), 247–263 (2013)
6. Franco-Bedoya, O., Ameller, D., Costal, D., Franch, X.: Open source software ecosystems: a systematic mapping. IST **91**, 160–185 (2017)
7. Iansiti, M., Levien, R.: The Keystone Advantage: What the New Dynamics of Business Ecosystems Mean for Strategy, Innovation, and Sustainability. HBP, Boston (2004)
8. Immonen, A., Palviainen, M., Ovaska, E.: Requirements of an open data based business ecosystem. IEEE Access **2**, 88–103 (2014)
9. Jansen, S.: Measuring the health of open source software ecosystems: beyond the scope of project health. Inf. Softw. Technol. **56**(11), 1508–1519 (2014)
10. Jansen, S.: A focus area maturity model for software ecosystem governance. Inf. Softw. Technol. **118**, 106219 (2020)
11. Kitsios, F., Papachristos, N., Kamariotou, M.: Business models for open data ecosystem: challenges and motivations for entrepreneurship and innovation. In: 19th Conference on Business Informatics, vol. 1, pp. 398–407. IEEE (2017)
12. Lindman, J., Kinnari, T., Rossi, M.: Business roles in the emerging open-data ecosystem. IEEE Softw. **33**(5), 54–59 (2015)
13. Mhamdia, A.B.H.S.: Performance measurement practices in software ecosystem. Int. J. Product. Perform. Manag. **62**(5), 514–533 (2013)
14. Munir, H., Wnuk, K., Runeson, P.: Open innovation in software engineering: a systematic mapping study. Empir. Softw. Eng. **21**(2), 684–723 (2015). https://doi.org/10.1007/s10664-015-9380-x
15. Najafabadi, M.M., Luna-Reyes, L.: Open government data ecosystems: a closed-loop perspective. In: Proceedings of 50th HICSS (2017)

16. Nakakoji, K., Yamamoto, Y., Nishinaka, Y., Kishida, K., Ye, Y.: Evolution patterns of open-source software systems and communities. In: Proceedings of the International Workshop on Principles of Software Evolution, pp. 76–85. ACM, Orlando (2002)
17. Oliveira, M.I.S., Lima, G.D.F.B., Lóscio, B.F.: Investigations into data ecosystems: a systematic mapping study. Knowl. Inf. Syst. **61**, 1–42 (2019)
18. Riehle, D.: The single-vendor commercial open course business model. Inf. Syst. e-Bus. Manag. **10**(1), 5–17 (2012)
19. Robles, G., Gamalielsson, J., Lundell, B.: Setting up government 3.0 solutions based on open source software: the case of X-road. In: Lindgren, I., et al. (eds.) EGOV 2019. LNCS, vol. 11685, pp. 69–81. Springer, Cham (2019). https://doi.org/10.1007/978-3-030-27325-5_6
20. Rudmark, D., Hjalmarsson-Jordanius, A.: Harnessing digital ecosystems through open data-diagnosing the Swedish public transport industry. In: European Conference of Information Systems (ECIS) (2019)
21. Runeson, P.: Open collaborative data - using OSS principles to share data in SW engineering. In: 41st ACM/IEEE International Conference on Software Engineering (ICSE): New Ideas and Emerging Results (NIER) track, pp. 25–28, Montreal, Canada (2019)
22. Runeson, P., Höst, M., Rainer, A., Regnell, B.: Case Study Research in Software Engineering - Guidelines and Examples. Wiley, Hoboken (2012)
23. Sieber, R.E., Johnson, P.A.: Civic open data at a crossroads: dominant models and current challenges. Gov. Inf. Q. **32**(3), 308–315 (2015)
24. Susha, I., Janssen, M., Verhulst, S.: Data collaboratives as "bazaars"? A review of coordination problems and mechanisms to match demand for data with supply. Transform. Gov.: People Process Policy **11**(1), 157–172 (2017)
25. Zuiderwijk, A., Janssen, M., Davis, C.: Innovation with open data: essential elements of open data ecosystems. Inf. Polity **19**(1, 2), 17–33 (2014)

Towards Generic Business Models of Intermediaries in Data Collaboratives: From Gatekeeping to Data Control

Iryna Susha[1,2](✉), Maartje Flipsen[2,3], Wirawan Agahari[2], and Mark de Reuver[2]

[1] Örebro University, 701 82 Örebro, Sweden
iryna.susha@oru.se
[2] Delft University of Technology, Jaffalaan 5, 2628 BX Delft, The Netherlands
[3] PwC Netherlands, Thomas R. Malthusstraat 5, 1066 JR Amsterdam, The Netherlands

Abstract. Data has become a core asset, as well as a "management fashion", of our time. It brings about unprecedented opportunities for data-driven decision making and innovation in various spheres of public life. This concerns data held by governments, as well as companies, academic institutions, non-profits, and citizens. In our study we investigate a novel form of cross-sector partnership called Data Collaborative, and namely the business models employed by intermediaries in data collaboratives. Based on an analysis of six cases, we derived four generic business models based on the level of openness and added value of the data: Data Gatekeeper model, One-stop-shop model, Information-as-a-service model, and Data Controls model. Our study contributes to the literature on data partnerships and on intermediation and information sharing more broadly.

Keywords: Data partnership · Data collaborative · Intermediary · Business model · Data innovation · Data intermediary

1 Introduction

Data has become a core asset, as well as a 'management fashion' [1], of our time. It brings about unprecedented opportunities for data-driven decision making and innovation in various spheres of public life. This concerns data held by governments, as well as companies, academic institutions, non-profits, and citizens. Often, collaboration is needed because data from different parties have to be combined to realize opportunities. The notion of Data Collaboratives captures this collaboration imperative and stands for "cross-sector (and public-private) collaboration initiatives aimed at data collection, sharing, or processing for the purpose of addressing a societal challenge" [31]. In the past five years the concept of data collaboratives, initially coined by The Gov Lab [34], has gained much interest (e.g. World Bank's Development Data Partnership, EU Commission's Expert Group on B2G Data Sharing).

There is a row of successful and less successful stories of data collaboratives. Data collaboratives face several rather specific challenges, such as balancing data control and

© IFIP International Federation for Information Processing 2020
Published by Springer Nature Switzerland AG 2020
G. Viale Pereira et al. (Eds.): EGOV 2020, LNCS 12219, pp. 304–315, 2020.
https://doi.org/10.1007/978-3-030-57599-1_23

ownership, governance challenges, legal constraints, privacy and ethics issues, competitive risks, technical challenges, to name a few [7, 16, 24, 32]. Different types of data intermediaries have emerged that view these challenges as opportunities. There is however little knowledge on how these data intermediaries operate and what business models they employ. Providing more clarity on this can create a better understanding of the roles that government can play in such data collaboratives. Therefore, our research question is: *What business models are employed by intermediaries to create value in data collaboratives?*

The paper is structured as follows: in Sect. 2 we review relevant literature on intermediation in data sharing and collaboration processes; in Sect. 3 present our analytical framework for intermediary business model analysis; in Sect. 4 we outline our multiple case study method; in Sect. 5 we present a comparative analysis of the cases; and in Sect. 6 we formulate generic business models from the case data; and in Sect. 7 we summarize and reflect on our findings.

2   Intermediaries in Data Collaboratives: Conceptualization

Data intermediaries in the context of data have characteristics that resemble well-known notions of infomediary, partnership broker, and innovation intermediary. Intermediaries that facilitate data sharing (also known as 'infomediaries') are well described in the open data literature. There are, however, different conceptualizations of the functions of these intermediaries. Open data intermediaries can develop products and services based on open data for citizens, government, or third parties [20] and can present complex datasets in a user-friendly way [22]. Meijer and Potjer [21] broaden the concept of open data intermediary to include actors facilitating the generation of data by citizens.

Inter-organizational collaboration literature puts forward the concept of 'partnership brokers' who have specific experience and capacity to facilitate negotiation and development of partnership arrangements [29]. Partnership brokers can create value by acting as matchmakers, connectors, facilitators, co-designers, conveners, mediators, or learning catalysts [19, 29].

Another relevant concept is that of an 'innovation intermediary'. Overall, innovation intermediaries create value by (1) connecting actors; (2) involving, committing, and mobilising actors; (3) solving, avoiding, or mitigating potential conflicts of interests; and (4) (actively) stimulating the innovation process and innovation outcomes [2]. Holzmann, Sailer and Katzy [14] discuss the role of innovation intermediaries in multisided markets, whereby innovation intermediaries are tasked with the matching process between demand and supply.

More recently, the term 'trusted data intermediary' (TDI) entered into circulation in the practitioner community [8, 9, 31]. Recently, a research agenda was formulated by Stanford researchers who recognized this as an emerging term [8, 9]. They defined TDIs as entities that have "a commitment to collect, aggregate, and make available large sets of digitized data for public purpose" [9]. The key distinguishing feature of TDIs is the suite of negotiations, ranging from data ownership, storage, access, analysis and security to ensuring privacy, regulations and legal conditions, and standards and practices (Ibid.). The intermediaries conduct these negotiations for different kinds of data, across sectors, and in various organizational forms (Ibid.).

These intermediation concepts provide the necessary depth for conceptualizing and grounding the notion of intermediaries of data collaboratives in existing academic research. Previous research [30] found that, compared to collaborations in general, data collaboratives face very specific collaboration challenges: the decisive role of trust between parties, data stewardship, data-related risk mitigation, and formulating value proposition to both sides. Intermediaries of data collaboratives, therefore, have a potential to create value by addressing these challenges. Our study aims to shed light on how they achieve this by analyzing emerging business models of select intermediaries in this context.

3   Framework for Business Model Analysis

The notion of 'business model' has been discussed in various streams of literature. Here, we follow the definition by Amit and Zott [4]: a business model depicts how the content, governance, and structure of transactions create value.

With the growing importance of data as raw material for the digital economy, there is an emergence of the data-driven business model (DDBM) as one specific type of business model [11] which emphasizes data as a key resource in firms' business models, particularly to establish value proposition [6]. The majority of scholars focused their research on identifying patterns and/or developing a framework/taxonomy for DDBM [11, 13, 26]. These classifications, however, apply primarily to companies in a commercial setting; they do not fully capture either the public value goals of data collaboratives or the non-profit motives of intermediaries in this context.

As for the intermediary business model, the literature in this domain is still scarce. Weill and Vitale [35] discuss the "generic business model" of electronic intermediaries. They argued that the provision of services in this business model (e.g., knowledge management, centralized management of applications, information search services) offers buyers and sellers (e.g., business, consumer, or other entities) lowered search and transaction costs. Similarly, Janssen and Zuiderwijk [15] explicate infomediary business models by formulating six types of business models based on the levels of data accessibility and dialogue between data users and data contributors. Most recently, intermediaries as marketplaces enabled by digital technologies were studied by Täuscher and Laudien [33], in which they developed a taxonomy of six types of web-based platform business models.

In sum, to describe a business model, many ontologies exist. A business model ontology is an explicit, simple specification of a conceptualization of components of a business model and the relationships between them [12, 17]. For our study, we needed a framework that is sufficiently broad to capture the description of kinds of value (for different customer segments), resources, governance mechanisms, and financial arrangement of intermediaries. Based on this rationale, we selected the Unified Business Model Framework (UBM Framework) by Al-Debei and Avison [3]. The framework is arguably one of the most comprehensive business model frameworks, as it was developed through the systematization of 22 other business model frameworks. This framework has also been applied in other similar studies [15, 23] that focus on entities that act as intermediaries.

The framework's ontological structure comprises of four dimensions, each explained by specific constituent elements. We follow the operationalization of this framework as proposed by Janssen and Zuiderwijk [15] since they focused on open data intermediaries which is a similar context to ours. See Table 1 for an overview of the four dimensions considered in this study.

Table 1. Framework for Business Model Analysis (adapted from Al-Debei and Avison [3] and Janssen and Zuiderwijk [15])

BM elements	Operationalization
Value proposition	Business logic for creating value by offering products and services for targeted segments (data providers on one side and data users on the other)
Value architecture	Architecture for the technological and organizational infrastructure used in the provisioning of products and services
Value network	Collaboration and coordination with other organizations
Value finance	Pricing and revenue breakdown associated with sustaining and improving the creation of value

4 Case Study Method

For our study we conducted an exploratory multiple case study [37]. We chose to sample cases by diversity. Data collaboratives can be categorized by their expected outcome into three arenas: (a) policy intervention, (b) data science, and (c) data-driven innovation [31]. In our case sampling we included two cases per each type to ensure diversity. We assumed that, based on these types, intermediaries create value for different target groups and therefore the value proposition, as well as value delivery and capture mechanisms, are likely to be different. As a result, the following cases were included in our analysis (Table 2).

The data was collected by conducting online desk research which included analysis of the case websites, documents, and applications. The number of data sources depended

Table 2. Selected cases with descriptions

Case	Since	Summary	Purpose
Social Science One (SSO)	2018	SSO is an initiative that enables social scientists around the world to analyze and use the increasingly rich troves of information amassed by companies to address societal issues. SSO is incubated at Harvard University (USA)	Data science

(continued)

Table 2. (*continued*)

Case	Since	Summary	Purpose
Vivli	2018	Vivli is an independent non-profit organization that provides a global data sharing and analytics platform for clinical research data	Data science
Humanitarian Data Exchange (HDX)	2014	HDX is an initiative of the UN OCHA to make humanitarian data easy to find and use for analysis across crises and organizations globally	Policy intervention
Global Forest Watch (GFW)	2014	GFW is an initiative of the research non-profit World Resources Institute that provides a real-time global forest monitoring and alert system	Policy intervention
Amsterdam Data Exchange (AMdEX)	2018	The Amsterdam Data Exchange (AMdEX) is a project under development, that aims to function as a secure and trusted open marketplace for data in the Amsterdam region of The Netherlands. The project was initiated by the Amsterdam Economic Board	Data-driven innovation
Civity City Innovation Platform (CIP)	2016	Civity's City Innovation Platform (CIP) is a Dutch product focused on enabling smart cities	Data-driven innovation

on the availability of information and ranged between 2 and 8 per case. In analyzing each case, we followed the qualitative content analysis approach [18] that is driven by the structure of the analytical framework, i.e. data for every case were coded and categorized into the value proposition, value architecture, value network, and value finance dimension. In cases when online research did not provide sufficient data, we conducted interviews with key informants of the projects to obtain clarifying information (CIP) or participated in observations during meetings and presentations (HDX, AMdEX).

5   Findings

In this section we present our analysis of the selected cases[1] through the lens of the analytical framework found in Table 1. We thus derive the business models of the intermediaries based on the four elements of the framework: Value Proposition, Value Architecture, Value Network, and Value Finance.

Our analysis shows that the intermediary model of data collaborative can be employed to address a wide range of needs and create value in different ways along the data value chain. Data intermediaries can facilitate access to previously closed data, provide an infrastructure for aggregating previously fragmented data, produce visualizations and targeted apps for eased use and understanding of data, offer interactive solutions for collecting and sharing data.

In terms of Value Architecture, the majority of the cases (except for SSO) rely heavily on pooling diverse data sources together, although they create value from that via different pathways.

Regarding Value Network, our analysis of the six cases shows that several roles can be identified. The intermediaries we analyzed have diverse organizational forms and various actors can be in the lead: academic institutions, companies, inter-governmental organizations, non-profit organizations; yet, the triple helix construction (government, industry, academia) is widely leveraged.

Finally, data intermediaries can be financially supported by different actors like non-profit foundations, industry, research institutions, government and can additionally create revenue themselves from fees for their products and services.

More nuance can be added by discussing pairs of cases according to our sampling strategy by three arenas: data science, policy intervention, and data innovation. Our analysis found that there are both similarities and differences among these types of cases.

As regards data intermediaries in the arena of data science, as evidenced by the cases SSO and Vivli, their core value proposition is facilitating easier access by researchers to valuable data from the private (and public sectors in case of Vivli). Industry-academia data intermediaries deliver value to researchers as data users by pre-negotiating data access agreements with data providers that otherwise cost researchers much time and effort. The rationale for the data provider differs depending on the context. In the case of SSO, data providers like Facebook may see it as a means to increase transparency and improve their reputation in the aftermath of negative data analytics publicity.

In the Vivli case, which provides a one-stop-shop of clinical trials data, the value for data providers is increased discoverability of their data and enhanced capacity for data sharing and reuse, thereby breaking down silos in medical research. Data contributors are offered services for secure data hosting, tools for anonymization and mapping of data, and the service of reviewing data requests on their behalf. Data users are offered a data search engine, a form to request data with data contributors, as well as an environment and tools for data aggregation (from various sources) and analysis of this data. Both

---

[1] The complete analysis of the cases per each element of the framework is uploaded as an open dataset to 4TU.Centre for Research Data repository and can be found using the following http://doi.org/10.4121/uuid:951848c4-6447-4fce-9f33-b1223b0c18e1.

data providers and users are asked to sign a Harmonized Data User Agreement prior to data sharing. In both cases, however, the intermediary support the scientific process by providing an organizational (SSO) and/or technical (Vivli) infrastructure for data access. Furthermore, they act like a "neutral broker" and perform a function of a data steward.

Data intermediaries in the arena of policy intervention are guided by slightly different objectives. Data resources created via these data collaboratives are a public good, therefore openness is at the heart of the value proposition of these intermediaries. In the case of HDX, the value of the intermediary, besides providing a technical platform and standardized process for sharing data, is providing quality assurance services to ensure risks to privacy are minimal. HDX exists since 2014 and during this time the focus has shifted from mere data aggregation to data transformations, such as visualizations. The value that this intermediary provides to data contributors is assistance with data processing and preparing data for publication, thereby tackling the data quality challenge in the humanitarian sector. Data contributors are offered services and tools that host data, impose access controls for published data sets, create metadata, and standardize, refine, statistically analyze and visualize data. For data users, services and tools for searching, following and requesting data are offered, as well as an API infrastructure to integrate the platform into user-own developments. The HDX team verifies data contributors and evaluates contributed data sets for data quality and sensitivity levels.

For both HDX and GFW, data visualizations form one of the core elements of the value proposition. The mission of the Global Forest Watch is to bring data insights to the society, including government decision-makers, companies, journalists, researchers and the public, to drive evidence-based action in forest management and conservation domain. This platform combines and overlays best available data from various sources (government, research, crowdsourced, proprietary) to produce targeted applications, such as Forest Watch and GFW Pro. There is also an open data portal for downloading datasets as open data. Both cases, HDX and GFW, add value by centralizing large volumes of data in one portal and by transforming data into actionable visualizations and insights to drive policy action. In this sense, they can be seen as 'infomediaries' [15] that help users manage vast amounts of information.

In the arena of data-driven innovation, the data intermediaries we analyzed were AMdEX and Civity. These intermediaries aim to provide a secure data infrastructure and 'rules' for data sharing among diverse parties from different sectors enabling data owners to remain in control of what data they share and with whom. Both cases are connected to international initiatives potentially feeding into the larger data innovation ecosystem in Europe. The CIP platform is limited to the smart city theme, while AMdEX has an open-ended scope potentially embracing a wide variety of data innovation use cases. Here intermediaries have to deal with issues of balancing competition and data protection with innovation and openness, therefore trust in the technical solution and in the members of the network play an important role in these cases. Both intermediaries create value to data contributors by offering a trusted data infrastructure. However, the difference is that in the case of AMdEX the business model is still a search process; it is emerging from consultations with stakeholders about their needs and challenges. Therefore, issues of standardization and interoperability are of concern, given the different demands and expectations of the wide range of stakeholders. While in the CIP case, the business model is very straightforward and determined by the company as a platform provider – 'take it or leave it'.

6 Discussion

Overall, we find that the business models described differ based on the following discriminating variables:

- Level of openness – stands for the extent to which data access is restricted or available. A high level of openness means that anyone can use the data provided through an intermediary; a medium level of openness means that there is a process in place to approve data requests; and a low level of openness means that the data is available to members only. Thereby, we place the business models on a continuum.
- Added value to the data – key activities that the intermediary performs along the data value chain to realize the value proposition.

Table 3 below shows how the six cases we analyzed are classified according to these variables. We observe that the level of openness in these six intermediary cases correlates with the three arenas based on which we selected the cases. Data science collaboratives, such as SSO and Vivli, have a medium level of openness due to the data access procedures that are put in place (call for proposals to researchers, data request forms). Policy intervention collaboratives, such as HDX and GFW, have a high level of openness due to the public nature of the issue and the fact that the platforms they provide are considered as public good. Data innovation collaboratives, such as AMdEX and CIP, have a low level of openness as in the former case data access can be controlled by the data provider and in the latter case the platform is offered on a for-profit basis.

Table 3. Variables for deriving generic business models from cases

Added value	Level of openness		
	Low	Medium	High
Data access		SSO	
Data aggregation		Vivli	HDX
Data visualization			GFW, HDX
Data exchange	AMdEX, CIP		

In terms of added value, some cases can be placed in several (more than two) categories (e.g. GFW provides data access through their open data portal, data visualizations through the Forest Watcher app, and data sharing tools for supply chain monitoring via its GFW Pro app). Nonetheless, in Table 3 below we highlight the activities that are at the very core of the value proposition of the intermediary. For some cases that are placed in two cells, namely HDX, this also shows the evolution of the business model (towards more data visualizations).

Based on these variables, we distinguish the following generic business models for a data intermediary in a data collaborative setting. Since we based our analysis on six cases, we allow the possibility that other cells in this table may be filled with other business models.

1. *Data gatekeeper model* (Social Science One): intermediary serves as a trusted third party that negotiates terms of access to previously closed data by users selected through a call for proposals. Value comes from the legitimacy of the process.
2. *One-stop-shop model* (Vivli, HDX): intermediary aggregates previously siloed data from multiple sources into a central data repository to ease discoverability, comparability, and analysis of data. Value comes from scale, therefore the intermediary is dependent on data providers contributing data.
3. *Information-as-a-service model* (GFW, HDX): intermediary provides data visualizations to targeted segments to ease the understandability of data for decision-makers. Value comes from ease-of-use and quality of decision support; therefore, the intermediary is dependent on users.
4. *Data controls model* (Civity CIP, AMdEX): intermediary offers a solution for sharing data (including sensitive data) in a secure, targeted, and controlled manner with full insight into who uses the data. Data owners are offered a menu of options what (parts of) data to share with whom and for what period. The value comes from the technical excellence of the product and the data expertise of the intermediary. Therefore, the intermediary is dependent on buy-in from key stakeholders and on standardization and interoperability efforts.

In the realization of these business models the intermediaries are dependent on interactions with other actors in the data ecosystem. In the Data Gatekeeper model, the data intermediary is dependent on the acceptance and trust of the wider (scientific) community. The role of government, at least based on the SSO case, is supporting, providing guidance and/or setting norms. In the One-stop-shop model, where more value comes from scale, the intermediary is dependent on data providers contributing data to build a comprehensive repository. In both Vivli and HDX government organizations can be data providers or users, as well as partners of the initiative. In the Information-as-a-service model, the intermediary is dependent on the users from different target groups. Governments can play multiple roles here by providing data, supporting the initiative, and consuming the data analysis products themselves. And in the Data Controls model, where value comes from buy-in from key stakeholders, government can be a facilitator, a data provider/client, data user, and funder. Overall, our study confirms and provides illustrations of the roles of government in data collaborations described in previous research [17, 27]: namely, government as a data provider, data user, facilitator of collaboration, supporter or funder, an active partner in the consortium, a guarantor of data quality, source of trust, public interest promoter. Our research however shows that it is rarely just one role that government organizations assume but a combination of roles.

When compared to the existing literature [15], there are some similarities and differences. For instance, the One-stop-shop model is an extension of three different business models, as this model aggregates siloed data from multiple sources (i.e. information aggregators) and stores those data centrally (i.e. open data repository) to make the data easier to search, compare and analyze (i.e. service platforms). Similarly, in the Information-as-a-service model, data intermediaries will act as service platforms that offer data processing and analysis services that can help decision-makers in making better policies. However, there are notable differences in a way that we also emphasize technical resources and the enabling environment to promote data transparency and sovereignty, as can be seen in the Data gatekeeper and Data control models. In this way, we allow the possibility to open up the data that are traditionally challenging to be open, especially data possessed by private entities.

7 Conclusion

Our study investigated how intermediaries create value and what business models they use to facilitate data exchange and collaboration in the context of data collaboratives. For our analysis we selected six cases representing three different arenas of data collaboratives: data science, policy intervention, and data-driven innovation. Based on the case analysis, we derived four generic business models that can be employed by intermediaries in data collaboratives. These generic business models are distinguished by two variables – level of openness and added value to the data. We labeled these business models as follows: Data Gatekeeper model, One-stop-shop model, Information-as-a-service model, and Data Controls model.

Our study shows that the intermediary model of data collaboratives can have different configurations and can follow various pathways for value creation. As evidenced by our cases, in their offerings intermediaries aim to tackle diverse challenges that data collaboratives face, such as balancing collaborative data sharing with control over data, overcoming fragmentation and creating data pools, brokering access to controversial data, matching data supply and demand though market rules, and more. The four business models further differ based on what the value comes from and who or what the intermediary is dependent on to realize the value proposition. We further discussed the implications of these findings for governments explicating the different roles in which they can step in these initiatives.

Our research contributed empirically derived knowledge about data intermediaries through the lens of data collaboratives. This adds to our understanding of emerging data ecosystems leveraging diverse data sources for creating public value through cross-sector collaboration. The limitations of our work are that our study is exploratory and was based on a limited number of cases. Future research can test and elaborate our findings in other empirical settings. Furthermore, much literature discusses trust as an important element of intermediaries (e.g. [5, 8–10, 25, 28, 29, 36]). In our study we did not explicitly interrogate whether and to what extent the conceptualizations of trust can be different across the various intermediary business models. We propose this research question for future investigations.

Acknowledgements. This research received funding from the Swedish Research Council under the grant agreement 2015-06563 "Data collaboratives as a new form of innovation for addressing societal challenges in the age of data". This paper is in part based on the work done by the second author in a scientific thesis. All copyrights on the prior work rest with the second author of the paper. Any views expressed by the second author in this paper are those of the author and do not necessarily reflect the views of her employer.

References

1. Abrahamson, E.: Management fashion. Acad. Manag. J. **21**, 254–285 (1996). https://doi.org/10.2307/258636
2. Agogué, M., Berthet, E., Fredberg, T., Le Masson, P., Segrestin, B., Stoetzel, M., Wiener, M., Yström, A.: Explicating the role of innovation intermediaries in the "unknown": a contingency approach. J. Strat. Manag. **10**, 19–39 (2017). https://doi.org/10.1108/jsma-01-2015-0005
3. Al-Debei, M.M., Avison, D.: Developing a unified framework of the business model concept. Eur. J. Inform. Syst. **19**, 359–376 (2010). https://doi.org/10.1057/ejis.2010.21
4. Amit, R., Zott, C.: Value creation in E-business. Strateg. Manag. J. **22**, 493–520 (2001). https://doi.org/10.1002/smj.187
5. Bailey, J.P., Bakos, Y.: An exploratory study of the emerging role of electronic intermediaries. Int. J. Electron. Commer. **1**, 7–20 (1997). https://doi.org/10.1080/10864415.1997.11518287
6. Benta, C., Wilberg, J., Hollauer, C., Omer, M.: Process model for data-driven business model generation. In: DS 87-2 Proceedings of the 21st International Conference on Engineering Design (ICED 17), vol. 2: Design Processes, Design Organisation and Management, Vancouver, Canada, 21-25.08.2017 (2017)
7. van den Broek, T., van Veenstra, A.F.: Governance of big data collaborations: How to balance regulatory compliance and disruptive innovation. Technol. Forecast. Soc. Change. **129**, 330–338 (2018). https://doi.org/10.1016/j.techfore.2017.09.040
8. Digital Civil Society: Trusted Data Intermediaries (2017). https://medium.com/the-digital-civil-society-lab/trusted-data-intermediaries-c58426c2c994
9. Digital Civil Society Lab: Workshop summary: Trusted data intermediaries (2018). https://pacscenter.stanford.edu/wp-content/uploads/2018/05/TDI-Workshop-Summary.pdf
10. Froomkin, A.M.: The essential role of trusted third parties in electronic commerce. Ore. Law. Rev. **75**, 49–115 (1996)
11. Hartmann, P.M., Zaki, M., Feldmann, N., Neely, A.: Capturing value from big data – a taxonomy of data-driven business models used by start-up firms. Int. J. Oper. Prod. Manag. **36**, 1382–1406 (2016). https://doi.org/10.1108/ijopm-02-2014-0098
12. Heikkila, J., Heikkila, M., Tinnila, M.: The role of business models in developing business networks. Electron. Commer. 221–231. https://doi.org/10.4018/978-1-59904-943-4.ch020
13. Hilbig, R., Etsiwah, B., Hecht, S.: Berlin start-ups – the rise of data-driven business models. In: ISPIM Innovation Symposium (2018)
14. Holzmann, T., Sailer, K., Katzy, B.R.: Matchmaking as multi-sided market for open innovation. Technol. Anal. Strateg. Manag. **26**, 601–615 (2014). https://doi.org/10.1080/09537325.2014.913786
15. Janssen, M., Zuiderwijk, A.: Infomediary business models for connecting open data providers and users. Soc. Sci. Comput. Rev. **32**, 694–711 (2014). https://doi.org/10.1177/0894439314525902
16. Klievink, B., van der Voort, H., Veeneman, W.: Creating value through data collaboratives. Inf. Polity. **23**, 379–397 (2018). https://doi.org/10.3233/ip-180070
17. Kort, C., Gordijn, J.: Modeling Strategic Partnerships Using the E3value Ontology. In: Handbook of Ontologies for Business Interaction, pp. 310–325 (2008). https://doi.org/10.4018/978-1-59904-660-0.ch018
18. Krippendorff, K.: Content Analysis: An Introduction to its Methodology. SAGE, Thousand Oaks (2004)

19. Lee, L.: Understanding the role of the broker in business non-profit collaboration. Soc. Responsib. J. **11**, 201–220 (2015). https://doi.org/10.1108/srj-05-2013-0050
20. Magalhaes, G., Roseira, C., Strover, S.: Open government data intermediaries: a terminology framework. In: Proceedings of the 7th International Conference on Theory and Practice of Electronic Governance (2013). https://doi.org/10.1145/2591888.2591947
21. Meijer, A., Potjer, S.: Citizen-generated open data: An explorative analysis of 25 cases. Gov. Inf. Q. **35**, 613–621 (2018). https://doi.org/10.1016/j.giq.2018.10.004
22. Mercado-Lara, E., Gil-Garcia, J.R.: Open government and data intermediaries: the case of AidData. In: Proceedings of the 15th Annual International Conference on Digital Government Research, pp. 335–356 (2014). https://doi.org/10.1145/2612733.2612789
23. Ranerup, A., Henriksen, H.Z., Hedman, J.: An analysis of business models in public service platforms. Gov. Inf. Q. **33**, 6–14 (2016). https://doi.org/10.1016/j.giq.2016.01.010
24. Robin, N., Klein, T., Jütting, J.: Public-Private Partnerships for Statistics: Lessons Learned, Future Steps. OECD Development Co-operation Working Papers, No. 27. (2016). https://doi.org/10.1787/5jm3nqp1g8wf-en
25. van Schalkwyk, F., Willmers, M., McNaughton, M.: Viscous open data: the roles of intermediaries in an open data ecosystem. Inf. Technol. Dev. **22**, 68–83 (2016). https://doi.org/10.1080/02681102.2015.1081868
26. Schüritz, R., Seebacher, S., Dorner, R.: Capturing value from data: revenue models for data-driven services. In: Proceedings of the 50th Hawaii International Conference on System Sciences (2017). https://doi.org/10.24251/hicss.2017.648
27. Schwabe, G.: The role of public agencies in blockchain consortia: learning from the Cardossier. Inf. Polity. **24**, 437–451 (2019). https://doi.org/10.3233/ip-190147
28. Skevington, P.J., Hart, T.P.: Trusted third parties in electronic commerce. BT Technol. J. **15**, 51–61 (1997). https://doi.org/10.1007/978-94-011-4918-1_4
29. Stadtler, L., Probst, G.: How broker organizations can facilitate public–private partnerships for development. Euro. Manag. J. **30**, 32–46 (2012). https://doi.org/10.1016/j.emj.2011.10.002
30. Susha, I., Gil-Garcia, J.R.: A collaborative governance approach to partnerships addressing public problems with private data. In: Proceedings of the 52nd Hawaii International Conference on System Sciences (2019). https://doi.org/10.24251/hicss.2019.350
31. Susha, I., Janssen, M., Verhulst, S.: Data collaboratives as a new frontier of cross-sector partnerships in the age of open data: taxonomy development. In: Proceedings of the 50th Hawaii International Conference on System Sciences, pp. 2691–2700 (2017)
32. Taddeo, M.: Data philanthropy and the design of the infraethics for information societies. Philos. Trans. Royal Soc. A. **374**, 20160113 (2016). https://doi.org/10.1098/rsta.2016.0113
33. Täuscher, K., Laudien, S.M.: Understanding platform business models: a mixed methods study of marketplaces. Euro. Manag. J. **36**, 319–329 (2018). https://doi.org/10.1016/j.emj.2017.06.005
34. Verhulst, S., Young, A., Winowatan, M., Zahuranec, A.J.: Leveraging private data for public good: a descriptive analysis and typology of existing practices. The GovLab (2019)
35. Weill, P., Vitale, M.: Portals, agents, auctions, aggregators and other intermediaries. In: Place to Space: Migrating to eBusiness Models, pp. 151–182. Harvard Business Press (2001)
36. Womack, R.: Information intermediaries and optimal information distribution. Libr. Inf. Sci. Res. **24**, 129–155 (2002). https://doi.org/10.1016/s0740-8188(02)00109-3
37. Yin, R.K.: Case Study Research. SAGE, Thousand Oaks (2003)

AI, Data Analytics, and Automated Decision Making

Generating Value from Government Data Using AI: An Exploratory Study

Yingying Gao[1](✉) ⓘ and Marijn Janssen[2] ⓘ

[1] Huazhong University of Science and Technology, Wuhan 430074, China
Y.Gao-2@tudelft.nl
[2] Delft University of Technology, Jaffalaan 5, 2628BX Delft, The Netherlands

Abstract. Open government data initiatives have gained popularity around the world. Artificial Intelligence (AI) has the potential to make better use of data. Combining the OGD and AI is crucial to generate more value from data. In this paper we investigate what kind of value was generated through AI and how. A context-input-process-output/outcome (CIPO) framework is developed to describe and compare three cases. The overview of cases shows the huge potential of AI, but it also suggests that AI is hardly used by the public to create value from open data. The objectives of the three cases are efficiency, innovation and crime prevention, whereas common open government objectives like transparency, accountability and participation are given less attention. By using AI, the risks of data privacy and arriving at biased or wrong conclusions become more prominent. With the rise of data collection from Internet of Things, complying with the 5-stars of Berners-Lee becomes more important. We recommend policy makers to stimulate AI projects contributing to the open government goals and ensure that open data meets the 5-star requirements.

Keywords: Open data · Open government · Artificial Intelligence · Internet of Things · Value creation · Smart cities

1 Introduction

Open government data (OGD) refers to publishing public sector data in open and reusable formats without restriction or charge for their use by society [1]. This movements have gained a great popularity across the world [2]. The public sectors generate and maintain a large amount of data [3], and its ability to collect data with application of low-cost devices enabled by Internet of Things (IoT), resulted in an explosion of digital data. Nevertheless, data is useless unless it is used to generate benefits from it [4]. Although policy-makers and smart cities could use these data, it needs to be opened and shared with the public in order to be able achieved the full potential of OGD.

Artificial Intelligence (AI) techniques have been extensively used to support the decision making and problem solving in different industries for many years [5–7]. AI can create new insights from combined datasets. Furthermore, AI systems can acquire their

G. Viale Pereira et al. (Eds.): EGOV 2020, LNCS 12219, pp. 319–331, 2020.
https://doi.org/10.1007/978-3-030-57599-1_24

intelligence by using data to understand how past problems were solved, and applying this learning for predictive purposes. With the advancement of open government data, it becomes possible to combine AI technologies and OGD to obtain more value from data.

Some articles focused on exploring the economic value of OGD [8, 9] and social, political value like transparency, innovation and so on [10, 11]. But the use of AI for OGD remains scarce. There are some examples of trying to employ AI processing open data. For example, Piscopo et al. [12] concluded that the prediction model of community capacity using machine learning is more accurate than other models built using conventional statistics. Saltos and Cocea [13] used the open crime data to test that decision trees can be used to reliably predict crime frequency. Kouziokas [14] forecasted high crime risk transportation areas in urban environment by application of AI to test the most efficient algorithm and optimal model. Most of studies combined different datasets and suggested to give an in-depth investigation of AI especially the application of AI in certain area such as public sector [15]. These studies are beneficial for us to understand how open government data could drive AI. However, most of these studies are conducted from a technical perspective and do not focus on understanding value creation from OGD based on AI.

In this study, we investigated the following research question: what kind of value was generated through AI application and how? For this, we conducted an exploratory study on OGD innovation cases through AI. The whole process from collecting data to creating value is analyzed. AI technologies facilitate data analysis and specific value generated.

2   Research Approach

To investigate the value created from OGD using AI, we employ the comparative case study research method. In such type of research, two or more cases are systematically compared through examination of a real-world phenomenon within its naturally occurring context [16]. In our work we follow the steps suggested by Yin [17]. (1) Identify specific research question to determine that it is appropriate to use comparative case study. (2) Select cases and design the case study. (3) Collect case data and analyze the case evidence. (4) Report case study.

Firstly, our research aim is to investigate how and what kinds of value was generated through AI. The type of research questions most appropriate for case studies are "how" and "why" questions since they focus on the underlying process and the causal relationship [16]. Accordingly, we focus on the cases of using AI to explore how value is created form OGD using AI. For this we examine the whole process from collecting data to evaluate its impact.

Secondly, we identified three cases. The cases should be in the public domain, employ AI and data should be available. We searched the European data portal for finding suitable cases. This portal covers more than 500 cases of OGD application or ideas from EU. Yet the number of cases employing AI is limited. Furthermore, we want to cover a diversity of AI applications, as for example there are several cases using chatbots. Finally, we selected three cases which reflect the three phases of AI application. In phase 1, AI could use structured data to automate simple and repetitive processes. In phase 2, AI is able to adapt to and learn from changes in the automated process. In phase 3, AI provides new and innovative insights by being able to analyze and learn from previous actions [18]. The first selected case is the AI parking which is a German application using real-time traffic data to help people find the parking space. And the second case is a chatbot application in Singapore. The last case is the crime prevention through artificial intelligence employed by Kent Police in UK.

For the third step, we construct a context-input-process-output/outcome framework in order to establish the logic of comparative study, which is discussed in detail in the next section. Finally, we analyze the cases according to the framework and report the results, which are presented in Sect. 4.

3   Towards a Comparison Framework

This section presents a comparative framework for OGD innovation cases using AI. Firstly, we describe the context-input-process-output/outcome (CIPO) model. Subsequently, a series of elements are derived referring to the CIPO model in order to construct the comparative framework of analyzing the AI-based innovation case.

3.1   Context-Input-Process-Output/Outcome (CIPO) Model

Systems theory offers an important insight to the role of the information systems or technology in this sequence from data to information to knowledge. Systems thinking especially soft systems thinking provides us a way to conceptualize the social process in a particular context [19]. Services or products like applications could be created by exploring OGD in which data is transferred into results. Any transformation process can be viewed as an input-output system [20]. This system was then developed to input-process-output model by other researchers and applied in project evaluation, team innovation management etc. [21, 22]. However, projects using government data or applied in public sector should be studied as a complex process because they are influenced by socio-political and other context factor [23]. In addition, a difference between output and outcome is often made in which output is the immediate result and outcome the long-term impact [24]. In this work, we study both the short-term and long-term impact. Therefore, we used the context-input-process-output/outcome (CIPO) framework to better understand the OGD innovation cases, which has been used in the past to analyze OGD policies [24].

3.2   Elements for Comparing Cases

In this section, we derive the elements for comparing the OGD innovation cases from literature, related reports and websites. The findings are sorted by four parts following the CIPO model, namely project context, project input, process and the output/outcome (see in Table 1).

Table 1. CIPO Framework elements for comparing cases

Framework	Elements	Explanation
Project context	Background	Country, stakeholders' overviews, who initiated the project, description of societal challenge and so on
	Project objectives	What aims the stakeholders want to achieve through the project
Project input	Type of data	Analyzing what kind of data was used and evaluating the data quality according to the 5-star model developed by Berners Lee [25]
	Type of AI	Specific AI technologies or algorithm
Process	Process	The process steps taken to transform inputs into outputs
Output/Outcome	Output	What type of application it generated, like an app, new insight into the situations etc.
	Outcome - type of value generated	The positive effects were derived according to the benefits of open data [3, 4, 26]
	Risks and challenges	The negative effects (like bias, discrimination) [3, 26, 27]

Project Context. The background describes the situation at hand, including the places, stakeholders and their contribution. The project objectives are referring the aims to be achieved through the projects. These projects may be set up to address multiple societal challenges. The OGD goals emphasized by different countries and different level of governments vary. So, it is necessary to investigate the context of the project to be able to evaluate the outcome.

Project Input. It mainly refers to the data and technology input since high quality data is the fuel and technologies are core part driving the innovation process with AI. It focuses on what kind of data is required to enable successful AI application and how the data is provided (batch or real time, using a file or API). We then evaluate the quality of data open according to the 5-star open data model developed by Berners Lee as shown in Table 2 [25]. In addition, AI technology takes often like a black box and it is unknown what type of AI technologies is used to process data and how the data is explored.

Process. The steps of process are analyzed about how datasets were combined, processed and explored to create value. Data can be analyzed from multiple perspectives, resulting many useful applications.

Output/Outcome. It comprehensively evaluates the immediate result and the long-term outcome which includes the value and the risks & challenges. The value refers more to

Table 2. The 5-star open data taken from Berners Lee [25]

Star	Explanation
★	Make your stuff available on the Web (whatever format) under an open license
★★	Make it available as structured data (e.g. excel instead of image scan of a table)
★★★	Make it available in a non-proprietary open format (e.g. CSV instead of excel)
★★★★	Use URIs to denote things, so that people can point at your stuff
★★★★★	Link your data to other data to provide context

the benefits of the AI applications. Although it is hard to identify what exactly values can gain from OGD because of different datasets and various application, some scholars tried to classify the benefits expected from leveraging open government data such as economic value and social value so on [4]. This classification provides us insight to identify the value of these projects.

4   Case Analysis Result

In this section three cases from Germany, Singapore and UK using AI to explore government data are compared. The cases are diverse in background, objectives, data used, AI tools and result (Table 3).

Table 3. Overview of each element of three cases

Framework	Elements	Case 1-AI parking	Case2-Chatbot	Case3-Crime prevention
Project context	Background	Germany project launched by Bliq company in which it was challenging to find a parking solution without sensors	Singapore project launched by The Government Technology Agency of Singapore in which citizens could not find an answer to their questions easily	UK project launched by Kent Police in which there were high levels of crime and people did not feel safe
	Project objective	Efficiency objective: Lower time to find parking place and reduce pollution through predicting the parking situation without installing sensors on a larger geographic scale	1. Efficiency objective: improve service delivery and quickly answer questions. 2. Social and political objectives: make citizens' lives better and improve the public satisfaction	Efficiency objective: fulfill an ever-expanding range of tasks for policies under the situation of reducing expenditure

(continued)

Table 3. (*continued*)

Framework	Elements	Case 1-AI parking	Case2-Chatbot	Case3-Crime prevention
Project Input	Types of data	1. Data content - Parking traffic data including parking locations etc. - Street-level imagery data about parking occupancy over time 2. Data quality ★ datasets include all kinds of formats like real time image data and the static parking location data. Only parking data uses open license	1. Data content - Unstructured Q &A and dialogue data - Service Catalog 2. Data quality: ★ Since most of Q&A and dialogue data is unstructured and need to be cleaned to be machine-readable data. The service catalog can be seen on the website, but not published in a machine-readable format	1. Data content - Structured current and historical crime data, including five data points for each incident 2. Data quality: ★ Crime data in Kent were available as an image. For privacy reason, not all the data points required by the prediction were published online
	Type of AI used	- Recurrent neural network	- Natural Language Processing -Machine learning	- Machine-learning prediction algorithm - Model–based on the causes of crime pattern formation
Process	Process steps from input to output	1. Combine data: aggregate parking traffic data of parking locations including street or dedicated parking lot to emulate virtual sensors 2. process data using AI: a deep learning model consisting of several artificial neural networks that process parking data 3. Test the model and applied: 14-month parking data collected with government validated the accuracy of the prediction model	1. Combine data - collect the Q&A between citizens and staffs in government and service catalog data 2. Process data using AI-The Natural Language Processing is used to analyzed the questions and answers and service catalog data. At last the basic Q&A pairs are derived. Supervised learning into which answers and data were fed 3. Feedback: The chatbot learn from the dialogues with citizens to increase its chat ability	1. Collect data -clarify crime types 2. Process-Use the patented algorithm developed by Predpol to predict where and when this kind of crime is most likely to occur, aiming to help precisely target a certain type of crime 3. Applied- The prediction algorithm is constantly learning from crime reports in the city and according the prediction can change at any moment
Impact	Output	A new app called AIPARK or Bilq park was developed to provide parking recommendation for users	A virtual assistant called Ask Jamie was implemented across 70 government agency websites to provide answers and service entry	A software system was applied in Kent Police from 2013 to 2018

(*continued*)

Table 3. (*continued*)

Framework	Elements	Case 1-AI parking	Case2-Chatbot	Case3-Crime prevention
	Outcomes of value generated	1. Economic value- The creation of the new company Bilq adding value to the economy 2. Social value – AI parking is an innovative service to decrease the searching time for parking consumed by end users	1. Social and political value- this application can improve the service capacity and the citizen satisfaction on public sector 2. Operational value- help call center agents to focus on resolving more complex citizen queries and optimize administrative processes	Social and Political value-create new insights for police and improve the police service for citizens
	Risks and challenges	1. Outdated data 2. Concerns of privacy by using number plates	Recommending wrong services	1. Lack of transparency of predictive algorithms 2. Entrenching pre-existing discrimination 3. Concerns about data protection and privacy

Note: The cases information is achieved from websites
https://bliq.ai/blog/
https://www.tech.gov.sg/products-and-services/ask-jamie/
http://blog.predpol.com/predpol-and-community-policing
https://www.bbc.com/news/technology-47118229

4.1 Project Context

There are many challenges faced by different stakeholders and their emphasized objectives also differ. In the first case, its main aim to lower the searching time for parking through prediction using AI. Whereas the latter two cases which are launched by governments, the main focus is on the social challenges like improving the service quality and decreasing the crime rate under the situation of reducing expenditure.

4.2 Project Input

Type of Data. In terms of data content, these three cases use traffic parking data, government Q & A data as well as the crime data separately. From view of data structure, unstructured text data is adopted in case 2 while structured data is collected in case 3 because there are five data points for each crime incident to generate predictions. The data source in case 1 is a mix of the structured location information and the unstructured picture information. This analysis shows the innovative potential of OGD.

In addition, we also evaluated the quality of data open. According to the 5-star model developed by Berners Lee, we give the three cases one star. Because in the case 1, part of data was shared with government. In the case 2, people might find question and answer and the service catalog on the Singapore government website, but the full Q&A data and the catalog data was not in an open and machine-readable format. In the case 3, the number and type of crime in Kent could be found in the website, but not all the data points needed by crime prediction are published due to data privacy.

Type of AI Technologies. There are several technologies namely neural network, natural language processing and machine learning adopted by these three cases. But it can be seen that algorithm models are a combination of scene-based knowledge and technology. For example, when conducting crime prediction, experts in related fields together created specific machine learning algorithm models based on the knowledge of criminal behavior. Similarly, in the application of parking and chatbots, developers construct various specific algorithm models for better applied in different fields.

4.3 Project Process

We analyzed the process steps taken to transform input into outputs by looking at three steps. (1) Data collection. After collecting the original data, the necessary clear data points are extract from combined datasets. (2) Using AI to process data. Using AI technologies to construct models and process data. (3) Applied in the certain field. At last, the data exploration processes are turned into applications.

4.4 Output/Outcome

Output. Three cases yield three applications namely AIPARK, Ask Jamie, Predpol. The first two applications are still under development and improvement. But for Predpol system, Kent Police decided to stop using it in 2018.

Outcomes of Generated Value. Previous literature summarized a variety of benefits of open data including social, political, economic and so on [3, 4, 26]. We derived the values generated by these cases according to the literature. For case 1, the main value is about economy since this team earned the investment and built a company in Germany. Moreover, the team also showed that this innovative service makes the time for searching to park three times shorter than the normal trip. For case 2, the chatbot improves service delivery, especially saving citizens' time for simple information consultation. The survey by government showed that 58% citizens considered it successful and 60% found the answers useful[1], which helped to improve the public satisfaction on government. On the operational level, it also saved the time of public servants and optimized the administrative process so that they focus on more complex tasks. In case 3, at four-month trial in Medway, street violence falls by 6%[2]. It has a social and political value of improving the police service delivery.

---

[1] Note: The data comes from https://www.tech.gov.sg/media/technews/winning-by-innovating.

[2] Note: The data comes from https://www.bbc.com/news/uk-england-kent-32529731.

Risks and Challenges. In the first case, the main challenge is about the data update since the outdated data could give a wrong parking suggestion. This application could also be extended by applying number plates data. And it is a similar challenge about the recommendation accuracy in the second case. There are only about 60% users think it useful. For the prediction application in UK, there are several challenges. First issue people concern is lack of transparency of how predictive algorithms reach their decisions. Another concern is the software entrenching pre-existing discrimination since the program had "learned" racism and bias. The last major risk is the data privacy. The principle of AI is that the more data an algorithm receives, the better it will become at its task. The more datasets mean less privacy generally.

5 Discussion

The framework was found to be useful for understanding the cases as a high level. It helps to systematically analyze the cases and enable us to compare them in the same dimension, which provides a comprehensive picture of the OGD innovation using AI. However, each innovation is a complicated process that include much detail like data collection, data cleaning and so on. The framework cannot cover all the process. It focuses on the critical process in the innovation cases. In this section, we discuss the case analysis result according the framework.

5.1 Context- Collaboration Between Government and Private Company

Although these projects were launched by different stakeholders, the entire implementation process of the project was based on the cooperation between government and private companies. In the first case, the company conducted a data collection project in cooperation with the local municipality to validate the parking prediction model. In the second and third cases, the government provided data and then hired technology companies to produce solutions. Therefore, private companies are an indispensable intermediary to create more applications and value for society from OGD using AI [28]. Future research about combining AI and OGD can focus on strengthening cooperation between government and enterprises.

5.2 Input- Improve the Data Quality and Technology Transparency

Improve the Data Quality. These three applications still provide relatively useful predictions although the datasets are rated as 1 star. Indeed, there are some AI mechanisms that can deal with low data quality. But AI applications are highly dependent on the data quality (accuracy, completeness, availability, timeliness) [29]. Whereas persons can spot easily mistakes in data, AI is not able to spot such mistakes which might result easily in incorrect findings [30]. Evaluating the information quality before using them with AI technology is therefore important. Furthermore, if data was formatted comply with the 5-stars model suggested by Berners lee [18], then the use of OGD based on AI is relatively easy, as the data is structured and well-described and has a persistent URI to ensure a continuous stream of data. Furthermore, there is a need for semantic descriptions of open data to explore the use of OGD. This is a condition for exploration of OGD to finding new insights and adds to representational information quality.

Improve the Transparency of AI Technologies. There is a wide variety of AI techniques and AI can be used to create various types of value. There seems to be no best AI techniques and which type of AI is used is dependent on the type of problem that is tackled. AI can be used to increase the efficiency (of parking) facilitate positive relationship with citizens (chatbots) and find anomalies (crime prevention). The use of AI might have negative effects like strengthening the discrimination since little information is given to understand how predictive algorithms reach their decisions, which need to be managed and clear accountabilities should be ensured. The need for guidance by a legal framework should be further explored.

5.3 Output/Outcome- Create More Value While Effectively Preventing Risks

Increase the Users' Take-Up Rate. In order to sustainably achieve the value from these project, it is necessary to increase the users' take-up rate [31]. No matter the AI parking or chatbots, they are still in the early stage of development. The number of users is limited. For the crime prediction software, Kent police has stop using it in 2018. So, developing the application is not the end. It is important to improve the service so that to increase the level of usage for sustainable value creation.

Objectives Value. OGD initiatives often focus on transparency, accountability, innovation for companies and participation [32]. In contrast, the objectives of the three cases were focused on efficiency, innovation and crime prevention. The objectives were often very specific and the value generated had limited contribution to the original OGD objectives. Also, some of AI projects were beneficial for governments instead of the public. This could be due to selection bias, but also that the public have limited capabilities to make use of AI. We recommend to stimulate AI projects for obtaining these general objectives of OGD initiatives.

The Balance Between Privacy and Utility. In the case of automatic parking, the application might be easily extended with vehicle number plate recognition or in the third case the names of criminals might be identified which might violate the privacy. The more data is released and available, there is a need for data privacy preserving techniques [33]. There is a tradeoff between privacy and utility of OGD publishing [33]. It might be a suggesting to release only the metadata including semantic descripting and only grant access once the purpose has become clear to avoid misuse. With the use of AI algorithm, the data collection and processing become less visible [34]. As such, mechanisms for dealing with the risks and AI-governance becomes more important.

6 Conclusion and Implication

This study developed a framework for comparing OGD innovation cases using AI that consists of the critical elements related to an AI project. The framework was useful to describe and compare the AI cases and draw the attention to the main value creation elements. This framework can be used to analyzed other cases, also outside the OGD or AI domain, which helps government to improve the data provide and adjust the objective.

AI is an area that can be used to create more value from OGD. Surprisingly, different types of value are created using AI than often what is aimed for by OGD initiatives. The cases show the high potential, but also challenges which complicates attaining the value. The analysis of three cases shows that it is necessary to strengthen the collaboration between the company and government since companies might have data and the capacity to process data using AI. In addition, the quality of the data is a key aspect for creating value using AI. This becomes more important as AI is less aware of the shortcomings in data, whereas data analyst can take this into account. Following the 5-stars model when opening data can simplify the use of AI.

There is a wide variety of AI techniques that can be used to create various types of value like neural network, natural language processing and machine learning. But it is important to improve the algorithm transparency and accountability to assess if there is bias or discrimination. Furthermore, the objectives of the project and value created in three cases hardly contributed to the ideals of the open government movement like transparency, accountability, innovation and participation. This can be explained as the projects investigated are initiated by governments. As further recommendation for policy-makers, we suggest more experiments with AI for OGD focused on the OGD objectives to facilitate learning.

References

1. Kalampokis, E., Tambouris, E., Tarabanis, K.: Open government data: a stage model. In: Janssen, M., Scholl, Hans J., Wimmer, Maria A., Tan, Y.-h. (eds.) EGOV 2011. LNCS, vol. 6846, pp. 235–246. Springer, Heidelberg (2011). https://doi.org/10.1007/978-3-642-22878-0_20
2. Saxena, S.: National open data frames across Japan, The Netherlands and Saudi Arabia: role of culture. Foresight 20(1), 123–134 (2018)
3. Kucera, J., Chlapek, D.: Benefits and risks of open government data. J. Syst. Integr. 5(1), 30–41 (2014)
4. Janssen, M., Charalabidis, Y., Zuiderwijk, A.: Benefits, adoption barriers and myths of open data and open government. Inf. Syst. Manag. 29(4), 258–268 (2012)
5. Androutsopoulou, A., Karacapilidis, N., Loukis, E., Charalabidis, Y.: Transforming the communication between citizens and government through AI-guided chatbots. Gov. Inf. Q. 36(2), 358–367 (2019)
6. Sun, T.Q., Medaglia, R.: Mapping the challenges of Artificial Intelligence in the public sector: Evidence from public healthcare. Gov. Inf. Q. 36(2), 368–383 (2019)
7. Lima, M.S.M., Delen, D.: Predicting and explaining corruption across countries: a machine learning approach. Gov. Inf. Q. 37(1), 101407 (2020)
8. Ahmadi Zeleti, F., Ojo, A., Curry, E.: Exploring the economic value of open government data. Gov. Inf. Q. 33(3), 535–551 (2016)

9. Bonina, C.M.: New business models and the value of open data : definitions, challenges and opportunities. In: NEMODE–3 K Small Grants Call (2013)

10. Jetzek, T., Avital, M., Bjorn-Andersen, N.: Data-driven innovation through open government data. J. Theor. Appl. Electron. Comm. Res. **9**(2), 100–120 (2014)

11. Lakomaa, E., Kallberg, J.: Open data as a foundation for innovation: the enabling effect of free public sector information for entrepreneurs. IEEE Access **1**, 558–563 (2013)

12. Piscopo, A., Siebes, R., Hardman, L.: Predicting sense of community and participation by applying machine learning to open government data. Pol. Internet **9**(1), 55–75 (2017)

13. Saltos, G., Cocea, M.: An exploration of crime prediction using data mining on open data. Int. J. Inf. Technol. Dec. Making **16**(5), 1155–1181 (2017)

14. Kouziokas, G.N.: The application of artificial intelligence in public administration for forecasting high crime risk transportation areas in urban environment. Transp. Res. Procedia **24**, 467–473 (2017)

15. de Sousa, W.G., de Melo, E.R.P., Bermejo, P.H.D.S., Farias, R.A.S., Gomes, A.O.: How and where is artificial intelligence in the public sector going? A literature review and research agenda. Gov. Inf. Q. **36**(4), 101392 (2019)

16. Kaarbo, J., Beasley, R.K.: A practical guide to the comparative case study method in political psychology. Polit. Psychol. **20**(2), 369–391 (1999)

17. Yin, R.: Case Study Research. SAGE Publications, California (2014)

18. Leveraging AI in the public sector with open data| European Data Portal. https://www.europe andataportal.eu/en/highlights/leveraging-ai-public-sector-open-data. Accessed 20 Mar 2020

19. Checkland, P.: Systems thinking: Rethinking management information systems (1999)

20. Starr, M.K.: Evolving concepts in production management. Acad. Manag. Proc. **1964**(1), 128–133 (1964)

21. David, S.: Bushnell: Input, process, output: a model for evaluating training. Train. Dev. J. **44**(3), 41–44 (1990)

22. Mathisen, G.E., Martinsen, Ø., Einarsen, S.: The relationship between creative personality composition, innovative team climate, and team innovativeness: an input - process - output perspective. J. Creat. Behav. **42**(1), 13–31 (2008)

23. Arfina Osman, F.: Public policy making: theories and their implications in developing countries. Asian Affairs **24**(3), 37–52 (2002)

24. Zuiderwijk, A., Janssen, M.: Open data policies, their implementation and impact: a framework for comparison. Gov. Inf. Q. **31**(1), 17–29 (2014)

25. Berners-Lee, T.: Linked data-Design issues (2006). http://www.w3.org/DesignIssues/Linked Data.html

26. Sébastien, M., Muriel, F., Slim, T., Madjid, I.: Open data: barriers, risks and opportunities. In: Proceedings of the 13th European Conference on eGovernment, pp. 301–309 (2013)

27. Sieber, R.E., Johnson, P.A.: Civic open data at a crossroads: dominant models and current challenges. Gov. Inf. Q. **32**(3), 308–315 (2015)

28. Bakici, T., Almirall, E., Wareham, J.: The role of public open innovation intermediaries in local government and the public sector. Technol. Anal. Strateg. Manag. **25**(3), 311–327 (2013)

29. Al-Hakim, L.: Information Quality Management: Theory and Applications. IGI Global, Hershey (2007)

30. Butler, D.: When Google got flu wrong. US outbreak foxes a leading web-based method for tracking seasonal flu. Nature **494**(7436), 155–156 (2013)

31. Osman, I.H., Anouze, A.L., Irani, Z., Lee, H., Medeni, T.D., Weerakkody, V.: A cognitive analytics management framework for the transformation of electronic government services from users' perspective to create sustainable shared values. Eur. J. Oper. Res. **278**(2), 514–532 (2019)

32. McDermott, P.: Building open government. Gov. Inf. Q. **27**(4), 401–413 (2010)

33. Li, T., Li, N.: On the tradeoff between privacy and utility in data publishing. In: Proceedings of the ACM SIGKDD International Conference on Knowledge Discovery and Data Mining, pp. 517–525. ACM Press, New York (2009)
34. Janssen, M., Kuk, G.: The challenges and limits of big data algorithms in technocratic governance. Gov. Inf. Q. **33**(3), 371–377 (2016)

Identifying Risks in Datasets
for Automated Decision–Making

Mariachiara Mecati$^{(\boxtimes)}$ (ID), Flavio Emanuele Cannavò, Antonio Vetrò (ID),
and Marco Torchiano (ID)

Politecnico di Torino, Turin, Italy
mariachiara.mecati@polito.it

Abstract. Our daily life is profoundly affected by the adoption of automated decision making (ADM) systems due to the ongoing tendency
of humans to delegate machines to take decisions. The unleashed usage
of ADM systems was facilitated by the availability of large-scale data,
alongside with the deployment of devices and equipment. This trend
resulted in an increasing influence of ADM systems' output over several
aspects of our life, with possible discriminatory consequences towards
certain individuals or groups. In this context, we focus on input data by
investigating measurable characteristics which can lead to discriminating
automated decisions. In particular, we identified two indexes of heterogeneity and diversity, and tested them on two datasets. A limitation we
found is the index sensitivity to a large number of categories, but on the
whole results show that the indexes reflect well imbalances in the input
data. Future work is required to further assess the reliability of these
indexes as indicators of discrimination risks in the context of ADM, in
order to foster a more conscious and responsible use of ADM systems
through an immediate investigation on input data.

Keywords: Bias · Data quality · Data ethics · Imbalance measures ·
Algorithm fairness

1 Introduction: Background and Motivations

Our daily life is profoundly affected by the development and adoption of automated decision making (ADM) systems [15]. This is due to the ongoing tendency
of humans to make decisions based on software-elaborated recommendations or
even to entirely delegate decision-making to machines. The adopted technical
approaches range from sophisticate neural networks to simpler software systems
that calculate and sort data according to predefined sets of rules.

A crucial enabling factor for these systems is the wide availability of data:
ADM systems are widely used to predict behaviours and classify individuals
depending on patterns extracted from the data collected about them or other
persons. The growing employment of these systems gives rise to both opportunities

G. Viale Pereira et al. (Eds.): EGOV 2020, LNCS 12219, pp. 332–344, 2020.
https://doi.org/10.1007/978-3-030-57599-1_25

and risks at the same time. Opportunities usually concern improved efficiency of the automated decision processes; on the other hand, one of the main risks is represented by data and algorithm bias, which usually induces systemic discrimination. Generally speaking, discrimination can be defined as an "unjustified distinction of individuals based on their membership, or perceived membership, in a certain group or category" [10]. Since biased software is software that exposes a group (e.g. an ethnic minority, gender, or type of worker) to an unfair treatment [21], an algorithm - often in order to achieve its optimization purposes - might discriminate and filter between people under consideration, with the result of a disparate impact on different population groups.

A large amount of evidence of discrimination by ADM systems has been recently collected in both scientific literature and journalistic investigations. Herein we rely on such body of evidence and we select only a few cases of discrimination caused by ADM systems; we are not proving here a complete review of the literature on automated discrimination, simply, we wish to highlight their impact on citizens' life. In a recent analysis of **risk assessment for juvenile justice** in Catalonia [22], the machine learning model marked male defendants and people of some specific national group as recidivist more frequently than others. Based on this discrimination problem, researchers suggested a method to assess predictive performance and unfairness in Machine Learning algorithms employed in the prediction of juvenile recidivism; then, the obtained results have been compared to Structured Assessment of Violence Risk in Youth (SAVRY), a widespread risk assessment tool employed to assess the risk of violence in juvenile justice. Researchers proposed two metrics in order to evaluate fairness: demographic parity and error rate balance. They discovered that machine learning algorithms become discriminatory when adopting SAVRY demographic features: male defendants were more likely to be classified as recidivists and foreigners were more likely to be labelled as high risk although they were non-recidivists.

Another example is represented by the "**Black box Schufa**" [18]. Schufa, which is the most well-known credit agency in Germany, asserts to have information on more than 67 million consumers and to output a score for each of them. Telecom providers, retailers, and even banks rely on these scores to support their business, ranging from determining which customers might get a loan, to which user get to see a certain ad. Thanks to a crowdsourcing project which involved 2,800 volunteers who asked Schufa for their free personal credit report, researchers reverse-engineered how Schufa works and found that younger people are often evaluated worse than older people. The same happens to males, worse ranked than females. The problem derives from the fact that the General Equal Treatment Act, whose purpose is to protect consumers from discrimination based on gender and age, is ineffective with regard to credit bureaus, so age and gender are legally but unfairly included in the score.

A third representative case is in the field of image classification, and specifically **facial recognition systems**, which has collected a lot of critics not only for the problem of discrimination, but also for the technology per se. The case concerns commercial gender classification: in [8] the authors revealed how automated facial image analysis is affected by performance disparity in gender and race: in particular, the gender classification on female faces works significantly worse than classification on male faces, and performance are better on lighter skin tones than darker ones.

Lastly, it is worthy to mention the "Report of the Special rapporteur on extreme poverty and human rights" [1], released by the United Nations clearly disapprove the way governments are actually automating welfare management, because the collected evidence showed that these systems systematically discriminate the weakest segments of society and exacerbate existing inequalities.

To conclude, the diffusion of ADM systems in a wide range of application domains has raised serious concerns about discriminatory impact towards certain individuals or social groups. Despite existing anti-discrimination laws in several countries forbid – for certain business and government services – unfair treatment of people based on the so-called sensitive attributes (i.e. specific traits of a person such as gender and race), this is not enough to mitigate the problem: fairness and bias in ADM systems remain an open and relevant issue [17]. These problems emerge in large part due to imbalanced datasets [6], mainly because machine learning systems search for certain patterns in the input data and apply them to new data.

In order to investigate this crucial aspect, in this paper we lay the foundations of a risk assessment approach based on quantitative measures to evaluate imbalance in the input datasets of ADM systems. Specifically, we use two indexes of heterogeneity and diversity to identify imbalance in two datasets that lead to disparate impact when used to feed an ADM. Our preliminary observations confirm that the indexes can be used as indicators of risks in datasets for ADM. The paper is organized as follows. In Sect. 2 we discuss the idea of imbalance metrics as risk indicators, motivated by the conceptual framework provided by the series of ISO/IEC standards on Software Quality Requirements and Evaluation (SQuaRE). In Sect. 3 we describe our approach, the selected metrics and the datasets we employed to conduct our exploratory study. Then, in Sect. 4 we report the results and discuss then. We take into account the limitations of this approach in Sect. 6 and, eventually, we highlight conclusions and potential future work in Sect. 7.

2   Imbalance in Datasets as Risk Indicator

Discrimination carried out by ADM systems is often due to imbalance in the frequencies of certain sensitive attributes in the datasets used as input (e.g., for training a machine learning algorithm) [6]. This chain of effects can be interpreted in light of the conceptual model of the series of standards ISO/IEC 25000, also known as SQuaRE [12], where both the internal software quality and the data quality have an impact on the external software quality, which in turn impact the users -active or passive- in the contexts in which the software is employed (quality in use). Figure 1 represents the chain of effects formalized in SQuaRE. A simplification of this concept is the well-known GIGO principle (i.e. "garbage in, garbage out"), which states that flawed input data produces garbage as output.

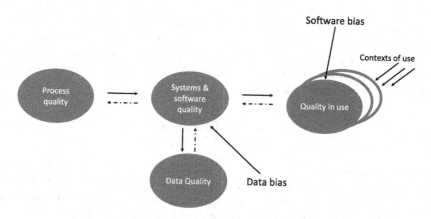

Fig. 1. Data/software bias in the context of quality effects conceptualized in SQuaRE

We use this concept and we propose that bias in the input datasets should be measured because it has the same propagation effects that data quality issues have, and can cause biased outputs, as most of today software-automated decisions are based on the analysis of historical data.

In practice, imbalanced datasets may lead to imbalanced results, generating problems of representativity when the data are sampled - therefore leading to an underestimation or an overestimation of the population groups - and of imbalance when the dataset used has not been generated using classical sampling methods.

Taking as reference this simple conceptual framework, we propose a metric-based approach to evaluate imbalance in a given dataset as a proxy of risk of biased output from ADM systems.

3   Exploratory Study

We conducted a study aimed at answering the following research question:

Are imbalance measures on a dataset able to reveal a discrimination risk when an ADM is trained with such data?

3.1   Metrics

In this study we focus on *categorical* and we propose two indicators of imbalance in data. The first one is the Gini index [9], a measure of *heterogeneity* used in many disciplines and often discussed with different designations: examples are political polarization, market competition, ecological diversity. Heterogeneity reflects how many different types (such as protected groups) are represented. In statistics, the heterogeneity of a discrete random variable R, which assumes m categories c_j with frequency f_j (with $j = 1, ..., m$), varies between a degenerate (=minimum value of heterogeneity) and an equiprobable case (=maximum value of heterogeneity, since categories are all equally represented). This means that for a given m, the heterogeneity increases if probabilities become as equal as possible, i.e. the different protected groups have similar representations. The Gini index is computed as follows:

$$I = \frac{m}{m-1} \cdot \left(1 - \sum_{i=1}^{m} f_i^2\right) \tag{1}$$

where we multiply by $\frac{m}{m-1}$ in order to normalize the index. According to the formula, the closer the index to 1 and the higher the heterogeneity is (i.e. categories have similar frequencies), and viceversa index closer to 0 means more concentration of frequencies in few categories, thus lower heterogeneity.

The second aspect used to measure imbalance is the *diversity*. Diversity indexes provide information about community composition taking the relative amounts of different species (classes) into account. We use the Shannon index, which is a measure of species diversity in a community and is calculated in this way: the proportion of species j relative to the total number of species (p_j) is computed, and then multiplied by the natural logarithm of this proportion ($\ln p_j$). The resulting product is summed across species and multiplied by -1. Then, we divide by $\ln m$ in order to normalize the index as follows:

$$H = -\left(\frac{1}{\ln m}\right) \sum_{j=1}^{m} p_j \ln p_j \tag{2}$$

Values of normalized Shannon index close to 1 indicate higher diversity (classes have similar frequencies) while values closer to 0 indicate less diversity (because frequencies are concentrated in fewer classes). To summarize:

> The closer the Gini/Shannon index to 0, the more data is affected by imbalance and the higher is the risk that such imbalance would cause effects in the output of an ADM system.

3.2 Data

We tested two datasets, each referring to a different application domain.

- **Credit card default dataset.** This dataset contains information on default payments, demographic factors, credit data, history of payment, and bill statements of credit card clients in Taiwan from April 2005 to September

2005 [14]. The dataset is composed by 25 variables of which four have demographic character and can be considered as protected attributes (i.e.: sex, age, education and marital status).

- **COMPAS Recidivism racial bias dataset.** Data contains variables used by the COMPAS algorithm in scoring criminal defendants in Broward County (Florida), along with their outcomes within two years of the decision. The original dataset contains 28 variables; in particular, eight of such variables are considered as protected attributes: first name, last name, middle name, sex, race, date of birth, spoken language, marital status [2].

We chose the COMPAS dataset because it is well-known it the scientific communities that study measures of algorithmic bias and related mitigation strategies. It was provided by the U.S. non-profit organization ProPublica that showed that the COMPAS algorithm is distorted in favor of white individuals, thus exposing black people to a risk of distorted recidivism. ProbPublica investigation[1] showed that one of the motivations for discriminations was that input data is highly imbalanced (e.g., black defendants are many more than white defendants).

The credit card default dataset was chosen because of the high impact of using ADM software in this domain (see motivations in the Introduction), and that particular dataset because of popularity: at the time of the research, it was ranked as the second most voted dataset on credit cards on Kaggle[2] and it fits better our study than the one ranked first (Credit Card Fraud Detection), which is based on transactions, while we are interested on datasets that collect data on persons. Differently than COMPAS, the credit card default dataset does not contain a pre-computed classification, so we trained a classifier with a portion of the data and ran it on the remainder, observing also in this case a problem of discrimination (although less evident than in COMPAS): details are reported in the next section and for reproducibility purposes we share data, code and environment in a permanent location [16].

4   Results and Discussion

We report results of applying the indexes on selected columns of the datasets in Table 1: the first two columns indicate the input dataset and sensitive attributes, while Gini index and Shannon index are reported in the third and fourth columns. Note that we normalize these two indexes between 0 and 1 in order to ensure their comparability, and we exclude missing values (NA) from our analysis. We report also the distributions of each class, as basis for interpretation and discussion in figures from Figs. 2, 3, 4 and 5.

---

[1] https://www.propublica.org/article/how-we-analyzed-the-compas-recidivism-algorithm, last visited on May 29, 2020.

[2] https://www.kaggle.com/datasets?search=credit+card&sort=votes, last visited on May 29, 2020.

For the credit card dataset, we report data for the following variables: sex, education, marital status and age, expressed as a percentage for each of their categories. For the COMPAS dataset we report data for the attributes ethnicity, sex and age category (which includes three age classes, i.e. "Less than 25", "25–45", "Greater than 45").

The rightmost two columns of Table 1 report the fairness test based on the separation criterion (equivalence of true positive and false positive for each level of the protected attributed under analysis, as formalized in [4]) and computed with respected to the protected attributes which lowest indexes (hence, higher risk of discrimination if bias is propagated): "marital status" for the credit card default dataset and "ethnicity" for COMPAS, which has a tie with "sex" but it is preferred because of the findings of the Pro Publica study. We found that the separation criterion was only partially met in the case of "marital status" -no difference between False Positive rates, but 8% difference for true positive- and not met at all in the case of "ethnicity" in COMPAS: computation is reproducible at [16].

Credit Card Dataset. In the literature, issues related to ethical decisions often appear alongside the field of creditworthiness [19,23]. For this reason, some studies have been conducted and have recently shown that access to credit is indirectly modulated by certain attributes such as race, rather than by information about the payer's status [5,7]. The dataset that we analyzed does not contain the protected attribute race, but contains other personal information, notably sex, level of education, age, marital status. The data show that 60.4% of individ-

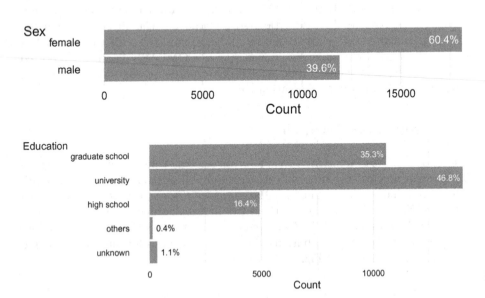

Fig. 2. Frequency histograms for the classes of the protected attributes SEX and EDU-CATION in the Credit card default dataset.

Table 1. Gini index and Shannon index for each protected attribute in the Default of credit card clients dataset and in the COMPAS dataset.

Dataset	Protected attribute	Gini index	Shannon index	Fairness (separation)	
				difference TP rates	difference FP rates
Default of credit card clients	*sex*	0.96	0.97		
	education	0.79	0.68		
	marital status	0.76	0.68	0.08	0
	age	0.98	0.88		
COMPAS	*ethnicity*	0.73	0.62	0.23	0.18
	sex	0.62	0.70		
	age category	0.87	0.89		

uals are women, 46.8% of individuals have attended university, the proportion of single individuals is predominant, and the most represented age is 29 years old. Looking at the single classes, for the protected attribute "**sex**" we found very high and similar indexes, suggesting a certain balance between the two classes (around 0.6 and 0.4 for female and male respectively). Then, we observe that categories "**education**" and "**marital status**" have most of data concentrated in certain categories (three out of five for education, two out of three for marital status): the corresponding two indexes assume values between 0.68 and 0.79, thus reflecting less heterogeneity and diversity than variable "sex". Finally, concerning the protected attribute "**age**", we note the presence of several categories with very different frequencies, which would lead to low values for Gini and Shannon indexes. By contrast, we obtained very high indexes: a feasible explanation is given by the fact that a very large number of categories is taken into account; as a consequence, occurrences are spread on all these categories, so that none of them present a distinct frequency on the whole. Indeed, in our frequency histogram we observe the typical shape of a right-skewed distribution. So, looking at such normal distribution, we can see the histogram as composed by several categories with high but similar frequencies (in the central region between around 20–25 and 40–45 years old), which may explain the high value indexes. Therefore, in presence of a large number of categories the behaviour of the indexes could be misleading and it would be recommended to aggregate - in a meaningful manner for the context at hand - the classes in fewer groups.

COMPAS Recidivism Racial Bias Dataset. Previous research has shown that the data in the COMPAS dataset is imbalanced in favor of white people and our investigation confirms the previous study [13]: the highest levels of reoffending are observed in black individuals. Indeed, analysis show very imbalanced data considering any of the selected protected classes. Concerning "**ethnicity**", about 34% of the dataset's observations refer to white people, while 51.4% refer to black people, indicating that there may be an overestimation of the race attribute -

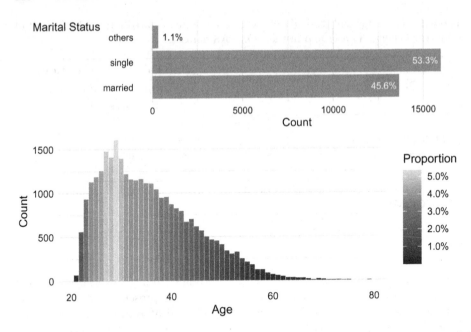

Fig. 3. Frequency histograms for the classes of the protected attributes MARITAL STATUS and AGE in the Credit card default dataset.

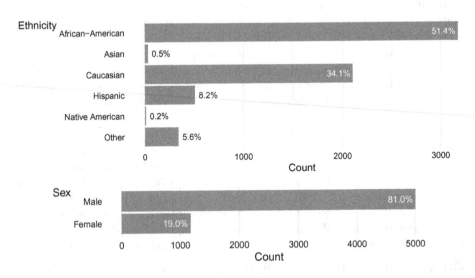

Fig. 4. Frequency histograms for the classes of the protected attributes ETHNICITY and SEX in the COMPAS dataset.

against black people - which would contribute to the estimation of recidivism, as suggested by the two indexes: 0.73 and 0.62 respectively for Gini and Shan-

Fig. 5. Frequency histogram for the classes of the protected attribute AGE CATE-GORY in the COMPAS dataset.

non confirmed medium level of heterogeneity and diversity. With respect to the protected attribute "**sex**", we note very different frequencies (81% and 19% for male and female respectively) that result in low value indexes, which reveal low heterogeneity and diversity. Finally, as regards "**age category**" we obtained 0.87 and 0.89 respectively for Gini and Shannon indexes: indeed, we observe that the distribution is principally concentrated on the class "25–45" (57.2%) but is almost equally distributed on the other two categories (~21% each one), so the indexes tend to be higher than expected.

5 Related Work

To date, approaches similar to ours are in the direction of labelling datasets for ethical indication purposes. One consists in a collaboration between MIT Media Lab and the Berkman Klein Center at Harvard University, which resulted in "The Dataset Nutrition Label Project" [20]. This initiative aims at avoiding that flawed, incomplete, skewed or problematic data have a negative impact on automated decision systems.

A similar approach is the "Ethically and socially-aware labeling" (EASAL) [6], in which authors propose a conceptual and operational framework to label datasets and identify possible risks of discriminatory output when used in decision making or decision support systems. Thus, it aims to plan and develop datasets metadata to help software engineers to be aware of the risks of discrimination.

Yet another labelling approach is proposed by Gebru et al., "Datasheets for Datasets" [11]: with respect to the previous proposals, this research work consists of more discursive technical sheets for the purpose of encouraging an increasingly clear and comprehensive communication between users of a dataset and its creators.

Finally, although in a different field, it is worth to mention "DataTags - Share Sensitive Data with Confidence" [3], a project conducted by members of the Privacy Tools project in collaboration with the IQSS Dataverse team. The goal of DataTags is to support researchers who are not legal or technical experts in investigating considerations about proper handling of human subjects data, and make informed decisions when collecting, storing, and sharing sensitive data.

6   Limitations

As limitations of our approach we could highlight two main aspects. The first issue is related to the amount of data that has been taken into consideration: it would be recommended to retrieve a wider number of datasets with all the concerning information, with the aim of further understanding and assessing the reliability of this approach. We are confident that investigating on a wider amount of data could help to interpret more profoundly the suitability of the adopted indexes. In the second place, for the purpose of improving our approach based on quantitative measures, it would be advantageous to take into account other kinds of metrics, examining and comparing their performance with the Gini and Shannon indexes. More datasets and more metrics are necessary to generalize the findings of this exploratory work and being able to deeply understand whether indicators of imbalance are reliable to anticipate the risk for potential emergence of discriminatory behavior by ADM software, as it should be accurately tested the chain of effects through which imbalance propagates.

7   Conclusions and Future Work

We presented a metric-based approach for detecting risks of biased output from automated decision making systems due to imbalance in the input data. The rational of this approach builds upon the conceptual framework of ISO SQuaRE standard series, in which a chain of quality effects is described: internal software quality and data quality have effect on external software quality, which in turn has effect on the quality in use and in the socio-technical context where software is used. Following this line of reasoning, and in line with the well known GIGO principle ("garbage in garbage out"), our hypothesis is that bias on input data will probably cause biased output data: in terms of automated decision systems, this would lead to potential discriminatory outputs.

We identified a heterogeneity index and a diversity index to measure the level of imbalance of the values of sensitive attributes and tested them on two datasets. The results showed that these indexes are able to represent imbalance in datasets that exposed problems of biased outputs. We also observed that the indexes are sensitive to the number of categories in the data: the indexes were not well reflecting the imbalance of attributes with a large number of classes.

In future work we want to test the indexes on a much larger number of datasets. Furthermore, we will enlarge the set of indexes and we aim to test this approach on real cases of automated decision making, with a view to understanding when the underlying hypothesis of the chain of effects holds.

References

1. Alston, P.: Report of the special rapporteur on extreme poverty and human rights, October 2019. https://undocs.org/A/74/493

2. Angwin, J., Larson, J., Mattu, S., Kirchner, L.: COMPAS Recidivism Racial Bias, propublica/compas-analysis (2016). https://github.com/propublica/compas-analysis/blob/master/compas-scores-two-years.csv
3. Bar-Sinai, M., Sweeney, L., Crosas, M.: Datatags, data handling policy spaces and the tags language. In: 2016 IEEE Security and Privacy Workshops (SPW), pp. 1–8, May 2016. https://doi.org/10.1109/SPW.2016.11
4. Barocas, S., Hardt, M., Narayanan, A.: Fairness and Machine Learning. fairmlbook.org (2019). http://www.fairmlbook.org
5. Bartlett, R., Morse, A., Stanton, R., Wallace, N.: Consumer-lending discrimination in the fintech era. Technical report, National Bureau of Economic Research (2019)
6. Beretta, Elena., Vetrò, Antonio., Lepri, Bruno, De Martin, Juan Carlos: Ethical and socially-aware data labels. In: Lossio-Ventura, Juan Antonio, Muñante, Denisse, Alatrista-Salas, Hugo (eds.) SIMBig 2018. CCIS, vol. 898, pp. 320–327. Springer, Cham (2019). https://doi.org/10.1007/978-3-030-11680-4_30
7. Breiling, L.: Opinion — The Race-Based Mortgage Penalty - The New York Times (2018). https://www.nytimes.com/2018/03/07/opinion/mortage-minority-income.html
8. Buolamwini, J., Gebru, T.: Gender shades: intersectional accuracy disparities in commercial gender classification. In: Conference on Fairness, Accountability and Transparency, pp. 77–91 (2018)
9. Capecchi, Stefania, Iannario, Maria: Gini heterogeneity index for detecting uncertainty in ordinal data surveys. METRON **74**(2), 223–232 (2016). https://doi.org/10.1007/s40300-016-0088-5
10. Friedman, B., Nissenbaum, H.: Bias in computer systems. ACM Trans. Inf. Syst. **14**(3), 330–347 (1996). https://doi.org/10.1145/230538.230561, http://doi.acm.org/10.1145/230538.230561
11. Gebru, T., et al.: Datasheets for datasets. arXiv preprint arXiv:1803.09010 (2018)
12. ISO: ISO/IEC 25000:2005 (2005). http://www.iso.org/cms/render/live/en/sites/isoorg/contents/data/standard/03/56/35683.html
13. Angwin, J., Larson, J., Mattu, S., Kirchner, L.: Machine Bias—ProPublica (2016). https://www.propublica.org/article/machine-bias-risk-assessments-in-criminal-sentencing
14. UCI Machine Learning: Default of credit card clients dataset (2016). https://www.kaggle.com/uciml/default-of-credit-card-clients-dataset
15. Matzat, L.: Atlas of Automation. Technical report, Algorithm Watch (2019)
16. Mecati, M., Cannavò, F.E., Vetrò, A., Torchiano, M.: Reproducibility package for identifying risks in datasets for automated decision-making (2020). https://dx.doi.org/10.24433/CO.5067135.v2
17. O'Neil, C.: Weapons of Math Destruction: How Big Data Increases Inequality and Threatens Democracy. Broadway Books, New York (2016)
18. Schufa: So funktioniert Deutschlands einflussreichste Auskunftei - DER SPIEGEL (2018). https://www.spiegel.de/consent-a-?targetUrl=https%3A%2F%2Fwww.spiegel.de%2Fwirtschaft%2Fservice%2Fschufa-so-funktioniert-deutschlands-einflussreichste-auskunftei-a-1239214.html
19. Rice, L., Swesnik, D.: Discriminatory effects of credit scoring on communities of color. Suffolk UL Rev. **46**, 935 (2013)
20. Ross, H., Bassoff, N.W.: The "Dataset Nutrition Label Project" Tackles Dataset Health and Standards (2019). https://medium.com/berkman-klein-center/the-dataset-nutrition-label-project-tackles-dataset-health-and-standards-658dc162dfbb

21. Rovatsos, M., Mittelstadt, B., Koene, A.: Landscape summary: bias in algorithmic decision-making. Technical report, Centre for Data Ethics and Innovation (CDEI) (2019)
22. Tolan, S., Miron, M., Gómez, E., Castillo, C.: Why machine learning may lead to unfairness: evidence from risk assessment for juvenile justice in Catalonia. In: Proceedings of the 17th International Conference on Artificial Intelligence and Law, ICAIL 2019, pp. 83–92. Association for Computing Machinery, New York (2019). https://doi.org/10.1145/3322640.3326705
23. Yang, T.: Choice and fraud in racial identification: the dilemma of policing race in affirmative action, the census, and a color-blind society. Mich. J. Race Law **11**, 367 (2005)

Using Government Data and Machine Learning for Predicting Firms' Vulnerability to Economic Crisis

Euripidis Loukis[1]([⊠]), Niki Kyriakou[1], and Manolis Maragoudakis[2]

[1] University of the Aegean, Samos, Greece
{eloukis,nkyr}@aegean.gr
[2] Ionian University, Corfu, Greece
mmarag@ionio.gr

Abstract. The COVID-19 pandemic is expected to lead to a severe recessionary economic crisis with quite negative consequences for large numbers of firms and citizens; however, this is an 'old story': recessionary economic crises appear repeatedly in the last 100 years in the market-based economies, and they are recognized as one of the most severe and threatening weaknesses of them. They can result in closure of numerous firms, and decrease of activities of many more, as well as poverty and social exclusion for large parts of the population, and finally lead to political upheaval and instability; so they constitute one of the most threatening and difficult problems that governments often face. For the above reasons it is imperative that governments develop effective public policies and make drastic interventions for addressing these economic crises. Quite useful for these interventions can be the prediction of the vulnerability of individual firms to recessionary economic crisis, so that government can focus its attention as well as its scarce economic resources on the most vulnerable ones. In this direction our paper presents a methodology for using existing government data in order to predict the vulnerability of individual firms to economic crisis, based on Artificial Intelligence (AI) Machine Learning (ML) algorithms. Furthermore, a first application of the proposed methodology is presented, based on existing data from the Greek Ministry of Finance and Statistical Authority concerning 363 firms for the economic crisis period 2009–2014, which gives encouraging results.

Keywords: Economic crisis · Economic recession · Data analytics · Predictive analytics · Artificial Intelligence · Machine Learning

1 Introduction

The COVID-19 pandemic is expected to lead to a severe recessionary economic crisis with quite negative consequences for large numbers of firms and citizens, as containment and social distancing policies adopted in most countries will on one hand 'flatten' the medical curve of virus spread (which is quite positive), but on the other hand will 'steepen' the resulting recession curve (which will have quite negative economic and

© IFIP International Federation for Information Processing 2020
Published by Springer Nature Switzerland AG 2020
G. Viale Pereira et al. (Eds.): EGOV 2020, LNCS 12219, pp. 345–358, 2020.
https://doi.org/10.1007/978-3-030-57599-1_26

social consequences) [1]. However, this is an 'old story': recessionary economic crises of various intensities and durations appear repeatedly in the last 100 years in market-based economies, and are recognized as one of the most severe and threatening weaknesses of them, having quite negative consequences for the whole economy and society [2–7]. The fluctuations that economic activity usually exhibits, and also some critical events, such as banking crises (like the one that gave rise to the 2008 Global Financial Crisis), epidemics (like the COVID-19 one), large increases in the prices of important goods (e.g. oil or gas), etc., can lead to significant economic recessions, meant as serious contractions of economic activity, resulting in economic crises. These contractions of economic activity can lead to big reductions of firms' production, procurement, investment, innovation and employment [5–7], and also closure of numerous firms, with serious social consequences, such as increase of unemployment, poverty and social exclusion, resulting in political unrest and instability.

For these reasons economic crises constitute one of the most severe and threatening problems that governments often face and have strong pressure to deal with them effectively in order at least to avoid catastrophic consequences. So it is imperative that governments develop effective public policies and make drastic interventions for addressing these economic crises. The most usual of these interventions is the provision of various kinds of support to the most vulnerable firms in the beginning of such crises, or even earlier, when an economic crisis is in sight (i.e. when there are serious forecasts that an economic crisis is going to occur, like the ones currently made by serious economists and economic research centers that the COVID-19 pandemic will give rise to a severe recessionary economic crisis [1]). This support usually includes the provision to firms of low-interest loans, subsidies, education or consulting services, co-finance of investments or employees' payroll, tax reductions, etc. However, since the available government resources (e.g. financial, human, etc.) for providing such support to firms are usually limited, much below than the ones required for meeting the high demands (from the numerous firms that submit applications for receiving this support), a selection among the applicant firms has to be made; it is based on some predefined criteria, which usually concern firm's sector and location (according to existing sectoral and regional priorities), as well as sales and profits in the last 3–5 years, market share, export activities, debts, etc. It would be very good if to these criteria could be added firm's expected vulnerability to the crisis, as an additional criterion, aiming to provide more assistance and support to the most vulnerable firms; this can increase substantially the effectiveness of such interventions, making them more focused, and improve public value generation from them towards the reduction of the negative consequences of recessionary economic crises. For the above reasons it would be quite useful if we can make a prediction of the vulnerability of individual firms to economic crisis.

Given the high importance of firm-level economic crisis vulnerability prediction it is necessary to exploit for this purpose to the highest possible extent: a) existing firms' data from economic crisis periods in various government agencies (such as Ministries of Finance and Statistical Authorities); and b) the most sophisticated algorithms for 'learning' crisis vulnerability prediction models from such data, and especially the most widely used Artificial Intelligence (AI) algorithms for such 'predictive analytics': the

Machine Learning (ML) ones [8–12]. In this direction our paper presents a methodology for using existing government data in order to predict the vulnerability of individual firms to economic crisis, based on their particular characteristics (concerning strategic directions, processes, human and technological resources, structures) using ML. Furthermore, a first application of the proposed methodology is presented, based on existing data from the Greek Ministry of Finance and Statistical Authority concerning 363 firms for the economic crisis period 2009–2014, which gives encouraging results.

In the following Sect. 2 the background of our methodology is outlined, while in Sect. 3 the methodology is described, followed by its abovementioned application in Sect. 4. The final Sect. 5 summarizes conclusions and proposes directions for future research.

2 Background

2.1 Economic Crises

As mentioned in the Introduction one of the most serious problems of market-based economies are the economic recessions that repeatedly appear, which cause significant disruptions and problems to the economy and the society in general, and have to be addressed by government through effective public policies including appropriate interventions [2–7]. The economic crises have negative both short-term as well as medium- and long-term consequences for the economy and the society. The short-term consequences include reductions of the demand for many goods and services, resulting in serious decrease of firms' sales, production and profits, leading to reductions in personnel employment (thus increasing unemployment) and materials' procurement (thus propagating the crisis towards the suppliers' sectors, etc., spreading the crisis to large parts of the economy). Furthermore, during economic crises firms usually reduce capital investment in production equipment, ICT, buildings, etc., and also in product, service and process innovations; this reduces the degree of renewal and improvement of their equipment, products, services and operation, as well as the exploitation of emerging new technologies, which causes serious medium- and long-term consequences for their efficiency and competitiveness.

Considerable research has been conducted concerning the negative impact of such recessionary economic crises on different aspects of firms' activities and performance, as well as the factors that affect the magnitude of this negative impact [13–19]. It has concluded that the above negative consequences of the economic crises differ significantly among firms, and depend critically on their individual characteristics, such as their human and technological resources, their strategic orientations, etc. Some firms have superior human and technological resources, as well as management structures, that allow them to be more efficient and effective during difficult crisis periods; these firms are able to offer higher value-for-money products and services during the crisis, and in general have higher capacity to make the required adaptations to the crisis conditions, which make them less vulnerable and more resilient to the crisis. Such firms have less negative consequences on their sales revenue, and therefore on their employment, procurement, as well as capital investment and innovation. For some other firms the opposite holds. Therefore it would be interesting to investigate the capabilities of

AI/ML algorithms to predict firm's vulnerability to recessionary economic crisis based on its particular characteristics, e.g. concerning its human and technological resources, management structures, etc.

2.2 Artificial Intelligence

Artificial Intelligence (AI) includes a group of techniques that enable computers to perform tasks of higher intelligence, approaching the human one, by learning from their environment, and then using the knowledge they have obtained from it for taking or proposing action [20–22]. The most representative and widely used AI techniques are definitely the Machine Learning (ML) ones [8–10]. They enable exploiting historic data we possess for a number of units (e.g. individuals, firms, etc.) concerning the value of an important dependent variable (usually an outcome one), and also a set of independent variables (that might be possible causes of this outcome or factors affecting it), by processing them through various algorithms, and finally extracting knowledge from them, usually having the form of a model or a set of rules, concerning the relationships between the independent variables and the dependent one (this is usually referred to as 'model training', while the historic data used for this purpose as 'training data'). This knowledge can be used then on one hand for gaining deeper understanding and insight about these relationships, and on the other hand for predicting the value of the dependent variable for new units, based on the known values of the independent variables, which can be quite useful for supporting relevant decisions or optimizing actions.

Initially AI was used successfully in the private sector, and these 'success stories' generated high levels of interest to exploit AI techniques in the public sector as well, in order to automate or support more sophisticated mental tasks than the simpler routine ones automated or supported by the traditional operational IS of government agencies [23–27]. Some first research has been conducted concerning the exploitation of AI in a variety of public sector thematic domains, such as education, policing, justice, public health, transport, etc. [28–33]. However, this research has revealed and investigated only a small part of the large potential of AI use in government. Therefore, much more research is required in order to exploit more this potential, in order to reveal and investigate more opportunities and methodologies for AI exploitation in government, in a wide variety of public sector thematic domains. Our study makes a contribution in this direction, by developing a methodology for using AI (ML algorithms) in a highly important domain of government activity: the intervention of government for addressing the quite threatening recessionary economic crises that repeatedly appear in market-based economies and cause major disruptions and problems.

3 The Proposed Methodology

As mentioned in Sect. 2.1 previous research concerning the negative impact of recessionary economic crises on firms has found that its magnitude differs significantly among firms, depending on their particular characteristics, such as their human and technological resources, management structures, etc. Furthermore, previous management science research has identified the main elements of a firm that determine its performance; so we can expect that these main elements might determine to a considerable extent firm's performance during the crisis in coping with the difficult recession conditions as well, and therefore the degree of its resilience/vulnerability to the crisis. Several conceptualizations of the main elements of a firm have been developed, the most widely validated and used among them being definitely the 'Leavitt's Diamond' framework [34]. According to it the most important elements of a firm that determine its performance are: a) task (=the strategies as well as the administrative and production processes of the firm); b) people (=the skills of firm's human resources of the firm); c) technology (=the technologies used for implementing the above processes); and d) structure (=the organization of the firm in departments, and the communication and coordination patterns them). An extension of it has been developed subsequently, which analyses the above 'task' element into 'strategy' and 'processes' [35]. Therefore we expect that firm's characteristics concerning the above five main elements (strategy, processes, people, technology and structure) might be good predictors of its crisis resilience/vulnerability. Government traditionally collects large amounts of data concerning firms' economic performance (the Taxation Authorities) and also firms' characteristics concerning human resources, use of various technologies (e.g. ICT or various production technologies), organization, innovation and other strategic orientations, etc. (the Statistical Authorities). It is quite useful to exploit these existing government data from economic crisis periods in order to construct firm-level crisis resilience/vulnerability prediction models based on firm's characteristics.

In particular, using government firm-level data from an economic crisis period concerning:

- on one hand firms' resilience/vulnerability to the crisis (e.g. data from Taxation Authorities concerning decrease of sales revenue, profitability, employment, etc. during the crisis)
- and on the other hand characteristics of the same firms concerning the above main elements (e.g. relevant data collected from Statistical Authorities),

We can train/construct prediction models of the resilience/vulnerability of a firm to recessionary economic crisis (to be used as dependent variable Y), based on the above characteristics of it (to be used as independent variables Xi); for this purpose we can use several different alternative ML algorithms [8–10], such as Decision Trees, Random Forests, Gradient Boosted Trees, Support Vector Machines, Generalized Linear Modelling, etc., and finally select among them the one providing the highest prediction accuracy. The constructed model can be used for predicting the value of the resilience/vulnerability of an individual firm to future economic crisis Y (taking into account that all economic crises, despite their differences, have in common their main characteristics: economic recession, contraction of economic activity and decrease of demand for products and services of most sectors) for which we have the values of the abovementioned characteristics Xi. The structure of the proposed methodology is shown in Fig. 1.

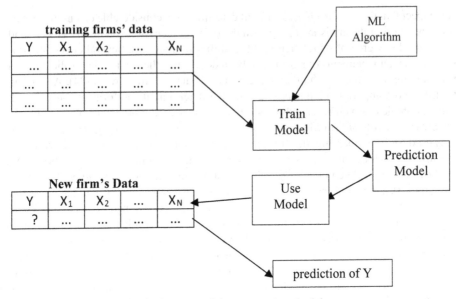

Fig. 1. Structure of the proposed methodology

Our methodology will use existing government data from two main sources:

I)   Data from Taxation Authorities for a large number of firms concerning the decrease of sales revenue, profits or other measures of economic performance during the economic crisis
II) Data from Statistical Authorities about characteristics of the same firms concerning the above five main elements of them:

- Strategic orientations: characteristics concerning the degree of adoption of the main strategies described in relevant strategic management literature [36], such as cost leadership, differentiation, focus, innovation, export, etc.
- Processes: characteristics of firm's processes, such as complexity, efficiency, formality, flexibility, etc.
- Human Resources: characteristics concerning the general education/skills level of firm's human resources (e.g. shares of firm's personnel having tertiary education, vocational/technical education, etc.), as well as the possession of specific skills concerning important technologies (e.g. concerning ICTs or various production technologies), the provision of various kinds of training, etc.
- Technology: characteristics concerning the use of the main enterpsise ICTs, such as Enterprise Resource Planning (ERP), Customer Relationships Management (CRM), Supply Chain Management (SCM), Business Intelligence/Business Analytics (BI/BA) systems, Collaboration Support (CS), e-sales, etc. systems, and also social media, cloud computing, or other technologies, or the use of various production technologies.

- Structure: characteristics concerning various aspects of the management structure of the firm, such as its main structural design (functional, product/service based, geographic, matrix), degree of differentiation, specialization, centralization-decentralization, or the use of organic structural forms (such as teamwork or job rotation) [37, 38].

Furthermore, we can also include general data about each firm, such as sector, degree of competiveness in this sector (in comparison with the other competitor firms), etc.

4 Application

A first application of the proposed methodology has been made, using firm-level data for the period 2009–2014 from the Ministry of Finance – Taxation Authorities as well as the Statistical Authority of Greece, in order to construct a prediction model of the most important measure of firm's vulnerability to the crisis, the reduction of sales revenue due to economic crisis, based on firm's characteristics. In particular, we used data provided by the Ministry of Finance – Taxation Authorities concerning the percentage of sales revenue reduction due to the economic crisis in the period 2009–2014 (dependent variable) of 400 Greek firms; these data were discretized by the Ministry of Finance (in order to avoid providing detailed firm's sales revenue data) into a variable with 13 possible discrete values (SALREV_RED): increase by more than 100%; increase by 80–100%; increase by 60–80%; increase by 40–60%; increase by 20–40%; increase by 1–20%; unchanged sales; decrease by 1–20%; decrease by 20–40%; decrease by 40–60%; decrease by 60–80%; decrease by 80–100%; decrease by more than 100%. For 363 of these firms from the Statistical Authority we found data concerning 43 characteristics of them (independent variables), which concern their strategic orientations (12 variables), human resources (9 variables), technology (16 variables), structure (1 variable) and also general characteristics (5 variables). The definitions – corresponding questions for our dependent and independent variables are shown in the Appendix. These 363 firms cover a wide range of sectors and sizes: 40.2% of them were from manufacturing sectors, 9.4% from constructions, and 50.4% from services sectors; also, 52.6% of them were small, 36.1% medium and 11.3% large ones.

Using the above data we constructed prediction models of SALREV_RED based on the above mentioned 43 firm characteristics. Since the dependent variable is ordinal, with a large number of values (13) and equal distances between them, it approaches a continuous variable, we have constructed and compared prediction models of SALREV_RED using the main alternative ML algorithms proposed by relevant literature [8–10] for the case that the dependent variable is continuous: the classical regression (termed as 'Generalized Linear Model') and also four alternative more advanced statistical methods:

- Decision Trees, which splits the initial training set into more homogeneous sub-sets using the most appropriate independent variables, and finally construct a decision tree with internal 'decision nodes' concerning some of the independent variables (the most useful as predictors) – actually tests concerning these independent variables – as well as leaf 'terminal nodes' that include predicted values of the dependent variable [9, 40];

- Random Forests, which creates a pool of decision trees based on sub-sets of the training data set, and then gets the prediction from each of them and finally selects the best prediction by means of 'voting' of these decision trees [39, 40];
- Gradient Boosted Trees, which is based on boosting prediction accuracy through the combination of a learning algorithm in a series, in order to achieve a 'strong learner' from many sequentially connected 'weak learners'; usually the weak learners are decision trees, and consequtive decision trees are constructed, with each new tree attempting to minimize the errors of the previous tree [41];
- Support Vector Machines, which mqp each training data item as a point in n-dimensional space, where n is number of independent variables; then, the algorithm tries to find hyper-plane that best fits the available training data [40, 42].

For each of these five ML algorithms we calculated its mean absolute error, which is according to relevant ML literature the recommended measure of prediction accuracy for the case that the dependent variable is continuous, using the k-fold cross-validation procedure (we selected k = 10), which includes the following steps [8–10, 40]:

a)   the data set is divided randomly in k equally sized partitions,
b)   then we estimate the prediction model k times, in each of them using one of these segments as test data, and the remaining ones as training data,
c)   and finally the absolute prediction error is estimated as the mean of the prediction errors over the test sets of the above k runs.

In Fig. 2 we can see the estimated mean absolute prediction errors of these five ML algorithms. We can see that the examined algorithms have similar levels of prediction performance/error (ranging from 1.422 to 1.572), with the Decision Trees algorithm exhibiting the lowest mean absolute error (1.422). This is a satisfactory prediction performance, given the small size of the dataset we have used (data from 363 firms), so

Absolute Error

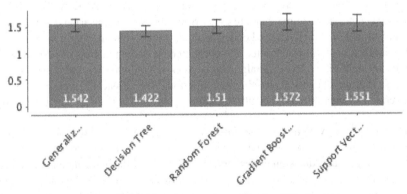

Fig. 2. Mean absolute prediction errors of the five ML algorithms

using a larger dataset (which is feasible, as Ministries of Finance – Taxation Authorities and Statistical Authorities have such data for quite large numbers of firms) can result in a smaller mean absolute error, and therefore an even more accurate prediction of the sales revenue reduction of a firm during an economic crisis.

5   Conclusions

In the previous sections has been described the development of a methodology for exploiting existing government data for economic crisis periods, in order to construct prediction models of individual firms' vulnerability to economic crises, based on Artificial Intelligence (AI) Machine Learning (ML) algorithms. In particular, it uses existing data for economic crisis periods, on one hand from Taxation Authorities (concerning firms' sales revenue, profits, employment, etc. decrease), and on the other hand from Statistical Authorities (concerning human and technological resources, structures, processes, strategic orientations, etc. of these firms); from these data prediction models can be trained/constructed, which enable the prediction of the vulnerability of a firm to future economic crises (e.g. in terms of sales revenue, profitability, employment, etc. decrease), based on firm's characteristics (concerning human and technological resources, structures, processes, strategic orientations, etc.). The prediction of the degree of vulnerability of a firm to economic crisis can be useful as a criterion in firm support programmes of government agencies, for the selection of the applicant firms that will receive support, as part of multi-criteria evaluation of applications, in combination with other selection criteria usually used in such programmes, such as sector, geographic location, sales, profits, market share, export activities, debts, etc.

The research described in this paper has interesting implications for both research and practice. With respect to research it creates new knowledge in the emerging areas of government data analytics and government AI exploitation, concerning a highly important domain of economic government activity/intervention, aiming to address the quite threatening recessionary economic crises that repeatedly appear in market-based economies and cause major disruptions and problems. With respect to practice it proposes a methodology of using existing historic government data for constructing prediction models of the vulnerability that individual firms will exhibit to future recessionary economic crises. These prediction models can be very useful to government agencies that implement firm support programs in the beginning of economic crises, or even earlier when crises are in sight, in order to use more effectively their available financial resources.

Future research is required towards: i) further application of the proposed methodology using larger datasets, in various different national contexts experiencing economic crises of different intensities, and also at sectoral level (using also sector specific independent variables); ii) investigation of the prediction performance of other ML algorithms, and especially Deep Learning ones; iii) analysis of the legal aspects of the practical application of the proposed methodology by government agencies, and especially with respect to the new EU GDPR (as the data used by our methodology have been collected by government for quite different purposes).

Appendix. Definitions/questions of the dependent and independent variables

Dependent variable	
SALREV_RED	Total percentage of change of your sales (increase or decrease) during the economic crisis of 2009–2014
Independent Variables – Strategic Orientations	
STRAT_CL	To what extent does your business strategy include low prices in comparison with the competition? (five levels ordinal variable)
STRAT_DIF	To what extent does your business strategy include high quality of products/services in comparison with the competition? (five levels ordinal variable)
STRAT_INNOV	To what extent does your business strategy include introduction of new products/services (with significant innovations)? (five levels ordinal variable)
INNOV_PRS	Over the last three years did your firm introduce product innovations (= new or significantly improved products)? (binary)
INNOV_PROC	Over the last three years did your firm introduce process innovations (= new or significantly improved processes)? (binary)
NEW_PS_P	What percentage of your total sales revenue (turnover) in 2014 came from new products/services that were introduced in the market during the three previous years? (continuous)
IMPR_PS_P	What percentage of the total sales revenue (turnover) in 2014 came from products/services that you had introduced before 2012, but were improved significantly over the last three years? (continuous)
INN_PRSD	Did you introduce methods/process innovation in the goods production or services' delivery processes in the last three years? (binary)
INN_SSWM	Did you introduce methods/process innovations in the sales, shipment or warehouse management processes? (binary)
INN_SUPP	Did you introduce methods/process innovations in the support processes (e.g. in the equipment maintenance ones) (binary)
R&D	Did your firm conduct R&D (Research and Development) in the last three years? (binary)
EXP_P	Percentage of exports in firm's sales revenue in 2014 (contin.)
Independent Variables – Human Resources	
EMPL	Number of employees at the end of 2014 (including any temporary employees, part-time, etc., who should be counted as full time equivalents) (continuous)
EMPL_TERT	Percentage of tertiary education graduates in the personnel of your firm (continuous)
EMPL_VOCT	Percentage of vocational/technical education graduates in the personnel of your firm (continuous)

(continued)

(continued)

EMPL_HIGH	Percentage of high school graduates in the personnel of your firm (continuous)
EMPL_ELEM	Percentage of elementary school graduates in the personnel of your firm (continuous)
EMPL_COM	What percentage of the employees of your firm use computer in their work (e.g. PC, terminal, or laptop)? (continuous)
EMPL_INTRA	What percentage of the employees of your firm uses the intranet (internal network) of the firm in their work the? (continuous)
EMPL_INTER	What percentage of the employees of your firm uses Internet in their work? (continuous)
EMPL_ICT	Percentage of qualified ICT personnel in the workforce of your firm (continuous)
Independent Variables – Technology	
D_ERP	To what extent are Enterprise Resource Planning (ERP) systems used in your firm? (five levels ordinal variable)
D_CRM	To what extent are Customer Relationship Management (CRM) systems used in your firm? (five levels ordinal variable)
D_SCM	To what extent are Supply Chain Management (SCM) systems (=systems that support the electronic exchange of information with customers, suppliers and business partners, such as inventory levels, orders, production, shipments, invoices, etc.) used in your firm? (five levels ordinal variable)
D_BIBA	To what extent are Business Intelligence/Business Analytics systems (=systems that support advanced forms of processing business data, which lead to the creation of useful reports, as well as various types of models that aim at the support of decision-making – this can be either a separate software, or a module of an ERP or CRM system) used in your firm? (five levels ordinal variable)
D_CS	To what extent are Collaboration support systems (=systems that support the internal collaboration between employees of the firm, and/or external collaboration with customers, suppliers and partners, offering capabilities of sharing various forms of content (e.g. text files, images), forum, instant messaging (and other forms of communication), project management, etc.) used in your firm? (five levels ordinal variable)
E-SAL	Do you conduct online sales of products/services through the Internet? (binary)
SM_SPRO	To what extent do you use social media for sales promotion? (five levels ordinal variable)
SM_OPCO	To what extent do you use social media in order to collect customers' opinions, comments and complaints about your products or services? (five levels ordinal variable)

(continued)

(*continued*)

SM_IMPS	To what extent do you use social media in order to collect ideas for improvements or innovations in your product or services? (five levels ordinal variable)
SM_PERS	To what extent do you use social media in order to search for and find personnel? (five levels ordinal variable)
SM_INTC	To what extent do you use social media in order to support the internal exchange of information and co-operation among the employees of your firm? (five levels ordinal variable)
SM_IPAR	To what extent do you use social media in order to support the external exchange of information and co-operation with other firms (e.g. partners, suppliers, customers, etc.)? (five levels ordinal variable)
CLOUD	Do you use cloud computing? (binary)
CL_IAAS	To what extent you use IaaS (Infrastructure as a Service = use of remote computing power and storage through the Internet)?
CL_PAAS	To what extent you use PaaS (Platform as a Service = remote use of the above plus database management systems and application development tools/environments/languages through the Internet)? (five levels ordinal variable)
CL_SAAS	To what extent you use SaaS (Software as a Service = use through the Internet of remote application software that run on provider's systems)? (five levels ordinal variable)

Independent Variables – Structure

ORG	Over the last three years did your firm use organic structural forms of work organization (such as teamwork and job rotation)? (binary)

Independent Variables – General

SECT	Firm's sector
COMP_PROF	How good was the financial performance of your firm over the last three years in comparison with your competitors in terms of profitability? (five levels ordinal variable)
COMP_SALR	How good was the financial performance of your firm over the last three years in comparison with your competitors in terms of sales revenue? (five levels ordinal variable)
COMP_MS	How good was the financial performance of your firm over the last three years in comparison with your competitors in terms of market share? (five levels ordinal variable)
COMP_ROI	How good was the financial performance of your firm over the last three years in comparison with your competitors in terms of ROI (return on investment)? (five levels ordinal variable)

References

1. Baldwin, R., Di Mauro, B.W.: Mitigating the COVID economic crisis: act fast and do whatever it takes. Center of Economic Policy Research Press, London (2020)
2. Keeley, B., Love, P.: From Crisis to Recovery - The Causes. Course and Consequences of the Great Recession. OECD Publishing, Paris (2010)
3. Knoop, T.A.: Recessions and Depressions: Understanding Business Cycles, 2nd edn. Praeger Santa Barbara, California (2015)
4. Allen, R.E.: Financial Crises and Recession in the Global Economy, 4th edn. Edward Elgar Publications, Cheltenham (2016)
5. Santana, M., Valle, R., Galanb, J.L.: Turnaround strategies for companies in crisis: watch out the causes of decline before firing people. Bus. Res. Q. **20**(3), 206–211 (2017)
6. Izsak, K., Markianidou, P., Lukach, R., Wastyn, A.: The impact of the crisis on research and innovation policies. European Commission, DG Research, Brussels (2013)
7. Arvanitis, S., Woerter, M.: Firm characteristics and the cyclicality of R&D investments. Ind. Corp. Change **23**(5), 1141–1169 (2014)
8. Russell, S., Norvig, P.: Artificial Intelligence: A Modern Approach, 3rd edn. Pearson, Essex (2020)
9. Murphy, K.P.: Machine Learning: A Probabilistic Perspective. MIT Press, Cambridge (2013)
10. Witten, I.H., Frank, E., Hall, M.A., Pal, C.J.: Data Mining - Practical Machine Learning Tools and Techniques. Morgan Kaufmann, Amsterdam (2017)
11. Blum, A., Hopcroft, J., Kannan, R.: Foundations of Data Science. Cambridge University Press, Cambridge (2020)
12. Siegel, E.: Predictive Analytics. Wiley, New Jersey (2013)
13. Latham, S.: Contrasting strategic response to economic recession in start-up versus established software firms. J. Small Bus. Manage. **47**(2), 180–201 (2009)
14. Latham, S., Braun, M.: Economic recessions, strategy, and performance: a synthesis. J. Strat. Manage. **4**(2), 96–115 (2011)
15. Wickramasinghe, V., Perera, G.: HRM practices during the global recession (2008–2010) - evidence from globally distributed software development firms in Sri Lanka. Strat. Outsourc. Int. J. **5**(3), 188–212 (2012)
16. Ahmed, M.U., Kristal, M.M., Pagell, M.: Impact of operational and marketing capabilities on firm performance: evidence from economic growth and downturns. Int. J. Prod. Econ. **154**, 59–71 (2014)
17. Lai, Y., Saridakis, G., Blackburn, R., Johnstone, S.: Are the HR responses of small firms different from large firms in times of recession? J. Bus. Ventur. **31**(1), 113–131 (2016)
18. Burger, A., Damijan, J.P., Kostevc, C., Rojec, M.: Determinants of firm performance and growth during economic recession: the case of Central and Eastern European count. Econ. Syst. **41**(4), 569–590 (2017)
19. Arvanitis, S., Loukis, E.: Factors explaining ICT expenditure behaviour of Greek firms during the economic crisis 2009–2014. In: 7th International Conference on eDemocracy, Athens, Greece (2017)
20. Craglia, M. (ed.), et al.: Artificial Intelligence - A European Perspective, EUR 29425 EN. EU Publications Office, Luxembourg (2018)
21. Duan, Y., Edwards, J.S., Dwivedi, Y.K.: Artificial intelligence for decision making in the era of Big Data – evolution, challenges and research agenda. Int. J. Inf. Manage. **48**, 63–71 (2019)
22. OECD: Artificial Intelligence in Society. OECD Publishing, Paris (2019)
23. Eggers, W.D., Schatsky, D., Viechnicki, P.: AI-augmented government. Using cognitive technologies to redesign public sector work. Deloitte University Press, New York (2017)

24. Desouza, K.C., Krishnamurthy, R., Dawson, G.S.: Learning From Public Sector Experimentation with Artificial Intelligence. Brookings, Washington D.C. (2017)
25. Desouza, K.C.: Delivering Artificial Intelligence in Government: Challenges and Opportunities. IBM Center for the Business of Government, Washington D.C. (2018)
26. Sun, T.Q., Medaglia, R.: Mapping the challenges of Artificial Intelligence in the public sector: evidence from public healthcare. Gov. Inf. Q. **36**(2), 368–383 (2019)
27. DeSousa, W.G., DeMelo, E.R.P., De Souza Bermejo, P.H., Sous Farias, R.A., Gomes, A.O.: How and where is artificial intelligence in the public sector going? A literature review and research agenda. Gov. Inf. Q. (2019, in-press)
28. Rockoff, J.E., Jacob, B.A., Kane, T.J., Staiger, D.O.: Can you recognize an effective teacher when you recruit one? Educ. Fin. Pol. **6**(1), 43–74 (2010)
29. Chandler, D., Levitt, S.D., List, J.A.: Predicting and preventing shootings among at-risk youth. Am. Econ. Rev. **101**(3), 288–292 (2011)
30. Kang, J.S., Kuznetsova, P., Luca, M., Choi, Y.: Where not to eat? Improving public policy by predicting hygiene inspections using online reviews. In: Proceedings of Empirical Methods in Natural Language Processing Conference 2013, pp. 1443–1448 (2013)
31. Camacho-Collados, M., Liberatore, F.: A Decision Support System for predictive police patrolling. Decis. Support Syst. **75**, 25–37 (2015)
32. Ku, C.H., Leroy, G.: A decision support system: automated crime report analysis and classification for e-government. Gov. Inf. Q. **31**(4), 534–544 (2014)
33. Kouziokas, G.N.: The application of artificial intelligence in public administration for forecasting high crime risk transportation areas in urban environment. Transp. Res. Procedia **24**, 467–473 (2017)
34. Leavitt, H.J.: Applied organization change in industry: structural, technical, and human approaches. In: Cooper, S., Leavitt, H.J., Shelly, K. (eds.) New Perspectives in Organizational Research, pp. 55–71. Wiley, Chichester (1964)
35. Scott-Morton, M.S.: The Corporation of the 1990s. Oxford University Press, New York (1991)
36. Johnson, G., Whittington, R., Angwin, D., Regner, P., Scholes, K.: Exploring Corporate Strategy, 10th edn. Financial Times/Prentice Hall, New York (2014)
37. Jones, G.R.: Organizational Theory, Design, and Change, 7th edn. Pearson Education Limited, Upper Saddle River (2013)
38. Donaldson, L.: The Contingency Theory of Organization. Sage Publications, London (2001)
39. Breiman, L.: Random Forests. Mach. Learn. **45**(1), 5–32 (2001)
40. Tan, P.N., Steinbach, M., Karpatne, A., Kumar, V.: Introduction to Data Mining, 2nd edn. Pearson, New York (2019)
41. Friedman, J.H.: Stochastic gradient boosting. Comput. Stat. Data Anal. **38**(4), 367–78 (2002)
42. Hastie, T., Tibshirani, R., Friedman, J.: The Elements of Statistical Learning: Data Mining, Inference, and Prediction. Springer, New York (2011). https://doi.org/10.1007/978-0-387-84858-7

Smart Cities

Towards Data-Driven Policymaking for the Urban Heat Transition in The Netherlands: Barriers to the Collection and Use of Data

Devin Diran(✉) and Anne Fleur van Veenstra

Netherlands Organization for Applied Scientific Research TNO, Anna van Buerenplein 1,
2595 DA The Hague, The Netherlands
{devin.diran,annefleur.vanveenstra}@tno.nl

Abstract. The transition of our society towards a sustainable, low-carbon reality is challenging governments at all levels to establish, implement and monitor policies that can realize this transition. In the Netherlands, cities are developing data-driven policies to ensure that the urban environment will make the transition from the use of natural gas to sustainable alternatives. However, the collection and (re-)use of data is not without its challenges, which may hamper policymaking, and thereby the ambitions for the transition. Therefore, this paper explores barriers to the data collection and use for the urban heat transition, based on literature and practice. First, an overview of barriers is derived from literature. Subsequently, we interview policy makers of eight frontrunner cities to explore which barriers they encounter in practice. We find that cities need different data in different phases of the strategy development, and that the main barriers for the collection and re-use of data are the required amount of effort and time, and the experienced difficulties to take decisions based on data that is poor in quality, level of detail and topicality.

Keywords: Energy transition · Data-driven policymaking · Open data · Data sharing · Data collaboration · Barriers · Smart cities

1 Introduction

The Netherlands is on a journey towards climate neutrality in 2050. The Dutch Climate Agreement, following the Paris Agreement and EU policy, is aiming to transform 1.5 million dwellings into sustainable dwellings by 2030 [1]. This transition in the built environment entails the shift from the natural-gas dominated heat supply, towards the supply of sustainable heat, commonly known as the *heat transition*. For this transition cities are in the lead on the local level, with decisions to be made regarding the timing when districts will be made subject to the transition, the new infrastructure for sustainable heating, and the support towards citizens to adopt the new technologies [1].

To develop effective heat transition strategies and implementation plans, cities aim to use data from different stakeholders to improve the quality of their policies [2–4]. *Data-driven policymaking* aims to use new data sources and data analytics for policymaking

© IFIP International Federation for Information Processing 2020
Published by Springer Nature Switzerland AG 2020
G. Viale Pereira et al. (Eds.): EGOV 2020, LNCS 12219, pp. 361–373, 2020.
https://doi.org/10.1007/978-3-030-57599-1_27

[5–7]. However, this is not without its challenges [8, 9] which may hamper the ambitions for the heat transition in local governments. For the heat transition in the Netherlands, local governments are making efforts to gather and utilize new data sources to support their decisions. However, in these early stages various, the implementation of data-driven policymaking for the heat transition is very challenging [2]. Therefore, the goal of this paper is to investigate the barriers local governments experience regarding data collection and utilization for the heat transition, and how this may impede data-driven policymaking. So far, we have not found any papers investigating the barriers experienced by local governments to data-driven energy policymaking.

First, we identify barriers to data collection and use for data-driven policymaking based on literature. Then, we explore the barriers that cities encounter when they develop data-driven policy for natural gas-free districts by examining eight frontrunner cities in The Netherlands using a combination of interviews and desk research. This paper is structured as follows. In Sect. 2 the theoretical background on data-driven policymaking for the energy transition, including its barriers, will be presented. This is followed by the methodology for the empirical study among eight frontrunner cities in Sect. 3, and the presentation of the results of our empirical study in Sect. 4. In Sect. 5 we discuss the findings, and the paper is concluded in Sect. 6.

2 Theoretical Background

2.1 Data-Driven Policymaking

Data-driven policymaking uses new data sources and data analytics to improve the 'evidence-base' of policy [5–7]. It, thus, builds on the notion of evidence-based policymaking [10, 11], but it can be distinguished by its focus on the use of big and open data and data analytics for policymaking [5–7]. Before elaborating on data-driven policymaking, it should be mentioned that the implementation of evidenced-based policymaking is still facing challenges. Widely reported challenges include: the access to validated and accurate evidence [12, 13]; the transformation of quantitative and qualitative evidence to policy [14]; the increasing complexity of policy challenges, the related evidence, and the stakeholders involved in establishing the evidence [12, 14]; the lacking skills of policymakers to derive insights from the evidence [13, 14]; the high up-front costs [13]; and the cultural difference between policymakers, scientists and other practitioners [15].

While data-driven policymaking aims to increase the quality and legitimacy of policymaking, it faces additional challenges to evidence-based policymaking [2, 7, 9]. Challenges include those related to: the use and integration of data from different domains and stakeholders [2, 8, 9]; the impact on policymaking [9]; and the involvement of relevant stakeholders and citizens [7]. Data-driven policy adoption differs between domains and sectors; sectors that have actively picked up on it include the safety and security domain, including the police [16], while others are slower to adopt data-driven approaches [17, 18].

To accelerate the urban energy transition, ample research is conducted on data-driven methods and tools, e.g. to predict energy demand and building energy performance, to optimize asset management and operation of energy infrastructure, and to test energy saving measures [19–22]. In addition to these technical aspects, research targets the social and behavioral aspects of an energy transition [23]. For instance, [24] study a method to derive citizen perception of energy solutions from social media data, and [25] derive the energy cost load for households through energy audit data. However, these models and tools are not always used to support local governments' energy policies, implying a gap between the state of the art in data-driven methods and tools and its adoption in energy policymaking [2, 17, 18].

2.2 Barriers to Data Collection and Use in Data-Driven Energy Policymaking

In literature, several barriers that local governments encounter when developing data-driven energy policies were found. These barriers cover different phases, including data collection, and data use consisting of the processing and analysis of data. These barriers are displayed in Table 1.

Table 1. Barriers found in literature on data collection and use in heat transition policymaking.

Category	Challenge or barrier	Source
Data collection	Poor or missing meta-data	[21, 26, 27]
	Scattered distribution of data	[21, 26, 27]
	Data access restrictions and costs	[21, 26, 27]
	Inconvenient interfaces	[21, 26, 27]
	Data providers limited by human and financial resources	[26]
	Data providers lack domain expertise, and policymakers lack data expertise	[26]
	Decentralized energy data challenges data agencies	[26]
	Real-time collection and (pre) processing of data	[28]
	Lacking willingness and trust to share data	[2]
	GDPR and privacy restrictions	[2, 29, 30]
Data processing and analysis	Lack of, or insufficient data formats and standards	[2, 19, 22, 26, 27, 30–32]
	Poor data quality	[26]
	Data lacking detail level	[23]
	Missing or incomplete data	[21, 26, 27, 33, 34]
	Large computing capacity required	[28, 30, 35]
	High paced technological development	[2, 20]
	Outcome difficult to comprehend	[2, 35]
	Resource intensive data preparation	[27, 36]
	Lacking inclusion and involvement of stakeholders	[2]
	Organizational immaturity for data	[2, 30, 36]
	High perceived investment costs	[2, 30, 36]

Barriers to data collection may lead to inconvenient data access, availability and findability; [21, 26, 27] report several barriers contributing to this, such as poor or missing meta-data, data dispersed among different actors, restricted or inconvenient data access, availability and findability, and inconvenient interfaces. Barriers to data collection can be related to challenges faced by the data provider [26]. Data providers, such as statistics organizations, can be challenged by limited resources, resulting in trade-offs between quality and quantity, and the need to coordinate distributed energy data [26]. Moreover, the lack in trust and willingness to share data [2], e.g. among citizens towards the government, and inexperience with GDPR legislation [2, 29, 30] are barriers towards data collection. Furthermore, a lack of energy domain expertise by data providers and a lack of data expertise by policy makers was found to be a barrier [26], as well as the collection and processing of real-time data [28].

Data processing and analysis include many barriers related to the interoperability [2, 19, 22, 26, 27, 30–32], quality [26], and level of detail [23] of the often incomplete data [21, 26, 27, 33, 34]; and to the lack of processing power [28, 30, 35] or the high paced technical developments [2, 20]. This leads to resource intensive data preparation or limitations in data analysis [27, 36], and eventually reluctance to take decisions based the data [2, 35]. Furthermore, barriers were found on stakeholder involvement [2], organizational immaturity [2, 30, 36], and the perceived high investment costs [2, 30, 36].

3 Research Methodology

The goal of this study is thus to explore the barriers to data collection and use in data-driven urban heat transition policymaking in the Netherlands. To this end a multi-case study among eight frontrunner Dutch cities was carried out: Utrecht, Rotterdam, Amsterdam, Groningen, Nijmegen, Haarlem, Hengelo and Den Haag. These cities were selected based on their leading role pertaining to the policies put in place and the role of data in that policymaking process for the heat transition. This selection was done in collaboration with the National Program on Natural gas free Districts which monitors the progress of cities [3]. Interviews are the main method used for data gathering, in combination with desk research of background information, e.g. policy documents, provided by the case cities. The semi-structured interview protocol was established by taking into account the barriers in data-driven policymaking derived from literature, and as presented in Sect. 2.2. The interview protocol was built around the following questions: *For which activities in the urban heat transition do local governments use data?, Which barriers complicate data collection?,* and *Which barriers complicate data processing and analysis?* The interviewees, were selected based on their mandate in heat transition policymaking, reflected in a direct and active role, and their experience with the collection and use of data for this process. Functions range from Policy advisers, Process managers, Project leaders, to staff working with data.

All interviews took place online during December 2019 and January 2020, lasting around 60 min. The analysis combines a structured approach as proposed by [37], with a semi-structured approach to give meaning to the qualitative data by means of the researchers' impression as proposed by [38]. The initial framework with barriers for data collection and use derived from literature, functions as the primary data analysis protocol. In line with [38], analysis occurred in-between interviews, and the framework of barriers could be tested and adjusted based on the empirical findings. The empirical findings also included the activities and decisions for which data is used. With all interviews conducted, categorical aggregation based on the combined theoretical and empirical framework was the chosen strategy towards the final findings.

4 Empirical Exploration and Findings

4.1 The State of the Dutch Urban Heat Transition

For the urban environment in the Netherlands, space heating, warm water and cooking are mainly fueled by natural gas, making up 82% of the energy demand [39]. Currently, regulated network operators maintain a fine-mazed network to supply natural-gas to dwellings for the generation of heat through individual installations. The heat transition entails the transition towards a situation with a mix of various infrastructure and technologies, both centralized and decentralized, for sustainable heat supply. Examples are collective district heating networks fed with heat from biomass, geothermal or aquathermal sources; or individual electricity powered heat pumps or infrared panels in dwellings substituting the gas boilers [1, 2]. As mentioned in the introduction, the city will be in the lead to facilitate this transition and ensure that the goals are met with a shift from national policymaking towards more local policymaking [1]. In other words, the municipal governments are assigned with new responsibilities regarding energy policy. They are considered to be positioned best with local knowledge and with strong ties to the local stakeholders necessary to realize the heat transition.

4.2 The Use of Data for Heat Transition Policymaking by Cities

The digitalization of the energy sector and cities is picking up pace in the Netherlands [4, 40, 41]. The role of data is acknowledged within energy transition policymaking, e.g. the theme on data-driven planning in the National Program on Natural-gas free Districts [3]. Related to the newly assigned responsibilities of cities, Table 2 presents an overview of activities by a city government, and data needs derived from the interviews.

Table 2. An overview of activities and data needs of the cities

Phase	Main activities	Data use/needs
Phase 1: Strategy development, entailing the sequence of districts to disconnect from natural gas by 2030 and the preferred alternative for sustainable heating	-Exploration of the current situation, e.g. with GIS tools and dashboards -Technical-economic analysis of heating alternatives to decide on the heating solution, with assessment models	-The heat demand, based on the number and type of dwellings and users -Dwelling ownership, type, age and technical installation -Energy infrastructure (e.g. natural gas, electricity and district heating networks) and its characteristics (e.g. location, age and capacity)

(continued)

Table 2. (*continued*)

Phase	Main activities	Data use/needs
Phase 2: Implementation plans for districts	-Developing district implementation plans. This calls for detailed data on the heterogenous building stock and citizens -Implement, monitor and adapt plans	-The technical state of dwellings and sustainability measures taken -The state of energy infrastructure, e.g. capacity and connections -The potential capacity and location of sustainable heat sources -Residents' and large consumers' behavior

4.3 Barriers to the Collection of Data

From the interviews with the eight case municipalities, the barriers experienced during the process of finding and collecting the relevant data are presented in Table 3.

Table 3. Barriers to data collection among the eight cities.

Barrier to data collection	Experienced by
GDPR and privacy restrictions	8/8 cities
High investments in time and costs	6/8 cities
Lack of expertise and skills	3/8 cities
Scattered distribution of data	7/8 cities
Poor data findability and access	5/8 cities
Lacking access rights	2/8 cities
Many formats and standards	5/8 cities
Lack of awareness, trust and openness in data sharing	3/8 cities

GDPR and privacy restrictions: ensuring data protection is a challenge shared by all eight cities. It takes a lot of time and legal expertise to deal with this properly. Risk-averse behavior, and unknowns about privacy legislation, result in assumptions that data, e.g. smart-meter data, is not available or very difficult to obtain. Moreover, data with potential commercial sensitivity is not widely shared, although necessary, and thus difficult to obtain. "How to deal with privacy sensitive data? There are significant obstacles to access and share data. Address linked data cannot be shared" - Utrecht.

High investment in costs and time: is mentioned as a barrier by six cities. "It takes a lot of time and effort to acquire the necessary data. How do you ask the right questions, to the right people to get the right data?" - *Utrecht*. Moreover, costs are high. These include payment for external data and hiring data specialists and consultants. Several cities state that costs can be saved if the city itself, or together with other cities, collect and process data. "Setting up the collective knowledge center is expensive, but worth it. A regional data authority was founded with the benefits of scale" - *Hengelo*.

Lack of Expertise and Skills: Three cities mention that expertise and skills to collect and (pre)process data is not always available internally. In Rotterdam, Amsterdam and Haarlem external experts are hired, while the other cities primarily rely on internal data expertise, often supplemented with external expertise.

Scattered Distribution of Data Sources: Six cities state that fragmentation of data sources within the city and among various external parties means that a lot of time is needed to find and collect data. The lack of data standards and agreements about which data is needed, combined with the fragmentation of data, leads to ad hoc data collection, whereby the data must be requested from various parties. For some parties this is not a priority and it takes a long time; for other parties, data must be paid for. "You really need to search within the city for which information is already available." - *Groningen*. "The fragmentation of data over the various parties involved in collecting the data and building models is immense" - *Haarlem*. "A lot of data has not been digitized yet within the city. This knowledge and data is in people's minds and is conveyed orally." - *Rotterdam*. "A lot of data is available, but the problem is to know where it is" - *Nijmegen*.

Poor data findability and access, as a result of, among others, the scattered distribution of data. Five cities mentioned this barrier.

Lack of Data Access: Two cities mention this as a challenge, particularly for the detailed district implementation plans. Here more detailed and potentially more sensitive data is needed, relative to the city scale. To share this data, it is essential to have mechanisms in place that 1) guarantee data security, and 2) control access and use.

Different Formats and Standards: Five cities mention missing data standards or questions on how to deal with standards, making data collection and processing resource intensive. "There is no routine in data supply, you have to be precise on what you need, and external data providers do not think along" - *Nijmegen*.

Lack of Awareness, Trust and Openness in Data Sharing: Three cities state that creating openness and trust takes time; a good relationship with data owners is essential. In these relationships it is necessary to explain what a city will do with the data. "External stakeholders are commonly reluctant to share data. Openness is essential, but many parties remain cautious. It took six months to get data on the natural gas network" - *Rotterdam*. "Housing corporations often find it difficult to share data, they often fail to recognize that it is also in their best interest to share data" - *Haarlem*.

4.4   Barriers to the Processing and Analysis of Data

Table 4 presents the barriers experienced during the actual utilization of data.

Table 4. Barriers to data use among the eight cities.

Barrier to data use	Experienced by
Cautious to make decisions based on insights from data	4/8 cities
Data lacking quality and consistency	4/8 cities
Incomplete and missing data	1/8 cities
Data not up to date	5/8 cities
Data is not always validated	6/8 cities
Data lacking detail level	1/8 cities
Lack of supporting tools	4/8 cities
Difficult to determine the value and purpose of data	2/8 cities
Data preparation is resource intensive	3/8 cities
Difficult to link, analyze, and visualize data	3/8 cities
Resources at the limits to process the quantity of data	2/8 cities
Legal limitations to data use	2/8 cities

Caution to make decisions based on insights from data is mentioned by four cities. This barrier is related to the cultural challenge for cities to take decisions based on data. Moreover, the following five barriers pertaining to data quality and reliability may contribute to this barrier.

Lacking data quality and consistency, is mentioned by four cities. The quality of the data is influenced by the technology used and the human involvement in generating the data, but also in cleaning and processing data and the choices made for generalizing, calibrating, formatting data, etc. "We used the Cadaster database for the surface of buildings, but these surfaces are incorrect. Important decisions are to be made based on this information, it must be correct. I spend a lot of time cleaning the data." - *Nijmegen.*

Incomplete and Missing Data: While several cities underline missing and incomplete data, one city mentions it explicitly as a barrier. In the Cadaster databases, with data used by all cities and considered essential for heat transition policy, there are approximately 8% missing values.

Data is not up to Date: This is mentioned by five cities. For many relevant data, there is a significant delay between data generation and publication. As a result, the analyzes are based on outdated data. "The reality changes quickly, but data is not adjusted as quickly. You make a plan for districts based on old data that is currently available, whereas it is a dynamic reality" - *Rotterdam.* "A major challenge is the lack of timeliness of data, e.g. energy labels and energy consumption. Especially during the implementation, it is crucial that this data is up to date" - *Hengelo.*

Data is not Validated: Six cities mention that many data sources cannot confirm whether the data is validated. The quality of insights derived from the data is difficult to assess if the data is of insufficient quality or not validated.

Data lacking detail is mentioned by one city, limiting analysis opportunities.

Lack of supporting tools for data-driven policymaking is mentioned by four cities, or they mention that the available resources do not meet requirements. Resources provided by the national government, were often found to arrive late, and to require additional resources to be enriched with local data. Each city interviewed uses its own (developed or purchased) tools. "We use our own tools, we have the internal capacity to develop our own tools, such as GIS maps." - *Rotterdam.*

Difficult to Determine the Value and Purpose of Data: This barrier is mentioned by two cities and relates to 1) the challenge to describe the purpose of data, and 2) a lack of data analysis expertise to give value and meaning to the data.

Data Preparation is Resource Intensive: Three cities mention that processing data takes a lot of time. "My time consists of 80% preparing data and 20% data analysis. Many cities outsource this" - *Nijmegen.*

Difficult to Link, Analyze, and Visualize Data: Three cities mention that the diversity in data formats and standards makes it difficult to link and analyze data. This is common, due to the great diversity in heterogeneous data sources, between which there are no agreements about data standards.

Resources at the Limits to Process the Quantity of Data: Two cities address that even in the early phases of data-driven analysis, the local hardware is at the limits to facilitate the volume of data available. "We see the technical limits of our equipment: we receive 90,000 records, but the spreadsheet only facilitates 60,000" - *Nijmegen.*

Legal Limitations to Data Use: Two cities address that data may not be used due to restrictions on the purpose, e.g. citizen data on social services. This data is available within a city, but cannot be used for energy transition purposes, where it also is relevant.

5   Discussion

Considering the increasing amount and variety of data becoming available, local governments in the Netherlands are starting to use data in their energy transition policymaking, in particular for the urban heat transition. Data-driven models and tools, such as economic assessment models and dashboards are developed to support decision-making and inform citizens and stakeholders on the progress and need for action. As presented by [19–22, 24, 25], there are many opportunities for data-driven energy policymaking. However, based on literature, several barriers and challenges are identified both for data collection and data processing and analysis.

The eight case cities that were investigated in our empirical study follow an iterative 'learning-by-doing' process for collecting and analyzing data and encounter many barriers in this process. The main obstacle for cities is that data collection and processing costs them a lot of time and effort, often because of the fragmentation of data between a myriad of stakeholders. Barriers include a lack of agreements on data formats and standards, skills for data processing, and a lack of proper tools. Data quality, detail and topicality are also often an obstacle. To make decisions with significant social and economic impact, it is essential that there is confidence in the data quality, so that decisions can be justified based on data. These barriers complicate data-driven policymaking among the frontrunner cities and may hamper further adoption of data in the policymaking process. While most of the barriers identified in our empirical study among eight cities validate the barriers found in literature, we also identified some other barriers. Barriers pertaining to data quality, detail level, scattered distribution and heterogeneity, inconsistent data standards and formats, resource intensity to find and prepare data, and GDPR legislation are mentioned in literature and common among the eight case cities. Barriers identified in the empirical study that have not been widely reported on in literature include policymakers' reluctance to formalize policy based on insights from data. Respondents mention several causes for this, e.g. the challenge to explain how insights are derived from the data and the lack of data reliability and quality due to the lack of quality assurance mechanisms. While this is not widely mentioned in literature on data-driven energy transition policymaking, it was mentioned by e.g. [9, 14, 42]. Other barriers found in the literature, e.g. on meta-data and barriers pertaining to data suppliers, were not confirmed in our study, which may be explained by the outsourcing of much of the work on data processing and on the limitation of this study to only interview representatives from local governments. Moreover, in literature a myriad of tools and their barriers can be found to support energy transition policymaking in a wide range of styles, e.g. [19–22]. This study finds that many of the available tools are considered superfluous due to a lack of detail, inclusion of social aspects, and poor timing in when these tools are made available, relative to the policymaking timeline of local governments. This points to the importance of timeliness and fitness for purpose of tools, building on insights from evidence-based policymaking, which not only includes systematic research, but also 'practice', and political judgement [43].

Our study was limited to interviews with representatives of local governments. While this resulted in an extensive overview of barriers and a rich interpretation of those barriers, the outcome could benefit from expanding the interviews towards data providers. The extended insights on the data providers' perception of barriers, could benefit the identification of structurally effective measures to tackle the barriers. Moreover, from the variety in approaches to incorporate data-driven policymaking in the heat transition found among the eight cases, including the intensive interaction with stakeholders, future research is recommended to understand the factors influencing the chosen data governance structure, such as described by [44, 45]. Developing data governance models and policymaking processes that cope with the recurring barriers, based on the lessons learned by the frontrunners, will be of great practical value, especially to cities which lack resources to experiment with these efforts.

6   Conclusion

This study investigates the collection and use of data for policymaking in the urban heat transition and the barriers local governments encounter based on literature and practice. The local governments in The Netherlands are in the lead for the urban heat transition and need to develop binding heat transition strategies and implementation plans. For this, local governments embark on data-driven policymaking. Based on an empirical study among eight frontrunner cities we find that their main challenge is related to the effort that goes into collecting and using data for heat transition policymaking. Furthermore, we find that a number of barriers, such as data quality, topicality and detail level, and lack of data-driven expertise among policymakers, affect the confidence of cities to use data and data-driven tools for energy policymaking, which has great economic and social impact. This calls for collaboration and standardization between data providers and users for these barriers in heat transition policymaking. This study is initially limited to the local governments, however, heat transition policymaking is a joint effort of the policymakers together with stakeholders such as utility companies and citizens. Barriers encountered by other stakeholders along the ecosystem, influence data use by the local governments. Further research is thus recommended to investigate the ecosystem-wide barriers, to work towards comprehensive data governance models and process designs for effective and supported data-driven policymaking.

Acknowledgement. Knowledge and Learning Program, as part of the National Program on Natural gas free Districts, and its commissioned study entitled "Data for the Transition Vision Heat and District Implementation Plans".

References

1. Ministry of Economic Affairs & Climate Policy: Climate agreement, The Hague (2019)
2. Diran, D., Hoppe, T., Ubacht, J., Slob, A., Blok, K.: A data ecosystem for data-driven thermal energy transition: reflection on current practice and suggestions for re-design. Energies **13**, 444 (2020)
3. Programma Aardgasvrije Wijken: Datagedreven planvorming. https://aardgasvrijewijken.nl/klp/dp/default.aspx
4. Di Silvestre, M.L., Favuzza, S., Sanseverino, E.R., Zizzo, G.: How decarbonization, digitalization and decentralization are changing key power infrastructures. Renew. Sustain. Energy Rev. **93**, 483–498 (2018)
5. Höchtl, J., Parycek, P., Schöllhammer, R.: Big data in the policy cycle: policy decision making in the digital era. J. Organ. Comput. Electron. Commer. **26**, 147–169 (2016)
6. Giest, S.: Big data for policymaking: fad or fasttrack? Policy Sci. **50**(3), 367–382 (2017). https://doi.org/10.1007/s11077-017-9293-1
7. van Veenstra, A.F., Kotterink, B.: Data-driven policy making: the policy lab approach. In: Parycek, P., et al. (eds.) ePart 2017. LNCS, vol. 10429, pp. 100–111. Springer, Cham (2017). https://doi.org/10.1007/978-3-319-64322-9_9
8. Clarke, A., Margetts, H.: Governments and citizens getting to know each other? Open, closed, and big data in public management reform. Policy Internet **6**, 393–417 (2014)
9. Janssen, M., Helbig, N.: Innovating and changing the policy-cycle: policy-makers be prepared! Gov. Inf. Q. **35**, S99–S105 (2018)

10. Head, B.W.: Toward more "evidence-informed" policy making? Public Adm. Rev. **76**, 472–484 (2016)
11. Haskins, R.: Evidence-based policy: the movement, the goals, the issues, the promise (2018)
12. Young, I., et al.: Experiences and attitudes towards evidence-informed policy-making among research and policy stakeholders in the Canadian agri-food public health sector. Zoonoses Public Health **61**, 581–589 (2014)
13. Oliver, K., Innvar, S., Lorenc, T., Woodman, J., Thomas, J.: A systematic review of barriers to and facilitators of the use of evidence by policymakers. BMC Health Serv. Res. **14**, 2 (2014)
14. Head, B.W.: Reconsidering evidence-based policy: key issues and challenges (2010)
15. Head, B.W.: Policy analysis: evidence based policy-making (2015)
16. Poel, M., et al.: Data for Policy: A study of big data and other innovative data-driven approaches for evidence-informed policymaking. Report about State-of-the-Art. Amsterdam technopolis, Oxford Internet Institute, Center for European Policy Studies (2015)
17. Pfenninger, S., DeCarolis, J., Hirth, L., Quoilin, S., Staffell, I.: The importance of open data and software: is energy research lagging behind? Energy Policy **101**, 211–215 (2017)
18. Poel, M., Meyer, E.T., Schroeder, R.: Big data for policymaking: great expectations, but with limited progress? Policy Internet **10**, 347–367 (2018)
19. Mathew, P.A., Dunn, L.N., Sohn, M.D., Mercado, A., Custudio, C., Walter, T.: Big-data for building energy performance: lessons from assembling a very large national database of building energy use. Appl. Energy **140**, 85–93 (2015)
20. Linder, L., Vionnet, D., Bacher, J.-P., Hennebert, J.: Big building data-a big data platform for smart buildings. Energy Procedia **122**, 589–594 (2017)
21. Hong, T., Yang, L., Hill, D., Feng, W.: Data and analytics to inform energy retrofit of high performance buildings. Appl. Energy **126**, 90–106 (2014)
22. Chen, Y., Hong, T., Piette, M.A.: Automatic generation and simulation of urban building energy models based on city datasets for city-scale building retrofit analysis. Appl. Energy **205**, 323–335 (2017)
23. Carlson, D.R., Matthews, H.S., Bergés, M.: One size does not fit all: averaged data on household electricity is inadequate for residential energy policy and decisions. Energy Build. **64**, 132–144 (2013)
24. Li, R., Crowe, J., Leifer, D., Zou, L., Schoof, J.: Beyond big data: social media challenges and opportunities for understanding social perception of energy. Energy Res. Soc. Sci. **56**, 101217 (2019)
25. Kontokosta, C.E., Reina, V.J., Bonczak, B.: Energy cost burdens for low-income and minority households: evidence from energy benchmarking and audit data in five US Cities. J. Am. Plan. Assoc. **86**, 89–105 (2020)
26. Liu, B., Evans, M., Yu, S., Roshchanka, V., Dukkipati, S., Sreenivas, A.: Effective energy data management for low-carbon growth planning: an analytical framework for assessment. Energy Policy **107**, 32–42 (2017)
27. Pervaiz, F., Vashistha, A., Anderson, R.: Examining the challenges in development data pipeline. In: Proceedings of the 2nd ACM SIGCAS Conference on Computing and Sustainable Societies, pp. 13–21 (2019)
28. Khan, A., Hornbæk, K.: Big data from the built environment. In: Proceedings of the 2nd International Workshop on Research in the Large, pp. 29–32 (2011)
29. Hemerly, J.: Public policy considerations for data-driven innovation. Computer (Long. Beach. Calif.) **46**, 25–31 (2013)
30. Cavanillas, J.M., Curry, E., Wahlster, W. (eds.): New Horizons for a Data-Driven Economy. A Roadmap for Usage and Exploitation of Big Data in Europe. Springer, Cham (2016). https://doi.org/10.1007/978-3-319-21569-3

31. Di Corso, E., Cerquitelli, T., Piscitelli, M.S., Capozzoli, A.: Exploring energy certificates of buildings through unsupervised data mining techniques. In: 2017 IEEE International Conference on Internet of Things (iThings) and IEEE Green Computing and Communications (GreenCom) and IEEE Cyber, Physical and Social Computing (CPSCom) and IEEE Smart Data (SmartData), pp. 991–998 (2017)
32. Göçer, Ö., Hua, Y., Göçer, K.: A BIM-GIS integrated pre-retrofit model for building data mapping. Build. Simul. 9(5), 513–527 (2016). https://doi.org/10.1007/s12273-016-0293-4
33. Estiri, H.: Energy planning in a big data era: a theme study of the residential sector. In: Thakuriah, P(., Tilahun, N., Zellner, M. (eds.) Seeing Cities Through Big Data. SG, pp. 219–230. Springer, Cham (2017). https://doi.org/10.1007/978-3-319-40902-3_13
34. Amasyali, K., El-Gohary, N.M.: A review of data-driven building energy consumption prediction studies. Renew. Sustain. Energy Rev. 81, 1192–1205 (2018)
35. Reinhart, C.F., Davila, C.C.: Urban building energy modeling–a review of a nascent field. Build. Environ. 97, 196–202 (2016)
36. Li, F.G.N., Bataille, C., Pye, S., O'Sullivan, A.: Prospects for energy economy modelling with big data: hype, eliminating blind spots, or revolutionising the state of the art? Appl. Energy 239, 991–1002 (2019)
37. Yin, R.K.: Case Study Research and Applications: Design and Methods. Sage publications, Singapore (2017)
38. Stake, R.E.: The Art of Case Study Research. Sage, Thousand Oaks (1995)
39. "Energie Beheer Nederland": Energie in Nederland (2018). Accessed 27 July 2020. https://www.ebn.nl/wp-content/uploads/2018/04/EBN-poster-cijfers2016.pdf
40. Ringenson, T., Höjer, M.: Smart city planning and environmental aspects: lessons from seven cities. In: ICT for Sustainability 2016 (2016)
41. Leal-Arcas, R., Lesniewska, F., Proedrou, F.: Prosumers: new actors in EU energy security. In: Amtenbrink, F., Prévost, D., Wessel, R.A. (eds.) Netherlands Yearbook of International Law 2017. NYIL, vol. 48, pp. 139–172. T.M.C. Asser Press, The Hague (2018). https://doi.org/10.1007/978-94-6265-243-9_5
42. der Voort, H.G., Klievink, A.J., Arnaboldi, M., Meijer, A.J.: Rationality and politics of algorithms. Will the promise of big data survive the dynamics of public decision making? Gov. Inf. Q. 36, 27–38 (2019)
43. Head, B.W.: Three lenses of evidence-based policy. Aust. J. Public Adm. 67, 1–11 (2008)
44. van den Broek, T., van Veenstra, A.F.: Governance of big data collaborations: how to balance regulatory compliance and disruptive innovation. Technol. Forecast. Soc. Change 129, 330–338 (2018)
45. Susha, I., Janssen, M., Verhulst, S.: Data collaboratives as "bazaars"? Transform. Gov. People Process Policy. 11, 157–172 (2017)

Identifying Strategic Planning Patterns of Smart Initiatives. An Empirical Research in Spanish Smart Cities

Manuel Pedro Rodríguez Bolívar[1]([⊠]), Cristina Alcaide Muñoz[2], and Laura Alcaide Muñoz[1]

[1] University of Granada, Granada, Spain
manuelp@ugr.es
[2] International University of La Rioja, Logroño, Spain

Abstract. The Smart Cities' projects favor the improvement and efficiency in public services, as well as the dis-closure and access more information, offering extraordinary opportunities for cities to spark a new wave of wealth creation. However, despite the relevance and complexity of designing strategic planning for smart city development, it continues to be ignored. This research contributes to prior research through the analysis of the demographical and citizens profile of SCs, identifying key patterns in the strategic planning processes of the smart initiatives in city governments in order to ensure the success of SCs initiative implementation. To achieve this aim, this paper has sought to analyze strategic planning process in a number of Spanish SCs under the microscope examining a total of 1,635 smart initiatives with the aim at identifying patterns in the strategic planning design. Findings show that smaller-size cities with a higher proportion of older people usually perform formal strategic planning processes.

Keywords: Smart cities · Strategic planning · Smart initiatives · Planning patterns · Citizens' profile

1 Introduction

In the last decades, cities have had to face numerous challenges concerning the adoption of technological advances, economic growth, urban development, operation processes, governance or environment sustainability, giving place to the so-called smart cities (SCs) [1]. These cities have been involved in undertaking new socioeconomic environments based on the introduction of emergent and new information and communication technologies (ICTs) to face these challenges for all residents [2]. This way, public managers and politicians have designed and planned new strategies implementing smart initiatives, which are based on ICTs to enhance city performance and sustainability with the aim at providing efficient public services and improving citizens' quality of life [3, 4].

Thus, the SCs provide infrastructure and services that improve its citizens' lives in a sustainable way [5], undertaking smart initiatives in different domains (mobility,

G. Viale Pereira et al. (Eds.): EGOV 2020, LNCS 12219, pp. 374–386, 2020.
https://doi.org/10.1007/978-3-030-57599-1_28

economy, governance, environment, living and people) [1]. These projects favor the improvement and efficiency in public services, as well as the disclosure and access more information, offering extraordinary opportunities for cities to spark a new wave of wealth creation [6].

However, despite the relevance and complexity of designing strategic planning for smart city development, it continues to be ignored [1], considering an abstract idea and a largely unknown field [3]. So, Yigitcanlar [7] and Mora et al. [8] are promoting prospective research and further critical debates and report of current practices about strategic planning tools used in smart city development because it needs to be carefully and critically revisited.

Although these smart strategies and initiatives could be implemented in different levels of public administration, like in national or in local governments [3], special attention should be paid to strategies that can be applied by city governments because, according to Harrison and Donnelly [9], the focus on cities is relevant to analyze the functions assigned to them like the construction of urban infrastructures, the performance of strategic planning and process as well as the implementation of local policies and investment of financial resources.

Based on these previous comments, this study aims to analyze the smart city phenomenon and its current strategic planning practices on smart initiatives with the aim at identifying patterns in strategic planning approaches. In order to achieve this aim, we have analyzed smart city strategies and planning approaches of 1,635 smart initiatives undertaken by a number of the Spanish SCs (n = 12) through the lens of the demographic and citizens' profiles of sample SCs, which have demonstrated to be relevant attributes that could influence on public policies regarding both the introduction and use of new technologies [10, 11].

The remainder of this paper is as follows. The next section presents the demographical and citizen' profile's attributes of SCs and shows the research questions of our research. Then, we describe the research methodology and data collection methods, analyzing the sample selection and the attributes examined in this research. Also, we describe the main results of our study. Finally, the discussion and conclusions bring the paper to an end.

2   Strategic Planning of Smart Initiatives for Smart Governance

The development of SCs is a complex procedure, as it involves multiple interactions between several stakeholders and dimensions into a "networking" strategy of governance [12], which requires an integrated view of technology, processes, products, services and participants [13]. Due to this complex structure, scholars emphasize the need of a road map to guide stakeholders and dimensions involved in the development of SCs to reach the ambitious target efficiently [13].

Nonetheless, the different demographic urban profile could lead to different patterns in governing smart cities [14] and, therefore, in the strategic planning processes in these cities. In this paper, strategic planning processes are understood as the organization's process of defining its strategy, or direction, and making decisions on allocating its resources to pursue this strategy. It may also extend to control mechanisms for guiding the implementation of the strategy (Wikipedia). Prior research has demonstrated that the planning objectives and the type of smart city initiatives that cities implement in these cities are highly diverse [7]. This way, it could be interesting to analyze how strategic planning in SCs are being performed under different demographic profile of these cities.

To begin with, several research studies have shown that population size affects both the adoption of new technology in public sector [10] and the innovation of city governments [15]. On one hand, larger SCs are engaged in the development and delivery of more complex and efficient services [16], which makes necessary the engagement of citizens with different competing interests into the public sector delivery [10]. By contrast, smaller communities often possess their own powerful sense of place and identity, which helps in obtaining consensus and collaboration [17]. In brief, according to prior research, it is expected to find different patterns in strategic planning of SCs according the municipal size (based on the Cambridge dictionary, a pattern is defined as a particular way in which something is done, is organized, or happens). Therefore, our first research question in this study is the following:

RQ1 – Are there patterns in the strategic planning of smart initiatives based on population size?

The citizens are increasingly an active part of the development of SCs [18, 19], which makes us to question about the profile of citizens that demands the implementation of new technology as well as their participation in the strategic planning process of SCs.

In addition, recent prior research has put emphasis on the need of digital awareness of citizens [13]. In this regard, several scholars have showed that young people increasingly demand the adoption of new technologies to enable their quality of life [11]. In fact, they have a more proactive attitude to use and test new technology than elder people because young people are aware that the learning of using ICTs and its use leads to a greater accessibility to labor market and education, resulting in better work opportunities and, in turn, an increased per capita income [20].

Therefore, it seems that strategic planning of SCs could be different according to the different citizen age structure of the city. Hence, the following research question is derived:

RQ2 - Are there patterns in the strategic planning of smart initiatives based on the age of inhabitants?

Finally, both education and income per capita are the most powerful predictors for the adoption of new technology to improve services delivery efficiently [21]. Local governments with a well-educated and higher income population demand the adoption of new technology to access information and the development and delivery of services efficiently [22]. Additionally, these local governments obtain more resources to implement projects on ICTs into their cities [23].

As with e-government, SCs growth has a closely relationship with education and income per capita, since availability of finance play a significant role in building this human capital and lead to the development of smart city [24]. Local governments with higher skilled people experience stronger growth in the quality of life, and have a proactive attitude towards the implementation of smart initiatives [25]. In fact, different research studies show that cities with more educated population have better employment opportunities, resulting in a more growth in quality of life [26]. As indicated by Foth [18], in order to make cities smarter, we need to make people smarter in the first place.

As for income per capita, in a specific case, Basu [11] showed that the upper middle-income and middle-income groups (30% and 28.75%, respectively) were mostly inclined in the use of mobility application aimed to smart mobility improvement in India. However, the lower income group used less this service comparatively. Based on these prior findings, the last research questions in this study are:

RQ3 - Are there patterns in the strategic planning of smart initiatives based on the level of education?
RQ4 - Are there patterns in the strategic planning of smart initiatives based on the income per capita?

In brief, this study analyses smart cities strategy and planning approaches of smart initiatives in Spanish SCs from the demographic lens and citizen's profile, since it might be significant to identify patterns of behavior in smart initiatives planning experiences in SCs in order to ensure the success of SCs initiatives implementation.

3   Research Methodology

3.1   Sample Selection

Prior research [27] has showed that SCs in Spain, UK, Germany, Italy and France are those that have undertaken a higher number of smart initiatives and projects into their cities. It makes interesting to focus our attention in SCs in these countries and collect evidences from the analysis and exploration of their smart initiatives. Thus, this paper is focused on the analysis of the smart initiatives implementing in SCs in Spain as a first approach of this issue, which could be interesting for SCs in other countries.

According to Harrison and Donnelly [9], we focused on the large-size SCs because it allows a more efficient innovation development that creates many challenges for the planning, design, finance, construction, governance and operation of urban infrastructure and services. Also, these cities are highly competitive economies and get a higher knowledge about urban problems and more flexibility of governance models to face them, as well as the possibility to get insights of smart solutions from others similar cities [3]. Finally, our sample selection is composed by cities having globally recognized as a SCs in the different leading world rankings.

In this sense, with the aim at collecting a wide range of Spanish cities, data collection of this research has been gathered following two steps. Firstly, we analyzed a sample composed of large-size Spanish cities (cities from 200,000 to 4 million inhabitants), which have been labelled "smart" by a European project sponsored by Asset One Inmobilienentwicklungs AG -see http://www.smart-cities.eu. Taking into account the information, classification and factors considered from this European SCs ranking [28], we collected seven Spanish SCs to the sample selection.

Secondly, we also analyzed large-size Spanish cities that are members of the EUROC-ITIES network (http://www.eurocities.eu). This network is composed of the local governments of the major European SCs with the objective of strengthening the important role that they should play in the adoption and implementation of smart governance structures. This second step allows us to collect five new Spanish SCs to our study aim. Therefore, our sample selection is composed of a total of twelve large-size Spanish SCs.

As for the methodology used in our research, based on Yigitcanlar [7], the selection criteria for determining the strategy documents of sample cities were: (a) The strategy or policy report having a specific focus on SCs and developed for a particular city -rather than a part of the city, region or nation-; (b) The full-text report being available for download from an official website of the city -rather than an executive summary or highlights- and; (c) The report having listed the department responsible of the project in the smart city, the smart city domain, stakeholders involved, vision, objectives, policies or strategies on the smart city transformation of the city; (d) The search was conducted in August-September 2019—only including policies published and made available online until this date.

After a thorough web search, in total 1,635 case smart initiatives were determined fulfilling the mentioned selection criteria. The policy documents of these SCs were downloaded from the official city government websites and their vision or aims, smart domains and smart city strategies or policies were obtained and checked, i.e. we selected the projects taking into account their content and objectives. Table 1 lists the number of smart initiatives on each one of the sample SCs.

Table 1. Sample selection and number of smart initiatives included in this study.

City	Number of smart initiatives	City	Number of smart initiatives	City	Number of smart initiatives
A Coruña	127	Barcelona	56	Bilbao	40
Gijon	252	Málaga	204	Madrid	103
Murcia	28	Seville	132	Terrassa	499
Valencia	15	Valladolid	47	Zaragoza	132
TOTAL		**1,635 Smart Initiatives**			

3.2 Smart Initiatives Attributes and Variables Analyzed

As for getting insights about the way that sample SCs are performing strategic planning of smart initiatives, this research characterizes the smart initiatives examining whether the sample SC has a global strategic planning of the city in which the smart initiatives are included, the formal/informal approach used, the scope of the smart project application (horizontal/vertical pattern), the project development approach (bottom-up/top-down) and, finally, the responsible body of the smart project (the city government or the city government jointly with other stakeholders).

Although other variables could be relevant like the structure of the local government or the level of decision-making decentralization, in this paper, we focus our analysis on the demographical city and citizens' profile attributes with the aim at finding patterns in strategic planning of smart initiatives. In this regards, four attributes are used in this study and consistent with previous studies [12, 29]: population size of the smart city and age of inhabitants, as demographical city profile, and level of education and income per capita, as citizens' profile, due to their relevance in finding patterns in e-government policies, and online information disclosure [29].

As for the attributes analyzed, in this paper we focus our efforts in the main ones that characterize the different patterns of organizing the strategic planning of smart initiatives in a SC and, specially, regarding the type of strategic planning performed (formal/informal), the scope of the smart initiatives (vertical/transversal) and the stakeholders involved into the strategic planning process (collaboration). Table 2 shows the definition and calculation method of each of the attributes analyzed in this research.

Table 2. Definition of attributes analyzed in this study.

Attribute	Acronym	Definition	Calculation
Type of strategic planning	FSP[a]	Approach used for strategic planning into the Smart City	Formal Informal
Scope of smart initiative	TSP[a]	Smart initiatives can involve 1 department (vertical) or, 2 or more departments (transversal)	1 = Vertical 2 = Transversal
Strategic planning approach	APP[a]	Strategic planning approach when a Smart City initiative is implemented	Bottom-Up Top-Down
Collaboration	COB[a]	Responsible body of the smart initiative	City government/collaborative/public-private partnership
Population	POP[b]	Population residing in the municipality	Number of inhabitants
Age of inhabitants	AGE[b]	Age of inhabitants	Age 15 from 24 Age 25 from 34 Age 35 from 64

(*continued*)

Table 2. (*continued*)

Attribute	Acronym	Definition	Calculation
Level of education	SECEDU[b]	Level of inhabitants with secondary education	Inhabitants with secondary education
	SUPEDU[b]	Level of inhabitants with superior education	Inhabitants with superior education
Income per capita	INCO[b]	Income per capita	Income (thousand euros) per capita

Notes: [a]Local Government Website and [b]National Statistical Institute (INE) (www.ine.es/)

4 Analysis of Results

4.1 RQ1 – Are There Patterns in the Strategic Planning of Smart Initiatives Based on Population Size?

Table 3 shows the characterization of the main attributes of strategic planning in sample SCs based on the population size of the sample municipality. Results reveal that local governments with lower inhabitants mostly develop formal smart strategic planning and, in turn, offer the entire information to their citizens (97.95% of smart initiatives). By contrast, the no-formalization of smart strategies increases as the size of the municipality increases (cities with more 500.000 inhabitants show more than 90.80% of informal smart strategic initiatives).

As for the scope in the implementation of the smart initiatives, cities between 292,879 and 506,124 inhabitants develop smart initiatives involving more than one department or area (vertical versus horizontal) (97.50% of smart initiatives). However, local governments with lower inhabitants mainly adopt smart initiatives which do not involve multiple departments (28.21%). They focus all efforts on one single department, which leads the smart strategic initiatives.

Moreover, results show that local governments are the main promoters of strategic planning of SC initiatives in all cities regardless of its size (99.54% and 98.29%, respectively).

Finally, the last attribute related to strategic planning under study (collaboration), it seems to be that the local governments with between 292,879 and 506,123 inhabitants encourage collaboration public-private in smart initiatives (10.34%). By contrast, non-collaborative smart initiatives are mainly concentrated in both smaller-size and larger-size cities (94.08% and 93.68%, respectively).

Table 3. Characterization of main attributes of strategic planning in sample SCs based on the population size of municipalities.

Population	FSP		TSP		APP		COB	
	Formal	Informal	Vertical	Transversal	Bottom	Top	Yes	No
0–292,878	97.95%	2.05%	28.21%	71.79%	0.46%	99.54%	5.92%	94.08%
292,879–506,123	50.43%	49.57%	2.50%	97.50%	2.30%	97.70%	10.34%	89.66%
506,124–714,028	58.33%	41.67%	26.62%	73.38%	2.14%	97.86%	8.97%	91.03%
714,029–3,182,981	9.20%	90.80%	26.09%	73.91%	1.72%	98.28%	6.32%	93.68%

Note: Population has been catalogued by quartiles

4.2 RQ2 - Are There Patterns in the Strategic Planning of Smart Initiatives Based on the Age of Inhabitants?

In Table 4, we can observe that there are some patterns related to the relationship between formal/informal smart strategic planning and the age of inhabitants. In this regard, the information about smart initiatives is formalized and disclosed when the inhabitants are older citizens (92.45%), meanwhile that the information is not formalized in cities with young people (54.98%), in opposition to the related literature. It suggests that the teenagers are mostly engaged in the adoption and the use of ICTs and, in turn, demand more information from public institutions [11, 29]. This controversy can be caused by the fact that our study takes into account too young people (between 15 and 24), whose role is primarily applicant of delivery of services than contributor.

Although the related literature established that the teenagers have more proactive attitude to use and test new technology than elder people, because they have a positive perception of them related to the positive impact of ICTs in the improvement of the quality of life [20]; we can observe no patters concerning the age of inhabitants. In order words, smart initiatives are usually promoted by the administration, which takes the lead in implementing technological advances that favor the creation of a smart and sustainable environment in cities, regardless of the age of its inhabitants.

Table 4. Characterization of main attributes of strategic planning in sample SCs based on the population aging in sample municipalities.

Age of inhabitants	FSP		TSP		APP		COB	
	Formal	Informal	Vertical	Transversal	Bottom	Top	Yes	No
Young population	45.02%	54.98%	26.54%	73.46%	2.02%	97.98%	8.26%	91.74%
Older population	92.45%	7.55%	26.56%	73.44%	0.62%	99.38%	6.32%	93.68%

Note: We have calculated median and formed two groups: *Young population* (citizens over the median of inhabitants from 15 to 24 years old + citizens over the median of inhabitants from 25 to 35 years + citizens over the median of inhabitants from 36 to 64 years) and *Older population* (citizens under the median of inhabitants from 15 to 24 years + citizens under the median of inhabitants from 25 to 35 years old + citizens under the median of inhabitants from 36 to 64 years).

Finally, there are also no patters when we analyze the relationship between the scope in the implementation of the smart initiative and the age of inhabitants (vertical versus transversal) as well as the relationship between the collaboration model for implementing these initiatives and the age of inhabitants.

4.3 RQ3 – Are There Patterns in the Strategic Planning of Smart Initiatives Based on the Level of Education?

Table 5 shows that the information disclosed is mainly formalized when the level of education of citizens in the sample SCs are below the median (94.67% and 93.49%). However, in SCs with higher educated citizens, the information disclosed is not formalized (80.59%), contrary to the related literature. Higher educated people experience stronger growth in the quality of life, and have a proactive attitude towards the implementation of smart initiatives and the demand of public information [18, 25].

Table 5. Characterization of main attributes of strategic planning in sample SCs based on the level of education of the population in sample municipalities.

Level of education	FSP		TSP		APP		COB	
	Formal	Informal	Vertical	Transversal	Bottom	Top	Yes	No
Over the median	19.41%	80.59%	30.94%	69.06%	2.97%	97.03%	10.05%	89.95%
Intermediate	94.67%	5.33%	1.59%	98.41%	0.82%	99.18%	4.51%	95,49%
Under the median	93.49%	6.51%	28.21%	71,79%	0.43%	9.57%	6.38%	93.62%

Note: We have calculated median and formed three groups: SCs in which educated population is over the median in both secondary education and superior education, SCs in which educated population is under the median in both secondary education and superior education and a third group with the rest of the options

Regarding the score in the implementation of the smart initiative (vertical versus transversal) and the smart initiatives approach, there are no patterns. Local governments mostly develop smart projects involving multiples departments or areas; in addition, local governments are the main promoter of smart initiative, regardless of the education level. Similarly, the education has no influence over the collaboration model for implementing smart initiatives.

4.4 RQ4 – Are There Patterns in the Strategic Planning of Smart Initiatives Based on the Income Per Capita?

In Table 6, we can observe that the information about smart initiatives are formalized in SCs with a lower income per capita than the median (93.98%). By contrast, in SCs with an upper income per capita than the median, the information disclosed is no formalized (60.50%).

Table 6. Characterization of main attributes of strategic planning in sample SCs based on the income per capita of the population that live in sample municipalities.

Income per capita	FSP		TSP		APP		COB	
	Formal	Informal	Vertical	Transversal	Bottom	Top	Yes	No
Upper median	39.50%	60.50%	28.00%	72.00%	2.81%	97.19%	12.56%	87.44%
Lower median	93.98%	6.02%	26.06%	73.94%	0.20%	99.80%	3.79%	96.21%

Note: We have calculated median and formed two groups: SCs with an upper income per capita than the median and SCs with a lower income per capita than the median.

As for the score in the implementation of the smart initiative (vertical versus transversal), the smart initiatives approach and the collaboration public-private to develop smart initiative, there are no patterns. In this sense, smart initiatives are mainly leaded by the administration and involved multiple departments and, in turn, the no-collaboration public-private is predominant, regardless of the income per capital.

5   Conclusions and Discussions

Findings show that some patterns can be identified according to both the demographical city profile and the citizen profile living in the SCs. Regarding demographical attributes of the sample SCs, although prior research has demonstrated that formal strategic planning where public managers are involved in could have a strong positive relationship with strategy implementation success [30], our findings suggest that both smaller-size cities and those with a higher proportion of older people usually perform formal strategic planning processes. These findings seem to confirm prior research which points out that larger-size jurisdictions may make strategic planning more difficult for them to do so effectively [31], perhaps due to the presence of so many stakeholders with a multiplicity of goals and conflicting accountabilities [32], which makes these municipalities to adopt other different approaches.

As for the young people, the European Union, strongly from the beginning of the 2010s decade [33], has promoted the young people involvement into public decisions as a key aspect for building cities with the aim at ensuring that they have a say in the democratic processes that shape Europe's future. Our findings show that SCs with a high proportion of older population are used to undertake formal strategic planning processes, which is a novelty result of this research, because it is not linked to the highly education level of this section of the population [34] as it could be expected. Indeed, findings of our paper indicate that SCs with a high proportion of highly educated population seem to undertake informal strategic planning process.

Concretely, findings show that in SCs, where intermediate and low levels of both educated and low-income people live in, city governments usually undertake formal and transversal strategic planning processes. Therefore, citizen profile also seems to modulate the way that city governments are undertaking strategic planning process of smart initiatives.

As for the scope of the smart initiatives, Guenduez et al. [13] found that participants and interviewees in a sample survey highlighted the importance of aligning and embedding the smart government strategy in the overall strategy of the government body in question. Our research shows that although general nowadays, transversal type of strategic planning in smart initiatives (using the transversal approach) is mainly performed in medium-sized municipalities (between 292,879–506,123 inhabitants) and where intermediate and high level of education people are living in. This finding could be linked to the previous one because formal strategic planning process usually takes an integral view of the strategic planning process.

By contrast, prior research has not obtained consistent findings concerning the strategic planning approach to be conducted by public administrations. While some scholars advocate the top-down or centralized approach [35], others find the bottom-up or decentralized approach as preferable [36]. In any case, in both cases, scholars highlight that the more participation in the planning process (including citizens, external stakeholders and public managers at all levels of the public administration), better results will be obtained [37]. Nonetheless, recent research has demonstrated that these prior findings could be context-depend because in the Nordic context, the formal strategic planning and the strategic types may have had little impact relative to stakeholder involvement [38].

In brief, demographic and citizen profile seems to be attributes that could be relevant in the way of undertaking strategic planning processes into SCs. Nonetheless, this research is a first approach to this issue and some limitations are present such as, for example, the low number of sample SCs and the similar context in which the SCs are located.

Therefore, future research should extend this research to other SCs in different countries and contexts with the aim at identifying similarities and differences. In addition, future research could include other variables that could influence on the strategic planning patterns of smart initiatives in SCs. As recent research has indicated, successful smart initiatives should focus not only on new technologies, but also on managing organizational capabilities, addressing environmental requirements, building leadership, and developing common strategies and standards [13]. Finally, future research could analyze the impact of strategic planning patterns on both the efficiency and efficacy of the smart initiatives implemented, and on the outcomes produced by these smart initiatives.

Acknowledgement. This research was carried out with financial support from the Centre of Andalusian Studies (Research proj. No. PR137/19).

References

1. Letaifa, S.B.: How to strategize smart cities: revealing the SMART model. J. Bus. Res. **68**(7), 1414–1419 (2015)
2. Grossi, G., Pianezzi, D.: Smart cities: utopia or neoliberal ideology? Cities **69**, 79–85 (2017)

3. Angelidou, M.: Smart city policies: a spatial approach. Cities **41**, S3–S11 (2014)
4. Rodríguez Bolívar, M.P.: In the search for the 'Smart' source of the perception of quality of life in European smart cities. In: Proceedings of the 52nd Hawaii International Conference on System Sciences, January 2019
5. Brorström, S., Argento, D., Grossi, G., Thomasson, A., Almqvist, R.: Translating sustainable and smart city strategies into performance measurement systems. Pub. Money Manage. **38**(3), 193–202 (2018)
6. Anthopoulos, L.: Smart utopia VS smart reality: Learning by experience from 10 smart city cases. Cities **63**, 128–148 (2017)
7. Yigitcanlar, T.: Smart city policies revisited: considerations for a truly smart and sustainable urbanism practice. World Technolopolis Rev. **7**(2), 97–112 (2018)
8. Mora, L., Deakin, M., Reid, A.: Strategic principles for smart city development: amultiple case study analysis of European best practices. Technol. Forecast. Soc. Chang. **142**, 70–97 (2019)
9. Harrison, C., Donnelly, I.A.: A theory of smart cities. In: Kineman, J. (ed.) 55th Annual Meeting of the ISSS-2011, vol. 55, no. 1, pp. 1–15. Hull, UK (2011)
10. Bolívar, M.P.R., Muñoz, L.A.: Political ideology and municipal size as incentives for the implementation and governance models of web 2.0 in providing public services. Int. J. Pub. Adm. Digit. Age (IJPADA) **5**(1), 36–62 (2018)
11. Basu, A.: Viability assessment of emerging smart urban para-transit solutions: case of cab aggregators in Kolkata city, India. J. Urban Manage. **8**(3), 364–376 (2019)
12. Rodríguez Bolívar, M.P.: Characterizing the role of governments in smart cities: a literature review. In: Gil-Garcia, J.Ramon, Pardo, Theresa A., Nam, T. (eds.) Smarter as the New Urban Agenda. PAIT, vol. 11, pp. 49–71. Springer, Cham (2016). https://doi.org/10.1007/978-3-319-17620-8_3
13. Guenduez, A.A.: Smart government success factors. Swiss Yearbook Adm. Sci. **9**(1), 96–110 (2018)
14. European Parliament: Mapping Smart Cities in the EU. European Parliament, Directorate General for internal policies, Brussels (2014)
15. Bonsón, E., Torres, L., Royo, S., Flores, F.: Local e-Government 2.0: social media and corporate transparency in municipalities. Gov. Inf. Q. **29**(2), 123–132 (2012)
16. Cegarra, J.G., Córdoba, J.R., Moreno, J.L.: E-government and Citizens engagement with local affairs through e-Websites: the case of Spanish municipalities. Int. J. Inf. Manage. **32**(5), 469–478 (2012)
17. Bradford, N.: Creative Cities: Structured Policy Dialogue Report. Canadian Policy Research Networks, Ottawa (2004)
18. Foth, M., Brynskov, M., Ojala, T.: Citizen's Right to the Digital City: Urban Interfaces, Activism, and Placemaking. Springer, Singapore (2015). https://doi.org/10.1007/978-981-287-919-6
19. Rodríguez Bolívar, M.P.: Governance models and outcomes to foster public value creation in smart cities. Sci. Reg., Italian J. Reg. Sci. **1**, 57–80 (2018)
20. Priya Uteng, T., Turner, J.: Addressing the linkages between gender and transport in low-and middle-income countries. Sustainability **11**(17), 45–55 (2019)
21. Kiiski, C., Pohjola, M.: Cross-country diffusion of the internet. Inf. Econ. Pol. **14**(2), 297–310 (2002)
22. Cabas-Perez, M.C., Rodriguez-Bolivar, M.P.R., Hernandez, A.M.L.: The determinants of government financial reports online. Transylvanian Rev. Adm. Sci. **10**(42), 5–31 (2014)
23. Sol, D.A.D.: The institutional, economic and social determinants of local government transparency. J. Econ. Pol. Reform **16**(1), 90–107 (2013)
24. Arora, R.U.: Financial sector development and smart cities: the Indian case. Sustain. Cit. Soc. **42**, 52–58 (2018)

25. Winters, J.V.: Why are smart cities growing? Who moves and who stays. J. Reg. Sci. **51**(2), 253–270 (2011)
26. Shapiro, J.M.: Smart cities: quality of life, productivity, and the growth effects of human capital. Rev. Econ. Stat. **88**(2), 324–335 (2006)
27. Alcaide Muñoz, L., Rodríguez Bolívar, M.P.: Using tools for citizen engagement on large and medium-sided European Smart Cities. In: Alcaide Muñoz, A., Rodríguez Bolívar, M.P. (eds.) E-Participation in Smart Cities: Technologies and Models of Governance for Citizen Engagement, pp. 23–35. Springer, Heidelberg (2019). https://doi.org/10.1007/978-3-319-894 74-4_2
28. Giffinger, R., Gudrun, H.: Smart cities ranking: an effective instrument for the positioning of the cities? ACE: Archit. City Environ. UPCommons, Barcelona **4**(12), 7–26 (2010)
29. Esteves-Araujo, J.F.F., Tejedo-Romero, F.: Does Gender Equality affect municipal transparency: the case of Spain. Public Perform. Manage. Rev. **41**(1), 69–99 (2018)
30. Elbanna, S., Andrews, R., Pollanen, R.: Strategic planning and implementation success in public service organizations: evidence from Canada. Public Manage. Rev. **18**(7), 1017–1042 (2016)
31. Boyne, G.A.: Strategic Planning. In: Ashworth, R., Boyne, G.A., Entwistle, T. (eds.) Public Service Improvement: Theories and Evidence. Oxford University Press, Oxford (2010)
32. Bryson, J.M., Edwards, L.H., Van Slyke, D.M.: Getting strategic about strategic planning research. Public Manage. Rev. **20**(3), 317–339 (2018)
33. European Union (EU): An EU Strategy for Youth–Investing and Empowering. A renewed open method of coordination to address youth challenges and opportunities/Commission of the European communities (2009). https://eur-lex.europa.eu/LexUriServ/LexUriServ.do?uri= COM:2009:0200:FIN:EN:PDF
34. Beunen, R., Meijer, M., De Vries, J.: Planning strategies for dealing with population decline: experiences from the Netherlands. Land Use Policy **93**, 104107 (2019)
35. Poister, T.H., Streib, G.: Elements of strategic planning and management in municipal government: Status after two decades. Public Adm. Rev. **65**(1), 45–56 (2005)
36. Robert, N.C., Wargo, L.: The dilemma of planning in large-scale public organizations: the case of the United States Navy. J. Public Adm. Res. Theor. **4**(4), 469–491 (1994)
37. Blair, R.: Public participation and community development: the role of strategic planning. Public Adm. Q. **28**(1/2), 102–147 (2004)
38. Johnsen, Å.: Impacts of strategic planning and management in municipal government: an analysis of subjective survey and objective production and efficiency measures in Norway. Public Manage. Rev. **20**(3), 397–420 (2018)

Demographical Attributes Explaining Different Stages of OG Development in Spanish Local Governments

Manuel Pedro Rodríguez Bolívar[(✉)], Cinthia L. Villamayor Arellano, and Laura Alcaide Muñoz

University of Granada, Granada, Spain
manuelp@ugr.es

Abstract. In recent years city governments have rethought and changed their governing routines, procedures and processes, to better understand citizens' needs, implementing Open Government Strategies. Our study analyzes the use of technological channels available to citizens by local governments to improve transparency and citizens' participation and collaboration. Our empirical research selected 145 Spanish local governments with more than 50,000 inhabitants. Findings show that the size of the municipality, the population density, the population age and the level of education of the inhabitants could influence on the citizen participation models implemented in sample cities. On the whole, findings indicate that the level of OG development is still low in Spanish local governments, which means that there is much room for improvement in the future if local governments want to make citizen participation true.

Keywords: Open Government · Transparency · Citizen participation · Collaboration

1 Introduction

In the last decade, cities have been facing unprecedented challenges due to an increasing population in the urban areas, which has evidenced the need of implementing technology-driven initiatives as a means for improving information transparency and citizen participation in public decisions. Under this framework, city governments have tried to follow a collaborative path in the way of becoming smart, mainly creating smart cities networks [1].

One main smart policy is about the new governance models that these new city challenges require [2]. In this regard, smart cities have focused their efforts on public governance at different levels under the label of Open Government Partnership (OGP). This has become one of the goals to achieve with the ICTs implementation is to provide citizens a higher level of information transparency [3], and a greater accessibility to public services [4], improving, this way, the citizen interaction, its participation and collaboration in public affairs [5]. In fact, although there is still confusion regarding the

© IFIP International Federation for Information Processing 2020
Published by Springer Nature Switzerland AG 2020
G. Viale Pereira et al. (Eds.): EGOV 2020, LNCS 12219, pp. 387–399, 2020.
https://doi.org/10.1007/978-3-030-57599-1_29

Open Government (OG) concept, these three main aspects (information, participation and collaboration) have been widely considered in academic literature as the principles that constitute the OG [6]. In this regard, the OECD (2011) [7], has defined the OG as one culture characterized by transparency of its actions, accessibility of citizens to its services and information, and government responsiveness to new ideas, demands and needs.

Prior research has mainly focused on some attributes like urban population and citizen educational profiles as main incentives for city governments to implement ICTs [8]. However, according to the recent literature review undertaken by [9], to date contextual factors like demographical factors have not been analyzed in their impact on smart city governance, which is linked to the OG movement regarding a more informative, participative and collaborative city governments. Indeed, these incentives have not been analyzed as drivers for OG mature process in the different cities and the literature about differences on the stages of OG development in municipalities according determinants factors is recognized nowadays as relatively limited.

Therefore, based on the analysis of the different levels of the OG development (specially focused on information and citizen participation channels), this paper deepens the understanding of the main attributes of the demographical profiles of cities that could affect their level of OG maturity process. To achieve this aim, this paper is focuses on the Government of Spain, whose Central Government has issued several action plans to align this country with the EU guidelines [10] in order to achieve the objectives established in its Digital Agenda [11], and its focus on the modernization and openness of government systems based on the approach of transparency, participation and collaboration. In this sense, the Government of Spain has formulated numerous action plans and legislation has been enacted in this regard [11]. Accordingly, this study aims to contribute to this research gap by analyzing the use of the technological channels available to citizens by local governments to improve transparency and citizen participation, allowing collaboration between citizens and public administrations. Besides, based on main theories about the stages and models of citizen participation [12], we categorized the main aspects of OG into two stages of OG: transparency and engagement. This analysis has been undertaken under the demographical factors (concretely, population size, population density, population age and educational level of citizens) to know whether these attributes affect the different levels of OG development in a sample of 145 Spanish municipalities, with more than 50,000 inhabitants, under the microscope. This analysis will provide us with an overview of the practices carried out, so as to establish conclusions and public policy recommendations that could favor these initiatives by public managers.

The paper is structured as follows. Section 2 provides details of theoretical framework of the study whereas Sect. 3 details the empirical research undertaken in this paper. Section 3.3 describes the main results of our research and, finally, Sect. 4 conclusion and discussion will bring the paper to an end.

2   The OG Maturity Models and the Arnstein's Participation Ladder

The question of maturity models in OG is something confused. Prior research has identified the OG maturity models as e-government maturity models [13]. Nonetheless, the e-government field of knowledge goes beyond the OG concern which is focused on governance issues. This way, others have clearly identified OG maturity models as steps or stages for achieving a greater level of governance but only in specific areas, like innovation [14], or through the use of specific technological tools, like social media [15].

By contrast, despite the time passed by the Arnstein's ladder of participation (ALP) [12], although changed and evolved, her work can provide nowadays the foundations for the central concepts included in the new governance models to be implemented in smart cities [16]. Indeed, in the last years it is growing in the presence of the ALP in the urban planning literature [16], and it has been recently used as a framework for the assessment of participatory models [17].

According to [12], there are eight rungs on a ladder of citizen participation which can be categorized into three main approaches according to the level of interaction between citizens and governments: a) Nonparticipation; b) Degree of tokenism and c) Degree of citizen power. Whereas the first one is mainly driven to manipulate and learn the "non-educated" citizens, the second approach is mainly addressed to improve information transparency and inviting citizens' opinions but the power of making decisions keep at the government level. Finally, the third approach is that of really a participation one where governments delegate some level of power for citizens to participate in an associated or in an individual basis to the public policies and decisions.

As noted previously, the three aspects that build the OG concept are information, participation and collaboration [18] which deal with the concepts of transparency, citizen engagement and citizen cooperation with public entities [19].

The transparency (TRANS) includes the information and consultation rungs in the ALP (third and fourth rung) and is mainly addressed to achieve government accountability and, by this way, better democracy avoiding government corruption [20]. In this approach, there is a unidirectional (information) or bidirectional flows of information (consultation) that only offer the possibility of obtaining, requesting and sending information to the public managers through customer satisfaction survey [21].

Citizen engagement (CITENG) includes participatory mechanisms that give opportunities for open and transparent discourse among citizens and government officials [22]. In brief, although a participative stage, the citizen influence in public decisions is still indirect, showing a slight authority of those involved [23].

Finally, citizen cooperation (CITCOO) represents the collaborative environment with citizens where citizens' highest level of authority is exercised. Collaboration involves the interaction among citizens, interest groups and government in the search for solutions to solve complex urban problems in a shared power basis. It means the need of public administration for promoting public polices with a view to strengthen the role of citizens in the governance process [24].

In sum, recent prior research indicates that the ALP seems to be a good framework for analyzing new governance models implemented in modern cities [17]. These cities have been implementing in the last decades new technologies for facing the new challenges given rise with the increasing growth of population. As this population growth is recognized as one of the main problems of urban areas, in our research, we seek to analyze whether different demographical attributes could help to understand the OG development stage of sample Spanish cities.

3 Empirical Research on Large Spanish Municipalities

3.1 Demographical Attributes and Research Questions

Harrison et al., [25] point out that the OG projects must produce public value. Nonetheless, the eventual success of an open government initiative often depends on the environment and the context [26]. In fact, based on the different theories (agency, legitimacy, contingency, capability and neo-institutional theories), prior research has demonstrated that demographical attributes have influence on both the level of implementation of ICTs in municipalities [27] and the acceptance and use of technological advances by citizens [28].

Thus, based on prior research, it is expected that main demographical attributes like the municipal size, the population density, the age of the inhabitants and the level of education of citizens could affect the OG maturity models implemented in the urban areas.

Municipal Size (POP)
According to the agency theory [29], large-size governments with a high degree of information asymmetry are expected to disclose a higher level of government information [30], improving democracy. In addition, it is recognized that municipality size is a main incentive for municipal innovation [31] and technological advances [32]. Thus, if the transparency improves and technological advances are implemented in local governments, citizens will better understand and trust in public processes and will be more likely to e-participate in public decisions [33]. In these technological contexts, public participation channels favor immediate communication between citizens and governments, reducing agency costs [34]. Also, prior studies have found a significant influence between the municipality size and citizen participation channels (websites or social networks) [32]. Therefore, the following hypothesis is derived:

H1. The population size of municipality positively influences on the level of OG development

Population Density (PDEN)
Based on the theory of legitimacy [35], actions are influenced by the information disseminated among different stakeholders, as a result of their legitimacy [36]. In this context, previous studies have found that the higher and more concentrated population in urban areas, the higher availability and use of new technologies [37]. Thus, when the population density is higher, citizens will have more internet access avoiding face-to-face contacts with their local governments, which will be driven through the use of more diverse public participation tools [38]. Taking into accounting this finding, we propose the following hypothesis:

H2. The population density positively influences on the level of OG development

Population Age (AGE15_24; AGE25_35; AGE36_64)

The theory of contingency advocates that social structure variables about both the information users and the political-administrative system, as well as their implementation barriers affect the citizen participation in public decisions, politics and administration [39]. In addition, it is demonstrated that the design and performance of open data projects are mainly linked to the individual profiles and motivations of citizens [40], and not as a way for giving citizens the opportunity to require protests, complaints, common causes, social demands, etc. [41].

Indeed, the population age is a main characteristic of the information user that influences on both the preferences/behavior of citizens regarding their interest in the dissemination of information and his/her public participation, and on the use of new ICTs as channels to be connected with city governments [42]. In fact, [43] considered that the population age is clearly associated with the use of e-government services, and recent research has found that younger people plays an active role in the society through the use of new ICTs. Also, [44] found older population are those with a higher demand for online information and public participation. Based on these assumptions, we propose the following hypothesis:

H3. Cities with higher proportion of young people positively influence on the level of OG development

Level of Education (SECEDU; UEDU)

Based on the capability theory [28], the main interest to participate in public decisions comes mainly from citizens with higher levels of education [45], because it has been demonstrated that the level of education is statistically a significant predictor with respect to the attitude of citizens to participate in these decisions. Thus, citizens with a high level of education will actively play a decisive role in government decisions through the use of ICTs in their daily lives [30]. However, these findings are not consistent with other studies that did not find a significant relationship regarding this issue [46]. Therefore, the following hypothesis is derived:

H4. The level of education of the population living in a city positively influences on the level of OG development

3.2 Sample Selection

Spain has done through both the adherence to OG principles (for example, adherence to the OG Partnership in 2011 and recommendations of the OECD on the Digital Strategies of the Government [47] and the issuance of several domestic regulations and actions plans to transform all levels of public administration in open, receptive and accountable governments. Indeed, the Spanish Central Government has carried out three action plans, focusing on regulations about information transparency and financial sustainability [48], on the creation of transparency websites as permanent channels for information [49] and on favoring the citizen's participation in public issues through a participatory space on the transparency website and the opening of a dialogue between the political forces and citizenship (third action plan, 2017−2019) [50].

These OG Spanish public policies have taken special incidence in the local government sphere due to the great number of services provided and the impact of their public policies on their citizens' daily file. In addition, local governments are usually among the first to adopt new technologies [32] with the aim of providing efficient services to the public, and they are called to be key actors to create an interactive-, participatory- and information-based urban environment, reforming city governance in a framework to encapsulate collaboration, cooperation, partnership, citizen engagement and participation [2]. Therefore, this research is focused on large Spanish local governments with more than 50,000 inhabitants (145 municipalities) that represent more than 50% of the Spanish population (National Institute of Statistics 2018).

To analyze the initiatives of the sample local governments in the implementation of OG policies, we visited their official websites, and other channels that allow citizen participation during November-December 2019. Then, we collected information about the different levels of OG development (TRANS; CITENG and CITCOO) according to the channels offered by the sample municipalities (see Table 2).

3.3   Independent Attributes and Method

To identify the factors that affect the three key aspects of OG (TRANS; CITENG; CIT-COO), we have analyzed the official websites and other official channels for participation (like social media, apps and e-participation tools) as well as online information of each of the 145 sample municipalities. The authors of this paper have separately catalogued whether the sample municipality is: a) disclosing information about events and issues of public interest or carrying out surveys to collect the opinion of their citizens (TRANS) -stages 3 and 4 of ALP-; b) allowing citizens to participate in municipal plenary sessions (CITENG) -stage 6 of ALP-; and c) allowing citizens to participate in public discussions (CITCOO) -stage 8 of ALP-. To ensure objectivity, after this cataloging method, authors discussed their results to achieve a consensus of the examinations performed. If there were any significant discrepancies, the websites and other official channels for participation were jointly examined again by all authors.

Also, based on previous sections, we have analyzed four demographical attributes to answer the research questions posed in this research: population size (POP) -RQ1-, population density (PDEN) -RQ2-, population age (AGE) -RQ3- and level of education (SECEDU; UEDU) -RQ4-. In order to undertake our analysis, the population and the population density have been classified into quartiles (see Table 1). As for the population age and the level of education, we have classified sample municipalities into three groups according to the median score in each one of the subgroups included into these attributes (see Table 1). In brief, Table 1 shows the definition and calculation method of each of the dependent and independent attributes.

On another hand, it is a surprising result the intention of sample municipalities for allowing citizens to participate in public decisions (73.10% in partnership rung), which could help to understand the effort of municipalities in engaging citizens to participate in municipal plenary sessions either in person or through different online participation channels. However, there is a low relevance of citizen cooperation in sample municipalities. Only the 26.90% of sample municipalities allow citizens to participate in discussions about public affairs of the municipality.

Table 1. Definition of the attributes and total descriptive data on the rungs and stages achieved by sample municipalities

Attributes	Acronym	Definition	Calculation/Method used/Rung ladder of participation
Information and Consultation	TRANS	Information and Consultation phases	Rung 3. Informing Rung. 4. Consultation
Citizen Engagement	CITENG	Participation phase	Rung. 6. Partnership
Citizen Cooperation	CITCOO	Collaboration phase	Rung 8. Citizen control
Population	POP*	Population residing in the municipality	Percentage of quartiles of population size
Population Density	PDEN*	Population residing in the municipality per km^2	Percentage of quartiles of population density
Population Age	AGE_15-24*	Numbers of inhabitants from 15 to 24 years old	• Group 1: the cities with median score lower than 9.94% from 15 to 24 years old, lower than 11.96% from 24 to 35 years old and lower than 44.75% over 35 years old • Group 2: the cities with median score higher than 9.94% from 15 to 24 years old, higher than 11.96% from 24 to 35 years old and higher than 44.75% over 35 years old • Group 3: all other cities that: do not comply with the above conditions
	AGE_24-35*	Numbers of inhabitants from 24 to 35 years old	
	AGE_35-64*	Numbers of inhabitants from 35 to 64 years old	
Education Level	SECEDU*	Number of inhabitants with secondary studies	• Group 1: cities with median score lower than 10.72% in secondary studies and lower than median score of 24.74% in university studies • Group 2: cities with median score higher than 10.72% in secondary studies and higher than 24.74% in university studies • Group 3: all other cities that: do not comply with the above conditions
	UEDU*	Number of inhabitants with university studies	

Notes: *INE (Statistic Institute of Spain) www.ine.es.

As for the influence of demographical attributes on the level of OG development (RQ1, 2, 3 and 4), results seem to confirm a relationship between large municipalities and higher level of OG development (RQ1). In this regard, data seems to indicate that large-size cities are more prone to promote citizen engagement (stage II) and citizen cooperation (stage III) than small-size cities (see % in q4 for CITENG and CITCOO).

Concerning the relationship between citizen concentration in urban areas (PDEN - RQ2-) and level of OG development, our empirical data seems to indicate that the higher citizen concentration in urban areas, the higher level of OG development, especially regarding citizen consultation, engagement and cooperation (see % in q3 and q4 in TRANS -rung 4-, CITENG and CITCOO). Nonetheless, both rung 4 and rung 8 have obtained a low level of accomplishment, which indicates a high potential to improve these aspects in the future. In brief, analyzing population variables (POP and PDEN),

Table 2. Descriptive data about different stages and all demographical attributes

Stage and Question	Q	POP % (H1)	PDEN % (H 2)	Group	AGE % (H 3)	SECEDU/UEDU % (H4)
Transparency stage (TRANS)						
3. Is information disclosed about events and issues of public interest to be produced by the municipality?	1	23.45%	22.76%	1	17.24%	31.03%
	2	24.14%	24.14%	2	18.62%	34.48%
	3	23.45%	24.83%	3	60.00%	30.34%
	4	24.83%	24.14%			
	TOTAL	**95.86%**	**95.86%**		**95.86%**	**95.86%**
4. Are surveys carried out to collect the opinion of citizens?	1	10.34%	8.28%	1	4.83%	13.79%
	2	12.41%	11.72%	2	11.72%	17.24%
	3	11.72%	13.10%	3	30.34%	15.86%
	4	12.41%	13.79%			
	TOTAL	**46.90%**	**46.90%**		**46.90%**	**46.90%**
Citizen Engagement stage (CITENG)						
6. Are citizens allowed to participate in municipal plenary sessions?	1	16.55%	15.17%	1	11.03%	19.31%
	2	18.62%	16.55%	2	15.17%	26.90%
	3	17.24%	20.00%	3	46.90%	26.90%
	4	20.69%	21.38%			
	TOTAL	**73.10%**	**73.10%**		**73.10%**	**73.10%**
Citizen Cooperation stage (CITCOO)						
8. Are online discussions held?	1	6.90%	4.83%	1	2.07%	3.45%
	2	6.21%	4.83%	2	4.83%	11.03%
	3	5.52%	8.97%	3	20.00%	12.41%
	4	8.28%	8.28%			
	TOTAL	**26.90%**	**26.90%**		**26.90%**	**26.90%**

Notes: "Q" adopted two values → population classified by quartiles: 1 (0–67,640); 2 (67,641–88,096); 3 (88,097–172,816) and 4 (172,817–3,182,981) and population density classified by quartiles: 1 (0–506); 2 (507–1,478); 3 (1,479–3,211) and 4 (3,212–18,895)

"Groups" adopted different values →

1) We have calculated median and formed three groups: 1 (citizens over the median of inhabitants from 15 to 24 years old + citizens over the median of inhabitants from 25 to 35 years + citizens over the median of inhabitants from 36 to 64 years); 2 (citizens over the median of inhabitants from 15 to 24 years old + citizens under the median of inhabitants from 36 to 64 years); and (citizens under the median of inhabitants from 15 to 24 years + citizens under the median of inhabitants from 25 to 35 years old + citizens under the median of inhabitants from 36 to 64 years.

2) We have calculated median and formed three groups: SCs in which educated population is over the median in both secondary education and superior education, SCs in which educated population is under the median in both secondary education and superior education and a third group with the rest of the options.

our data reveals that public managers in larger and more densely populated cities are more motivated to implement OG initiatives.

In the particular case of the AGE attribute (RQ3), results seems not to indicate a preference for a particular young (group 1) or old citizenry (group 2), except for the citizen consultation rung (rung 4), although it seems clear that older people are more prone to participate and collaborate than the younger ones (see % in rungs 6 and 8). Indeed, cities with a medium-aged citizenry achieve a higher level of OG development (see % in group 3 in all rungs).

Finally, results showed that cities where low-educated people live in are those with low scores at consultation, engagement and, significantly, cooperation rungs (see Table 2). Indeed, results show a low percentage of OG development in these rungs in cities where low-educated people live in. However, cities where medium and highly-educated people live in, the level of OG development is much higher. Besides, results seem to indicate that cities where highly-educated people live in are those where the consultation rung is highly achieved by city governments (see % in Table 2). It could mean that city governments are usually more prone to collect the opinions of their citizens, sharing knowledge and capacities for problem-solving issues in the city.

4 Discussion and Conclusion

This study contributes to understanding the level of OG maturity development in Spanish large-size cities (those with more than 50,000 inhabitants) and deepens the understanding of the main attributes of the demographical profiles of cities that could affect their level of OG maturity process (and concretely, the analysis of the population size, population density, population age and citizens' level of education). On the whole, findings indicate that the level of OG development is still low in Spanish local governments, which means that there is much room for improvement in the future if local governments want to make citizen participation true.

Findings indicate that the informing rung is fully achieved in all sample cities. Therefore, the information phase is already overcome in cities, disclosing a high level of information about events and public interest affairs through the use of different technological tools like official websites, social media, etc. This finding confirms prior research that indicates that city governments are mainly focused on unidirectional information disclosure [51].

Also, findings show the intention of city governments to make citizens to participate in plenary sessions of the Council Board of the city (rung 6 of ALP). Nonetheless, this finding is mainly present in large-size and highly-densely populated cities, where city governments promote both the citizen involvement in the plenary sessions of the Council Board of the municipality and the online discussions, but the online discussions are nowadays almost inexistent. Indeed, city government are not worried about collecting opinions of nor having discussions with the citizenry (rungs 4 and 8, consultation and cooperation). Therefore, findings seem to confirm that city governments are more concerned to both achieve the legitimacy of their actions and reduce agency costs than an effective participation of the citizenry -agency and legitimacy theory- [34].

Also, findings show that there is not preference in city government to achieve a higher level of OG development where young people is living in. This result is not on the way of prior research concerning the younger people to be more prone in using ICTs than older people [52]. Indeed, our finding confirm [43] study where medium-aged population used ICTs at the same grade. In addition, it could indicate that, nowadays, the cultural and generational gap regarding the implementation of ICTs has been solved and all citizens are used to utilize the ICTs for interaction with the government, avoiding the digital divide, which represents an active role of all citizens in the information age since they are immersed in new ICTs.

Finally, findings have confirmed that city governments are more prone to promote citizen consultation, engagement and cooperation where medium and highly-educated people are living in. Especially, the consultation rung seems to be linked to cities where highly-educated people are living in.

As this is a first approach to this research field, this study has some limitations, including the analysis of the information quality disclosed or the will of citizens to participate and/or cooperate with city governments. Therefore, future research should deepen in these issues and widen the sample selection to other countries and different contexts with the aim at analyzing if our findings are context-dependent. Also, other attributes could be analyzed seeking to know the whole factors and barriers in the OG development models. Finally, statistical test could help us to strongly support this first approach to this topic.

Acknowledgement. This research was carried out with financial support from the Centre of Andalusian Studies (Research proj. No. PR137/19) and Ministry of Science, Innovation and Universities (Spain) (Research proj. No. SmartGov_Local RTI2018-095344-A-100).

References

1. Eurocities: Eurocities Network (2020). http://www.eurocities.eu/eurocities/home. Accessed 25 March 2020
2. Rodríguez Bolívar, M.P.: smart cities: big cities, complex governance? In: Rodríguez-Bolívar, M.P. (ed.) Transforming City Governments for Successful Smart Cities. PAIT, vol. 8, pp. 1–7. Springer, Cham (2015). https://doi.org/10.1007/978-3-319-03167-5_1
3. Rodriguez, P.B., Alcaide, L.M., Hernandez, A.L.: Trends of e-government research. contextualization and research opportunities. Int. J. Digit. Account. Res. (2010). https://doi.org/10.4192/1577-8517-v10
4. Cordella, A., Paletti, A.: Value creation, ICT, and co-production in public sector: bureaucracy, opensourcing and crowdsourcing. In: Proceedings of the 18th Annual International Conference on Digital Government Research, pp. 185–194. ACM, June 2017
5. Taylor, J., Lips, M., Organ, J.: Information-intensive government and the layering and sorting of citizenship. Public Money and Manag. 27(2), 161–164 (2007)
6. Chang, Y.H., Wu, T.H., Cheng, C.R., Lin, S.W., Tu, J.K.: U.S. Patent Application No. 10/273,140 (2019)
7. OCDE: Government at a Glance 2011. In Government at a Glance 2011 (2012). https://doi.org/10.1787/9787515002620-zh
8. Rodríguez Bolívar, M.P.: Governance models and outcomes to foster public value creation in smart cities. Sci. Regionali, Italian J. Reg. Sci. 1, 57–80 (2018)
9. Wilhelm, R., Ruhlandt, S.: The governance of smart cities: a systematic literature review. Cities 81, 1–23 (2018)

10. European Commission: The Digital Agenda in the Europe 2020 Strategy (2015). https://eur opa.eu/european-union/file/1501/download_es?token=3l7D0Fil

11. Alcaide Muñoz, L., Rodríguez Bolívar, M.P., Alcaraz Quilez, F.J.: Policies and strategies for digital inclusion: regional governments in Spain. Prescott, J. (ed.). Handbook of Research on Race, Gender, and the Fight for Equality, pp. 1–29. IGI Global (2016)

12. Arnstein, S.R.: A ladder of citizen participation. J. Am. Inst. Plann. **35**(4), 216–224 (1969)

13. Almuftah, H., Weerakkody, V., Sivarajah, U.: Comparing and contrasting e-government maturity models: a qualitative-meta synthesis. In: Electronic Government and Electronic Participation: Joint Proceedings of Ongoing Research and Projects of IFIP WG, vol. 8, pp. 69–79 (2016)

14. Ham, J., Lee, J.N., Kim, D., Choi, B.: Open innovation maturity model for the government: an open system perspective. In: Proceedings to the 36th ICIS 2015. USA: Fort Worth, Texas (2015)

15. Lee, G., Kwak, Y.H.: An open government maturity model for social media-based public engagement. Gov. Inf. Q. **29**(4), 492–503 (2012)

16. Slotterback, C.S., Lauria, M.: Building a foundation for public engagement in planning: 50 years of impact, interpretation, and inspiration from Arnstein's Ladder. J. Am. Plann. Assoc. **85**(3), 183–187 (2019)

17. Contreras, S.: Using Arnstein's ladder as an evaluative framework for the assessment of participatory work in Postdisaster Haiti. J. Am. Plann. Assoc. **85**(3), 219–235 (2019)

18. Ruvalcaba-Gomez, E.A., Criado, J.I., Gil-Garcia, J.R.: Discussing open government as a concept: a comparison between the perceptions of public managers and current academic debate. In: Proceedings of the 19th Annual International Conference on Digital Government Research: Governance in the Data Age, pp. 1–10, May 2018

19. McDermott, P.: Building open government. Gov. Inf. Q. **27**(4), 401–413 (2010)

20. Piotrowski, S.J.: The "Open Government Reform" movement: the case of the open government partnership and US transparency policies. Am. Rev. Public Adm. **47**(2), 155–171 (2017)

21. Nabatchi, T.: Putting the 'public' back in public values research: designing public participation to identify and respond to public values. Public Adm. Rev. **72**(5), 699–708 (2012)

22. Coleman, S., Gøtze, J.: Bowling Together: Online Public Engagement in Policy Deliberation, pp. 39–50. Hansard Society, London (2001)

23. Miller, S.A., Hildreth, R.W., Stewart, L.M.: The modes of participation: a revised frame for identifying and analyzing participatory budgeting practices. Adm. Soc. **51**(8), 1254–1281 (2019)

24. Routzouni, A., Deligiannis, A.P., Peristeras, V., Gritzalis, S.: An intercountry survey of participatory practices used for open government partnership national action plan development. In: Lindgren, I., Janssen, M., Lee, H., Polini, A., Rodríguez Bolívar, M.P., Scholl, H.J., Tambouris, E. (eds.) EGOV 2019. LNCS, vol. 11685, pp. 82–93. Springer, Cham (2019). https://doi.org/10.1007/978-3-030-27325-5_7

25. Harrison, T.M., et al.: Open government and e-government: democratic challenges from a public value perspective. Inf. Polity **17**(2), 83–97 (2012)

26. Galasso, G., et al.: Analysis of the value of new generation of eGovernment services and how the public sector can become an agent of innovation through ICT. Directorate-General of Communications Networks, Content & Technology, European Commission, Luxembourg (2016)

27. Rodríguez Bolívar, M.P., Alcaide Muñoz, L.: Political ideology and municipal size as incentives for the implementation and governance models of web 2.0 in providing public services. Int. J. Public Adm. Dig. Age (IJPADA) **5**(1), 36–62 (2018)

28. Heres, J., Mante-Meijer, E., Turk, T., Pierson, J.: Adoption of ICTs: a proposed framework. In: Mante-Meijer, E., Klamer, L. (eds.) ICT Capabilities in Action: What People Do, pp. 19–48. Office for Official Publication of the European Communities, Luxemburg (2005)

29. Zimmerman, J.L.: The municipal accounting maze: an analysis of political incentives. J. Account. Res. **15**(Suppl.), 107–144 (1977)
30. Serrano-Cinca, C., Rueda-Tomás, M., Portillo-Tarragona, P.: Determinants of e-government extension. Online Inf. Q. **33**(3), 476–498 (2009)
31. Gonzalez, R., Llopis, J., Gasco, J.: Innovation in public services: the case of Spanish local government. J. Bus. Res. **66**(10), 2024–2033 (2013)
32. Bonsón, E., Torre, L., Royo, S., Flores, F.: Local e-government 2.0: social media and corporate transparency in municipalities. Gov. Inf. Q. **29**(2), 123–132 (2012)
33. Zheng, Y., Schachter, H.L.: Explaining citizens' e-participation use: the role of perceived advantages. Public Organ. Rev. **17**(3), 409–428 (2017). https://doi.org/10.1007/s11115-016-0346-2
34. Cárcaba, A., García-García, J.: Determinants of online reporting of accounting information by Spanish local government authorities. Local Gov. Stud. **36**(5), 679–695 (2010)
35. Suchman, M.C.: Managing legitimacy: strategic and institutional approaches. Acad. Manag. Rev. **20**(3), 571–610 (1995)
36. Archel, P., Husillos, J., Larrinaga, C., Spence, C.: Social disclosure, legitimacy theory and the role of the state. Account. Audit. Account. J. **22**, 1284–1307 (2009)
37. Garcia-Murillo, M.: International broadband deployment: the impact of unbundling. Int. J. Digit. Econ. **57**, 83–105 (2005)
38. Guillamón, M.D., Ríos, A.M., Gesuele, B., Metallo, C.: Factors influencing social media use in local governments: the case of Italy and Spain. Gov. Inf. Q. **33**(3), 460–471 (2016)
39. Lüder, K.: A contingency model of governmental accounting innovations in the political-administrative environment. Res. Gov. Nonprofit Account. **7**(1), 99–127 (1992)
40. Janssen, M., Charalabidis, Y., Zuiderwijk, A.: Benefits, adoption barriers and myths of open data and OG. Inf. Syst. Manage. (ISM) **29**(4), 258–268 (2012). http://dx.doi.org/10.1080/10580530.2012.716740
41. Gértrudix, M., Gertrudis-Casado, M.-C., Álvarez-García, S.: Consumption of public institutions' open data by Spanish citizens. El profesional de la información **25**(4), 535–544 (2016). http://dx.doi.org/10.3145/epi.2016.jul.03
42. Alcaide Muñoz, L., Rodríguez Bolívar, M.P.: Demographic Profile of Citizens' Interest, Evaluation and Opinions of Local Government Apps in Smart Cities. In: Lindgren, I., Janssen, M., Lee, H., Polini, A., Rodríguez Bolívar, M.P., Scholl, H.J., Tambouris, E. (eds.) EGOV 2019. LNCS, vol. 11685, pp. 313–325. Springer, Cham (2019). https://doi.org/10.1007/978-3-030-27325-5_24
43. Belanger, F., Carter, L.: The impact of the digital divide one-government use. Commun. AC **52**(4), 132–135 (2009)
44. Lowatcharin, G., Menifield, C.E.: Determinants of Internet-enabled transparency at the local level: a study of midwestern county web sites. State Local Gov. Rev. **47**(2), 102–115 (2015)
45. Bearfield, D.A., Bowman, A.O.M.: Can you find it on the web? An assessment of municipal e-government transparency. Am. Rev. Public Adm. **47**(2), 172–188 (2017)
46. Rodríguez-Domínguez, L., García-Sánchez, L.M., Gallego-Álvarez, L.: From emerging to connected e-government: the effects of socioeconomics and internal administration characteristics. Int. J. Digit. Account. Res. **11**(1), 85–109 (2011)
47. OCDE: Recommendation of the Council about OG (2014). https://www.oecd.org/gov/Recommendation-Open-Government-Approved-Council-141217.pdf
48. Government of Spain: Digital Agenda for Spain (2013). http://www.agendadigital.gob.es/agendadigital/recursos/Recursos/1.%2520Versi%25C3%253n%2520definitiva/Agenda_Digital_para_Espana.pdf
49. Government of Spain: Second National Action Plan of Spain 2014–2016 of The OG Partnership (2014). http://transparencia.gob.es/transparencia/dam/jcr:336c4f45-7d4a-4425-b9cf-70ba8fa2b454/II_Plan_Accion_Espana.pdf

50. Government of Spain: Third National Action Plan of Spain 2017–2019 of the OG Partnership (2018). http://transparencia.gob.es/transparencia/dam/jcr:7bcfaa1f-e2c0-482f-8913-12a45a8bc62e/SPA-ENG_III_Plan_OGP_v2018_vf.pdf

51. Rodríguez Bolívar, M.P.: The influence of political factors in policymakers' perceptions on the implementation of Web 2.0 technologies for citizen participation and knowledge sharing in public sector delivery. Inf. Polity **20**(2, 3), 199–220 (2015)

52. Van Dijk, J., Hacker, K.: The digital divide as a complex and dynamic phenomenon. Inf. Soc. **19**(4), 315–326 (2003)

Identification of Competencies and Teaching Models for the Governance of Smart Sustainable Cities in the South American Context

Aurora Sanchez-Ortiz[1(✉)], Mauricio Solar[2], Elsa Estevez[3],
and Gabriela Viale-Pereira[4]

[1] Universidad Católica del Norte, Antofagasta, Chile
asanchez@ucn.cl
[2] Universidad Técnica Federico Santa María, Valparaíso, Chile
msolar@inf.utfsm.cl
[3] Universidad Nacional del Sur, Bahía Blanca, Argentina
ece@cs.uns.edu.ar
[4] Danube University Krems, Krems, Austria
Gabriela.viale-pereira@donau-uni.ac.at

Abstract. This study is developed in the context of the Strengthening Governance Capacity for Smart Sustainable Cities (CAP4CITY) Project, part of the Erasmus + Programme. The study aims to support the design of teaching materials to address the human-capacity related needs for the governance of Smart Sustainable Cities (SSC) in South America. This article identifies the competencies and instructional design for the design of smart sustainable cities courses adapted to the South American context. Applying a scenario-building approach and the CAP4CITY roadmap for smart sustainable city initiatives, we conducted two workshops in Chile and two in Argentina attended by representatives from academia, NGOs, government agencies, and private companies. Using the data about competencies and teaching models gathered during these events, the study clustered the data and identified the major areas of competences and instructional methods. Lastly, we compared the results from both countries.

Keywords: Smart cities · Sustainable cities · Governance · Human-capacity · South America

1 Introduction

The use of innovative digital technologies to improve the quality of life of residents in urban contexts has been a goal for many local-level governments around the world and it is known as smart city efforts. However, the concept, that has gained popularity in the academic and practitioner world during the last decade, is still at an infancy stage in terms of current governance capabilities of urban centres [1] and available education programmes. Many frameworks, rankings, and technical standards have been conceived

© IFIP International Federation for Information Processing 2020
Published by Springer Nature Switzerland AG 2020
G. Viale Pereira et al. (Eds.): EGOV 2020, LNCS 12219, pp. 400–411, 2020.
https://doi.org/10.1007/978-3-030-57599-1_30

to assess the level of smartness of cities but, a uniform approach or a single recipe that can fit for all cases is difficult to be envisioned, in part due to the multidisciplinary nature of the field and the uniqueness of different countries and cities [2–8]. Many cities in developed countries are transiting towards being considered smart and sustainable in those rankings. Yet, cities in the Global South, and in particular, in South American countries, face a completely different reality compared with the former, mainly considering the technological, cultural and geographical perspectives [9].

The design of smart sustainable cities (SSC) training modules contextualized to the Latin American region is one of the main goals of the CAP4CITY Project. To address the problem, several workshops were conducted in Argentina, Brazil, Chile, and Colombia to assess the training needs for each country. In this research, we identified the main competences and training needs concerning planning, development and management of smart sustainable cities in Chile and Argentina. This article therefore describes and discusses the main competences and teaching methods identified as most relevant during the workshops with stakeholders from government, academia, private companies, and third sector, conducted in Chile and Argentina.

The rest of this article has the following structure. Section 2 presents some background concepts in SSC and discusses related work. Section 3 explains the methodology applied to conduct the workshops and to gather data. Section 4 discusses the major findings of the workshops in Chile and Argentina as well as lessons learned. Finally, Sect. 5 summarizes conclusions and future work.

2 Literature Review

2.1 Smart Sustainable Cities (SSC)

The term 'smart city' has become trendy to distinguish or promote cities that are considered advanced in the deployment and use of digital technology, and many cities are currently developing long term plans to become one. However, the concept of a 'smart city' is still ambiguous and complex since efforts for its development have to integrate multiple disciplines behind the city and the smartness dimensions, ranging from the urban and social related issues, through economic and environmental, to the technological areas. Additionally, we need to see the need to adapt it to cultural, social and geographical differences [10, 11]. Some commonly used definitions are the following:

- A smart city is one that utilizes Information and Communication Technologies (ICT) to meet the demands of the market (residents of the city), and to promote community involvement in the process. Thus, a smart city would be a city that not only possesses ICT technology in particular areas, but has also implemented this technology in a manner that positively impacts the local community [12].
- A smart city promotes regional competitiveness, transport and ICT economics, natural resources, human and social capital, quality of life, and participation of citizens in the governance of the city [5].
- A smart city brings together technology, government and society to enable the following characteristics: smart economy, smart mobility, smart environment, smart people,

smart living, smart governance (Institute of Electrical and Electronics Engineers Smart Cities Community)[1].

- A city can be defined as 'smart' when investments in human and social capital and traditional (transport) and modern (ICT) communication infrastructure fuel sustainable economic development and a high quality of life, with a wise management of natural resources, through participatory action and engagement [10].
- A developed urban area that creates sustainable economic development and high quality of life by excelling in multiple key areas: economy, mobility, environment, people, living, and government. Excelling in these critical areas can be done so through strong human capital, social capital, and/or ICT infrastructure[2].

The CAP4CITY Project, part of the Erasmus + Programme of the European Union, defines Smart Sustainable Cities (SSC) as a progression of how cities apply digital technology to serve their populations, pursue sustainable socio-economic development, and transform themselves. The urban development that leads SSC requires a growing number of roles and competencies to work together in order to plan, design, implement and manage the ongoing transformations of the city, enabled by technological innovation. A large number of competencies are needed for pursuing SSC efforts, mainly related to areas such as Business Administration, ICT, Computer Science, Engineering, Architecture and Urbanism, Urban Planning, Law, Political Science, Sociology, and Communication, among others. In addition, although the SSC concept has gained considerable attention in Latin America, there is a need for improving old and developing new teaching and learning tools, as well as curricula in all levels of higher and continuous education to build the needed qualified human resources able to develop SSC in the region.

The smart city concept integrates ICT, and various physical devices connected to the IoT (Internet of Things) network to optimize the efficiency of city operations and services and to connect citizens [13]. Such infrastructure enables to integrate data collected from citizens, devices, and assets. This data is processed and analyzed to monitor and manage traffic and transportation systems, power plants, utilities, water supply net-works, waste management, crime detection, information systems, schools, libraries, hospitals, and other community services [14]. Technology deployed in a smart city allows city officials to interact directly with both community and city infrastructure and to monitor what is happening in the city and how operations and daily activities in the city evolve. ICT is used to enhance the quality, performance, and interactivity of urban services, to reduce costs and resource consumption, and to enhance interactions between citizens and government. Smart city applications are developed to manage urban flows and allow for real-time responses [15]. Therefore, a smart city is more prepared to respond to challenges than one with a simple "transactional" relationship with its citizens [16]. Yet, the term itself remains unclear to its specifics and therefore, open to many interpretations [17]. When considering the sustainable dimension to the smart city concept, we could see that there is no general consensus since most frameworks are not integrating all the

---

[1] https://www.ieee.org/membership-catalog/productdetail/showProductDetailPage.html?product=CMYSC764.

[2] http://www.businessdictionary.com/definition/smart-city.html.

areas that should be assessed. Ahvenniemi, Huovila, Pinto-Seppä and Airaksinen [18] compared the frameworks and standards to assess smart sustainable cities and suggested that the initial target of sustainability of a city is not sufficiently addressed in some of the smart city frameworks with environmental indicators clearly underrepresented and a large variety of indicators considering economic and social aspects of a city.

2.2 Competencies and Massive Online Open Courses (MOOCs)

Researchers in many fields agreed about the importance of identifying competencies in the development of new curriculums rather than only focus on the knowledge itself. This change in perspective is characterized by a change in emphasis from teaching to student learning [19]. Then the words competencies, competence and competent become relevant when talking about learning and performance in education. These words mainly refer to a perso's state or quality of being able and fit. Katane and Selvi [20] defined competencies as "the set of knowledge, skills, and experience necessary for future, which manifests in activities" (pp. 44). Although Selvi [21] proposed the existence of various competencies for teachers, most researchers grouped the competencies in only three main areas: field competencies, pedagogical competencies and cultural competencies. Field competencies are related to the question of "what should school teach." In the past, field competencies were considered as the most important ones based on the concept that teachers were the only actor responsible for transmitting the content. However, today, other competencies, such as pedagogical competencies, are also necessary. The UK Training Agency [22] defines competence as a broad concept which embodies the ability to transfer skills and knowledge to new situations within the occupational area. It includes those qualities of personal effectiveness that are required in the workplace to deal with co-workers, managers, and customers.

Elam [23] sustained that under the Performance-Based Teacher Education program the main characteristics for the assessment of the student's competency should include i) using performance as the primary source of evidence, ii) taking into account evidence of the student's knowledge relevant to planning for, analyzing, interpreting, or evaluating situations or behavior, and iii) striving for objectivity. Another relevant approach to the understanding of design learning was made by Bloom [24] who proposed a taxonomy of cognitive domains that has been extensively used in competence-based learning. Bloom's taxonomy structured educational goals into the 'cognitive', 'affective' and 'psychomotor' domains, a structure which is closely related to the contemporary concept of competency as made up of knowledge, attitude and skill components.

The massive adoption of technology in education has given birth to various approaches, including Massive Open Online Courses (MOOCs), who materialize the interest in providing tools to support distance education and company training. Kalz [25] acknowledges the importance of technological advancements in MOOCs to remove existing barriers in lifelong learning. Castaño-Muñoz, Kreijns, Kalz and Punie [26] emphasize the importance of MOOCs to provide access to education for people who could not access to this opportunity for financial reasons or because they lack the necessary qualifications. Most MOOCs today are free and open to any interested participant. They provide the opportunity to numerous students to access simultaneously to online educational resources, without charge, in highly recognized institutions such as

MIT Open Courseware, Stanford Engineering Everywhere, Khan Academy, and others. MOOCs are based on the principles of open learning with the student at the center and a strong focus on learning rather than teaching. MOOCs provide students with flexibility and choice in meeting their educational goals. They comprise various non-traditional learning opportunities, from short courses to degrees.

3 Methodology

The main purpose of the study documented in this paper was to identify the perception of main stakeholders in the South American community about knowledge, skills, and competencies that should be present in courses building human capital for SSC. Such courses include elective courses at the undergraduate level, at the postgraduate level, including a Specialization and a Master degree programs, as well as MOOCs for continuous education. Applying the roadmap for SSC developed by the CAP4CITY Project, the study collected data and information through eight workshops conducted in the region – particularly in Argentina, Brazil, Chile, and Colombia. In this paper, we focus on the four workshops conducted in Chile and Argentina with representatives from government, NGOs, private companies, and academia. The study collected quantitative and qualitative data. Quantitate data was analyzed using IBM SPSS, and qualitative data was analyzed using logical tools and a computer-aided word-driven analysis with the software KH Coder. KH Coder recognizes patterns in word co-occurrence [27].

3.1 Workshop Activities

To conduct the workshops in Argentina and Chile, we apply the same methodology comprising the following three activities:

1) *Raising awareness* – delivering presentations about results of preliminary work explaining the state of the art on educational programs related to SSC
2) *Identifying knowledge areas and competencies* – conducting group discussions about knowledge areas and type of competencies to be delivered by new courses.
3) *Proposing pedagogical models* – conducting group discussions to identify innovative pedagogical models suitable to deliver the proposed competencies.

The workshops conducted in Chile took place in Antofagasta and Valparaiso, while the ones in Argentina, in La Plata and Bahia Blanca. All workshops were conducted in Spanish, and one researcher from the CAP4CITY Project presented the "Raising awareness" activity, explaining the partial results of the project and the methodology for the workshop. Following, participants were divided into groups to have team discussions. At the end of this activity, each group presented and discussed in plenary sessions the knowledge areas and competencies that they found necessary to be included in SSC courses. The third activity was conducted following the same approach previously used for the second one, but the theme to discuss and present was the pedagogical models most suitable for delivering the knowledge and developing the already identified competencies. The workshops followed the same methodology to allow for a combined analysis of the results.

3.2 Population and Sample

In total, 113 participants attended the workshops in Chile and Argentina. In Chile, there were twenty-eight representatives from academia (58%), fourteen from the private sector (29%), and six from the government (13%); while in Argentina, fifty-four representatives from academia (83%), five from the private sector (8%), and six from the government (9%). Figure 1 shows the number of workshop participants per sector. In each workshop, the organizers requested participants to assemble into teams, each of them constituting round tables with 6 to 8 attendees.

4 Results

Based on their experience and understanding, participants identified knowledge areas and competencies needed to develop SSC in their cities. The study classified the competencies based on the participants´ contributions respecting their main ideas but syntactically rephrased them. The researchers used the conventional style for defining competencies, i.e., starting with a verb in the infinitive. The identified competencies were organized according to the knowledge areas that appeared in the group presentations. In both countries, a total of 270 SSC competencies classified in 14 knowledge areas were identified by participants as relevant for SSC. Table 1 summarizes the identified knowledge areas and, for each country, the number of competencies per area. Similarities in the results of each country include the relevance of three topics: 1) *Technology and Apps*, ranked second in Argentina and first in Chile; 2) *Urban and Territorial Development*, fourth in Argentina and second in Chile; and 3) *Governance and Citizens*, third in Argentina and fifth in Chile. Some differences refer to: 1) the high position of the knowledge area *Management and Projects* in Argentina, ranked first, and the lower level in Chile, ranked seventh; 2) the high relevance of *Communication and Ethics* in Chile, ranked third, and the lower appearance in Argentina, ninth; and 3) the high relevance that Argentina gives to Society and People, ranked sixth, and the low level in Chile, eleventh.

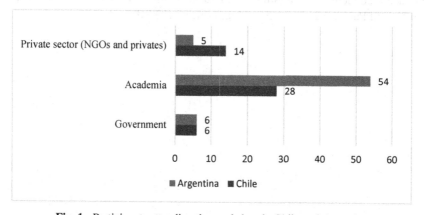

Fig. 1. Participants attending the workshop in Chile and Argentina

Table 1. Number of competences by area of knowledge

Knowledge areas	Chile	Argentina
Urban and territorial development	23	9
Laws and regulations	15	6
Entrepreneurship and innovation	7	1
Technology and apps	28	10
Data	18	5
Environment and sustainability	16	8
Governance and citizen participation	17	10
Management and project	16	14
Security and privacy	5	3
Social media and marketing	9	0
Communication and ethic	20	5
Society and people issues	6	8
Education	2	5
Information	0	4
Total	182	88

The CAP4CITY project team grouped the competencies in nine major themes according to their similarities. Figure 2 shows the percentage of competencies mentioned by the workshop participants in the nine themes by country. We could see that Argentina mainly mentioned competencies in the following themes: Governance (20.5% of the total competencies), Urban Studies and Sustainability (19.3%), and Public Administration and Management (15.9%). Meanwhile, in Chile, the themes in which more competencies were identified include Urban Studies and Sustainability (21.4%), Socio Technical ICT (15.4%), and Public Administration/Management" (13.7%).

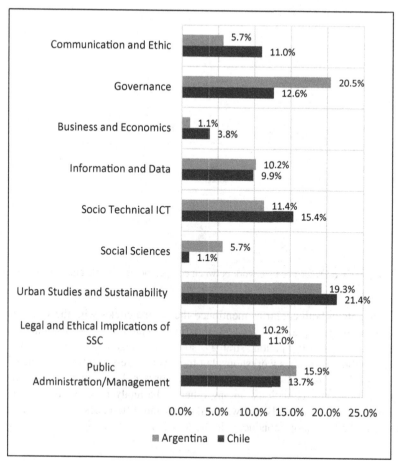

Fig. 2. Percentage of competencies identified by SSC theme

4.1   Comparison of Knowledge Areas Using Co-occurrence Analysis

This part of the study analyzes similarities and differences among the knowledge areas and competencies mentioned during the workshops conducted in Argentina and Chile.

Initially, we clustered the competencies identified by the workshop participants and coded them in the fourteen knowledge areas enumerated in Table 1. Later, a word analysis using the KH Coder software was performed to analyze and conceptualize the text. This software analyzes the structure of a text using statistical tools [27]. We applied the co-occurrence network [28] to analyze the similarities and differences among the competencies mentioned by the workshop's participants. This analysis showed that even though both countries share some competencies, many others were different, as we see in Fig. 3.

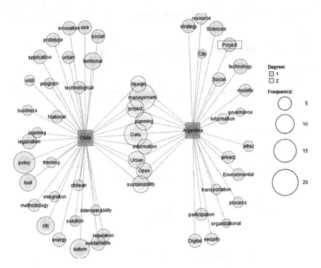

Fig. 3. Co-Occurrence Network between competencies in Chile and Argentina

Participants in both countries mentioned the competencies with the words design, management, project, planning, data, information, urban, open, and sustainability. The words governance, participation, strategy, social, organizational, and environmental stood out in the Argentina's workshops, but they were barely mentioned in the Chilean workshops. Chile, individually, mentioned the words policy, datum, interoperability, tool, legislation, and regulations, among others. The analysis of pedagogical models are shown in Fig. 4, which also shows similarities and differences between the models identified in the workshops conducted in the four cities.

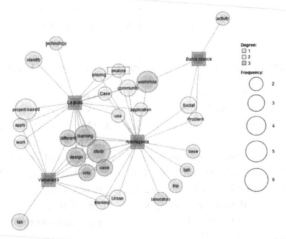

Fig. 4. Co-Occurrence Network between pedagogical models identified in Chile and Argentina.

The analysis clearly identified more similarities than differences in the suggested pedagogical models.

5 Discussion

The workshops organized in Chile and Argentina, aimed at identifying competencies and teaching models for the governance of smart sustainable cities in the South American context, enabled to collect more than two hundred competencies in various knowledge areas. The four workshops were conducted applying the same methodology and attracted a wide variety of participants from government, private companies, and academia. One essential requirement related to the participants was to include professionals from different areas of expertise – e.g. lawyers, IT professionals, urban planners, economists, and sociologists, among others, to cover the multiple dimensions and views needed for governing SSC efforts.

Results showed that even both countries being geographically close; their perception of the competencies needed for SSC development is not similar. The main differences between both countries can be summarized as follows. The Argentinian community emphasizes Governance and Social Sciences more than the Chilean community, but the Chilean community emphasizes Communication and Ethics, Socio Technical ICT, and Business and Economics more than the Argentinian community. Despite the differences, some similarities we found is the shared interest in areas such as Information and Data; Urban Studies and Sustainability; Legal and Ethical Implications of SCC; and Public Administration/Management. In addition, the pedagogical models identified by the participants were very similar in both countries. For instance, in the workshops conducted in the cities of La Plata, in Argentina, Valparaiso, and Antofagasta in Chile, participants identified the use of case studies and project-based learning as suitable learning methods for building competencies for SSC. Workshop's results were the first stage for the envisioned implementation of the courses – elective undergraduate courses, postgraduate courses and postgraduate programs – Specialization and Master, and MOOCs. Currently, the consortium defined a portfolio of 31 courses to develop the total set of the identified competencies. The usage of such courses will be open to the community. Moreover, acknowledging that each city has its own values, and one recipe does not fit all cases, we argue that each university, government or actor willing to use the courses, will need to select those that best fulfills the need of the local context.

6 Conclusions

Cities around the world are rapidly evolving, and they need to become smart and sustainable, adapting to the technological changes and the new demands of their citizens. Policymakers at the country and city level in South America need SSC programs that are adapted to their geographical and cultural condition. The series of workshops in South America, in the context of the CAP4CITY project, provided insights for developing a suite of courses that any city can adopt, customize, and use depending on their training needs. The successful implementation of such workshops allowed the researchers to identify the competencies and pedagogical models that could be both general but adapted to the South American context. This approach can be repeated to assess the training needs in a city. The findings of this study are of key importance for government, private companies, and academia to drive towards finding a balance between knowledge areas, pedagogical models, and SSC programs adapted to their environment.

The study has some limitation. We were able to consider only two cities per country, and a limited number of participants. Therefore, the methodology used in the workshops can be replicated by other cities to identify their specific training needs before implementing an educational programme in SSC. In this sense, the contribution of this study is mainly oriented to present a methodological approach that any city can adopt rather that claiming any generalization of the results.

Future work includes completing the design and content development for the courses, designing the most appropriate implementation mode of the curricula, and designing and establishing postgraduate programs based on the courses. We believe that this work may lead to new approaches for training city leaders to better govern their cities, addressing the challenges of the South American cities in the 21st century.

Acknowledgements. The research presented in this paper is part of the CAP4CITY Project, co-funded by the Erasmus + Programme of the European Union. Grant no: 598273-EPP-1-2018-1-AT-EPPKA2-CBHE-JP.

References

1. Ruhlandt, R.W.S.: The governance of smart cities: a systematic literature review. Cities **81**, 1–23 (2018)
2. Albino, V., Berardi, U., Dangelico, R.M.: Smart cities: definitions, dimensions, performance, and initiatives. J. Urban Technol. **22**, 3–21 (2015)
3. Anthopoulos, L.: Defining smart city architecture for sustainability. In: Proceedings of the 14th IFIP Electronic Government (EGOV) and 7th Electronic Participation (ePart) Conference 2015. Presented at the 14th IFIP electronic government and 7th electronic participation conference 2015, pp. 140–147, IOS Press (2015)
4. Chourabi, H., et al.: Understanding smart cities: an integrative framework. In: 2012 45th Hawaii International Conference on System Science (HICSS), pp. 2289–2297. IEEE (2012)
5. Giffinger, R., Fertner, C., Kramar, H., Kalasek, R., Milanović, N., Meijers, E.: Smart cities - ranking of European medium-sized cities (2007)
6. Marsal-Llacuna, M.L., Colomer-Llinas, J., Melendez-Frigola, J.: Lessons in urban monitoring taken from sustainable and livable cities to better address the Smart Cities initiative. Technol. Forecast. Soc. Change **90**, 611–622 (2015)
7. Nam, T., Pardo, T.A.: Conceptualizing smart city with dimensions of technology, people, and institutions. In: Proceedings of the 12th Annual International Digital Government Research Conference: Digital Government Innovation in Challenging Times, pp. 282–291 (2011)
8. Ramaprasad, A., Sánchez-Ortiz, A., Syn, T.: A unified definition of a smart city. In: Janssen, M., et al. (eds.) EGOV 2017. LNCS, vol. 10428, pp. 13–24. Springer, Cham (2017). https://doi.org/10.1007/978-3-319-64677-0_2
9. Viale Pereira, G., et al.: South American expert roundtable: increasing adaptive governance capacity for coping with unintended side effects of digital transformation. Sustainability **12**, 718 (2020)

10. Caragliu, A., Del Bo, C., Nijkamp, P.: Smart Cities in Europe. VU University Amsterdam, Faculty of Economics, Business Administration and Econometrics, Serie Research Memoranda 18 (2009)
11. Han, H., Hawken, S.: Introduction: innovation and identity in next-generation smart cities. City, culture and society **12**, 1–4 (2018)
12. Deakin, M., Alwaer, H.: From intelligent to smart cities. Intell. Build. Int. **3**, 140–152 (2011)
13. Peris-Ortiz, M., Bennett, D., Pérez-Bustamante, D.: Sustainable Smart Cities: Creating Spaces for Technological, Social and Business Development. Springer, Cham (2016). https://doi.org/10.1007/978-3-319-40895-8
14. McLaren, D., Agyeman, J.: Sharing Cities: a Case for Truly Smart and Sustainable Cities. MIT Press, Cambridge (2015)
15. Komninos, N.: What makes cities intelligent? In: Smart Cities, pp. 89–107. Routledge (2013)
16. Bhatt, J.G., Jani, O.K.: Smart development of Ahmedabad-Gandhinagar Twin City Metropolitan Region, Gujarat, India. In: Vinod Kumar, T.M. (ed.) Smart Metropolitan Regional Development. ACHS, pp. 313–356. Springer, Singapore (2019). https://doi.org/10.1007/978-981-10-8588-8_5
17. Cavada, M., Hunt, D., Rogers, C.: Smart cities: Contradicting definitions and unclear measures. In: World Sustainability Forum, pp. 1–12. MDPI AG, (2014)
18. Ahvenniemi, H., Huovila, A., Pinto-Seppä, I., Airaksinen, M.: What are the differences between sustainable and smart cities? Cities **60**, 234–245 (2017)
19. Prøitz, T.: Learning outcomes: What are they? Who defines them? When and where are they defined? Educ. Assess. Eval. Account. **22**, 119–137 (2010)
20. Katane, I., Selvi, K.: Teacher competence and further education as priorities for sustainable development of rural school in Latvia. J. Teach. Educ. Train. **6**, 41–59 (2006)
21. Selvi, K.: Teachers' competencies, cultura. Int. J. Philos. Cult. Axiol. **7**, 167–175 (2010)
22. Agency, T.: Development of accessible standards for national certification guidance. In: Note No. 1, Sheffield Employment Department/Training Agency (1989)
23. Elam, S.: Performance Based Teacher Education. What is the State of the Art? (1971)
24. Bloom, B.S.: Taxonomy of Educational objectivesn: Cognitive Domain, vol. 1, pp. 20–24. McKay, New York (1956)
25. Kalz, M.: Lifelong learning and its support with new technologies, 7 (2015)
26. Castaño-Muñoz, J., Kreijns, K., Kalz, M., Punie, Y.: Does digital competence and occupational setting influence MOOC participation? Evidence from a cross-course survey. J. Comput. Higher Educ. **29**(1), 28–46 (2016). https://doi.org/10.1007/s12528-016-9123-z
27. Higuchi, K.: A two-step approach to quantitative content analysis: KH coder tutorial using Anne of Green Gables (Part I). Ritsumeikan Soc. Sci. Rev. **52**, 77–91 (2016)
28. Palmer, S., Campbell, M.: Text analytics visualisation of Course Experience Questionnaire student comment data in science and technology. In: AAEE 2015: Proceedings of the Australasian Association for Engineering Education 2015 Annual Conference, pp. 1–10. School of Engineering, Deakin University (2015)

Author Index

Printed in the United States
By Bookmasters